"KEEP 'EM IN THE EAST"

FILM AND CULTURE
A series of Columbia University Press

Edited by John Belton

For a complete list of titles, see page 531

"KEEP 'EM IN THE EAST"

*Kazan, Kubrick, and the Postwar
New York Film Renaissance*

RICHARD KOSZARSKI

Columbia University Press
New York

Columbia University Press
Publishers Since 1893
New York   Chichester, West Sussex
cup.columbia.edu

Copyright © 2021 Richard Koszarski
All rights reserved

Library of Congress Cataloging-in-Publication Data
Names: Koszarski, Richard, author.
Title: Keep 'em in the East : Kazan, Kubrick, and the postwar
New York film renaissance / Richard Koszarski.
Description: New York City : Columbia University Press, 2021. |
Series: Film and culture | Includes index.
Identifiers: LCCN 2020051651 (print) | LCCN 2020051652 (ebook) |
ISBN 9780231200981 (hardback) | ISBN 9780231200998 (paperback) |
ISBN 9780231553872 (ebook)
Subjects: LCSH: Motion picture industry—New York (State)—New York—
History—20th century.
Classification: LCC PN1993.5.U77 K68 2021 (print) | LCC PN1993.5.U77 (ebook) |
DDC 791.4309747/1—dc23
LC record available at https://lccn.loc.gov/2020051651
LC ebook record available at https://lccn.loc.gov/2020051652

Cover image: Ray Milland, photographed on Third Avenue near 103rd Street, for *The Lost Weekend*, October 1946. No hidden cameras. Bison Archives.

Cover design: Chang Jae Lee

0.1. Martin Balsam (who was barely visible in *On the Waterfront*) supporting George Justin's "Keep 'em in the East" campaign on the set of *12 Angry Men*. Fox Movietone studio, June 1956. Photo by Muky Munkacsi. George Justin Collection, Museum of Modern Art Film Stills Archive.

CONTENTS

Introduction 1

PART I: ROOTS

1. Not Just Another Location 11
2. The Pathé Studio: Miniature Hollywood or Just Another False Dawn? 31
3. Now It Can Be Told: Louis de Rochemont, Henry Hathaway, and the Birth of Docudrama 51
4. Race Movies: New York's Original Independent Cinema 93

PART II: REVIVAL

5. Eight Million Stories 147
6. The O'Dwyer Plan 188
7. Joe Lerner's New York Noir 206
8. Just Passing Through 232
9. Pictures and Politics 254

PART III: RENAISSANCE

10. Crime on the Waterfront 293
11. Obsessed with Film 313

12. The Golden Warrior 341
13. Kiss Me, Kill Me 356
14. "And the Winner in New York Is . . ." 372
15. Happy Ending 402
16. Thank You, Hollywood! 419

List of Abbreviations 429
Notes 433
Index 499

"KEEP 'EM IN THE EAST"

INTRODUCTION

By most accounts, the creation by John V. Lindsay of the Mayor's Office of Motion Pictures and Television in 1966 marks the official beginning of New York's postwar film renaissance. This era of *Midnight Cowboy, The Godfather, Annie Hall,* and *The French Connection* has long been hailed as a local production triumph. But no matter how appreciative they are of individual films, studies of this period have never been very interested in exactly why and how this renaissance happened the way it did. They never ask the big question: Exactly where did this renaissance come from?

Was it really true that not much happened in the east after D. W. Griffith left New York to join the bulk of American film producers in southern California? Textbooks said that the sun had set on New York and risen in Hollywood, a geographically absurd metaphor. Allowing for an exception here or there, that was still the way they explained it to me in graduate school—even at NYU. But basic research showed that this narrative was clearly inadequate, and my previous book, *Hollywood on the Hudson: Film and Television in New York from Griffith to Sarnoff,* detailed a rich interwar history that had been excluded from traditional accounts. It also showed that existing explanations were unable to account for a sudden revival of film production in New York in the 1960s and '70s because they were based on an incorrect historical premise: unless you understand that the motion picture industry never did abandon New York, you will have a great deal of difficulty explaining its return. While the production of feature-length narrative films did fall to historic lows during World War II, every other industry function—executive office, exhibition, advertising and distribution, and short subject, newsreel, animation, sponsored, and industrial film production—continued to flourish. An unbroken filmmaking tradition has operated here since the days of Thomas Edison, and demonstrating this was one of the goals of that book.

"Keep 'Em in the East" shows how this continuing tradition and the industrial infrastructure and trained cadres of technical workers that came with it made New York—not Texas or North Carolina—the only possible location for that 1960s renaissance. In doing so, New York provided a model that even Hollywood would follow in the poststudio era, as long-term contracts and brick-and-mortar facilities were supplanted by the strategies of a new, "independent" commercial cinema. And because even New York filmmakers saw feature-length theatrical narratives as synonymous with "the movies," that is where this book finds its focus. Some were written, produced, and directed entirely by local talent; others were the work of outside film crews just passing through. Therefore, any concentration on features here is not intended to slight the work being done in theatrical and nontheatrical shorts, experimental cinema, sponsored and commercial films, and both live and filmed television, where the bulk of local filmmaking activity actually took place. All of these had significant input on the development of New York's feature picture business, a fascinating history of hybridization and reciprocity that is one of the defining elements of our local history. But with over two hundred local features already under discussion here, a complete account of all those other genres will have to wait for the next volume.

On the Waterfront is a landmark in any history of New York filmmaking. It startled Hollywood by winning eight Academy Awards in 1955, but it was not alone that season. That was the same year Stanley Kubrick released *Killer's Kiss*, which he had shot simultaneously with Elia Kazan's film in the winter of 1953–54. They may have been made at the same time, each on local streets on different sides of the Hudson, but the production histories of the two films are radically different. One marshalled some of the greatest talents in the American motion picture industry while the other was a precocious indie financed on lab credits and salary deferments. But different as they are, both films emerged from the same cultural and economic traditions that had already shaped New York cinema for a generation. And both clearly belong to "New York," despite all the time Kazan spent shooting in Hoboken. Remember that the New York we are talking about here is not so much a matter of plot line or location but a sensibility, an overdetermined cultural perspective shaped by everything from population patterns to trade union regulations. As we will see, each film broke new ground in terms of financing, production, and distribution, strategies that would be widely adopted by future filmmakers but at the time were still largely unrecognized or ignored by the Hollywood majors. Accordingly, the final third of this book presents detailed production histories of each film, interwoven not only to highlight their differences and similarities but also to indicate how and why they came to be made at this particular time and place, and to suggest the range of influence that both films had on the subsequent development of American cinema, in both New York and Hollywood.

The first two parts of the book document what led up to this. For example, it is obvious why local films featured more cops than cowboys but why so few conventional musicals during a golden age of musicals on Broadway? Part of the explanation comes from the tastes and talents of key local personnel, such as Elia Kazan, Sidney Lumet, Boris Kaufman, Paddy Chayefsky, Richard and Paul Sylbert, John Cassavetes, and Ralph Rosenblum, whose work in the developing New York film industry was in all cases built on their prior experience in theater, television, documentaries, industrial films, and other aspects of the city's diverse cultural life. Some of these people I was able to interview over the years, but others I know only through their personal papers and business records, archived in special collections in libraries all across the country (or in Stanley Kubrick's case, London). But in addition to such relatively familiar figures, there were many others whose significant contributions have generally been relegated to the "noncreative" category. George Justin, for example, was a production manager and the public face of New York's filmmaking community during this period, launching a "Keep 'em in the East" campaign that he promoted at every opportunity—in the press, of course, but also exhorting his crews by plastering the slogan on large banners he would hang in the handful of functioning stages whose survival he was helping ensure. Indeed, the full page "Keep 'em in the East" ad Justin placed in *Variety* following *On the Waterfront*'s remarkable Oscar victories not only marks the official start of his campaign but also serves as a title for this book.

Equally invisible were the many women working behind the cameras in New York during this period, most of whom, like Faith Elliott Hubley, Martha Pinson, and Roberta Hodes, belonged to Script Supervisors' Local 161. When I started this research I was surprised to discover that many of them had kept—at home, in their closets—the daily production reports and annotated shooting scripts for dozens of key films, including *The Miracle Worker*, *Splendor in the Grass*, and *Odds Against Tomorrow*. Unlike the situation in Hollywood, New York's independent production companies, operating no permanent facilities of their own, depended on these women to keep track of all the paperwork personally—which they did, often for decades. The information contained in records like these, unavailable elsewhere, helps us understand how such disparate talents—never under long term contract to anyone—were able to work together as a unified cohort, transforming what might simply have been a loose collection of more or less interesting films into a coherent regional cinema with its own stylistic hallmarks and technical capabilities.

These men and women certainly deserve full credit for their accomplishments, but no matter how brilliant their individual skills, the films they subsequently created would never have existed (at least not in anything like the same form) if New York did not already support some level of professional filmmaking. Since Hollywood all but monopolized the production of feature-length narratives with broad audience appeal, New York had to specialize in something else, and by 1945 it had captured two marginal genres that occupied a very narrow commercial niche: documentaries and race movies.

Between 1942 and 1971 the U.S. Army Signal Corps made thousands of films at the old Astoria studio. Almost all of those films were made by civilian employees, not GIs, who came to see nonfiction film production as something more than Hollywood's stepchild; when they moved back to the private sector they took with them not only a degree of respect for "informational" film but also a working knowledge of the techniques that went with it. Jack Arnold, for example, went directly from the Signal Corps to a long stretch as an industrial film director (including *With These Hands*, an Oscar nominee for Best Documentary feature in 1950) and then to Hollywood. Ralph Rosenblum spent many years editing industrial films at shops like MKR with his partner Gene Milford (editor of *On the Waterfront*) before teaming up with Sidney Lumet and Woody Allen. Boris Kaufman, who won the Academy Award for his photography of *On the Waterfront*, had spent a decade making sponsored and industrial films for a host of local producers.

Still, it has never been easy to move directly from commercials and documentaries to a career in dramatic features. What made it work this time? The newsreel business had always been centered in New York, and producer Louis de Rochemont pioneered one solution when he adapted his "March of Time" style to a string of postwar docudramas, beginning with *The House on 92nd Street* in 1945. His director, Henry Hathaway, who also made films like *Kiss of Death* and *Fourteen Hours* here, told Scott Eyman that there was nothing neorealist about this. If he was making a film away from the studio, he claimed, he treated it just like a western. With studio space at a premium, the filming of documentary-inflected police procedurals soon became a familiar sight on the streets of Brooklyn and Manhattan. But this did not mean that subsequent New York–produced films, like *The Hustler* or *The Pawnbroker*, would simply mimic the look of a newsreel. That could have been done anywhere, at any time, but New York always had other cultural resources to draw on. The Broadway director Elia Kazan, annotating his working script of *On the Waterfront*, knew that he had to find a way of blending the authenticity of "the street" with what he had already discovered on the stage. "Don't be objective! This is not a documentary," he wrote to himself. "Be *subjective*, be Terry."

But what really laid the groundwork for the theatrical postwar feature film business in New York was something unpredicted and, even now, unrecognized—the race movie. Relics of a segregated cinema, these "all Black" productions, intended for African American audiences in urban ghettoes or the rural South, had been produced in and around New York since 1920. For various reasons, this branch of the local motion picture business had quickly bounced back after the war, even as race movie production in Florida, Chicago, and Los Angeles never recovered from the War Production Board's draconian rationing of motion picture stock. Of thirty-three theatrical feature films made in the New York area from 1946 through 1948, seventeen were race movies, all filmed on impossibly low budgets. The director Josh Binney recalled spending a record $43,000 on Cab Calloway's *Hi De Ho!* This cycle not only revived many of New York's moribund stages but provided early feature film credits for a core group of writers, directors, designers, and technicians. For years, historians simply ignored the production of race movies in their accounts of American film history. More recently, this "separate cinema" has been allotted its separate corner in a number of standard textbooks, but even these seem at a loss on how to integrate their story into the larger narrative of American cinema. This book is not the first to discuss race movies, but it is the first to see their contribution as integral to the development of the motion picture industry as a whole—at least that part of it that came to flourish in New York just after the war. By the time the race movie genre collapsed in 1948 (only three were among the thirty-eight features made in New York from 1949 through 1951), the local talent base had developed an infrastructure that would allow it to continue working on more mainstream material for years to come.

Street photography, portable equipment, low-budget cost-cutting strategies, disregard of established narrative conventions, making and marketing films to otherwise ignored audiences, the use of local actors and technicians, a lack of concern for "studio" perfection, 16 mm for production or distribution—all of this we now see as characteristic of New York independent cinema. The fact that these strategies—seen in films as different as *Killer's Kiss* and *Little Fugitive*—originated in the local nonfiction and race movie business is not a coincidence and is crucial for understanding why this postwar film renaissance could only have happened there.

And then there is the political dimension. When his old friend Mark Hellinger told him of the troubles he was having filming *The Naked City*, Mayor William O'Dwyer began the first organized campaign to lure theatrical film production back to New York. O'Dwyer was later run out of town because of his alleged association with the mobster Frank Costello, but in 1947 he appointed his top labor advisor, Edward C. Maguire, to spearhead a program to reform "archaic and obsolete" municipal laws and regulations. This was the sort of announcement that may have sounded good at a news conference but initially did little to sway anxious producers (and issues of blatant municipal corruption were left for another day). Yet just a few months later, on August 28, 1947, the *New York Times* announced an agreement even more startling than Maguire's recent action in the city's crippling transit strike. Under the headline "Movie

Unions Sign Peace Pact Here," the paper revealed that "A five-year guarantee that New York picture makers will not be plagued by the jurisdictional strikes that have produced picket lines, broken heads, and long production delays in Hollywood movie studios was signed in Mayor O'Dwyer's presence by the heads of the thirteen principal film unions in this city."

It was true, as Maguire was quick to point out, that the New York film industry never suffered the degree of labor violence that marked the notorious Disney or Warner Bros. strikes in the 1940s, but the exact role of New York's motion picture unions in this story has always been controversial. The issue of labor reciprocity, for example, always cut both ways. Boris Kaufman had not shot a conventional feature since escaping occupied France in 1941 and had spent a decade in New York working in the nonfiction sector, developing a style that would later be recognized as innovative and "realistic." He won the *On the Waterfront* assignment only because New York unions would not allow a Hollywood cameraman to work in their jurisdiction without being covered by one of their own members; when producer Sam Spiegel refused to pay for this second cameraman, the company settled on Kaufman. But even after winning the Academy Award, Kaufman could not work in Hollywood because the West Coast local would not accept a New York member. Kaufman's papers at Yale are filled with warnings of "the irrevocable conclusion that no out-of-state cameramen or nonmembers would be given special dispensation for employment here" (a glum report sent in by his Hollywood agent). So Kaufman stayed in New York, making films there and training crews in the style he had developed to suit the insular working conditions in New York, which were not those of Hollywood. In this period, it seems, American cinema was already far from monolithic.

There is no argument among historians of American cinema that a transformative post-1966 New York film renaissance really happened. What remains unexamined is exactly why this local filmmaking community proved so successful in accommodating itself to changing industry conditions and whether the local cultural and economic climate informed the films they made in any special way. The music industry understands how and why Nashville is not New Orleans. Can the same sort of thing be said about New York's local filmmaking community? In any case, no one makes movies there in order to save money. Just how this local filmmaking community overcame its obstacles—and set the stage for that fabled renaissance—is a story of art and politics, big business and labor history. It is also a story that, until now, no one has ever really attempted to tell.

Acknowledgments

While working my way through the papers of cinematographer Boris Kaufman (twenty-five well-indexed boxes at the Beinecke Library), I came across a telegram inviting him to introduce *On the Waterfront* at a film festival in Brooklyn. Although others had made good use of these papers before me, I doubt that anyone had paid much attention to the Young People's Film Festival, a series of five features screened at Brooklyn College's Walt Whitman Auditorium in July 1964. As it turned out, Kaufman couldn't make it, and *On the Waterfront* was never even shown, so who could blame them?

But the telegram certainly meant something to me because I was one of the 1,500 New York City high school students who did manage to wrangle an invitation. Organized by Father John Culkin, the director of Fordham University's Communication Arts department, the festival was sponsored by Mayor Robert F. Wagner's Office of Cultural Affairs "to stimulate recognition by young people of the medium of film as a serious reflection of the contemporary scene."

Serious movies were suddenly the next new thing, and festivals like this were sprouting up everywhere. I still remember how grown up it made me feel to be there as the lights went down. Unfortunately, I don't remember much else about it, other than sitting way in the back at a screening of *The Hustler*, introduced by Robert Rossen, the first real movie director I ever laid eyes on. Was I there to see Frank and Eleanor Perry introduce *David and Lisa*, or Arthur Penn with *The Miracle Worker*? And did anyone in charge take the trouble to point out that all three of those films—as well as *On the Waterfront*—were not just good movies but great examples of the postwar film renaissance that was taking place right here in New York? Indeed, the two "Hollywood" films shown that week were probably slipped in as honorary New York productions, courtesy of the local celebrities who introduced them, the screenwriter Horton Foote (*To Kill a Mockingbird*) and the actor Howard Keel (*Seven Brides for Seven Brothers*).

I can't claim that Mayor Wagner's film festival was what turned me on to the art of the motion picture because I had already found my way to MOMA and Dan Talbot's New Yorker. But the organized festivity probably did help convince me that my passion for movies was not just a personal obsession but part of something big, a movement that Stanley Kaufmann would soon label "the film generation." And by 1977 I was actually getting paid to study New York's film history, first as an assistant to Thomas and Nancy Hoving, who had been hired to develop a proposal for the creative reuse of the abandoned Astoria studio, then as a curator for the Museum of the Moving Image that grew up out of its ruins. Some of that personal history I outlined in *Hollywood on the Hudson*, which told the story of what happened here in the 1920s and 1930s. This book takes the story up through 1955, when Stanley Kubrick released his DIY feature *Killer's Kiss* and Elia Kazan's *On the Waterfront* went home with eight Oscars. That may have seemed an improbable success to some—except for people like George Justin, who would build an entire "Keep 'em in the East" campaign around it—but by the time John Lindsay got to City Hall even better things were on the horizon.

For helping me find out about this history and understand why it was important, I have forty years of names to thank, and space is already running short. My model here will have to be Eva Marie Saint, accepting her Oscar for *On the Waterfront*, who managed to thank as many people as time allowed and still wrapped up everyone else with a gracious nod to "all the longshoremen."

First, of course, the immediate family—my wife, Diane, who lived through this entire adventure with me, and our daughter, Eva, who did much the same, except that she missed the part that happened before she was even born. My brother and sister, Ted and Elizabeth. And the memory of our mother, Janina Koszarski, and our sister, Maria Knight, to whom this book is dedicated.

Thanks also to those who made this history and took the time to share their stories, stills, and documentation with me, including Larry Barr, Laslo Benedek, Stanley Cortez, Lee Garmes, Tommy Hanley, Tom Hanlon, Henry Hathaway, Alan Heim, Gerald Hirschfeld, James Wong Howe, Valerie Sharaff Justin, Joseph and Geraldine Lerner, Don and Karl Malkames, Edward J. Montagne, "Muky" Munkacsi, Sol Negrin, Frank J. Payne, Martha Pinson, Sam Robert, Budd Schulberg, Leo Seltzer, Paul Sylbert, Charles Turner, and Bernard Vorhaus.

And those who helped me understand what I was hearing, which took a whole lot longer, included Steve Abrams, Donald Albrecht, Richard Allen, Rita Altomara, Lou Azzollini, Eric Barnouw, Lisa Barrier, Jeanine Basinger, Rachel Bernstein, Michael J. Bowen, Geoff Brown, Kevin Brownlow, Joe Burtis, Lea Carlson, Paolo Cherchi Usai, Ian Christie, Joseph Clark, Anne Coco, Thomas Cripps, Dave Davidson, Lou DiCrescenzo, Noah Eisenberg, William K. Everson, Karen Falk, Susan Felleman, Moira Fitzgerald, Tag Gallagher, Joseph Gelmis, Erika Gottfried, Eric Goldman, Bruce Goldstein, Christopher Gray, Joanne Hanley, Jan Harlan, Louise Hilton, Jake Hinkson, J. Hoberman, Jan-Christopher Horak, Eric Hoyt, Mary Huelsbeck, Ron Hutchinson, Paula Klaw, Robert Kosinski, Mark Lackowski, Bruce Lawton, James Layton, Dan Leab, John Libbey, Ron Magliozzi, Richard Mason, John McElwee, Linda Mehr, Tom Meyers, Barbara Miller, Joan Miller, Eddie Muller, Charles Musser, Nelson Page, Mark Phillips, David Pierce, Gary Rhodes, Thelma Schoonmaker, David Schwartz, Rick Senat, Anthony Slide, Aubrey Solomon, Cathy Surowiec, Richard Ward, and Marc Wanamaker.

Philip Leventhal of Columbia University Press.

John Belton, for believing in this project and pushing it up a very long hill.

Andre S. Kaufman, for permission to use materials in the Boris Kaufman Collection at the Beinecke Library.

Reid Cinema Archives, Wesleyan University, for permission to quote from materials in the Elia Kazan Collection.

And all the longshoremen.

PART I
ROOTS

CHAPTER 1

NOT JUST ANOTHER LOCATION

Fiorello La Guardia was the first New York mayor to realize the full significance of the motion picture industry to the city's economic well-being. The few hundred jobs directly at stake in the late 1930s were not unimportant, but ever since the turn of the century, the movies—along with broadcasting and publishing—had also been doing something else for New Yorkers. Where the twentieth century had begun with a range of great American cities competing for world and national attention, it was now clear that modern America was no longer so flat a landscape. Now there was New York—and all those other places. Pittsburgh, Chicago, and San Francisco were all great cities, but New York was *the* city. It was large and it was wealthy, but its importance in banking or shipping or manufacturing was not enough to explain so dramatic a shift in the popular imagination.

This perception of New York—a New York of the imagination that featured in everything from Hart Crane's poetry to William Randolph Hearst's newsreels—was a useful ideal, an illusion. On stage and screen, on the printed page and over the air, the world had been told that this was our city of opportunity—not just the heart of America's modern economy but its undisputed cultural and artistic capital. By midcentury, "New York" had come to enjoy its status as a modern myth and accepted the benefits that came with the title as if they had been bestowed by right. It had taken years for the media to create this image, and the movies were only a part of the equation. But cultivating an image requires attention, and controlling that image is not a responsibility best left to others (even if the Hollywood studios were only factories operating at the behest of a handful of corporate bosses, all of them based in New York).

La Guardia had had other concerns when he first arrived at City Hall in 1934. True, the once-healthy local film industry was in rapid decline, but so were many other industries with greater claims on the mayor's attention. The movies, hardly a priority, were even seen by some locals as tainted goods. The playboy mayor "Broadway" Jimmy Walker, who had defeated La Guardia in the 1932 election, had been attacked (by Patrick Cardinal Hayes, for one) for the immorality of his showbiz lifestyle, which included a very public affair with Ziegfeld showgirl Betty Compton. Trying to position himself as far as possible from Walker, La Guardia closed New York's burlesque houses and personally smashed its slot machines. So it was not until his second term that he suddenly made the revival of New York's local film industry a municipal priority.

La Guardia traveled to Los Angeles in September 1938 for an American Legion event and avoided all invitations to visit the major studios. But he did spend a considerable amount of time with Walter Wanger, a personal friend from World War I days when they had both flown with the Army Air Corps on the Italian front. At a luncheon with Wanger, La Guardia, as expected, criticized the "cheap thrillers" from Hollywood that were poisoning young audiences back home. "That's the kind of picture we want to keep out of our neighborhood houses," he told local reporters.[1] Their wartime experiences may have brought them together in Hollywood, but La Guardia soon found an even stronger bond connecting him to his one friend in the motion picture business: both men had a deep distrust of bankers. The mayor had long seen the banks as selfish and obstructionist, standing in the way of New Deal policies promoted by the Roosevelt administration. Wanger, an independent producer struggling at the edges of the system, was hundreds of thousands of dollars in debt to A. H. Giannini's Bank of America and regaled his old friend with the injustice of it all. If La Guardia wanted to know what was really wrong with Hollywood, a few hours with Wanger would have given him the answer: not the objectionable content of its films but the objectionable behavior of its bankers. As soon as La Guardia returned to New York he began to listen, for the first time, to the complaints of the local filmmaking community, who he now began to feel had been battling his old enemies all along.

Over the next two years the mayor tried everything he could think of to lure motion picture production back to New York. He created a Department of Commerce and ordered its first director, Clendenin J. Ryan, to make this movie business a top priority. He considered creating a municipal "Cinema City," a film industry version of the public markets he had constructed around the city. He negotiated with unions and talked up the city to visiting producers, calculating that New York deserved to be the home of at least 10 percent of domestic motion picture production.[2] He dangled the power of the purse, insisting that "there will be no taxation difficulties here, because New York is not a hick town," a not-so-subtle reference to the threat of a new film-related tax in California.[3] And if that didn't work, his office leaked plans for "starting a motion picture company to compete with Hollywood" a scheme identified by one source as "the Mayor's own idea and . . .his 'pet baby.' "[4]

"There's no reason for a monopoly of the motion picture industry in any one city," La Guardia told one reporter:

> As a matter of fact I think it would be a healthy thing right now to break the monotony of isolation in which the film business has been steeped too long. How can the powers of such an industry assimilate new ideas when they are not subject to any, huddled as they are all in one spot. A shift at this time would create a rivalry of standards. That's always good.
>
> And why shouldn't the shift be to New York? This city is the greatest market in the world for the movie product, is it not? Then why shouldn't it have a hand in the making, too? We have every conceivable advantage. What do movie producers want?[5]

But for every step forward the project fell two steps back. The outbreak of war in Europe shut off key foreign markets and made Hollywood producers wary of any change in production procedures. Government restrictions put in place after Pearl Harbor favored studios with large back lots and scenic warehouses stuffed with interchangeable set elements—Hollywood studios, not the kind they had in New York. Distracted by his new position as national head of the Office of Civilian Defense, La Guardia was only too happy when the largest and finest studio in the city was sold to the federal government for use as a training film facility. Adolph Zukor and Jesse Lasky had opened their Astoria studio in 1920, and while activity ebbed and flowed over the years it had remained the center of New York's production activity for the past two decades. Even when Paramount stopped making its own films in Astoria, the studio remained active as an independent rental facility under Western Electric's auspices.

Reporters, military brass, and a few local celebrities gathered there to celebrate the formal dedication of the Signal Corps Photographic Center (SCPC) on September 22, 1942. "I've been trying to get motion pictures back in this shack for a long time now," the mayor told the radio audience listening in on the festivities.[6] Of course, these wouldn't be the kind of motion pictures he had been thinking about, but there would certainly be enough work to keep up local production skills for the duration. After the mayor left the microphone, SCPC staff screened a clip reel featuring Rudolph Valentino, Gloria Swanson, Claudette Colbert, Noel Coward, and other "Hollywood" stars who had once graced the stages. They followed this with a recent Army training film, in color. The juxtaposition was intended to highlight the gulf separating the two distinct realms of filmmaking: fiction and nonfiction, fantasy and reality, entertainment and instruction. No one at the event that day could have predicted it, but the Astoria stages wouldn't see another Hollywood-style feature picture until 1975.

No matter how many individual shooting days might be involved, La Guardia had not simply been trying to sell New York to Hollywood producers as just another attractive location site. While those streetscapes were part of his argument, what he was really interested in was a wholesale revival of the local motion picture industry, meaning an increased production of films that would draw on New York's own writers, actors, directors, and designers. "This is the art center of the world," he announced while enumerating local advantages, envisioning filmmaking as an integral part of New York's cultural landscape.[7]

So he would have found the fate of *Beyond Tomorrow* especially galling. In September 1939, producer Lee Garmes announced that he would soon begin shooting the film at Eastern Service Studios in Astoria (the old Paramount studio), the start of a three-picture deal he had negotiated with RKO. Then the financing he had arranged with a local bank suddenly collapsed, due either to "concern over the war's effect on the market" or the bank's general inexperience with film underwriting. RKO stepped in with financing from a California bank, but only "on condition the film be made on the West Coast." To rub salt in the wound, the Hollywood-based *American Cinematographer* later ran a shot of Garmes and his crew on the cover of their February 1940 issue. Standing before a painted backdrop of the Manhattan skyline, ankle deep in artificial snow, they are hard at work on the film's "Central Park" episodes inside a Hollywood soundstage. "Garmes said the film would have cost $25,000 more had it been made in New York, but he felt it would have been worth the difference," the *Times* reported.[8]

But independent productions like this would always be hit-or-miss affairs, so La Guardia's real hope had been to duplicate Paramount's "miniature Hollywood in Astoria," where its full-service operation had produced thirty-eight features between 1928 and 1932.[9] He knew that Warner Bros. had shot hundreds of short films at their Flatbush studios from 1928 to 1939 under the same conditions—with all interiors and exteriors, as well as postproduction, being done locally. Even with studios that chose not to maintain the overhead of their own East Coast operation, if any principal photography had to be done in New York, then *all* the principal photography could be done in New York. That was what had happened in 1933, when Columbia shot *Social Register* here and Universal made *Moonlight and Pretzels*: everything was done locally, with no return to the coast for additional photography. The only exceptions were occasional inserts of musical numbers for revue-style films like *International House* (1933) or *The Big Broadcast of 1938* (filmed at Astoria in 1937), in which an East Coast sequence was dropped like a plum into a Hollywood pudding.

That was the situation in the early days of sound, although things had worked a bit differently with silent pictures. In addition to those major producers like Paramount and First National, who operated their own full-service studios here, many others would send their leading actors to New York for days or weeks of principal photography then bring them back to the coast for the rest of the film. Harold Lloyd's *Speedy* (1927) and King Vidor's *The Crowd* (1928) were just two of the more prominent examples. Hollywood had been the nation's film production center since before World War I, but with so many of its best stories taking in place in New York it made sure to put that city on-screen in the most convincing way possible. Until around 1933 that almost always meant "in the flesh," but things had changed.

Except for films like *The Scoundrel* (1935) or *One Third of a Nation* (1939), which were completely made in New York studios, what La Guardia would now have observed on-screen was a virtual New York evoked by the crafty manipulation of editing, stock shots, and back projection, as in *King Kong* (1933) or *Nothing Sacred* (1937). No matter how important New York might be to the storyline, Hollywood producers were no longer authorizing lengthy New York location jaunts for their leading actors. This had little to do with local chauvinism or problems with location sound recording but was instead the result of a revolution in the special effects department. Hollywood technicians had made tremendous strides in the use of rear-screen projection beginning around 1930, fueling a rapid increase in the use of back-projection plates and transparencies. By 1942, Paramount alone was processing up to 2,000 such setups a year, "and hardly a picture goes out without some of these scenes in them."[10] Decrying the "fantastically expensive" cost of location filming, Farciot Edouart argued that

> if a comparable location result can be achieved in the studio, with the only added expense involved being that of sending a skeleton transparency background crew, with perhaps an assistant director and such supernumerary players as doubles, for the principal actors, extras, stunt riders, and the like, to the location, and thereafter completing the scenes with the principals in the studio, it is obvious that worthwhile economies must result.[11]

Of course, the more a studio invested in technology like this, the more department heads like Edouart would be able to argue that it made good economic sense to never set foot outside the studio at all.

In 1933, Columbia had sent a crew of specialists to film background footage of New York locations for Frank Borzage's *Man's Castle*. The director and his stars, Spencer Tracy and Loretta Young, never set foot in New York, and the work was carried out by anonymous technicians with cryptic instructions to film the city only from certain angles at specific times of day.

The wily cinematographers even try to persuade their audiences that Mr. Tracy goes swimming in the East River. There one sees the Queensboro Bridge and Mr. Tracy approaching the river and jumping into the water. But the water that Mr. Tracy entered was California water. . . . When he is swimming he looks up and sees the city, and again the audience sees Manhattan through his eyes. This sequence was photographed from the river in New York. When the scenes are joined in their proper sequence the illusion is complete.[12]

The crew spent five weeks filming 6,000 feet of inserts, POV, and reaction shots, of which 450 feet (about five minutes) were said to have been used in the film.

Audiences had previously associated such techniques with fantasies like *The Lost World* (1925) or spectacles like *Ben-Hur* (1925), but what was new this time was that a high degree of movie magic was being employed on an intimate romance set among the unemployed residents of an urban shanty town. It would be the preferred style of establishing location authenticity throughout the decade. After the war, New York filmmakers would show Hollywood the advantages of avoiding so manipulated a mise-en-scène. But until then, American films would typically represent New York through little more than a process shot.

Wartime Blackout

Movie attendance would soar during the war years, but no one in Hollywood had predicted this sort of benefit in 1939. Instead, the first thing producers began to prepare for was the expected collapse of the European market. With such a large percentage of the international gross coming from Germany and France, budgets were reduced to account for the projected loss of revenue. Stories and even stars whose core appeal was thought to be essentially European were now considered potentially risky. Unfortunately, the films most frequently produced in New York were the ones most seriously affected. The first genre to suffer was the Yiddish film, a significant part of the New York feature film business since the mid-1930s. Even as Maurice Schwartz was putting the finishing touches on *Tevya* in September 1939, the *Times* reported that the studio in which he was working, the Biograph, was closing because of "curtailment of the activities of independent producers because of the European war," code for the collapse of the international Yiddish film market.[13] The few subsequent Yiddish pictures, like Edgar G. Ulmer's *American Matchmaker* (1940), were now aimed primarily at a domestic audience.

The production of both Yiddish films and race movies, another major component of New York's local film industry, was effectively eliminated by government decree in 1942. When rationing of 35 mm film stock came into effect that year, the major producers were able to protect their own operations at the expense of independents serving marginal audiences. "Producers who make pictures on speculation, without definite release arrangements, makers of road show features for small theaters, of dialect films, negro pictures with colored casts and the like, will get no more 35 mm film under conservation orders of the WPB," Lowell Mellett of the War Production Board decreed.[14] Hollywood studios were ordered to restrict their purchases to prewar levels, but these niche producers were simply put out of business for the duration.

Less obvious, but with tremendous long-range impact on the future of New York production, was another dictate issued by the War Production Board that placed a $5,000 cap on the cost of new construction materials used on any single set.[15] This handicapped independent producers and favored studios whose back lots contained acres of standing sets representing everything from Southern plantations to Brooklyn brownstones. There were no such back lots in the east. And when an elaborate interior setting was created at Universal or MGM, the windows, doorframes, staircases, and furnishings could be taken apart and stored for reuse in vast scenic warehouses. New York had very few of those, either. Consequently, Hollywood studios were able to build "new" sets simply by creative reuse of the old ones, giving them a significant head start when confronted with the same $5,000 budget cap.

Although a surprising number of inexpensive musical shorts continued to be produced locally, the only feature-length theatrical film known to have been shot entirely in the New York area during the war was *Follies Girl*. This low-budget independent production, little more than a compendium of musical numbers and comedy routines wrapped around a flimsy wartime romantic plot, stands as a link between New York's indigenous prewar and postwar feature film industries. It was produced and directed by William Rowland at Ideal Sound Studios in Hudson Heights, New Jersey, in October 1942, with other sequences "shot at night spots in New York."[16] Where a Hollywood musical would make use of talent already under contract, Rowland brought in a mix of local performers recruited from those same theaters and night spots, including the band leader Ray Heatherton, the musical comedy star Doris Nolan, and the modern dance pioneer Charles Weidman—who can be identified in the film but receives no screen credit.[17] Confronted with the War Production Board's materiel restrictions, Rowland appears to have taken full advantage of existing theatrical locations, spending well under $5,000 each on the few threadbare studio sets built at Ideal. The staging of one musical number consists of two characters sitting in a car and smoking while they listen to a song over the radio. In another number, Fritzi Scheff, a popular musical performer of the World War I era, entertains GIs at the "Broadway Swing Canteen" by singing "I Knew Your Father, Son," accompanied by a montage of newsreel footage that runs from the Great War up to the era of Chiang Kai-shek and

Joseph Stalin. Although *Motion Picture Daily* praised *Follies Girl* as "an ambitious effort at a smart musical production," it also criticized an overall lack of "cohesive continuity."[18]

An innovative low-budget producer whose prewar New York musicals included both *Moonlight and Pretzels* (1933) and *Sweet Surrender* (1935), Rowland understood that filmmaking in New York was intimately connected with the rest of the local entertainment industry, especially radio broadcasting and Broadway. So to make *Follies Girl* he covered as many bases as possible by partnering with Donald Flamm, the former managing director of radio station WMCA, and W. Horace Schmidlapp, a wealthy young investor from Cincinnati who had recently taken an interest in bankrolling Broadway musicals.[19] They called their new operation Associated Producers, Inc. and immediately sold their first feature to an appropriately low-end Hollywood distributor, Producers Releasing Corporation.[20]

Rowland soon picked up his career in Hollywood (and Mexico), but Horace Schmidlapp decided he liked producing movies in New York. After leaving his day job at Chase Bank's foreign division, he had begun investing in Broadway shows in 1939. He was one of many backers to profit from *Cabin in the Sky* (1940), and his production of Cole Porter's *Let's Face It* (1941–1943) ran for 547 performances. But Schmidlapp was not just another playboy investor; he had been operating a successful "commercial" film studio, making industrials and other sponsored films, even before joining Associated Producers. Along with two film industry veterans, Leon Leventhal and Stanley Neal, he had incorporated Associated Filmakers as early as September 1941, suggesting that his later partnership with Rowland was to some degree an outgrowth of his existing industrial film operation.[21] Yet the glamour of working on *Follies Girl* was obviously more appealing than supervising the production of industrial films. Associated typically rented stage space at the Fox Movietone studio, where *Follies Girl* originally hoped to shoot. But as soon as work on the feature wrapped—in New Jersey—local trade papers announced that Associated would be expanding into a studio of its own.[22]

In March 1944 Associated Filmakers released through Astor a forty-nine-minute film called *The Meadville Patriot*, directed by another sponsored film veteran, B. K. Blake. Although three of the actors were carried over from *Follies Girl*, including Cora Witherspoon and Gordon Oliver, the film was not a musical but a conventional melodrama about a big-city reporter who takes over a small-town newspaper.[23] Inserts of newspaper headlines shown in the film are all dated April or May 1942, suggesting that *The Meadville Patriot* might never have been intended for theatrical release at all and had instead been filmed much earlier and targeted at an entirely different market.

A 1945 article in *Film Daily* makes no mention of Associated Filmakers having produced anything but sponsored films (eighty of them, in fact) and notes that it is currently working on three full-length features "for commercial firms."[24] There are a few examples of feature-length industrial pictures being released into the theatrical market—like *The Middleton Family at the New York World's Fair* (1939), an extended commercial for Westinghouse—but what client would have commissioned *The Meadville Patriot*? When Gordon Oliver arrives in Meadville to take over its local newspaper he soon finds himself at odds with a coterie of old women, censorious puritans who pressure him to support their prohibition crusade. Although the Twenty-First Amendment had repealed federal prohibition in 1933, ten states had either voted against repeal or continued to enforce their own prohibition statutes. A decade later the "liquor interests" were still fighting this battle, and they or their allies could easily have fostered the production of *The Meadville Patriot*, hoping to circulate it in those states still debating the issue of repeal. Indeed, the only review I was able to locate dismisses the film as "more a preachment against prohibition than anything else."[25] But for its national advertising campaign in 1944 Astor bypassed the liquor angle and tied the film to Roosevelt's more popular "Four Freedoms" campaign ("Freedom of the Press Was More Than a Phrase to This Country Editor").[26] Desperate for product, Astor was happy to put anything new on the screen, even if they had to repurpose a "wet" promotional film as a theatrical feature to do so.

The "Broadway Swing Canteen" referred to in *Follies Girl* was modeled on the American Theater Wing's "Stage Door Canteen," which had opened in the basement of the Forty-Fourth Street Theater in March 1942. Frank Borzage began filming *Stage Door Canteen* in Hollywood in December 1942 on a detailed reproduction of the forty- by eighty-foot club. But five weeks later the production moved to New York—not to shoot at the actual club ("because of lighting difficulties") but to work at an identical recreation built at the Fox Movietone studio at Tenth Avenue and Fifty-Fourth Street. "The trek to Manhattan was necessary to shoot sequences in which Broadway figures such as Katherine Cornell, Tallulah Bankhead, Alfred Lunt and Lynne Fontanne, Helen Hayes, Gertrude Lawrence, Dorothy Stickney and Ilka Chase will appear."[27] Steve E. Fitzgibbon, manager of the studio, was still using the production of this film to drum up business in the summer of 1944 when he announced plans for construction of a third sound stage, "which will start going up after the war."[28]

Despite rare exceptions like these, one would expect that restrictions on travel and transportation would limit New York's appearance on wartime screens to a series of stock shots, a trend which was already in place during the 1930s. Conventional wisdom has it that producers were forced onto their back lots, not only to make better use of those standing sets but because of the logistical problems of extensive location shoots. For example, Carlo Gaberscek's detailed examination of location sites used for the filming of American westerns shows that wartime production in places like Arizona, New Mexico, and Colorado dropped to almost zero after Pearl Harbor. Westerns were still being made but on less picturesque locations a lot closer to Hollywood.[29]

But there was another side to this coin, the side that limited the amount of money that could be spent on set construction. Once filmmakers grew tired of rearranging the studio's standing sets, some degree of filming on location began to seem like a reasonable option. Far-flung locations would still be off-limits, but even a trip to downtown Los Angeles was still a location shoot, often requiring busloads of actors and trucks full of technical apparatus. One location that would stand to benefit from this realization was New York, which had structural advantages that made it far more attractive than Arizona or New Mexico.

The first "Hollywood" film to do any principal photography in New York after December 7 was *Tarzan's New York Adventure* (originally *Tarzan Against the World*), for which traffic on the Brooklyn Bridge was tied up for an entire morning in early January.[30] When Boy is kidnapped, Tarzan and Jane track him to New York, only to find he is being forced to work as an elephant wrangler for a circus. Johnny Weissmuller is clearly established at the bridge, and in a nicely staged scene we see him (and his stunt double) evade the NYPD as Tarzan makes a spectacular dive into the East River. The film contains plenty of New York back projection, but the money shot here looks at least as good as a newsreel.

Twentieth Century Fox sent director Irving Pichel to New York in July 1942 to film location scenes for *Life Begins at Eight-Thirty*—not just back-projection plates but scenes with the principal actors, Monty Woolley and Ida Lupino.[31] Pichel did not need to bring along his own extras, nor did he need to drag in truckloads of studio apparatus from Hollywood. Instead, he simply hired New York crews and local Fox cinematographer Larry Williams. They shot their exteriors, mainly around East Fifty-Second Street and near the Queensboro Bridge, and went back to Hollywood. Unfortunately, by the time the film was released nearly all of this footage had disappeared. Monty Woolley, as a washed-up ham reduced to playing Santa Claus at the "Marcy Herald Square" store—a role once envisioned for John Barrymore—does his best to carry the film with a string of acidulous insults. Channeling his trademark *Man Who Came to Dinner* performance, Woolley taunts a waiting crowd with a sneering chorus of "How I hate you, one and all!" But what could have been a sharp-tongued precursor to *Miracle on 34th Street* then goes straight downhill, trapped in a few small studio interiors. Woolley finally leaves his apartment and walks out into the city (two shots, maybe), but by then the film is just about over. One or two well-placed location exteriors might have relieved the film's air of claustrophobia, but whoever was responsible for assembling *Life Begins at Eight-Thirty* had not yet learned the lesson George Seaton would demonstrate so clearly only a few years later.

From Hitchcock to Wilder

Producers now had to decide if the added value of location filming—increased realism plus reduced set-construction costs—might offset some of its associated headaches. But whatever the economic benefits, leaving the studio would have a lasting effect on American films and filmmakers. Alfred Hitchcock, for example, was already well known for his extensive use of studio settings and special-effects technology, a tendency that had only increased on his arrival in Hollywood. But *Shadow of a Doubt*, the first film he put into production after the announcement of the War Production Board's materiel restrictions, sent him off in a new direction. "Right from its original conception," Hitchcock's friend and biographer John Russell Taylor would write, "*Shadow of a Doubt* was built on a principle new to Hitch's American films, and indeed new to his sound films altogether—that of detailed location realism."[32] The decision had aesthetic consequences as well as economic benefits. "With the government limit on new sets," the *New York Times* reported, "Hitch was virtually forced out into the open." Four weeks of this location shooting took place in Santa Rosa, California, which was not just a convenient small town but one that had been "cast" by Hitchcock and his writer, Thornton Wilder, during preproduction. The anonymous *Times* reporter immediately connected this style of shooting with silent film technique:

> Hitchcock soon discovered advantages in this older and more informal method of making a film, for it offered opportunities that could never have occurred within the well-guarded gates of a modern Hollywood studio. There was a wider latitude for the extemporaneous, for the impromptu touch; even the accidental sometimes found itself accepted.[33]

Shadow of a Doubt not only can serve as a model for postwar location shooting in cities like New York (sometimes by Hitchcock himself) but also should be recognized as one of the earliest wartime films to do some of its own filming there. The opening scenes of the film, where "Uncle Charlie" escapes from two detectives who have been shadowing him, were shot there by Hitchcock in August 1942, even before Joseph Cotten had been cast in the role. "For the atmospheric opening shot of the Pulaski Skyway over the Hackensack River, Hitchcock dressed a couple of neighborhood factory workers as bums sitting on a dock in the foreground," George Turner wrote in *American Cinematographer*. "The scene was filmed on an old residential street in Newark, with another actor doubling for Cotten in the long shots. Wooden dolly tracks were quickly knocked together and silvered light reflectors of the kind used on Western locations served as boosters."[34] The *Times* highlighted Hitchcock's development of an improvisational style, describing his incorporation of a gang of kids he found playing ball in a Newark street, or a tricky shot, taken in a Manhattan parking lot, with the action framed between the shoes of a sleeping "Uncle Charlie" (ultimately not used here, but the idea was saved for similar effect in *The Trouble with Harry*).[35]

For *Saboteur*, shot before the War Production Board's edict, Hitchcock had famously assembled his climax from a montage of back projections, matte work, and studio photography on full-scale mock-ups of the Statue of Liberty (or at least its head and arm). But Bill Krohn reminds us that crucial to making audiences accept this fanciful concoction was a simple piece of establishing footage that could only be shot in New York. "Norman Lloyd, who had been hired to play [Frank] Fry on the basis of a screen test made while he was still in New York, was filmed by [John] Fulton's second-unit crew before the start of production going up the steps to the real statue, followed by a double for Priscilla Lane's Pat."[36] With the statue rising prominently in the background, Lloyd turns his head and looks directly at the camera so we can be sure to see that he is really there.

In addition, Lloyd is also visible very briefly in the crowd outside Radio City Music Hall and while traveling on and exiting from the Statue of Liberty ferry. All these shots are remarkably brief, as if Hitchcock wanted to keep the use of Fulton's location footage to an absolute minimum. For example, a quick flash of Lloyd on the actual ferry, his hair blowing wildly in the wind (he seems to be the only man without a hat) is immediately followed by a far less windblown close-up of Lloyd in front of a studio back projection.[37]

Nothing accidental or impromptu here, but it is interesting to see the progression from *Saboteur*'s use of location photography as one element of an overdetermined mise-en-scène to *Shadow of a Doubt*'s reliance on the real world—whether Santa Rosa or Newark—as the core around which a new kind of Hollywood movie might be constructed. (But only the core: Hitchcock still had a full-scale replica of the main Santa Rosa location constructed back at the studio.)[38]

The best remembered (and least understood) wartime location shoot involved Billy Wilder's *The Lost Weekend*, a hard film to sell that Paramount decided to promote on the strength of its "realism." Part of this involved publicizing the crew's New York location trip, where Ray Milland was filmed wandering along Third Avenue, outside Bellevue Hospital, and opposite the Church of St. Agnes at 143 East Forty-Third Street. Billy Wilder had previously shot parts of *Double Indemnity* at various locations around Los Angeles, so he was

1.1. Ray Milland, photographed on Third Avenue near 103rd Street, for *The Lost Weekend*. October 1946. No hidden cameras. Bison Archives.

familiar with the benefits of getting away from the back lot. In fact, he had employed that innovative filming style on his earliest European films, *Menschen am Sonntag* (1929) and *Mauvaise Graine* (1934). But in his detailed account of the production, Ed Sikov notes that the actual number of shooting days in New York was quite small—only about nine working days over the period October 1–15, 1944, and on several of these days the company was only able to make one or two usable shots.[39]

The most memorable sequence in the film is a three-minute segment in which Milland, trying to raise enough money for a bottle of rye, staggers along Third Avenue with his typewriter, searching for an open pawn shop. After walking, apparently, for miles, he is finally told that the shops are all closed because of Yom Kippur. In fact, there are only four or five shots of Milland in this sequence that actually show him on Third Avenue, and even those were difficult to get. Local cameraman Bill Kelly was operating for John F. Seitz, the director of photography brought in from Hollywood. "To get the shots of Ray Milland wandering up Third Avenue in the pawn shop sequence, the camera was set up before dawn in a large packing case with an aperture [sic] for the lens. Knocks on the case would tip off Kelly when Milland was coming within camera range."[40] All the shots of Milland trudging toward the camera were taken before a back-projection screen in Hollywood. All the shots containing dialogue were photographed on sets built on the Paramount lot, including the bit where he learns the date of Yom Kippur; the reverse angle there shows Milland in front of another back projection. Numerous POV shots of various building facades and a montage of street signs documenting his progress fill out the sequence. As soon as the New York locations had been selected, construction crews back in California began to rebuild two representative blocks on the Paramount lot, intending to "match the area near 55th Street, between 2nd and 3rd Avenues, in New York, described in the book, and including Don Birnam's apartment house, the rear garden, shops, Sam's Saloon and Geraghty's Liquor Store."[41] The sets are well built, but the California lighting on these "Third Avenue" inserts simply does not match the footage shot in New York.

Nonetheless, the episode is so skillfully cut together that audiences at the time reacted to the scene as if it had come out of a newsreel. The film's other major location episode, in which Milland is seen emerging from Bellevue at dawn, climbing the steps of an elevated station, and eventually entering a liquor store on Forty-Third Street, has much less process work but far more documentary flavor.[42] Great care seems to have been taken with the photography here. Ed Sikov notes, "Light was an enormous problem. The dawn sequences really had to be shot at dawn, which means that even under the best conditions only an hour or so of work could possibly be done."[43] These were the shots—impossible to obtain on even the most detailed back-lot setting—that would justify the entire trip.

All in all, the difference between Ray Milland's New York in *The Lost Weekend* and Spencer Tracy's New York in *Man's Castle*, is only about a dozen shots of the principal actor actually filmed in Manhattan. But it was enough. Tom Wood and Gene Phillips, otherwise conscientious Wilder biographers, both write that close to one-third of the picture was filmed there. Maurice Zolotow, a Hollywood journalist whose colorful biography usually takes Wilder's claims at face value, concluded that "most of it was shot on location in New York." Zolotow, overcome by enthusiasm, also says that the film begins with "helicopter shots of Manhattan" and a "zoom in to a whiskey bottle."[44] However, these technologies were not in use in 1944. Even Ed Sikov writes that Wilder insisted on "no back lot New York street scenes, no generic Hollywood sets."[45] Many biographies focus on the same stories of hidden-camera photography originally sent out by Paramount's press office. Milland's walk up Third Avenue, Zolotow tells us, "*was filmed in a single day with the actor actually walking all that time, while a camera, concealed in a bakery truck, followed him.*"[46] Stories like this suggest some sort of extended Wellesian tracking shot that is completely unlike anything we see in the film.

The last wartime film to take advantage of New York locations in this way was not a visitor from Hollywood but a transplant from England's Denham studios: Michael Powell and Emeric Pressburger's *A Canterbury Tale*. The film told the story of an American GI in England who discovers the shared values underpinning Anglo-American culture while retracing the route of Chaucer's pilgrims. Powell and Pressburger cast John Sweet, an American army sergeant with no professional experience whom they had seen in a GI production of *The Eve of St. Mark*.[47] Blending mystical nationalism with a curious dose of slapstick comedy, the film was rejected by critics and audiences when it opened in London in May 1944. One year later, Powell and Pressburger were in America trying to cast their next film, *A Matter of Life and Death*, while still looking for someone to distribute *A Canterbury Tale* there. Although the Production Code Administration gave the film a Code Seal, contingent on "deletion of all profanity and references to marijuana," there were still no takers.[48]

In Hollywood, Alfred Hitchcock had introduced Powell to Kim Hunter, who would not only star in the new film but also, in a flash of inspiration, be used to help update and "Americanize" a fresh version of *A Canterbury Tale*.[49] A frame story would be created to help postwar American audiences connect with the

1.2. Sgt. John Sweet working with Kim Hunter's stand-in atop 30 Rockefeller Center. Location footage for the American version of *A Canterbury Tale*. August 1945. Frame enlargement.

old film, which would now begin in America, atop the observation deck at Rockefeller Center, where the demobilized GI would begin to tell his new bride of the wonders he experienced during his pilgrimage. More new scenes would be shot in a recreation of the "Canterbury Tea Room" set at Denham. Sgt. Sweet was still in England in July 1945 and shot the tea room scenes there with Kim Hunter. The pair also shot key footage for the opening sequence on "a mock-up of the railings at the top of Rockefeller Center." Sweet was discharged from the military and returned to New York, where he appeared in establishing shots taken atop the real 30 Rock later that summer.[50] The effect is completely convincing, all the more remarkable because the woman in the scene is not Kim Hunter (who was still working on *A Matter of Life and Death*) but a New York extra wearing the same clothes and hat.[51]

It seems that the idea for remaking the film in this manner only occurred to Powell and Pressburger in Hollywood after they failed to sell the Americans their original version. But what else did Hitchcock tell his friend Mickey Powell? Did they talk about *Saboteur* and how Rockefeller Center was an iconic part of New York not yet overexposed as a film location? Movie magic allowed Hitchcock to leave Priscilla Lane at home while filming only Norman Lloyd in New York, a lesson Powell could duplicate with John Sweet (and just as Hitchcock stayed home, leaving the location work to John Fulton, Michael Powell would turn over those chores to Jock Laurence).[52] But even Hitchcock had not used the observation deck, which, if only briefly, makes its first screen appearance in *A Canterbury Tale* years before its "discovery" in *On the Town* and a host of subsequent New York location films.[53]

Of course, the bulk of Hollywood's wartime "New York" films, from RKO's *Cat People* to Universal's *Lady on a Train*, would never take the time and trouble to send any of their stars to New York for the benefit of local color. Prewar practice discouraged the idea, and melodramatic thrillers like these hardly seemed to call for the dose of realism Billy Wilder picked up on Third Avenue. Universal did have a crew, and an extra dressed as Deanna Durbin, film scenes along the New York Central tracks on Upper Park Avenue for *Lady on a Train*. But the effect of Durbin, gamely trying to keep pace with the back projection as she shuffles along on a treadmill back in California, is laughable. MGM spent a lot more money on *The Clock*, but despite New York's central role in this important boy-meets-girl romance it saw no need to send its stars there, even for a few days. Simply announcing to the press that 30 percent of the film had been shot in New York seemed good enough.[54] *The Clock* incorporates a massive amount of back projection and—now that set construction limitations had been lifted—the first of a series of colossal MGM reproductions of New York landmarks. According to James Sanders, whose *Celluloid Skyline* exhaustively documents the history of Hollywood's back lot New York, the Pennsylvania Station set alone cost $66,450.[55] Scenes of Central Park and the Metropolitan Museum of

Art are created through an artful blend of editing, studio recreations, and the photography of doubles standing in at the real spots. In one audacious long take, the real Judy Garland and Robert Walker sit atop the mock-up of a Fifth Avenue double-decker bus as the back projection behind them unspools a panorama of the west side of the Avenue, from Wallach's department store on Forty-Fourth Street to the University Club on Fifty-Fourth. MGM did its best to cue dialogue references to Radio City and St. Patrick's Cathedral at appropriate intervals, but for native New Yorkers the effect carries about the same level of authenticity as the "train ride" enjoyed by Louis Jourdan and Joan Fontaine in *Letter from an Unknown Woman* would for the Viennese. The director Vincente Minnelli, whose cinematic "New York of the imagination" would later include such hothouse creations as *The Band Wagon* and *Bells Are Ringing*, probably did not lose any sleep over this.

Back in New York, crews from Local 644, the union representing motion picture cameramen, continued to film required location footage to order. Each studio maintained a short list of preferred talent, with Bill Kelly generally on call for Paramount, Warner Bros., and the larger independents, like Selznick or Goldwyn. Larry Williams, who had worked on *Life Begins at Eight-Thirty*, still had the Twentieth Century-Fox franchise. Bill Miller shot Universal's New York footage, while MGM favored Charles Harten. George Webber and Don Malkames picked up whatever business remained. Because only first cameramen received screen credit, and all first cameramen on Hollywood productions belonged to the West Coast Local, none of this work was ever officially credited.

This was a trade union issue intended to protect at least some New York jobs. In order to allow John Seitz and the *Lost Weekend* crew to work in their jurisdiction, Local 644 insisted that one of their own men, in this case Bill Kelly, also be put on at full first cameraman's salary (the Hollywood Local was even more exclusive and far more powerful). Sometimes this man would simply stand by, with little or nothing to do. In the case of *The Lost Weekend*, Kelly functioned as camera operator—locked inside that crate—but at the higher salary. As we have seen, there were very few of these jobs to be had, and most work, as in the days of *Man's Castle*, did not involve the principal actors. Kelly, for example, had been filming such odd bits and pieces as far back as *King Kong*, when he photographed the skyline from the mooring mast of the Empire State Building. For Hunt Stromberg's *Young Widow*, shot in the spring of 1945, Kelly filmed "a subway tunnel sequence with special lights and hundreds of extras while the train continued to repeat its route for the camera," an effect impossible to achieve on a Hollywood "subway" setting.[56]

In October 1945 Kelly was shooting New York footage for *The Sin of Harold Diddlebock*, a Howard Hughes/Preston Sturges production. Neither Sturges nor his star, Harold Lloyd, came to New York for this work, which the *New York Times* reported took eleven weeks. "Kelly received a copy of the script from the West Coast with a detailed outline of the required footage, specifying height, camera angle and other factors, but allowing him sufficient latitude in obtaining his shots."[57] Scenes were shot "around Lafayette Street" and a ten-foot platform was constructed outside the twentieth floor of 61 Wall Street as a vantage point.[58] Another eight-foot platform was constructed outside the twenty-second floor of 40 Wall Street, from which "the camera was swung on a twelve-foot pendulum to photograph the street crowds supposedly gaping up at Lloyd." Because New Yorkers refused to gape on cue, 150 extras were hired to do the job.[59]

More interesting was John Berry's *From This Day Forward*, an almost nostalgic look back at the hardships of working-class life in Depression-era New York, for which second-unit material was shot there that fall. The adaptation of a 1938 proletarian novel by Thomas Bell, it was updated with a postwar frame story set in a veterans' employment office, a ploy that hardly disguises its (by then unfashionable) examination of urban tenement life.[60] Although one critic claims that Berry "shot the film on location and in the studio in New York," this is clearly not the case.[61] There doesn't appear to be any principal location photography in the film, but there are three separate visits to the High Bridge in the Bronx, where the main characters enjoy several significant interludes; long shots are filmed with doubles, and the stars appear only in closer shots staged in Hollywood. The oldest bridge in New York, High Bridge was still a functioning part of the Croton Aqueduct system in 1945, as well as a popular esplanade for local residents (the characters live on East 189th Street). At the film's climax, Joan Fontaine and Mark Stevens embrace a shared vision of their working-class future while a spectacular trick shot ascends to the heavens, leaving the audience with an impressive view of the century-old Harlem River span. *From This Day Forward* treats it with the sort of reverence usually reserved only for the Brooklyn Bridge.

Just Visiting? Or Here to Stay?

By 1945 Fiorello La Guardia would have been able to recognize several distinct categories of "New York" movies, which we can differentiate by how they used their actors and recorded their sound. The gold standard would be a film shot and recorded entirely in and around New York—interiors as well as exteriors—with a local creative team both before and behind the camera. Until the early 1930s such films were not uncommon, but recent examples (think *Follies Girl*) had been rare and not especially inspiring. It seems unlikely that even La Guardia, looking at a film like that, could have imagined local crews producing *12 Angry Men*, *Splendor in the Grass*, or *The Miracle Worker*, much less the wave of indigenous production that would mark New York's great filmmaking renaissance of the 1960s and '70s. In retrospect, of course, it is easy to see that the roots of that renaissance were planted in the postwar decade under consideration here and that while independent productions like *Carnegie Hall*, *Guilty Bystander*, and *Killer's Kiss* may not have attracted much attention from critics or audiences, they did succeed in demonstrating that "American Cinema" was not always synonymous with "Hollywood."

But such an ideal still seemed a long way off. The films La Guardia was counting on right now were transient Hollywood productions that might devote just a portion of their budgets to New York location scenes (he had plans to fix the studio problem, but never acted on them). Taxis, hotels, and restaurants would benefit, as would the small number of local personnel lucky enough to be signed on as extras or electricians. Any "New York content" would be decorative at best, as all the creative shots would be called by the same Hollywood minds that had generated the project in the first place. In that case, there would be no need for any indigenous filmmaking infrastructure here—labs, equipment houses, or trained cadres of film workers—because all these visiting producers really wanted was a scenic backdrop: Brooklyn Bridge today and maybe the Golden Gate tomorrow. Like good campers, the West Coast crews would take everything back home with them when they left, leaving nothing behind to alter the landscape.

These "drive-by" productions reflected quite a wide range of commitment on the part of their producers. The most ambitious, like *The House on 92nd Street* or *The Naked City*, spent weeks filming their principal actors in New York and tried to record at least some direct sound there. Less ambitious projects, like *The Lost Weekend* or *Cry of the City*, sent a few actors but didn't bother about a sound crew, either looping these scenes back in Hollywood or avoiding the semblance of direct dialogue altogether. This work generally required only a few location days. The least interesting, especially for anyone looking for some degree of authentic New York content, are those films that sent only a second-unit crew and, at best, a few doubles for the principal actors. *The Clock* and *The Secret Life of Walter Mitty* were done in this fashion, the principal actors working before a virtual New York conjured up on a back-projection screen (when they weren't emoting on the studio's sunbaked "New York Street").

Films like these had little interest in the history and tradition of New York's own filmmaking culture, from which they drew nothing and contributed less. But from the city's point of view—where the number of "permit days" was seen as a quantifiable standard—one shooting day was as good as another. Rebuilding New York's indigenous motion picture industry must have seemed like a pipe dream in 1945, but luring those Hollywood camera crews, with or without their principal cast members, was a goal that actually seemed achievable.

By the end of the year the war was over, and the city had a new mayor. Fiorello La Guardia, the maverick Republican, was feuding with the party establishment, which had nominated the former Democrat Jonah Goldstein (who also appeared on the Liberal-Fusion line). La Guardia created the No Deal party to split the Republican vote by nominating its own Republican, Newbold Morris. This left a clear path for Brig. Gen. William O'Dwyer, currently executive director of the War Refugee Board, but better known to the electorate as the prewar prosecutor responsible for bringing the crime syndicate known as Murder, Inc. to justice. La Guardia had defeated O'Dwyer in the hotly contested 1941 election but was now more interested in sabotaging Republican chances. For his part, O'Dwyer had been using his recent position to good effect within the film community. As early as May 5, the *Motion Picture Herald* referred to him as the "New York mayoral possibility" when describing his meeting with Hollywood producer William Goetz (nominally to discuss support for the Jewish Welfare Fund).[62] In September, when Spyros Skouras and J. Edgar Hoover hosted a VIP screening of *The House on 92nd Street*, O'Dwyer appears to have been the only politician on the guest list, mixing with the likes of Cornelius Vanderbilt Jr., Dorothy Kilgallen, Toots Shor, and Will Hays.[63] O'Dwyer's candidacy also seems to have appealed to the labor vote, with nearly a quarter of his support coming from his presence on the American Labor Party line. In a three-way race, O'Dwyer won 55 percent of the vote. A week after the election, a small group of local filmmakers, sensing a change in the air, held the first organizational meeting of what would become the Screen Directors Guild (not yet affiliated with the similar Hollywood group). At the time, most of them were still directing documentaries and race movies.[64]

Warner Bros. celebrated the New York opening of its big Technicolor western, *San Antonio*, with a "Wild West parade" down Broadway. New York's mayor is sworn in on January 1, but when Warner's cowboys and Indians marched past City Hall on December 28, 1945, one prominent trade paper boasted that *both* the outgoing mayor and mayor-elect were expected to be on hand to greet them.[65] The message was clear: there would be no change in policy regarding the importance of the motion picture industry to the cultural and economic well-being of New York. "Fiorello La Guardia in 1939 lighted a whopper of a candle in New York's window, but the war rained it out," *Film Daily* later reported, weighing the city's success in luring the motion picture industry "back home."[66] Now it would be O'Dwyer's turn.

CHAPTER 2

THE PATHÉ STUDIO

Miniature Hollywood or Just Another False Dawn?

The handful of wartime features shooting in and around New York between 1942 and 1945 displayed nearly the entire range of production strategies to be employed there after the war. The 1930s "back projection only" approach was most spectacularly illustrated in *The Clock*, while *The Lost Weekend* featured the hybrid 1920s style, with a Hollywood crew coming east for just a bit of principal photography. *Follies Girl* continued the prewar New York tradition of an independent production unit pulling together a feature with whatever local resources were available. What did not develop was an integrated full-service studio operation affiliated with one of the major Hollywood producers, a tradition that died when Warner Bros. shut down its Brooklyn studio in 1939. But when postwar labor issues began to affect the operations of Hollywood's own stages this alternative suddenly became a lot more interesting.

The war in the Pacific officially ended on September 2, 1945, but within a few weeks a new war, a labor war, had already broken out in Hollywood. By October 14 the total number of Hollywood studios shut down by labor violence had grown to five. In the day's most violent demonstration, the toll outside the RKO studio was five wounded—four strikers and Maurice Cantion, chief of the studio's private police force.[1] Worse would follow. Jurisdictional disputes between the International Alliance of Theatrical Stage Employees (IATSE) and the Conference of Studio Unions (CSU), on hold for the duration, soon marred Hollywood's hopes for postwar expansion, poisoning labor-management relations on the West Coast for years.

That month the Society of Motion Picture Engineers (SMPE) held its first postwar meeting at the Hotel Pennsylvania on Eighth Avenue. Only a few days after the riot at RKO's Hollywood studio, Ralph B. Austrian, the president of RKO Television Corporation, revealed the parent company's ambitious plans for "a complete motion picture production plant"; incorporating a full complement of state-of-the-art facilities, it would be built not in Hollywood but in Harlem.[2]

RKO had been thinking about a studio in New York for some time and was prepared to act immediately now that wartime building restrictions would finally be relaxed. The current labor war in Hollywood may only have been a coincidence, but it was just the sort of coincidence that would help move this project off the drawing boards. Fourteen months and $1 million later, their new Park Avenue studio at 105 East 106th Street was finally open for business.

The eleven-story building had been constructed in 1928 as an Odd Fellows Temple and then acquired by Diesel Electric in 1932. Its 180- by 200-foot plot allowed ample room for additional construction, and a four-story laboratory annex would go up in 1947. Samuel R. Firestone, who brokered the deal, received a $1,000 prize for "the most ingenious, constructive and beneficial real estate sale of 1945."[3] The Odd Fellows' spacious ballroom was converted into a 90 × 80 × 27 foot sound stage occupying the bulk of the second and third floors; a glass enclosed "sponsor's box" allowed interested parties to observe production from on high. Two smaller sound stages, each 30 × 60 × 18 feet, were available on the fifth floor, and the rest of the building housed dubbing and recording stages, editing suites, film vaults, screening rooms, and executive offices. The building, owned by Pathé Industries, Inc. and formally known as Television Center, Inc., was generally referred to as the Pathé studio. Eight of the floors were leased to RKO Pathé for motion picture studio operations, with most of the remaining space occupied by Pathé Laboratories, another subsidiary. RKO promoted it as "the first vertical studio in the United States," with all studio facilities contained in one multi-story structure (although Fox had built its own vertical studio on West Fifty-Fifth Street in 1920).[4]

Austrian's original announcement contemplated using the studio "for the production of the several series of theater shorts [RKO] is currently making, for the increased production of commercial pictures, for the production of documentary pictures, and for the production of other specialized and varied subjects it has long contemplated making."[5] "Industrial" and "educational" films were highlighted, and Austrian recognized that "the just awakening field of television will require film producing facilities of some magnitude." RKO Pathé News would stay in its old offices at 625 Madison Avenue, and there was no mention at all of feature films, the backbone of Hollywood studio production. The long contemplated "specialized and varied subjects" remained undefined.

It should be noted that RKO Pathé was not the only film producer interested in building a full-service rental studio in New York as soon as the war was over. Associated Filmakers finally announced the future location of their new facility—Mount Vernon, just north of the city—even before Ralph Austrian revealed RKO's plans to the SMPE convention.[6] Horace Schmidlapp had shifted his interests away from musical theater. His last Broadway production was *Polonaise*, an ambitious historical epic based on Chopin's music, which managed 113 performances during the winter of 1945–46 (in the middle of the run he married Hollywood starlet Carole Landis). By then he and his partners had located a site at the intersection of Central and Tuckahoe Avenues in Yonkers, where they planned to spend $350,000 on "the largest studio [complex] outside of Hollywood," a project that would grow to include eight sound stages and a dedicated film laboratory spread over eighteen acres. As with RKO, the plan was to produce sponsored films and make the studio available to "Hollywood companies wishing to shoot scenes in and around New York."[7] In 1946 he organized Colonial Pictures Corp. to make a dozen features here under its own banner, claiming to have raised $3 million to pay for them.

In fact, Colonial hoped to convince members of the Allied States Association of Motion Picture Exhibitors, a loose affiliation of independent theater owners, to put up this money in the form of distribution guarantees.[8] But the Civilian Production Administration, a remnant of wartime industrial policy, suddenly rescinded its prior approval of Colonial's Yonkers studio plans, sending it back for "reconsideration."[9] Despite earlier press accounts indicating that the studio was ready for operation, *Motion Picture Daily* reported in December 1946 that "an investigation shows that the Yonkers N.Y. studio which had figured in early talks concerning the production at present amounts to only a sign on a vacant lot which proclaims that a 'motion picture studio will be erected here.'" That was the same month RKO Pathé held the gala opening of its own New York studio; when combined with news of the vacant lot in Yonkers, press coverage of Colonial's plans suddenly evaporated. The twelve feature pictures were never made, but Associated Filmakers continued in the industrial film business, opening a West Coast office while still listing Yonkers as its "studio address" for several years.[10]

Industry trade papers soon began describing the 106th Street studio as "the brainchild" of Frederic Ullman, Jr., president of RKO Pathé since 1942. In his new state-of-the-art facility (which, unlike most Hollywood studios, would be fully climate controlled), Ullman prepared to centralize and expand short film production, produce sponsored films under contract, and rent out the stages to any available clients. All of this was easier said than done in the postwar era because, even if restrictions on civilian use of crucial materiel had been lifted, there were still no stockpiles available. The opening date was postponed "because the company is facing considerable difficulty in obtaining equipment.

Unable to get cameras, lights, plywood for sets, etc., in the east," RKO Pathé had to strip the West Coast RKO studios. "Most of the equipment is being trucked back to N.Y.," *Variety* reported in July.[11] Failure to open on schedule meant that several likely feature prospects, including *Carnegie Hall* and an untitled James Cagney production, had to go elsewhere. A subsequent opening date of August 1 was also missed.

The studio would not formally open its doors until December 11, 1946. *Motion Picture Daily* cited the average cost for producing an entire feature here as $2,250 a day, yet clients with more limited interests might choose to rent only the big stage ($450 a day) or one of the screening rooms ($9 an hour). Of course, the main reason for building the studio was to house RKO Pathé's own productions, which had outgrown their old building at 35 West Forty-Fifth Street.[12] This meant that even without any rental clients, Ullman would have the studio busy turning out two issues of the RKO Pathé newsreel each week, one *Sportscope* and *This Is America* short every month, and eight *Flicker Flashbacks* every year.[13]

"We had to rip out a $25,000 bowling alley, but we managed to salvage six Wurlitzer organs," Ullman told a reporter from *The New Yorker*. "We set up a studio here in addition to what we have in Hollywood because there wasn't enough available studio space there—plenty of land, but no construction for a long time—and also because New York's the distribution center of the world and has a pool of acting talent second only to Hollywood's. Furthermore, radio performers and stage actors can make a film here and still hold their regular jobs. Some of them are doing that right now."[14]

To another journalist touring the new facility, Ullman admitted, "We won't be able to make a technicolor [sic] musical on our stages . . . but we will be able to provide the space and equipment to make an average full-length feature," a definite shift in corporate thinking since 1945.[15] But the first film shot at the studio, already in production on opening day, was *Mr. Bell*, a thirty-one-minute tribute to the inventor of the telephone. Produced for the Bell centennial by AT&T, it was directed by Richard Fleischer and designed by Albert Johnson, top-flight credits for an industrial film. The studio's resident art director, Howard Saulter, built fourteen sets for the picture, most of them representing Boston in the 1870s. Saulter had been head of the art department at Paramount's Astoria studio in the early 1930s, working on films for Ernst Lubitsch and George Cukor. Fleischer had begun his film career working for Ullman in New York on the *This Is America* and *Flicker Flashbacks* series. His career would later flourish in Hollywood, but at the moment he was just another young director between jobs.

Fleischer and Ullman cast the film with New York stage and radio actors, including Jed Prouty and Taylor Holmes; Raymond Edward Johnson, the host of radio's *Inner Sanctum*, was Bell. Less dependent on voice-overs than conventional dialogue sequences, *Mr. Bell* looks more like a low-budget feature than a typical sponsored or industrial film. Various sequences show Bell as a teacher of the deaf, pitching his invention to investors, and of course summoning Mr. Watson via telephone. A concluding lecture specifically links Bell's personal achievements to the general progress of science. Heavily promoted on the nontheatrical market, the film was broadcast in New York on WNBT television on March 3, 1947.[16] Within a few months Ullman had produced many other industrial films here, including *Where Profit Lies* (for *Pathfinder* Magazine);, *Long Range LORAN* (for the US Navy), *Help Yourself* (for Cities Service), *A Master Is Back* (for US Rubber), and *Energy for Americans* (for the National Confection Association).[17] All this activity was great for young acting talent. Eva Marie Saint, for example, worked in a Chevrolet film in 1948.[18]

For years, many of the Hollywood majors (especially Paramount and Fox) had used their East Coast facilities to produce a range of nonfiction subjects, with biweekly newsreel production as the core. The camera crews, editing rooms, dubbing studios, and archival film vaults already in place for newsreel production were exactly what were needed for sponsored films and documentary releases. While this business model was already in place during the 1920s, the explosion of interest in documentary film during World War II suggested that this would be a growth area in the postwar period. As early as 1945 Ralph Austrian had cited "the great success the Armed Forces experienced with training films" as an influence on the new studio's business plan. Those films had soon gone beyond the original target audience, and theater audiences had come to respect—even look forward to—the new documentaries that came out of the war. In 1941 the Academy of Motion Picture Arts and Sciences even began awarding Oscars for documentary film production. Things would change after 1945, but "documentary style," with its location photography, voice-over narration, and "realistic" subject matter and *mise en scène*, would affect all postwar American films, nonfiction or not.

Frederic Ullman had been a pioneer in the production of theatrical documentaries. In 1933 he and Gilbert Seldes produced *This Is America*, a feature-length compilation documentary drawn largely from Pathé's news film library. His *Flicker Flashbacks* series would later make use of Nickelodeon-era subjects and old news film to "explore nostalgic worlds of fashion, sport, and politics."[19] While rival series, like MGM's *Goofy Movies* shorts, mocked the obsolete styles shown in these films, *Flicker Flashbacks* was less a comedy reel than a historical documentary, a progenitor of such later television series as *The Twentieth Century* (CBS, 1957–1969).

In 1942 RKO had lost its contract to distribute Louis de Rochemont's innovative nonfiction series *The March of Time*. Like every other major producer-distributor, RKO offered theaters a package of features, shorts, cartoons, and newsreels, and Ullman moved to fill the gap in RKO's program by reviving *This Is America* as a monthly short subject reel. Always in the shadow of de Rochemont's groundbreaking series, *This Is America* worked to differentiate itself from *The March of Time*'s focus on big issues and important people, reliance on maps and charts, and stentorian "voice of doom" narration. Instead of Hitler and Roosevelt, the series focused on GIs and blue collar workers, "average Americans" doing their jobs in average American towns. Because there was no concentration on great events, a feature of *The March of Time*, there was no need to restage these events for the cameras or underscore them with attention-getting camera effects. Richard Meran Barsam, one of the few scholars to pay any attention to the series, found both its strengths and weaknesses in this focus on positive, almost clichéd, celebrations of small-town American life.[20]

To be fair, this emphasis changed after the war. Ullman produced films about life on the Bowery (*Street of Shadows*, March 1946), the postwar housing shortage (*No Place Like Home*, May 1946), the rising divorce rate (*Courtship to Courthouse*, July 1946), and Alcoholics Anonymous (*I Am an Alcoholic*, May 1947). Phil Reisman, Jr., who with Jay Bonafield took over the series in 1947, singled out these episodes as models for the sort of "honest" documentary RKO Pathé sought to produce. "Our scripts call for real people doing real things," he wrote in *Film Daily*, an obvious dig at de Rochemont. But just to make it clear, he also insisted that any documentary he made would not be "a film with long hair and dirty fingernails that strives to be Arty by being obscure ... a film that is photographed through the bottom of a beer mug and seven thicknesses of a Navaho blanket ... that has the hell montaged out of it, and then is scored to a musical saw and two guys blowing through opposing ends of one kazoo."[21]

As was the case with most of the studios, business had boomed for RKO during the war, and 1946 continued to show record profits. Dore Schary, a promising young producer, took over as vice-president in charge of production at the Hollywood studio on January 1, 1947, a few weeks after the formal opening of the studio in New York. But theater admissions had already begun to drop, and soon went into free fall. On July 28, the RKO Pathé newsreel operation was sold to Warner Bros., a move which rumor suggested had been in the works for years. Warner Bros. would continue to run the newsreel as Warner Pathé News, working out of the old offices at 625 Madison Avenue. They also acquired most of the key staff and the extensive Pathé film library, but not, however, "Pathe short subjects, commercial films, studio and other activities."[22]

Getting out of the newsreel business just before the bottom fell out proved to be a very well-timed business decision. But much of its postproduction editing, scoring, and dubbing had been carried out at 106th Street, and the studio clearly felt the loss of a steady customer. The Pathé laboratory operation moved up from its longtime home in Bound Brook, New Jersey, but the facility was now too large to justify the production of RKO Pathé's short subject releases and occasional commercial assignments. The immediate infusion of Warner cash certainly helped (Douglas Gomery reports the sale price as $4 million), but new clients had to be found, and they would have to be found in an area not considered when the studio was designed in 1945: feature film production.[23]

Since the 1930s, rental stages in New York and New Jersey would play host to a range of independent producers targeting marginalized audiences ignored by the major studios. Many of these were race movies and Yiddish pictures, but other religious and ethnic groups also produced occasional films. The major difficulty was not getting a film made but reaching its target audience in an efficient and economic manner. One such film was *Citizen Saint*, a biography of the newly canonized Mother Frances Cabrini, which became the first feature film shot at the new Pathé studio. Unlike the typical Hollywood feature of the classic era, it was not aimed at the general public but hoped to find its audience within a very specific niche market. On release, one industry trade paper noted that it "may be suitable for showing before audiences limited to Catholics."[24]

The canonization of Mother Cabrini in 1946 had attracted considerable media attention in the United States, largely because she was the first American citizen so recognized by the Catholic Church. With the enormous box-office success of *The Bells of St. Mary's* clearly in mind, Hollywood studios quickly announced plans to film the story of her life. Clyde Elliott, an independent producer, preemptively seized the market and outmaneuvered Bing Crosby, Bryan Foy, and Edgar G. Ulmer by buying and releasing *The Life and Miracles of Blessed Mother Cabrini*, a documentary-style Italian feature that blended staged recreations of scenes from Mother Cabrini's life, newsreel coverage of her 1938 beatification ceremony, and footage taken at various locations associated with her career, including "the chapel of Mother Cabrini High School [in New York], where Mother Cabrini's body can be seen."[25] The *New York Times* reported that 15,000 people had seen the Italian film during its first two days at the Ambassador Theater, encouraging Elliott to produce "a complete American remake" at a studio on the West Coast.[26]

But on December 16, 1946, *Citizen Saint* went before the cameras at 106th Street, under the direction of Harold Young, once a prolific poverty row director in Hollywood but more recently "one of the directors of the Denes Psychodramatic Theatre, [the] new adult education program at Washington Irving High School."[27] Shooting was completed by January 16 and Elliott announced the film would be ready for exhibition in February. He seems to have brought in his own crew, including a screenwriter, Harold Orlob, and an experienced local cameraman, Don Malkames. The large cast was mainly composed of unknowns (with the exception of a few B-movie veterans, like Jed Prouty and William Harrigan), but Elliott achieved a minor casting coup by finding a small role for Julie Haydon, who had created the role of Laura Wingfield in the original production of *The Glass Menagerie* only a few months earlier. Mother Cabrini was played by Carla Dare, a young actress from Chicago whose main qualification seems to have been her grandmother's personal acquaintance with Cabrini.[28]

Citizen Saint premiered at Constitution Hall in Washington, DC, on April 12, 1947, on a double bill with David Miller's *Seeds of Destiny*.[29] I have found two reviews of this version, one referring to it as "inexcusably inept," and the other as "poorly written, acted and directed [with] little entertainment value for commercial theaters."[30] These are very harsh reviews for a religious picture, and Elliott would later refer to this release as "the rough-cut version."[31] The film was sent back for major surgery, with whole sequences flying in or out, apparently at random. "Available descriptions of the picture's narrative are sketchy," the *American Film Institute Catalog* reports. A fragmentary continuity deposited for censorship purposes with the New York State Motion Picture Division in April describes a series of framing episodes that have little connection to a surviving sixty-four-minute print in the author's collection. *Citizen Saint* appears to have gone back into production in August (apparently in Chicago), adding twenty-three new speaking parts, a focus on the miraculous cure of Peter Smith, and an entire South American episode. These new scenes were inserted into the previous assemblage, which itself consisted of footage from the Italian film that had been intercut with scenes shot at Pathé.[32] Reviews were better, or at least more respectful. Like many such films produced at the margins, *Citizen Saint* has little regard for conventional narrative logic and shifts back and forth among several distinct generic modes, patching its plotline together from at least three separate (and stylistically dissimilar) release versions. Seen today, this might be considered either a bold and innovative collage of fiction and nonfiction styles or, as most of its original reviewers seemed to feel, amateurish and incomprehensible.

David O. Selznick's New York Adventure

Citizen Saint may have been the first feature shot in the new Pathé studio, but any memory of it quickly disappeared from studio publicity. On January 30, 1947, David O. Selznick announced that his next production, *Portrait of Jennie*, would be "filmed entirely in New York" (purportedly "at the insistence of Mayor William O'Dwyer"), 90 percent on exteriors, with all interiors to be shot at the Pathé studio.[33] Selznick had acquired rights to the novel in 1944 but still did not have a script that worked to his satisfaction. No matter. Within a week, Jennifer Jones, Joseph Cotten, and their director, William Dieterle, found themselves in New York, filming in the snow in Central Park. Selznick was attempting to do something almost without parallel: shoot an impressionistic romantic fantasy

2.1. The antirealism of *Portrait of Jennie*: magic and mystery of a New York location. Frame enlargement.

entirely on location, using highly realistic, even "documentary," production techniques. He would shoot the film in New York, he said, "because it will have an atmosphere it won't have here in the studio, thereby improving the quality of the picture immeasurably."³⁴

This was a fine idea, but Selznick and his producing organization were in over their heads. The company had still not recovered from the loss of its longtime production manager, Ray Klune, who had always been the one to cast a sober eye over expenses. Selznick was suing United Artists for refusing to distribute his films, and his wife Irene, another stabilizing force, was in the process of divorcing him over his flagrant affair with Jennifer Jones. Production of *Duel in the Sun* had been bitter and protracted, while *The Paradine Case*, which went before the cameras in December 1946, was regarded by everyone on the lot as a disaster in the making. As an independent producer, Selznick was particularly vulnerable to the wave of strikes that had been sweeping through Hollywood, and now his own contract talent, notably Ingrid Bergman and Alfred Hitchcock, were in open rebellion. On top of all this was the everyday anxiety of supplying the newly formed Selznick Releasing Organization with something to release. "I am on the verge of collapse and not thinking clearly," he wrote in December.³⁵

So the *Portrait of Jennie* company was sent to New York, thousands of miles away from Selznick's supervision, without a workable script, with inadequate location preparation, and with an associate producer, David Hempstead, whom the historian Ronald Haver has characterized as a competent, if unimaginative, alcoholic.[36] Selznick generated his usual barrage of memos, but try as he might, even he could not prevent the wind from blowing and the snow from falling. "The Selznick memos on *Portrait of Jennie* are among the longest and most anguished in his files," Haver wrote. "There is one telegram that unfolds to a length of nearly 8 feet."[37]

For example, New York partisans were proud of the snow that had fallen in Central Park for the first day of shooting—it meant that special-effects crews had no need to throw down an artificial blanket of it.[38] But in Hollywood, headlines read "*Portrait* Trouble in New York," with complaints that "production standards there are not up to Hollywood's norm." Jennifer Jones was suffering, it was reported, because the film was shooting in real snow and ice, while the star was wearing only "a skimpy skirt and lisle hose, a cotton jacket and no hat."[39] Without an experienced location manager, the shooting was dogged by a series of amateurish blunders. "A couple of months ago, somebody took a fancy to a field of daisies in Oldwick, and we made a lot of shots there," Joseph Cotten told one reporter.

> But then the daisies went away, which nobody had thought of, so now the only shots of Oldwick we can use involve a brook there. Then there was a fine old brownstone somebody discovered in Tudor City last winter. Just the kind of thing we needed. But there were a couple of trees in front of the house, and by the time we got around to shooting it, the trees were all in bloom and you couldn't get a good shot of the damned place.[40]

The company began shooting studio interiors on March 10, and in April they went on a location trip to the Graves lighthouse in Boston in search of a hurricane (they were misinformed: hurricane season runs from June through November). By the end of the month Selznick had seen the rushes and suspended shooting for five weeks pending a complete rewrite of the script. In a memo, he complained about production waste and inefficiency—weeks spent waiting for the weather in Boston, tens of thousands of dollars spent on casting and costuming extras in the Central Park scenes ("merely specks in the distance!"). Too late to make any difference, he wrote, "If I can get the time, I will see if we can't get a script that makes sense."[41] What he did not do is suggest moving the production to Hollywood. Whatever the costs, the "atmosphere" seemed worth the effort. Working from the new script, shooting resumed in New York on June 10.[42] Aline MacMahon, who had left for New York at the end of March to play the role of the art dealer, Miss Spinney, would be one of the film's first casualties. Ethel Barrymore took over the part, but Selznick could not swap out Jennifer Jones or Joseph Cotten quite so easily.⁴³

Most commentary on *Portrait of Jennie* takes Selznick's early "90 percent on exteriors" claim at face value and treats the film as some kind of predecessor to *The Naked City* (which came into town just as *Portrait of Jennie* was wrapping up). But *The Naked City* built no sets in New York, while Selznick's film shot for weeks at Pathé on settings designed by Joseph Platt and built by William Saulter's technical crews. "Three draughtsmen translate the scenic designer's ideas from watercolor sketch to dimensional and constructional drawings. Ten or more scenic artists do the paint job after as many as 15 carpenters and plasterers have completed building," one promotional account boasted.⁴⁴ The most interesting of these sets, from Saulter's perspective, was the artist's studio, but the busiest and most frequently shown off to reporters and visiting celebrities was the Irish bar, which shared the main stage with the mock-up of Miss Spinney's art gallery.⁴⁵ (To people this bar Selznick recruited local character actors like David Wayne and Albert Sharpe, borrowed from the cast of *Finian's Rainbow*.) "This bar came from a place on Second Avenue, and we're going to take it back to Hollywood with us," one of the prop men boasted. But as usual in New York, there were problems. "The big picture over the bar is supposed to be Michael Collins, the Irish patriot. Now that we got the thing in all kinds of scenes, it turns out the painter made Collins look like Stalin. Wouldn't that kill you?"⁴⁶

Selznick could only carp and complain. He hated the rushes, damning the photography as "wretched beyond words."⁴⁷ But director William Dieterle knew exactly what was happening. "The camera technique is changing," he told a reporter on the set. "Don't shoot for the moon. Just take it so I don't know there's a camera."⁴⁸ Cinematographer Joseph August had previously worked with Dieterle on *All That Money Can Buy*, another hard-to-handle fantasy with supernatural overtones. But during the war he had been shooting documentaries for the Navy, and then went straight into John Ford's remarkable *They Were Expendable*, an elegiac war movie that mixed dramatic and documentary camera technique in the new postwar style. He was looking forward, trying to find another new blend of styles, while Selznick was still thinking in terms of prewar photography. August would be nominated for an Oscar for his work on *Portrait of Jennie*—losing to *The Naked City*.

Dieterle complained that he couldn't stomach the food in New York, so he had his mother fly in three home-cooked meals a day from Beverly Hills (or at least that's what the *Wall Street Journal* reported).⁴⁹ "But I suffer with pleasure making picture in New York," he told another reporter, who did his best to suggest the German-born director's shaky command of English. "Here is the new talent, the new faces—excitement. The last picture, we had to put games on the set, so the actors wouldn't go away and get lost. Here, they love to stay on the set. And the backgrounds we get in New York could never be duplicated in Hollywood. All the money Hollywood has couldn't build Central Park."[50] Central Park, the irreplaceable centerpiece of *Portrait of Jennie*, would always be the major factor in everything that was said about the picture, good or bad.

By midsummer the company thought they were finished in New York and went back to the coast, where they rebuilt some of the sets, including the bar, in Culver City.[51] Selznick continued to add new scenes and retake the old ones. Joe August, now accustomed to working in the air-conditioned New York studio, had trouble readjusting to Hollywood conditions. On September 25, 1947, he left the set to visit the production office, "where he complained of the heat and a moment later toppled to the floor."[52] Filming continued for a full year after his death, off and on, but August still received sole screen credit (and a posthumous Oscar nomination).

Portrait of Jennie opened in Los Angeles on Christmas Day, 1948, and proved a financial disaster, losing nearly all of Selznick's $4 million investment. Typically described as Selznick's last "Hollywood" production, it was the New York element that would be blamed for its fatal cost overruns. David Hempstead, who had supervised the New York shoot, felt the locations alone had "justified the trek" but that New York "will remain little more than a location site to Hollywood producers" unless stage space and support facilities were brought up to Hollywood standards.[53] In fact, it was Selznick's own lack of preparation, not any deficiency in technical resources, which would sink the picture—that, and the essentially unfilmable nature of the original material. Impossible for audiences to swallow, mysterious, beautiful, and stuffed with a remarkable amount of pretentious hokum, it was just the sort of film that Selznick must have known would never make money. "The movie seeks to invoke the dreamy, creepy context of 'another kind of distance' to conceal its gulfs in narrative credibility," David Thomson writes. He suggests, and I would agree, that it might have worked better as a silent picture, or in a foreign language, with subtitles.[54]

When Selznick originally came to New York he was said to have taken an option for three additional features at Pathé. He never made the films, but he certainly stayed long enough. "We came here from the Coast expecting to stay six weeks, and now we're in the sixth month," Joseph Cotten told *The New Yorker* in July. Pathé must have been delighted to have every inch of space booked for most of 1947, but their other customers found themselves locked out as *Portrait of Jennie* hogged the stages. In March, and again in May, the trades reported that *Close-Up*, a feature produced by one of Pathé's subsidiaries, would shoot at 106th Street—but with stages occupied indefinitely by Selznick, space had to be rented elsewhere.[55] *Motion Picture Daily* reported on May 29 that Edward A. Golden would produce *Texas, Brooklyn and Heaven* at New York's Pathé studio, but that film also had to relocate—to Hollywood.[56] The biggest impact, of course, was on the studio's projected core business, the production of shorts and industrials. "Realizing the great business potential of the commercial film Pathé builds a nice, modern plant where quality pictures can be turned out, and what happens?" asked Sumner Lyon, who made his living writing such films. "Eastward flows the tide of Hollywood feature production units. Selznick moves into the studio for his *Portrait of Jenny* [sic]."[57]

Silence Is Golden

One film that got in under the wire was *Man About Town*, the "English version" of René Clair's *Le Silence est d'or*. Distributors of foreign language films had long hoped to crack the distribution barrier created by dubbing and subtitling, strategies that had never been embraced by American audiences. In a "frankly experimental" move, RKO-Pathé Cinema now decided to explore the potential of "bilingual pictures and special versions prepared for the American public" and chose Clair's film as the test case.[58] A romantic comedy that recreated the early days of French cinema, it brought Maurice Chevalier back to the screen after a long absence and was Clair's first French film in over a decade.

Screenwriter Robert Pirosh, who had worked with Clair in Hollywood on *I Married a Witch* (1942), was sent to Paris to collaborate on a script that could serve as the template for a true bilingual production. It was not uncommon in smaller export markets for foreign-language films to be released in narrated versions, where the original dialogue remained but was overlaid with an additional soundtrack that provided both commentary and translation (Clair referred to its use here as "verbal subtitling").[59] But this approach was nearly unknown in the United States. Sacha Guitry's *Le Roman d'un tricheur* (1936) might have been an inspiration, but in that film the actors never speak and the narrator does *all* the talking. *Le Silence est d'or/Man About Town* would be far more ambitious.

Clair finished principal photography in Paris in January 1947, building in long pauses designed to accommodate a spoken voice-over, and shooting as many as one hundred "special takes" to facilitate the English version. At a press screening in Paris of the French-language version in May, Clair seemed happy with the idea, announcing that "an experimental type of English narration will be used" to avoid conventional dubbing or subtitling in English language markets.[60] To complete this version, Pirosh had come to the Pathé studio in New York at the end of March, where he directed Chevalier in a special prologue sequence and supervised his recording of the narration (his credit reads "Associate in Production and English Adaptation").[61] William Saulter constructed a large set representing a theatrical stage and proscenium, with segments of a pit orchestra and auditorium. "Pathé carpenters and painters began construction on a complete theatre interior for *Man About Town* on [a] Friday. By Monday morning tests were made, and cameras were turning on Chevalier early Tuesday."[62]

After the RKO logo and credits, Chevalier strides onto this set as if he were performing his popular stage act—which is how he was then best known to American audiences. In his trademark style he sings "Place Pigalle" and announces that "it's a great pleasure to appear before you again and to present my latest film." The film will be in French, but the audience needn't worry because "love is the universal language," and "if at any time you are in the dark, I'll be right here to help you out." A curtain pulls back and *Le Silence est d'or* is projected on screen, with Chevalier still on stage, translating the French credits and desensitizing the audience to the strangeness of it all. As the action begins the English-speaking Chevalier continues as an off-screen voice, a sort of Gallic *benshi* interpreting all the French-language performances, including his own. The original French version ran 106 minutes; the Pirosh version, even with the additional musical number, only ninety (according to *Film Daily*, *Man About Town* was also distributed here in subtitled and conventionally dubbed versions).[63] Clair and Pirosh were both pleased with the results, at least on a technical level. But when they screened the film for audiences they realized that breaking the fourth wall in this manner had "destroyed the illusion of reality" audiences of narrative cinema had come to expect. As Clair wrote in the published edition of his screenplay, "An invisible and omniscient being intervening between the heroes of the film and the spectators seemed to remind the latter, continuously, that what was being presented to them was nothing more than the shadow of a fiction . . . [T]he public understood everything happening on the screen but lost interest in it at the same time."[64]

Philip K. Scheuer, in a supportive review in the *Los Angeles Times*, noted that he had seen both versions of the film and preferred the "pure French" edition. Apparently, so did the management of the Laurel Theater in Los Angeles, which chose to run the French version with conventional English subtitles. "These do not get in the way of the picture as often as the star's bilingual accent did."[65]

The international market had taken on much greater importance in the postwar period, especially in light of the decline in domestic box office. Frederic Ullman spent a considerable amount of time in Europe in 1946, nominally on *This Is America* business, but clearly concerned with other tricky issues of international production and distribution (the Clair project had been funded by blocked RKO export revenues). The sophisticated dubbing and recording studios he installed at 106th Street testify to the importance attached to this business, which was not going to be subcontracted to outside vendors. The RKO Foreign Versions Department, under Raoul De Leon, was ensconced on the seventh floor, and when a *New Yorker* reporter toured the studio in April he was shown not only the Selznick sets but also a dubbing crew preparing the "Mandarin Chinese" version of *King Kong*.[66] When not in use by RKO, a sixty-three- by fifty-two-foot recording studio, also with top-of-the-line RCA equipment, was leased to Capitol Records for commercial recordings of anything up to "full size jazz bands."[67]

Crime on the Streets

When RKO sold off its newsreel operation to Warner Bros. on July 28, 1947, it triggered a major executive shift in the East. Some of the staff was absorbed by Warner Bros., but Ullman decided to move to the West Coast, resigning as president of RKO Pathé, Inc. as of August 9 to work as a producer under Dore Schary.[68] His first project was *The Window*, an adaptation of a Cornell Woolrich story to be filmed in the New York studio. "It is understood that Ullman will employ the same documentary technique in *The Window* that he used during the five years he was turning out the *This Is America* series," the *Times* reported.[69]

Shooting began in New York on November 12 under Ted Tetzlaff, once a cameraman (*Notorious*) but now focusing on direction as part of Schary's scheme to upgrade the studio's B-product and develop new talent. Tetzlaff had entered the business in the last days of silent cinema, a background *American Cinematographer* felt explained his concern that "the visual aspect of moviemaking has not received sufficient attention in recent years." As he put it to Ezra Goodman (another silent film aficionado), "The producers of motion pictures . . . have forgotten the technique of silent films when you had to speak with the camera and tell with pictures what people stand in the middle of the room and talk about today. There is entirely too much dialogue in pictures. The essential, visual principle of the screen is too often neglected. In *The Window*, dialogue will be held to a minimum, sufficient to explain attitudes and the progression of the story."[70]

Bobby Driscoll plays a small boy who sees a murder through a tenement window, but his reputation for tall tales means that no one believes him—except the killers. A taut, nightmarish thriller with no subplots and only a handful of characters, it was an ideal first film for the new producer. Bill Steiner, a local cameraman, and the art directors, Walter Keller and Sam Corso, were prewar veterans of the New York studio system, and the spectacular grubbiness of their settings and locations are impressive, especially when compared to Hollywood's notion of urban working-class family life. The torpor of a 94° day is also well illustrated, despite outdoor filming in New York in November and December.[71] Deserted tenements on East 105th and 116th Streets, right near the studio, provide a children's playground more reminiscent of bombed out sections of London than anything available on a Hollywood back lot.

Scheduled for six weeks, *The Window* wrapped in New York within a month. Ullman announced that RKO had saved a million dollars by shooting there (although "only a fraction of 1 percent of all films" might achieve comparable benefits).[72] As if on cue, Josh Binney showed up as soon as Tetzlaff's sets had been taken down (maybe sooner). He began shooting *Killer Diller*, a Dusty Fletcher/Moms Mabley race movie, on December 15 and finished it in five days. This was not a good omen.[73] The *Window* company returned to Culver City for "a few days' run-through of process shots," special-effects sequences involving a collapsing tenement interior and much flying debris.[74] But when Howard Hughes acquired RKO on May 10 everything at the studio came to a halt.

A few days later, RKO Pathé announced that as of July 1 they were leasing all three of their New York sound stages to NBC "for the expansion of its television facilities," effectively ending any plans of their own for feature film production in New York.[75] Although Mayor William O'Dwyer and his film coordinator, Edward Maguire, tried to put a good face on this, *Variety* understood that the decision "cut off at one swoop the city government's chief drawing card in its bid to Coast producers."[76] Not only was RKO leaving, but any hopes that local film producers might be attracted to its state-of-the-art stages had also evaporated. Dore Schary resigned on June 30, and a week later Hughes announced a 75 percent cut in RKO personnel.[77] Ullman managed to hang on, now assigned to a new project, *Sam Wynne*, "a modern melodrama with New York City as its background."[78] By the time it went into production in November the title had been changed to *Strange Bargain* and the locale to Beverly Hills. Ullman died there of a heart attack on December 26, 1948, at the age of 45.[79] Ironically, this was the day after the long-delayed opening of *Portrait of Jennie*, a film whose production in New York he once described as "a step in ultimately breaking Hollywood's monopoly on film making."[80]

Release of *The Window* was delayed just as long, not opening in New York until August 6, 1949. In this case there were no costly rewrites or reshoots, only the chaos connected with the new Hughes regime at RKO. Hughes was in the process of dismantling RKO, which would become the first, and only, Hollywood major to put itself out of business. Ullman's ambitious New York studio operation was over, but at least *The Window* survived as a worthy monument. Reviews were terrific. "Categorically a 'sleeper,' this is as wide-awake a sleeper as movie audiences are likely to see for some time," wrote one West Coast trade paper: "A tense, exciting tale, fraught with almost unbearable suspense that never relaxes its hold on the spectator throughout its 73-minute running time. Performances are near perfection, and Director Ted Tetzlaff has achieved a realism that matches the finest of so-called "realistic" films to come from Europe."[81]

The *New York Times* found a different area of comparison, noting that "Tetzlaff has squeezed out every ounce of suspense in the story and, much after the fashion of those early Alfred Hitchcock thrillers, has managed to top one startling situation with another." But whether it was channeling Hitchcock or

2.2. Advertising art for *Close-Up*, a pioneering low-budget New York crime thriller filmed almost entirely on local streets and practical interiors. Author's collection.

neorealism, *The Window* was certainly, "a splendid tribute to its producer, the late Frederic Ullman, Jr."[82]

In the meantime, what had happened to *Close-Up*, the film RKO Radio Pictures had once announced would follow *Portrait of Jennie* into the new Pathé studio?[83] It had been squeezed out when Selznick's production ran farther and farther over schedule, and in August the project was acquired by Harry Brandt's Marathon Pictures, which was then shooting its first film, *Open Secret*, in Hollywood. Brandt was an important New York theater owner. Frank Satenstein, his young brother-in-law, was president of Marathon, but more significant were some of the other board members—the Rialto Theater manager, Arthur Mayer, and Robert L. Joseph, son of New York City comptroller Lazarus Joseph. Satenstein arrived in New York in September and announced that Marathon was moving its entire production operation to New York, "establishing the company as one of the first to heed Mayor O'Dwyer's invitation to producers to make the city a filming center."[84] New York was an especially good place to make Marathon's low-budget films, he claimed, because "union scales and studio rentals are 20 per cent less" than in Hollywood, and "more and better unknown actors are available in New York than in Hollywood."[85] Weather was no longer a problem because "it doesn't rain any harder on the roof of a studio in New York than it does on the roof of a studio in Hollywood."[86] Satenstein, the *Times* concluded, "thinks Marathon can avoid Hollywood clichés in castings, in writing, and in directing by leaving town."[87]

Marathon quickly hired a crew of experienced locals. Jules Bricken, who had recently worked on *Carnegie Hall*, became their New York production adviser. The cameraman was Bill Miller, of *Carnegie Hall* and *The Naked City*, while the rest of the crew consisted of such familiar faces as Jimmy Di Gangi, Ira Senz, and Faith Elliott. But to direct Marathon imported Jack Donohue, a Broadway hoofer and dance director who had been working at MGM on musicals like *Girl Crazy* (1943) and *Anchors Aweigh* (1945), mostly without credit. Donohue had never directed an entire film on his own, dramatic or musical, but did have one interesting credit: in 1946 he came to New York with Frank Sinatra and shot the "Brooklyn Bridge" number for *It Happened in Brooklyn*.[88]

A newsreel cameraman accidentally films a Nazi war criminal who is passing through New York en route to a South American getaway. The Nazi, and the "cheap American gangster" who works for him, do what they can to recover the footage before authorities realize that "Martin Beaumen" did not perish in the ruins of Berlin.[89] The gangster's duplicitous moll, a typically untrustworthy femme fatale, seduces the cameraman before switching sides and double-crossing her boyfriend. Marathon boasted about all the New York acting talent they were hiring, but most of the cast, including Alan Baxter and Virginia Gilmore, were better known in Hollywood than on Broadway (Gilmore did appear opposite Marlon Brando in the legendary 1946 production of *Truckline Café*). Richard Kollmar, "Radio's Boston Blackie," was the husband of Dorothy Kilgallen and the cohost of their popular "Dorothy and Dick" radio show. The role of the escaped Nazi would be his only motion picture appearance, but his most important contribution to the film was as the former theatrical partner of both Brandt and Satenstein.[90] Kollmar's involvement with those two suggests another reason for the dance director Jack Donohue's otherwise inexplicable assignment to this pulpy melodrama: he was a veteran of Kollmar's big Broadway hit of 1945, *Are You with It?*

Close-Up was not the first postwar feature shot in New York nor was it the first to be filmed entirely outside of a studio, as was also claimed at the time. Five days were spent at the West Coast Sound Studios, 510 West Fifty-Seventh Street, a small rental stage that had been home to short films and industrial producers for fifteen years. But in a remarkable demonstration of guerilla filmmaking, the other seventeen days were spent on the streets or working in practical interiors, always with live sound recording. One major sequence was shot at the Hoboken Ferry Terminal and onboard the *Elmira*, which Marathon rented for $35 a day; another was a well-staged shoot-out in the abandoned Rupert Brewery building followed by a final chase to the Army Engineers' seaplane landing at East Ninety-Third Street (this is one of the few films to spend much time emphasizing Manhattan's existence as an *island*). The budget, variously reported as either $135,000 or $165,000 was slim either way, even accounting for an extra $2,000 caused by the loss of five shooting days to bad weather. For $1,200, Marathon was able to rent a townhouse at 18 East Eightieth Street, saving the cost of seven studio sets. And the newsreel office, complete with screening and editing rooms, was actually the headquarters of the film's distributor, Eagle-Lion, on West Forty-Sixth Street.[91]

"Mayor O'Dwyer and a few of his aides visited one of the sets the other day to have a look-see and apparently to bestow his blessing," *Film Daily* reported. "Having no hull on which to crack a bottle of champagne there was no tense climax, but the evident interest displayed by the Mayor is symbolic of the rest of the metropolis as the increasing hum of production continues to be heard."[92] A good part of that hum was caused by the simultaneous production of *Close-Up* and *The Window*, but the hum ultimately did New York film producers little good. *The Window*, as noted, received excellent reviews but was not released until 1949. *Close-Up* opened in April 1948 to some of the worst reviews I have ever seen. Critics on both coasts panned the script, the direction, the acting, and even the sound recording. Cecelia Ager described it in *P.M.* as "merely some flotsam that washed up at the Globe," which "proves that a shoe-string quickie can be made as ineptly in our own home town as anywhere under the sun." The only good thing about it, she wrote, was that it "provides at least a solid rock-bottom; at least we know that the second feature-length picture to be made in its entirety in New York can't be worse." One of the only balanced reviews came from Lee Mortimer of the *Daily Mirror*, who recognized the film's "technical imperfections—visual and auditory," but still praised Frank Satenstein "for overcoming such difficulties as an austerity budget and a famine of technical talent in New York. His finished product gives hope that Gotham again can make major films."[93] Satenstein was so grateful for this rare accolade that he had Marathon purchase the rights to *New York Confidential*, a book that Mortimer had written with Jack Lait, for $5,000. Production, he promised, would begin in New York in the fall of 1948.[94]

RKO Pathé continued to operate their studio on 106th Street, if only for the support facilities needed by its foreign department and declining shorts operation. Ullman's *This Is America* series, now produced by Jay Bonafield and supervised by Phil Reisman, Jr., ran until August 1951. On May 28, 1948, they released an episode called *Crime Lab*, reviewed by *Film Daily* as "sort of a miniature *Naked City*."[95] In fact, it was *The Naked City* that had been drawing on the documentary techniques developed by series like *This Is America*. When a murdered girl is found in an abandoned car, detectives must "analyze slender clues that [will] finally bring a murderer to justice," before the end of the seventeen-minute reel.[96] RKO Pathé was now producing nothing but shorts here, but the success of *The Window* encouraged the organization to produce a feature length spin-off of *Crime Lab*, *The Tattooed Stranger*, also written by Reisman, produced by Bonafield, and directed by Edward J. Montagne. Press accounts acknowledged that it would "follow the on-the-spot realistic quality of *The Window*," which had finally opened in New York a few weeks earlier.[97] Montagne, working with a budget of only $124,000, made *The Tattooed Stranger* a model of low-budget location shooting.[98] He shot at the Brooklyn Navy Yard, the Bronx Botanical Gardens, the American Museum of Natural History (location of an earlier *This Is America* subject), Central Park, Palumbo's Stoneworks, St. Raymond's Cemetery, and Fort Tryon Park. Dialogue at these locations was all wild, the words being looped by the actors back at the studio. The RKO Pathé crew knew this technique from their dubbing business, but it would soon become standard for low-budget location work. Using the same technical crews that had worked on *The Window* (Bill Steiner, Sam Corso, and the inevitable William Saulter) and a cast of complete unknowns (a young Jack Lord is not even billed), Montagne made a film that one fan magazine said could be "classified as somewhere between a documentary and a murder mystery."[99] A late entry in the postwar police procedural cycle, *The Tattooed Stranger* made little impact at the time. "The thrills are few and far between in this manhunt," the *Times* wrote, "but the authenticity is obvious."[100] A more recent film noir encyclopedia puts it another way: "One of the seediest films ever made, *The Tattooed Stranger* remains a unique testament to independent film makers. Taking to the streets, the film is populated with non-professional actors [*sic*] who suggest, rather than act out, the intrinsic fear and loathing found in many urban slums."[101]

Two art directors are credited, but the film uses actual locations whenever possible, more likely to cut the cost of set construction than for any concern over documentary authenticity. When that was not possible, it made use of whatever was at hand. At one point, Capt. Lundquist (Frank Twedell) sends his detectives out to locate the source of an unusual type of grass found at the crime scene. It is a brief scene, too short for a location trip and not long enough to justify building even a rudimentary set. So Saulter and Corso repurpose another space, probably an office of some sort right at the studio. In what I like to think of as a veiled homage to their old boss, Frederic Ullman, Jr., they leave the pictures on the wall intact. Prominently located in the middle of this police captain's office is an architectural rendering that was widely distributed to the local press a few years earlier: an imposing image of RKO Pathé's state-of-the-art "vertical studio" on East 106th Street. Although *Variety* reported that the "pic is first of a series of low-budgeters which RKO plans to make in the east," it was, in fact, the last.[102]

CHAPTER 3

NOW IT CAN BE TOLD

Louis de Rochemont, Henry Hathaway, and the Birth of Docudrama

Pathé saw the end of the war as an opportunity to recreate New York's prewar studio system, only bigger and better. Across town, their newsreel rivals at Fox and *The March of Time* saw the future differently.

Louis de Rochemont had revolutionized the theatrical nonfiction business in the 1930s. Once the short subjects editor of Fox Movietone News, he left Fox in 1934 to develop *The March of Time* for Henry Luce at RKO. Their "new pictorial journalism" disdained scoop-chasing in favor of longer, more reflective analyses of the Dust Bowl, the League of Nations, or some other topic not amenable to a forty-five-second sound bite. *The March of Time* stunned Hollywood, which awarded the reel a special Oscar in 1936, an unprecedented honor. Dramatically scored, powered by the portentous narration of Westbrook van Voorhis, and freely mixing "authentic" actuality footage with "authentic recreations" staged by *March of Time* crews, it blurred the line between fiction and fact in ways that seemed outrageous even then.[1]

The restaging of newsworthy events was already a fixture of the *radio* version of *The March of Time*, on the air since 1931. But the film version required a different level of theatricality—lights, sets, costumes, makeup—which necessarily led de Rochemont and his crews farther and farther away from the simple assemblage of news clips offered by the earliest newsreels. If Huey Long or Haile Selassie failed to get themselves photographed during crucial moments in their careers, *The March of Time* simply restaged the events back at the studio, making good use of celebrity look-alikes.

In August 1940 RKO released de Rochemont's *The Ramparts We Watch*, an elaborately staged feature film designed to juxtapose America's current lack of preparedness with the situation in 1914. Shot mainly in the streets, factories, public buildings, and private homes of New London, Connecticut, it recreated the life of a typical American small town as it had existed twenty-five years earlier. But without a specific historical setting or incident for his model, de Rochemont depended on the authenticity of this location to establish the film's aura of "realism" (he denied to the *New York Times* that *The Ramparts We Watch* was a documentary, already a dirty word in theatrical circles). De Rochemont also avoided professional actors, casting the film with 1,400 locals (of which 73 were said to have important speaking parts), "because they happened to represent types called for in the story."[2] A few years later the use of nonprofessional actors and the abandonment of studio settings would emerge as key elements of postwar Italian neorealism. Vittorio de Sica is known to have acknowledged the influence of a silent American film like King Vidor's *The Crowd* on his neorealist masterpiece, *Bicycle Thieves*, but it is unclear if he had also previously been aware of de Rochemont's use of this technique in more recent dialogue films.[3]

De Rochemont saw *The Ramparts We Watch* as the prototype of a new style of dramatic feature, a hybrid of fictional and nonfictional elements. But the production itself was an extraordinary gamble: his budget ballooned from $200,000 to around $400,000, and while making a film to warn Americans of a coming war, his production schedule was overtaken by the arrival of that very war. Stuck with an out-of-date preparedness polemic (*not* a documentary, at least), de Rochemont saw a way to add news-headline relevance by pirating a reel of battle footage from the Nazi propaganda documentary *Feldzug in Polen*. Although he fought off claims of copyright infringement from the German UFA organization, de Rochemont left himself open to charges of inserting raw Nazi propaganda into his film, an affront that led the film to be banned from exhibition in the state of Pennsylvania.

In the summer of 1942 a management decision transferred distribution of *The March of Time* from RKO to Twentieth Century-Fox.[4] Ned Depinet, the head of distribution at RKO, had been seen as supportive, even indulgent, in his attitude toward the series, which seemed like a big fish in RKO's relatively small pond. At Fox, the pond was much bigger and *The March of Time* had to justify its content, and its budget, every month. This change of distributors would have major consequences, and not just for the career of Louis de Rochemont. Within weeks, Darryl F. Zanuck resigned his position as Fox's vice-president in charge of production to take on his duties as a lieutenant colonel (later colonel) in the U.S. Army Signal Corps. Zanuck's main job over the next nine months was overseeing the production of Army documentaries on the North African campaign, and he spent most of November and December in the desert, the only studio head to serve anywhere near the front lines. How successful these films were is open to question, but Zanuck was eager to put his Hollywood expertise to use for the war effort and made sure the public knew all about it. Fox had been making its money with cheerful entertainments starring Shirley Temple and Betty Grable, but Zanuck was also proud of having produced *The Grapes of Wrath* (1940) and of greenlighting *I Am a Fugitive from a Chain Gang* (in 1932, when he was head of production at Warner Bros.). Both films were critical and commercial hits that Hollywood honored as benchmarks of "realism," and—unlike his peers at Paramount or MGM—Zanuck seemed to believe that both kinds of film would still have a place on his studio's postwar production schedule.

The published record of his military exploits, *Tunis Expedition*, is a simple diary account in which Zanuck describes what he saw in North Africa while posted with the Signal Corps. The only extended reference to film technique occurs in the entry for November 21, 1942:

We are using 16 mm cameras with Kodachrome magazine clips. They are light and simple to reload in a hurry. For combat action there is nothing to compare with them. Thirty-five mm Eyemos are fine behind the lines, but when you must grab action "on the fly" you cannot spare the time to reload. Furthermore, in 16 mm we can carry on our person two and one-half times as much film as we could in 35 mm, and this is a vital factor.[5]

Note that Zanuck prefers 16 to 35 mm for this work not because it allows the cameraman to shoot in Kodachrome color, or because it is cheaper (it wasn't), but because it saved time and weight. As postwar studio shooting became more encumbered by rising costs and labor issues, Zanuck would begin to think seriously about the speed and efficiency of this "on the fly" documentary technique. Incorporating it into established studio technique would not be easy, but perhaps Louis de Rochemont was the man to solve the problem for him.[6]

De Rochemont's second *March of Time* feature, *We Are the Marines*, was released by Fox in December 1942, when Zanuck was still in North Africa. Raymond Fielding describes it as "a competent if not artistically distinguished documentary that traced the training of marines from boot camp to battleground." The film contained recreations of Pacific island battles so convincing that generations of stock film researchers thought they were looking at the real thing.[7] Zanuck was placed on inactive status by the Army at the end of May 1943 and immediately returned to his job at the studio; three months later de Rochemont quit his job at *The March of Time* and began working as a producer for Fox.[8] The first project he supervised was *The Fighting Lady*, a documentary feature about the operation of an aircraft carrier, notable today for the work of its chief cameraman, Edward Steichen. Fox released it in December 1944, but by then de

Rochemont had outgrown the constraints of traditional documentary and was looking for something new.

The first *March of Time* episode de Rochemont delivered to Fox was *The FBI Front* (September 1942), an account of how the Federal Bureau of Investigation infiltrated a band of Bundist agents. The film blended behind-the-scenes revelations of FBI procedure with a dramatized espionage plot. "It has all the qualities of a melodramatic thriller, even more so because it presents fact instead of fiction," said *Film Daily*, relishing this odd marriage of melodrama and documentary.[9] In chapter 2, we saw how RKO would spin one of its *This Is America* subjects, *Crime Lab* (1948), into the CSI police procedural *The Tattooed Stranger* (1950). But this seems to have been another idea first developed by de Rochemont, who would soon transform *The FBI Front* into the prototypical docudrama, *The House on 92nd Street* (1945).

The House on Ninety-Second Street

De Rochemont always began one of his projects by compiling mountains of research, and in preparing what he first called *Now It Can Be Told* he drew on his FBI contacts to create a composite narrative highlighting various FBI counterespionage successes already known to the public. Although cobbled together with other events, the FBI's arrest of a New York–based spy ring in 1941 was the core around which the rest of the narrative would grow.

Warner Bros. had already made *Confessions of a Nazi Spy* (1939), based closely on published records of an earlier espionage case. *Now It Can Be Told* would have to go farther than that, using bits and pieces of various cases to create a "best of" feature highlighting FBI accomplishments throughout the war. In *March of Time* fashion it would be shot, whenever possible, on the actual locations referenced in the plot, and J. Edgar Hoover would make a host of agents available to "play themselves" in the film, himself included. But de Rochemont now began to regret his earlier belief that nonprofessionals could play themselves, or someone like themselves, in a dramatic film. "This time I'm not going to repeat the mistakes I made in filming *The Ramparts We Watch*," he told the *New York Times*. "When a character has to do real acting or speak important lines, that will be done by an experienced actor."[10] Like all good New York documentarians of the 1930s, de Rochemont would have been familiar with Eisenstein's notion of typage, in which nonprofessionals might be cast according to their *visual* suitability for a role. But line readings now made a hash of this silent film technique, which even Eisenstein had abandoned once talkies arrived. While Vittorio de Sica was able to cast *Bicycle Thieves* (1948) with nonprofessionals who happened to look right for the part, it was only because Italian films always had their dialogue rerecorded back at the studio.

Unfortunately, treating dialogue this way was not acceptable in American features, especially in a film "founded on fact and made with genuine realism."[11] De Rochemont solved the problem by finding professional actors who would not be recognized as such by movie audiences and cast even the smallest roles with Broadway actors, most of whom, like Vincent Gardenia and E. G. Marshall, had never appeared in features. "And when we work with our characters," de Rochemont told a reporter in 1951, "we have them talk as people in the locale would talk, not simulated accents, necessarily, but with the simplicity of speech in ordinary situations."[12]

The Ramparts We Watch had been signed by de Rochemont as producer-director, but Raymond Fielding notes that "there were several directors on the film—simultaneously—with de Rochemont telling them what to do."[13] This was also not going to work on a major studio feature. Director Henry Hathaway claimed that he saw the Now It Can Be Told script at Fox and asked Zanuck for the assignment, seeing more in the project than the "cheap documentary" he felt de Rochemont was proposing.[14] Hathaway had almost no experience with urban crime dramas, his reputation resting on a series of Zane Grey westerns at Paramount in the early 1930s, and a few A-pictures like *Lives of a Bengal Lancer* (1935) and *The Trail of the Lonesome Pine* (1936), the first three-color Technicolor western. But over the next few years he would dominate the postwar urban docudrama, working with and without de Rochemont on such films as *13 Rue Madeleine* (1946), *Kiss of Death* (1947), and *Call Northside 777* (1948). "People are always shocked that I did those urban documentaries," he told Scott Eyman. "Christ. Aren't Westerns documentaries? It's the same thing; you learn to work outside."[15]

Hathaway's assignment to the project appears to have coincided with a decision to shoot much more of the film on location than had originally been intended. On February 12, the chairman of the Producers' Committee had written to Walter Lang, business representative of the New York cameramen's union, about an upcoming FBI project that Fox thought would require a bit of New York location photography. "There is, as I understand it, no acting; it will simply be what we all would consider background shots."[16] A few days later, Lang informed him that "if this is to be a production we would require a full crew, that is, First Cameraman, Operative Cameraman, Assistant Cameraman, and a Still Cameraman; if this is just backgrounds, or inserts, we would require a First Cameraman and an Assistant Cameraman."[17] This was the union's standard deal; the only room for negotiation involved the distinction between backgrounds and inserts and whatever might be defined as "a production." That seems to have been settled by March 18, when Lang scribbled a note for his files outlining his meeting with the film's director of photography, Norbert Brodine, "who advises they will be in about April 15, 1945—requested permission to bring in his asst, which was granted not to work—D. of P. operative man asst & Still will be put on from the local."[18] This was going to be a real production.

Pooling their knowledge of outside work, de Rochemont and Hathaway made almost the entire film on location. Hathaway shot at FBI headquarters, even in J. Edgar Hoover's own office (Hoover had to wait in the corridor until Hathaway was satisfied with the lighting).[19] A plant in Great Neck served as the factory infiltrated by German spies, while a townhouse at 55 East Ninety-Third Street doubled for the eponymous Ninety-Second Street building.[20] *American Cinematographer* would later describe Brodine's "trial and error" approach to lighting such practical settings as "an almost complete reversal of previously standardized studio techniques." Brodine worked the locations without a generator, tapping into the local electrical mains to power the photoflood lamps he used for most interior illumination.[21] He would perfect this "documentary style" later on *Boomerang!*, *13 Rue Madeleine*, and *Kiss of Death*. "In lighting these actual locales," he explained, "we were striving to maintain studio finish, plus a newsreel authenticity." The secret of this approach, he felt, was to avoid not just the presumed artlessness of the newsreel but the stylized artiness that later audiences would associate with film noir:

> Those of us in the industry, along with theatregoers in the large key cities, recognize and appreciate the artistry of low-key, cross-lighting, and the more extreme mood effects. However, in making pictures we must think of the people in the small towns who make up the majority of our audiences. The butcher, the baker and the candlestick-maker who pay their 35 cents to go to the movies on Saturday night are anxious to watch certain stars and to be able to *see* their faces. I personally believe in avoiding effects that are too dark and extreme, and might prevent the audience from seeing the faces of their favorites.[22]

The film achieves such results not only through Brodine's lighting effects but also with a highly conscious manipulation of mise en scène, which Hathaway took pains to explain to the *Los Angeles Times*:

> Like the newsreels, he employed stationary cameras—no trucking or dolly shots. Believing that the medium shot is too far away for the spectator to see facial expressions and too near for effective composition, he confined his setups to close-ups and long shots. And to emphasize the confinement of small spaces, he permitted his cameraman to photograph people who were not "full in" the frame—a cardinal sin in orthodox Hollywood.[23]

"Whether the experiment succeeds or not," the paper concluded, "Hathaway is convinced it will accelerate a migration back to real locations and away from the faking and 'processing' of backgrounds."

Unfortunately, grabbing so much footage in public places brought with it problems of its own. "There is a New York 'right to privacy' law which makes you liable to prosecution for photographing anyone without permission," Hathaway admitted. "If he is recognizable on screen, he can slap an injunction against the picture." Whenever a "civilian" drifted into a shot, assistants would run after him or her, armed with a release form and an offer of financial compensation. If this approach failed, "we have to make the shot all over again."[24] This was just the sort of legalistic complication that caused Hollywood to embrace "faking and processing" in the first place, but Hathaway still believed the final result was worth the effort.

Although the principal actors were frequently filmed on various New York locations, there is no direct sound recording on exteriors. To compensate for this, the film uses a considerable amount of voice-over narration, a style from *March of Time* that Hathaway embraced. Indeed, he later suggested that the opportunity to use so much voice-over was one of the things that had attracted him to the project in the first place, "telling the story with half-narration that could work over scenes so that you don't have to have on-camera people talking too much."[25] When the *New York Times* suggested to him that the use of voice-over "seems to pop into everybody's mind with the mere mention of a fact film," Hathaway insisted that it would only be used here to cover time lapses. "We won't use as much narration as there was in *How Green Was My Valley*," he promised, somewhat defensively.[26]

With the exception of the office used by an FBI agent, Lloyd Nolan, the limited number of dialogue scenes in *The House on 92nd Street* were nearly all shot on studio sets. The Nazi spy school in Hamburg was constructed at the West Coast studio (exteriors courtesy of another German film appropriated by de Rochemont), but the interiors of "the house," as well as a diner used for spy meetings, were sets constructed at the Fox Movietone studio on West Fifty-Fourth Street.[27] This was a significant shift from the procedure on *Life Begins at Eight-Thirty* or *The Lost Weekend*, where filming on New York sound stages was not even considered. Although Brodine received sole credit for photography, Fox also used several New York cameramen, including Larry Williams and George Stoetzel, who would continue to work on Fox's New York location shoots for almost a decade. In the postwar era many American cities would host visiting Hollywood film crews, but only New York had the infrastructure to entice them to work on its soundstages as well as its streets.

Where *The March of Time* mixed "documentary" footage of floods or political rallies with dramatized reenactments, *The House on 92nd Street* went one better by incorporating previously unseen FBI surveillance film, 16 mm footage of likely suspects entering or leaving the German embassy in Washington, shot with telephoto lenses from an apartment across the street.[28] Unlike a 1930s "G-Man" movie, the agents here seldom draw a gun and spend most of their

3.1. Traffic problems on the George Washington Bridge in Louis de Rochemont's *The House on 92nd Street*. Museum of Modern Art Film Stills Archive.

time recording conversations, filming spies through trick mirrors, and threading 16 mm projectors. Much of the film's documentary credibility comes from this foregrounding of the very act of documenting, with cameras and microphones proving their value as the ultimate weapons in a new kind of warfare. Of course, more emphasis on "just the facts" reportage means less room for things like conventional characterization. Hathaway and de Rochemont do as little as possible to break the illusion that the film is simply an unmediated reflection of real world events. There is no shading here regarding heroes or villains, and we sit back in passive admiration as the FBI methodically rounds up the spies and traitors.

A film that celebrates surveillance and policing can never be understood as part of the film noir cycle, but *The House on 92nd Street* is a transitional work that occasionally suggests the dark tone of what would soon follow. The most interesting characters, such as they are, are the two key German spies, a chain-smoking female Gestapo agent, and an exotic spider-woman type (code named "Mr. Christopher") who dons male attire in a futile last-minute effort to escape FBI justice.[29] As for the dreaded voice-over narration, that narrative technique would become one of the most characteristic of all film noir mannerisms.

The House on 92nd Street focuses entirely on German espionage activities— Italy and Japan are hardly referred to. (Nor is the Soviet Union, ironic in light of the film's bold claim that the FBI was completely successful in preventing the theft of any scientific or military secrets during the war.) The 1941 espionage trial that largely inspired the film was concerned with attempts to steal traditional military secrets, like shipping schedules and plans for the Norden bombsight (which the Nazis had already stolen in 1938).[30] For dramatic purposes, the film focuses instead on a single, mysterious "Process 97," which the script treats like something out of *The 39 Steps*. Given de Rochemont's previous history, it seems strange that he would base this important feature on some generic MacGuffin. If not the Norden bombsight, what was Process 97 supposed to be? According to the *American Film Institute Catalog*, "script files reveal that as late as April 2, 1945, the name of the atomic bomb was not allowed to be printed in the studio's copy of the screenplay 'until release from proper authority can be obtained.' "[31] If true, this suggests that de Rochemont and his staff knew about the atomic bomb before Harry Truman did—at least enough to know not to say anything about it. By September 1945, with the bomb dropped and the war over, Fox was letting it be known that Process 97 was really "a part of the atomic bomb formula."[32] Although there seems to be nothing nuclear about the material these spies are pursuing, the narration on the release print does reference "the atomic bomb" and "20,000 tons of TNT," the first time these words would have been heard in a feature picture. Was this just a vulgar bit of Hollywood exploitation added after the fact to take advantage of the public's fascination with the bomb? Or had de Rochemont really been on to something here?

Getting Zanuck's Attention

Hathaway's next film, *The Dark Corner*, was a typical New York noir with more than a passing resemblance to Fox's current hit, *Laura*. This time Clifton Webb played a gallery owner instead of a columnist, and the idealized female portrait he treasures is four hundred years old and attributed to Raphael. But Mark Stevens's detective, here a private investigator, resembles a neurotic Alan Ladd hero more than *Laura*'s brooding Dana Andrews (he does get to deliver at least one iconic film noir line: "I feel all dead inside. I'm backed up in a dark corner and don't know who's hitting me"). Larry Williams shot inserts and back-projection plates with Hathaway in New York in October 1945, and the director wrapped up principal photography back at the studio between November and January.[33] Like many another Fox "New York" picture, the film begins promisingly with Alfred Newman's familiar "Street Scene" on the soundtrack. A real elevated train roars past and the camera tilts down to reveal the corner of Third Avenue and Grand Street, or at least what a sign tells us is the corner of Third Avenue and Grand Street (there is no such place). We cut to a closer view of a suspicious character loitering under a lamp post, but that first cut takes us far away from New York and straight to the Fox studio in Los Angeles, where, for the most part, we will remain for the rest of the film. Clearly considering it just another studio assignment, Hathaway hardly mentioned the film in later interviews, but it contains something that had not been seen in a New York picture since silent movie days: a high-speed automobile chase up the east side of Manhattan. The detective steals a cab downtown, rushing past landmarks like the Customs Building and the Criminal Court, eventually eluding his pursuers by pulling into a taxi garage tucked underneath the Queensboro Bridge, where his vehicle is indistinguishable from dozens of others. Unlike *The House on 92nd Street*, none of the principal actors came east for the film, so the sequence depends entirely on the back projections and doubles shot by Hathaway in New York.[34] Taking up less than ninety seconds of screen time, the chase is modest compared to what we will see in a film like *Side Street* (1949). But it lets a breath of fresh air into a rather claustrophobic, studio-bound noir, while launching a tradition that would climax years later with *The French Connection*.

The Dark Corner, produced not by de Rochemont but by Fred Kohlmar, was a straight crime melodrama with a bit of location window dressing. But when *The House on 92nd Street* proved a surprising critical and commercial success, Fox began to see de Rochemont's production style as an end in itself. Indeed, they began referring to any film with more than the usual amount of location shooting as a "documentary," a genre on which they seemed to claim the copyright. Hathaway remembered that Zanuck was delighted to see his faith in their new genre validated, not least because his distribution chief, Tom Connors, had originally declared *House on 92nd Street* "a disaster" that would probably lose the studio over half a million dollars. Instead, the low-budget sleeper (which cost less than a million dollars) would earn two and a half times its negative cost in domestic rentals alone, an excellent return.[35] Zanuck agreed with de Rochemont that they should follow up their FBI film with a tribute to the Office of Strategic Services (OSS), a project that would allow for the incorporation of location shooting in England and France. But he also felt that the earlier film's box office results would have been even greater with a star more potent than Lloyd Nolan in the lead.[36] De Rochemont had dropped the idea of "real people playing themselves" as artistically impractical, settling for relatively anonymous contract talent like Nolan. Now Zanuck decided that even documentaries needed some star power. In January he had announced that Mark Stevens would play the lead, but the actor's lackluster performance in *The Dark Corner* may have given him second thoughts.[37] Reaching out to one of the most recognizable stars in Hollywood, he signed James Cagney to play the head of a secret OSS unit training American operatives for service in occupied France. Cagney was now an independent producer with his own production slate to worry about, but after a good deal of negotiation he agreed to give Zanuck twelve weeks for what was then called 32 *Rue Madeleine*. The problem with this casting coup was that Cagney refused to travel by air, and sending him back and forth to Europe by ocean liner would eat up too much of the allotted twelve weeks. In the old days, this might have been overcome through the use of back projection and studio construction, but not for a de Rochemont "documentary." Hathaway claimed that he was the one who found the solution. "I said I'd do England in Boston and France up in Quebec and on the Ile d'Orleans, which I knew very well."[38]

Ironically, postwar rationing still affected the company's ability to move around the country as quickly and efficiently as de Rochemont had hoped. What was set to be the first "all-air location trip" stalled on May 25, 1946, when the studio's chartered plane was grounded in Los Angeles "because of the government's restrictions on fuel and use of planes."[39] Filming began in Washington, with most of the location work done in and around Boston.[40] After filming the "French" sequences in Quebec, the company returned to Hollywood on August 10, completing fifty-six days on location (an additional four days were required in California for the "secret landing sequence").[41] De Rochemont informed the press that location filming was saving $400,000 over the cost of a studio shoot, and had reduced the projected schedule by three weeks.[42]

While only a few shots were actually taken in New York (Twenty-First Street near Broadway being transformed into "a typical London street scene"), de Rochemont did keep as much of the production as possible within range of his home in Newington, New Hampshire, just outside Portsmouth.[43] But Hathaway claimed that the producer began to lose interest in the film by the time the company moved to Quebec and had to be coerced into visiting the location.[44] De Rochemont did continue the tradition of hiring as many "unknown" New York stage actors as possible, finding small parts for actors like Karl Malden, Red Buttons, and E. G. Marshall. But what these fresh faces might have supplied was largely offset by Cagney's high-powered star turn. The performance is clearly too big for the picture. De Rochemont was still grumbling about this five years later. "I think *13 Rue Madeleine* would have been a more convincing picture if Darryl Zanuck hadn't forced me to star James Cagney," he complained to Maurice Zolotow. "Cagney is one of our greatest actors, but he's wrong for my kind of picture."[45] Perhaps the reason de Rochemont appeared to have lost interest in the film was because he was focusing his energy on a project with a bit less star power. Not a spy thriller, *Boomerang!* would be the case study of a miscarriage of justice narrowly averted. It would star no one more electrifying than Dana Andrews and Jane Wyatt and would be directed not by the formidable Henry Hathaway but by a younger man de Rochemont probably felt he could control more easily: Elia Kazan. Best of all, it could all be shot on location in Connecticut, almost as close to home as the Boston shoot.

Father Hubert Dahme, a Catholic priest in Bridgeport, Connecticut, had been shot to death on Main Street, assassination style, on February 4, 1924. Public outrage over the killing demanded action by the authorities and a drifter named Harold Israel was soon arrested for the crime. He was identified by seven eyewitnesses, owned the murder weapon, and signed a full confession. The State's attorney, Homer S. Cummings, first declared it "a perfect case" but grew suspicious over the confession, extracted after two full days of grilling by the police. He created an uproar at the arraignment (and raised the ire of fellow Democrats) by discrediting all the evidence and allowing Israel to go free.[46] "It is just as important for a State's attorney to use the great powers of his office to protect the innocent as to convict the guilty," Cummings argued, in a frequently studied summation that made his legal reputation.[47] In 1933 he was appointed Franklin D. Roosevelt's first attorney general.

De Rochemont assigned a writer named Richard Murphy to develop the story as early as December 1945, clearly intending it as the third of his Fox docudrama series. Garson Kanin was announced as director in July, but a few days later the project was abruptly handed to Kazan, who was just completing a complicated and unsatisfying Tracy-Hepburn film at MGM, *Sea of Grass*.[48] Murphy proved to be the ideal writer for these location-centric melodramas, elegantly balancing the need for "the facts" with a flair for characterization that delivered exactly what Zanuck found missing in a film like *House on 92nd Street*. His later scripts included *Cry of the City*, *House on Telegraph Hill*, and *Panic in the Streets*. He kept *Boomerang!* very close to the legal facts of the case but fleshed out the clinical "law and order" elements with a surprisingly political personal story, winning an Oscar nomination for his efforts.

The film begins with an introductory title typical of postwar docudrama: "The story you are about to witness is based on fact. In the interests of authenticity, all scenes, both interior and exterior, have been photographed in the original locale and as many actual characters as possible have been used." Only the first part of this is true. Although de Rochemont had negotiated with the Bridgeport authorities for months, permission to shoot there was abruptly canceled in June, even before a director had been signed.⁴⁹ Clearly irked, de Rochemont informed a reporter for the *Times* that John Lyddy, Bridgeport's police superintendent, "chose to regard the film as casting a reflection upon his department and could not see his way clear to guarantee the movie company the 'protection' it required."⁵⁰ De Rochemont scrambled to relocate the production to Stamford, some twenty miles west, with courthouse scenes to be shot in the Westchester County Courthouse in White Plains, New York. No one thought it necessary to change the printed prologue, but as the camera pans over Stamford's downtown at the start of the film, the voice-over narration makes a flatly contradictory statement, insisting that what we will see could be the generic story of any American town: "That's why it doesn't make much difference that we have brought you to this small town in Connecticut. The basic facts of our story actually occurred in a Connecticut community much like this one. But they could have happened anywhere. . . ."

The idea that a film crew would visit a specific location to illustrate a generic narrative ("could have happened anywhere") is an indication of just how different de Rochemont's notion of realism was from what the Italians were doing (Rome, Milan, and Naples generally play themselves in neorealist cinema). Indeed, it suggests the opening of Anatole Litvak's *The Long Night*, a remake of *Le jour se lève* being shot simultaneously on the West Coast, which opens with footage of three specific mill towns—Youngstown, Ohio, Bethlehem, Pennsylvania, and Gary, Indiana—before a voice-over tells us that specificity of location doesn't matter very much here because the story being told involves "average human beings living in an average American town."

Production began in Stamford only a few weeks after *13 Rue Madeleine* had wrapped. De Rochemont and his unit manager, "Boots" McCracken, were pleased to find that they had no trouble recruiting the hundreds of extras that were needed to populate the town (250 for the funeral of the priest alone). "I went out on Saturday afternoon, stopped about ten people on the street and told them we were making a movie and would pay them to appear in it," McCracken recalled. The pay was $10 a day; with meals, hotel bills, and other ancillary costs, he estimated that Fox would add some $250,000 to the local economy—money that could have gone to Bridgeport.⁵¹ "We used real cops—they talked the way they do in real life," Kazan told a reporter. "Actors talk phony. We wanted a man making love to a girl in the doorway. I stopped a girl on the street and said, 'Want to be in pictures, honey?' She said no, but I persuaded her. She was great."⁵²

Zanuck would have approved the key casting, setting the reliable Dana Andrews for the lead and Jane Wyatt, a veteran performer whose career had been stalled for years, as his wife. "It is nearly all to be produced in Stamford, Connecticut, and we will use the facilities that are right there," she told one reporter. "I mean if we seem to be working in a room in a house it will actually be a room in a house and not a set. All the backgrounds will be 'documentary'—or so they might be called—rather than make-believe."[53]

Other than the stars, Kazan felt free to cast as many of his Broadway associates as possible. While shooting *Boomerang!* Kazan was also working with Arthur Miller on a new play, *All My Sons*, which would go into rehearsal as soon as work in Stamford was over. Miller would hang around the location and discuss plans for a script he hoped to write about labor problems on the waterfront. Kazan even used him as an extra, one of the "suspects" in a police lineup.[54] Miller was so taken with the production that he urged Kazan to cast *All My Sons* with actors he was using in *Boomerang!* Ed Begley, Arthur Kennedy, Karl Malden, and Dudley Sadler all went straight from the film to the play.[55] In the film (his first), Ed Begley played a scheming real estate developer who kills himself when his shady plans are exposed; in the play, he is a profiteering aircraft parts manufacturer who kills himself in similar circumstances.

In fact, *Boomerang!* is the most directly political of all the postwar docudramas. It begins and ends not with "Street Scene," but with an orchestration of "America the Beautiful." De Rochemont saw it as "a tribute to American justice," and the attention it pays to the workings of small-town government recalls several of the best *March of Time* episodes.[56] But there is a worm in this apple. The population is easily swayed by the media, seen here as controlled by politicians for whom justice and democracy are little more than slogans. A "reform party" has come to power, and its leaders want a conviction for selfish personal and political reasons. "The "opposition party" and its newspaper support the defense, if only to embarrass the incumbents ("I don't care whether he's guilty or not"). They may be on the right side but for all the wrong reasons. On the other hand, the incumbent reformers are funded by smiling businessmen who use their access to power in order to facilitate shady business deals of their own. Dana Andrews, playing the State's attorney, manages to stand up to the pressure from his own side, and by courage and skill assures that justice is done. As in Frank Capra's *Mr. Smith Goes to Washington*, the institutions are solid, but unless every citizen stays vigilant, the structure could easily be eaten away by criminals and profiteers.

Kazan suggested to Michel Ciment that this was the moment he lost his faith in the perfectibility of American institutions. He had come to feel that the triumph of the State's attorney was "almost a matter of luck," and that the forces of corruption surrounding him were, in the long run, irresistible.[57] Of course, unlike de Rochemont, Kazan had spent a very disillusioning period as a member of the Communist Party. A few years later he would testify that he joined because he hoped this *was* the reform party. When he named names, he felt he was calling out the bad apples that had spoiled the barrel. *Boomerang!* suggests that this sort of corruption is not necessarily the province of political extremists but can be found, as the voice-over tells us, in any American community.

Kazan worked well with de Rochemont, "an affable and intelligent man, agreeable enough and intelligent enough to leave the filmmaking to the filmmakers."[58] Darryl F. Zanuck, on the other hand, still exercised control in the traditional top-down Hollywood studio manner. He was unhappy with the film they delivered to him late in 1946, in which the real killer is made known to the audience in the first reel. By "making some deft eliminations" he did what he could to turn a critique of the American justice system into a more conventional suspense film.[59] Kazan's experiences in Hollywood, especially on *Sea of Grass* (where Louis B. Mayer had told him they were in the business of making "beautiful pictures about beautiful people"), had left him doubting his own talent and suspicious of any sort of big studio production. But working in this new style energized him, perhaps recalling the youthful enthusiasm of projects like his 1938 documentary, *People of the Cumberland*.[60]

> Another thing I learned from *Boomerang!* was that it cut through a lot of bullshit about photography. On *Sea of Grass* I was initiated into all that careful back-lighting and line-lighting and so on. But the cameraman on *Boomerang!* was an old guy who just put the camera down and turned the box on. And it looked better to me than the other! It was so simple, really—so much simpler than that enormous mechanism of making "beautiful pictures about beautiful people."[61]

"I've called *Boomerang!* my cure," he wrote in his autobiography. "It was. I walked the Stamford streets—they were my stage—as master of it all. Call it arrogance. I call it confidence, and it had come flooding back, filling the cavity that was emptied in Culver City. . . . Work was a joy again. I'd found my way of making films."[62]

Boomerang! opened in February 1947. It did prove a turning point in Elia Kazan's career, but it also assured Louis de Rochemont's status as master of this new narrative form, whatever it might be called. *Home Movies*, which reviewed films from the perspective of an ambitious amateur filmmaking community, saw *Boomerang!* as "particularly inspirational" because of the way it "intertwines documentary and 'stage' shots so well that it is often difficult to tell one from the other." Praising the way Kazan handled his extras as well as his streetscapes, this is the only review I know that critiques the film entirely in terms of its revolutionary mise-en-scène.[63]

Where Did It All Come From?

The Naked City had not yet gone into production and only one Italian neorealist film had been released in the United States—to great critical acclaim and small audiences. But one British film journal, bemoaning the sorry state of postwar British cinema, understood the importance of *Boomerang!* immediately:

> It appears probable that, if producers wish to counter the present signs of defeatism, of escape into sadistic crime or puerile romance, then they can do it best by a concentration upon the kind of documentary techniques that Louis de Rochemont is so brilliantly developing in the United States and Rossellini in Italy in their films *Boomerang* and *Open City*.[64]

This is one of the first published statements connecting de Rochemont, or de Rochemont style, with Italian neorealism, but it would not be the last. Historians writing years later (and even some filmmakers, like Jules Dassin) would cite neorealism as a major influence on postwar American docudrama, but it should be remembered that very few of these Italian films were seen in the United States early enough to have made any difference. *The House on 92nd Street*, of course, was shot before the end of the war. The *New York Times* did not review *Open City* until February 26, 1946. *Shoe-Shine* followed eighteen months later, on August 27, 1947. By that point, *13 Rue Madeleine* and *Boomerang!* had long since come and gone, and Jules Dassin had already shot most of *The Naked City*. Rossellini's *Paisan* was reviewed by James Agee in *The Nation* on the same day as *The Naked City*, April 24, 1948. By the time Bosley Crowther's review of *The Bicycle Thief* appeared on December 13, 1949, audiences had seen so many de Rochemont-style docudramas that the cycle seemed played out.[65]

It is clear that only one neorealist film, *Open City*, could have had any significant influence on the de Rochemont "school," already well along in adapting the techniques of documentary production for narrative purposes on its own. Reviewing the films of 1946 from a Hollywood perspective, *Los Angeles Times* critic Philip K. Scheuer found that Rossellini's "vivid Italian resistance semi-documentary, *Open City*, fostered a whole cult of followers," but identified no one in particular as a cult member.[66] And what was it, exactly, that had attracted them? Historian Peter Lev suggests that someone on de Rochemont's team had clearly taken note of the film, since the shot of James Cagney at the end of *13 Rue Madeleine*, "strapped to a chair and bleeding from his wounds looks similar to the torture scene near the end of Roberto Rossellini's Italian neorealist film *Open City*."[67] As it happens, the observation accords with that of an editorial writer in the December 1947 issue of *The Screen Writer*, who was comparing the artistic levels of European and American films. Of the "three superb Italian pictures" then attracting attention, he found that "the one that got much the furthest, *Open City*, was luridly advertised as a red-hot sex-and-horror item, crammed with lesbians, dope, and torture-by-blow-torch."[68]

This is not to say that *The Bicycle Thief* (as it was called in America) failed to impress Hollywood filmmakers, only that its influence came at the *end* of the de Rochemont cycle, not the beginning, and not exactly for the reasons so many would later recall. In January 1950, with the film in its fifth week at the Laurel Theatre, the *Los Angeles Times* reported that "Many movie directors and producers" were in the audience, "studying . . . de Sica's technique." The house manager predicted that within a matter of months, "Hollywood movie makers would turn out the first American-produced films using nonprofessional actors; simple, inspirational stories and natural out-of-door sets." Hollywood was already filming on location, but those inexpensive Italian actors were something new, an alternative to "stars who worry about their profiles and whether or not their dressing rooms are complete with bed, television and hot and cold running water." The lesson, the manager concluded, was that "the cost of turning out a picture like *The Bicycle Thief* is so low as compared to the regular Class A Hollywood product that the Italian technique cannot be ignored by us."[69]

Of course, if we look harder for European influences we will also have to consider films like Lazar Wechsler's *The Last Chance*, shot in Switzerland just before the end of the war and released here by MGM in November 1945. Bosley Crowther's review in the *Times* cited "the directness and simplicity of the semi-documentary account, the sharp photographic fidelity and the honesty of performance of the cast—some members of which were recruited from untrained actors," as responsible for the film's power and authenticity.[70] He had praised de Rochemont for these same qualities, and would use almost identical terms to describe neorealist films, as soon as he was able to see them. Crowther would put both *The House on 92nd Street* and *The Last Chance* on his "top ten" list for 1945. The following year he was even more taken with *Open City*, which he felt had a "sharply realistic and deeply compassionate quality" suggestive of *The Last Chance* and a few other European films he had seen recently.[71] In 1946 *Variety* reported that Wechsler would be the first independent producer "financed by the floating of a public stock issue," a more flexible funding option than the usual bank loan guaranteed by the negative. Noted for his use of nonprofessional actors and low production budgets ("He aims to do the same thing in this country"), Wechsler was said to be interested in establishing a U.S. production base in the East, perhaps at the new Associated Filmakers' Studio in the Bronx.[72] But Wechsler never made a film in the United States, continuing to produce such later films as *The Search* (1948) in Europe.

Instead of trying to draw hierarchies of influence here, it might be better to conclude that the increasing prominence of documentary production during the war made it inevitable that narrative filmmakers in every market would see advantages in hybridizing fiction and nonfiction strategies. Stylistically, of course, de Rochemont and the Europeans adjusted the proportions of this formula to suit their own tastes and abilities. As Charles and Mirella Affron point out, "Whereas neorealist directors were steeped in the traditions of the melodrama, and only punctuated their postwar films with the practices of nonfiction, de Rochemont had made his mark as a producer of newsreels and documentaries and only accented his fiction films with the trappings of melodrama."[73]

Some of the more severe examples of the American style do lean so heavily on a just-the-facts approach that today they seem hopelessly flat, hardly in the same class with their warmly humanistic Italian rivals. "In their concern for the situation of the individual in modern society, the Italian neorealists were fundamentally opposed to the focus on abstract institutions, technology, and consensus that runs through the semi-documentary police procedural," Rebecca Prime argues.[74] But while this conclusion seems spot on in describing the police procedurals, it works less well in helping us understand *Boomerang!* or *Lost Boundaries*, films not produced with the support of some government policing agency. The most interesting of Louis de Rochemont's films have very little to do with hidden cameras, wiretapping or counterespionage but focus on intimate personal interactions in ways that Hollywood seldom found time for. And those are the films that would serve as models for a generation of postwar independent filmmakers in New York.

For his part, by 1947 Louis de Rochemont had already given up on Hollywood. There were rumors that Zanuck had been charging studio overhead against the cost of de Rochemont's films, films that were heavily publicized as *not* having been shot at the studio.[75] And perhaps the real problem wasn't working with Fox, or even Darryl F. Zanuck, but the nature of the Hollywood studio system itself. "I feel that I am closer, in my home in Newington, to the heart of this country than I would be in Hollywood, a community that has somehow isolated itself even from the city in which it is located, Los Angeles," he told the *Los Angeles Times* a few years later. "In Hollywood, moreover, because of its remoteness, we tended to view society either from the top or bottom. Life was viewed as either beautiful beyond words or sordid beyond description. I find real drama where I am—and the people here are neither millionaires nor gangsters."[76] His departure was not amicable. Publicity had already gone out announcing that Fox had bought Ruth Moore's novel *Spoonhandle* for de Rochemont, but after his break with Zanuck the project stayed behind, its title changed to *Deep Waters*. It was shot in the autumn of 1947 by Henry King, with all exteriors photographed in the state of Maine, "in the locale associated with the story," an indication of the project's de Rochemont roots.

Kiss of Death

Back on the West Coast, Fred Kohlmar, the producer who had put together *The Dark Corner*, was called in to work with Henry Hathaway again on a project that would synthesize the stylistic innovations of his last three pictures. Zanuck had purchased a story called *Stoolpigeon*, an insider account of dealings within the New York district attorney's office, which had been written by a New York assistant DA named Eleazar Lipsky. This was the sort of thing that had served as the source for many prewar "straight-from-the-headlines" melodramas, such as *Marked Woman* (1937) or *Confessions of a Nazi Spy* (1939). But now Zanuck would go one better. "All scenes in this motion picture, both exterior and interior, were photographed in the State of New York on the actual locale associated with the story," an introductory title card boasted. Of course, like similar claims on many other films, this statement is not literally true in the case of *Kiss of Death*, as the film was eventually called. But the intention is what counts here—especially as the film was not even founded on any specific case and always admitted to being nothing more than a "story" compiled by Lipsky out of various events and observations.[77]

Covering this story with the veneer of reality did not come cheap. Years later Hathaway told me that it was more expensive to shoot the film in New York than on the back lot, which would have shaved an entire week off the production schedule.[78] One news report mocked the studio's "curious economy drive" with the story of an Eighth Street "bachelor girl" who had been renting Fox her $70 a month apartment for $140 a day for the past two weeks, and felt that "Hollywood in New York is a Very Good Thing."[79] But location shooting could justify its additional cost by contributing added value, not just aesthetically, but in terms of publicity and promotion. As with all the postwar Fox docudramas, the studio publicity mill worked overtime emphasizing the unique qualities of location shooting and the great efforts that had been made to achieve it. Away from the studio, it seems, film technology itself had become a burden, with forty tons of technical equipment loaded onto six heavy trucks, all shuttling lights, cameras, and sound equipment among seventy-six different locations. How much of this material had to be shipped from California, and how much was available from local suppliers, is unclear.[80] Press reports highlighted the work of Charles Hall (a busy West Coast production manager who had also worked on *The Dark Corner* and *13 Rue Madeline*), who was responsible for identifying and managing work on these locations. Filming began on March 10 at the "Louisa May Alcott House" on MacDougal and Third Streets and continued for two very busy months.[81] The Fox unit shot at a small Italian grocery store at 156 Sullivan Street, several court houses and prisons (including Sing Sing), the Chrysler Building, the Hotel Marguery, the Convent of the Holy Angels in Fort Lee, the Greyhound Bus Terminal on 180th Street, a nightclub on West Third Street, an apartment building at 66 West Eleventh Street, and a town house on East Eighteenth Street.[82] A modest home on Fourteenth Street in Astoria, with the Triborough and Hell Gate bridges prominent in the background, was rented for $200; the family who lived there moved themselves into one room for the duration of the shooting.[83]

The sound recording on these locations, "both exterior and interior," is excellent, with very little of the telltale echo that marks (and certifies) most location sound in this period. Cameraman Norbert Brodine, an industry veteran who had specialized in low-budget assignments for decades (and who also shot *House on 92nd Street*, *13 Rue Madeleine*, and *Boomerang!*) packed himself into a Chrysler building elevator for a suspenseful sequence where a team of jewel robbers endure an endless trip down from the twenty-fourth floor. To achieve this he used a 16 mm camera loaded with Kodachrome reversal stock (as Zanuck had done in North Africa), which was then blown up to 35 mm black and white for release.[84]

"Melodrama must be believable to be effective," Hathaway told a reporter from the *Times*. "That's where atmosphere is of the utmost importance, and no matter how we may age buildings at the studio they don't have the authority of the real thing." Audiences could now see the difference, he argued. "They can sense real backgrounds and faked ones."[85] To achieve the necessary look, unit manager Charles Hall had to do his own field research, climbing steps and ringing doorbells. "His toughest job was finding a tenement with a third floor flat opening directly onto a steep stairway as called for in the script," the *Times* reported. "This was important because a crippled old lady in the story . . . had to be pushed out of the door in her wheelchair and killed in this brutal fashion." Hall found just the spot but lost it when he explained the nature of the scene to the landlord. " 'I thought for a while I shouldn't have said anything,' he remarked, 'but I had to take that chance. You have to be honest with people in this business, or else you won't get anywhere, not the second time, anyway.' "[86] Mark Philips, one of the most diligent online location detectives, has identified the building used in the film as 142 East Eighteenth Street, just west of Third Avenue and long since demolished.

Hall received no screen credit for *Kiss of Death*, but neither did D. A. Doran, the local outside prop man hired for the production. While West Coast studios like Paramount or Fox depended on their own warehouses to supply any necessary physical object, there were no such depots in the east. What prop houses existed were independent rental operations available to all and generally geared to the requirements of stage producers. Doran had been in the business since the heyday of the Fort Lee studios, and had worked for Paramount at Astoria in the 1930s. While an inside prop man would be brought in by the art department to dress studio sets, someone like Doran would be called on to dress locations, a role he had recently filled on *The Lost Weekend*. Although the company did shoot at the real Greyhound Bus Terminal, the telephone booth used in the scene was a prop supplied by Doran. If Charles Hall arranged to film the cells of actual inmates at Sing Sing, it was Doran who decorated each one with personal effects. Doran had the responsibility of disguising building facades (the Squibb Building became "the Chaffee Building") and transforming plain automobiles into police cars, "which are not allowed to be shown on the screen." While Doran generally drew on the stock of local prop houses and furniture dealers, the *Times* reported that "he sometimes takes furniture and props, from rugs to cocktail shakers, out of his own ten-room colonial house in Flushing when time is pressing."[87] There was not a lot of local behind-the-camera talent used in *Kiss of Death*, but the expertise of many uncredited workers, like Doran, could not be duplicated in other American towns used by Hollywood as "documentary" locations. It would be that wealth of experience, not iconic locations like Central Park or the Chrysler Building, on which the coming New York film renaissance would be based. That, and the pool of theatrical talent that New York could always supply in abundance.

Soon after production started, trade papers reported that Hathaway had signed twenty Broadway actors for "supporting parts," among them Karl Malden (who had already appeared in *13 Rue Madeleine* and *Boomerang!*) and Anthony Ross (also in *Boomerang!* and *The Window*).[88] But in line with Zanuck's desire for star power, the leads were all familiar Hollywood names.

3.2. Patricia Morison (right) with Victor Mature and Coleen Gray in *Kiss of Death*. Morison's entire role was cut from the film by Darryl F. Zanuck, but publicity stills had already been released and it was too late to remove her billing from the film's posters and advertising. Museum of Modern Art Film Stills Archive.

Victor Mature was Nick Bianco, a misunderstood hoodlum—prejudice against ex-cons keeps him from legitimate employment—who is arrested following a jewelry heist he undertook in order to buy Christmas presents for his daughters (or so the unreliable, self-interested narrator informs us). Brian Donlevy was the crafty assistant DA for whom Bianco turns informer, and Patricia Morison played Nick's wife Maria, who puts her head in an oven after her husband is sent up to Sing Sing. The *New York Times* named Mature and Morison as the film's featured players in at least two different articles published during production, and the *Los Angeles Times* also highlighted Morison's role, which was "important dramatically."[89] But she was cut out of the film entirely by the time *Kiss of Death* was released in August, as was Henry Brandon, who played Pete Rizzo, one of Nick's criminal associates, and at least three other actors the *AFI Catalog* identifies as having worked in the film. Zanuck thrived on this sort of postproduction reimagining of a film's narrative line, but sometimes unintended consequences developed. In this case, never seeing anything of Nick's relationship with Maria makes his subsequent passionate attachment to the family's former babysitter (Coleen Gray) a bit startling, especially for 1947. *Los Angeles Times* critic Philip K. Scheuer (whose perplexed review was headlined "Informer Vindicated") felt that all this reediting made it "seem that a section of the film had been lost somewhere."[90] As for Morison, she abandoned her film career soon after her nonappearance in *Kiss of Death*, returning to Broadway in 1948 to create the role of Lilli Vanessi in *Kiss Me, Kate*.

The most serious postproduction revision involved the entire ending of the film, which (despite Fox's claims) was reshot on the studio back lot in June and July. The squealer, Nick Bianco, is being stalked by the psychopathic hood Tommy Udo (a legendary performance by Richard Widmark, the film's most successful local hire), who earlier had sent that old lady down the stairs in her wheelchair. Hathaway claims that he protested the original ending, in which Bianco holes up in Astoria, baiting Udo to track him down and kill him. According to Hathaway's account, after seeing the rough cut Zanuck agreed that the hero was too passive and that "the wrong guy is chasing the wrong guy."[91] Philip Dunne was brought in to write a new ending, in which Bianco does not simply wait for Udo to show up at his house but instead trails him to "Luigi's," an Italian restaurant on 125th Street. Like Clint Eastwood's character at the end of *Gran Torino*, Nick goads the villain into shooting him down, knowing that Udo will then be arrested by the DA and the threat to his loved ones will be over.

This involved redoing all the scenes after Nick had sent his family off to safety. Because it was considered impractical to return to New York for these reshoots, Hathaway duplicated the Astoria house to show Donlevy arriving there, not Widmark. A set for "Luigi's" had to be built, along with a street exterior. Like the "New York" street sets built by Paramount for *The Lost Weekend*, the construction was realistic enough by Hollywood standards, but obviously fake when compared to the real New York seen in the rest of the film. Unlike Eastwood, however, Mature survives the villain's bullets, smiling triumphantly as he lies wounded on the back lot sidewalk, with Alfred Newman's "Street Scene" swelling up on the soundtrack.[92] Ironically, the new ending was a perfect illustration of exactly what Hathaway had told the *New York Times* only a few weeks earlier:

> There is something about an apartment or a bank or a jail that is honest to goodness what it is which somehow doesn't show through in tailored sets no matter how perfect we may duplicate them. I don't want to sound as though I'm discrediting the talents of our art directors, but a room that has been lived in has a certain intangible quality which comes through on the film.[93]

Zanuck vs de Rochemont

Kiss of Death opened in August 1947. In September, after four "New York" films in a row, Hathaway found himself in Chicago working on another "straight-from-the-headlines" location documentary. But this time his producer was not Louis de Rochemont but Otto Lang, who had recently been serving as Darryl F. Zanuck's ski instructor.[94] Lang had been trying to make the leap from Sun Valley to Hollywood and had once been announced as director of *13 Rue Madeleine* before Henry Hathaway took over; now Zanuck decided he was just the right man to step in for the troublesome de Rochemont.[95] His documentary experience consisted of a single short subject, *Ski Flight* (1938), but this would not be a problem with Hathaway directing and Zanuck himself calling the shots back in Hollywood. The success of de Rochemont's *Boomerang!*, which would go on to gross double its negative cost, was a challenge that Zanuck set out to meet with *Call Northside 777*.[96]

"Unless we top *Boomerang* by a very wide margin, we are going to take a severe beating," Zanuck wrote to Quentin Reynolds, whom he had hired to punch up the script. "I happen to have personally originated the so-called de Rochemont touch. It came out of my noodle and no one else's, and therefore I consider myself to be personally on a spot in this venture."[97] At this point Zanuck was fed up with hearing about Louis de Rochemont. James Agee had just reviewed *13 Rue Madeleine* in *The Nation*, and the clipping was probably still on Zanuck's desk. According to Agee, "Louis de Rochemont, the producer, is not the only man making movies in this country who knows the great value of getting outside the studio and shooting in highly specific places; but he is getting more of it done, more effectively, than anyone else, and if the idea spreads, and becomes a practice, I expect that most of the credit will be due to him." As if this wasn't bad enough, Agee had twisted the knife by adding a rare postscript to the column: "One seldom has the pleasure of expressing a hope and being thankful for its fulfillment in virtually the same breath.... I have just seen Mr. de Rochemont's *Boomerang!* It is too late to say more about it in this issue than that it enlarges my respect for him and exceeds my hopes."[98]

But even Agee had praised *13 Rue Madeleine's* "backgrounds" more than its plot and characters. Zanuck got the point, and just days after that column appeared he sent off a memo to Reynolds and Lang, warning them:

> The story [of *Call Northside 777*] lacks any genuine semblance of dramatization.... If we do not have a vital personal story and characters whom we understand and appreciate, then our film becomes as impersonal as a *March of Time*.... Almost like a cold, stenographic report, we tell the facts which we want the audience to know in each separate episode, but we fail to take advantage of the opportunities to dramatize these facts.[99]

As with *Boomerang!*, the facts that needed dramatizing here involved a miscarriage of justice already familiar to audiences from earlier media accounts. A Chicago policeman named William Lundy had been gunned down during a delicatessen robbery in 1932. Two Polish Americans were quickly arrested and given ninety-nine year sentences on the strength of a single eyewitness identification. In 1944 a *Chicago Daily News* editor noticed a classified ad offering a reward for information leading to the identity of the real killers of Officer Lundy and assigned a reporter to investigate. What began as a local human interest story (the mother of one of the convicts had been scrubbing floors for years to raise the reward money) ultimately lead to the impeachment of the eyewitness testimony and freedom for the innocent men.[100]

There is, of course, little direct "New York" input in *Call Northside 777*, which was filmed under the jurisdiction of the Chicago union local. Unlike the situation in New York, the Chicago local had few members with experience in theatrical production, so Fox crews simply took over all technical responsibilities the same way they did, for example, when shooting *Margie* on location in Reno, Nevada, the year before. But the influence of de Rochemont's East Coast docudramas is all over the film, beginning with the familiar claim of having been photographed (whenever possible) on "the actual locales associated with the story." Zanuck was determined to show that he could beat de Rochemont at his own game, filming both interiors and exteriors in and around Chicago, recording as much dialogue on location as possible, laying in just a bit of voice-over narration, and occasionally intercutting what looks like archival footage with new photography. A celebration of investigative journalism and state-of-the-art crime fighting technology, the film highlights the use of gadgets like polygraphs and fax machines in a way that suggests *The House on 92nd Street* more than *Boomerang!*

Zanuck's main problem with de Rochemont's approach seems to have involved the casting of stars, familiar faces who could solve the problem of "characters whom we understand and appreciate" just by showing up. But while Cagney's performance in *13 Rue Madeleine* simply amped up his prewar persona, James Stewart agreed to be cast off-type as a cynical reporter who isn't even convinced of the truth of his own stories. *Call Northside 777* is a strange hybrid, a film that wants to celebrate the virtues of a free press and the American justice system, but can't avoid noticing a residue of corruption in both spheres. Bringing out Stewart's dark side, years before *The Naked Spur* or *Vertigo*, helps audiences understand a world that is far more complex than the Manichean battleground of *The House on 92nd Street*. A fine idea, of course, but *Boomerang!* had already suggested as much the year before.

Zanuck continued to assert his proper ownership of "the so-called de Rochemont touch," putting *The Iron Curtain* into production in Quebec in November 1947 and *The Street with No Name* (filmed on Los Angeles locations doubling for a generic "Center City") in December. Both films were produced with extensive cooperation from J. Edgar Hoover and the FBI.[101] Not an FBI film, but equally supportive of law enforcement, was *Cry of the City*, filmed quickly at the studio between December 26 and February 24, with four days of New York location work in March. Zanuck produced some notable film noir critiques of postwar American society, including *Nightmare Alley* (1947) and *Thieves' Highway* (1948), but was always careful about his treatment of law enforcement. Any slight ambiguity regarding American law or justice, as seen in films like *Boomerang!* and *Kiss of Death*, disappears in films shot after the raucous House Un-American Activities Committee (HUAC) hearings of October 1947. *Cry of the City*, based on a 1947 novel, is set in a world of sinister criminals and benevolent policemen more typical of 1930s gangster films. Victor Mature (the cop) and Richard Conte (the criminal), play characters who were both born and raised in the slums but have taken different paths in life. Like a religious allegory (Italian Catholicism is heavily emphasized), the film juxtaposes the situation of these characters throughout. Conte has been shot and wounded but escapes his hospital ward and wanders the nighttime streets of the city; later Mature is shot and wounded and, bleeding profusely, flees his hospital room to continue the search for Conte. The film ends as Mature shoots Conte in the back, in front of a church, and in a final image embraces Conte's impressionable younger brother, who has now decided to reject the temptations of the dark side.

A blurb in the film's pressbook boasts, "Audiences will be treated to the new photographic technique called 'news-realism' which has been designed to give the moviegoer himself a direct eyewitness position in the story's happenings."[102]

Reviewers generally accepted this line, the *New York Times* describing the film as "of the documentary-like style of film fiction" due to its "authenticity of scene and dialogue and expert characterizations by stars and subordinates."[103] In addition to director Robert Siodmak's clever use of studio settings and back projections, this effect was achieved through a brief New York location trip (March 17–20, 1948) that allowed Mature, Conte, and Hope Emerson to be "established" in recognizable New York neighborhoods. As far as I can tell, only three such shots remain in the film: one of Mature buying a paper on the corner of Cherry and James Streets, another of Conte and Emerson entering the Eighteenth Street IRT station on Fourth Avenue, and an additional shot of Emerson walking past the Third Avenue El (an angle also used in *The Dark Corner*). None of these shots have any narrative significance, and numerous other locations cited in press accounts do not appear to have made the final cut.[104]

Although all the American studios made more feature pictures on location after the war, Fox was especially busy, having put around two dozen such films into production by the end of 1950. One reason may have been the excessive overhead charges laid on at the Fox studio, said to be as much as 52 percent, nearly double the overhead charges at RKO and U-I.[105] *The House on 92nd Street* stands at the head of this line, closely followed by two other de Rochemont docudramas, *13 Rue Madeleine* and *Boomerang!*, which emphasized his newsreel-centric approach to location filming. But this was not the only way of using a location. Zanuck made *Margie* (Reno, Nevada) and *My Darling Clementine* (Monument Valley, Arizona) early in 1946 and then had *Miracle on 34th Street* (New York) and *The Captain from Castile* (Mexico) before the cameras by Thanksgiving. These films all have extensive location work but seem closer to prewar Hollywood genres than to whatever it was that *House on 92nd Street* might have started. Working without de Rochemont from 1947, Zanuck greenlighted several "de Rochemont style" crime thrillers, including *Kiss of Death*, *Call Northside 777*, and *The Iron Curtain* (not to mention the one-time de Rochemont project, *Deep Waters*, shot in Maine). But where de Rochemont valued this style because he felt it provided his films with a special quality of *authenticity*, Zanuck, whose commercial instincts were much better, turned to it for *spectacle*, as he had done with Technicolor and would soon do again with CinemaScope.

This becomes very clear following de Rochemont's break with Fox in 1947. While de Rochemont on his own continued to make films like *Lost Boundaries* and *The Whistle at Eaton Falls*, Zanuck abandoned headline-hunting docudrama almost entirely. Working with blocked European capital, he sent Henry King to Italy for *Prince of Foxes* in 1948 and Henry Hathaway to Morocco for *The Black Rose* in 1949. He made heavy use of Britain's Shepperton studios, not only for *The Forbidden Street* (1948) and *Night and the City* (1949) but also for one of Fox's only "location" comedies, *I Was a Male War Bride* (1948–1949).

Domestically, location filming was usually chosen for reasons of production efficiency, like proximity to airfields, which is why *Slattery's Hurricane* (1948) and *Twelve O'Clock High* (1949) were both shot in Florida. Zanuck felt that he owned not just the docudrama genre but pretty much any sort of location-based narrative, from renaissance costume epic to Hawksian service comedy. In his mind, what de Rochemont was doing only addressed a sliver of these possibilities, while he, Zanuck, was using the lessons of location filming to add value to whatever genre the public was clamoring for.

In December 1949 Zanuck sent Elia Kazan to New Orleans to shoot *Panic in the Streets*, but in New York the studio's "documentary" impulse was already running out of steam. Just after Christmas, Otto Preminger began shooting two weeks of location footage here for *Where the Sidewalk Ends*. The *Times* claimed that twenty-two locations would be used but that Preminger had already been "harried by delays and other encumbrances" while trying to get the first scenes at a pier on Twenty-Third Street.[106] Although the film's pressbook boasted of "its authentic New York location scenes," what we see are a few back-projection plates and a handful of inserts featuring doubles getting in and out of taxicabs.

Henry Hathaway returned to New York in the summer of 1950 to film portions of *Fourteen Hours*, and we can see how Fox's take on location filming had changed entirely. Although generally understood by critics and audiences as an account of the notorious July 26, 1938, suicide of John Warde, the film does not open with any claims of documentary verisimilitude but instead announces that everything and everyone depicted are "entirely fictional," a clear indication that interest in such "actual location" stories had evaporated. Warde had spent eleven hours perched on a seventeenth-story ledge outside the Gotham Hotel before evading would-be rescuers and plunging to his death. The spectacular suicide not only made the papers but also made history when it was broadcast live by NBC's experimental television station, W2XBS.[107]

The film uses the fourteen-hour standoff (in this version) as the framework for investigating the lives of three other characters affected by events on the ledge, a device taken from Joel Sayre's fictionalized account of the tragedy, *The Man on the Ledge*.[108] In what would become a commonplace tradition in 1950s melodrama, the reason for the central character's "cuckoo" behavior is laid entirely on his parents' child-raising strategies. "It starts early, usually. Something that happens between children and parents," a helpful psychiatrist explains. The screenplay fully embraces the postwar obsession with "Momism," a notion promoted by Philip Wylie in his pop-Freud classic, *A Generation of Vipers* (1942). Agnes Moorehead, playing the Mom in question here, has turned this pitiful example of American manhood into a nervous wreck. Audiences were expected to need no further evidence of motivation for the threatened jump.

Because no hotel cared to be associated with the tragedy, the Guaranty Trust Company building at 128 Broadway doubled as the "Rodney Hotel," with curtains added to the office windows to lend a more homey quality. Hathaway and the main camera unit were positioned a block away in a fifteenth-floor corner office at 111 Broadway. A $32,000 mock-up of the hotel had been built on Stage 8 back at the Fox studio, but a bit of location work was thought needed for long shots and crowd scenes. This work was scheduled for a three-day weekend, but when it turned out that the available ledge was only three inches wide, scenic artists were brought in to build it up to fourteen inches,stretching the shoot out for two weeks.[109] As in his other location films, Hathaway was quite clear about how each space would need to function dramatically, choosing this site for the ability it offered to force the visual perspective. "First of all, a narrow building looks higher—and the Guaranty's only three rooms wide," he told one reporter. "Also, it's an offset building, so the side streets go off from it at an angle. The street in front is one-way and narrow, with room for only one car at a time. We heightened the perspective by lining up three taxicabs, one in the street and two on the sidewalks!"[110]

Years later Hathaway told Charles Higham that Richard Basehart, who played the jumper, spent many hours on this ledge, secured by a hidden steel cable.[111] In fact, Basehart's work on the ledge all took place inside that Fox soundstage, although he was still twenty feet above the studio floor. "At first we had a platform and mattresses rigged below him," Hathaway admitted, "but we decided that made him too careless and took them away."[112] In New York, Basehart was doubled by Richard Lacovara, a twenty-five-year old father of two small children who was "regularly employed as a porter in the stereo-type room of *The Daily Mirror*."[113] Construction workers who also responded to Fox's call for someone daring enough to work on the ledge all backed off when told they would have to do it without a rope. Lacovara proved his grit by accepting the challenge, "but that was just a bit of strategy on the part of the director to see how far he could go with his prospective stuntman." Lacovara had no previous climbing experience but seems to have needed the money (ten days of work at $55 a day, with double time on Sunday). He also seems to have had hopes for a career in Hollywood. "I keep wondering whether Mr. Hathaway likes my work good enough to give me a chance in his next picture," he told a reporter for the *Times*. From his camera position across the street, Hathaway would direct action on the ledge by murmuring, "Tell the boy he's wonderful, wonderful," into a telephone mouthpiece dangling from his neck. Years later he had forgotten all about the amateur stuntman he picked up through a New York newspaper ad, but he did remember an incredible story about how the studio ruined the ending of his picture.

Following the facts in the case (and Sayre's story version), Hathaway prepared an ending in which Basehart falls to his death. Then something else happened. "The day *Fourteen Hours* was shown in New York with the proper—suicide—end to it, Skouras's daughter jumped out of the eighth-story window of a hospital she was in and committed suicide," he recalled.¹¹⁴ In fact, Spyros Skouras's twenty-four-year-old daughter Dionysia did plunge to her death from the penthouse apartment of her uncle Charles, head of Fox's theater operations, but that happened on July 17, 1950, while the film was still in production.¹¹⁵ Whatever the chronology, Spyros Skouras, president of Twentieth Century-Fox, vowed that the corporation would never release such a film as long as he had any say in the matter. At Zanuck's insistence, Hathaway reworked the ending. "I shouldn't have done it. I should have said, 'To hell with you, then we won't show the picture.' "¹¹⁶ But Hathaway, a good studio soldier who never questioned a corporate order, was not the man to take that sort of position.¹¹⁷

According to a December 8, 1950, cutting continuity cited by the *AFI Catalog*, Basehart was to fall to his death accidentally after being startled by floodlights turned on by local news crews. In an alternate "happy" ending also shot by Hathaway, he is caught in the safety net stretched below him by the police. *Life* magazine ran a photo spread on the film that focused on the two endings, running stills from both versions as well as a shot of John Warde on his ledge outside the Gotham Hotel for comparison. "Movie producers debated six weeks before choosing climax," they reported, saying nothing about the Skouras family.¹¹⁸ Happy ending or no happy ending, audiences rejected the picture. Hathaway never shot another film in New York, and the studio turned its back on the docudrama genre. Fox was not through with *The Man on the Ledge*, however. On December 28, 1955, they aired another version as one episode of their television anthology series, *The Twentieth Century-Fox Hour*. Cameron Mitchell and Vera Miles starred. The producer was Otto Lang.

Trials of an Independent

Louis de Rochemont's Fox contract had included a loophole allowing him to produce nontheatrical or "educational" films on the side. In May 1947, as his relationship with Fox was deteriorating, he had signed with United World Films to produce a series of *Your World and Mine* shorts, the first of which, *Jungle Nomads* and *Farmer-Fishermen of Norway*, were on the market by July 1948.¹¹⁹ From this point on, Louis de Rochemont Associates would make use of its documentary credentials in all manner of sponsored or nontheatrical productions. To take just one example, *New Tobacco Land*, a one-reel Cinecolor short made for Liggett & Myers, appeared to be just another agriculture documentary, at least until audiences noticed all the references to Chesterfield cigarettes. Theater owners were paid as much as ten dollars for every thousand patrons who saw it.¹²⁰

Classroom films and cigarette commercials must have seemed a real comedown for the producer of *Boomerang!* and *The House on 92nd Street*, but de

Rochemont needed to keep busy while trying to extricate himself from his Fox contract. "I hired a big Hollywood agent, Sam Jaffe, to get me out of my contract with Zanuck," he told columnist Maurice Zolotow. "I think I'm the only guy in Hollywood who ever hired an agent to make him lose a job."[121] By February 1948, trade papers announced that de Rochemont had signed with MGM to produce another feature, *Lost Boundaries*, signaling the final break with his old studio.[122] Partnering with *Reader's Digest*, he then formed the RD-DR Corporation to make "documentary films, both features and shorts," based on material from the magazine (it had already provided his literary source for *Boomerang!*).[123] That summer MGM agreed to distribute a series of "factual shorts" to be produced by RD-DR, while de Rochemont spent many weeks working on the *Lost Boundaries* script, traveling back and forth between Hollywood and the prospective New England locations, trying to solve the problem of casting a film in which an entire African American family "passes" for white.[124]

The studio seemed very high on the project, boasting that it would be "the first film of its kind to deal with problems of the Negro," clearly hoping for something in the line of *Crossfire* and *Gentleman's Agreement*, critically and commercially acclaimed treatments of anti-Semitism that were the talk of Hollywood that summer.[125] But suddenly, in November, MGM shut it all down.[126] De Rochemont told a reporter for the *Times* that once studio overhead was factored in, the film's budget would have been higher than his contract allowed (the fact that the film was not going to be shot at the studio remained unsaid). It also turned out that MGM already had two "Negro problem" films of its own in development, *Stars in My Crown* and *Intruder in the Dust*, making this independent RD-DR production much less of a priority.[127] The short subjects deal also evaporated. De Rochemont later told another reporter that he left MGM because studio head Dore Schary had insisted on "big stars" for *Lost Boundaries*. In any case, extricating himself from this contract proved just as difficult as the situation with Fox, so de Rochemont was forced to bring in Sam Jaffe again.[128]

Part of the deal allowed de Rochemont to buy back the property but not until *after* his current MGM contract expired in January. Realizing that he did not want this to be the third or fourth "Negro" film to reach theaters, de Rochemont moved very quickly. He already had a script and had spent the summer of 1948 scouting locations; in a matter of weeks he found backers (Elliott Hyman and Harry Levine), a new distributor (Film Classics, Inc.), and managed to trim MGM's estimated budget of $1,250,000 down to only $650,000.[129] *Lost Boundaries* began shooting in Portsmouth, New Hampshire, on February 28, 1949, and wrapped on April 29. Except for a brief sequence in Harlem, the entire film was shot within a fifty-mile radius of de Rochemont's home in Newington, and the producer economized by calling in favors from friends and neighbors who had seen him do this before on *The Ramparts We Watch* and *We Are the Marines*.

Appeals went out over WHEB radio for "dresses and suits" from the 1920s and 1930s, which were all supplied locally, not from costume rental houses.[130] Where Dore Schary had inflated the budget by demanding the use of big-name stars, de Rochemont saved money by insisting on the value of fresh faces, a decision that was not just economic but a key element of "the de Rochemont touch."

To this date, no one has uncovered evidence of which stars Dore Schary might have wanted to use in *Lost Boundaries*. De Rochemont's director, Alfred Werker, apparently cast Mel Ferrer in the lead after seeing his headshot in a pile of photos on a casting director's desk. Ferrer was then under contract to David O. Selznick, trying unsuccessfully to convince him to produce a film adaptation of *Strange Fruit*, a drama of miscegenation and lynching in which Ferrer had appeared on Broadway.[131] It was conventional to cast white actors in such "passing" roles, but audiences always knew that Susan Kohner (in *Imitation of Life*) or Ava Gardner (in *Showboat*) were not black; Ferrer was an unknown quantity. Although he told *Negro Digest* that "I always felt that, ideally, a Negro should have had [the part], and not an actor playing a role," Ferrer did succeed in representing the required racial ambiguity. In that same interview he spoke of encountering fans who would quietly approach him and say, "I'm passing, too." And in a bizarre instance of life imitating art, he revealed that his sister Terry, an associate editor at *Newsweek* who had been engaged to deliver the commencement speech at "an exclusive boys' school in the East," found the invitation withdrawn after someone saw *Lost Boundaries* and "discovered she was a Negro."[132]

Screen Director, the newsletter of New York's local Screen Directors Guild, was ecstatic at the nearly "all New York production" and devoted several pages to the film in its April 29, 1949, issue. The Guild was justifiably proud that out of a crew of sixty, only four men needed to be brought out from the coast: the director, Alfred Werker; the unit manager, Percy Ikerd; the assistant director, Horace Hough; and the sound mixer, Hugh McDowell. The only downside to this degree of local production, the Guild confessed, was the $27,000 bill the company ran up at Portsmouth's Rockingham Hotel (other scenes were shot in Durham, New Hampshire, and Kennebunkport, Kittery, and Yorke, Maine).[133] Everything was a location: the exterior of the family's home was represented by the local Pepperill house; interiors were shot in the Sparhawk mansion. De Rochemont had the "sets" decorated with furnishings from his own home.[134] The cast was composed of thirty New York stage actors, few of whom had ever been seen on screen before. Beatrice Pearson's only other film credit was opposite John Garfield in *Force of Evil*, shot a few months earlier. De Rochemont cast his own pastor, Rev. Robert A. Dunn, as the town's local minister, and made good use of Parker Fennelly, an iconic New Englander then known to audiences only as the voice of Titus Moody on Fred Allen's radio show. The most remarkable performance was certainly that of Richard Hylton as the tortured adolescent son, possibly the first appearance of the "anguished teenager," a character who would later become a cliché of 1950s Hollywood cinema. But on release, one otherwise admiring trade paper realized that "the only name of much value in the cast is Canada Lee in a small part."[135]

Lost Boundaries was the story of Dr. Albert C. Johnston, a light-skinned black radiologist, who with his wife and children "passed for white" in a small New England town during the 1930s. Johnston had applied for a commission in the Navy, but when his racial background was discovered he was rejected for failing to meet "physical qualifications." The subsequent public revelation of this secret was all the more dramatic because Johnston and his wife had kept this information from their children.[136] De Rochemont knew this local story (the Johnston's home in Keene, New Hampshire, was not far from his own place in Newington) and had Walter L. White work it up for *Reader's Digest* before convincing MGM to buy it for him.

Historian Donald Bogle categorizes *Lost Boundaries* as part of the "tragic mulatto" genre, overshadowed today by the various versions of *Showboat* and *Imitation of Life* (not to mention Darryl F. Zanuck's *Pinky*, which was filming simultaneously on the West Coast).[137] The unfortunate situation of the characters in these films stems not from any conventional dramatic problem but from the fact that in a world of white privilege an accident of skin color has allowed them to play the role of white, if only at the cost of denying their own racial heritage. The African American filmmaker and novelist Oscar Micheaux had often made use of "passing" in his own books and films because it allowed him to critique issues of color and caste *within* this community. De Rochemont understood this as well, but by placing his story in the whitest part of America he shifted much of the focus away from his "black" characters onto the white culture that he, and most of the movie audience, traditionally took for granted (the film's voice-over narration, apparently speaking for the town, addresses the audience as "we"). Indeed, Bosley Crowther, in a feature essay in the *New York Times*, found that "the usual environments of the Negro are only incidentally glimpsed in the film. This is actually a picture—and a story—of the working of caste in a New England white society which prides itself on its democracy."[138]

Highly praised on release, *Lost Boundaries* was not without its critics. The delay in production meant that Stanley Kramer's *Home of the Brave* got into theaters first, stealing some of the thunder from de Rochemont's film, which by contrast seemed to deal with an issue that affected only one segment of the black population. Why deal with "passing" when more pressing aspects of racism and discrimination remained unaddressed?[139] But the larger issues raised in *Home of the Brave* are only there because the film is a generic entry in the "antidiscrimination" cycle, swapping out the Jewish protagonist of Arthur Laurents's play for an African American character. "It didn't pretend to solve the problems of the Negro," Ferrer said of *Lost Boundaries*, "but made its point more subtly than a pile of documentaries. It was just what it pretended to be, a story about an individual, not rigged like the others had been."[140]

De Rochemont no longer had Darryl F. Zanuck vetting his scripts, but he still understood the need for outside input. Among the readers who commented on various drafts was Ralph Ellison, then still at work on *Invisible Man*. According to Thomas Cripps, Ellison found the hero too passive and encouraged the writers to make him more "forthright, energetic, and clearly the master of his milieu." But another reader warned that a more forthright script might "damage . . . people you will never know."[141] De Rochemont was still tinkering with the script in Portsmouth, even accepting good ideas from the actors. Mel Ferrer claimed that he rebelled at filming a conclusion in which his character "should be a bit humble at the end, that he had made a mistake in trying to pass, that perhaps he should be punished, slapped on the wrists and be allowed to return to his home town but on terms dictated by his white neighbors." The night before the scene was to be shot Ferrer succeeded in arguing for a rewrite.[142] The doctor returns to the community on his own terms, but despite the minister's "we are all God's children" sermon, the audience is not left with the feeling that goodwill can paper over this amount of pain. The family's troubled young daughter leaves the church in the middle of the service and walks outside, alone. We have no idea what she is thinking or what she plans to do.

Ferrer also spoke of being impressed by "the Negroes in the cast," who worked closely with him on his interpretation of the part. "Quietly but firmly they spoke to de Rochemont, Werker, and the writers about misconceptions in the script and with a great deal of intelligence made recommendations which were adopted and which helped make the picture great."[143] Although he mentions no names, Ferrer may be talking about William Greaves, who played the small role of the college buddy who comes to dinner. Greaves was associated with both the American Negro Theatre and the Actors Studio. He appeared on Broadway in *Finian's Rainbow* (1947–1948) and *Lost in the Stars* (1949–1950) and starred in some of the last race movies shot in New York.

> De Rochemont was an inspiration to me, an aspiring young, black filmmaker in the 1950s. He knew of my interest in filmmaking and allowed me to "hang out" and apprentice in his editing rooms. . . . In the early 1950s, the de Rochemont studio was the only white-run film studio where a black man could be treated with respect and given a chance to develop in the forbidden skills of motion picture production. This, too, was a de Rochemont milestone in an industry that was, at that time, entirely hostile to black people.[144]

Soon after, Greaves was up for a role in Fox's *No Way Out*. "I didn't get it because I had done *Lost Boundaries*: Zanuck didn't want to use anybody from one of Louis de Rochemont's films . . . he was feuding with de Rochemont at the time."[145] Sidney Poitier won the career-defining role, while Greaves, with de Rochemont's support, joined the National Film Board of Canada and began a new career as a producer of documentaries.

According to Ferrer, by 1951 *Lost Boundaries* had already grossed $2.5 million, an excellent return on negative cost and a phenomenal amount for an independent production.[146] But producing a film was one thing and maximizing its distribution potential was another. When de Rochemont bought back *Lost Boundaries* from MGM he lost access to the Loew's distribution network and turned instead to Film Classics, Inc., a start-up that seemed well positioned to handle the growing wave of independent features. Unfortunately, Film Classics took on too many such films at the wrong time and was soon caught up in the general box-office collapse of the late 1940s. In 1950 it was absorbed by a rival, Eagle-Lion, and the year after that the merged remains were folded into the United Artists operation. De Rochemont had invested nearly everything he had in the film and "was left with very little in the end," according to Daniel Leab.[147] Film Classics was also the distributor of record for several other New York independent productions, including *Project X* (1949), *Cry Murder* (1950), and *Guilty Bystander* (1950), and its collapse crippled the producers of those films and sent control of their negatives into legal limbo.

Such distribution problems were not uncommon for independent producers trying to gain access to American theater screens. What *was* uncommon was the progress of the lawsuit RD-DR and Film Classics filed against the city of Atlanta, Georgia, whose motion picture censor, Christine Smith, had banned the exhibition of *Lost Boundaries* because it was "likely to have an adverse effect upon the peace, morals, and good order of the city."[148] Although the federal district court was unhappy that Atlanta was exercising this authority "without any standard other than the censor's personal opinion," it upheld the ruling in light of the U.S. Supreme Court's 1915 *Mutual* decision. In that landmark case, the Court had ruled that "the exhibition of moving pictures is a business pure and simple," not to be regarded as "part of the press of the country or as organs of public opinion."[149] That decision related to the state of Ohio's authority to license or regulate the exhibition of Nickelodeon films, which the Court described as merely another example of the "multitudinous shows which are advertised on the billboards of our cities and towns." By categorizing films as simple commercial spectacles, as opposed to books, newspapers, or stage plays, the decision allowed for prior restraint of their exhibition on the part of local authorities. The court of appeals agreed with the district court, sending *RD-DR v. Smith* up to the Supreme Court for final decision. The time seemed right for a history-making turn, but in a surprising move the high Court declined to take up the matter. Ira A. Carmen, in his account of the Supreme Court's involvement with motion picture censorship and free speech issues, is at a loss to explain why Justice Hugo Black, "who had talked with so much conviction about the rights of motion pictures being coequal with those of other media of expression, did not join [Justice William O.] Douglas in a desire to hear oral argument." This seemed especially odd because only two years later, in *Burstyn v. Wilson*, a unanimous Court would completely dismantle *Mutual* in what came to be known as "the *Miracle* decision."[150] Black's unexpected reticence in *RD-DR v. Smith* meant that it was Roberto Rossellini's *Il miracolo*, and not Louis de Rochemont's *Lost Boundaries*, that broke the back of film censorship in the United States.

De Rochemont extricated himself from the Film Classics debacle and signed a three-year contract with Columbia in January 1950. His first project was *Dormitory 7* (later known as *Lift Up Your Hearts*), an illustration of the success modern penal practices were having in rehabilitating the prison population.[151] But that was soon put on hold in favor of *The Whistle at Eaton Falls*, a labor-management saga that he again decided to film in and around Portsmouth. To direct he hired Robert Siodmak, remembered today as a master of Hollywood film noir. But Siodmak had begun his career in Germany with *Menschen am Sonntag* (1929), "shot entirely in the public parks of Berlin, to take advantage of the local atmosphere," as the *New York Times* put it, suggesting an early affinity for de Rochemont's own style.[152] Siodmak was one of the most successful wartime refugee filmmakers, working steadily for many studios since arriving in 1940, but *Whistle at Eaton Falls* would be the last film he would make in America.[153] Like de Rochemont, he was bitter about Hollywood's creative restrictions, where "the director is nothing more than a glorified cameraman" and "the studio always wanted to change my psychological endings into physical ones."[154] Although the *Times* felt that "Siodmak was excited by the idea of continuing in the naturalistic genre he had forsaken," he had already done this in his previous film, *Deported*.[155] A neglected link between film noir and Italian neorealism, *Deported* was recognized at the time as a thinly veiled dramatization of events in the career of Charles "Lucky" Luciano. Produced by Robert Buckner and photographed by William Daniels (who had just won the Oscar for *The Naked City*), its extensive Italian location shooting was designed to take advantage of blocked currency Universal-International was otherwise unable to access. "Roving the streets and waterfront docks of Naples and the historical countryside between Siena and Florence, Buckner, Daniels, and Siodmak have ground out thousands of feet of film at comparatively small cost," one of the *Times*' stringers reported, underscoring the budgetary advantages of filming a dark crime narrative on naturalistic locations.[156]

James Petrie, de Rochemont's location manager, arrived in Portsmouth in May 1950 and began scouting locations. He knew the area well, having done the same job here on *Lost Boundaries* and *The New England Story*, a documentary de Rochemont had made for the State Department three years earlier. "It is rumored by the awed natives that he can drive down the main street and rattle off a description of every stick of furniture in any house in town," the *Times* reported.¹⁵⁷ The story was set in a small town whose economy was linked to a single, dying, plastics factory. *Lost Boundaries* was daring in presenting a hero who lived on both sides of the color line; *The Whistle at Eaton Falls*, the fictional story of a union leader who becomes head of that plastics factory, recast this notion of racial doubling as a labor-management allegory. According to de Rochemont, the film "is the story of a young president of a labor union in New England who attempts to save his community from becoming an industrial ghost town. It is our purpose . . . to dramatize in documentary fashion that labor is an indispensable ingredient in our capitalist system."¹⁵⁸

Siodmak arrived at the Rockingham Hotel in late September and finalized the locations. A working factory in Exeter was used for exteriors, while interiors were shot in an abandoned factory in Dover, dressed for the part with "light wooden replicas of the cumbersome [machinery]" called for in the script. The film captures a liminal moment in American industrial history: the workers in this factory town raise an unemployment fund by staging a square dance (called by Parker Fennelly), but the eventual solution to their problems involves a more efficient way of manufacturing plastic knobs for television sets. Robert Cushman, de Rochemont's local casting director, was surprised at how easy it now was to cast young men in their twenties or thirties for extra work. "Last year, males in this age group were reluctant to apply, on the grounds that movie acting was a sissified occupation." The *Times* reported that he had "about 1,000 names and faces in his Portsmouth files."¹⁵⁹ Putting so many nonprofessional actors on screen was not just cost effective but essential to creating the realistic sense of community de Rochemont was after. "We spend months picking out those locations because we feel there's an added element in the finished product if in the background of the material you can bring out the real flavor of the community," de Rochemont told a reporter from *Theatre Arts*. But any comparisons with neorealism went only so far. "De Rochemont does not agree with Roberto Rossellini's practice of allowing his characters to ad-lib dialogue as they go along," the article noted.¹⁶⁰

Shirlee Weingarten, who cast the principals (she also worked on *Lost Boundaries* and *Walk East on Beacon*), came up with the mix of fresh faces and dependable, anonymous, acting talent that de Rochemont preferred. If Canada Lee was the biggest name in *Lost Boundaries*, Lloyd Bridges, who played the union leader, would be de Rochemont's star in this picture. He had appeared in more than seventy films over the past decade but had just graduated from B-pictures with films like *Home of the Brave*. Some in the audience might have recognized Dorothy Gish, a star whose silent career began at the Biograph Company with D. W. Griffith, but who had only been seen in two previous talking films. Carleton Carpenter, who made his screen debut in *Lost Boundaries*, was now back with de Rochemont after a brief career as an MGM juvenile.

Anne Francis (*So Young, So Bad*) and Arthur O'Connell (*Naked City* and *Force of Evil*), had already appeared in films on both coasts, while Ernest Borgnine and Murray Hamilton, whose screen careers would extend for decades, were at this point practically unknown. Several actors, including Parker Fennelly, John Farrell, and Rev. Robert A. Dunn, were locals who had worked on de Rochemont's last Portsmouth film.

One of the ways in which de Rochemont had been able to cut costs was by dispensing with the services of a well-paid screenwriter. The idea for the project had originally been presented to him by a professor at Harvard Business School, who subsequently developed a treatment along with de Rochemont and his wife. This went on for many weeks, with a host of consultants and one "former Fox screenwriter" being brought in for short periods to merge all of their good ideas into a coherent script. A. Barton Palmer quotes one of de Rochemont's associates explaining to a potential investor that "Louis has found by experience that in the making of his kind of real life pictures it is too costly to give the basic idea to a Hollywood screenwriter . . . and prefers to do the preliminary work with less expensive (and less experienced) writers."[161] Once in front of the cameras, de Rochemont's team felt free to ignore the script as the film began to take shape on location. "Since both the producer and [director] agreed that only by working with their characters through seeing the daily rushes could they get to know them thoroughly, there were frequent last-minute script changes," a challenge for both cast and crew faced with the daily delivery of revised script pages.[162] Palmer refers to this process of "bargain basement development" as "a huge mistake." It would not have happened in Hollywood.

Nor was there any movie star nonsense from the actors, which is exactly what de Rochemont wanted and could afford. "It has reminded me so much of the way we made pictures back in the old days of Mr. Griffith," Dorothy Gish told one reporter.

> To me, there's too much spit-'n'-polish about today's film technique. When Lillian and I were in silent films, we did everything for ourselves—mother made our costumes, we did our own hair, put on our own make-up. It gave one a feeling of being intimately a part of what was going on. Nowadays, you have a couple of people getting you into a costume, another couple fussing around on your hair, others with your face. You feel, somehow, like Marie Antoinette—even with the best will in the world, rather aloof and removed.[163]

This, too, was part of the de Rochemont style. "The clothes worn by actresses in a de Rochemont production are not the output of big-name designers," one reporter noted, "but are mostly inexpensive ready-to-wears bought by Herb Andrews, de Rochemont's designer, in a department store in Portsmouth, New Hampshire. Twenty-five dollars is about as much as Andrews ever lays out for a dress. The result is that characters in a de Rochemont picture look like people who really walk around on streets in suits and dresses that do not fit them too perfectly." De Rochemont was known to dress the sets with furniture from his own home and feed the cast and crew with apples from his orchard. His wife, Virginia, collaborated on the scripts of his films, and if food was required for a particular scene, she and daughter Gingy often prepared it themselves.[164]

Like Kazan working on the streets of Stamford, Siodmak seems to have drawn energy from de Rochemont's New England locations. He "bounced around" Portsmouth in a Tyrolean hat ("for comic effect"), "gesticulating and grimacing like a super-animated Punch in an outdoor puppet show."

> He put on an especially lively performance for several hundred stoic New England extras gathered together for a climactic union hall scene, trying to arouse in them the feeling that they were participating in a stormy workers' meeting. "After half an hour," he recalled recently, "they were yelling like the crowds in *Potemkin*!"[165]

The Whistle at Eaton Falls was shot in October and November 1950, but Columbia did not release it until August 1951, and it did not open in New York until October (*Lost Boundaries*, despite its distribution problems, was in theaters two months after the end of principal photography). De Rochemont claimed that Columbia "hesitated to distribute the picture at first," and asked him, "Why don't you make something less controversial?"[166] It is not surprising that Columbia reacted this way. In their comprehensive catalogue of American feature films, the American Film Institute tags each entry with a series of key words. One of the terms used for *The Whistle at Eaton Falls* is "trade unions." According to the AFI, only two such films had been made in the previous fifteen years: *Native Land* (1942), produced by the left-wing cooperative Frontier Films, and *With These Hands* (1950), a sponsored film made for the International Ladies Garment Workers Union. Neither was handled by a major studio. No subsequent films on this subject would appear until 1954, when a group of Hollywood blacklist victims produced *Salt of the Earth* and Columbia released *On the Waterfront*. Given the political climate in 1951, Hollywood executives would have seen any film dealing with organized labor, no matter how even-handed, as potentially troublesome. By comparison, the year *Lost Boundaries* was released there were four major studio releases dealing with "racism" (according to the AFI's categorization). Five more followed in 1950 and seven in 1951. *Lost Boundaries* may have been controversial, but *The Whistle at Eaton Falls* was radioactive; no one wanted to go anywhere near this subject.

To navigate these dangerous waters, "de Rochemont contended that the picture would present both sides of the labor-management question so fairly that nobody would be offended." After test screenings, he claimed that representatives of both union and management felt it supported their own positions. "The premise I was working on was that there are people who are prejudiced against both sides, and people have blind spots."[167] But for many at the time, this "on the one hand/on the other hand" approach made *Whistle at Eaton Falls* seem more like an educational film intended for classroom discussion. Valorizing the actions of reasonable men and blaming extremists in both camps was not considered dramatically compelling. The film lost points for its attempt at even-handedness because, unlike *Salt of the Earth*, it was not easy to see who the good guys were supposed to be. Bosley Crowther, otherwise a supporter of "message pictures," wrote that de Rochemont and Siodmak "have got a weak picture because they have run from the issues they have raised, either from lack of convictions or out of sheer timidity."[168] One Hollywood trade paper saw it as "a dull, plodding, lifeless exhibit filmed in New England. . . . de Rochemont himself takes to a neutral corner and allows the story to spread itself ambiguously through ninety minutes of tiresome, talky material." The same reviewer even turned on the film's signature visual style, complaining that "the drab atmosphere of a factory town is concentrated on so grimly that characters, plot and movement, which might bring some lift, are totally submerged."[169] Tastes had clearly shifted. As the *Hollywood Reporter* put it, "Some day a law will be passed, we hope, abolishing films featuring 'native types'—i.e., amateur actors whose gnarled faces are given huge close-ups while they utter a colloquialism absolutely unintelligible except to their next door neighbors." Describing its characters as "downright bores," the *Reporter* blasted the film as "the longest ninety minutes this reviewer has ever spent in a projection room."[170] De Rochemont later recalled that "this feature encountered more resistance than any I ever made" and admitted that "we have taken a staggering loss on the project."[171]

As with Fox, de Rochemont's Columbia contract allowed him to make "educational" films on the side, and he took advantage of this to produce an adaptation of George Orwell's *Animal Farm*. Britain's Halas & Batchelor animation studio began work on the film in 1951 under the careful supervision of de Rochemont and his secret "financial sponsors," the Central Intelligence Agency's cold war propaganda arm, the Office of Policy Coordination. Daniel Leab, in his study of the US government's involvement in this film, concludes that de Rochemont's "dire need for funds" may have made him more receptive to the OPC's offer, but that "given his interests and ambition, he would have been equally receptive even without financial problems."[172] De Rochemont had made films directly for the government before this, and as a producer of sponsored films he knew how to take orders from a demanding client. But while the production of *Animal Farm* lies outside the scope of this study, the apparent shift in de Rochemont's political position is also evident in his next film for Columbia, *Walk East on Beacon!*

Even at the time, *Walk East on Beacon!* was seen as a sequel to *The House on 92nd Street*. But while the earlier film was nominally created and controlled by de Rochemont, developed by his staff from various incidents in FBI files, *Walk East on Beacon!* was said to be based on a story directly attributed to J. Edgar Hoover, with whom de Rochemont had had a good working relationship for over a decade.[173] "The Crime of the Century: The Case of the A-Bomb Spies" had appeared in *Reader's Digest* under Hoover's byline, making it available for filming under the RD-DR contract. Hoover was paid for motion picture rights, but de Rochemont used little of this material, which dealt with the Julius and Ethel Rosenberg case. Apparently, dramatizing a notorious incident in which successful espionage did occur would not have shown the FBI in the most favorable light, something that should have occurred to de Rochemont, or Hoover, before the story was acquired. Instead, a refugee German scientist whose family is still trapped behind the Iron Curtain is blackmailed into revealing the secret of "Falcon," a mysterious whatzit that has something to do with computers, rockets, or a space station. As in *The House on 92nd Street*, he turns double agent and helps the FBI round up the spy ring.

The film was shot in and around Boston in the fall of 1951, with location trips to Portsmouth and Dover, New Hampshire, and a return visit to Hoover's office in Washington. Hoover assigned two agents to the film for the entire production, and de Rochemont put them to work as technical advisors, especially when authentic FBI jargon was required. They can be seen in the film playing two FBI agents who tail a Russian spy through Boston's South Station.[174] Indeed, Tony Shaw claims, "The FBI had a hand in virtually all aspects of production: story and screenplay, selection of cast and director, shooting schedule, editing, publicity, and advertising."[175] George Murphy, in his final screen appearance, took the Lloyd Nolan part, while the supporting cast featured an unusually large array of familiar European types (Finlay Currie, Karel Stepanek, Paul Andor). Among the newcomers was George Roy Hill, his only screen credit as an actor before a long career as a television and film director.

Alfred Werker was again brought in to direct, perhaps because de Rochemont knew his earlier location noir, *He Walked by Night* (1948). But there was not much Werker could do with a script that lacked even the narrative coherence of *The House on 92nd Street*. As if to compensate, de Rochemont returned to the heavy use of voice-over narration to patch everything together, even bringing back Westbrook van Voorhis from *The March of Time*. There is the usual focus on teletypes and microscopes, but where *House on 92nd Street* showed FBI agents secretly filming spies with 16 mm cameras, *Walk East on Beacon!* ups the ante by giving them a television camera. Even critics who enjoyed the film saw it as out of date. "Expertly turned melodrama, but melodrama in a familiar format," the *New York Times* reported.[176] Other than the excellent low-key photography of Joseph Brun (who shot *The Whistle at Eaton Falls*), it seemed that de Rochemont's film contributed nothing new to a genre he himself had largely invented.

And why was de Rochemont so late with an anti-Communist docudrama, a subject Columbia had already handled as far back as *Walk a Crooked Mile* (1948, the same year as Zanuck's *The Iron Curtain* at Fox)? While Hollywood was making films like those, de Rochemont had made two socially conscious films in a row, talking not about Communist infiltration but American racism and labor-management issues. But after *Whistle at Eaton Falls* his penal reform film was canceled and he turned instead to *Animal Farm* and *Walk East on Beacon!* When Howard Hughes ran RKO he tested the political loyalty of his directors by offering them projects like *I Married a Communist*. De Rochemont never worked for Hughes, but the apparent shift in the politics of his films after 1950 suggests a certain degree of "self clearance," as the acceptance of such projects was sometimes called during the blacklist era. In any case, he was now in bed with both J. Edgar Hoover *and* the CIA.

If political clearance was de Rochemont's goal, he certainly succeeded. Sen. Karl Mundt, who, while a HUAC member, had taken a leading role in the committee's investigation of communism in Hollywood, thus helping to launch the blacklist, praised *Walk East on Beacon!* on the floor of the Senate.[177] It is impossible to know if this shift in the political flavor of de Rochemont's films was a sincere reflection of his own beliefs or a defensive reaction to changes in the American motion picture industry, but one clue might be found in an extraordinary outburst de Rochemont delivered in a feature article published in the *Saturday Evening Post*. Nominally promoting *Walk East on Beacon!* he starts with the familiar strategy of distancing himself and his films from the general understanding of "documentary," a position he had been taking since at least 1940. But this time he doesn't stop there:

> De Rochemont hates the word "documentary." "It's the kiss of death at the box office," he groans. "An exhibitor hears you're selling a documentary, and right away he thinks of one of those arty *avant-garde* films like the Department of Agriculture used to put out, plugging itself. You know the stuff—long shots of wheatfields, close-up of a broken door on a barn that's falling to pieces, a rusty bedspring in a dried-up river, the busted silo. To make it really poison, these things always had some off-screen commentary, somebody spouting some phony stuff like an imitation of Carl Sandburg. Most of these documentaries usually tried to sneak in a little message; they were usually trying to sell us the idea that our private-property system was all washed up and we should buy some kind of government ownership."[178]

Now it comes out. Sixteen years earlier, de Rochemont's *March of Time* had gone head-to-head in many venues with films like *The Plough That Broke the*

Plains and *The River*, produced by Pare Lorentz for Franklin D. Roosevelt's Resettlement Administration. De Rochemont's catty characterization is close enough to hurt, but he forgets that his *March of Time* handled the Dust Bowl and the Tennessee Valley Authority in the same New Deal–friendly fashion. Nonfiction film had experienced an active and wide-ranging critical debate in the years since de Rochemont had entered the business; one season he and his films might be held in high regard, while the next year they might be dismissed as brash and manipulative. Distancing himself from this entire debate was one way of handling the situation, although complaining about propaganda films powered by voice-over narration does seem a bit disingenuous. But the attack on sneaking socialism is something new, a distinction tailor-made for the age of J. Edgar Hoover and the CIA.

Walk East on Beacon! would be the last de Rochemont film made in the classic "de Rochemont" style. His various companies continued to work on sponsored films and television productions, as well as wide-screen travelogues like *Cinerama Holiday* (1955) and *Windjammer* (1958). In 1953 he optioned rights to the story of Guy Burgess and Donald Maclean, British moles who escaped to the Soviet Union, though nothing came of it.[179] But he did succeed in completing a film on Hollywood's own double agent, Boris Morros, that he called *Man on a String* (1960).

For years, de Rochemont had taken every opportunity to insist that his theatrical features had nothing to do with those pesky documentaries. "They aren't documentaries, but they aren't fiction, either," he told one reporter. "I guess the closest thing to describe them would be the phrase 'pictorial journalism.' Actually, they're a new breed of cat, they're what I want to do, they're what I can do best."[180]

CHAPTER 4

RACE MOVIES

New York's Original Independent Cinema

John Kisch uses the term "separate cinema" to describe a corner of the American film industry that catered to segregated audiences during the height of the Hollywood studio era.[1] While racial segregation was then the norm in many American movie houses, the separate cinema that he and others have described was not simply an artifact of racist theater policies, but included all aspects of producing, distributing, and exhibiting motion pictures. The "race films" that were produced to service these audiences were not a subgenre of Hollywood cinema but a distinct business enterprise involving production companies and distribution exchanges that often dealt in nothing but race movies; creative and technical personnel who seldom worked on Hollywood-style features; and a collection of theaters that may also have shown Hollywood pictures (like most other theaters on the planet) but were still separate enough to be relegated to their own section in the back of the industry's annual trade directories. The 1944 *Film Daily Yearbook*, for example, named 431 "Negro Theaters," but by 1947 another industry source claimed the number of theaters "catering exclusively to Negro audiences" was actually 684, despite the continuing effects of wartime manufacturing controls that had shut down the production of race movies almost entirely.[2]

Between June 1945 and December 1947 a handful of specialized producer/distributors made a heroic effort to revive America's moribund race film industry. Working with a small group of technicians and an even smaller list of local studio facilities, they produced most of the theatrical films made in New York immediately after the war—something they accomplished without benefit of tax incentives or mayoral commissions. But in those thirty months the way that films were made and shown in the United States would undergo a series of seismic shifts, and small-time operations like theirs would be among the first casualties. History has forgotten them and their films, a fate that would not have surprised the critics or audiences who experienced them on the screens of America's segregated motion picture theaters over sixty years ago. The lessons they learned, however, were not so easily forgotten.

New York had been the major producer of race movies until the late 1930s, when it was challenged by a surge of production in Texas, Florida, and California. Prewar race movie audiences enjoyed a wide range of dramas and comedies, and while musicals and gangster pictures were the most popular genres, producers also made westerns and even occasional horror films. Wartime film conservation measures imposed by the War Production Board would shut this business down for the duration, but when it came back to life in 1945 it was in a radically changed form that struggled to adapt to postwar economic conditions.[3] Except for a handful of features coming out of Texas and Chicago, New York was now the only functioning race movie production center, and the only films it seemed interested in producing were musicals. But to understand just how this happened, and why it would matter to the future development of independent film production in New York, we need to look first at the history of an even more marginal film product, one so separate that its output was not even designed for exhibition in theaters: Soundies.

Soundies: The Motion Picture Jukebox

The Mills Novelty Company dominated the manufacture of vending machines, jukeboxes, slot machines, and other coin-operated devices in the prewar period. In 1940 they partnered with James Roosevelt, son of President Franklin D. Roosevelt, to promote a motion picture jukebox device called the Panoram.[4] Mills, acting through the Soundies Distributing Corporation of America, would manufacture and service the devices, as they did with conventional jukeboxes. But while jukeboxes like the Dancemaster or the Zephyr could be stocked with 78s turned out by America's vast recording industry, Panorams needed a constant supply of *filmed* musical numbers, which Roosevelt's Globe-Mills Productions was created to produce. Although the first few were produced by Globe on the West Coast, a New York unit known as Cinemasters began producing Soundies at the Fox Movietone studio in December 1940, with Arthur Leonard directing and Don Malkames behind the camera. A few months later Minoco Productions supplanted Cinemasters, working first at the Eastern Service Studios in Astoria but from 1942 at the old Edison studio on Decatur Avenue in the Bronx.[5]

The Panoram itself was somewhat smaller than a telephone booth and projected its Soundies on the rear of a translucent 18- by 22-inch ground glass screen. As with a conventional jukebox, each selection consisted of a single song or other musical performance running no more than three minutes. Soundies were issued in fixed programs of eight separate selections, strung together on an endless loop of 16 mm film. An automated RCA projector was programmed to go through each item in order, one at a time, then start again at the beginning; customers could not select individual titles and took their chances as to what number was up next, one reason the Panoram failed to supplant the conventional jukebox in popularity. Although Roosevelt originally hoped for 100,000 units in bars and restaurants across the country, the actual total never exceeded 4,500. Indeed, RCA stopped manufacturing 16 mm projectors for the consumer market entirely during the war.[6] Yet somehow, despite facing the same restrictions that had affected other marginal producers, Soundies continued to be produced in large numbers all through the war. One source lists over 2,000 titles copyrighted and released through the end of 1946, at which point the bars and clubs that had been its customer base began replacing their Panorams with television sets and production abruptly stopped.[7]

Although the major studios had produced many low-budget band shorts of their own during the 1930s and 1940s, to maintain this level of production Soundies producers needed to industrialize the filmmaking process beyond anything dreamed of in Hollywood. Some of the earliest Soundies had been directed by ambitious figures like Dudley Murphy (director of *The Emperor Jones*) and Fred Waller (later the creator of Cinerama). Both had experience directing theatrical shorts for studios like RKO or Paramount but were unable, or unwilling, to stay with the Soundies operation after budgets and schedules were pared down in 1942. When business fell off that year following the initial wave of interest, Roosevelt and Gordon Mills reorganized their West Coast operation as RCM Productions, teaming with Hollywood producer and songwriter Sam Coslow. A third production center in Chicago, called Filmcraft, was run by William Forest Crouch. Crouch soon moved the operation to New York, supplanting Minoco at the Edison studio (Mills Industries eventually purchased the Edison studio and named it after Filmcraft). While maintaining professional quality in terms of image and sound, the most important thing now was to produce the films as efficiently as possible, on a sort of motion picture assembly line. Sound recordings were made in the morning, and the musicians would lip-synch to playback after lunch. Crouch was not shy about producing several films a day in this manner, usually on the same set. His record was eleven.[8]

Soundies programs always consisted primarily of white acts, but even in 1941 they were issuing a small but consistent percentage of black acts as well (around 10 percent or so), making this the only integrated filmed entertainment program available at the time. These numbers offered many crossover performers likely to attract both black and white audiences, including Duke Ellington, Cab Calloway, Nat "King" Cole, Fats Waller, Count Basie, and Louis Armstrong. This did not happen by chance. James Roosevelt had given "the exclusive contract in the casting of Negroes" to Fritz Pollard's Sun Tan Studios, described as "the clearinghouse of Negro theatrical talent in Harlem." Sun Tan Studios was not a film production facility—more like a booking agency married to a dancing academy.[9] And while Fritz Pollard was not a director, his role in the casting of locally produced race movies made him a significant player, especially as music came to be their dominant element. Indeed, because A-list white singers and musicians could usually find more lucrative gigs elsewhere, the average quality and interest of the black subjects was probably higher than what the average white Soundie could offer. Stan Kenton, Gene Krupa, Spike Jones, Hoagy Carmichael, and Jimmy Dorsey all appeared in Soundies, but the vast majority of white acts featured mid-level talent (Lawrence Welk or the young Walter Liberace), house bands, or energetic unknowns.

Although the percentage of black acts remained about the same in 1946, the last year of Soundies production, the makeup of these acts, and how they were distributed, had changed significantly. Crouch began to work more directly with producers and distributors of traditional race movies, especially Astor Pictures and Sack Amusement Enterprises, who licensed a number of Soundies for theatrical release on the race movie circuit. And black-cast Soundies began to look more like conventional race movies, as Crouch turned to stars with little or no crossover appeal, such as Pigmeat Markham (*Pigmeat Throws the Bull*, 1945) and Vanita Smythe, whom he featured in a series of raunchy numbers, including *They Raided the Joint* and *Back Door Man* (both 1946). Most important, he turned over much of the black-cast production to William Alexander, an African American producer who had recently entered the theatrical race movie market. Crouch would continue to direct a few of the black-cast subjects himself, while still maintaining responsibility for the rest of Filmcraft's product line, everything from polka bands to country-western performers.

A Separate Cinema?

When Mills Industries offered the Edison studio for sale in March 1948, long after production of Soundies had come to an end, *Film Daily* reported that 1,500 of the three-minute musicals had been shot there.[10] Whatever the actual number, Soundies had somehow kept the near-derelict facility afloat all during the war, its survival allowing it to play a more significant role in the production renaissance of the 1950s and 1960s. What was left unsaid in that report was that most of the feature films made in New York since then had also been made there, and that all of them were race movies.

If Soundies carried the studio through the war, race movies would push it into the era of postwar feature film production. And what happened at Edison affected the rest of the local industry as well, since the Filmcraft operation provided dependable employment for a core group of local technicians and served as a useful business model for other independent producers looking to create their own "separate cinema" in New York.

The importance of this achievement, of course, does not rest on the films' critical or commercial value, of which there was little or none. The best of the prewar race films were culturally ambitious efforts that could hold their own against similarly budgeted Hollywood product, at least on the segregated screens targeted by their producers. Even today, critics and historians are impressed by such imaginative and innovative films as *Within Our Gates* (Oscar Micheaux, 1920) or *The Blood of Jesus* (Spencer Williams, 1941). But despite a rapid and enthusiastic postwar revival, the cultural and economic climate had changed so dramatically that within a few years race movie production would shut down entirely.

How could this have happened? In 1945 and 1946 industry trade papers were filled with hopeful announcements from race movie producers old and new. *Ebony* magazine published an enthusiastic piece called "Negro Movies Hit Pay Dirt," detailing a host of ambitious production schemes.[11] Few at the time could have predicted the imminent integration of Hollywood cinema (however limited), which would steal away promising stars like Ruby Dee. And even more punishing was the same rise in production costs that battered Hollywood producers. The major studios responded by doing what they could to increase average film grosses, but race movie producers were still looking at the maximum gross of $40,000 to $60,000 cited by *Ebony* in 1946. The difference had to come from crucial below-the-line costs: technicians, technology, and production values. Where prewar race films might look and sound like low-end Hollywood product from Mascot or PRC, the threadbare appearance of so many later films from Ted Toddy or Alfred N. Sack now seemed to fall short of any professional standard.

"After 1939, each one seemed more meretricious than its forebear," wrote historian Thomas Cripps. "Critics and audiences gave up on them, consuming them as 'camp' at the bottoms of double bills, warning their children against their excesses, complaining of them in the press, and always voting with their feet for the Hollywood article."[12] *Ebony* soon began to downplay its coverage of race movies, spending more time on films like *Lost Boundaries* or even Roberto Rossellini's *Paisan*, which featured African American actor Dotts Johnson in a significant role. The magazine ran photo spreads on Rex Ingram or Josh White having won small roles in this or that Hollywood film, but low-budget comedies and musicals starring "Moms" Mabley and Pigmeat Markham were generally ignored.

The last feature article on race movies to appear in *Ebony* was published in March 1947 and was actually a self-promotional plug for Crouch's *Ebony Parade*, in which an array of stars "will be introduced by coming to life out of the pages of *Ebony* magazine."[13] The article is illustrated with behind-the-scenes shots taken during the production of *Reet, Petite and Gone* in October 1946 because *Ebony Parade* consisted of nothing but a collection of old Soundies loosely pasted together with bits of interstitial material. The reporter seemed dazzled by the speed and efficiency of Crouch's Filmcraft operation ("movie-making at break-neck speed"), his low shooting ratio (three feet of negative used to get one foot of finished film, where the industry average was closer to fifteen to one) and the fact that he never made more than one or two takes of anything, a strategy credited to the years he spent producing Soundies.

Today, few scholars of African American cinema have anything good to say about postwar race movies like *Ebony Parade*, where nothing seems to have mattered but time and money. Race movies had never been produced on comfortable budgets, but a strategy developed to mass-produce jukebox movies was no solution to the financial woes of low-budget feature film production. Still, the remarkable thing about any of these films is the fact that they managed to get made in the first place. Written off at the time by critics and audiences alike, they at least deserve to be acknowledged for their one real accomplishment: before the RKO Pathé studio opened its doors, and while Louis de Rochemont was still under contract to Fox, a handful of race movie producers managed to kick-start the production of independent features in postwar New York. William Forest Crouch would certainly play a major role here, but the key figure, at least at the start, was someone in front of the camera: Louis Jordan.

"Mr. Personality"

A dynamic musical star who fronted his own band and composed many of his own hit singles, Jordan was at the peak of his career just as the war ended, releasing five straight number one records between July 1946 and May 1947. According to one Wikipedia entry, Jordan "still ranks as the top black recording artist of all time, in terms of the number of weeks at #1," his total of 113 weeks far surpassing Stevie Wonder's record of 70 weeks.[14] Jordan formed his first band in 1938, but his career took off after signing with his new manager Berle Adams at General Artists Corporation in 1941. Innovative marketing and distribution strategies at Decca, often aimed directly at the lucrative coin-operated music market, made Jordan "king of the jukeboxes" during the early war years. While racial segregation continued to damage the visibility of even the best touring black bands, the relative color blindness of this new distribution technology made it far easier for an act like Jordan's to break through to wider audiences.

The Mills Novelty Company serviced those jukeboxes, so when they began distributing jukebox musicals they knew exactly who to sign up. What clinched the deal was that Jordan, "Mr. Personality," was a highly physical performer in the Cab Calloway tradition—mugging, dressing up, sometimes even leaping into the audience. Unlike Vincent Lopez or Duke Ellington (who also made Soundies), this man was not going to sit at the piano or stand up front waving a baton around. Louis Jordan and His Tympany Five made their first batch of Soundies in Los Angeles in 1942, including *Down, Down, Down* and *Old Man Mose*. A year-long ban on the recording of instrumental music, organized by the American Federation of Musicians, did little to slow Jordan's growing popularity, as he had stockpiled enough recordings to see him through. The ban affected Soundies as well, and as soon as it was lifted he filmed another series, this time in New York, beginning with *G.I. Jive*, released on March 13, 1944. Most artists saw their Soundies gigs simply as easy money, but Berle Adams saw something else. Adams told *Billboard* that after studying the response to Jordan's last few Soundies, he realized that the films were more valuable as promotional tools, plugging Jordan's records and road appearances and bolstering the value of his music catalog—what the trade paper referred to as "a 3-Way Payoff."[15] Years later, music videos would serve much the same function. Another manager might simply have encouraged the production of more Soundies, but Adams decided to take a proactive approach: with his client Louis Jordan and the director William Forest Crouch, he formed Adams Productions and made a two-reel short called *Caldonia*.[16]

According to one biography, the music publisher BMI, eager to get a piece of Jordan and his work, "subsidized the making of the film in the certain knowledge that it would be able to recoup revenue from music-license earnings when the short was shown in cinemas."[17] The innovative financing scheme (actually too clever by half, as it led to a damaging lawsuit from Jordan's existing publisher) was matched by an equally original distribution plan. While a few Soundies had already been extracted from preexisting theatrical features, and there were times, as with *Ebony Parade*, when Crouch would work in the opposite direction and patch together a theatrical release by dipping into his Soundies backlist, *Caldonia* was designed from the start to function simultaneously as both a theatrical short *and* a repository for the harvesting of future Soundies.

Caldonia was shot at Filmcraft in December 1944, photographed by Don Malkames on sets designed by Sam Corso. Containing four separate musical numbers joined together with a bit of narrative, it was considerably more ambitious than the three-minute musicals they had all been working on lately. As originally produced, the musical numbers fleshed out a plot in which "a would-be film producer convinces Louis and the band to make films in Harlem rather than their scheduled Hollywood destination, but the lack of resources is a running joke."[18] Considering the film's significant position at the dawn of postwar independent production in New York, a joke like this is quite startling, although no one would have thought much about it at the time.

The trades had announced that *Caldonia* would be available in January, but Decca held back Jordan's recording of the song until April, and a releasing deal with Robert Savini's Astor Pictures was not signed until May.[19] Several more months would go by before the film finally appeared in theaters, and by then the various component numbers had all appeared on the screens of local Panorams. A hit from the start, *Caldonia* played one Southern theater six times in as many months and was billed as the cofeature when Jordan played a two-week run at Chicago's Oriental, a 2,200 seat picture palace—remarkable placement for an independent short.[20] And in addition to the Soundie and the Astor short, Jordan reprised the number in *Swing Parade of 1946*, which he shot at the Monogram studio on July 30–31, 1945, while on a West Coast tour. Compared to Crouch's staging, this Monogram musical looks like something from MGM's Arthur Freed unit. Audiences would have certainly been aware of the painful difference in production values—and the *Caldonia* short even did its best to make a joke of the situation. But in Hollywood, while Jordan lights up the screen in a couple of numbers, he soon disappears entirely, leaving the audience with Phil Regan, Gale Storm, and The Three Stooges. Only in race movies could Jordan carry an entire film, and those films were going to be made in New York, regardless of budgetary limitations. So instead of killing the market, the use of the song across all these different platforms has to be seen as an innovative marketing ploy that pioneered the kind of synergy perfected by the recording industry years later.

Robert Savini

"Encouraged by the spirited response to their first effort at independent flicker production," *Billboard* reported, Adams and Jordan decided that the next logical step was to make their own feature picture, *Beware*. Robert Savini's Astor Pictures Corp., which had distributed the short, would now also function as producer. "Because the first short proved such an excellent promotion gimmick for tunes, two of which, 'Caldonia' and 'Buzz Me,' have reached hit proportions, [they] have inserted seven ditties from the catalog of their own firm, Preview Music, a BMI affiliate."[21] Promoting the catalog may have been the main justification for making the film, but once the decision was made to produce a feature, Jordan—and to a lesser extent his new partner, Robert Savini—clearly felt the need to differentiate *Beware* from the general run of race movies. Readers of *Ebony*, for example, were being told that "most [race movies] are still crude, corny tales about gangsters and night clubs. Acting is stilted, unimaginative and story material is on a par with what Hollywood presented a quarter of a century ago. . . . Many of the Negro films are full of zoot suits, dice, fried chicken and other stereotypes, [and] do not pretend to be interested in 'Negro Uplift.' "[22]

In an interview with *The Chicago Defender*, Savini made it clear that films like *Beware* were something else entirely. "Bob anticipates much success for his pictures, because he has gotten away from the 'Uncle Tom's Cabin' characterization of colored people," the *Defender* reported, approvingly.[23] Savini, of course, was talking to an African American newspaper, but he also understood that he was in partnership with a valuable crossover talent whose persona was neither corny nor stereotypical.

Savini had founded Astor Pictures Corp. in 1933, and most of its business was devoted to repackaging and reissuing previously released material.[24] Astor handled *Tumbleweeds, Hell's Angels, Scarface*, and a compilation of Shirley Temple's shorts for Educational, along with many lesser titles. In 1945 they were very successful with a compilation of Danny Kaye's Educational shorts, which they distributed as *The Birth of a Star*. Apparently assembled by Bud Pollard, this cutting together of earlier short subjects prefigures what Crouch would later do, for Astor, in *Ebony Parade*.[25] Astor had put money into a few films of its own in the 1930s, including *The Terror of Tiny Town* (1938), but the company was not part of the prewar race film business. Nonetheless, after picking up *Caldonia* and a few other shorts, Savini decided to enter the race film market with a new kind of feature. Where earlier producers saw only an African American audience, Savini looked instead at the race record business, which by the 1940s was marketing a significant portion of its product to white listeners as well. A crossover race movie might play in theaters all over the country, grossing far more than even the best prewar productions. In September 1945 Savini announced that Astor would soon begin production on two feature-length Negro musicals.[26] Of course, such films would have to feature talent already familiar to white audiences. Like Louis Jordan.

For his part, Jordan saw these films as a way to correct what he felt was an unfair characterization of his act within the black community. To some, even in his own band, Jordan's crossover success was built on comic routines never intended for white audiences, an accusation that infuriated him. A fastidious bandleader who demanded a high level of professional discipline from his men, Jordan had no tolerance for drugs, drunkenness, or unpolished shoes. He also resisted incorporating the newer bebop sound in his repertoire. This attitude did not always go over very well with those who had to work for him: Paul Quinichette, who played tenor sax for Jordan, described him as "a dictator with Uncle Tom qualities."[27] According to his biographer, John Chilton, "Louis countered such allegations by pointing out that all of his showmanship had been learnt from black performers, all of his tricks of the trade mastered while he was playing to black audiences. If, later, white audiences found them funny this was not, in his eyes, a disgrace."[28] *Beware* would make clear to both black and white audiences that Jordan, and Savini, were not interested in peddling the usual stereotypes.

Like *Caldonia, Beware* contains only enough plot to justify its musical numbers. It was shot at Filmcraft in December 1945, photographed by Don Malkames and designed by Frank Namczy. William Forest Crouch had never directed a feature picture, so *Beware* was produced, directed and edited by low-budget veteran Bud Pollard (no relation to Fritz Pollard). Unlike any other race movie, the film is set on the campus of a historically black college in the South. As in a Judy Garland-Mickey Rooney musical, funds need to be raised to save the school and resolve a melodramatic romantic dilemma. Supporting characters consist largely of deans and university professors. Prof. Drury was played by Frank Wilson, a distinguished African American actor who had appeared on stage in *Porgy* and *The Green Pastures* and in films like *The Emperor Jones* and *Paradise in Harlem* (which he co-wrote with Vincent Valentini). Paging through the alumni directory for likely donors—a lawyer, a congressman, and a millionaire are good prospects—Drury sees the name of Lucius Brokenshire Jordan (Louis Jordan), a graduate of whom not much had been expected. Now a phenomenally successful bandleader, Jordan arrives in the nick of time, hosts the benefit concert, and manages to perform as many numbers from the Preview Music catalog as possible.

Savini would make three features with Louis Jordan, but their production was dependent on Jordan's musical output (new songs to plug) and his touring schedule. Jordan needed to be in New York to make the films, which Savini felt was "the ideal place to make all-Negro pictures because most of the good colored talent is to be found here, in theaters and night clubs."[29] The acts could appear in his films during the day while performing live in the evening. In October 1945 Jordan was playing the prestigious Café Zanzibar, above the Winter Garden on Broadway, sharing a bill with Mantan Moreland (described by John Chilton as "Louis's old favorite").[30] As it happened, the first of the two black musicals Savini put into production that fall featured not Louis Jordan but Mantan Moreland. Bud Pollard had *Tall, Tan and Terrific* before the cameras in Fort Lee by October 31 and only started on *Beware* after he had finished the Moreland picture.[31] Barely feature length (available prints are even a bit short of the announced forty-eight-minute running time), *Tall, Tan and Terrific* concerns itself with gamblers and gangsters and is set almost entirely in a night club, suggesting exactly the sort of film Savini claimed he was trying to avoid. The locale justifies the inclusion of seven musical numbers, which are interspersed with stand-up comedy routines delivered by Mantan Moreland, playing himself. Moreland also anchors the floorshow, helps unravel a murder, and unites the film's young lovers.

The villainous rival club owner in *Tall, Tan and Terrific* was played by the American Negro Theater veteran Dotts Johnson. Historians have described a network of influences running back and forth between the postwar New York cinema and the concurrent Italian neorealist movement, but Johnson's work in 1945–1946, while largely unheralded, is especially interesting. Soon after completing Savini's film he was hired by Rod Geiger, who was assembling a cast of American actors for a film he was producing for Roberto Rossellini. Geiger had been unable to come to terms with Canada Lee (or any of the other well-known American actors Rossellini thought he was sending him) and returned instead with Johnson, Lee's understudy in "Anna Lucasta." (The Bud Pollard film would not have been mentioned.) Johnson's performance as an American MP in Naples whose shoes are stolen by Italian urchins would be a highlight of the film, which was released as *Paisan*.[32]

But if Savini was really trying to move his films away from traditional "Uncle Tom" stereotypes, what was he doing with Mantan Moreland? The historian Donald Bogle later tagged Moreland as "one of the few pure coons to attain popularity at a time when the humanized toms had taken over."[33] In other words, Moreland's persona, which he carried with him from film to film, was closer to that of Stepin Fetchit than to someone like Eddie "Rochester" Anderson. While not nearly as popular as Louis Jordan, Moreland (unlike Dusty Fletcher or Pigmeat Markham) was also well known to white audiences, especially for his role as Charlie Chan's comic sidekick, Birmingham Brown. Years later he claimed, with only slight exaggeration, to have played the part over eighty times.[34] His Hollywood films had established him as the stereotypical stammering coward, fleeing at the first hint of danger ("Feet, don't fail me now . . ."), and he would continue to play the role in most of the films he made for the postwar race market as well. But not this one.

In much the same way that Louis Jordan is used in *Beware*, Mantan Moreland appears here as a real-world superstar, dropped into the world of this film to resolve the various difficulties plaguing the other characters. And in both films it is *those* characters who are the stereotypes—nightclub owner, college professor, gambler, young lovers, or what have you. Moreland is comfortably at ease in every situation, the center of all attention, and beautifully dressed—just the way he and Louis Jordan must have appeared while on stage at the Café Zanzibar (indeed, one wonders if the entire floorshow performance, which takes up all but ten or fifteen minutes of the film, was lifted intact from the stage of the Zanzibar). Whatever is happening here, Savini made sure that the Mantan Moreland seen in this film has little in common with the pop-eyed stereotypes he created in films like *King of the Zombies* (Monogram, 1941) or *Return of Mandy's Husband* (Toddy, 1947).

Although they featured different stars and were shot in different studios, Savini clearly saw *Beware* and *Tall, Tan and Terrific* as a matched set. The films were made one after another by the same producer/director/editor (Bud Pollard) and were both written by one of Pollard's associates, John E. Gordon.

Both found ways of repackaging an existing nightclub act so the results could be advertised as a new feature picture. At one point, Savini even told a reporter that producing the two films in New York had been a test to determine "the practicability of producing musicals here for other types of theaters" (i.e., non-Negro theaters), suggesting that Astor might be looking to raid the New York club scene for white acts as well.[35]

While the films may have done some crossover business, the reaction from the black press was disappointing. *Ebony* dismissed *Tall, Tan and Terrific* as "stilted ... an oft-told yarn done half a dozen times in Hollywood but usually done much better" and was dubious of Savini's claims that the two films were "proof that Astor is intent on giving decent roles to Negroes. While both are a notch above the average in Negro movies, they are not what might be termed 'the best' that the Negro race has to offer."[36]

Southern theaters, accustomed to paying flat rentals for race movies, refused to accept the more costly percentage deals Astor now demanded. In response, Savini took the unusual step of going into competition with these houses by striking 16 mm prints and hosting local premieres in churches, lodge halls, or even in tents. But these 16 mm roadshows were also available to "those localities where there are no theaters which will book Negro pictures for the Negro population."[37] The use of 16 mm as a theatrical distribution medium had been tested by Bud Pollard as far back as 1931, when his independent production of *Alice in Wonderland* was released simultaneously in both 16 and 35 mm.[38] The scheme failed to catch on at the time, but the widespread use of 16 mm during the war had now changed the situation entirely. Indeed, the use of 16 mm for both production and exhibition would be a key element of New York's independent film scene in the postwar era.

Whatever its problems, *Tall, Tan and Terrific* is a landmark in the history of independent New York cinema. Although some might quibble on the matter of length, this was the first theatrical feature shot in the New York area after the war. Financed and distributed by a local producer, it was filmed in Fort Lee by a local crew, using talent drawn directly from Broadway. *Beware* followed in a matter of weeks, but by then Ted Toddy and E. M. Glucksman already had features of their own in production.

Savini, who was always more of a distributor than a producer, spent most of 1946 repackaging the films he already owned—most of which were not race movies—and studying the potential of television. He picked up a few shorts and at least two features (*Swanee Shuffle* and *That Man of Mine*) made by others. Louis Jordan continued a grueling national tour schedule (thirty shows a week at the Apollo alone), interspersed with occasional recording dates. While in New York in June he cut four new sides for Decca, including "Ain't Nobody Here But Us Chickens," which would spend eighteen weeks on *Billboard*'s jukebox race records chart, and "Let the Good Times Roll," a feature of his next

Astor production, *Reet, Petite and Gone*. Jordan's status as "king of the jukebox" was celebrated on a 1948 magazine cover, where he poses with Berle Adams and Bud Pollard on the set of his latest film. Behind them is a gigantic billboard documenting his dominance of the chart in 1946–1947. Over a seventy-eight-week period, Jordan's music held the number-one spot for sixty-six weeks.[39]

Reet, Petite, and Gone was shot at Filmcraft in October 1946, this time with William Forest Crouch as director, his only feature credit.[40] With production of Soundies winding down, Crouch was looking for work (he directed a few shorts locally for Universal, including the *Juvenile Jury* series in 1946–1947, but has no more credits after 1948). Dotts Johnson, who had just returned from Italy after completing his scenes in *Paisan*, was again cast by Savini in a heavy role.[41] With a more complicated narrative than Savini's two earlier films, *Reet, Petite and Gone* still manages to showcase fourteen musical numbers, including "Wham, Sam (Dig Those Gams)," a fetishistic tribute to female anatomy. Indeed, the film was shot under the title *Wham, Sam*, which suggests that Savini was no longer "heeding the call for dignified, full-length feature films," a claim reported in the black press only a few months earlier.[42]

While there was always a sexual element in Jordan's music, Crouch emphasizes this in the staging and not just in double entendre numbers like "That

4.1. Milton Woods and Louis Jordan check out the chorus line in Robert Savini's *Reet, Petite and Gone*, shot at the Filmcraft studio in October 1946. Museum of the Moving Image.

Chick's Too Young to Fry." In one number, in which Jordan does not even appear, June Richmond and Bea Griffith are roommates, waiting in a hotel room for their big break. Bea sits at her dressing table, wearing only bra and panties, with June brushing her hair and offering encouragement. June sings "I've Changed Completely" (accompanied by a handy phonograph) as Bea crosses and uncrosses her legs and very slowly puts on a pair of stockings. The "big break" appears to come in an audition (which involves no singing or dancing and is held not in a theater but a private apartment), where a stream of swimsuit-clad models step up to have "their measurements" taken. Attempting to find a woman with an ideal figure (there is a complicated plot justification for this), Milton Woods, playing Louis Jordan's manager, pulls a tape measure across each woman's breasts, waist, and hips. Crouch simply turns the camera on this parade, which the *American Film Institute Catalog*, in a lengthy plot summary, describes as "interminable." Such imagery would never have appeared in a 1947 Hollywood musical, and like most race films, *Reet, Petite and Gone* does not display a Code Seal. The AFI reports that censors around the country "ordered the elimination of a number of suggestive songs and dance sequences featuring 'indecent' abdominal movements."[43] Those cuts do not seem apparent in currently available copies of the film, which also features Jordan's notoriously misogynistic hit, "Ain't That Just Like a Woman."

For some reason, Savini held off releasing *Reet, Petite and Gone* for over a year. Not until September 1947 was the film described as "complete" and available for worldwide distribution, packaged with a trio of musical shorts: *Ebony Parade, The Dreamer,* and *O'Voutie O'Rooney*.[44] We have already seen how *Ebony Parade* was slyly positioned as a new film, but none of these shorts could be said to have had conventional production histories. *The Dreamer* was a Mantan Moreland film that Crouch apparently made at the same time as *Reet, Petite and Gone*. Contemporary production accounts list Moreland among the *Reet* cast, but he is nowhere to be seen in the completed film.[45] What seems to have happened was that Crouch, or Savini, did not want to waste Moreland in the feature—which already had a bankable star—so they gave him his own short instead. The fact that the same supporting cast (June Richmond, Bea Griffith, and Pat Rainey) also appears in *Reet, Petite and Gone* is what ultimately gives the game away.

O'Voutie O'Rooney was a Slim Gaillard short that Savini had acquired from Jack Rieger, a low-end packager whose day job involved distributing old prizefight footage. It is unclear just where Rieger got his hands on this film, but we know that in 1946 he had joined the "executive staff" of the new Lafayette Television and Motion Picture studio, which was about to build "the largest independent studio outside of Hollywood."[46] Having taken over an old Elks lodge at 144–48 South Oxford Street in Brooklyn, Lafayette planned to exploit the projected boom in East Coast production by building 16,500 square feet of motion picture sound stages and a 7,500-square-foot television stage. To equip the new studios they turned not to RCA or General Electric but to William Bundy Still's Jamaica Radio-Television Mfg. Co.[47] The son of African American composer William Grant Still, Bill Still was a largely self-taught electronics engineer who earned spare cash as a child by "recording the music of orchestra leaders known to himself and his father," including Clarence Williams, Fats Waller, and James Johnson. Fascinated by television, he custom built receivers for industrial clients and claimed he could set up a small local transmitter for less than $20,000, a tenth the going price. Still had applied to the FCC for a television broadcasting license as far back as 1940 and was preparing to put W2XJT on the air over local channel 13 by the end of 1945. But W2XJT failed to launch and in May 1946 Still joined Rieger at Lafayette, signing on as consulting electronics engineer.[48]

Robert Savini gradually moved Astor away from the race film market, relocated to Hollywood, and became more involved with traditional B-movies—first westerns and then science fiction films. In March 1948 he produced the last Louis Jordan feature, *Lookout Sister*, again written by John Gordon and directed by Bud Pollard.[49] Shot under the title *Dude Ranch*, the film is a musical western in which an ailing Louis Jordan, heavily medicated, dreams himself into the plot of a traditional B-western (he awakens just after saving the heroine's ranch from foreclosure). Savini had formed the Astor Publishing Company in January to handle the music used in his films, so Jordan managed to include eleven potential hits, including at least one Bob Willis "country swing" number.[50] A West Coast production, many of the film's exteriors were shot near Jordan's home in Phoenix, Arizona.

There is one curious footnote to Savini's race movie operation, and that involves his distribution of Oscar Micheaux's *The Betrayal*. Micheaux had been based in New York all through the 1920s and 1930s, but in the summer of 1947 he turned away from his current publishing interests and self-financed a comeback picture at All-American's modest studio in Chicago.[51] According to the *Chicago Defender*, what was apparently a "deserted house" was really a production facility that had "turned out many successful news shorts [and] has a well equipped studio with suitable lighting effects and scenery that should keep the flicker in the professional groove."[52] *The Betrayal* was a remake of his first film, *The Homesteader*, which had been made in Chicago in 1918—although why Micheaux made the fatal decision to abandon New York at this time is unclear. E. M. Glucksman used this small studio for his own "Negro newsreels" and short subjects, but made his feature-length race movies at Filmcraft in New York. If Micheaux hoped to arrange a distribution deal with All-American, he was bound to be disappointed—Glucksman had product of his own to worry about. The Chicago shoot was elaborate enough to have included three or four weeks of rehearsal, but post-production dragged on for months, some say at a studio in Fort Lee. Micheaux announced to the trades in February that his new film would be road shown at advanced prices, at the extraordinary length of 195 minutes (a three-part edition, "to be shown on successive engagements," was also being prepared).[53] Since he had no distributor, he was preparing to take on this task himself, as he had in silent movie days.

Unlike any other postwar race film, *The Betrayal* was an ambitious return to the socially conscious, race-based melodramas of the classic era. It is also the final chapter in the biographical legend that Micheaux had been developing even before he began making films, a film intended to be read as an illustration of his own early years as a prairie pioneer. A serious work, it seems to have been one of the few Micheaux talkies without a single musical number. Neither critics nor audiences had any idea what to make of it. Some modern critics (who have never seen it—the film has been lost since 1949) feel that Micheaux's focus on skin color and "passing" was obsolete, and led to *The Betrayal*'s violent rejection by the black press. The film was excoriated by *The Amsterdam News*, for example ("bad . . . amateurish . . . ridiculous . . . downright stupid"), but not, apparently for reasons of outdated content.[54] If anything, Micheaux was ahead of the curve here, too early in the market with a film whose basic concerns would also be addressed in *Pinky* and *Lost Boundaries*. Both those films were still in production on June 24, when *The Betrayal* opened at the Mansfield Theatre, a legitimate Broadway playhouse that had been booked by the only distributor interested in handling it, Robert Savini's Astor Pictures.

What actually seems to have sunk *The Betrayal* were its technical deficiencies, with most reviewers complaining about the physical look and sound of the picture and the performances of its nearly all-amateur cast. The three-hour length did not help matters (the *Chicago Defender* headlined its review, "Thousands of Dollars Wasted Annually On Production of Negro Films").[55] Oddly enough, the film's best reviews can be found in the trade papers. The *Motion Picture Herald*, for example, while conscious of the film's slow pace, crude direction, and "excessively detailed" story, still rated it as "Fair," a far cry from the diatribes in the black press. Impressed by some "scattered moments of engrossing drama," the *Herald* felt that whatever its shortcomings, *The Betrayal* was "obviously a labor of fervent conviction."[56] Subsequent histories have conflated the film's poor critical reception with a lack of commercial success, seeing it as an "elephantine flop" which "played for only a few days."[57] But Patrick McGilligan's research suggests that it played all over the country for months, possibly to good houses.[58] In fact, there are no financials for this film, and we have no idea what it cost, or what it may have taken in. What is clear, however, is that it did not disappear as quickly as some would have it. On September 17, 1949, fifteen months after the premiere, Robert Savini still needed to buy space in the trades warning exhibitors against illicit screenings. "NOTICE," the small display ad read. "Oscar Micheaux is NOT authorized to book the picture

THE BETRAYAL. ALL bookings MUST be approved by ASTOR PICTURES CORPORATION, who control exclusive distribution rights."[59]

Distributing *The Betrayal* was Savini's last contact with race movies. He had started in the picture business in 1904, and had been involved in every sort of marginal operation from nickelodeons to tent shows.[60] He had never worked with Oscar Micheaux but must have known about his reputation for creative accounting, the decades of lawsuits from actors, investors, and distributors, and the fact that Micheaux and his films had been banned from the most important chain of Harlem theaters since 1932.[61] Micheaux, not one to easily let go of a dollar, was still playing the same cat-and-mouse game that independent producers, distributors and exhibitors had always played with one another—only this time it was Savini who caught him at it.

William Alexander and the Associated Producers of Negro Motion Pictures

Bill Still was not the only African American entrepreneur looking for ways to enter the film and television business in New York. William Alexander had spent the war in Washington, doing public relations work for the Office of War Information. E. M. Glucksman's All-American News, a Chicago-based operation, had begun distributing a weekly newsreel for black audiences in 1942 and was soon heavily dependent on free footage channeled to them by the OWI. All-American took as much black-themed material as the government could supply, and Alexander appears to have been the point of contact between Glucksman and Washington.[62] At the end of 1944 All-American decided to expand into the production of theatrical shorts, which would be made for them in New York by Bud Pollard.[63] Alexander had worked with Pollard during his OWI days and was credited as "presenting" *Invasion* (1942), a six-reel compilation of war film material Pollard had assembled largely from government-supplied footage. Feeling he could do at least as good a job as Pollard, Alexander moved to New York and formed the rival William Alexander Productions, making what seems to have been his first theatrical film, *The Vanities*, sometime in 1945. Three single acts—a singer, a dancer, and an impressionist—perform on a very small stage space. There are no technical credits on the surviving print. The camera never moves (it does tilt a bit to follow the dancer) and each act is recorded in a single long take.[64] The film seems to have been shot in a small local club, possibly using a single-system newsreel camera. It is the only postwar race film I know that displays so limited a stylistic vocabulary. Indeed, there would be little else to say about it but for the Bette Davis impression performed by Charles Keith. Instead of *The Little Foxes* or *Jezebel* or *Of Human Bondage*, Keith does Leslie Crosbie in *The Letter*. Celebrity impressions of any kind are very rare in surviving race movies, and this example of cultural appropriation is possibly unique. But why this film? There are plenty of Bette Davis performances to choose from, but Keith picks the one that deals with sex across the color line, and its explosive consequences. One wonders if Oscar Micheaux, whose films frequently returned to the issue, got the joke.

In March 1946 the International Sweethearts of Rhythm (billed as a "Negro" all-girl orchestra, but actually carrying a few white musicians) brought their popular act to the Apollo Theater in Harlem. By the end of the month Alexander was announcing to the press that Associated Producers of Negro Motion Pictures, his new production company, would be releasing the group's first motion picture.[65] The new company was seen as a challenge to the racial hierarchy of the established race film community. "Alexander has made white producers uneasy by his open claims that his company is the only all-Negro owned enterprise in the field," *Ebony* reported. "He plans to use Negro technicians where other firms use whites predominantly."[66] In June he sold *Sweethearts of Rhythm* and two military themed documentaries left over from his OWI days, *The Call of Duty* and *In the Highest Tradition*, to Astor Pictures for national distribution (*The Vanities* was not mentioned). The documentaries would go only to "Negro houses," while Astor would try to book the musical everywhere.[67]

But by that time Alexander had also entered into a relationship with the Soundies Corporation of America, which would release at least fifteen numbers produced by Alexander and directed by race movie veteran Arthur Leonard before the end of the year. Alexander made the films do double duty, producing them as theatrical subjects for Astor while preselling rights to the films' musical numbers for screening on the Panoram (*Rhythm in a Riff* alone would be pillaged for half a dozen Billy Eckstine Soundies). But while Soundies were too short to bother with anything resembling a plot, Alexander quickly realized that audiences for the theatrical shorts were more impressed by films that offered some kind of narrative framework. So in *Love in Syncopation*, for example, Ruby Dee is trying to convince her father (Powell Lindsay) to book Henri Woode's band into his club. While the film is still little more than a collection of musical numbers, that one story idea let audiences know that *Love in Syncopation* was more ambitious than the average jukebox musical.

Later that same year Alexander made his first feature, *That Man of Mine*, directed by Leonard Anderson. As with his earlier films, most of the eleven musical numbers soon wound up on the Panoram. Or perhaps we should say that this group of Soundies also had another life as a theatrical feature: the copyright registration for *That Man of Mine* covers only the three-minute Soundie clip; no one even bothered to copyright the feature. That may demonstrate that the Soundies operation was the dominant element in this business plan, but it could also indicate just how disorganized Alexander's operation was in terms of ordinary business practice. Indeed, he even forgot to include the name of the male lead, Harrel Tillman, in the screen credits (although he was properly listed on the poster art).

The plot of *That Man of Mine*, such as it is, hinges on the problem Associated Motion Picture Studios is having in casting the female lead in its new picture. Low-end Hollywood producers frequently took advantage of movie studio settings, but the lack of traditional back lots and standing sets made them rare in any East Coast production. In this film we see no cameras or microphones, the location being suggested only by a few floor lamps and director's chairs. Lem Coles (Tillman) is a popular singing star about to turn producer. Joan, his costar and fiancée (Ruby Dee, in her first feature), has to remind him that he is "admired by young and old alike not only for your fine performances as an actor but for the dignity and meaning you've insisted on in your work." Joan feels he has gone commercial, but Lem sees his new hip-swinging musical project differently. "When people enter into a movie house to see a musical, they don't care about fine acting," he tells his director (Powell Lindsay, who

4.2. Race film distributors like William Alexander often used 16 mm prints, like this copy of *Jivin' in Be-Bop*, to reach beyond traditional theatrical venues. Frame enlargement.

wrote the film's screenplay). "What they want to see is beautiful girls and hear fine music. The box office is where the payoff is." Lem feels that he needs to replace Joan with "a ravishing beauty," regardless of all he has previously said about the art of moving pictures. Joan, disgusted and angry, tells him that "the only pictures you care about are on dollar bills. Go ahead, take your sex, your glamour," she tells him before storming out of the studio. "I'm not losing *my* principles." After a series of illogical plot twists and a great many "rehearsals" of the film's musical numbers, Lem comes to his senses in a paroxysm of self-criticism. "I know now that I shouldn't try to concentrate completely on the box office," he admits to his collaborators. "I should try to make great pictures with the help of fine artists such as you two." The film ends as the three of them happily shoot the same musical number that had caused all the trouble in the first place.

Alexander followed *That Man of Mine* with *Jivin' in Be-Bop*, a straight concert film, again photographed by Don Malkames and probably shot at Filmcraft. A reversion to the plotless format of his earliest work, it does serve as a showcase for Dizzy Gillespie and his orchestra, who play their own hits (like "Salt Peanuts") and accompany the other acts. A very young Gillespie even gets the chance to sing "He Beeped When He Shoulda Bopped." Not picked up by Astor, the film was distributed by Alexander himself. One wonders if Gillespie's music was considered commercial enough for the established race film distributors.

If so, Alexander's next film was loaded with commercial elements. Early in 1947, when the future of race movies still seemed bright, he signed Joe Louis, Ruby Dee, and the Mills Brothers to appear in a film dealing with serious issues of poverty and juvenile delinquency, *The Fight Never Ends*. Unfortunately, he had only $25,000 to make it. In a very rare move for a race movie producer, instead of hiring one of the small group of local race movie specialists, he turned to a fledgling outfit called Visual Arts Productions. Joseph Lerner was the creative partner in Visual Arts, and he agreed to deliver the entire film for this sum (including writing the script and serving as line producer), so long as they could keep any part of the budget that remained unspent. Years later, he was still proud of having brought in the film for $18,000.[68] Lerner realized that the best way to keep down the budget was simply to avoid renting a studio. At a time when other race films were locked inside studios in New Jersey or The Bronx, *The Fight Never Ends* was shot entirely on practical locations, primarily a redecorated warehouse in the East Fifties. De Rochemont and Rossellini were already doing this, but Lerner knew how to shoot a sound film on location because he had spent the war years at the Signal Corps Photographic Center in Astoria, serving as a writer, director, and head of special productions. He also had B-movie skills picked up at Columbia and RKO in the 1930s.

He knew by experience that most Signal Corps-trained cameramen ("kids") would be too slow to handle the fifty or sixty setups a day required by a five-day feature, so he turned to seventy-one-year-old George Webber, a grizzled veteran with thirty years behind the cameras in New York. During the silent era he had been one of Paramount's leading cameramen, working with stars like Gloria Swanson and Louise Brooks, but like everyone else in the business he would learn to do his best with whatever work was available. Webber shot Soundies. He shot the notorious sex education film, *The Birth of a Baby* (1938). He even shot *Follies Girl*. He also knew about race films, of course, and had just finished one called *Sepia Cinderella* at Filmcraft. "They had told me he was very quick," Lerner remembered. "He wasn't good, he was just quick." Lerner offered him $300 for a week's work then struggled to keep up with him on the set. "But I always felt if I wasn't close to him he'd fall over 'cause he was so old!"

Lerner claimed to have written the script to suit the available talent. Joe Louis (playing himself) is troubled by poverty and crime in Harlem, so he sets out to establish a Boys Athletic Club to keep the young folks out of trouble. At one point he sets up a projector and shows them "Highlights from the Best of Joe Louis's Fights Presented in the Interest of Clean Sportsmanship" to get the point across. Ruby Dee plays a concerned older sister. The Mills Brothers play at the fundraiser thrown to raise money for the project (the film's working title was "Benefit Performance"). Lerner was aware of the growing postwar concern with juvenile delinquency, a subject only a handful of low-budget films had previously addressed (Nicholas Ray's *Knock On Any Door*, for example, was shot more than a year later). He was also unafraid of providing an explanation for this crisis, creating a scene in which young black men discuss the pros and cons of becoming crooks or settling for racially coded dead-end jobs as bellhops. They decide to form a street gang.[69]

Alexander was able to book the film onto the Loew's circuit in New York, an unprecedented accomplishment for a race film.[70] *The Fight Never Ends* was well received by industry trade papers, one critic hailing it as "a very creditable production made in New York with an all-Negro cast" and singling out "some very good acting, with a well-drawn characterization of the sister . . . portrayed by Ruby Dee."[71] For even a positive review of a race film to praise the quality of the acting was at least as rare an achievement as winning Loew's time. The race film director Josh Binney put it this way in 1948:

> When a cast is selected a couple of complete run-through readings suffice to give each character a pretty clear conception of what is expected. Then, at the time the scene is to be photographed, one quick rehearsal is indulged in to acquaint all concerned with tempo and timing, but interpretation and expression, also dialogue (as long as it is appropriate) is left to the actor and it is really surprising that satisfactory results are usually obtained.[72]

Binney blamed limited schedules and budgets for any deficiencies in the acting in his films, as well as any flaws in photography or sound recording. Any success along these lines he accepted as a pleasant surprise.

In her memoir, *With Ossie and Ruby*, Ruby Dee speaks passionately of her involvement in *The Fight Never Ends*. "Well, we've got to begin to make the films ourselves," she told her future husband, Ossie Davis. "This man, Alexander, is trying to do right. We've got to begin to control, to have some input into the kind of images that govern us—."[73] Perhaps she still remembered some of the idealistic rhetoric Alexander had inserted into *That Man of Mine*. In any case, he talked her into a loan of $5,000 to cover "an emergency," a sum that would be paid back in a week. After that money disappeared, Dee convinced Ossie Davis to throw in his life savings of $3,000 as well. Neither of them saw any part of this money again. Dee cites "the lawsuits, the cessation of filming, and the seizure of footage" and notes that the picture (in which she had an unofficial proprietary interest) "had been seized by creditors and that Bill Alexander could only come to New York on weekends if he wanted to avoid arrest."[74] Davis and Dee claimed to have spent years trying to locate Alexander and his

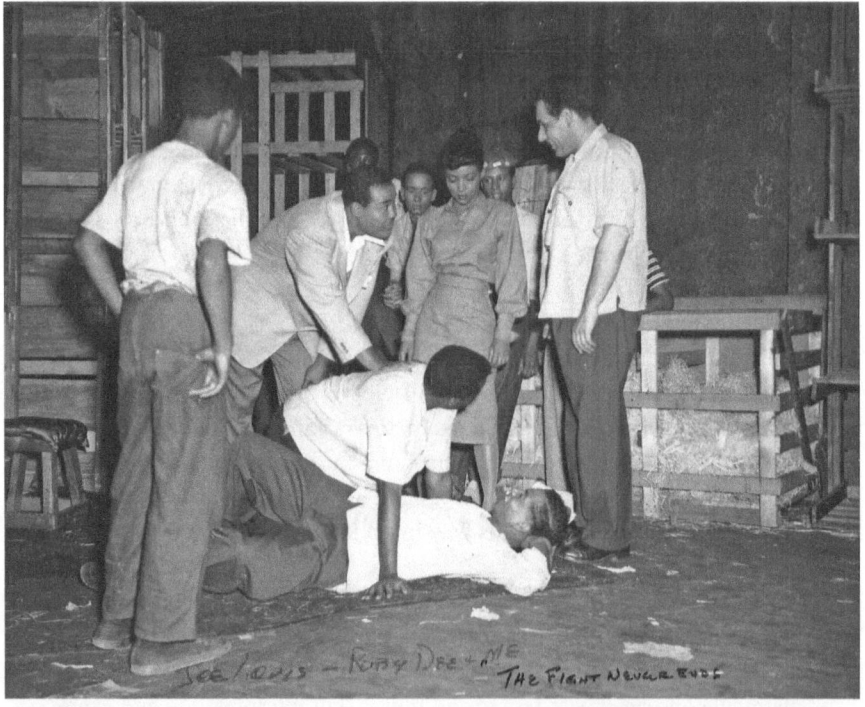

4.3. Joseph Lerner directs Joe Louis and Ruby Dee in *The Fight Never Ends*. A disused warehouse was repurposed to serve as a studio. Author's collection.

financial partner, Ted Parisi (or even a print of the film), without success. Nevertheless, Alexander remains an honorable figure in the memoir, struggling against everyone from film labs to labor unions; the director of the film, Joseph Lerner, is not mentioned in this book.

Sometime in 1948 Alexander was able to produce an even more serious film, *Souls of Sin*, an allegorical drama of three men (a gambler, a writer, and a musician) who share space in a Harlem basement. The film was written and directed by Powell Lindsay, who also appears in a small role. Lindsay was a serious actor (he would star in the brief all-black Broadway revival of *Tobacco Road* in 1950), and while he had written the script of *That Man of Mine*, he had never directed a film before. Perhaps Alexander was finally making good on his earlier promise to employ more black talent behind the camera on his films, but if so, he failed to give the inexperienced Lindsay any proper professional support. The action transpires mainly on two sets, the basement apartment and a local bar, both painted and constructed as if by amateurs: a small fight in the bar almost causes the entire back wall to collapse. Camerawork and editing are rudimentary, and the technicians responsible (Louis Andres and Walter Cruter) have no other known credits. There are a few promising exteriors, including an opening montage ("This is New York . . .") reminiscent of *The Naked City* and a brief sequence in which the fatally wounded gambler stumbles home through the streets. But all too soon we find ourselves back inside those two cheap sets. This is unfortunate, because the story material is promising and even a competent hack like Leonard Anderson might have made something interesting out of it. But Alexander was obviously pinching pennies again. If *The Fight Never Ends* was really made for $18,000 (including the salaries of well-known talent), one shudders to think what *Souls of Sin* actually cost.

Alexander made one last race feature, possibly the last one ever made. He directed *Burlesque in Harlem* himself, though the rest of the film's technical credits, except for editor Nathan Cy Braunstein, an exploitation film specialist, consisted of another roster of unknowns. The emcee, Dick Barrow, introduces a series of burlesque acts, from strippers to baggy pants comics. Where films like *Tall, Tan and Terrific* or *Jivin' in Be-Bop* replicate middle-class entertainments, *Burlesque in Harlem* is heavy on exotic dancers, apparently influenced by the plotless West Coast burlesque features that began to circulate in the late 1940s. Films like this, and Hugh Prince's *Harlem Follies* (1949), can be seen as edging over into more promising territory: the sex exploitation market. Pigmeat Markham's "love-making bureau" sketch here, while hilarious, is also much bluer than his other filmed material. Alexander retreated to the documentary and nonfiction side of the business, targeting Black audiences with the By-Line Newsreel in the mid-1950s.[75] In 1974 he produced (in Hollywood) a notorious adaptation of William Bradford Huie's *The Klansman*, starring Lee Marvin, Richard Burton, and O. J. Simpson.

E. M. Glucksman and the All-American Newsreel

Alexander's connection to the All-American Newsreel is frequently cited but not at all clear. Pearl Bowser quotes him as saying, "We formed the All-American Newsreel Company and used to take OSS crews all over the world," something that happened either during or after his stint with the Office of War Information.[76] Although some historians suggest otherwise, the "we" seems to indicate that Alexander did not see this as his personal accomplishment but rather a group action involving his employer, the OWI, working in association with E. M. Glucksman. Joseph Clark indicates that Alexander worked as "a cameraman, director, on-camera interviewer and, for a time, as All-American's Washington Bureau chief."[77] The later By-Line Newsreel does seem to have been co-produced by Alexander (with Biddy Wood), but All-American News, Inc., was a Chicago corporation headed by E. M. Glucksman, who had once produced Mentone musical shorts for Universal and had been trying unsuccessfully to launch a sports newsreel in the months before Pearl Harbor.[78] The Office of War Information, a propaganda agency whose domestic arm was charged with promoting and clarifying the nation's war aims, was not universally loved by either Congress or the American press, both of which were suspicious of its political motives. OWI did manage to cooperate with several Hollywood newsreel producers to create 267 episodes of "United News," essentially a filmed news release supplied to theaters by the government at no charge. But the studios were not happy to see the government wading into their business, and there were tensions over editorial control, providing an opportunity for Glucksman.[79]

With Joseph Loewy, Glucksman formed the All-American Features Corp. in June 1944, and in December hired Bud Pollard to direct a dozen theatrical shorts for the "Negro market," not using their Chicago studio but somewhere "in the East."[80] This is one of the first announcements of any type of renewed theatrical film production in the New York area. Pollard was to deliver six one-reel "All-American Varieties" and six two-reel "All-American Gems." In January Glucksman announced the imminent release of the first short, Ida James in *Romance on the Beat*, but the films were slow to appear and received little or no press coverage (*Romance on the Beat* seems not to have arrived in Baltimore, for example, until July 7, 1946).[81]

Glucksman may have been holding the films off the market until he had a reasonable number on hand, or at least something of better quality to anchor the program. In July he announced a fairly ambitious cast for his latest, *Big Timers*, now upgraded to "All-American Streamlined Feature" with the addition of a much more important headliner, Stepin Fetchit.[82] With the war in the Pacific just winding down, a wartime ambiance is still in the air. The hero is a GI who appears in uniform, and a Harlem billboard encourages residents to buy war bonds. The setting is the African American community of Sugar Hill, "where the rich folks live," but the focus is mainly on the lives of the less-rich folks who serve them. Francine Everett is in love with her wealthy boyfriend but fears he may discover that her mother is a simple domestic worker in a Sugar Hill apartment hotel. After a certain amount of confusion and misrepresentation, reminiscent of a 1930s two-reel comedy, an excuse is found to stage a variety show in the apartment, and this takes up the entire second half of the film. The thirty-six-minute three-reeler was directed by Pollard at "the All-American Studios in Fort Lee, NJ," and in addition to the studio work there is a bit of comedy shot on the street, without synchronized sound (stills from some of Pollard's other All-American shorts indicate that they also included exteriors, rare among postwar race films).[83]

Stepin Fetchit had never appeared in race movies but was struggling to salvage a career that had been specifically targeted by Walter White and the NAACP.[84] In an interview with the *Baltimore Afro-American* two months earlier he had insisted that his indolent theatrical persona was "no Uncle Tom role" and explained that "I look as if I'm always trying to get out of something, but you can see that I have a soul and that I'm thinking fast."[85] At the start of *Big Timers* he is seen working as a comic porter but is later identified as the famous Stepin Fetchit and agrees to perform in the show (his remarkable proto-rap number is a highlight). The fact that Fetchit's persona shifts between two characters here—he is simultaneously a bumbling janitor *and* a celebrity entertainer—is typical of the more casual approach to narrative and characterization employed in many race films, although *Big Timers* is otherwise shot and edited in conventional low-budget style.

All-American announced a major change in their production plans in December 1946, which would now be anchored by six "all-Negro" features, including four westerns, and a dozen short documentaries. The documentaries were all to be on cultural topics (*Negro Colleges, The Negro in the Field of Art*) and were to accompany "the weekly newsreel schedule."[86] Joseph Clark, who has copies of several of these titles, reports that they were hosted by Claude Barnett, head of the Associated Negro Press, and were apparently underwritten by Liggett & Myers, maker of Chesterfield cigarettes ("worth watching for the hilarious product placement").[87] A dozen "short features" were also listed, including films made by Bud Pollard in New Jersey, some "Streamlined Features" like *Chicago After Dark, Lucky Gamblers*, and *Midnight Menace*, all directed by Josh Binney, and Joseph Seiden's *Stars on Parade*. Like *Big Timers, Stars on Parade* was filmed at the All-American Studios in Fort Lee and used four of the same cast members, including Francine Everett and Milton Wood, but its technical credits are entirely different from Glucksman's other films. It was written by Vincent Valentini, Jack Goldberg's writer, and photographed by J. Burgi Contner, who had worked on Yiddish films for Seiden and others before the war.

It seems likely that the All-American Studios was actually the same Palisade Avenue facility (either a rented loft or converted garage) that Seiden had been operating since 1939 as Cinema Studios.[88] Between 1939 and 1941 the Sepia-Art Pictures Co. produced four Eddie Green shorts here, which Green also wrote, produced, and directed; Don Malkames was the cameraman. The first of these, *The Dress Rehearsal*, was credited as the first race movie ever broadcast on television (December 1939).[89] Closed during the war while Seiden "was devoting his time to the manufacture of recording equipment for the U.S. Air Force," by January 1945 it had been refurbished and was said to be used by *The March of Time*.[90] This was the studio Glucksman rented for Pollard, with the slightly longer *Stars on Parade* (forty-three minutes) part of a side deal he made with Joe Seiden. The radio station background of the film would have made good use of any sound recording apparatus Seiden still had on the premises.

Josh Binney

In the 1947 *Film Daily Yearbook* entry for All-American News, Josh Binney is listed as "Director of Features" at their "Eastern Studio" at 1010 Palisade Avenue in Fort Lee.[91] In addition to three of the "streamlined" features, Binney also made four full-length features for Glucksman, the last of them not released until 1949.[92] One of the first men into the postwar race movie scene in New York, he would also be one of the last men out. Like Bud Pollard, Josh Binney was a veteran of silent slapstick comedy (he had his own studio in Jacksonville in 1918, where he directed Fatty Filbert two-reelers). He also had studios in Portland, San Francisco, Los Angeles, Milwaukee, Butte, and San Antonio, or at least raised money for them from local investors. The trade press, which had an interest in purging the industry of various cons and scams, documented Binney's career in articles like "Josh Binney Arrested" or "Hollywood Producers Arrested in *News* Expose," which generally included lines about "taking money under false pretenses."[93] Living in New York when the race movie bubble hit in 1945, Binney smelled money in the air and found himself a home with All-American. Of course, he had never been in the race movie business before, and since 1918 had not actually directed much of anything. But he still had the skills Glucksman was looking for.

Having proven himself on the "streamlined" features, Binney took the reins of All-American's most elaborate production, a $43,000 musical starring Cab Calloway. *Hi De Ho* was shot in January 1947 at Filmcraft, not Cinema Studios, with an especially large camera crew.[94] Don Malkames was director of photography, while cameramen George Stoetzel, Sid Zucker, and Lester Lang also received screen credit. Like all the features Binney directed for Glucksman, the script of *Hi De Ho* is credited to Hal Seeger, better known as an animator who had worked for the local Fleischer studio and later had a successful television career (e.g., *Batfink*, 1966–1967). The plots all center on some excuse for an assortment of headliners to come together in a performance and differ mainly in what proportion of comedy and drama are mixed in. They are Seeger's only feature credits as a screenwriter, and I have no idea how he, Binney, and Glucksman found one another. *Hi De Ho* is the most single-minded in its focus on one star, Cab Calloway, who plays a struggling bandleader of the same name.

As the film begins he is growing tired of his current lady friend, a frowsy alcoholic named Minnie, played by Jeni Le Gon, who is jealous of Cab's attractive new manager, Nettie (Ida James). The first scene shows Cab summoning her from their hotel bedroom. Despite her seductive appearance *en déshabillé*, all he wants is to have his drink freshened up, which annoys the woman. He tries to placate her with an a cappella version of "Minnie's a Hep-Cat Now," but things quickly go from bad to worse. "I'll see you dead before I let anybody take you from me" she swears, at which point Calloway hits her so hard that she flies off the sofa they are sitting on and rolls across the room. She is still crying when the manager appears at the door, catches sight of the hysterical woman on the floor, and is greeted by Cab's blandly cheerful "Hi, Nettie!" Even today, the effect of this opening sequence is shocking, especially as we have no reason to suspect a dark side to Calloway's bandleader. But the film piles on. Minnie turns to a rival club owner and convinces him to take out a hit on Calloway, but when she presses too hard, he also flattens her. Violence against women, especially in a masochistic "blues" context, was not unknown in race films. In *St. Louis Blues* (1929), Bessie Smith is cruelly abused by the low-life scum she supports, but in *Hi De Ho* the sympathies (in both cases!) are with the men. Minnie eventually regrets her actions and takes a bullet for Cab, allowing him a happy future with Nettie—who has now taken off her glasses.

As always with these films, most of the running time is devoted to musical numbers, highlighted here by an impressive performance of "St. James Infirmary Blues." Calloway, like Dean Martin or Maurice Chevalier, plays himself (in this case, literally), but Binney has no idea what to do with the two talented women in the cast. Jeni Le Gon, an experienced dancer who partnered Bill Robinson at MGM, was hailed as "the sepia Cinderella girl who set London agog with her clever dancing."[95] Here she does no dancing but is instead made to act "drunk" and deliver pages of badly written dialogue. Realizing the danger she has created for Cab, she turns to the camera and exclaims, "Oh, gosh. What shall I do?" Playing a singer, she also does no singing. Ida James, who plays Nettie, was a singer. She appeared with Nat "King" Cole in William Forest Crouch's 1944 Soundie, *Is You Is, or Is You Ain't My Baby?*, and was long associated with the song. But under Binney's direction, Le Gon never dances and James never sings.

In another peculiar move, Glucksman chose to remove *Hi De Ho*'s main comic set piece almost as soon as it was released. Playing the Apollo a few months earlier, Cab Calloway had topped the bill with his dramatic "St. James Infirmary" number, and was supported by the Peters Sisters and the specialty tap dance act of Miller Bros. & Lois, all of whom would soon appear with him in the new film.[96] But the comedy portion of that bill, the team of Moke and Doke, were replaced on screen by Dusty Fletcher and his "Open the Door, Richard" routine. *Hi De Ho* was released at a length of seventy-seven minutes but was soon reduced to about sixty-three, the version now generally available on DVD.[97] Fletcher disappeared from the film, and an entire credit card, which also included the film's other specialty acts, the Peters Sisters and Miller Bros. & Lois, was spliced out. Why would Glucksman bother to do this? Pigmeat Markham had been using "Open the Door, Richard" as a comedy skit on the chitlin' circuit for years, but Dusty Fletcher and others had also used the routine. It was musicalized by Jack McVea, who recorded it in October 1946, and subsequent covers by Count Basie, Louis Jordan, and Dusty Fletcher himself (there seem to have been fourteen recorded versions) were topping the charts all through the early months of 1947.[98] Despite the fact that his film featured the skit, not the song, Glucksman suddenly realized that he was onto a good thing, and in February quietly extracted the "Richard" segment from *Hi De Ho* and announced that he had completed a new short.[99]

Variety had published an extensive summary of the act when Fletcher played it on Broadway the year before, and from this we know that the film provides an almost unmediated transcript of this remarkable piece of African American vaudeville.[100] It begins as Fletcher's character, dressed in his usual rags and obviously drunk, is being thrown into "the street" by a disgusted saloonkeeper who threatens to "kick your teeth out, one by one" if he ever catches him in that bar again. "Why don't you get yourself a job and go to work," he says, not really expecting a satisfactory answer. The barkeep later returns to deliver a key prop, a ladder Fletcher has left behind. (Fletcher says that it must have been Cab Calloway who left the ladder behind, a likely ad lib inexplicable outside the context of the feature.) The physical action in the rest of the nine-minute skit consists of Fletcher's crawling from stage left to stage right, where the proscenium represents a door that Fletcher's supposed roommate, Richard, never opens for him. Fletcher does get up to do an amazing bit with the ladder but otherwise plays the entire scene from the floor. What led *Variety* to describe this act as "different than most comedy turns on the boards today" is Fletcher's stream-of-consciousness monologue, like some W. C. Fields mumblings stretched out for an entire reel and culturally reimagined. Fletcher talks about drinking paint (and asks for paint remover as an antidote) and of going off relief because government staffing cuts have made it too time consuming to wait in line for his check. Stepin Fetchit usually made it plain that his character's sluggish demeanor masked something else entirely, and that it isn't work he is avoiding so much as what comes with it: the need to jump to someone else's orders (often a white man but sometimes an exasperated spouse or just about anyone in authority). Critics may disagree about Fetchit, but with Fletcher there is nothing to argue about: the character employs no mask and *defines* shiftlessness and irresponsibility. One hesitates to project a modern critical sensibility onto this midcentury vaudeville. This is not Samuel Beckett. But anyone looking at the film today will need to reassess their opinion of traditional 1940s burlesque performance.

Soon after, Astor released *I Ain't Gonna Open That Door*, sometimes known as *Richard's Answer*. Earl Bostic and his band perform a spin-off number called "Lazy Richard." Failing to get "Richard" to open the door, they try the phone; cutaways reveal him to be Stepin Fetchit (who answers the phone as "Richard Perry"). According to Mel Watkins, "the short offers what is perhaps the best example of Fetchit's humor or 'audible pantomime' available in pictures. In its tone and spirit, it vividly captures his style, deceptive wit, and near-perfect timing."[101] Between choruses of the song, Fetchit raps out another stream-of-consciousness monologue while firmly refusing to get out of bed. The film is much slicker than Dusty Fletcher's version, not just technically but also in the presentation of its main character. Fletcher plays an alcoholic wastrel who delivers his number from the gutter. Fetchit, neatly dressed for bed in a comfortable B-movie bedroom, answers his own phone and seems more sleepy than lazy. The class differences between these two characters suggest they could never be roommates but also that the filmmakers involved were aiming at two different audiences. The IMDb indicates that William Forest Crouch directed this film in 1949. While it does look like Crouch's work, the 1947 date suggested by the Library of Congress is more convincing. And though Astor eventually picked it up, it is anyone's guess who produced it.

After *Hi De Ho*, Binney may have worked on short films again, including one called *Cow Town* with Red River Dave. This was to have been made in San Antonio, where he had dabbled in the studio business before the war. *Motion Picture Daily* reported that this was "said to be a Western picture with Negroes," although Red River Dave was a white cowboy singer.[102] Binney did go to London in 1947, where he directed an hour-long feature, *Merry-go-round*, for Federated Film Corporation. Or at least assembled it, using a familiar cut-and-paste technique. A "distracted film producer" in need of ideas is given some by his janitor, which appear as "second rate musical turns . . . with alternating scenes of very poor comedy and badly played music."[103] Historian Geoff Brown reports that "the footage in the film must have come from other material controlled by Federated or the distributor Butcher's, another bargain basement operation," suggesting that Binney was trying to go international with this strategy.[104]

He returned to New York in December just in time to direct Glucksman's next feature, *Killer Diller*, which was shot at the Pathé studio the week of December 15, 1947.[105] The RKO unit producing *The Window* vacated on a

Friday, and Binney began work on Monday. This is one of the few race films known to have been shot at Pathé, the most modern studio facility in the country, although that is impossible to tell from looking at the film. Abandoning the fairly dramatic narrative line of *Hi De Ho*, *Killer Diller* reverts to the simpler revue format, showcasing "Moms" Mabley, Dusty Fletcher, and Butterfly McQueen in a series of loosely organized scenes. The action is set in a theater, where a harassed producer is trying to put on a variety revue starring the King Cole Trio and Andy Kirk's orchestra. Establishing shots of the Lincoln Theatre on West 135th Street are used, and we see lobby posters advertising "All-American News/Latest News of the Day." There are even a few bits staged out of doors, as a group of comedy policemen chase Dusty Fletcher around the building (Fletcher has far more screen time than Butterfly McQueen, who is wasted in a throwaway bit). Binney also hated exteriors because they "involve weather conditions which frequently cause long, costly delays," something he could not abide.[106] The "Keystone Kops" quality of these scenes—in which the pursuers periodically stop running in order to leap in the air—recalls the slapstick comedies of Binney's youth, and the editing and camerawork seem equally old school. Again, Binney films a master shot and splices in close-ups when required, but his touch is clumsy and disruptive. Most of the film is shot and recorded in this "live" manner, but some numbers appear to involve playback. When "Moms" Mabley is on stage the film lurches from one recording style to the other in the middle of the sequence, with a noticeable effect on sound quality. *Killer Diller* was banned by the Chicago police censor, although press reports provide no explanation.[107]

Considerably more interesting was *Boarding House Blues*, which has better variety acts and a more developed frame story taking up nearly half the running time. "Moms" Mabley runs a theatrical boarding house but is always short of money because the tenants fail to pay. The landlord threatens to foreclose and throw everyone into the street unless a beautiful young singer, Lila Foster (Marie Cooke), will agree to marry him. The motley assortment of tenants stages a variety show to raise cash in an attempt to save both their homes and her honor (Seeger seems to have gotten this plot from an old Betty Boop cartoon). Dusty Fletcher plays the most troublesome tenant, who insists on sharing his room with his partner, a chattering primate named Steggy, who swings from the chandeliers. The role is played by a man in a threadbare monkey suit (Jack Riano, an acrobat who had a long stage career specializing in stunts and eccentric dancing). The audience assumes that—with the aid of this cheap, B-movie costume—the men are conning everyone in the boarding house, all of whom believe that Fletcher's partner really is a scruffy animal of some kind. That's one level of joke. But eventually we realize that Steggy continues to chatter and leap on the furniture even when he and Dusty are alone. He isn't supposed to be *playing* an animal, he is supposed to *be* an animal. So as with Nana in a stage production of *Peter Pan*, we agree to accept this theatrical representation because we understand how theatrical conventions work. But in the last five minutes of the film, Dusty and Steggy are discovered quarreling and playing cards, and we see that Steggy is half out of his costume ("hot in there!"). If Steggy can remove this mask, what do we make of this whole role-playing business? This third-level gag tops, and transforms, the other two. While there is much about the comedy in these films that is both crude and conventional, there are also times when they demand to be read as very conscious exercises in theatrical style. The actors, and their original audience, are sharing a joke about masks, image, and performance.[108]

The bulk of the film's music was supplied by Lucky Millinder and His Orchestra, featuring Bull Moose Jackson, Anistine Allen, and Paul Breckinridge, who were all appearing with him at the Apollo.[109] But the film also features specialty numbers from Lewis and White, whose stand-up routine is laced with drug references (cocaine, marijuana, Benzedrine . . .), the remarkable "Crip" Heard, a one-armed, one-legged theatrical dancer making his only film appearance, and several other acts. Then, as with "Open the Door, Richard," Glucksman found he had gotten lucky again.

Lucky Millinder was chosen to anchor the only all-black radio show airing on a national network. As the *Chicago Defender* put it, "Wednesday, July 7, will go down in the history of show business as the day that the 'National Minstrel Show' made its debut on the NBC network."[110] Years before Spike Lee's *Bamboozled*, NBC did plan to air a weekly minstrel show that season, a summer replacement for Dennis Day's Wednesday night broadcast. "The National Minstrel Show" was intended as an homage to black entertainment. Millinder would be supported by Jackson, Allen, and Breckinridge, who all played with him at the Apollo and in Glucksman's film. "Moms" Mabley was also picked for the radio show but not Dusty Fletcher, who was replaced by the team of Miller and Lee. As might be expected, there was immediate pushback on this from the NAACP, which resulted in the sudden cancellation of the July 7 premiere, a quick series of negotiations, and a new name and starting date.[111] "Swingtime at the Savoy" premiered on July 28, now fronted by Noble Sissle and written by Langston Hughes, with guest star Ella Fitzgerald joining Millinder's crew.[112] The focus on black entertainment history was still there: "Moms" Mabley delivered a tribute to Bert Williams, but even *Variety* thought that Miller and Lee's routine "was strictly out of the minstrel end men book, long since discarded."[113] The show ran successfully all summer.

On September 11, it was announced that Lucky Millinder's new film, *Boarding House Blues*, "will be released nationally early in September."[114] The film was obviously shot in New York around the time of the radio show, but did this happen before, during, or after the NBC booking? It is clear that Fletcher, Mabley, and Millinder's people are part of one narrative line, while the specialty acts were shot on an entirely different stage and spliced in to bring the running time up to eighty-seven minutes. Binney directed in his usual style, using several cameras and a minimum of editing. Once again three cinematographers are credited: one as director of photography and two simply as cameramen. Of course, at one point Binney still covers a conversation by panning back and forth between close-ups of the actors. But the editing, while simple, lacks the off-balance quality of his earlier films; no editor is credited, which under the circumstances probably means that someone did not wish to be identified. This added polish might also be due to the work of a better assistant director, Sal Scoppa, Jr. Scoppa has no other race movie credits, and generally worked on films with much higher budgets, like *Carnegie Hall*, *Portrait of Jennie*, and *The Window*. His presence, and that of art director Sam Corso, who also worked on *The Window* and *Killer Diller*, suggests that the Pathé studio was used again, once more with a minimum of publicity.[115]

That fall Josh Binney directed his last film, *The Joint Is Jumpin'*, which he claimed at the time was the cheapest race movie he ever made, a $9,000 feature.[116] Waiting for their dates in a small restaurant, two penniless schemers (John Mason and Jimmy Short), devise a plan to avoid paying the bill: when the check comes they will start a fight and get themselves thrown out. One wonders if this ploy is some kind of inside joke on Hal Seeger's part, a subtle reference to the way Binney and Glucksman actually paid for films like this. In the aftermath of the fight the pair wind up running the restaurant and listen to a pitch from a TV salesman, who demonstrates the machine for the customers. "The salesman switches channels and together they watch a variety of singers and dancers on the different channels."[117] After the set is turned off, the leader of the house band suggests that the diners continue the entertainment on their own. Binney had won the race to the bottom but at the cost of driving the last nail into the race movie coffin.

The restaurant action was filmed at All-American's Chicago studio. "What for many years was thought to be a deserted house, palatial as it must have been at one time, located at Twenty-Ninth and Prairie, is in reality the home of All-American News," wrote local reporter Al Monroe.[118] His surprise suggests that the facility had not been used very much recently. As the reader must suspect by now, the bulk of the musical numbers were shot elsewhere and presented "on the television." Monroe was told that all the scenes with Bob Howard, Una Mae Carlisle, Hadda Brooks, Slick and Slack, and various others had already been filmed in New York. In fact, some of them had been filmed three years earlier by Joseph Seiden, who used the numbers in *Stars on Parade*.[119] Hadda Brooks (unforgettable at the piano in Nicholas Ray's *In A Lonely Place*) was part of some fresh footage that Binney had shot in New York. While he had her in the building he also squeezed out a ten-minute short called *Boogie Woogie Blues*, in which she sits at a piano in a living room set and performs three numbers. The first two appear to be recorded "live," and the third incorporates some rudimentary playback effects, including a 180-degree change of angle and another shot framed in a baroque mirror. It is clear that no one knew how this material was going to be used while they were shooting it. Introducing her first number, Brooks says, "I'd like to do another favorite of mine." The ending is signaled by a voice shouting "Cut!"

Back in Chicago, Binney filmed local performers on the "restaurant" set, including Olivette Miller, Mildred Kirk, and Stewart Hampton. "Just what all these performers do, in the picture, your guess is as good as ours," Monroe warned. "However, there is every reason to believe they've been given plenty to do and with Josh Binney directing they should do their parts well."[120]

In December 1948, after his experience of race movies was over, Binney published an essay on "Movies for and with Negroes" in the local Screen Directors Guild newsletter. He spent much of his time discussing the relative advantages of shooting musical numbers to playback or staging them live, the way the first talkies were produced in the early days of sound. While his most expensive film, *Hi De Ho*, was clearly shot to playback, as his budgets shrank Binney decided that this was an unnecessary luxury, at least as far as race films were concerned. He now preferred to cover a musical number with multiple cameras, as if he were filming a televised variety show. Binney said he used this technique because of the actors, or more exactly, the black actors. He felt that he "had a great deal of experience with Negroes and has found them as responsive and capable as artists of any other race or nationality, particularly if they are allowed the opportunity to be creative, to interpret the character and situations as they feel it and are not held to a strict adherence to the author's or director's conception." Conventional shot breakdowns, or worse, the filming of a sequence out of order, are a problem for the black actor, Binney argued, because "if he is interrupted, he likely cannot repeat what he has done, nor can he hit the tempo, expression nor action to make possible good cutting of long shots, medium shots and close-ups if he has done them separately. For this reason many complete sequences [in Binney's films] are photographed with two or three synchronized cameras, *and very rarely is a 'retake' made*."[121]

To be fair, Binney admits that this problem with black actors "does not apply where long periods of time have been given to rehearsal, but long periods of time cannot be given to rehearsal where a feature is produced in a few days, at a cost of around $35,000." And rehearsal was something that he, or Glucksman, could not afford. "Prerecording, with action done to 'playbacks,' was resorted to as little as possible, even though all of these pictures would be classified as musicals. Because of the difficulty Negroes have in doing things twice in the same way, 'lip synchronization' is not resorted to as a usual thing."[122] By this time Binney's musical numbers were generally shot live (he gives a figure of 80 percent), with cameras peering over the heads of "the audience" and microphones recording whatever came their way.

It is hard to know where to begin with this.

On one hand, Binney is talking about problems that affect every low-budget picture: no time for rehearsals or retakes means that not much should be expected of such a film or the man responsible for it. "Pictures made under such circumstances cannot help but fall far short of perfection, 'sound' can never be perfect, neither can photography, because it is next to impossible to 'light' a set, or action for three cameras, three angles at one time, but results meet the requirements of the Negro market," he writes in the rambling conclusion to his essay on making race movies.[123] And that dovetails with his other problem, producing low-budget films with performers who are talented ("Negroes Are Good Artists" is a subhead in this essay) and observant ("the Negro can grasp a situation quickly") but temperamentally unsuited to the mechanical routine of conventional film production technique. This, he says, is what forces him to avoid playback and conventional scene dissection.

Even if we could put aside the racist component of this argument, the fact still remains that Bud Pollard, Arthur Leonard, and Joseph Seiden do not seem to have expressed any misgivings about black actors being able to do things twice in the same way. William Forest Crouch directed hundreds of Soundies, with both black and white performers, and insisted that playback was the *only* way to shoot such musical numbers quickly and efficiently. But as far as Binney was concerned, it was still not efficient enough. So while Crouch would record audio in the morning and shoot to playback in the afternoon, Binney decided to skip that first part, effectively doubling Crouch's rate of production. Quality might suffer, of course, but to avoid the amateurish look of something like William Alexander's *Vanities*, he could simply add a few more cameras, and that would have to be good enough. Not perfect, of course, but good enough to "meet the requirements of the Negro market." Binney was not the only race film director to understand that he was in a race for the bottom as far as production standards were concerned, but he seems to have been the only one to address this in print—if only as a way of excusing his own limitations. One suspects that he employed the same sort of twisted logic in earlier days, when angry investors in one of his studio promotions complained about a lack of results. It was always somebody else's fault.

Sack Amusement Enterprises

When the production of race movies was frozen during the war, the veteran distributor Alfred N. Sack continued to circulate titles he had stockpiled before 1942, including Spencer Williams's extremely popular *The Blood of Jesus*. In 1944

Sack broke the freeze with *Go Down, Death!* and *Of One Blood*, also directed by Williams, who in 1946–1947 would become the house director at his "Harlemwood Studios" in Dallas (the earlier films had also been shot in Texas).[124] Films shot at Harlemwood, including *Juke Joint, Girl in Room 20*, and *Dirty Gertie from Harlem, USA*, represent the only significant body of postwar race films *not* made in New York.[125] Sack, one of the key players in New York's prewar race film industry, now had plans to get his films elsewhere—except where people like William Forest Crouch or George Quigley were concerned.

Crouch had directed Louis Jordan's two-reel *Caldonia* in December 1944 with the idea of taking it apart and processing it into a series of Soundies. But in January it was announced that he was also hard at work on a series of one-reel musicals for Sack Amusement Enterprises, some also featuring Louis Jordan and his band. This work actually consisted of reediting and relabeling a selection of popular Soundies—including Jordan's *Ration Blues* (originally released March 27, 1944), *Rocco Blues* (with Maurice Rocco, December 31, 1943), and *Toot That Trumpet* (Francine Everett, October 18, 1943)—so they could now be sold into the theatrical market. Sack, like Astor, was in the business of retitling and reissuing used goods, and Crouch had access to an unlimited supply. Press accounts were generally careful to avoid the claim that these were new productions, and the eight films in the package were typically described as "completed and in the cutting room," never "before the cameras."[126] Sack swept them all into its own release schedule, and their provenance has been confusing film and music historians ever since.

Even more confusing was Sack's 1947 deal with George P. Quigley's Century Productions for a trio of Bob Howard films.[127] A lively piano vocalist in the Fats Waller tradition, Howard was already a well-known radio personality with his own show since 1937. In July 1948 he would become the first African American with his own television program on a network affiliate, the daily "Bob Howard Show" on WCBS in New York, which ran until December 1951.[128] Quigley appears to have fallen heir to a prewar (1941?) New York race movie called *Mistaken Identity*, a crime drama with a few musical numbers. He added several new numbers featuring Howard and the Noble Sissle band, shot wraparound footage of Howard explaining much of the missing backstory, and changed the name to *Murder with Music*. The second feature, *Junction 88*, featured Howard and Pigmeat Markham as a pair of New York music promoters who drive to the small town of Junction 88 in search of a songwriter. This film is also assembled from disparate material but in a very different way. Scenes shot in Howard's New York office are professionally lit and edited, probably filmed in a small New York studio. Pigmeat Markham wears his traditional comic outfit and plays his familiar low-comedy character as the men sing "Poor Lulu." But most of the film appears to have been shot in some rural location (Texas?), using many exteriors and a few rudimentary sets. The visual quality of these scenes appears suddenly degraded, as if the footage had been blown up from 16 mm; indeed, the photography credit is split between Don Malkames and John Visconti, an industrial film cameraman.[129] But the tone of the film also changes. Pigmeat Markham now wears a business suit, stops clowning, and sings the dramatic "Eagle Eye Blues" instead of one of his bawdy burlesque numbers. In place of some snappy Harlem atmosphere, the film offers a credible image of the rural black south, seen as a real community whose members are affected by postwar price hikes but glad to be rid of "GI haircuts." Everything centers on the church. The fundraising plot is served here by Noble Sissle (who apologizes for appearing with only six members of his band), but the church choir also performs and a talented eight-year-old sings "My Country 'Tis of Thee" as if he were in a Leo McCarey picture. Despite an obviously low budget, the film does not limit itself to a series of studio interiors but also makes nice use of direct sound recording on exteriors, rare in a race film. Indeed, some scenes played on studio interiors move back and forth between live recording and playback, technically sophisticated for any low-budget production in this period.

One suspects that this film was begun in New York and completed at Sack's Harlemwood studio. But did George Quigley really direct it? Or is it mainly the uncredited work of Sack's house director, Spencer Williams? Sack was never very concerned about credits, in any case. While "Noble Sissel" is credited on the main titles, Sack's one-sheet poster calls him "Nobel Sissle," and only the lobby cards actually spell his name correctly. The third film in the package was a two-reel short called *Bob Howard's House Party*, perhaps a spin-off of his radio program—or an unintended trailer for his upcoming television show?[130]

Jack Goldberg

Just two weeks after the announcement that Jack Rieger had signed on at Brooklyn's Lafayette studio, Jack Goldberg's Hollywood Pictures announced that it would make three "all-Negro" films there "due to the company's failure to get studio space on the coast."[131] The Lafayette studio project soon fell into the same dark hole that swallowed a number of other potential New York studios that year, and Goldberg did not make his "Negro films" in Brooklyn, but it seems curious that the only producer who even expressed an interest in shooting at Lafayette was hoping to make race movies there. Who tried to bring in this business? Was it Jack Rieger? Was it Bill Still, who had been working with people like Fats Waller since he was a teenager and whose ambitions probably went beyond installing the electrical equipment? Or was Goldberg already so interested that he didn't need to be sold on the idea of making race movies in New York?

Jack Goldberg boasted that he had "made some twenty-five all-Negro pictures in Florida, Hollywood, and the East" over the past twenty years.[132] He had been booking black acts around the country since the 1920s and expanded into films when he prepared the sound version of Josephine Baker's *La Sirène des tropiques* in 1929.¹³³ According to Judith Weisenfeld, that was also the year he married famed blues singer Mamie Smith.¹³⁴ Goldberg's approach to the race film market was unique. Using newly available Signal Corps footage, he had assembled *The Unknown Soldier Speaks* in 1934, a feature-length documentary that was produced in both "white" and "black" versions, the latter emphasizing accomplishments of the 369th Infantry Regiment. That same year he organized The Negro Marches On, Inc., with the intention of producing a newsreel-style series of nonfiction films for distribution to black theaters. "This, he says, will be a Negro version of what is being done by the publishers of *Time Magazine* with their 'March of Time,' " the *Motion Picture Herald* reported in 1936. "Mr. Goldberg plans to present a reenactment of incidents in the history of the American Negro, such as the recent 'Scottsboro Case' in Alabama."¹³⁵ Goldberg seems to have left the newsreel idea to E. M. Glucksman, but after producing two features in Miami in 1941 he announced an even more ambitious "creative center for the development of Negro films and screen talent," to be known as the Liberty City Motion Picture Studios. Both a studio and a school for training black screen talent, this was to have been part of a vast Miami "social welfare" project headed by Capt. James E. Scott. "Negro audiences want pictures that have a more realistic approach to their own problems," he told one reporter, noting that they were "tired of the kind of fare they have been given in the past," and he was preparing to offer them something new.¹³⁶ How serious this scheme really was is impossible to say, as the war soon put civilian projects like this on permanent hold. But after Pearl Harbor Goldberg did assemble another military compilation film targeted at black audiences, *We've Come a Long, Long, Way*, which his Negro Marches On company released in 1944. Unfortunately, the government had its own film on the same subject, *The Negro Soldier*, using much of the same footage (their own). Goldberg's reputation suffered when he attempted to enjoin the government from releasing their "competing" film, and he was attacked in some corners of the black press as mercenary and opportunistic.¹³⁷

Unlike Robert Savini or Alfred Sack, race films were not a side issue for Jack Goldberg but the core of his business for over twenty years. In 1944 he formed Hollywood Pictures Corp. to produce theatrical subjects, although he also maintained a full staff at The Negro Marches On until at least 1950.¹³⁸ He acquired an unreleased Lena Horne short, *Boogie-Woogie Dream*, which had been shot in New York by Czech refugee director Hans Burger in 1941.¹³⁹ Hollywood Pictures released the short in 1944, and it often played on the same bill with Michael Curtiz's Warner Bros. musical, *Janie*, suggesting an encouraging postwar future for crossover talent like Horne (or Louis Jordan).¹⁴⁰ Goldberg's Television Motion Picture Company also cut the film up into three-minute musical segments, and he squeezed further mileage out of it by splicing in some other shorts he controlled and releasing the result as *Harlem on Parade* in 1946.[141]

Even before the war was over, Jack announced that he and his brother Bert would begin work on a series of twelve "Negro features" as early as June 15, 1945—but in Hollywood, not Florida.[142] In spring 1946 he appears to have agreed to make these films in partnership with Alfred Sack (various studio locations were mentioned, including the Lafayette studio in Brooklyn), but *Beale Street Mama* seems the only feature to have come of this.[143] Goldberg soon broke with Sack and formed Herald Pictures in August, announcing that director Arthur Leonard would begin shooting their first $50,000 feature, *Boy! What a Girl!* at the Movietone studio on September 16. Not eager for a long-term lease at the relatively upscale Movietone, Goldberg announced that Herald was already converting a building in Harlem for use as its future studio home.[144]

Arthur Leonard was an experienced New York director who had gone from Vitaphone shorts to race movies to Soundies, mirroring the general decline of the entire local film industry over the past decade. *Boy! What a Girl!* and Goldberg's follow-up feature, *Sepia Cinderella*, would mark the end of Leonard's theatrical directing career, but the production of these two features in 1946 provided further evidence that independent filmmaking was finally beginning to take root in New York. In fact, *Boy! What a Girl!* and Edgar G. Ulmer's *Carnegie Hall* were in production at Movietone simultaneously. According to one planted news story, Ulmer (who also directed race movies in New York before the war) saw Sheila Guyse working on Leonard's set and quickly cast her in his own film.[145] She appears as Marsha Hunt's maid, "Margaret," putting a record on a turntable and announcing that she has organized a "Tony Salerno fan club." Despite the fact that she plays a named character and shares a brief scene with the star, she is unbilled. An attractive singer and dancer in the Dorothy Dandridge mode, she was a frequent cover girl for *Jet* and *Hue* and later appeared on Broadway in *Finian's Rainbow* and *Lost in the Stars*. Guyse would star in all three features Goldberg made in New York, but these (and *Carnegie Hall*) are the only films she ever made.

Boy! What a Girl! is set in a Harlem apartment house, where a hopeful theatrical producer is trying to raise money for his new show while romancing the daughter of one of his potential investors. The plot involves a lot of mistaken identity and female impersonation (Tim Moore, who later starred as Kingfish on television's *Amos 'n' Andy*, plays most of the film in drag, hence the title). More complications are introduced via a trio of burlesque "Frenchmen," who are usually accompanied on the soundtrack by the strains of "La Marseillaise." Rehearsals and a boisterous rent party provide the excuse for several musical numbers featuring the Slam Stewart Trio and Big Sid Catlett's Band. At one point in this otherwise "all black" film, drummer Gene Krupa shows up at the rent party and takes over from Slam Stewart. "I know who you are—you're Gene Krupa," Stewart exclaims. "Yeah. And don't forget, I want you to do the same for me in one of my pictures," he responds, a self-referential gag not atypical of low-budget cinema in this period. Elwood Smith, who plays the promoter, talks aloud to himself when the plot requires it and once even addresses the audience. If the seams were going to show anyway, why not make a joke of it?

Goldberg was hoping to reach a crossover audience here (hence the Krupa appearance), so he made sure that *Boy! What a Girl!* was more than just a pack of musical numbers. The film offers a romantic plot and plenty of broad comedy, while the numbers are well shot, to playback, and dialogue sequences are competently edited together from multiple angles. True, the comic characters are far more interesting than the romantic leads and the sets show very little of the touted $50,000 budget, but Leonard does a proper job of delivering a B-movie feature on a Z-movie budget. By comparison, Edgar G. Ulmer's notoriously inexpensive *Detour* cost $117,226.80 in Hollywood the year before.[146]

Sepia Cinderella was shot in December 1946 at the Filmcraft studio in the Bronx, which seems to have provided more commodious accommodations. In one scene a character enters the door of his apartment and the camera tracks with him as he plays a scene with another actor while they both walk into the adjacent room, the camera "passing though the wall" as if this were a James Whale film. This may not seem like much of an accomplishment, but it shows that this $50,000 feature is trying to look like a real movie and not an overproduced Soundie. While Goldberg had to use Filmcraft's resident art director, Frank Namczy, he employed the same director (Leonard), cameraman (George Webber), writer (Vincent Valentini) and editor (Jack Kemp) he used on the earlier film. This is a black-cast film, but there is little here that audiences of the time would have considered stereotypically "black." Although it starts in another theatrical boarding house, most of the action unfolds at a high society soiree and the elegant Cinderella Club. A trio of comedians supplies some laughs, but there is little humor of the "chitlin' circuit" variety, and the burlesque Frenchmen are replaced by a caricatured "Chinaman" named Ah Foo, played by Al Young. The nominal star, Billy Daniels, was a popular nightclub singer in the late 1940s but did not record his million-selling hit, "That Old Black Magic," until 1948. So instead of appearing as "himself," as Louis Jordan was doing, he plays a popular bandleader named "Bob Jordan." Because Daniels was a balladeer, the numbers are smoother and more romantic than what we see in the funkier *Boy! What a Girl!* pushing the musical closer to romance than comedy. Goldberg may have had an eye for this rising talent in 1946, but Daniels is better at singing than acting and lacks Louis Jordan's screen presence. In a startling five-minute interpolation, the former child star Freddie Bartholomew shows up at the Club, appearing as himself. He plugs his current personal appearance tour, delivers a couple of bad dialect comedy jokes and recites a bit of Shakespeare. As with Gene Krupa's cameo in *Boy! What a Girl!* this token integration would have allowed Goldberg to distinguish his film from conventional race movies by putting a white name or face on his posters.[147] Although Goldberg must have been pleased to land Krupa and Bartholomew, he apparently never knew that he had also hired Sidney Poitier, whose one day as an extra marked his first appearance in a theatrical film.[148]

Another way of announcing that these films were higher value products was to avoid the "states' rights" distribution market, where race movies had always been sold. Goldberg—who had worked for the Loew's organization—created Screen Guild Productions, Inc. to distribute the films and announced that *Sepia Cinderella* was "the first Negro picture to be distributed by a national releasing organization for general showing."[149] Of course, this company was simply another of Goldberg's subsidiaries, and the film still seems to have made little headway with traditionally white theaters, a number of whom had always been willing to screen a race movie under certain circumstances. If this approach fell short, he had also set up 16 mm mobile units to road show the films.[150]

Goldberg had not given up on the possibility of converting the Brooklyn Elks Lodge into a studio complex, and after the Lafayette Studio project collapsed he formed Federal Motion Picture Studios, Inc. to get it up off the ground again. "When completed the plant will have three sound stages," *Motion Picture Herald* reported soon after *Sepia Cinderella* had wrapped. "Preparations are being made to utilize the top floor for television. Facilities will permit all types of films from features to industrial and educational shorts."[151] The *Brooklyn Eagle*, praising Goldberg for starting "the first large-scale organization to provide feature-film opportunities for the large body of Negro players in the city," reported that he would spend $500,000 on these stages by the time they opened on July 1.[152] But he never did open them.

While his first two films had been shot back-to-back in late 1946, *Miracle in Harlem* did not go before the cameras (at Filmcraft, not Federal) until September 1947 and was not released until the following summer, allowing Goldberg time to reassess his production strategy. He described the film to the black press as a "new departure" in race movies because, "unlike other pictures, the plot is very heavy drama and mystery, with strong religious overtones."[153] Instead of foregrounding its music and dancing, *Miracle in Harlem* simply adds these elements to a heavily plotted murder mystery. The advertising clearly downplays any music, and while Stepin Fetchit is given featured billing, he only has one real scene, and even that is tied to a necessary plot point. By this point in his career Fetchit and his theatrical persona were coming under attack from all sides, a situation he found incomprehensible. "He kept to himself and seemed very serious about what he was doing," recalled his costar, William Greaves. "It was in that context that I realized how talented he was."[154]

Aunt Hattie (Hilda Offley) operates a successful candy manufacturing business out of her Harlem apartment. When the sinister retail magnate who has swindled her out of her business is poisoned ("this chocolate has a nice, rich flavor . . .") there are plenty of suspects. Sheila Guyse and William Greaves provide the romantic interest; he is just back from a stint in the army, where his chemical warfare experience briefly puts him under suspicion. The film's religious overtones are supplied by Aunt Hattie, who complains about the younger generation and holds religious services in her home. The hymns sung there, by the Juanita Hall Choir, are in contrast to the jazzy torch songs performed at a house party thrown by one of the other suspects, where Savannah Churchill and other entertainers appear as themselves. But there are relatively few of these numbers, and while "performed" (for an on-screen audience), there is no theatrical setting here, no nightclub or recording studio. One number, in which Juanita Hall sings "Chocolate Candy Blues" while stirring a gigantic pot of batter, is even integrated into the plot in the style of a Rodgers and Hammerstein musical.[155]

Creating Screen Guild meant that his product would be distributed differently than other race movies, but *Miracle in Harlem* was also produced differently. Don Malkames took over from cameraman George Webber, and Goldberg's editor, Jack Kemp, replaced Arthur Leonard as director. Kemp had worked on many race films and ethnic pictures in New York and New Jersey, including five Edgar G. Ulmer films, notably *Green Fields* (1937), *Cossacks in Exile*, and *Moon Over Harlem* (both 1939). This would be his only directorial credit. What did remain constant was the script provided by Vincent Valentini, who had written all of Goldberg's race movies since *Paradise in Harlem* (1940). Valentini started writing vaudeville skits and songs in the 1920s, and later turned to the exploitation market with the nudist film *Back to the Sun* (1933) and Joseph Seiden's *Sex Madness* (1938). While never terribly sophisticated in terms of plot or characterization, his real flaw was a tin ear for colloquial speech, a problem his actors and directors never seemed able to overcome. But whatever his degree of talent, by the time Jules Dassin arrived in New York to begin shooting *The Naked City* in the summer of 1947, Vincent Valentini had already written four locally produced features.[156]

Mayor William O'Dwyer had begun a campaign to bring order to New York's slowly reviving motion picture industry, and Herald Pictures, interested in "using the streets of Harlem for authentic backgrounds and locations," acquired twenty location filming permits.[157] In fact, there are only a handful of exterior shots in the entire film, but such bureaucratic niceties must have seemed a far cry from the buccaneering days of Oscar Micheaux. Goldberg even hired "a major scorer," Jack Shaindlin, to produce a full musical score for the film, making this "the costliest colored feature made in the East to date."[158] The trade papers were generally supportive of *Miracle in Harlem*, and were especially impressed by its more elaborate production values and sepia-tinted release prints. One noted that "it employs extensively combination sets making it possible for the story to gravitate from scene to scene with a continuous flow of action."[159] This apparently refers to several long takes in which camera movements follow action through a series of adjacent rooms, an expansion of a similar effect used in *Sepia Cinderella*. The larger Filmcraft stages encouraged the construction of sets like this, which were not only attention-getting but could also minimize labor costs by reducing the number of setups.

But Goldberg's most risky innovation was probably the decision to mix religious values, represented by Aunt Hattie's hymns and gospel music (which appealed to Southern audiences) with a film-noirish plot involving murder, shady business practices, and a dangerous (but attractive) urban lifestyle, elements targeted at race movie audiences living in cities. Producers like Toddy and Sack had known for years that their audience was not monolithic, that films appealing to urban audiences seldom drew as well in the South, and vice versa.[160] The race movie market was so small, however, that neither sector could be entirely ignored. Goldberg appears to have been aiming at both audiences at once—hence the title stressing both *Miracle* and *Harlem*—but the result may not have been what he expected.

Film Daily found it "one of the best all-Negro productions," while another industry paper praised it as "a modern drama of serious proportions far removed from the average person's idea of a Negro picture," griping only about the "uneven quality" of the acting.[161] On the street, however, the response was quite different. "The opening night's audience at Harlem's Apollo Theater didn't take too kindly to *Made in Harlem* [sic]," *Variety* reported. "Sequences which were intended to impart a warm glow were actually laughed at, and the gauche acting, directing and production were never taken seriously."[162] What scenes were these? *Miracle in Harlem* is a film in which "Nobody Knows the Trouble I've Seen" plays under the main title and a beatific Aunt Ellie inspires the young folks in her charge to better their behavior ("Swing Low, Sweet Chariot" also makes an appearance). This material would have worked fine in Spencer Williams country, but the crowd on 125th street wasn't buying it. How rural audiences in the South—still the backbone of the race movie business—reacted to all the cheating, lying, and poisoning in the murder mystery plot is an open question. At least the presence of Stepin Fetchit didn't seem to have been a problem. In announcing the comedian's "return to the screen," the *Chicago Defender* noted approvingly that he "will play the same type of comedy role that has endeared him to millions of movie fans" and later praised his "fine comedy" as just about the only good thing in the picture.[163] "In an entirely black setting, [Fetchit] comes across purely as a comedian . . . not as a racial symbol but as a skilled artist," Mel Watkins wrote in a revisionist biography of this "doleful clown." "But we also glimpse that, well, perhaps total dedication to labor is not all it's cracked up to be."[164]

Herald's ambitions were highlighted by a page one story in *Variety* announcing that a "tolerance short" featuring Canada Lee and Lena Horne would begin shooting at their "eastern studio" on September 10. Written by Bob Condon, a publicist for Eagle-Lion, and directed by Leigh Jason, the unnamed public service short concerned "a Negro butler [who] dreams of a turnabout with his white master and then puts him through all the clichés usually reserved for colored people in films and radio."[165] Goldberg hoped to find a commercial release for the film, but there is no record that it was ever produced, much less distributed. Films attacking racism and anti-Semitism were briefly popular that season, but the radical approach suggested in this comedy would have gone far beyond anything seen in *Pinky* or *Gentleman's Agreement*.

Miracle in Harlem, Jack Goldberg's most expensive and ambitious race movie, was also the last one he ever produced, though that had never been the plan. As soon as it finished shooting, Goldberg announced he was about to start work on the greatest crossover picture ever—a Jackie Robinson biopic starring Jackie Robinson as himself.[166] Joe Louis had done something similar when he appeared in the 1938 race movie *Spirit of Youth*, but this would be no "all Negro" production. Goldberg would coproduce *Courage* (later known as *Brooklyn, USA*) with Eagle-Lion's Benjamin Stoloff, with Arthur Leonard directing. Indeed, Goldberg announced he was moving his entire operation to Hollywood, where he would make six additional films for the struggling independent.[167] Robinson arrived on the coast in January, but there was no script and no releasing deal: Eagle-Lion had suddenly backed out. Goldberg blamed script delays, which meant the picture could never be finished before the start of spring training. But *Variety* suggested that Eagle-Lion was scared off by "the problem of presenting a Negro on an equal plane with whites" and a possible boycott of their entire product line by angry Southern theater chains.[168] Perhaps it was racism, or perhaps Eagle-Lion's shaky finances were to blame. That summer Goldberg was making news in Florida again, announcing that he would turn Miami's Amelia Earhart airport into the Hialeah Motion Picture Studios, where he would make westerns and "four to six Negro films" a year.[169] That didn't happen either. A year later Eagle-Lion did make *The Jackie Robinson Story* but without Jack Goldberg or Arthur Leonard, apparently unconcerned about the wrath of Southern exhibitors. When Robinson went to court about this it was Goldberg he sued, winning a $14,500 judgment in 1954 when the producer failed to show up to defend himself.[170] I don't know if he ever collected.

Ted Toddy

With Robert Savini concentrating on his partnership with Louis Jordan, and Alfred Sack apparently more interested in Bob Howard, stars like Pigmeat

Markham and Mantan Moreland were hardly at the center of the Astor or Sack race movie catalogs. But Ted Toddy had other ideas, and despite the low regard many already had for these veteran vaudevillians, they would star in all the race films Toddy would produce in New York after the war.

Toddy operated the Dixie Film Exchange out of Atlanta and entered the race movie business by purchasing Leo Popkin's Million Dollar Productions in 1940, consolidating his various production and distribution interests under the Toddy Pictures Company banner in 1941.[171] This gave him a backlog of existing films to distribute during the war, but in 1945 he announced that he would begin production on ten all-Negro features and two series of shorts, all in the east.[172] To make these films he hired Sam Newfield, the fastest director in the business. If the *AFI Catalog* is to be believed, Newfield directed 146 features between 1937 and 1946, approximately one every twenty-five days for nine years. (Newfield might hold the record over distance, but William Forest Crouch's personal best of eleven band shorts in one day seems equally impressive.) Toddy booked space at the Ideal Studio in Hudson Heights, New Jersey, an obsolete facility built for silent movie director Herbert Brenon in 1916 and subsequently refurbished for talkies. *Follies Girl* had been shot here in 1942, but since the coming of sound it had been used mainly for race movies and Yiddish pictures.[173] Was it simply a coincidence that when Toddy decided to make his big move into race pictures he hired the one man who had directed both of his two new stars before—Mantan Moreland in the first all-black musical western, *Harlem on the Prairie* (1937), and Pigmeat Markham in a small role in *Am I Guilty?* (1940).

Pigmeat Markham had one of the longest and most controversial careers of any African American comedian. A burlesque trooper who continued to play in full blackface until 1943, his exaggerated, low-class comedy fascinated Langston Hughes (for whom he was one of the "golden dozen" black comedians) but was considered vulgar and embarrassing by many others.[174] In his younger days, Markham was known as a singer and dancer as well as a stand-up comic, and he claimed to have introduced "Truckin' " on stage in Washington in 1935. Although he had never enjoyed the crossover success of Mantan Moreland or Eddie "Rochester" Anderson, Markham's career experienced a sudden revival in 1968 following a sensational series of television appearances on *Rowan & Martin's Laugh-In*. The retro appeal of his vintage "Here Come Da Judge" routine, where he would shout out politically incorrect punchlines while slamming the bench with an inflated pig's bladder ("Sock it to me!"), was completely at odds with the cooler, more sophisticated style of revisionist comedians like Bill Cosby or Dick Gregory. When contemporaries like Mantan Moreland were long forgotten, Pigmeat Markham found himself in the vanguard of a cultural rebellion boiling up from underneath. Indeed, his 1968 Chess Records recording of "Here Come the Judge," a chanted narrative released by the label that usually handled his comedy albums, is seen by some music historians as a progenitor of rap.[175]

As might be expected, Newfield worked quickly. By the end of November 1945, he and cameraman Jack Etra (who had just finished *Tall, Tan and Terrific* at a nearby Fort Lee studio), had completed *House-Rent Party* and were already at work on *Fight That Ghost*.[176] Both films feature Markham as a small businessman (first a barber, then a tailor), a trickster with an eye for women and a talent for financial chicanery. A stock figure familiar to all prewar vaudeville and burlesque audiences, the trickster was often given a particular ethnic slant, as in many of Groucho Marx's most characteristic roles. John "Rastus" Murray appears in both films as Markham's comic foil, "Shorty." In *House-Rent Party*, Pigmeat finds various clever ways to cheat his friend and employee out of any money that comes their way, a manipulative relationship that suggests the cruel comedy of a team like Wheeler and Woolsey. As business partners they are on more equal terms in *Fight That Ghost*, joining forces to trick their landlord and later pocket an inheritance by staying the night in a haunted house (the plot of *House-Rent Party* also turns on scoring an unlikely financial windfall). Sam Newfield is credited with the story and screenplay for both films—but since this is the only time he ever took such a credit, one suspects that his real narrative contribution was finding a way of stitching together a series of preexisting vaudeville routines developed by Markham and Murray (and a few musical numbers, of course). Actually, the writing credit is shared with Ted Toddy, who also took broadsheet billing as producer—again, unique instances in both cases. Herman Abrams, who was in charge of Toddy's Dallas distribution office, later told an audience at Southern Methodist University that Toddy was especially interested in these films. "Much of the money that he earned in distributing his other pictures, such as his westerns and other specialty pictures, he invested in making the black films, because he simply loved to make black films. He had a certain feeling in his heart for black people."[177]

It would be interesting to see how Markham's character was played here, but no prints of these films appear to survive. In *Junction 88*, made a year later, he morphs from baggy pants to business suits by the second reel, suggesting an effort to reinvent his controversial stage persona.[178] But were we still getting the original Pigmeat in Newfield's films? The *Chicago Defender*, reporting that Markham had just finished these two features for Toddy, said the company was also handling some earlier films made on the West Coast, "and one is a Pigmeat Markham 'Extreme Comedy.'"[179] "Extreme Comedy" seems a very modern phrase, suggesting something edgy and provocative. But perhaps its use in 1946 was more of a warning?

Giving himself producer credit on the advertising material indicates that Toddy was personally invested in these films to an unusual degree, and soon after they were completed he announced the names of his next seven Negro features (among them *A Night with the Devil* and *Prairie Comes to Harlem*).[180] No prints of these films can be found today either, and we also lack any stills, posters, or contemporary accounts of their production. Independent producer/distributors would frequently float the titles of films they were *going* to make as a way of inflating their stature in the marketplace, but the sudden cancellation of this entire program suggests a major shift in Toddy's business plan by spring 1946.

Before Sam Newfield returned to Hollywood in December 1945 he had completed a third film for Toddy, *Mantan Messes Up*.[181] Set in a television station where Mantan Moreland has come looking for work, this forty-three-minute feature is padded out with footage taken from earlier films controlled by Toddy, allowing the posters to advertise names like Lena Horne, Buck and Bubbles, and Nina Mae McKinney. Did Sam Newfield actually complete this film? Or did Ted Toddy push him aside so that he could assemble this pastiche himself? Press reports at the time say that Newfield finished the picture, but when it appeared his name was not on the credits. Nor did Ted Toddy choose to list himself as producer.

Instead of producing a broad array of race movies in an assortment of genres (crime, comedy, western, musical), Toddy decided to focus on the work of one established talent. Robert Savini had gone into business with Louis Jordan; now Toddy would do much the same thing with Jordan's old friend, Mantan Moreland. Unlike the Pigmeat Markham titles, *Mantan Messes Up* (and three subsequent Moreland-Toddy pictures) was issued under the label of Lucky Star Productions, an entity apparently created by Moreland and Toddy for this purpose. Those films, *What a Guy*, *Return of Mandy's Husband*, and *Mantan Runs for Mayor*, were announced as "ready for release" in March 1947, more than a year after *Mantan Messes Up* was shot. No director or other technical credits were given, so it is difficult to say who made these films or where they were produced. A September 1947 survey in *Film Daily* says that half of Toddy's films are being made in New York and the rest on the West Coast, without going into detail.[182] One internet source suggests that Sam Newfield may also have directed these three films, as he still maintained a relationship with Toddy.[183] But why no credit?

Mantan Runs for Mayor and *Return of Mandy's Husband* teamed Moreland with Flournoy Miller, a vaudevillian long established on the West Coast, where I suspect both films were shot. But *What a Guy* is another matter. Among the supporting cast is Ruby Dee, who can be seen in several postwar New York race movies (but no Hollywood films until 1950), and at least three actors who later in 1947 would appear in *Miracle in Harlem*—Monte Hawley, Lawrence Criner, and Kenneth Freeman. "I remember working without a script," Dee recalled. "The director, who was also the producer, would lay out the story and break out the specifics as we went along. The entire film was shot in a room about twenty-five by thirty feet, and it starred Lawrence Criner. He gave me pointers on improvisation as well as telling me exactly what to do and say."[184] If the director was also the producer, does that mean Ted Toddy was handling this job himself, using a veteran like Criner to tell the cast "exactly what to do and say"? Criner had been acting in race movies since the silent era and had recently worked in a few films at Monogram with Mantan Moreland, so between him and Ted Toddy why bother hiring someone else to direct?

A few weeks after announcing the availability of these films, Toddy acquired distribution rights to a very different item, *Going to Glory, Come to Jesus*.[185] Said to have been made by Royal Gospel Productions over a six-month period in 1946, the film illustrated the transformative power of religion through an attack on worldliness and materialism, and it would seem to have been inspired by Spencer Williams's highly successful *Blood of Jesus*. As in Williams's film, Satan appears in full theatrical regalia, collecting wayward souls by tempting them from the path of righteousness. The settings are modest, with considerable use of exteriors, and dreams are used to justify almost anything.[186] But where did this film come from? And who made it? Could there be any connection with the revivalist films Williams had been making in Texas for Alfred Sack? Royal Gospel Productions had a New York business address and posters claimed the film was "From the Successful New York Play by Wesley Wilson and Leola Grant." In larger type, the advertising lists eight spirituals sung by the "Royal Gospel Choir," but Wesley Wilson and Leola Grant had nothing to do with the gospel movement. The husband and wife team were jazz and blues singers—and composers—who had worked with Louis Armstrong, Fletcher Henderson, and Sidney Bechet (quite a few recordings of their "dirty blues" from the late 1920s and early 1930s still circulate online). Sometimes he worked as Sox Wilson or Kid Wilson; she usually appeared as Coot Grant or Miss Coot. When not performing, Wilson had been writing new material for Mezz Mezzrow's King Jazz label. His most famous number was the 1933 Bessie Smith classic "Gimme a Pigfoot (and a Bottle of Beer)."[187] His catalog doesn't seem to have included any gospel numbers.

According to information provided in the *AFI Catalog*, censors in Ohio and Pennsylvania ordered the deletion of one number sung by Irene Williams ("Regardless") and another performed by "Miss Coot and Sox [Wilson]," unusual demands for the score of a gospel picture. None of these performers are credited on the film's posters, nor do the songs "Regardless," "I Was Glad," and "You'd Better Watch Out," also cited in the *Catalog*, appear on the list of gospel numbers. According to a continuity script deposited with New York's motion picture censorship office, there were at least two sequences set in honky-tonks designed to illustrate the degraded lifestyle of hedonistic jitterbugs. Here is where Sox Wilson and Miss Coot did their stuff and where the numbers found objectionable in Ohio and Pennsylvania must have occurred. One can see why the posters, which tout the film as "The Spiritual Masterpiece," include no mention of them or their music. But if these two did write enough of this film to earn that credit, and appeared in it as well, could the final effect really have been so negative in its portrayal of their music? In any case, can this oddity even be considered part of the postwar New York race movie scene? Given the fact that both performers were no longer touring by the late 1940s, instead depending on a few regular gigs in New York, it is unlikely that they would have made this film anywhere else. If the film had been made in Texas or Florida, there would have been no need to import blues singers from New York and even less reason (in budgetary terms) to go up there just to shoot footage of them. True, at first glance those exteriors do resemble Spencer Williams's Harlemwood. But nothing we see here couldn't have been shot just as easily in New Jersey.

Toddy understood that any real money to be made in this business would be made by the distributor, so he sought innovative ways of reaching his target audience, four million of whom were without access to conventional motion picture theaters. "He predicts that within the next few years there will be a boom in Negro exhibition," the *Motion Picture Herald* reported in 1947, "but expects this expansion to come from the development of 16 mm Negro theaters and roadshow units throughout the South."[188] He could see that other producers were already taking up the slack in the race film market and that there was no pressing need for him to keep generating product on his own. When William Alexander needed a national distributor for his Joe Louis feature, *The Fight Never Ends*, Toddy added it to his catalog in 1948, as he had done earlier with *Going to Glory, Come to Jesus*. These were both fairly serious films, however, and not the sort of picture Toddy was interested in putting his own money into. "Negro audiences do not care for the heavy emotional dramas," he told the *Motion Picture Herald*. "Their choice in film entertainment is the pictures which feature light comedy, outdoor adventure, musical comedies with an abundance of singing and dancing, and comedy-romances."[189]

He produced only two more race features—*She's Too Mean for Me* and *Come On, Cowboy!*—both starring Mantan Moreland. Moreland played a conventional comic lead, but he was supported by the team of Miller and Lee, who were in New York in summer 1948 for NBC's "Swingtime at the Savoy." This time Ted Toddy clearly directed the films himself, shooting exteriors for the western at a dude ranch in Suffern, New York, and building small sets at the Hartley Productions studio, a commercial facility at 20 West Forty-Seventh Street. The films were photographed by Irving Hartley, whose work was generally limited to commercials and industrial films.[190] Toddy had the films ready for release by October 1948, but bookings were scarce; all that survives of them today is some tattered promotional material.[191] A year after that he announced that his 1949–50 distribution calendar would include twenty-eight features and thirty-two shorts, a total that could rival the output of a Hollywood major. The list was impressive, but these were not new films. Hardly anyone was producing race movies anymore.

Finished

A genre that seemed so hot in 1945 was finished by 1949. Historians have suggested many reasons for this, often blaming the integration of Hollywood cinema and other cultural factors. Some compare the fate of race movies to that of the Negro leagues, the inevitable result of a transfer of talent from one cultural sphere to another. In this equation, the defection of Jackie Robinson and Larry Doby is said to be echoed by that of performers like Lena Horne and Ruby Dee, who had worked in the race film market but left it when wider opportunities arose. This may be part of an explanation, but we should be careful in comparing movies and baseball.

In assessing the problem of casting well known stars, race movie director Josh Binney offered his own explanation. "Some of the most outstanding Negro artists are not at all popular with Negroes," he claimed.

> They often are classed as "white man's entertainers" and when so considered they cease to be "Box Office Draw" personalities in the strictly Negro theatre, except in a very few of the bigger and better theatres in the large cities. . . . Some of the "top" Negro artists will not consider appearing in an all-Negro, independently produced picture at any price . . . because they realize they will not draw in the Negro field and that their reputations and standings would suffer as a result.[192]

Binney may simply be rationalizing the lack of stars in his own films, but an aversion to "all-Negro, independently produced" films might have been a real consideration for crossover talent in this period, especially if those films had come to be regarded as toxic and second rate. We need to pay attention to the negative reviews appearing in black newspapers and to published accounts of Harlem audiences laughing these films off the screen. And we also need to understand how the parallel "race record" industry responded to many of these same changes.

Billboard eliminated its "race record" chart in 1949, but this did not mark a decline in the importance of the music (they simply renamed it the "Rhythm and Blues" chart). R&B labels like Atlantic (founded in 1947) and Chess (1950) flourished for years, developing new stars and musical genres out of the same African American musical traditions. Given the even broader integration of the recording industry in the postwar period, why did these labels succeed in maintaining a racially specific identity while every race movie producer went out of business?

William Greaves, who started as an actor in race movies and became an award-winning independent filmmaker, felt the answer was less cultural than economic:

> A further complication in the production of black independent films at that time was the rising costs. You could no longer make a feature for from eight to twenty thousand dollars. The actual theaters themselves in the black neighborhoods were being torn down because of escalating real estate values and other kinds of structures were going up. The union costs were going up. Costs all across the board were going up, so that while you might be able to get a certain amount of financing—say fifteen to thirty thousand dollars—to do a black film in 1947, by 1953 that money had to be somewhere in the vicinity of eighty to a hundred thousand dollars.[193]

And remember that race films had a very low potential earnings ceiling. Binney estimated a maximum return of $48,000 to the producer, but only for "a mighty good Negro picture."[194]

Here one also has to consider the catastrophic drop in theater attendance that affected the entire industry beginning in 1947. While the impact of this on traditional Hollywood product has been well studied, race movies would seem to have been hit especially hard. Noting the "hard times" affecting all theaters in 1949, the *Showmen's Trade Review* found that "the loudest squawks about poor business are coming from theaters catering to patrons in low income brackets. Especially is this true of Negro theatres, where the pinch is really bad. In addition, the smaller communities are faced with competition from itinerant 16-mm. outfits who frequently beat the exhibitor to the punch."[195] It seems ironic that 16 mm, embraced by Savini, Goldberg, Toddy and Glucksman as a solution to their distribution problems, appears to have played its own role in the ultimate destruction of their fragile race movie business. But while it might play the role of villain here, 16 mm would have a much more positive effect as far as the overall growth of independent cinema in postwar film culture was concerned.

Finally—and particularly because we are talking about an industry that was centered in New York—we need to acknowledge the impact of a very New York problem: real estate. During this entire period the largest studio facility in the New York area was operated by the U.S. Army Signal Corps in Astoria and not available for commercial production. The second largest, Warners' Vitagraph studio in Flatbush, had been mothballed in 1939 and would not be reopened for feature film production until 1955. The Bronx Biograph studio, also closed in 1939, would not see another feature picture until 1956. When film production did resume in the East in 1945, the first available studios were Ideal in Hudson Heights (*Fight That Ghost*) and All-American in Fort Lee (*Tall, Tan and Terrific*), but both studios were so ill-equipped that they were quickly abandoned. *Boy! What a Girl!* was shot at Movietone in 1946, but that facility was not favored by race film producers, who never seem to have used it again. Two or three race movies were shot at the RKO Pathé studio in 1947–48 (*Killer Diller*), but that facility was then acquired by NBC Television. Indeed, the sudden need for television stages absorbed nearly every available theater, warehouse or lodge hall, putting all these spaces out of reach for any local film producer. That leaves the Bronx Edison studio, operated as Filmcraft by Mills Industries from the early war years. It was this studio, home to the production of hundreds, perhaps thousands, of Soundies, that became the center of New York's postwar race film production (and in fact the busiest of any of its commercial studios). Soundies production tapered off during 1946, but as early as December 1945 Bud Pollard had been able to shoot *Beware* at Filmcraft. The bulk of subsequent race film production—Goldberg's *Sepia Cinderella*, Glucksman's *Hi De Ho*, Alexander's *Jivin' in Be-Bop*—would take place on its stages. When Filmcraft was sold in early 1948 there were few remaining rental studios available, and none that were so commodious, well-equipped, and inexpensive.[196] We can see the result in *Souls of Sin*, produced somewhere in New York in 1948, which looks as if it had been shot in a high school auditorium.

When the Pathé and Filmcraft studios closed their doors to local film producers in 1948, the race movie business moved from marginal to homeless. With *The Fight Never Ends*, Joseph Lerner had shown that through skill and imagination, race movies could be shot on location in the already familiar style of Louis de Rochemont or Roberto Rossellini. *On the Waterfront, Killer's Kiss* and many other local productions would soon follow this lead, but race movie producers did not. Perhaps the films they were making were too dependent on music, or perhaps, as William Greaves suggested, the economics of race movie production had already turned against them. Or maybe their audience had simply written them off entirely regardless of content or quality. In July 1948 *The Chicago Defender* ended a dismissive review of *The Betrayal* and *Miracle in Harlem* by grumbling, "We've seen two all-Negro films within a fortnight. We hope they are the last of the season."[197] The conclusion seems designed to discourage anyone from getting into this field, but the *Defender* had no need to worry. Although race films continued to be released for some months after this, production had essentially stopped. In the end, it made little difference whether critics and audiences supported these films or not, because after 1948 there was no place left to make them.

PART II
REVIVAL

CHAPTER 5

EIGHT MILLION STORIES

On the day William O'Dwyer took over at City Hall, most industry analysts would have predicted that New York's future as a film production center depended on whatever happened on 106th Street. Ralph Austrian had laid out Pathé's plans for America's most modern studio back on October 17, 1945. He had the real estate, and he had the blueprints, with full details on air conditioning and dubbing studios that made rival schemes look like the usual smoke and mirrors. Whatever success the Movietone studio might be having, it was too small to support a viable local film industry all by itself. Not one industry analyst noted that in the weeks between Austrian's speech and O'Dwyer's inauguration, local producers had shot four feature-length race movies.[1]

In March 1946 *Variety* noted that within a few months New York would see the opening of three new studios offering twenty modern stages: Pathé; Schmidlapp's Associated Filmmakers operation in Yonkers; and that "former Elks hall being converted in Brooklyn." Story Productions, run by the independent producers Hal Horne and Armand Deutsch ("more or less a N.Y. setup"), was preparing Taylor Caldwell's *This Side of Innocence* for immediate production and was said to be giving these facilities "some serious eyeing."[2] Erwin Lesser, who operated the Little Carnegie art house, had already been dabbling in the production of "true crime" shorts featuring former Police Commissioner Lewis Valentine. Within a few months he expected to go into production on a feature, *Blood on the Horn*, as well as a series of musical shorts.[3] But none of these features were ever made, and Lesser's four completed *Crime Newsreel* shorts were neither distributed nor copyrighted.

Pathé was not to open for another year, and (with one big exception) everything of consequence that might be shot in New York in 1946 was going to be shot on the street. At first, this began to look like a replay of the work Bill Kelly had done on *The Sin of Harold Diddlebock* in 1945: the principal actors stay home in Los Angeles, while a satellite crew films bits and pieces of the city to order. That is just what Kelly was doing again in the spring of 1946 for Samuel Goldwyn. In *The Secret Life of Walter Mitty*, Danny Kaye, while playing a character from Perth Amboy, New Jersey, never left Hollywood. All the Fifth Avenue imagery that would later be used as back-projection footage in Hollywood was shot to order by Kelly and a crew from Local 644. An occasional insert might show a double for one character getting out of a real cab in New York. Later, in Hollywood, a closer view would show the proper actor standing in front of a process screen. Kelly worked under the direction of John Fulton, the special-effects expert Goldwyn had shipped to New York to supervise the footage. In fact, Fulton had arrived with a party of eight technicians of his own, as well as doubles for Danny Kaye and Virginia Mayo and also stunt doubles for those doubles. "Hollywood's film libraries have millions of feet of celluloid showing New York from every possible angle," Fulton told one reporter. "The old system was to use those stock shots for everything, including close-ups, using complicated process photography to put the actors in the right location. Producers have now discovered that they can get better and cheaper results by sending director, stars and crew east."[4] This seems an odd thing to say, especially after Fulton revealed that none of the principal *Walter Mitty* actors had actually traveled to New York. But he did shoot forty taxicabs greeting the arrival of a ship at Pier 72 because if Hollywood had such footage it was probably either prewar, in black and white, or both. This sort of minor trickery would hardly be worth mentioning here but for the fact that *Walter Mitty*, like *The Clock* the year before, is a story in which the cultural geography of New York plays an important role. Unlike *Harold Diddlebock*, these films really could not have been set anywhere else.

The first postwar "Hollywood" film that did any principal photography in New York was Walter Wanger's *Smash Up—The Story of a Woman*, which shot here for two weeks in May 1946. One Hollywood trade paper saw this as "in line with the trend for on-the-spot location shooting," although that trend was only starting to make itself felt in New York.[5] Susan Hayward, in the first of her five Oscar-nominated performances, played an emotionally insecure cabaret singer descending into alcoholism. Sometimes dismissed as a soap opera or mere "female *Lost Weekend*," *Smash-Up* (to use its working title) was an ambitious attempt to propose a series of interrelated cultural conflicts as a root cause of alcoholism. Previous efforts, from *The Lost Weekend* itself to D. W.

Griffith's *The Struggle* (filmed in New York in 1931), either saw the condition as inexplicable or suggested some moral failing. *Smash-Up* offers both a psychoanalytic explanation and a critique of American consumer society, especially as it affected a postwar American housewife recently displaced from her position in the workforce.[6]

According to Wanger biographer Matthew Bernstein, *Smash-Up* reflected the producer's current interest in " 'adult realism,' as seen in the Italian neo-realists and the British cinema of quality."[7] The film's " 'realism' was visually emphasized through its 'semi-documentary' sequences, with location shooting in New York," he notes, although *Smash-Up* is too slick (and too early) to suggest much influence from the Italians.[8] Wanger's *Scarlet Street* had created a nightmare New York on the Universal back lot, but *Smash-Up* is closer in tone to some of his later, more socially conscious melodramas, like *I Want to Live!* (1958, also with Susan Hayward). In order to believe in this character's plight the audience has to have some reason to believe in the world she lives in, but such efforts came at a price.

The *New York Times* reported on a series of "minor though annoying difficulties" that plagued the production, most involving the same issues of organization or access that would bedevil David O. Selznick a year later.[9] Attempts to film Susan Hayward striding across Broadway and into the Fifty-Seventh Street branch of the National City Bank were foiled by "curious onlookers who appeared at the wrong time" and then by "a capricious sun which didn't appear at the proper time." Wanger was even "stymied for a while by the reluctance of Sutton Place property owners to cooperate in the interests of cinematic art" until one friendly tenant, the playwright Rose Franken, allowed access to her apartment at 2 Sutton Place South. In the film, Hayward and her husband (Lee Bowman), land an apartment with a picture-postcard view of the Queensboro Bridge, already a convention of Hollywood's "New York" movies, and in this case symbolic of the success Hayward's character will be unable to handle. The bridge is a back projection, but Wanger's crew did film cars driving up and down in front of the real building.

The main location sequence remaining in the film was shot at the Central Park Zoo, where Hayward's character, who has lost custody of her child due to her own bad behavior, kidnaps the infant while her nanny is otherwise occupied. Hayward was clearly filmed in New York for this sequence, although some use of doubles and back projection (for closer shots) is also evident. But even this simple action did not go smoothly; small children employed as extras "just stared into the camera" while a flock of pigeons, "suspicious because there were so many peanuts" thrown around as bait, refused to appear on cue. The director, Stuart Heisler, had been expecting more cooperation all around. "We think we've gotten what we came for," he told a reporter, not especially happy.[10] Hollywood filmmakers could not understand why New Yorkers would not simply do what they needed them to do. It would take another year or two for the city to develop a cadre of experienced location managers capable of organizing such work in a professional manner, but even then the movements of the sun, and the behavior of the pigeons, continued to remain a problem.

One step in this direction was MGM's on-location filming of a key musical number for Frank Sinatra's *It Happened in Brooklyn*.[11] In July 1946, almost three years before he would return to the city to film *On the Town*, Sinatra performed Sammy Cahn and Jule Styne's romantic ode to the Brooklyn Bridge, a love letter to the wind whistling through her strings and the clouds floating overhead "like a crown." The groundbreaking number was simply but effectively staged right on the bridge itself by dance director Jack Donohue. Donohue had previously worked with Sinatra and Kathryn Grayson (also his costar in this film) on *Anchors Aweigh*, and in 1947 he would direct a significant "all New York" production of his own, *Close-Up*. This sequence, filmed to playback on location and shot with multiple takes in proper MGM-musical fashion, seems to have been made with a minimum of publicity, if only to avoid the curious onlookers who had recently dogged Susan Hayward. MGM crews were here for ten weeks, but despite regular reports in the *Brooklyn Daily Eagle* detailing the company's progress on the film, the paper never told readers when or where it was being shot.[12]

The *AFI Catalog* tells us that the first postwar Easter parade (April 21, 1946) was filmed for Allied Artists' *It Happened on 5th Avenue*, but there are no such scenes in this film. In fact, the production seems to have had significant crowd-control problems, one report noting "an unruly afternoon crowd [that] forced the scrapping of 1,000 feet of film" during the shoot.[13] Like *It Happened in Brooklyn*, which was made at the same time, this little film also addresses the problems of returning veterans but with a surprisingly political slant—like a leftover populist comedy of the 1930s—and with a far more candid treatment of class issues. Should an abandoned military base be used for industrial development or turned into housing for returning veterans? The simultaneous production of these two "It Happened . . ." films suggests a growing interest in the modern life of this city, especially highly recognizable spots like Brooklyn or Fifth Avenue. What the trade papers were already calling "the trend for on-the-spot location shooting" was a fashion ripe to be exploited, and by the summer of 1946 New York was ready for its close-up.

Edgar G. Ulmer Plays Carnegie Hall

Boris Morros and William LeBaron organized Federal Films, Inc. as an independent film and television producer in September 1945.[14] LeBaron had recently been producing musicals for Fox (including *Stormy Weather* and *The Gang's All Here*, both 1943) and had a lengthy career as composer, magazine editor, and studio executive dating back to the 1920s. He had begun his film career in New York with Hearst's Cosmopolitan Productions and had been head of production at Paramount's Astoria studio in the early sound years. Boris Morros is best known today as a Soviet agent, codenamed "Frost" in the Venona intercepts. The longtime musical director at Paramount, where he had been nominated for three Oscars, Morros was now operating as an independent producer. His most ambitious previous film was the all-star anthology *Tales of Manhattan*, which he made with Sam Spiegel in 1942. J. Edgar Hoover later managed to turn Morros, who became a double agent in 1947, but at the time he made *Carnegie Hall* he was still working for the NKVD, not the FBI.[15] Politics aside, given their shared musical backgrounds it is no wonder that Federal Films had four musicals in development during the two years it operated as an active producer. *Babes in Toyland* would have been a Technicolor production starring Ezio Pinza and Lily Pons, along with George Pal's animated Puppetoon characters; *Carmen from Kenosha* was an updated, Americanized version of the Bizet opera, with music by Victor Young, also for Pinza and Pons; *My Immortal Beloved*, a Beethoven biography, never seems to have advanced to the casting stage; and *Carnegie Hall*, a catalog of high-brow musical culture, would be told against the background of New York's famed concert venue. It would be the only film Federal ever actually completed.[16]

What might seem like an overly "classical" production slate today would have looked very different at the time. *Film Daily*, reviewing expected public reaction to *Carnegie Hall*, saw the film arriving at the peak of a resurgence in popularity of "long-haired" music, noting "the increasing box office returns being garnered by such enterprises as the concert stage, the ballet, [and] the opera," greater radio air time, and a reputed tripling of classical record sales. "Once a drug on the market, classical and serious music has now developed unusual box office appeal."[17] They might also have mentioned the current wave of "classical music" films inspired by the success of *A Song to Remember* in 1945, including Frank Borzage's *I've Always Loved You* and the Joan Crawford-John Garfield *Humoresque* (both shot just before *Carnegie Hall*) and MGM's Schumann biography, *Song of Love*, with Katharine Hepburn and Robert Walker, filmed right after it. *The Red Shoes* would follow a few months later.

All those films were able to maintain a successful balance between music and plot, except for *Carnegie Hall*, which has always been seen as a disproportionate pastiche of narrative and nonnarrative elements. Morros and LeBaron had conceived the film as an all-star lineup of the world's greatest musicians right from the start, and any narrative thread would have to be subservient to musical performance. The final cut includes Bruno Walter, Gregor Piatigorsky, Rise Stevens, Artur Rodzinski, Artur Rubinstein, Jan Peerce, Ezio Pinza, Jascha Heifetz, and Leopold Stokowski (among others), with a popular music component represented by Vaughan Monroe and Harry James.[18]

For *Tales of Manhattan*, Morros had been able to stuff a similar all-star lineup into one two-hour feature by breaking the structure down into a series of discrete episodes. But in that case each separate tale still served to move the story of the fugitive dress suit toward a satisfying climax. In *Carnegie Hall*, each musical number stops the film in its tracks. As the film's director, Edgar G. Ulmer, later told Peter Bogdanovich, "What are you going to do after Rubinstein plays Chopin? You're going to have a scene where *actors talk?* It's impossible. It's as impossible as putting Hepburn and Walker into a picture about Schumann."[19]

The storyline for *Carnegie Hall* is credited to Seena Owen, a silent movie actress who had worked for William LeBaron at the Hearst studio. Borden Chase was hired to turn this into a film script on the strength of his work on *I've Always Loved You*, but his draft was rejected and the final script was credited to Karl Kamb, a minor writer of B-movies with none of Chase's wit or imagination.[20] Edgar G. Ulmer, who had just gotten out from under his PRC contract, was first announced as director on June 18 and left for New York ten days later.[21] He clearly had very little input into the selection of artists used in the film, but he did have a few weeks to do what he could with the screenplay. "I wanted to do a documentary, which they wouldn't let me do. . . . Couldn't put it across—had to have that silly story," he remembered.[22]

What he filmed instead was an all-star variety show, a feature-length excuse to string together a group of musical set pieces and still be able to think of your final product as something more than a collection of high-class Soundies. Hollywood had pioneered this style of musical in the 1930s—think of the way Kirsten Flagstad is dropped into Paramount's *The Big Broadcast of 1938*, a film on which both Morros and LeBaron had worked. The strategy had more recently been relegated to lower-budget musicals, like Columbia's *Reveille with Beverly* (1943), where we see musical numbers featuring Frank Sinatra or Count Basie simply because a disc jockey, Ann Miller, put one of their records on a turntable.[23] Ironically, it was also the style of musical then being produced in abundance by New York's race movie industry.

Ulmer wanted the Hall itself to function as both witness and catalyst, observing the infusion of Europe's musical traditions into the new world while this great tide of cultural appropriation ebbs and flows on its own stages. To personify this, the film creates the figure of an immigrant Irish cleaning woman, played by Marsha Hunt, who observes the history of the Hall over the decades from backstage. "Nora, you *are* Carnegie Hall," Jascha Heifetz eventually tells her. As many Ulmer scholars have pointed out, all the "classical music" greats seen in the film are Europeans, as is all the music they perform. They have come to our shores bringing with them this gift of great music, with the Hall functioning as a cultural stand-in for Ellis Island, New York's usual locus of immigration narratives.[24] American music is represented as simple entertainment, in need of a good musical education, at least until the performance (by Harry James, introduced by Stokowski) of a "new modern rhapsody" at the climax. The recent release of Warner's highly successful George Gershwin film, *Rhapsody in Blue*, seems a clear influence here, and at one point Morros claimed to have signed Benny Goodman, a coup that would have instantly recalled Goodman's historic Carnegie Hall jazz concert of 1938.[25]

Ulmer himself was one of many Hollywood immigrants. But while most of the others never looked back, Ulmer remained in the thrall of European high culture for the rest of his life, nostalgically invoking his personal and professional friendships with men like Max Reinhardt, F. W. Murnau, and Leopold Stokowski. That he could only eke out a Hollywood career on poverty row (or worse), grinding out films with titles like *Girls in Chains*, he saw as a profound and painful irony. His greatest films, notably *Detour* (1945), picture an America whose grotesque popular culture inevitably snuffs out any lingering vestige of elite cultural traditions. That this attitude suggests the sour vision of American culture developed in the work of fellow exiles like Max Horkheimer and Theodor Adorno is probably no coincidence.[26]

Detour's Al Roberts, a bummed-out drifter who has failed in his own ambition to play the Hall, is often seen as the quintessential Ulmer hero. The difference here is that this protagonist *does* make it to Carnegie Hall, and the classical European tradition informs, but does not smother, his new style of indigenous American music.[27] That makes for a much sunnier film than Ulmer's supporters might usually expect, which partially explains the film's low standing in the Ulmer canon. Perversely, the film's sixty-two-day shooting schedule and comfortable budget (claimed as between $1.5 and $1.7 million, according to various period accounts) also functions as a strike against it. Ulmer's critical profile often shows him at his best when working with the most meager resources, but even though it was made by independent filmmakers in New York, *Carnegie Hall* can hardly be considered a marginal production. The fact that Ulmer was enjoying a brief flush of success that season, and clearly enjoyed working on a million-dollar film with so many of his musical idols, must have put him in too good a mood. Things would soon get back to normal for him, however.

Carnegie Hall was the most expensive (and most heavily publicized) film shot in New York since the early days of talkies. In an advertising insert United Artists placed in the trade papers, it was called "the greatest music picture of all time, and a far cry from the trite and usual."[28] The film was promoted as an elite experience, and even the way its musical icons were recorded was touted as superior to anything previously seen or heard on screen. These numbers were recorded in twelve-channel stereophonic sound by Walter Hicks and Richard Vorisek of Reeves Sound Studios, using a special mobile recording unit assembled by Western Electric just for this film.[29] Sensing some good free publicity for both the film and the recording process, these original multichannel tracks were played back in the Hall for anyone who would listen. *Film Daily*'s gossip columnist, running into Ulmer at the Russian Tea Room (which served as the film's unofficial commissary) found him "raving about the recording made by the famous cellist Piatigorsky on the new stereophonic sound system." After a quick trip next door, "we listened to a playback of Jan Peerce singing some Italian number.... Yep, that stereophonic sound is terrific!"[30] Many of these accounts also contained an element of high-tech boosterism, noting that the new apparatus "is at present available in New York but not in Hollywood for another 18 months," a reminder to readers that similar technological advances, especially in the sound realm, were historically the product of East Coast engineering.[31] Even the artists themselves were impressed. Boris Morros told one reporter that stereophonic recording would "render obsolete" present recording methods and claimed that when Rise Stevens first heard herself in stereo "she did not recognize the voice of Rise Stevens she had come to know in other movies and in phonograph records."[32] Most of these listeners had never heard a stereophonic recording—the technology was still in the developmental stage—and they wouldn't be hearing this one again, either. Although recorded in stereo, all the numbers were mixed down to conventional mono tracks for theatrical release, as no theaters were equipped to play them back. Even the original soundtrack album, "Night at Carnegie Hall" (Columbia ML 2113) was, of course, released in mono only. The fate of these stereo tracks is unknown today.[33]

Federal Films had been created in the heady days just after the end of the war, one more independent operation trying to negotiate a share of Hollywood's limited amount of stage space. But William LeBaron soon confessed to *Film Daily*, "The expanding field of independent production has put a very heavy burden on all existing studio facilities." It seems that several independent producers were already eyeing "two big San Diego aircraft factories for quick conversion into sound stages" and even considering filming in New York.[34] While location shooting at Carnegie Hall itself had always been in the cards, Federal at first assumed it would build any required sets at a West Coast rental facility and later put in a bid for space at New York's still uncompleted Pathé studio. Final selection of the Fox-Movietone studio for "small-set shots" was not announced until just before the start of shooting.[35] Although offering only two sound stages against Pathé's three, the largest stage at Movietone was slightly bigger than anything Pathé could offer.[36] But what would always make Pathé a first choice for visiting producers was its brand-new RCA sound installation, something even Hollywood was hard-pressed to match after years of wartime shortages.

Shooting began in a blaze of publicity on August 5, 1946. As if he were tossing out the first ball of the season, Mayor William O'Dwyer showed up at the Hall to "direct" the film's opening shot; he was given a miniature megaphone, a

5.1. In a ceremonial visit on *Carnegie Hall*'s first day of shooting, Mayor William O'Dwyer goes over the script with Marsha Hunt and Frank McHugh. Courtesy of Marsha Hunt Collection/Carnegie Hall Rose Archives.

copy of the script, and an honorary Screen Directors Guild card (this was the New York guild, not the Hollywood-based Directors Guild of America). NBC News covered the event, running film on WNBT television that same evening.[37] The photo op was deemed worthy of two pictures in the *New York Times* the next morning, and a few weeks later a larger photo spread was featured in the Sunday *Times Magazine*.[38] From their headquarters in the Hampshire House, Morros and LeBaron made sure to let everyone know how well things were going in New York and how "strike ridden" the production situation in Hollywood had become. While the Conference of Studio Unions had shut down several Hollywood studios due to a jurisdictional strike, all the film unions in New York were hard at work.[39] Crews from Local 52 and sister unions were praised for the speed with which they were able to wire the Hall for interior shooting ("on two weeks' notice as compared with the wider time latitude afforded the West Coast workers") and their skill in installing $20,000 worth of steel girders "to reinforce part of the auditorium ceiling and the flies . . . to support the scaffolding and additional weight of the lighting equipment." Details were provided on the extent of the electrical service required by the filming operation, all smoothly assembled by union crews and the local Edison Company.[40] Even the film editing was now being done in local laboratories, *Film Daily* reported, "an important factor since the Hollywood laboratory technicians are the latest screen workers to remain outside the picket lines, making impossible the development, printing or editing of Hollywood produced films."[41] De Luxe Laboratories, heir to the old Fox studios lab at 850 Tenth Avenue, handled all the film's processing and printing. When elevator operators pulled an unauthorized wildcat strike of their own at the Hall, a quick call to union bosses by Morros and LeBaron immediately brought "the 'big boys' " down from union headquarters to put things right.[42] Ulmer later told the press that the sixty-two-day shooting schedule (as against 90 to 112 days if the film had been shot in Hollywood) was only possible because all New York craft workers were under a single authority, reducing the jurisdictional friction that slowed things down on the coast.

The company moved into the Movietone studio by September 15, working on sets created by art director/costume designer Max Ree who, along with editor Fred Feitshans, was one of the few key technical people brought in from the West Coast. Ulmer was also considered a Hollywood import because he had been working for PRC since 1942—this despite the fact that he had previously been one of the most active directors in New York during the late 1930s, specializing in Yiddish pictures, race movies, and a wide array of sponsored films (needless to say, none of that history was repeated for the press). Bill Miller, who had worked on many of those Ulmer films, was the cameraman, although the famed (but nonunion) cinematographer Eugen Shuftan was credited for "Production Technique." In the middle of shooting, Jules Bricken, a local producer and director of short subjects and sponsored films, was added to the payroll as "Dialogue Director."[43] Unless Morros and LeBaron were feeling generous, this seems like a case of contractual "coverage" intended to make up for the replacement of a local union man by someone brought in from Hollywood (Ulmer?). Publicity for this film was very careful to note how many local film workers had been hired (about 150), and how few job-taking Hollywood technicians needed to be brought in. Samuel Rheiner, Federal's production manager, had "assured labor leaders that there would be no wholesale importations from Hollywood and that local workers would always get the preference. The result was a wholehearted support from the many IATSE unions and from the New York branch of the Screen Actors Guild."[44] SAG was happy because they supplied all the extras for the film, but unlike the films of Louis de Rochemont, almost every speaking role in *Carnegie Hall* was assigned to a familiar Hollywood face. There are no Karl Maldens or Ed Begleys here.

Ulmer wrapped up the film after another six weeks at Movietone. The settings were modest but appropriate, the studio apparently being large enough to accommodate not only *Carnegie Hall*'s needs, but those of Jack Goldberg's race movie, *Boy! What a Girl!* (it had started at Movietone just as *Carnegie Hall* was in its final weeks). As noted earlier, Sheila Guyse appeared in both films. The only African American with a speaking part in *Carnegie Hall*, it is she who represents contemporary American culture. Like Nora decades before, she is a domestic worker in one of the Carnegie Hall apartments but also serves as president of the pop star Tony Salerno's fan club. It would be interesting to know if this small role had been written for an African American or if the casting really was a last-minute inspiration on Ulmer's part, as the *Chicago Defender* claimed.[45]

Even after shooting had ended, William LeBaron continued to go out of his way to say nice things about production conditions in New York. "I had been told that the producer would run into costly snags and delays if he attempted to shoot his picture in the East," he told the *New York Times* in December, "because the procuring of sets, props, costumes, and so forth, would be difficult. We didn't find it so. Such things were easily obtained, usually on competitive bidding and usually at prices cheaper than Hollywood quotes." He planned to shoot *Babes in Toyland* in Hollywood because it required a Technicolor plant nearby, but *Carmen from Kenosha* was still to be made "entirely in New York."[46] Ulmer, already signed to direct, was not so sure. He understood the limitations of New York's filmmaking infrastructure much more clearly, especially when it came to shooting a complex musical feature. That would require a studio with at least three big sound stages, and he suggested that O'Dwyer "continue his efforts to make the Army Signal Corps' studio in Astoria, L.I., available to feature producers."[47]

Probably the greatest encomium *Carnegie Hall* (and New York's production chances in general) ever received came in the form of a seven-page advertising insert in *Film Daily:* "Not only have Morros and LeBaron shattered the decade old myth that a top notch, high budget picture cannot be made in its entirety away from the Hollywood scene, but they have given new heart to the hundreds of men and women who, through choice or circumstance, have been loyal to the production of Gotham."[48]

Of course, this insert was an extended advertisement disguised as editorial matter, but it is touching, and revealing, that the copywriters saw fit to lead their major promotional piece with a tribute to New York as a production center. The trade papers continued to be kind to the film when it opened in May 1947, focusing on the star presence of the musical performers, the quality of the recordings, and the way in which it had all been put together in New York. Those attributes, unfortunately, were not what the New York critics wanted to talk about. They focused instead on what even Ulmer dismissed as "that silly story," praising the music but damning the familiar immigrant saga that framed and supported it. In the *New York Times*, Bosley Crowther found the story not only "trite and foolish" but "hackneyed and maudlin" as well (for good measure, he also dismissed the concluding "modern rhapsody" as "a pretentious piece of musical claptrap").[49] But this was nothing compared to James Agee's blast in *The Nation*, one of the cruelest reviews this influential critic ever published. "*Carnegie Hall* is about the thickest and sourest mess of musical mulligatawny I have yet had to sit down to, a sort of aural compromise between the Johnstown flood and the Black Hole of Calcutta . . . a gnarled mirror of American musical taste at its worst," he wrote. Unlike Crowther, Agee gave no specifics—he just didn't like the film—but even when he tried to soften the blow he couldn't resist going nuclear. "I am sorry to be writing this way about *Carnegie Hall*, for I can't avoid feeling that some rather good intentions were involved in it. But then I can't doubt that Hitler had good intentions. He and I just didn't see eye to eye."[50] Dropping the Hitler bomb seems a bit excessive here, especially in light of the role that refugee culture plays in the film. A more judicious response appeared in the *Times* a few weeks later when their music critic, Olin Downes (who appeared briefly on-screen as "himself") was at least able to articulate just why the film seemed so leaden.[51] It was not so much the fault of the backstage story, he argued, but of the way the musical numbers themselves had been staged and photographed. Why couldn't these lengthy sequences have looked more like *Hymn of the Nations*, he asked, citing Alexander Hammid's remarkable Toscanini short, produced for the Office of War Information in 1944 and photographed by Boris Kaufman? Downes didn't like *Carnegie Hall* very much either, but unlike Crowther or Agee, at least his comments were informed, constructive, and rational.

Regardless of any negative critical opinion, *Carnegie Hall* did succeed in selling a lot of tickets. After one year in release, the film had grossed $1.1 million, but given the realities of independent distribution even this apparently healthy figure proved inadequate.[52] After UA took its distribution fee, Federal Films' share was only $768,000. And Federal was still responsible for $412,000 spent on domestic prints and advertising and $128,000 in foreign distribution costs. European profits, which might have provided a cushion, were slim or non-existent: the net profit from all of England was only $2,504.70. This left Federal with $128,000, barely enough to have covered the cost of a film like *Detour*. But *Carnegie Hall* had cost much more—maybe not the million dollars claimed at the time, but at least the $600,000 minimum demanded by the distribution contract Federal signed with UA on April 3, 1946. With a bank indebtedness of $720,000, Federal found itself more than half a million dollars in the red, which explains why *Carmen from Kenosha* and *My Immortal Beloved* never went before the cameras. It is certainly true that changes in the postwar motion picture business encouraged independent producers like Moross and LeBaron to enter the marketplace. Given the way this marketplace was still rigged, it is also true that only a handful of them would ever make any money at it.

In a peculiar footnote to this story, Artur Rubinstein returned to Carnegie Hall in April 1947 as part of his appearance in another musical feature, RKO's *Night Song*. Under the baton of Eugene Ormandy, Rubinstein accompanied the New York Philharmonic in the performance of a short concerto composed by Leith Stevens (in the film, the work of a blinded GI played by Dana Andrews).[53] But while *Variety* reported the shooting to have gone without incident, two months later the *New York Times* revealed something else entirely.

> A camera crew accompanied the sound crew to New York in the hope that the Carnegie Hall scenes could be photographed in their actual locale, but the difficulty of moving lighting equipment in and out between concerts persuaded Harriet Parsons, producer of the picture, that the best solution was to build a replica set [in Hollywood] and bring Rubinstein and Ormandy to the coast.[54]

The lesson most of Hollywood took from this fiasco was that there was nothing sacred about any potential New York locale and that everything of interest the city had to offer might be more efficiently recreated inside a sound stage. Fortunately, not every producer in Hollywood was paying attention.

The Bill O'Dwyer Story

During his 1945 mayoral campaign, William O'Dwyer had been endorsed by the Unaffiliated Independent Exhibitors of New York, insurgents who supported the Justice Department's investigation into the unfair distribution practices of the integrated Hollywood majors.[55] As soon as he was sworn in, O'Dwyer announced his intention to set up a special PR bureau, attached to the office of his secretary, William J. Donoghue, designed to boost New York as "a center of art, culture, entertainment, fashions and commerce."[56] These were fine words, but before he managed to do anything practical about the city's cultural profile, he had more important political issues to deal with.

O'Dwyer had made his reputation as the Brooklyn DA responsible for the prosecution of Murder, Inc. in 1940. Along with his chief assistant, Burton Turkus, he obtained a series of convictions, most famously that of Louis "Lepke" Buchalter, who in 1944 became the only American mob boss ever executed for murder. Turkus and O'Dwyer were able to convict Lepke (and several others) through the testimony of a hit man, Abe Reles, who had turned state's evidence. On November 12, 1941, Reles was due to testify against Lepke's partner in Murder, Inc., Albert Anastasia.[57] Although guarded by five policemen, Reles managed to fall to his death from a sixth-floor window of the Half Moon Hotel in Coney Island. Despite holding other evidence against Anastasia, O'Dwyer subsequently dropped the investigation. Frank Costello, head of the Luciano crime family, was suspected of having engineered Reles's death, but O'Dwyer never pursued Costello, either.[58] Even worse, it was later discovered that O'Dwyer had met with Costello on more than one occasion, apparently to gain his political backing within the Tammany Hall organization. This embarrassing association only surfaced after Miles McDonald, the newly elected Brooklyn DA, empaneled a grand jury in October 1945 to look into the Murder, Inc. investigation—too late to affect that fall's election but the start of a series of revelations that would eventually help force O'Dwyer from office in 1950.[59]

What really burned up local exhibitors, however, was the enforced shutdown of all New York's theaters, suddenly ordered by O'Dwyer's Disaster Control Board on February 12, and just as suddenly lifted eighteen hours later.[60] This was a response to the effect of a ten-day tugboat strike, which had cut off the city's coal supply and forced the rationing of heat and electricity (and directed special attention to the extraordinary power held by a small number of politically connected waterfront powerbrokers, like Big Bill McCormack). Losses over those two days were said to have cost the film industry $300,000. On top of this, O'Dwyer had proposed an additional 5 percent "luxury tax" on theater admissions, a levy that independent exhibitors, who served the most marginal audiences (and who had supported his campaign a few months earlier) felt would fall disproportionately on them. Although the tax hike was eventually killed by Democrats in the State Assembly, local film interests were shocked at the way O'Dwyer had begun his reign over the nation's center of art and culture.[61] There were even rumors that he was considering the sale of the city's municipal radio station, WNYC, a civic institution closely identified with his predecessor, Fiorello La Guardia. "In not much more than a month in office," *Variety* reported, "New York's Mayor O'Dwyer has scarcely endeared himself to the various branches of the amusement industry in this 'entertainment capital of the world.'"[62]

Surprisingly, one of those branches was the increasingly vocal number of independent film producers, so far all in the commercial and nontheatrical field. Led by Stanley Neal of Associated Filmakers, they had taken O'Dwyer at his word when he promised to "ballyhoo" the city as a multifaceted center of cultural production. Appealing to the mayor directly, Neal listed five local studios currently active in commercial production: Fox Movietone, Soundmasters, Filmcraft, West Coast, and Reeves, all said to be booked to 95 percent of capacity. In addition to several additional studios planned or under construction (notably Pathé), Neal raised the possibility of reopening the mothballed Warner Bros. studio in Flatbush and recapturing the Signal Corps Photographic Center in Astoria. Although he was writing from the perspective of a healthy nontheatrical industry, Neal also pointed to *The House on 92nd Street* "as evidence that theatrically successful features can also be produced here." He seems to have specifically associated his request with La Guardia's prewar initiative, which may have been one reason O'Dwyer apparently gave it "a brushoff," sending the letter down to George Sanders in the Division of Commerce and failing to issue any sort of personal response to Neal or his group.[63]

In fact, Neal was prescient in suggesting that the availability of new studios would spur on the revival of New York's theatrical motion picture industry: the Pathé, Warner Bros., and Astoria studios would all be central to the coming film renaissance (as would Movietone and Filmcraft). Yet few at the time thought this was anything but a press agent's fantasy. Even Sal Scoppa, business manager of Local 52 and a longtime supporter of local filmmaking, now publicly "doubted whether eastern production would ever encompass more than its current crop of commercial pix" because the major studios were all firmly ensconced on the West Coast and unlikely to divert any of their production to New York.[64] What Scoppa could not predict, in February 1946, was the extent of the turmoil that was about to disrupt the business model of the American film industry.

O'Dwyer first began to pay attention to the local motion picture business in April, when he appointed his personal attorney, Edward C. Maguire, to resolve a jurisdictional dispute involving coverage of United Nations sessions being held at Hunter College, which was city property. Newsreel crews covering the event were IATSE members, but when CBS sent in a television crew, those men were members of the International Brotherhood of Electrical Workers (IBEW), sparking the first of many intramural labor disputes between local film and television unions. Maguire's eventual solution was to eject the television crews, a decision that suddenly made O'Dwyer a figure of great interest in film industry circles.[65] By July, the mayor had become such a favorite that he was issuing denials to the press that he was set to take over from Will Hays as head of the industry's main trade group, the MPAA.[66]

The mayor seems to have had no involvement with the filming of *Smash-Up* and *It Happened in Brooklyn*, but the production of *Carnegie Hall* was a different matter. He was so prominent on August 5, the first day of shooting, that *Film Daily* cited him as "an 'extra' special friend of the film industry" for the amount of face time he gave reporters.[67] But O'Dwyer himself had had little to do with bringing the film to New York or facilitating its production here. Indeed, he was riding on the publicity barrage organized by Morros and LeBaron, a fact generally recognized by industry analysts who knew just how long it had taken *Carnegie Hall* to "bring to reality a dream of former Mayor La Guardia to make New York a motion picture production center."[68] O'Dwyer could now see that this was no pipe dream but a potential goldmine, politically as well as economically. The only question was how to rebrand La Guardia's dream as his own.

Out on the West Coast, screenwriter Malvin Wald had been looking to reestablish himself in the business after spending the war years writing training films for the First Motion Picture Unit of the Army Air Forces (when not moonlighting on low-budget filler like Edgar G. Ulmer's *Jive Junction*). While working on these documentaries Wald had fallen under the influence of Ben Maddow, a veteran of New York's prewar documentary movement whose credits included such films as *People of the Cumberland*, *Heart of Spain*, and *Native Land*. Realizing that the raw recruits brought in to write these training films were completely unfamiliar with the history and traditions of documentary production, Maddow organized lunchtime screenings of masterworks by Robert Flaherty, John Grierson, Joris Ivens, and other nonfiction pioneers. Wald decided to call on someone he had known slightly before the war, the independent producer Mark Hellinger, a "professional New Yorker" who had given up his career as a newspaper columnist to make films like *The Roaring Twenties*, *The Killers*, and *Brute Force*. "Hellinger listened patiently to my story about Ben Maddow, Robert Flaherty, and the documentary film and asked what this had to do with Hollywood," Wald remembered years later, still surprised that Hellinger had actually sat still for the pitch. He was asking Hellinger to fund a research trip to New York, where he would delve into unsolved homicide records and bring back a story (to be called *Homicide*) that could be filmed on the streets of the city. He admitted that he knew little or nothing about the sources and methods used by homicide detectives but planned to research this dramatic police procedural in the same way he had researched military documentaries. When faced with the responsibility of writing a film on ditching B-17s or assembling radar units, he would immerse himself in primary materials until he found the most efficient way for these "facts" to tell their own story. As a clincher, his pitch concluded by noting that someone else had already succeeded with this same basic idea: Louis de Rochemont's *The House on 92nd Street*. In the best Hollywood tradition, their movie would be the same, only different.[69] Hellinger's biographer, Jim Bishop, has a similar account of their meeting, but claims that it was Hellinger who proposed that Wald go to New York to research a realistic mystery or crime film. "It had to be so New Yorkerish that it would look like a documentary."[70]

Hellinger was intrigued by the New York angle but, in Wald's account, suspicious of everything else. He felt that de Rochemont could get away with these "semi-documentaries" because he had spent years working on *The March of Time* and knew exactly what might best be filmed on actual locations and how to go about doing it. He didn't believe that the police would let some Hollywood screenwriter rummage through their files or shut down streets and bridges so his crews could find the most compelling camera angles. And because—as an independent producer in postwar Hollywood—he was spending his own money, he had little interest in pioneering a new narrative form just because people like Ben Maddow saw some dramatic potential in it.

But Bill O'Dwyer's opinion was something else again. According to Bishop, Hellinger admitted to Wald, "I've got a little in with Mayor O'Dwyer and Police

Commissioner Wallander."[71] He remembered O'Dwyer from before the war, when he was still a Broadway columnist and Bill-O was working his way up the political ladder of Democratic politics. Now O'Dwyer was making noises about encouraging film production in New York, and Hellinger had a New York project in development that would need a great deal of encouragement. In early October—with *Carnegie Hall* still shooting at Movietone—Hellinger made a quick trip to New York for a meeting with the mayor and his police commissioner. O'Dwyer saw the opportunity to get on the right side of this film production issue and reached for it. There were no tax incentives on the table, but the two men promised Hellinger all the cooperation they could possibly offer, and not only during the long weeks of location shooting. Wallander would open the department's files to Hellinger's "researcher" and allow him unfettered access to line-ups, morgue procedures, and ballistics labs. When Hellinger said he would film at least half the picture in New York, Wallander agreed to allow "many scenes [to be] taken directly in the police department's homicide squad."[72] *Variety* claimed that Wallander and O'Dwyer were being so cooperative "because they are convinced that [the film] will help to discourage crime."[73] A few days later Malvin Wald arrived from the coast to begin his research project.

Hellinger, of course, was a creature of New York's bathtub gin era and would have remembered exactly how things got done in New York. Having "a little in with the mayor" had always worked back when Jimmy Walker was in office. Had things really changed in the few years since he had gone Hollywood? Indeed, the situation was notorious. In 1979 I interviewed Ed Baldwin, who worked in the casting office at Paramount's Astoria studio in the early 1930s. "Mayor Walker was the mayor [and] Betty Compton was his girlfriend," he remembered. "So we at Paramount put her on the payroll. See? And any time we wanted to take any shots in Manhattan, block off Forty-Second Street and Broadway, 'think nothing of it, just call up the mayor's office, sure, go ahead.' And they used to pay off the police, too."[74] Hellinger would not have had to get this information from Ed Baldwin, assuming that as long as he could get Bill O'Dwyer on the phone, everything would be under control.

While Hellinger's writer sifted through the records of New York's homicide squad, *Variety* published an analysis of the "production move away from Hollywood." The completion of *Carnegie Hall* and the imminent opening of the "elaborate" RKO-Pathé studio had focused attention on New York, but the runaway movement had already begun to spread overseas, fueled by "strike-bound Hollywood studios, high domestic production costs and foreign quotas on U.S. pix imports."[75] According to this analysis, New York's greatest advantage was in the relative labor peace it offered at a time when Hollywood studio operations were frequently disrupted by raucous picket lines. But in an adjacent article on the same page, Edgar G. Ulmer, while praising the "speed and low cost" that had facilitated his production of *Carnegie Hall*, admitted that New York lacked the stage space and technical resources necessary to compete with Hollywood; he urged Mayor O'Dwyer to find some way of privatizing the Signal Corps studio in Astoria, "the only setup that provides sufficient space for full-scale production" in the city.[76]

A Miracle on Thirty-Fourth Street

But New York did have one other advantage that *Variety* left out: the "million dollar backlot" that included everything from Central Park to the Manhattan skyline. Darryl F. Zanuck had just approved George Seaton's request for twenty-two days of New York location shooting on a script he had written called *The Big Heart*, crucial scenes that required all four principal actors, a minimum of back projection, and the Macy's Thanksgiving Day Parade. Unlike most of Fox's other location-based features, this was not a crime film and was certainly not based on a true story. *Miracle on 34th Street*, as it was finally called after a series of name changes, came into town on November 26. Two days later they shot the parade (as did local television crews—it was the first one to be televised) but also remade it for their own purposes, transforming a real staged event into a "realistic" scene from Zanuck's latest picture. When "a somewhat frostbitten Santa Claus, in the person of Edmund Gwenn," stepped down from his sleigh to unveil Macy's seasonal display windows, few in the crowd of two million realized that this was not the actual Santa Claus but a ringer—an actor playing a part in Fox's latest New York location picture.[77] To make things even more interesting, they were not just watching this show but working in it themselves, an army of unpaid extras on New York's million-dollar backlot.

Seaton was said to have been carrying this story around with him for years but had been having trouble raising any interest in it. A funny little man who believes he really is Santa Claus changes the lives of a single mother and her little girl, two modern New Yorkers for whom belief in anything does not come easily ("Those two are a couple of lost souls," Santa, aka Kris Kringle, says at one point). The film was heartwarming but also a little bit edgy, suggesting a conflict between the progressive postwar ethic of rational capitalism and a folksy humanism grounded in some nebulous concept of "faith" (but not religious faith, as Christ has completely vanished from Seaton's vision of Christmas). "Loss of belief in Santa Claus, in fact, is equated with loss of belief, period," critic Gavin Lambert later wrote, "and when the consequences of no more Santa are pointed out, material interests and spiritual values hold hands at the thought of toy business and Christmas business in general falling off, and workers being laid off."[78]

Zanuck found Seaton's first draft "excellent, fresh, exciting, and delightful," but disliked the character of the mother, a busy young woman who sees no benefit in feeding her little girl whimsical Santa Claus fantasies. "I feel that she is so cold, so cut and dried, that an audience will have a difficult time forgiving her," he wrote to the producer on November 6. "It was impossible for me to believe that any mother could be as heartless as she appeared to be.... Any man who ever heard [a mother] give her child the kind of advice that Doris does would start running in the other direction."[79]

Regardless of his feelings, after a quick look at the calendar Zanuck resisted the temptation to tinker with the script. Unwilling to give up the (essentially free) spectacle value of the famous parade, he ordered Seaton to begin shooting in New York in less than three weeks. He called an angry Maureen O'Hara back from a long-delayed Irish holiday, teamed her again with a familiar costar, John Payne, for box office insurance and gambled on the casting of a sixty-nine-year-old veteran, Edmund Gwenn, and an eight-year-old newcomer, Natalie Wood.[80] Realizing that they would have no opportunity for retakes, Seaton

5.2. For *Miracle on 34th Street*, Fox planted their own Santa Claus, Edmund Gwenn, in the 1946 Macy's Thanksgiving Day Parade. Note cameraman with 35 mm Eyemo at lower left. Museum of Modern Art Film Stills Archive.

(who had gone to New York many times over the previous two years trying to set up the film) dotted the parade route with camera crews, covering every point of interest from Seventy-Seventh Street to Herald Square, and even playing the film's key opening sequence at the parade assembly point behind the American Museum of Natural History.[81]

What Fox did not do was depend on any New York studio facilities for even a part of their constructed interiors—something done by *The House on 92nd Street* and *Carnegie Hall*, which had both built sets at the Fox Movietone studio. Seaton did follow the de Rochemont pattern by hiring unfamiliar local faces for occasional bits. For example, Guy Thomajan and Jack Albertson played a scene (shot in the general post office) where two postal employees decide to deliver to the Edmund Gwenn character thousands of dead letters addressed to Santa Claus.[82] But otherwise the "New York" input here was mainly geographic.

"New York remained bitterly cold that winter," Maureen O'Hara remembered, "so cold the cameras froze on one occasion and wouldn't turn over."[83] But Seaton was able to film indoors as well, not just at the post office, but in Macy's back offices, locker rooms, cafeteria, and main sales floor. Filming on the sales floor usually took place at night, but even daytime interiors were extremely difficult to light, given the size of "America's largest store." Extra electrical cables were draped around pillars and decorated with Christmas bunting, as if they were part of the holiday lighting scheme.[84] And all of this had to be done during the busiest time of year, the few weeks between Thanksgiving and Christmas. By comparison, when Blake Edwards needed to film inside Tiffany's in 1960 he had fewer pages of script to shoot and much less floor space to worry about.

Arthur Jacobson, the assistant director, had no complaints about the store or its staff but was still fuming about problems with the film's "irresponsible unit manager" more than forty years later. "He was somebody's friend, and that's how he got the job," he grumbled. But just who was this unnamed miscreant who wouldn't do what Jacobson told him to do? Was it the production manager, Ray Klune, who also held this job on *The Dark Corner* and *The House on 92nd Street* (as well as *Gone with the Wind*)? Or was it another experienced hand, the location manager, Charlie Hall, whose other films included *Kiss of Death* and *13 Rue Madeleine*?[85] Or was it simply a matter of three uncredited assistants all struggling to demonstrate who was really in charge under very difficult circumstances? The final result may appear smooth and effortless, but managing a New York location of this size and complexity had never been done before. Indeed, at a time when filmmakers generally avoided showing the names of real products, corporations, or trade names on screen, the extent of this film's association with Macy's was unprecedented, marking some sort of landmark in on-screen product placement. Significantly, the press interpreted this at the time not as a simple commercial tie-in but "a documentary expedient, imbuing with more reality what happens."[86]

Miracle on 34th Street was a fairly expensive film for Fox, eventually costing $1,570,000, about the same as *Kiss of Death* but half a million dollars more than *Boomerang!* Yet despite the fact that it did very well at the box office, grossing $2.65 million on initial release (better than *Boomerang!* but less than *13 Rue Madeleine*) Zanuck was never very excited about it.[87] Arthur Jacobson recalled Seaton telling him before production that "Zanuck can't see it," until one day he was authorized to "shoot it if you can arrange it," a level of enthusiasm that suggests that the head of the studio was busy with more promising material.[88] The company continued to work in New York for almost a month before returning to California, where they officially finished production on February 22. But studio records indicate that something was still not right, and additional scenes were ordered on February 28 and March 1, with further retakes on March 24.[89]

Today, the most surprising aspect of this film is the strong characterization of the mother by Maureen O'Hara, the feisty heroine of innumerable costume pictures. In modern dress as a Macy's executive in charge of producing the annual spectacle, Doris Walker is also a devoted single mother (of Susan, played by Natalie Wood) and a divorced woman, a remarkable combination for a 1946 American film. But Zanuck always felt that the character in the original script was "overdrawn." "You get the feeling that she is a bit of a fanatic on the subject of Santa Claus when she is merely a modern woman who doesn't believe in feeding a child a lot of silly, antiquated fairy stories," he had written back in November. He also suggested, "Perhaps if there were a way to bring out quicker the hurt in her background and past life we might be able to understand her."[90] The hurt was essential to the character: as John Payne eventually tells Santa, "she hasn't really believed in anything for years." But by the time the film was released the sources of her existential anxiety had not been clarified but eliminated. "My father and mother were divorced when I was a baby" little Susan matter-of-factly tells her Mom's prospective suitor, a line that passes so quickly that the otherwise reliable *American Film Institute Catalog* refers to Doris not as a divorcée but "a widow." Gavin Lambert, citing an earlier script draft, notes that "by eliminating the character of the alcoholic ex-husband, who's only referred to in the final version, they made her insistence on 'life's harsh realities' less understandable."[91] Whatever Zanuck had been unable to fix before Thanksgiving he quickly tried to patch up in Hollywood during the retakes. But he never did solve the problem of this complicated modern woman and seems to have washed his hands of the picture. He didn't even bother to show up for the preview.[92] Instead, the studio arranged for a feature article in the *Los Angeles Times* in which O'Hara came out in favor of motherhood and religion and distanced herself as much as possible from the divorced career woman she played in the film. "Maureen hopes she won't be held up as a horrible example when *Miracle on 34th Street*, her next movie, is released," the paper made clear.[93]

O'Hara also recalled Zanuck's uncertainty about what to do with the film, a Christmas movie he decided to release in June.[94] The advertising campaign downplayed any association with Christmas or Santa Claus, and no holiday imagery appeared on the generic one-sheet poster. The spectacularly uninformative five-minute trailer (available on YouTube) must be seen to be believed. What were they thinking? *Miracle on 34th Street* was made and released about six months after another Christmas classic, Frank Capra's *It's a Wonderful Life*. This was too soon to have affected the style or content of Seaton's film, although one could easily imagine Edmund Gwenn and Henry Travers swapping roles as each film's cherubic deus ex machina. But the disappointing box office returns of Capra's fantasy must have validated Zanuck's earlier doubts about the picture, and instead of saving it for the holidays he tossed it out as soon as it was ready, just in time for the Fourth of July. He must have been as surprised as anyone when he saw the film's grosses, not to mention its three Oscars.[95]

Seaton would return to New York in the summer of 1951 to shoot two weeks of principal photography for *Anything Can Happen*, a contemporary immigrant saga starring José Ferrer as an endearing Georgian folk singer. America is seen as a welcoming land where Georgians, Turks, and Armenians find they can all assimilate quite painlessly, while local folk-music fanatics record the songs of their homelands at rousing jam sessions. Unlike so many others, Seaton and Ferrer filmed their "immigrant's arrival" scene right in New York's harbor, although one technician worried aloud that the Statue of Liberty "looked awful skinny" and would have to be replaced by "a stock shot out of the library."[96] This was all too sweet for the *New York Times*, which felt that "the cozy picture Mr. Seaton presents of a band of genial eccentrics singing songs and having feasts in old-country style, as of the present, is in the realm of myth."[97] Notable for casting such underused actors as Kurt Kaszner, Oscar Beregi, and George Voskovec, *Anything Can Happen* is a well-meaning effort that plays like a piece of UNESCO propaganda, perhaps one reason the film was picketed on release by the American Legion (who were also taking issue with José Ferrer's politics).[98]

After signing off on Mark Hellinger's film, O'Dwyer paid little attention to the city's movie business in the winter of 1946–47. City Hall appears to have taken no advantage of *Miracle on 34th Street* or any of the other visiting films shooting here in November. A scheduling glitch forced Lewis Milestone to shoot retakes for *Arch of Triumph* in a hastily rented Manhattan studio. Charles Laughton had replaced Michael Chekhov midway through production, but by the time Laughton showed up Ingrid Bergman had already finished her scenes and left for Broadway to star in *Joan of Lorraine*. Milestone and Laughton went to New York to redo all the Bergman-Chekhov scenes, working in front of the same Parisian back projections the company had used in Hollywood.[99] *Arch of Triumph* was so heavily publicized that even these two days of retakes made the papers, but Paramount's *Blaze of Noon* seems to have avoided local press coverage entirely. An early aviation saga, the film featured one hazardous sequence in which the stunt pilot, Paul Mantz, "flew a B-23 just over the George Washington Bridge and twenty feet over the water in lower New York bay, barely grazing the ships' masts, with the camera shooting out of the plane's nose."[100]

As 1947 began, all local attention was focused on the Pathé studio, where *Citizen Saint*, *Man About Town*, and *Portrait of Jennie* would be produced, and on Fox's current location noir, *Kiss of Death*. A drive-by production like MGM's *The Hucksters*, which shot for four nights at the Fulton Fish Market at the end of March, hardly seemed worth mentioning. The second unit director, John Waters, had arrived around March 17, recruited a local crew, and sent out a call for extras. Many of these, apparently, were recruited at the Lambs Club, "a sort of post office and grapevine combined," where actors at liberty might pick up tips regarding casting calls. "The scene itself was incredibly boring," wrote one reporter who also followed a tip. "About 40 players walked around in front of the market—where Al Smith spent hours in his youth. They walked until seven in the morning, looking like ordinary passersby. Each extra got about $15 for the night's work."[101] The finished film reveals a few shots of the market, with doubles substituting for the principal actors, and a lot of back projection.

Portrait of Jennie was the most heavily publicized of all these films, but the fact that its production was mired in New York for six months was not necessarily a good thing. As noted earlier, Selznick had not properly prepared for the shoot and the unit producer, David Hempstead, was barely competent. Of course, he tended to blame New York, New York weather, and New York officials for any and all problems, and eventually his complaints wound up on Mayor O'Dwyer's desk. George Sanders, a "personal friend and traveling companion" of the mayor, should have been attending to such matters in his capacity as head of the Department of Commerce, but he seems to have been otherwise occupied. O'Dwyer had created a blue ribbon Business Advisory Committee, chaired by Nelson A. Rockefeller, to create a plan for the general "betterment of business, labor and industry" in the city. Their proposal for a two-year effort, to be paid for mainly by private industry, was delivered on August 8, 1946, but after months of inaction Rockefeller resigned the following March 24 and the rest of the members went with him.[102]

Sanders himself soon became a liability. On May 10, 1946, at 4:30 a.m., he had run over and killed a pushcart peddler on the corner of Fifty-First Street. Because there was "no proof" of his culpability, he was not charged; the *Times* noted in its report that he was "a personal friend of the mayor and police commissioner Arthur W. Wallander."[103] Then he was caught up in a corruption and bribery scandal uncovered by Frank Hogan, the New York County DA, who was investigating abuses in the granting of pier space to excursion boat operators (Sanders had previously been an official of the Dutton Line, operating boats to Bear Mountain and the Statue of Liberty). Although he challenged the accusations as "absurd," he was forced to resign from his dollar-a-year position at the Commerce Department on May 2, 1947.[104]

The timing of all this was terrible. Hellinger was coming to town with *The Naked City*, and the city had just begun to negotiate with union and industry representatives on the creation of a municipal "film liaison," whose job it would be to facilitate such production. At the instigation of the IATSE president, Richard Walsh, Sanders had met twice with this group in April in an effort to eliminate "red tape" resulting from "overlapping responsibilities of various city departments, and the necessity for securing approval for location shootings from several quarters."[105] Encouraged by the progress, O'Dwyer issued "a renewed invitation" to film producers, pledging the city's "full cooperation to the industry."[106] But Sanders's sudden resignation, it was reported, would now put a "temporary crimp" in plans for the creation of this municipal film coordinator.[107] In fact, it would be six months before the city would have a new commerce commissioner.

Mark Hellinger's Naked City

Just a few weeks after Sanders's departure, *Variety* published a remarkably thoughtful analysis of the real reasons behind the current wave of runaway production. "While the ostensible reason for the sudden splurge of eastern production is the realism to be gained by on-the-scene shooting, there's a more basic factor. It's not that it is cheaper to film a picture on location than it is to build sets in a studio. It often isn't. Transportation of personnel and equipment 3,000 miles can easily eat up that differential."

> What's causing the move out of Hollywood is that the pictures that can best be made on eastern locations are by their very nature pictures that cost comparatively little to produce—whether on the lot or on location. They're stories about everyday people in everyday surroundings. They require no expensive costumes or elaborate sets—at least no elaborate sets that can't be better shot with the real thing. . . . Some erudite Hollywood observers view the present towering production costs as a blessing in disguise, since they are forcing this swing to more simply conceived pictures. They see it changing the whole art form of the film in a few years to put emphasis on realism and everyday life, rather than continual phantasy. Thus, with more variety in types of pix, they see a larger audience for them.[108]

This trade paper analyst doesn't go so far as to say that stories of "realism and everyday life" will one day supplant the audience's desire for "continual phantasy," but he does have a good sense of where the future New York film renaissance will come from. Not from films like *Portrait of Jennie*, then in production at the Pathé studio, but from things like *The Naked City, On the Waterfront*, and *Killer's Kiss*—no elaborate costumes or sets; contemporary situations; everyday people and ordinary surroundings. The "whole art form of the film" is about to change, he realizes. And while this may sound like Cesare Zavattini's neorealist manifesto, Italian neorealism seems to have had nothing to do with it.

When Malvin Wald arrived back in New York (he had grown up there and worked for two years as a postal clerk in Brooklyn) he found that Commissioner Wallander's good graces only went so far. The men who were supposed to instruct him in the history and practice of homicide investigation "did not welcome me with open arms."

> I began to feel like a criminal as the various detectives eyed me with cold appraisal. They informed me in their own quiet way that they didn't harbor much affection for screen writers—especially those who write murder mysteries. Slowly they poured out their bitter complaints. In too many movies they were shown as lazy, stupid characters who couldn't find a sailor in the Navy Yard. In the films they were unable to solve even the simplest murder without the assistance of a handsome private eye and his blonde secretary. And this in the face of the fact that not a single murder had been solved by a private detective in New York in the last quarter-century.[109]

The cops were right to think this way. Police in American films had long been pictured in exactly this fashion, and not just in Mack Sennett's Keystone Cops comedies. FBI agents were always treated positively, but local police were more likely to be represented by hapless Inspector Oscar Piper (James Gleason), whose cases were always solved by the schoolmarmish Hildegarde Withers. The men complaining to Wald were fed up with Nick Charles and Philip Marlowe, and they had no use at all for slapdash B-movies like Columbia's *The Homicide Squad* (1939). Things only began to change for Wald when word got around that he was working for Mark Hellinger, whose *The Killers* they found "100 percent accurate."[110]

Wald also impressed the locals with his intimate knowledge of Brooklyn streets (he knew Pineapple from Orange ever since his days in the post office). He won over Inspector Joseph Donovan, head of the Statistical and Criminal Identification Bureau, who not only allowed him access to the files but provided an off-the-record tutorial. Donovan in turn led him to Deputy Chief Cutrayne at the Police Academy, and by the time Wald finished his research he had personal experience of everything from the ballistics lab to the city morgue.[111] But most of his time was spent reading detective reports, on which he dutifully reported back to Hellinger. The two thousand reports collected in the triple-murder Veronica Gedeon case were tantalizing but too time consuming. So Wald also looked into the murders of Harry Nichols, Fritz Gebhardt, Nancy Titterton, Bummy Davis, and a host of others before settling on the unsolved 1923 murder of "Broadway Butterfly" Dot King. The public was not supposed to have access to the files of unsolved killings, but Donovan had made an exception.

"Hellinger was excited because he was on the case," Wald remembered. "He and [Walter] Winchell were riding with the police one night when the homicide call came. He had visited the murder apartment and had seen the corpse—and he had known the victim when she was alive."[112] Much of this may actually have been true—Hellinger's career as a columnist had just started in 1923, and he really was a friend of Winchell. But even more important was that the Dot King story had so many elements of a good Hellinger column: crime, Broadway, and an acute sense of New York as a community divided socially, economically, and geographically. And no happy ending. Although the writer Luc Sante characterized Hellinger as "Damon Runyon with an extra dose of schmaltz," the reality was far different.[113] Hellinger's *Daily Mirror* columns are not easy to track down, but he did anthologize many of them in collections like *Moon Over Broadway*. These are not heartwarming stories of Damon Runyon's little people but cynical tales of men and women on the margins—dupes, suicides, and self-deluded losers who often deserve everything that happens to them. One story, "Handsome Boy," begins as follows: "If you're not in the mood for an ironic story, it would be better for you to skip this yarn. There is bitterness here—and plenty of it. I've written of many twisted lives, but never have I struck one quite so cruel as this. . . ."[114] The stories often feature "O. Henry endings," but the surprise is usually that things turn out *worse* than we expected. Or as Hellinger might put it, more cruel and ironic.

Indeed, even *American Cinematographer*, after praising the "graphically journalistic, often staccato approach of the camera," noted that "one can see the Mark Hellinger of fifteen years ago doggedly following up the story of a socially insignificant young woman who was strangled and left floating in a bath tub."[115] I do not know if Hellinger had previously used the Dot King murder as fodder for his column, but "Front Page," collected in the same volume, suggests how he might have handled it. It tells the story of a murder committed in New York in the winter of 1917. "On 23d st., just off 10th av., a young woman was found beaten to death. She was neither pretty. Nor wealthy. Nor interesting. Just a woman—like millions of others."[116] Forensic police work identifies the killer through the teeth marks he leaves on an apple. While Hellinger was no Hemingway, prose like this suggests why the two men might have bonded. The novelist announced that he "was proud" of the job Hellinger had done on *The Killers*, and just weeks before the producer's death had contracted with

Hellinger to adapt four more of his stories in the next year, with an option on all of Hemingway's other short fiction.[117]

Hellinger was attracted to the new style of reportorial fiction he saw in the story synopsis Wald had prepared, but "doubts suddenly overwhelmed him about the whole project."[118] Things seemed to be going well for him, but he was leery of producing another *Moontide* (1942), a failed Jean Gabin vehicle he had made at Fox. Richard Brooks, who wrote two films for him, described him (in a memorial piece!) as "secretive, suspicious, frantic, fearful," a classic paranoid who felt that jealous rivals were "conniving against him, pulling off secret deals against him, planning to push him out of the movie business."[119] He wasn't about to give them the chance. And anyway, this time it was his own money. Two full screenplay drafts made him no happier, so he paid Wald off and consigned *Homicide* to his graveyard of unproduced properties. Then Jules Dassin got a look at it.[120] In the spring of 1947 Dassin had been shooting *Brute Force* for Hellinger, another powerful film noir steeped in as much existential despair as *The Killers*. "I hated the scenario," he later said of *Homicide*, "but I agreed to make the film despite the story because I thought I would be able to make the film I had always dreamed of. I said that I would do it if they let me film in the streets of New York, in real interiors, with unknown actors."[121] As that had been the plan all along, all that was needed was a more polished script, and for that Dassin brought in Albert Maltz, a friend he had known in New York before the war.

Maltz was now one of the hottest writers in Hollywood, with credits on *This Gun for Hire*, *Destination Tokyo*, and *Pride of the Marines*. But he was also hot for other reasons. A Communist Party member, in February 1946 Maltz had published a notorious essay called "What Shall We Ask of Writers?" in *New Masses*. He announced that he found current left-radical literature "sterile" because it was tied to an obsolete "art is a weapon" aesthetic. He praised instead the work of social novelists like James T. Farrell, who did not sacrifice their personal vision for the sake of a predetermined political end, and claimed to have long since adapted this strategy in his own work. Maltz's position, itself a relic of the popular front era, was now in disfavor following the expulsion of Party chief Earl Browder, so attacks from fellow comrades began immediately. Two months later, after being excoriated by John Howard Lawson, Howard Fast, and a string of other Party members at a raucous fraction meeting, he took space in the same journal to recant his previous position.[122]

While the Maltz affair sent a shockwave through the liberal community (and was diligently noted by professional Communist hunters), what would it have meant to someone like Mark Hellinger? Maltz had been finishing his work on Fritz Lang's *Cloak and Dagger* when all this happened, and when that film opened in September 1946 he shared a screen credit with Ring Lardner, Jr. He would not receive another such credit until 1970—except for the one

Mark Hellinger would give him on *The Naked City*. It is true that it was Jules Dassin, a fellow traveler (if not an active Party member), who brought Maltz onto the picture, but Dassin himself had been handpicked by Hellinger, as had Frank Tuttle, another Communist, who was directing Hellinger's other current project, *Swell Guy*. Whatever Hellinger's own politics might have been (and *Swell Guy* certainly deserves another look here), he does not seem to have been uncomfortable working with writers, actors, and directors he must have known were prominent members of the Hollywood left.[123]

In a memo to Hellinger written on April 7, 1947, Maltz seemed to evoke Dziga Vertov more than Rossellini, suggesting "that the CAMERA EYE, whenever possible, reflect the rich and infinite detail of the daily life of New York: the small boy hitching on the back of a truck; the alley cat digging for its food in an open garbage pail . . . the architectural beauty and squalor that exist side by side."[124] The one European film he did suggest as a model of "dramatic handling" was *Brief Encounter*.[125] The use of flashbacks, subjective narration, professional actors, and studio settings would seem to mark this British "film of quality" as the opposite of something like *Open City*—but the insistent use of the word "ordinary" in *Brief Encounter*'s voice-over suggests one element that Zavattini, Maltz, and Noel Coward all understood as central to the new postwar cinema.

Malvin Wald, who spoke out about the film far more than Albert Maltz ever did, tended to diminish Maltz's contribution (on the DVD commentary track, he refers to him as the "dialogue writer"). Recent scholarship tends to agree with Wald. Carl Richardson, who compared the various drafts, found no major structural changes, concluding only that Maltz's rewrites had "humanized" and "lightened" Wald's work, which was at times either too dry or laden with obvious symbolism (a detective searching a suspect's office discovers a volume of Nietzsche, for example).[126] Rebecca Prime saw a "clear imbalance between Maltz's and Wald's contributions," with Maltz's changes evident mainly in "the film's introductory narration."[127] Citing an interview with Wald, she suggests that Hellinger granted Maltz a shared screenplay credit, "the better to capitalize on Maltz's renown." But the value of this renown (which in 1947 might be better described as notoriety) is open to question. It seems more likely that Hellinger, or Dassin, awarded this credit as a gesture to a man in trouble, something that Wald—who conceived the idea and spent six months on the project—was forced to accept as best he could.[128]

Neither Wald nor Maltz accompanied Hellinger when he arrived in New York on June 2, the first official day of shooting.[129] Dassin and William Daniels, his director of photography, had already been there for two months, scouting locations and casting the film with the "unknown actors" Dassin had always wanted. The only familiar faces would be their star, Barry Fitzgerald, playing Lt. Dan Muldoon, and Frank Conroy in the small role of Capt. Donahue. Howard Duff, who played "Sam Spade" on the radio, had been in *Brute Force*, but that

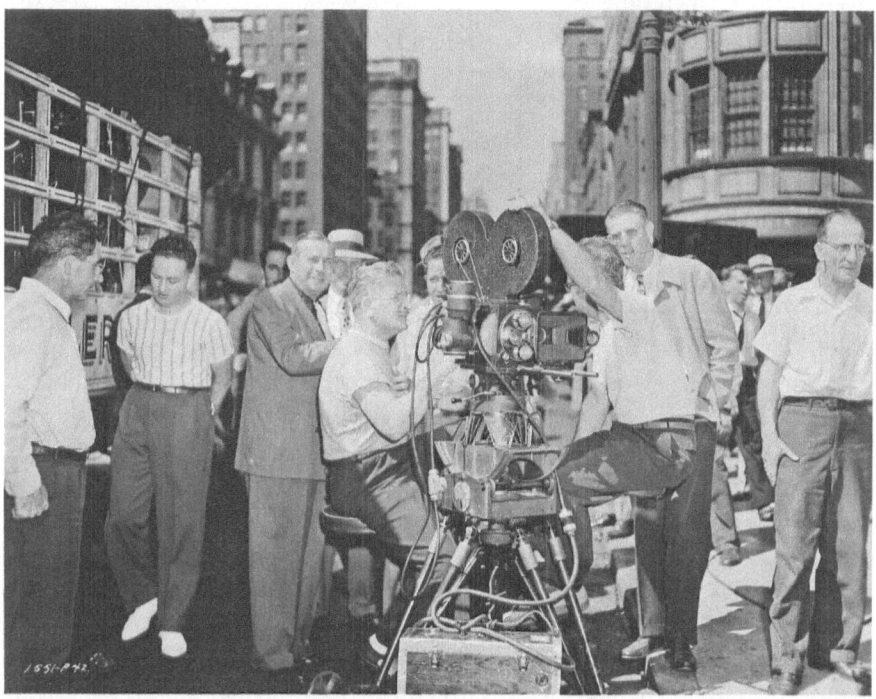

5.3 Producer Mark Hellinger, not dressed for warm weather, poses between the cinematographer, William Daniels, and the director, Jules Dassin (in striped shirt), on one of the *Naked City* locations. Author's collection.

film hadn't been released yet. Enid Markey was a veteran silent screen actress who had only appeared in one film since 1920. Dorothy Hart, Don Taylor, and Ted de Corsia had each played in one or two films, often without credit. The rest of the cast was composed of New York stage and radio actors, people like Tom Pedi, David Opatoshu, Paul Ford, Arthur O'Connell, Celia Adler, and John Marley.

Hellinger still considered himself primarily a writer, and all revisions to the final May 20 shooting script were handled by him alone, working in consultation with Dassin. For example, the conclusion of that script has the villain, Garza (eventually referred to as Garzah), racing across the Williamsburg Bridge. Climbing a fence while attempting to escape across the subway tracks, he is shot by a police sniper, falls on the third rail, and dies "in a shower of sparks."[130] Later it was decided instead to have Garza, in a panic, climb up one of the bridge's towers and be shot down by the police, but Hellinger was still unhappy. In a memo to Dassin he warned that the sequence they were about to film spent too much time personalizing Garza, "a man who was merely incidental to our entire yarn," by including too many big close-ups and a melodramatic "UFA situation atop the superstructure." Like all industry professionals, Hellinger knew the dramatic visual style of the old German Ufa studio, which Robert Siodmak had conjured for him on *The Killers*. But what he now wanted was a "newsreel effect" achieved by use of "the long-shot notion wherever possible" and greater reliance on the narrator. All this, of course, would make the sequence play more like a documentary while avoiding "entering into situations that have been done ever since the movies began."[131]

The longer Hellinger worked on the film, the more attached he became to this narration, which he eventually decided to speak himself. His first real film success, *The Roaring Twenties* (1939), was one of the earliest dramatic narratives to feature a third-person voice-over narration, although it was delivered by an unnamed, "objective" narrator. Nevertheless, Hellinger did brand that film with a signed introductory prologue, and its script is based on a collection of his old stories.[132] Indeed, Hellinger was not ignorant of the use of voice-over narration in dramatic features, but had pioneered the strategy well before Orson Welles even arrived in Hollywood. What he did borrow from *The Magnificent Ambersons* was the personalizing of this narration as the voice of the filmmaker himself, something not at all indicated in the final shooting script.

The film as released begins with two full minutes of additional narration plainly written by Hellinger, who starts off by introducing himself ("I was in charge of the production") and the key members of the cast and crew. In *The Magnificent Ambersons*, Welles delivers this same information ("I wrote it and directed it") at the end. "As you see, we're flying over an island, a city, a particular city, and this is a story of a number of people and a story also of the city itself," he tells us. The sound of airplane engines in the background suggests that this is not some disembodied authorial voice (like Welles) but a fellow passenger bending our ear as we fasten our seatbelts for the descent into LaGuardia. "I may as well tell you frankly that it's a bit different from most films you've ever seen.... It was not photographed in a studio," he boasts. "Quite the contrary." *Portrait of Jennie* also begins with an aerial shot of Manhattan, but no two films could be more different. "This is the city as it is," Hellinger claims. "Hot summer pavements; the children at play; the buildings in their naked stone; the people, without makeup." None of this is in the shooting script. His other major change to the narration occurred at the very end. While the script completes the cycle of life and death by closing with the birth of a baby at Presbyterian Hospital ("naked into a naked city"), Hellinger the storyteller instead reminds us that what we have seen was really just another one of his stories. "There are eight million stories in the naked city. This has been one of them."

The opening narration of *The Naked City* famously asserts its objectivity. But what it really announces is local boy Mark Hellinger's intimate, almost proprietary relationship to life in the big town, and his pride and excitement at being part of this scene. That aspect of the narration is one of the most iconic elements of the film, but Hellinger and his writers were only tapping into a magical Manhattan zeitgeist that was already well established in American popular culture. New Yorkers were understood to have a peculiar affection for this noisy, vibrant, cosmopolitan island, which the rest of the country saw as floating in isolation somewhere off the East Coast. Of course, Hollywood had already done its part in helping to create this image. *Nobody Lives Forever*, to take just one example, had been produced at Warner Bros. in 1944, while Hellinger was still on the lot, but had yet to be released when *The Naked City* began filming in New York. John Garfield plays a Broadway hustler, wounded at the front and now returning after three months of rehabilitation in a military hospital. The film opens to stock shots of Manhattan from his point of view on Governor's Island. His voice-over narration tells us he has been studying the skyline hungrily, like "a guy who waits for a girl he loves. And that's the way I felt about New York." With eyes full of anticipation he takes the short ferry ride home (back projection of the skyline), racing back to Manhattan's embrace. "It was getting dark as we rode up Broadway, right from The Battery to Times Square," he tells us, "and every light in the city seemed to be turned on just to welcome me." The film suddenly cuts to a high-angle picture-postcard view of the city at night, glittering like a tray of diamonds (second-unit work). The moment looks and sounds an awful lot like something out of *The Naked City*, and Mark Hellinger certainly saw *Nobody Lives Forever* before shooting it. But since Hellinger himself had spent a lifetime helping to create this seductive Manhattan image, it would be hard to say exactly who was influencing whom.

As noted earlier, Hellinger had decided to shoot most of the film in New York soon after his October 1946 meeting with O'Dwyer and Wallander. The project had been known as *Homicide* ever since, but Warner Bros. had priority for use of a similar title and Jack Warner was no friend of Hellinger's. Malvin Wald appears to have been the one who brought the New York street photographer Weegee's 1945 volume *Naked City* to Hellinger's attention, and a title change was announced just before the start of shooting.[133] Weegee was employed as a still photographer, location expert, "technical adviser on the workings of the Homicide Bureau," and even "appeared in a few scenes" himself, according to at least one source.[134] But Universal did almost nothing to publicize this connection, and stills from *The Naked City* credited to Weegee are surprisingly scarce. *Look* magazine's nineteen-year-old staff photographer, Stanley Kubrick, was also assigned to cover the shoot (and even grabbed one shot of Weegee working from a ladder), but his employer used none of the eighty-one prints he handed in.[135] Universal's own stills man did get a shot of Kubrick and Barry Fitzgerald on the Williamsburg Bridge location, eating watermelon.

Dassin and Daniels were certainly familiar with Weegee's work, but other than the use of his title there is nothing in the film that suggests any specific influence.[136] Daniels had spent twenty years at MGM, first working with Erich von Stroheim on films like *Greed* (1924), then mastering a different style as Greta Garbo's favorite cameraman. Out of work from 1944 to 1946, he was able to reestablish himself by contracting with independent producers—first Hunt Stromberg (*Lured*) and then Mark Hellinger, who teamed him with Dassin on both *Brute Force* and *The Naked City*. Any reviews of the film that did mention the photography were more likely to mention *Greed* as a source for its visual style.[137] Indeed, there already was an established "documentary look" for filming in New York, as can be seen in the 1941 MGM "Passing Parade" short *This Is the Bowery*, directed by Gunther von Fritsch and photographed by Bill Miller (Miller was hired as the local cameraman on *The Naked City* and would shoot some of the film himself when Daniels was ill or otherwise unavailable).[138]

It should be remembered that Daniels, coming from Hollywood, would have taken pains to disassociate himself and his style from anything to do with the word "documentary," which he told one photography journal was now synonymous with "badly shot 16 mm films." "To give the search the smacking reality of a newsreel," they reported, "Daniels used a camera technique which he termed 'what we call realism.' " This involved using small banks of GE RSP2 Photospots, coated Baltar lenses (from 25 to 150 mm), and a disguised panel truck that allowed him to shoot on the streets through one-way glass (although this bit of trickery resulted in a loss of two full exposure stops). All of the unit's camera and sound equipment had been brought in from Hollywood, bypassing New York's local equipment houses. And while *Carnegie Hall* had used the local De Luxe lab for all its developing and printing, Daniels flew his film back to Universal City every night. Using Universal's own lab was probably part of Hellinger's deal, but all this air freighting was expensive and resulted in significant production delays on the eighty-four-day shoot.[139]

While *Portrait of Jennie* and *The Naked City* shot in and around the city that spring and summer, Hollywood continued to send a few hit-and-run units to bring back crucial establishing shots. Universal-International was simultaneously shooting parts of *The Senator Was Indiscreet* in New York but only during the first two weeks of June. Although the star, William Powell, remained at the studio, director George S. Kaufman (his only film) brought supporting players Ella Raines, Peter Lind Hayes, and Arleen Whelan to New York for a few establishing shots of Grand Central Terminal. But by June 19 they were back at Universal City, working on a train station set meant to match the footage shot on location.[140] And Paramount had already finished capturing whatever New York scenes it required for *The Big Clock* and *Dream Girl* even before Hellinger's crew arrived.[141]

Fox, as usual, was more active. *Kiss of Death* was heavily publicized while filming here in March, April, and May, but Henry Hathaway was not even the only Fox director in town. *Daisy Kenyon* sent no principal actors to New York, but in this case director Otto Preminger and cinematographer Leon Shamroy came east to handle all the location work personally.[142] Joan Crawford's character lives on West Twelfth Street in the Village (a Hollywood back-lot set), and in one scene Henry Fonda waits for her in a restaurant across the street from her local movie house, the Greenwich (a real theater, really located on West Twelfth Street). He is seated by a large window through which we can see this theater, then playing a double bill of *Mr. Lucky* and *Woman in the Window* (it is tempting to make something of this programming, but this is simply what the Greenwich was playing on May 28, 1947, when Shamroy shot the footage).[143] Fonda did not go to New York for this film but played his scene at a table in Hollywood, in front of a window, behind which was a back projection of the Greenwich. At one point he puts down his coffee and exits screen left, apparently going out an off-screen door. A moment later a double dressed as Fonda is seen through the window entering the filmed back projection from screen left and heading toward the theater, a bit of basic movie magic seamlessly linking the foreground and background action. This may sound simple enough, but it indicates far more preproduction planning than was seen in most contemporary New York grab shots. While Preminger did not care to bring his actors to New York, neither did he want to create the impression that they were simply working in front of a backdrop.

    A different approach to salting some "New York" sequences into a film can be found in *Gentleman's Agreement*. The director, Elia Kazan, had argued that "we do the film as I'd done *Boomerang!*, in real locations." Zanuck apparently agreed, but then Moss Hart delivered a script that consisted of "a series of dialogue scenes rather than action scenes. The idea of flinging the story into the streets, offices, and apartments of New York City had to be relinquished."[144] The company worked in New York for three weeks in the beginning of June (although actual filming took only "about a week") but returned for more shooting two months later.[145] Instead of spreading its valuable location shots throughout the picture, the New York footage in *Gentleman's Agreement* is concentrated in the first five minutes. The film begins with a shot of the New York skyline underscored by Alfred Newman's "Street Scene." Gregory Peck and Dean Stockwell are seen walking among the pigeons near the Plaza Hotel. They sit down on a bench and discuss Peck's new job in New York (aided by some back projection for the close-up dialogue portions). Then they walk down Fifth Avenue, stopping to look at the statue of Atlas in Rockefeller Center; a reverse angle looks back at them, through the exposed grid work of Atlas's globe. They meet Anne Revere in Sak's Fifth Avenue, just across the street from the statue. She will do some shopping with Stockwell while Peck disappears into a Rockefeller Center elevator bank. One later scene does show Peck at Gracie Square, overlooking the East River Drive around Eighty-Fourth Street, but the rest of the film appears to be shot on studio sets representing New York restaurants, offices, and apartments, including at least one with the obligatory killer view of the Fifty-Ninth Street Bridge. A visit to the suburbs does take Peck and Dorothy Maguire to the Darien train station, but it is doubtful that interiors were actually shot at Libbey Holman's Connecticut estate, as one press account indicated.[146] Although both Zanuck and Kazan won Academy Awards, *Gentleman's Agreement* is not highly regarded today, with most complaints falling on the screenplay (Hart lost his Oscar to George Seaton and *Miracle on 34th Street*).[147]

The *Naked City* unit continued their work in New York throughout a hot and wet summer. Mark Hellinger was not well, and he had plenty of reasons, both personal and professional, to stay home in Hollywood and let Jules Dassin shoot the location footage for this picture by himself. But it was obvious that David O. Selznick had made a serious error with *Portrait of Jennie*, which was months behind schedule and still before the cameras at Pathé when Hellinger and his people arrived. Hellinger needed to be hands-on with this picture, not just because it was his own money, but because this was New York and his triumphant return was something that needed public celebration. Every night. There were said to be 107 locations packed into this eighty-four-day shoot, and Hellinger felt he needed to be at every one, dressed like a character in one of his own Broadway stories: pin-striped suit, dark blue shirt, white tie. Every night, soaked to the skin, he would have just enough time for a quick change of clothes before making a celebratory appearance at one of his old haunts. He was able to keep up this routine until July, when he returned from a long day on the Williamsburg Bridge location feeling especially low. But some good brandy improved his spirits, and he headed to "21" for a bowl of spaghetti with clam sauce. That's when the "indigestion" caught up with him. Quietly hustled back to the Sherry-Netherlands by his wife, Gladys Glad, a former Ziegfeld showgirl, Hellinger collapsed with a coronary. Keeping him alive required the efforts of three cardiologists and two weeks in an oxygen tent.[148]

This was going to be the last film on his Universal-International contract, because on December 22 he would begin doing business as Mark Hellinger Productions, with financing and distribution arranged by David O. Selznick.[149] But this deal had not yet been formally announced, and Hellinger was terrified that word of his near-fatal heart attack would quickly spread all over Hollywood, tainting the forty-four-year-old producer as a poor insurance risk. According to his friend Jim Bishop, Hellinger told his publicists to blame it all on the clams, a freak case of ptomaine poisoning somehow brewed up in "Jack and Charlie's" kitchen. Finally, after three weeks out of sight, he began to be seen again at Toots Shor's, and even "21" (no hard feelings). On August 15, popping nitroglycerine pills, he left New York for the last time "to complete the film in Hollywood."[150]

There was a lot to complete. Although the film is famous for its well-publicized exteriors, much of it was quietly shot on studio interiors constructed at

Universal City. Edward Dimendberg, in his study of the presentation of urban space in classic film noir, analyzed the scenic department budget for two of Hellinger's most important U-I films, *The Killers* and *The Naked City*:

> The former, mostly filmed in the studio, spent $113,675 on set construction, operations, striking and dressing. The latter utilized extensive location cinematography and spent $95,500 on these same expenses plus a $10,000 contribution to the Police Athletic Fund and $7,500 in gratuities and entertainment for the New York Police Department. These expenditures resulted in a nearly identical total of $113,000.[151]

The fact that the scenic department spent almost the same amount on *The Naked City* as it had for the studio-bound *The Killers* is quite interesting (although some of those costs may represent payments to property owners for the use of their premises; Dimendberg does not break out those figures separately). What is more remarkable, especially given the active support of both Mayor O'Dwyer and Commissioner Wallander, is the acknowledgment of the large sum devoted to paying off the NYPD, either above board (the athletic fund) or under the table (gratuities and entertainment, a charitable way of describing retail bribery). The widespread recognition in Hollywood of the extent of such corruption would be a drag on New York's film economy until the Lindsay administration.

Any interior that would require a significant amount of dramatic action (or dialogue) would have been built back in the studio. Muldoon's office at the Tenth Precinct on West Twentieth Street is a set because a great deal of exposition needed to be laid out here. But Muldoon's tiny apartment was shot on location at 7 West Fifteenth Street. The wealthy Mrs. Hylton's apartment belonged to one of Hellinger's cronies, Toots Shor, but the murder victim's apartment, where much forensic police activity plays out, is another set. One of the most interesting practical interiors was the home of Detective Halloran and his wife. The crew did a heroic job of recording live sound in the living room of this modest row house, with only a trace of reverberation remaining on the track. Oddly enough, Dassin later demeaned the value of shooting in such locations. "All that did was to limit the movements of the camera and, consequently, the staging of the scene," he said, suggesting that the actors didn't like this very much, either.[152] To make matters worse, Dassin had to be hospitalized after stepping on a rusty nail while working in "Garza's apartment" (252 East Houston Street), which must have further soured him on the rigors of location shooting.[153] But it may have been these same challenges that forced him to work more imaginatively at the Halloran location than, for example, in Muldoon's office, where he settles for a conventional fourth-wall Hollywood studio mise en scène.

Hellinger loved New York, but he was publicly complaining about the cost of shooting there, blaming most of his problems on the weather (in August alone the city was swamped with twice as much rain as normal).[154] But Harold Lewis, manager of the RKO-Pathé studio, countered that it was his own fault for not having a cover set in reserve, leaving his company at the mercy of the elements. Lewis was quick to point out that such well-equipped studio space was now easily available at his own facility.[155] Of course, even when the weather cooperated, local residents might not. The daily production reports are filled with accounts of delays caused by the failure of police to manage the crowds. One day on Rivington Street, for example, Dassin had been rehearsing actor Don Taylor's short scene with the owner of a candy store for much of the morning and was finally ready to shoot.

> He had forgotten it was noon. A moment later the reminder was vivid. P.S. 160, a block away, had loosed its kids for lunch. They swarmed over the sound mixer, shouted mocking answers to Mr. Taylor's spoken lines, wormed through the crowd and clambered up Bill Daniels' platform. Even the cops were helpless, until at 1 p.m., the principal and a half dozen teachers led the kids back to classes by their ears.[156]

As soon as the kids had left, adult hecklers took over. Dassin finally distracted them with the aid of a professional juggler, a shill he had planted at the other end of the block.

By August the film was very late and far over budget. Malvin Wald thought it was half a million dollars over and was afraid that he might be blamed for talking Hellinger into the costly location expedition. "The police were not as cooperative as they should be," he recalled, suggesting that the assistance promised by Commissioner Wallander never materialized.[157] Daniels and Dassin followed Hellinger back to the coast on August 19, leaving Bill Miller and the second-unit director, Jack Hively, to complete the Williamsburg Bridge sequence with Ted de Corsia and Kermit Kegley.[158] They were still working in October, having spent many weeks filming various points of interest in and around the city, not just for this film, but for anything else Universal might have needed (for example, on October 14 they filmed the Elizabeth Street police station for use in *A Double Life*).[159] By then Dassin had finished shooting interiors at the studio and returned to New York with Daniels, working on last-minute inserts and skyline shots as late as October 20.

After the main unit finally wrapped in New York, Dassin joined Hellinger on the coast and assembled a rough cut of the film with Paul Weatherwax (who would win an Oscar for Best Film Editing). Hellinger's most successful recent films, *The Killers* and *Brute Force*, had been scored by Miklós Rózsa, but this time, according to Rózsa's autobiography, he had acceded to Dassin's request that they hire a deserving friend of Dassin's who had been let go by MGM. As

5.4. In an unprecedented promotional move, Universal-International commissioned dozens of atmospheric photographs documenting the work of the *Naked City* crew. This extreme high-angle view of a brief encounter outside the Essex Street market suggests the continuing influence of prewar documentary photography. Author's collection.

Rózsa remembered it, "when Hellinger heard this man's score at the recording session he almost had another heart attack. He ranted and raved and swore that, come what may, that music would never go into his picture."[160] In Jim Bishop's biography, this negative reaction occurs at a December 17 preview, where

Hellinger is pleased with everything about the picture but the music (too loud and not "in mood with the scene"). Three days later Hellinger is on the line with Universal, "screaming into the phone about the music for *The Naked City*. It was going to be changed, by God, whether he was still at Universal or not at Universal and it had better be changed goddamn quick."[161] He got Rózsa on the phone, too, and talked him into returning to write a new score. "That was our last conversation together," Rózsa remembered. "Next morning I heard on the radio that he had died during the night from another heart attack."[162]

Control of the picture now swung, suddenly and decisively, over to Universal. The studio agreed to replace the original score but insisted that there was now no time for Rózsa to compose a new one all by himself; staff composer Frank Skinner would handle "the less important dialogue sequences" while Rózsa concentrated on "the 'foreground' areas." Skinner was better known as an arranger, but he had recently written the music for *Swell Guy* and his work would have been familiar to Hellinger and his people.[163] There was also the problem of the voice-over narration that framed the film and occasionally intruded on the action. Unlike the case of Orson Welles and *The Magnificent Ambersons*, this highly personal narration was coming from a recently deceased celebrity whose death had been in the papers for weeks (even the appearance of Mayor O'Dwyer at Hellinger's funeral made minor headlines).[164] Would audiences be put off by listening to the voice of this dead man? It would have been simple to find a new voice, but eventually the studio decided to keep the soundtrack just the way it was.[165]

As it happened, these turned out to be minor issues. Hellinger had already told Dassin that Leo Spitz, the head of production at U-I, thought that *The Naked City* was nothing but a travelogue and should be cut up for stock footage.[166] And he didn't like it any better now that Hellinger was dead. In fact, the studio had no faith in the picture, which had been made for them with his own money by an independent producer who was no longer around to defend it or help publicize it. Dassin had respected Hellinger as "a producer who took care of the director," and looked forward to continuing their partnership under the Selznick deal.[167] But the film was now an orphan, and Dassin was in no position to protest once Universal got their hands on it. "I worked myself on the editing for ten weeks, day and night," he told a reporter from *Sight and Sound*. "It was very difficult, demanding work, but they cut it all. When I saw *Naked City* for the first time, I could have wept."[168]

Dassin implies that between Hellinger's death on December 20 and the January 20, 1948, press show Universal destroyed the film that he and Hellinger had created.[169] "They got their hands on it after Mark died," he announced at a 2004 screening, and made multiple changes intended to soften the film's political vision of New York as a city of contrasts, divided along lines of power and wealth.[170] Hellinger had died at a very inopportune moment. On October 28,

1947, Albert Maltz had refused to testify before the House Un-American Activities Committee and become hopelessly entangled in the "Hollywood Ten" affair. Both the film's director (Dassin) and its associate producer (Jules Buck) would soon be working in exile, while Howard Duff, who had second billing to Barry Fitzgerald, would find himself featured in the pages of *Red Channels*. According to Dassin, Universal seriously considered not releasing the film at all.[171]

In fact, the studio had only a few weeks to do anything practical about all this. If cuts were made, how severe were they, and just who made them? Malvin Wald and his wife attended a preview screening just before Hellinger's death and were "dismayed that the audience laughed at some of the opening documentary scenes." Hellinger told them not to worry—"We'll cut some of those scenes. It will be all right."[172] Wald does not mention Dassin attending the screening, and one suspects that he had already left the project, happy with the cut he had delivered to Hellinger.[173] When he did see the film again, after Hellinger's death, he made the assumption that Universal-International had changed it. But it was Hellinger who removed the musical score that Dassin's friend had supplied and Hellinger who ordered cuts in some of the documentary material because of audience reaction at the preview.

The original script was filled with visual suggestions underscoring the gap between New York's highest and lowest citizens, not so far from the urban ironies Hellinger himself had dramatized in his Depression-era columns. In the opening montage, we were to see "A DRUNKEN, UNSHAVEN BUM" razzing a window dresser in "A SMART FIFTH AVENUE DRESS SHOP" as he tries to slip a girdle over one of the mannequins. "Hey, buddy, do they pay you for that...."[174] An added scene that Dassin remembered shooting included a pan from a sign reading "Hotel Progress" down to a derelict sleeping in the street below. But as Rebecca Prime shows, that footage had been discarded as far back as June, when the production manager realized that no release had been obtained from the hotel.[175] Such blunt juxtapositions suggested the stylized agit-prop of left-wing classics like *Pie in the Sky* (1935) or *Footnote to Fact* (1933) and were probably introduced by Dassin and Maltz for just that reason. Hellinger may even have been sympathetic, at least at first. But when the preview audience began laughing, he knew that the 1930s were over.

Hellinger was not a political filmmaker, but that does not mean he was unaware of the political realities that were starting to affect the way any Hollywood producer could operate. On December 3, 1947, Eric Johnston and leading members of the Motion Picture Association of America issued the Waldorf Declaration, which "deplored" the actions of those writers and directors who had been cited for contempt by HUAC for refusing to testify as to their political affiliations. The members also announced, proactively, that they would suspend without pay or blacklist any of the Ten who failed to acquit himself of the contempt charges and swear under oath that he was not a Communist.

Hellinger's writer, Albert Maltz, was now unemployable. Two weeks later, entertainment journalist Ezra Goodman interviewed Hellinger at his office at Universal, surrounded by the boxes of paperwork he was about to ship off to his new operation, Mark Hellinger Productions. Pacing back and forth in his office, Hellinger exploded. "Hollywood is gutless," he told him. "You can't make an honest, forceful picture here. Hollywood is the whipping boy, the natural target for all kinds of pressure groups, and the industry does not stand up to them." He blamed industry leaders for failing to unite against these outsiders, a function of internal squabbling and the corruption of "easy money." "No matter what you do in pictures, you're wrong," he said. "*Going My Way* got squawks from the Protestants. *The Best Years of Our Lives* was attacked for its presentation of bankers." He attacked the restrictions of the Production Code, claiming that "*Open City*, about which many people are shouting, could never have been made here under any circumstances." Turning to his own films, he complained that Hemingway's short story, "The Killers," had met no opposition but that the film version "was criticized for those very things that highlighted the Hemingway original."

> The trouble with *Brute Force* was that it was not brutal enough. At the time the picture was being released and being made the subject of all sorts of criticism, the papers carried headlines about sixteen Negroes being killed for talking back to a warden. If I put that stuff in a picture tomorrow, what would happen?[176]

With his new partner, Humphrey Bogart, Hellinger was about to put *Knock on Any Door* into production, but he was certain that "eighty million people will be after my scalp if I make a faithful picturization of the book." This does not sound to me like "Damon Runyon with an extra dose of schmaltz." That night, Hellinger and his wife took Barry Fitzgerald to the *Naked City* preview at the sleek new Loyola Theatre on Sepulveda Boulevard. Three days later Hellinger was dead.

Leo Spitz was wrong about *The Naked City*, which became one of Universal's highest grossing releases of 1948.[177] It won Academy Awards for editing and cinematography, and Malvin Wald was nominated for the best original story. Although other films had been sold on the strength of their location realism, Universal's ad campaign went beyond this by exploiting Hellinger's personal identification with the city. One poster, for example, not only boasted that it was "Filmed on the streets of New York with a cast of 8 Million New Yorkers!" but that it was "Terrifically told By Manhattan's Modern O. Henry." Most reviewers quickly fell in line, either praising the film as "one of the most realistic crime dramas ever filmed" or personalizing it as "the kind of a story that Hellinger, one of the great tabloid crime reporters of the bath-tub gin era, used to write."[178] The picture was so closely identified with Hellinger ("a virtual

Hellinger column on film," the *Times* reported) that the name of the director, Jules Dassin, seems to have appeared only when contractually required. During the 1940s, most writers reviewing movies for the daily newspapers saw themselves primarily as journalists, and many seem to have identified immediately with fellow scribe Mark Hellinger's "fond tribute to his big-town newspaper beat."[179]

But the more discriminating of these scribes, especially those based in New York, were not so easily satisfied. "The most serious criticism of the picture," wrote Howard Barnes in the *New York Herald Tribune*, "is the fact that it tries to dress up an ordinary murder melodrama with a lot of fancy talk about Manhattan."[180] *New Movies* complained of "the unreality implicit in Mark Hellinger's wholly romantic view of New York," while James Agee dismissed everything but the photography as "mawkish and naïve."[181] "Mr. Hellinger's remarks are about as penetrating as the spiel of a guide on a sight-seeing bus," carped *The New Yorker*, "and the film resorts to all kinds of flummery to force the real complexities of New York to conform to the simple and sentimental concept of the city so often set forth on the Broadway columns."[182] Bosley Crowther attacked the film in the *Times* more than once, first damning it as "superficial, being no more than a conventional 'slice of life'—a routine and unrevealing episode in the everyday business of the cops," then coming back a week later to again dismiss it as "a curiously superficial film [that] for all its surface observations . . . fails to look very closely at anyone."[183] For Crowther, the film appeared old-fashioned and unrealistic, especially when compared to a European *policier* like H. G. Clouzot's *Jenny Lamour*, which had recently opened in a local art house.

When the New York Film Critics Circle announced its annual awards for 1948, *The Naked City* was shut out, citations going instead to *Hamlet*, *Paisan*, and *The Treasure of the Sierra Madre*. Hollywood, as noted, was more impressed, but sometimes such largesse created issues of its own. Malvin Wald reports how *Photoplay* magazine hosted an awards banquet honoring the year's best films and found itself facing an embarrassing Albert Maltz problem:

> They could not refuse to invite Maltz, but they saw to it that he and I were seated out of sight of the photographers, behind a palm tree, near the kitchen. That was nearly thirty years ago, and it was the first and last time I was to meet Albert Maltz. But as I recall it now, the rest of the banquet room was enthusiastically responding to the introduction of the stars who were being honored, and there sat Albert Maltz, one of America's most gifted writers, quietly sipping champagne, on his way to prison for defying Congress and pleading his First Amendment rights. . . . It could easily have been one of the "eight million stories of The Naked City."[184]

CHAPTER 6

THE O'DWYER PLAN

"In Hollywood the movie industry is a big frog in a little puddle," Edward Ellis wrote in 1947. "In New York the movie industry is a little frog in a big puddle. While Mayor O'Dwyer wants to fatten the New York frog, it is bigger now than one might think."[1] Ellis then outlined the city's importance in executive operations, financing, distribution, and exhibition, also sketching in its role in both fiction and nonfiction film production. Surprisingly, the *Los Angeles Times* more than agreed with him. "Film patrons generally are unaware that New York already leads Hollywood in virtually all phases of the film industry except feature production," they admitted.[2] Of course, feature production was one hell of an exception, but O'Dwyer and his team still believed that these "other phases" could serve as the basis for a real renaissance of theatrical film production in New York.

The role that Bill O'Dwyer played in easing the production of *The Naked City* had not gone unnoticed. In June, Harry Thomas, the president of PRC, announced that its new Marathon Pictures Corp. subsidiary would soon film *The Pride of New York*, the life of Mayor William O'Dwyer. "From Ireland to America, the old tale; from immigrant to mayor of the world's greatest city, a brilliant tale; from ignorance to brilliance as lawyer, soldier and politician, a fascinating tale."[3] Harry Brandt, the head of New York's powerful Brandt Theater circuit, was board chairman of Marathon and a political supporter of O'Dwyer. He expected to begin shooting in Brooklyn the following summer. Pat O'Brien was being considered for the role of the mayor; a few months earlier O'Dwyer had flown to the coast to stand as godfather to O'Brien's daughter, Kathleen.[4]

Marathon eventually did shoot a film in the city, but they never went ahead with *The Pride of New York*. Instead the project went into turnaround, available to other interested parties. A year later *Variety* reported that the Warner Bros. producer Milton Sperling was developing *From Stoker to Mayor*, which would concentrate on O'Dwyer's role in the Murder, Inc. investigation. The mayor was said to be asking $200,000 for the rights.[5]

Of greater consequence was the shuffling of administrative roles at City Hall in the wake of George Sanders's forced resignation in May 1947. Not only had this left a vacancy at the top of the Commerce Department, but it also left the position of film coordinator unfilled. The mayor turned again to Edward C. Maguire, "a soft spoken, white-haired man, whose integrity has always been respected by labor and management alike."[6] Maguire, a labor lawyer, had been appointed city magistrate by Fiorello La Guardia in 1942, resigning the following year to serve as deputy transportation commissioner. But he also served as La Guardia's chief labor adviser, a role he continued to fill for O'Dwyer. He was crucial in resolving over two dozen threatened strikes that year, involving everyone from tugboat operators to drivers of hearses. Maguire essentially created "The O'Dwyer Plan," in which various labor-management problems were addressed through ad hoc industrial committees; the film industry committee on which he served with Sanders was only one of these.

Maguire had been serving as the salaried director of the Division of Labor Relations since October 1, 1946, and planned to return to private practice on August 31, 1947. But on July 9 he agreed to take on the role of film coordinator, for which "he will study prospects of bringing a substantial portion of the motion picture industry to New York City."[7] The mayor, noting the recent increase of film production in New York, announced, "We want to encourage such a trend and are prepared to extend every reasonable cooperation to this great industry. . . . No city in the world provides such a reservoir of talent or more satisfactory labor conditions." But he also admitted that in order for this movement to continue, the city needed to reform its administrative bureaucracy.

> It has been called to my attention that some delays and inconveniences have been encountered by the motion picture industry in New York because of unfamiliarity with our departmental requirements and that we in the city are not fully cognizant of the needs of the industry. . . . If this city can obtain through encouragement and cooperation its proper share of motion picture productions, it will mean additional employment for our citizens.[8]

"Mr. Maguire didn't know anything about moviemaking when he started in on the job, but he went through the works with a crew shooting twenty local scenes of a Ronald Colman picture and came out educated," *The New Yorker* revealed.⁹ The film was *A Double Life*, produced by Michael and Garson Kanin for Universal-International release and directed by George Cukor. Cukor was one of the Broadway directors recruited for talkies in the early 1930s, when he had made *The Royal Family of Broadway* and *Tarnished Lady* for Paramount in Astoria, although he came to prefer the comfort and lifestyle of Hollywood.¹⁰ But *A Double Life* would be the first of a series of postwar films in which Cukor made the decision to return to New York for location work rather than pose his actors in front of studio back projections.

Although Universal's historic "*Phantom* stage" was used for most of the theatrical interiors, Colman was also filmed walking around the city (especially the Broadway district) and into the lobby of the Empire Theatre. According to a feature article in *American Cinematographer*, Universal "set up a miniature studio in Manhattan, and was thus able to get realism with a minimum of blood, sweat and tears."¹¹ Exactly what this "miniature studio" consisted of was left unsaid. Other scenes are reported to have been shot inside the Lyceum Theatre and downtown at Houston and Elizabeth Streets, with the Gran Festa di San Ciro Protettore Marineo serving as background.¹² Unfortunately, nothing of this festival survives in the final cut. The same could be said of the New York footage in Anthony Mann's *T-Men*, in which Dennis O'Keefe, standing on the steps of New York's City Hall, was filmed asking a bystander for a light—that bystander "accidentally" being Mayor O'Dwyer.¹³ The O'Dwyer part sounds like press-agentry, but the fact that a leading actor was taken to New York for principal photography suggests that the city once had a much more important role in this classic noir.

Maguire learned fast. He found that "moviemakers shooting an outdoor scene are classified by city officials as street fairs and have to get up to half a dozen permits to conduct a street fair on public property." One solution was to consolidate the need to collect daily permits from multiple agencies, but outdated municipal regulations were only half the problem. More intractable was the "senseless friction between movie men and New York civil servants," some of whom "took a bureaucrat's delight in making screen officials wait around a couple of hours for permission to, say, strangle an ingénue at the southeast corner of Broadway and Pine."¹⁴ This is a polite way of characterizing an atmosphere of bribery and corruption. Drafting new permit guidelines was a simple matter in comparison; changing the city's administrative culture was much more difficult, and once Maguire and O'Dwyer were out of office, the situation would quickly revert to normal.

By the end of August Maguire was meeting with the mayor nearly every day, plotting the city's future as a motion picture center. A skilled negotiator, he saw the current wave of labor violence in Hollywood as a gift to New York filmmakers and understood that if O'Dwyer could promise labor peace, everything else should fall right into place. On August 27, "speaking in the glare of newsreel floodlights," O'Dwyer rolled out Maguire's report, "the most dramatic and positive step yet effected in the mayor's all-out campaign to attract motion picture production to the city." New York would facilitate motion picture production by appointing a full-time film coordinator to work with producers on issues ranging from studio space ("facilities available here are not fully used," was one surprising conclusion) to the perennial location permit nightmare. An ad hoc commission of film industry representatives would be assembled to study and streamline a host of other production problems. The report even claimed that "labor costs in the movie field were lower here than in Hollywood."[15]

While Maguire was stepping down as director of the Division of Labor Relations to enter private practice, he agreed to volunteer his services as temporary film coordinator; he expected it would only take about two months to get everything set up and running smoothly. This was extraordinary. No city had ever established a municipal motion picture office, and even La Guardia's grand schemes had ultimately gone nowhere. But the icing on this cake, the part of O'Dwyer's announcement that made national headlines, was a declaration of union peace. In Hollywood, the United Brotherhood of Carpenters and Joiners and the International Alliance of Theatrical Stage Employees had been at each other's throats for the past ten months, throwing competing picket lines around most of the West Coast studios, the latest manifestation of a jurisdictional squabble that had been going on for twenty years. In New York, Maguire had somehow gotten both of them to join ten other local film unions in a five-year peace pact, promising that any differences between them would be settled through negotiation, not fistfights and walkouts.

Maguire's film industry commission included representatives of local unions and major studios with an interest in New York production, namely MGM, Columbia, RKO, and Universal-International. Over the next two months word of their deliberations was periodically leaked to the press. Where shooting in the streets was previously licensed under street festival regulations and required approvals from police, water, gas, electricity, and housing and building departments, as well as the local borough president's office, the new "motion picture permit" would now be obtained from one individual in the police department.[16] Other rules under examination barred bringing more than two reels of nitrate film into a building, which "practically makes shooting interiors impossible," and demands that electricians licensed by the city install all electrical lines going into a location. "All it amounts to," one source declared, "is that we pay fat fees to hook up cables which our technical crews, already on the payroll, are competent to do."[17]

Obsolete or irrelevant regulations like these could always be addressed, but the leak that really hurt suggested something more systemic. *Variety* reported that one Hollywood producer testified that "attachés of New York City's police and fire departments, and others, were 'on the take' from Hollywood producers attempting to shoot films in Gotham." It seems that too many hands were collecting "contributions to welfare funds," an accusation the administration denounced as "absurd" and "ridiculous."[18] A few years later, revelations as to the full extent of this culture of corruption would essentially drive the mayor out of office and even, for a time, out of the country.

On October 20, 1947, Maguire summarized his efforts to date while addressing the Society of Motion Picture Engineers on the topic of New York motion picture production.[19] First he made clear what he and the mayor did not intend to do: "We do not envision lifting Hollywood from the West Coast and dropping it into New York City," he announced, a goal that needed to be clarified, given some of the outrageous expectations that had been floated in the press. O'Dwyer, for his part, felt that 20 percent of American film production sounded like "a fair share for New York City for the time being."[20] Maguire discussed their current study of "unreasonable restraints and restrictions" and the establishment of the film coordinator's office. He raised the issue of "the only complaint" so far received, dismissing it in a cloud of positive feedback supplied by friendly producers who swore that cooperation from city agencies was just fine.

> At this time any production manager who wants to take scenes in the City of New York has only to contact directly the office of the Co-ordinator. If in certain situations permits are required, those permits are procured for the unit by that central office. We have worked the thing down to the point now where only a very short time is necessary to obtain clearance. As an example of it, one morning a major motion picture company called; they wanted to take certain pictures. It was just a telephone call. The thing was arranged for them within a half hour.[21]

Ever since O'Dwyer first released Maguire's original report, both local newspapers and the industry trade press had devoted extensive coverage to the city's sudden interest in the motion picture business. The *New York Times* film critic Bosley Crowther wrote an entire *Sunday* magazine piece about how "the new proposal to bring a large part of the movie industry here revives many old arguments." Crowther had been around long enough to see that "His Honor was hopefully repeating a familiar thought which has tickled the commercial fancies of certain burghers in this area for many years."[22] Indeed, much of this 1947 article recapitulates the arguments in a similar piece he wrote about the La Guardia initiative in 1939.[23] Certainly the conclusion was the same: the motion picture industry was so invested in Southern California that nothing short of an act of God could force it to shift even a portion of its production activity back east. He added a few new arguments this time, suggesting that the production heads in Hollywood "are happy to keep the breadth of the country between themselves and the 'home offices' in New York," so that company executives and eastern bankers can be kept at a comfortable distance, "in the manner of a tourist in Soviet Russia. What they don't see won't hurt them is a tacit axiom. If the studios were too close to New York, the 'money men' might meddle too much."[24] True, he does mention the string of recently produced A-pictures, from *The Lost Weekend* and *The House on 92nd Street* to *Portrait of Jennie* and *The Naked City* but refers to all of this as "marginal activity."

Crowther, like every other industry analyst in 1947, was too impressed by the apparent stability of Hollywood's business model and the overwhelming scale of its real estate investments. New York's filmmaking community was calling for a few crumbs from Hollywood's table, but like many others he saw little chance of this ever happening. Because he failed to predict the effects of the Paramount Decrees, broadcast television, and the catastrophic drop in theater attendance, he assumed that the industry would continue to operate as he had always known it to operate, and that the geographic decentralization of this industry was inconceivable. No disruption of the Hollywood studio system would mean no renaissance of film production in New York, a conclusion that was simple and logical, not just to Crowther but to everyone else in both New York and Hollywood. O'Dwyer and Maguire also had no crystal ball, and they were certainly not planning to launch any sort of renaissance. But neither were they willing to write off the chance of grabbing at least a few of those crumbs if that could mean "additional employment for our citizens."

As film coordinator, Maguire understood that he faced three separate problems. He had already dealt with the labor issue, but "facilitating" the ability of producers to shoot on the streets was not going to be so simple. O'Dwyer had been able to help his friend Mark Hellinger by personally cutting through much red tape, once interrupting a City Hall conference to take a call from an exasperated Hellinger in Los Angeles. Because of Fire Department foot-dragging on the Rivington Street location, the unit stood to lose the equivalent of $15,000. "Well, we straightened that out quickly," the mayor wrote in a bylined fan magazine piece, "because, as Mayor, I'm very anxious for Hollywood to realize New York offers advantages on making pictures that can't be matched by any other city."[25] Finding a permanent solution to the city bureaucracy's "street fair" mentality would require a lot of care and attention but at heart was simply a matter of better management. Indeed, every city had similar labor and management issues, but what made New York different, Maguire understood, was the power of its local real estate industry.

The mayor, with Maguire and "a group of industry members" in tow, had already made an official visit to the Pathé studio, a "first stop in his planned schedule for probing the potentialities of the city as a major film producing center."[26] The most modern studio in the country, its construction suggested that starting from the ground up would always be preferable to refurbishing the city's stock of old silent movie studios. As if in response, the theater architect

John Eberson immediately dusted off his plans for a 1,000-acre Telecity studio complex, a $60 million project containing two dozen stages, each 150 × 250 × 75 feet, that he had created for developer Lawrence B. Elliman in 1946. If O'Dwyer really wanted to encourage the industry to relocate, Eberson suggested, it was time to build some new stages.[27]

Three major projects quickly made the headlines that fall, each targeted at a slice of what seemed to be a growing local production market. The first of these, Fort Lee Studios, Inc., leased the World Film studio site in Fort Lee and announced plans to renovate its main 85 × 125 foot studio, while also adding additional stage space and two dozen dressing rooms. Facilities would be available to interested parties at below market rates. The group behind this move also formed Gateway Productions, which they claimed would produce three features per year there, budgeted at $500,000 to $750,000 each. Construction appears to have started, but the project collapsed even before its scheduled April 1948 completion date.[28]

A far more ambitious proposal was floated by an unnamed Manhattan developer who submitted over one hundred blueprints for Maguire's approval. Located on a disused but "centrally located" Manhattan plot, this involved construction of a forty-story tower that would be leased to a consortium of six major Hollywood producers. Each of the tenants would occupy six stories in this building, space that would include massive sound stages and a full range of support facilities. All that was needed for the $20–25 million project to proceed was for "the six major motion picture companies to sign 10-year leases." *Variety* noted that none of the majors had expressed any interest "because of uncertain conditions existing within the industry, [a] result of the general snafued condition of the foreign market."[29]

Most visionary of all, though lacking funding, blueprints, tenants, or anything other than a few pencil sketches, was the Cinema City promoted by Sal Scoppa, longtime business manager of Local 52. Scoppa had been pushing such a project since the days of Mayor Jimmy Walker and had once even gained the support of Fiorello La Guardia.[30] This iteration required the purchase of "a certain private airport in New York," on which would be constructed a $25 million complex of buildings available to both independent and major producers. The business plan involved not just studio rentals but the income generated by guided tours similar to those featured at Radio City. "A moving observation platform could be built in a gallery around the stage," Scoppa declared, channeling the 1939 World's Fair as much as anything offered at the Music Hall. "This platform would travel entirely around the stage in, say, an hour. Spectators could stand on this moving platform and watch movies actually being filmed." One-way glass would grant some privacy to "sensitive actors doing a love scene."[31] Note that Universal City, which had featured such tours in the early silent movie days, would not take up the practice again until 1964.[32]

None of these projects went anywhere. Even Maguire cautioned that "only about 50 per cent of the studio space in and around New York is now in use," suggesting that increasing the amount of square footage might not be the solution to anything.[33] For his part, O'Dwyer had already made it clear that large capital expenditures were out. "I am not necessarily thinking in terms of colossal projects," he told reporters. "I see no reason for needlessly making extravagant expenditures. The motion picture industry has enough white elephants on its hands."[34] Political and economic realists, both men would say what needed to be said in May 1948, when RKO-Pathé "tossed in the sponge" on local feature film production at their 106th Street studio.[35] But by then it was clear to almost everyone that neither real estate interests nor Hollywood producers cared to risk an investment in new motion picture stages for New York filmmakers. If the movies really were going to take root here again, attempting to rebuild the Hollywood studio system was not the way to go.

Force of Evil

The successful release of *The Naked City* in January 1948 had surprised Universal-International as much as the rest of Hollywood. Fox, as discussed earlier, was already beginning to cut back on its "de Rochemont style" location projects but in March suddenly decided to add three days of New York location work to *The Law and Tony Rome*. They also decided to change the title to something with the word *city* in it, releasing it as *Cry of the City* after much of the original publicity had already gone out. But there was no rush to film in New York that year, and the only other significant Hollywood visitors were John Garfield's independent production company (*Force of Evil*) and Universal-International itself, whose adaptation of *The Amboy Dukes* would appear as *City Across the River*.

John Garfield and his producing partner, Bob Roberts, were riding on the success of *Body and Soul*, a landmark prize-fight drama written for Garfield by Abraham Polonsky and directed by Robert Rossen. Now Polonsky would both write and direct their next film, *Force of Evil*, an adaptation of Ira Wolfert's politically inflected tale of the New York numbers racket, *Tucker's People* (1943). Press reports document a series of location trips in March, April, and May of 1948, including one in which "Richard Day, art director on the project, went to New York . . . and returned with a series of still pictures which have influenced Roberts, Garfield and Polonsky to go East as soon as the work here [in Hollywood] is finished to shoot two climactic sequences in Manhattan."[36] They were also auditioning Broadway actresses, but the one they found, Beatrice Pearson, was already in Hollywood under contract to David O. Selznick.[37]

Mark Hellinger had employed many Hollywood leftists who would soon find themselves blacklisted or greylisted, but they left few political traces on any of his films. The situation with Roberts Productions, on the other hand, was quite different. Polonsky's two films with Garfield, according to one biography, "quite simply embody the highest achievement of the American Left in cinema before the onset of repression."[38] The irresistibly corrupting "force of evil" is capitalism, which destroys humanistic traditions of honor, selflessness, and family loyalty. Wall Street (and we will have to see the real Wall Street here, not some Hollywood back lot) is just a dressed-up version of the old numbers racket, where corrupt lawyers, brokers, and politicians prey on hapless suckers. The most attractive people are old-school gangsters running storefront numbers parlors; the worst are class traitors like the Garfield character (Joe Morse), concerned with nothing but "making my first million dollars."

Body and Soul had been a critical and commercial success, although its view of prize-fight managers as "thieves, gangsters and double-crossers" and its "pro-Negro" storyline made it a target of right-wing suspicion in 1947.[39] Soon after its release, California State Senator Jack Tenney had accused Garfield of Communist sympathies, a charge that would follow him until his death in 1952, so doubling down on the social content of their next film was a risky move. Hiring a first-time director and a female lead with no screen experience suggests other problems, as did a sudden change of distributor from Columbia to Enterprise just weeks before the start of production.[40] Did the Waldorf Declaration (December 1947), in which Hollywood studios announced they would fire or blacklist suspected Communist Party members, already have a hand in this? Enterprise Productions had been formed in 1946 as a packager of independent film projects and had done well with *Body and Soul*. But it was now struggling financially and would go out of business in 1948, leaving the distribution of *Force of Evil* in the unsympathetic hands of Loew's/MGM.

Production started on the Enterprise Studios lot in Hollywood at the beginning of June, with one week of exteriors in New York scheduled for July 31. Garfield and Pearson rehearsed their parts while on board a train from the coast with Polonsky, Roberts, and their cameraman, George Barnes. Barnes had shot Marion Davies films in New York in the 1920s and was an eight-time Oscar nominee whose recent work included *Spellbound* and *The Bells of St. Mary's*. Polonsky suggested in interviews that Barnes was delivering "standard romantic photography" until he took him aside and showed him a book of Edward Hopper paintings ("Third Avenue, cafeterias, all that back-lighting, and those empty streets. Even when people are there, you don't see them."). After looking at the paintings, Barnes replied, "Oh, that!" and delivered the needed alienated streetscapes from then on.[41] This is a good story, but I suspect that Richard Day, who had already returned from New York with that valuable "series of still pictures," also played a role here. Day's location filming experience included everything from *Greed* to *Miracle on 34th Street*, and he would win an Oscar for *On the Waterfront*.

The O'Dwyer Plan   197

6.1. An icon of 1930s modernism, the George Washington Bridge provides a suitable backdrop for John Garfield in *Force of Evil*. "I just kept going down and down there," he says of his journey to the rocks below. "It was like going to the bottom of the world." Museum of Modern Art Film Stills Archive.

Anticipating problems with recording sound on location, the company announced that they would "record all the dialogue of the New York scenes in advance," with the actors "governed by a wire recorder which recorded the dialogue simultaneously with the usual sound system."[42] Using prerecorded dialogue would have required cumbersome playback apparatus on location, a technique used on the musical *It Happened in Brooklyn* two years earlier but unlikely here. Perhaps this garbled report means that a small wire recorder on location was used to create a wild track, a guide to proper synchronization in a dubbing studio later on. That strategy would be used on a range of lower-budget independent films, from *Jigsaw* to *Killer's Kiss*. In any case, the "two climactic sequences" that were crucial to the production—Wall Street and the George Washington Bridge—feature no direct sound and are covered only by the narrator's voice-over commentary.[43] More innovative was the use of a Zoomar lens, originally brought from Hollywood as a cost-cutting device that would allow close-ups as well as long shots to be taken from the same camera position.[44] But Polonsky and Barnes do employ at least one precocious "zoom shot," moving in to a close-up of Garfield and Pearson as they lean over a parapet near the George Washington Bridge.

In an interview with the *Los Angeles Times*, Polonsky pointed out a few of the changes that had occurred while compressing Wolfert's novel, notably "eliminating the Negro angle," significant in a film about the numbers racket. But he did not mention the new ending, in which the Garfield character does not hang himself in his jail cell while awaiting trial but agrees to cooperate with the mysterious prosecutor by telling everything he knows about his former criminal associates (*Kiss of Death*, in which squealing also plays a significant role, had been released a few months earlier). Instead of the "essentially cynical and defeatist" tone of the book, the character's decision to inform is given an upbeat and empowering fig leaf: "I decided to help."[45] Years later, Polonsky would try to explain away this ending as the only way to obtain a Code Seal, claiming that he really "didn't want Joe to be cooperating with the law in any way or to be seen doing so," and that Joe's decision to testify should be seen more as vengeance than moral redemption.[46] But he only said this after *On the Waterfront* had made the issue of squealing central to any political reading of postwar American cinema.

Polonsky had filmed scenes of Joe testifying in court but eventually decided to use only the audio, which functions as the film's voice-over narration. "And naturally I was feeling very bad there as I went down there. I just kept going down and down there. It was like going to the bottom of the world. . . ." The poetic tenor of this monologue seems at odds with the character we see in the film, and it comes as a surprise to discover that this account of his venal career is somehow connected to the help he is giving the public prosecutor. Informing is ultimately the strongest link between *Force of Evil* and *On the Waterfront*, but it's one that is seldom brought up by supporters of either picture. Indeed, it seems clear that Budd Schulberg knew *Force of Evil* quite well and at least unconsciously absorbed much of its dramatic structure as he struggled to develop the script of *On the Waterfront* a few years later.

Inspired by the highly publicized "crime-busting" tactics of prosecutors like Thomas E. Dewey, each film makes use of a government prosecutor or crime commission as a way of examining corruption in the public sphere. A personal story involving a contrast between two brothers dramatizes questions of morality and ethics, while the romantic angle is provided by a strong-willed innocent who is simultaneously attracted to and repelled by the rugged male at the film's center. The murder of a brother motivates the protagonist's redemptive behavior in both films. All the characters are manipulated by a powerful off-screen figure, either special prosecutor Link Hall (voiced by Arthur O'Connell), whose wiretapping provides some of the creepiest moments in Polonsky's film, or the plutocratic "Mr. Big" who no longer takes Johnny Friendly's calls at the end of *On the Waterfront*.

Although he died well before production started, John Garfield was the actor Budd Schulberg had in mind while creating the character eventually played by Marlon Brando in *On the Waterfront*. Garfield had turned down the role of Stanley Kowalski in the original production of *A Streetcar Named Desire* because he had promised Lee Strasberg and Cheryl Crawford to appear in a play for them, *Skipper Next to God*. That show had a limited run (January 4–March 27, 1948), which allowed him to get back to work on *Force of Evil*. If Garfield had taken the role in *Streetcar*, which opened on December 3, 1947, and ran for two years, *Force of Evil* would have had to wait. But with Garfield out of the picture, *Streetcar*'s director, Elia Kazan, needed to find a new Stanley: Marlon Brando.

Generally ignored by critics at the time, *Force of Evil* quickly developed a cult following and was occasionally used as a club with which to attack Kazan's film. Lindsay Anderson may have been the first, denouncing the moral reformation of Terry Malloy ("what he does, he does for himself, to avenge his brother's murder, and for the *beaux yeux* of Edie") as opposed to Joe's genuine "acknowledgment of moral responsibility" expressed with "integrity and a true passion" in Polonsky's film.[47] As noted, Polonsky himself might have been uncomfortable with this interpretation. Andrew Sarris, never a big Kazan fan, took a sly dig at the director (whom he found "less than meets the eye") by bringing up yet another plot coincidence. "*Force of Evil* stands up under repeated viewings as one of the great films of the modern American cinema," he wrote, "and Garfield's taxicab scene with Beatrice Pearson takes away some of the luster from Kazan's Brando-Steiger tour de force in *On the Waterfront*."[48]

The five minutes of New York location footage in this film barely exceeds what can be found in *The Lost Weekend*, but its relevance to the plot gives it far more dramatic weight. Billy Wilder's film might have been set anywhere, but the social and political allegory driving *Force of Evil* draws on New York's historic immigrant culture as much as its role at the center of finance capitalism. Like Mark Hellinger and Malvin Wald, Polonsky and Garfield were New Yorkers born and bred who had made their mark in Hollywood because that's where the American film industry was based. What might have happened if their careers had continued to develop through the 1950s and 1960s is unknowable. Polonsky was blacklisted after refusing to testify before HUAC in 1951. He subsequently wrote film and television scripts with the aid of various fronts, notably *Odds Against Tomorrow* (1959), one of the most important New York productions of the late 1950s. His name would not appear on screen again until 1968.

The "Naked City" of Brooklyn

Universal purchased *The Amboy Dukes* in March 1948, intending to use Irving Schulman's best-seller as the next entry in a continuing series of New York location pictures. If it is a success, they announced, "other stories will be written to deal with life in other New York boroughs, Queens, the Bronx, and Staten Island."[49] With Mark Hellinger gone, the project was handed to Maxwell Shane, a prolific writer of radio dramas and B-pictures whose directorial debut, the Cornell Woolrich adaptation *Fear in the Night*, had won him a rare writer-producer-director deal with U-I. "It would be impossible to match Schulman's realism on a set in Hollywood," Shane announced, "so we came to Brooklyn." *The Amboy Dukes* was the story of a Jewish gang in Brownsville whose oppressive slum environment inevitably sets them up for a life of violence and crime. The novel's naturalistic portrayal of the details of immigrant existence and its single-minded focus on slum clearance as the cure for most urban ills was a relic of prewar ethnic literature. *City Across the River* would not be ethnically specific (although characters are still likely to ask for "a glass tea"[50]) and would instead place greater emphasis on the details of juvenile delinquency, a growing postwar concern. Schulman, who adapted his novel, would later write an early draft of *Rebel Without a Cause*.

Following de Rochemont's strategy of casting unfamiliar faces as one way of making a film look less like a Hollywood movie, Shane auditioned two hundred New York actors as gang members.[51] Many would never be seen on screen again, but exceptions included Richard Jaeckel, Mickey Knox, and Tony Curtis (in his first speaking role). Unable to film on Amboy Street because it was "so narrow and confined that there was not enough light for the camera," he moved the production to Williamsburg, taking over a stretch of South Third Street near the intersection of Havemeyer. "He spent almost three weeks absorbing the sights and sounds of Brooklyn, visiting the candy stores, markets, poolrooms and dance halls of the Third Street-Havemeyer area, taking pictures and recording conversations and bits of dialogue with a concealed microphone and tape recorder."[52] This hardly compares with Malvin Wald's extensive research trip, but *City Across the River* was a much less prestigious effort, shot on a smaller budget with a far less expensive production unit (the B-movie specialist Maury Gertsman instead of the famed cinematographer William Daniels, for example).

Shane began filming in Brooklyn on September 24 and was due back at Universal City by October 11.[53] Production delays in New York caused by everything from rainy days to rusty nails had pushed *Naked City* far over budget and U-I was not about to repeat the same mistakes here. "Time was when if some little thing went wrong on location, or if the weather wasn't quite right, the whole company would sit around and wait until things returned to normal, meanwhile adding quite a chunk onto the budget," Gertsman told *American Cinematographer*. "Nowadays, with economy very much a factor in the production of films, we can no longer afford to do this. The cameraman has to take whatever conditions exist and work around them, often in newsreel fashion."

Where Daniels had brought everything with him from the studio in an effort to *avoid* looking like a newsreel, Gertsman admitted he was traveling light, bringing only "a skeleton crew of technicians from Hollywood" and "the barest necessities of equipment." Everything else was rented locally. "Working so far from our studio facilities, we had to make every light count," he remembered. Instead of supplemental lighting units, reflectors were used whenever possible, and some tenement interiors were filmed with as little as 70 amps of illumination; one tiny bathroom, too small for any of the company's standard lighting units, was lit with a 150-watt bulb. But the cast and crew still had to contend with the same unruly bystanders that dogged Hellinger's company. "They came piling out of houses and tenements, ganging up in front of the camera despite the efforts of police to hold them back," Gertsman told a reporter from Hollywood. "Some of them weren't very polite, either. One gang of kids kept throwing prune pits in the dolly tracks." But Shane still made all of the exteriors and process plates, along with a small number of practical interiors, in only eight working days.[54]

Where some films just dropped in their New York scenes right at the start, Shane skillfully blended his location footage, back projections, and studio recreations throughout the picture. Dialogue is also cleverly looped, further blurring the line between studio and location work. Replacing Hellinger as narrator was columnist Drew Pearson, who appears behind a desk (and an ABC microphone) just after the main title. This hoary educational film technique seems designed to push the film away from Hellinger's chatty little narrative and move it closer to the world of news and documentary. Pearson returns at the end, not only delivering the film's moral but introducing the cast of unknowns, including "Anthony Curtis," who played the Dukes. Shane joked that the title had been changed from *The Amboy Dukes* because "people began to ask if it was a historical romance," but there may have been more political reasons as well.[55]

Unlike *The Naked City*, in which the police solve the crime and the entire story is quickly disposed of as yesterday's news, *City Across the River* is a very bleak tale that ends with the root causes of crime and delinquency—living conditions in the slums—entirely unresolved. While so many other films of the period were quick to blame improper mothering for the problems of youth, Schulman and Shane implicitly suggest governmental action to clear out this breeding ground of delinquency, a New Deal–style solution out of favor in postwar America. Where films like *The Blackboard Jungle* and *Rebel Without a Cause* end with some hope for the survivors, there are no potential winners in *City Across the River*: one of the main protagonists falls to his death and the other is hauled off by the police. Not surprising, perhaps, in a film where teenagers manufacture zip guns in shop class and use one to murder their teacher, a burnt-out case who had earlier suggested dropping an atom bomb as the only way of cleaning up the mess. Where was this awful place? Brooklyn, of course.

In large display ads, U-I advertised the film as "*The Naked City*—of Brooklyn!" and an "Exposé of Brooklyn's Cellar-Club Hot-Beds of Juvenile Delinquency."[56] If anyone missed that, Drew Pearson tells us from the screen that "this story happens in Brooklyn . . . where Flatbush meets the slums . . . in the city of churches." Politically connected Brooklynites "kicked up quite a fuss" at this public shaming and pressured O'Dwyer for action. The *Times* reported that all such negative references to Brooklyn were cut from the print—and the print ads—immediately.[57] In any case, existing prints of the film still give Brooklyn full credit.

The mayor, along with Maguire, local journalists like Bosley Crowther, and most developers of potential New York studio sites, continued to think of New York as a glorified location, a would-be satellite of the Hollywood studio system. *Portrait of Jennie* and *The Naked City* had won a lot of press attention, not all of it good, and the cost overruns associated with both films—largely the result of poor production management—had been blamed on the city's bad weather, bureaucracy, and municipal corruption. Maguire's 1947 report was designed to address these problems, but very few Hollywood production units filmed in New York in 1948.[58] Joseph Mankiewicz shot suburban scenes along the Hudson, and at Cold Spring, Mahopac, and Hook Mountain for *Letter to Three Wives* but did nothing in New York City itself.[59] But at least he brought his leading actors with him; *Mr. Blandings Builds His Dream House* settled for a conventional montage of "harried New Yorkers" with no principal photography in the east at all. Instead, the year was full of bad news for local film producers, from the loss of the Pathé and Filmcraft studios to the collapse of the race film business. Nonfiction and sponsored film production remained strong, and television seemed to hold great promise, but the idea of reviving the theatrical film industry in New York seemed as fanciful as ever.[60]

The Danzigers in New York

In retrospect, however, the seeds were already there. From *The House on 92nd Street* to *Carnegie Hall* to *Close-Up*, producers were becoming increasingly comfortable with local talent, technicians, sound stages, labs, and equipment houses. Still, while New York boasted the finest directors of stage plays and radio dramas, and had formed its own Screen Directors Guild in 1945, none of those films was entrusted to a local director. That changed in the spring of 1948, when the Danziger brothers hired Fletcher Markle to direct *Jigsaw*. Edward and Harry Lee Danziger had been in the amusement park business (they owned Luna Park for a time in the 1940s) and had dabbled as investors on Broadway.[61] But those were chancy businesses dependent on variables that were hard to control. Edward had been a captain in the Signal Corps and perhaps, like many others, he hoped to make some use of that experience in civilian life.[62]

The brothers also owned Eastern Sound Studios at 550 Fifth Avenue, which had been dubbing features for Paramount and other Hollywood studios since 1944.[63] Eventually they expanded this business and began shooting second-unit material under contract to Hollywood producers.

The Danzigers made their first move into features in February 1948, when they purchased the negative of *Sarumba* at public auction. The film had been shot in Cuba in March and April 1947 by George P. Quigley of Century Productions but was seized by the lab when he was unable to pay them a back bill of $5,831.[64] Quigley had been making industrials and race movies (like *Junction 88*) and told *Variety* that "this pic represents his company's first white feature." It was also one of the first postwar American features to be shot completely in Cuba, Quigley being attracted to Havana's National Studio because their posted rates were half of what American studios were charging. Unfortunately, poor management, the language barrier (cameraman Don Malkames was unable to converse with his head electrician), and the skill displayed by local merchants in "cooking up phony invoices" quickly broke the budget. Quigley also complained that Cuban dancers, while individually "tops," were "unable to adjust themselves to precision terping as in a chorus line."[65] This was a real problem in a musical (*Sarumba* = Samba + Rumba) designed to show off the talents of Tommy Wonder and Doris Dowling.[66] The Danzigers may have bought the negative, but Quigley managed to tie them up in court for years. The film was reviewed in the trades as an Eagle-Lion release in March 1950, but the notices were terrible, *Harrison's Reports* dismissing it as "mediocre . . . amateurish . . . weak in story, dialogue and acting, and presented with little imagination."[67] The collapse of Eagle-Lion later that year killed any chance of distribution. Two years later the Danzigers were finally able to unload it on Bob Savini's Astor Pictures, but they would have been lucky to get their lab costs back. The five-year-old film was still being described as unreleased in the American market.[68]

Far from being discouraged by this fiasco, the Danzigers plowed ahead with *Jigsaw*, having learned a number of valuable lessons. Keeping an eye on the budget was very important, but avoiding the loss of control that accompanies the accumulation of debt was crucial. "They're spending their own money on the picture and they're certain they can make a good picture," an inside source told the *New York Times*, "but until they see what they've got they honestly do not want to publicize it or even discuss a releasing arrangement."[69] In other words, the Danzigers self-financed *Jigsaw* without a distribution guarantee, a very risky move.

In the course of running their dubbing studio, the Danzigers had seen the finest European filmmakers "produce complete pictures on actual locations [and] they decided to go all out themselves. They had been filming parts of pictures in New York for years, so they decided to produce full-length films."[70] The Danzigers also realized that "with the acceptance of their highly successful method of dubbing for foreign versions, the same method could be applied to the production of films for domestic use."[71] They would abandon Hollywood's insistence on the use of live sound and copy what Roberto Rossellini and Vittorio De Sica had been doing: shooting everything on location wild and dubbing in all the sound back at the studio. That would allow their actors and directors to work unencumbered by microphones and recording booms and save the Danzigers the cost of set construction and studio rentals. "The picture is certain to be studied with interest by producers of low-budget films," *American Cinematographer* reported, because the approach "can materially reduce production costs whether the picture is made in Hollywood or New York."[72]

Fletcher Markle was also interested in using sound in a new way but for very different reasons. An artistically ambitious acolyte of Orson Welles, Markle was a talented Canadian radio broadcaster who had come to New York in 1946, invited by Norman Corwin to work on the groundbreaking *Columbia Workshop* series at CBS. Welles soon hired him as a producer/director on *The Mercury Summer Theatre of the Air* and, some claim, to collaborate on the script of *The Lady from Shanghai*.[73] Heavily influenced by Welles's radio work, Markle created the ambitious dramatic series *Studio One* in 1947, moving it to television the following year.

Jigsaw (originally *The Time Is Now*) was shot in six weeks, from late April through the beginning of June 1948.[74] The Danzigers described it as "a topical suspense drama on a political theme," but the story soon drifts away from the activities of The Crusaders, a generic hate group whose specific targets are never made clear. Instead, most of the film follows a one-man murder investigation undertaken by the assistant DA, played by Franchot Tone. Interesting suggestions of widespread corruption involving the mafia, right-wing vigilantes, and political power brokers who operate out of Manhattan penthouses are never developed in any satisfactory way. Tone appears to have been an investor in the film, which co-starred his wife, Jean Wallace. Most of the cast consisted of unfamiliar New York faces, but Markle and Tone did convince quite a few of their friends to pop up in oddball cameos. John Garfield appears as a man in the street reading a newspaper (Tone would reciprocate a few months later, making "a token appearance as a numbers collector" in *Force of Evil*).[75] Burgess Meredith, who would soon direct Tone and Wallace in *Man on the Eiffel Tower*, is a bartender. Henry Fonda, Marsha Hunt, Marlene Dietrich, and Everett Sloane are also there, along with columnist Leonard Lyons and Fletcher Markle himself, who is Dietrich's escort on a visit to the Blue Angel nightclub. Critics were not impressed by this clubby humor. "Several stars who happened to be hanging around the Main Stem appear in the picture as walk-ons," the *Los Angeles Times* grumbled. "Their presence, rather than furthering an already shaky illusion, only increases the conviction that Tone & Co. took the whole business as a lark."[76]

Markle and his cinematographer, Don Malkames, did not do too much exterior work, which would have made the company dependent on the vagaries of New York's weather and the crowd control abilities of its police force. Instead they filmed a series of practical interiors, including various offices and apartments, a pet shop, a restaurant, and the actual Blue Angel on East Fifty-Fifth Street. Because some of these spaces were quite small, Malkames lit them with large quantities of Mole-Richardson midget spots and small inky-dinkies, attaching them to ceiling beams and apartment moldings where possible and flooding the rest of the space with small portable broads.[77] He had the opposite problem with the film's dramatic climax, a shoot-out filmed at night inside the cavernous Brooklyn Museum. Impressively low key, these scenes earned high praise from at least one trade paper critic, who noted that "Don Malkames' excellent photography is at times reminiscent of *Citizen Kane*."[78]

While Fletcher Markle might have been pleased by the Welles reference, he would not have been happy with the response to his soundtrack, described variously as "bad" or "largely inaudible." Aware that they will all be dubbing their own lines later—a skill with which they would not have been familiar—the actors appear unusually stiff and uneasy. The synchronization is also off at times, but worse than this is the lack of ambient sound, an absence of room tone that suggests nothing more than the acoustics of a dubbing studio. Within a few years the ability to manipulate and rerecord dialogue tracks would advance significantly, and today very little of what we hear in a theater is actually recorded during shooting. But whatever its flaws, this pioneering work at least suggested that American independent (read: low-budget) filmmakers, like their European cousins, might do well to avoid the headaches associated with direct sound recording altogether. Stanley Kubrick, for one, was clearly paying attention.

CHAPTER 7

JOE LERNER'S NEW YORK NOIR

Joseph Lerner had directed *The Fight Never Ends* in 1947, the first race movie to be booked into the Loew's circuit in New York. But that was still a race movie, and in any case Lerner's name was seldom associated with it. When the war ended he decided to remain in New York, where he had been writing, producing, and directing army documentaries at the Signal Corps Photographic Center. "Directed everything from the love life of a storage battery (joke) to dramatizations of medical problems," he noted in his professional resume.[1] During the Depression, Lerner had worked as an actor and director, staging summer theater productions, making occasional radio appearances, and in 1935 even playing "the second lead" in Elia Kazan's first Broadway show, *The Young Go First* (whose cast also included future directors Jack Arnold and Nicholas Ray). By the late 1930s he was in Hollywood, directing screen tests and second units for Columbia, RKO, and "many quickie producers." This was where he met his wife, Geraldine (Geri), then working as a sound editor for MGM.

Sensing that film production was about to take off in New York, Lerner founded Visual Arts Productions with his partner Max Rosenbaum, "a very good salesman who knew how to open doors." In addition to *The Fight Never Ends*, they made a few industrials and even some short films for Universal but had their first high-profile success with *Kings of the Olympics*, a documentary feature on the 1936 Berlin Olympic Games. One of the doors Rosenbaum opened appears to have been that of the Office of Alien Property, which turned over to them both parts of Leni Riefenstahl's 1938 epic, *Olympia*. The Lerners trimmed all footage of Hitler, swastikas, or anything recognizably German, had Bill Slater record a new narration, and began screening the film under the aegis of the U.S. Olympic Committee.[2] *Kings of the Olympics* was picked up by United Artists and distributed widely in several different versions. Although Riefenstahl was not credited, reviewers generally knew who was responsible. *Motion Picture Daily* claimed that the film was newly assembled from outtakes and raw footage originally shot "under the direction and supervision of Leni Riefenstahl, actress friend of Hitler, Aryan by the Fuehrer's ukase, and director of Nazi propaganda films."[3] In a lengthy piece that only credits Riefenstahl, Arthur Daley of the *New York Times* admitted that "Leni Riefenstahl, a good-looking doll who knew der Fuehrer slightly better than somewhat, was in charge of the breath-taking camerawork. To give the Devil Her due, she did a truly magnificent job."[4] And Walter Winchell not only knew who had made the film but who had remade it. "Hitler never dreamed (when he had Leni Riefenstahl employ 600 Nazi photographers to 'shoot' the 1936 Olympics in Berlin) that one day that film footage would make a fortune for a non-Aryan," he wrote.[5] When I interviewed them in 1987, Geri was still delighted at having gotten her hands on the picture. As a compilation film, *Kings of the Olympics* did not achieve the same level of attention as other documentary features released that year, but Lerner had now made important contacts at UA. And even Leni Riefenstahl was happy. "More good news came from the United States," she wrote in her autobiography. "My *Olympia* film, distributed by United Artists, was having a highly successful run there under the title *Kings of the Olympics*."[6] It is unclear if she knew exactly what the Lerners had done to it.

As far as the postwar New York film industry was concerned, Joe Lerner had by now touched all the bases: some Broadway, a bit of Hollywood, SCPC, race movies, sponsored films, and documentaries. With a new partner, producer-promoter Rex Carlton, Lerner created Laurel Films and began to make features. Reviews for his two earlier films had been strong enough to attract a distributor, Film Classics, which in turn brought financing from Chemical Bank and Trust. Although negotiations for several Broadway plays fell through, by the end of 1948 Lerner was ready to begin work on *Customs Affair*, a "government agent" thriller written by one of his old Hollywood friends (the title was soon changed to *C-Man*, a nod to Eagle-Lion's recent government agent success, *T-Men*).[7] The official budget was still a modest $110,000, of which Chemical Bank agreed to put up 60 percent if Laurel Films could raise the rest. They did this by scraping together nearly $40,000 in deferments, promises from certain participants who agreed not to demand payment up front. Lerner's own salary as producer and director was deferred, and Reeves Sound Studios also deferred $6,000 of their fee.

Hazard Reeves agreed to defer this sum, which covered the rental of his small A stage at 304 East Forty-Fourth Street, only because Lerner agreed to do all of his sound recording on the Reeves Magicorder. While the magnetic recorders introduced by RCA and other manufacturers were adaptations of their existing optical recording technology, Reeves had designed the Magicorder from scratch, and it was well adapted to the special requirements of his clients. The Magicorder was a lightweight synchronous sound recorder using fully coated 16 or 35 mm magnetic film and had already been used by a few industrial film producers.[8] But Reeves wanted to break into the feature-film market, long dominated by optical recorders manufactured by RCA and Western Electric. Established producers were loath to experiment with magnetic sound, but Lerner found the proposition attractive ("I needed that six grand") and *C-Man* became the first dramatic feature anywhere recorded entirely on magnetic film. "Now magnetic film for recording is being used almost entirely throughout the film industry," Reeves wrote proudly a few years later. "But this development, which should have come from within the industry itself actually was developed independently and without industry aid."[9] By which he meant, without input from the *Hollywood* motion picture industry.

"Well, when we went into the projection room the next day and listened to the sound," Lerner remembered, "it was fantastic. It was so wonderful. You could hear the rustle of a jacket as a guy unbuttoned it. You could hear everything. I was in seventh heaven. The problem was, how do you cut it?" Sound editors could see the modulations on an optical track and were trained to use them as a guide, but this sprocketed brown ribbon showed nothing, a problem Reeves had not considered. While shooting went on in Studio A, Geraldine Lerner taught herself, and the staff, how to conform magnetic tracks in proper Hollywood fashion. Afterward, Joe remembered, "she came in with a score, with a whole breakdown all lined up and laid out where to go. They had never seen anything like that before in this city, with a real MGM-like breakdown of all the tracks and how they come in, and the footages and all that. . . . She must have walked into the mix with maybe 15 tracks. She had a loop for every frame of the goddamn picture. And Vorisek, Dick Vorisek, who was the mixer, would sit there and say, 'My God, you're using up every pot in all of Reeves!' " The introduction of the portable Nagra III magnetic recorder in 1958 would revolutionize independent cinema, but the Magicorder was the first step in bringing this new technology within the reach of low-budget producers.

The plot of *C-Man* involved an attempt to smuggle a stolen necklace into New York via KLM Royal Dutch Airlines (product placement) and the efforts of a customs agent, Dean Jagger, to bring down the gang and its ringleader, also responsible for the death of his old army buddy. Jagger was a known commodity, but he had not worked in a year and needed the job. John Carradine, another recognizable name, was already in New York; he has only two scenes in the picture but gets featured billing. Harry Landers, who trained with Jeff Corey at the Actors Lab in Hollywood, was hired to play the sort of psychopathic thug made popular by Richard Widmark in *Kiss of Death*. Landers had already appeared, uncredited, in both *Kiss of Death* and *Boomerang!* and would become a regular in Lerner's acting company and a fixture on innumerable television series, from *Capt. Video* to *Ben Casey* and *Star Trek*.

Lerner began another longtime association here, with cinematographer Gerald Hirschfeld. A Signal Corps cameraman who had never shot a feature before, Hirschfeld became an important figure in New York's industrial film business while also shooting such local features as *Fail Safe* (1964) and *Cotton Comes to Harlem* (1970).[10] Hirschfeld worked fast and like Lerner was fond of improvising. When no proper camera car was available, Hirschfeld took the hood off a Chevy, covered it with a plywood platform, and filmed their traveling shots that way. "It got a little hot from the engine it covered," Lerner remembered, "but what's a hot seat if you can get a good shot?"

C-Man was scheduled for four days of exteriors and six days of studio work, which called for a maximum of speed and improvisation. Some introductory footage of Jagger walking around downtown near the old Customs House appears to have been grabbed quickly with available lighting and a handheld camera, but scenes taken at LaGuardia Airport are more impressive—and not just because the same location also doubles as an airport in France. Although I assumed that the important dialogue sequences here were looped back at the studio, the Lerners both claimed that everything we see was shot live, and there was no dubbing of dialogue or sound effects in any of their films. This seems to have been a point of principle and not just another quickie shortcut. Geri insisted that proper room tone recordings be made for every sequence, a professional demand that added "about thirty or more minutes a day," a delay Joe still remembered forty years later ("I wouldn't have done it that way"). But fistfights in *C-Man*, unsweetened by the sound of theatrical punches, have always failed to impress audiences accustomed to even rudimentary Foley work. Still, the sound quality here is obviously superior to a film like *Jigsaw*, where the entire track was looped in a recording studio and sounds like it.

The Lerners freely admitted that as "children of the Depression," they were not just tight with a dollar but constitutionally unable to pay someone for work they might just as well do themselves, like location scouting or breaking down the script for budgetary purposes. Although William Saulter was hired as art director (he was available now that Pathé had cut back production), Lerner claimed that it was his own idea to "sandwich" the fifteen (or eighteen) sets that would be built at the Reeves studio.[11] Stage A at Reeves was an insert stage used for filming close-ups of products or other tabletop items. Lerner remembered it as only thirty or thirty-five feet square, with no room for constructing and storing multiple film sets. Instead, the sets were built one in front of the other. The smallest set was built in front, and after its scenes were completed it was hauled off and tossed into a dumpster, revealing the next smallest set right behind it. The largest set, requiring the full depth of the stage, was left for last. The space was so cramped that Hirschfeld had to paint shadows on some of the walls because there was no room for proper lighting. Furniture and props for the entire shoot were piled up along the fire stairs; when all these set dressing elements had been discarded, Lerner filmed several angles of Jagger climbing this same flight of stairs, which in the film are edited together to suggest a climb of several stories.

Given this proclivity for cost-cutting, it may seem surprising that Lerner dropped the original notion of scoring the film with library music ("the Czechoslovakian Symphony Orchestra, the Hungarian Band, or whatever the hell they had") and instead hired Gail Kubik, a student of Walter Piston and a 1944 Guggenheim Fellow. Kubik had never written a theatrical film score but during the war worked on many films for the OWI and the U.S. Army, notably William Wyler's *Thunderbolt* and *The Memphis Belle*.[12] Realizing that their film needed something out of the ordinary, the Lerners accepted the "crazy, way out kind of music" Kubik delivered, which at times required the use of an old railroad tie laid across the keys of the piano. "I thought that maybe he should play it on a garbage can cover, because it wasn't my dish of tea," Joe recalled. But Geri loved the music, and the challenge of recording and mixing it on Reeves's new equipment. The score even included a brief visit to a jazz club, already a film noir cliché, for which Kubik composed a suitably manic "shout song" called "Do It Now." At first even Hazard Reeves was dubious ("Oh, God! What are you doing to my magnetic tape!"), but eventually he realized that this cacophony was the best possible advertisement for the range of his Magicorder. Kubik later turned his *C-Man* score into the *Symphony Concertante for Trumpet, Viola, Piano and Orchestra*, further developing the contrasts he introduced in the film; it won the Pulitzer Prize in 1952.[13]

Few reviewers felt that *C-Man* was worth writing about, but those who did often focused on its discordant, highly untraditional score. "Dominating the soundtrack even more than the dialogue," wrote *Variety*, "the background music has a nervous, pounding, pulse-quickening quality which, combined [with] the headlong action, results in a powerfully stirring total effect."[14] A trade paper critic, reviewing a low-budget crime thriller, praising the score? In truth, while *C-Man* may be a milestone in the history of New York independent cinema for all the reasons brought out here, it remains a film for specialists. "Among the New York-filmed independent movies, I have a particular fondness for Joseph Lerner's *C-Man*," the archivist and historian William K. Everson wrote in 1979. "It was made on a miniscule budget, and it showed it—but it tried. . . . Threadbare it may have been, but I remember it far better than many major films of the period."[15]

While the government agents do solve the crime and round up the culprits, *C-Man* is no *Naked City*. The heroine is drugged into unconsciousness on a transatlantic flight, while the hero, several villains, and even an innocent landlady are all beaten within an inch of their lives, or worse. The National Legion of Decency cited it as morally objectionable on account of its "excessive brutality," a rating even *Kiss of Death* had avoided. Laurel Films calculated that *C-Man* would break even in less than eighteen months, but it was in distribution for only eight months before showing a profit. Yet the Lerners claimed never to have received a penny of their deferred salaries, instead using the unpaid sum as collateral against the production of their next film, another crime thriller with a much larger budget. If they took no salary for their work on *C-Man*, even after it went into profit, how did the Lerners support themselves during this period? As with *The Fight Never Ends*, where their payment consisted of whatever cash remained after filming was completed, the Lerners "lived off the budget." "Our budget [for *C-Man*] was $110,000, of which we watered a lot of it, because nobody knew. The banks didn't know how much was one and one," Joe admitted to me.

The bigger budget of that second film, $450,000, allowed for the purchase of a real book, a pulpy detective novel called *Guilty Bystander*. Partnering with Edmund L. Dorfmann, a successful shorts producer looking to get into features, Laurel Films announced the project as early as July 1948 but had set it aside to make room for the less demanding *C-Man*.[16] *Guilty Bystander* had been written by the team of Bob Wade and Bill Miller, writing as Wade Miller (other films adapted from their work would include *Touch of Evil* and *Kitten with a Whip*). It was the first of a short series featuring the very flawed hardboiled detective Max Thursday, a disagreeable, angry drunk working here as house detective in a skid row hotel little better than a Bowery flophouse. His estranged wife rouses him from a drunken stupor with the news that their young son has been kidnapped. Thursday begins an underworld investigation, but the villains find he can easily be distracted by a few stiff drinks. In the final reel the kidnapping is foiled and the underlying crime is solved, but the atmosphere of corruption and despair is so thick that the audience can hardly be expected to take the happy suburban conclusion at face value. In truth, *Guilty Bystander* is a mood piece so focused on delineating the dark corners of Max Thursday's life that very little attention is given to the details of its mystery plot. "The film suffers from a lack of clarity in its plot development and at times leaves the spectator feeling bewildered over exactly what is happening and why the events are taking place," one trade paper reported.[17]

Don Ettlinger, who wrote the screenplay, not only changed the locale of the story from San Diego to New York City but offered a different reason for Max's alcoholism and divorce. In the book, Max had been a respectable private eye before the war, but he emerged from a stretch in the Marines with a crippling case of PTSD, making it impossible for him to continue as he had in the old days. The film says nothing about the war, and Max is a former cop who has been "thrown off the force because he was drunk." Around this time there was a brief wave of films featuring damaged and dangerous war veterans, such as Edward Dmytryk's *The Sniper* (1952), where violent behavior was explained as a function of battle fatigue, a psychological problem that might be addressed by proper medical treatment. But Lerner's film suggests a far darker explanation: cop culture. Cops, Max explains, "like to shove people around. . . . They like violence, they like to carry guns. They're just muscle men who like to use their muscles." But when you are no longer on the force, things change. "You don't *tell* people, you *ask* them," a decline in status that seems to have turned the self-pitying Max into a hopeless alcoholic. As Jake Hinkson notes in a recent essay on Lerner's films, "Apparently, all Thursday misses about being a cop is the freedom to push people around, to use violence to get his way."[18]

To play this unlikable antihero, Lerner hired Zachary Scott, a specialist in weak and even unpleasant second leads (think Joan Crawford's husband Monte in *Mildred Pierce*). No longer under contract to Warner Bros., Scott had been trying to establish himself in the independent field by starring in films like Edgar G. Ulmer's *Ruthless*, but he was not really a big enough name to carry a major feature. To play opposite him Lerner hired Faye Emerson, another Warner veteran who had first worked with Scott on *The Mask of Dimitrios* (1944). Emerson had left Hollywood after marrying Elliott Roosevelt and was now in New York working in television, where she was already the star of her own show. Of course, as in *C-Man*, there is no traditional romantic relationship in this film, nor is there any comic relief, an unconventional dramatic decision not followed by films like *Close-Up*, for example.

The rest of the cast was stacked with familiar faces, from established stars like Mary Boland and Sam Levene to future favorites Kay Medford and Jesse White. But Lerner also hired J. Edward Bromberg and Elliott Sullivan, charity cases already on the run from a growing Hollywood blacklist. "Joe called me and said, 'Whattya got, I'll take anything,' " Lerner said of Bromberg, who he knew from Group Theatre days. In 1951 Bromberg, once a busy character actor, would refuse to name names when called before HUAC; he died six months later (Elia Kazan posthumously named Bromberg as a Communist during his own 1952 appearance). Elliott Sullivan, another blacklist victim, had been reduced to selling gadgets door-to-door. Lerner found a small part for him but then kept him on for additional days as an extra. "Be there, but stay the hell out of camera. Keep your back to the camera," he told both men. "There were, I guess, seven or eight other people who were getting extra work [on *Guilty Bystander*] who were actors who were marked lousy," he told me. "I was never a member of the C.P., although I was so goddamn close to being one that. . . . I just wasn't a joiner, that was what saved me, I think. Because I was very well known. I directed plays for the Hollywood Anti-Nazi League on radio, I knew all those people." Lerner remembered with some pride that he had given both

Bromberg and Sullivan screen credit when producers in Hollywood didn't even want them on the lot.

Scott flew to New York on August 8, 1949, to begin ten days of rehearsals at Reeves Sound Studios.[19] According to Lerner, *Guilty Bystander* had a twenty-three-day shooting schedule, with two sets built at Reeves while two full stages were occupied at the larger Fox Movietone Studio. Faith Elliott, who had been script supervisor on *Close-Up* (and was already committed to *So Young, So Bad*) recommended Dede Allen; they had both been messengers and apprentice editors at Columbia. Allen had never worked as a script supervisor but knew what a Hollywood-trained editor like Geraldine Lerner would need to see in the way of paperwork. She became a charter member of Script Clerks Local 161 and within a few years was established as one of New York's finest film editors (*The Hustler, Bonnie and Clyde, Serpico*).[20] *Guilty Bystander* followed *With These Hands* into the Fox studio in August 1949; Gerald Hirschfeld shot both films.

With William Saulter ill, Lerner hired Leo Kerz to design the sets. A theatrical designer with no prior film experience, Kerz struck Lerner as extremely well organized. He designed the sets with multiple breakaway walls and his scenic renderings included fabric swatches, luxuries Lerner had not enjoyed on

7.1. Ray Julian and Harry Landers menace Zachary Scott on one of Leo Kerz's stylized staircases. Kay Medford is *Guilty Bystander*'s femme fatale. Author's collection.

his earlier films. "Everything was working as if he'd made fifty pictures in his lifetime as opposed to none. I could get any angle I wanted." Even more impressive, Kerz had analyzed the script chromatically, describing Scott's character as "a kind of dark brown" while Faye Emerson was "a blue person." Once Lerner understood how this sensibility would function in dressing a black-and-white film, "I went hog wild for it." It was a big step from asking the actors to work in their street clothes or renting a few pieces from Eaves Costume Company.

Guilty Bystander makes better use of locations than *C-Man*, shooting at the Manhattan House of Detention on Centre Street (then known as "the New Tombs"); the shadowy side streets beneath the Brooklyn Bridge; what the *Brooklyn Eagle* described as "the fabled Gowanus Canal section in Brooklyn;" and the abandoned IND Court Street station, today home of the New York Transit Museum.[21] Everything looks dark and dangerous, and we see nothing of the picture-postcard New York featured in many other location films. Even the obligatory long shot of the Brooklyn Bridge shown under the credits is taken at night. The real coup was filming a battle between Scott and Sullivan on the platform at Court Street, closed since 1946. The Transit Authority charged only $25 to drive a five-car train into the station on cue, although two motormen still had to be hired at union scale. Running the train did require a live third rail, a problem that needed special attention once the battle continued onto the tracks. According to the *New York Times*, "company spokesmen were convinced that these few hours of labor had resulted in authentic background footage which would have cost infinitely more to reproduce on a fabricated studio set."[22] Comparison with similar scenes in *Cry of the City* and *The Glass Wall*, which do make use of back projections and studio sets, bears this out. The station would subsequently appear in many other film and television productions, including *The FBI Story* (1956) and both versions of *The Taking of Pelham One Two Three*. The city's cooperation in making available both Court Street and the New Tombs was duly noted by Lerner, who told the press that "there is nothing in Hollywood that New York cannot supply, unless it is studio space." He boasted that New York had the best sound equipment, young technicians, and "new faces in the acting profession." Even better, shooting on the streets turns a liability into an asset because it "eliminates the expensive item of constructing sets, and serves to heighten the realism of scenes" while offering "added stimulant to the actors, who when surrounded by authenticity, submerge deeper into their roles and give more natural performances."[23]

Laurel had promised Gail Kubik he would do the score of *Guilty Bystander*, but Lerner had never been happy with the music he delivered and went looking for someone else.[24] He first thought of his friend Alex North, who claimed to be too busy. Then Stanley Kramer, another friend from the SCPC, introduced him to Dimitri Tiomkin. Tiomkin had scored many of Frank Capra's wartime documentaries, but unlike Kubik he was a big Hollywood name whose recent work included *Duel in the Sun*, *Red River*, and *Portrait of Jennie*. When I asked Lerner how he could have afforded Tiomkin, he told me a long story about promising to find him the "real fancy toilet seats" he was looking to add to the seven or eight he already had at home. "This may sound unusual to you," he said, but "Isn't it part of a filmmaker's education to know things like that?" Such shenanigans, he was telling me, were par for the course when trying to make movies in New York during the last days of the O'Dwyer administration. And then there was the clincher: "When I suggested that I might even get him a discount, I knew I had him." In the end, it was Tiomkin who gave Lerner a discount, charging him only two-thirds of what Stanley Kramer had been paying him.

But Tiomkin also bonded with the Lerners over more technical issues, especially their mutual appreciation of the Schillinger System, "a musical theory based on mathematics" created by Joseph Schillinger that could be applied to all genres of music.[25] On the first day of shooting Lerner had decided to direct the actors according to a tempo dictated by a metronome, in this case largo. "We rehearsed Scott and Emerson to the beat which in a way dictated how they moved and how they looked and paused between lines," he remembered. But when the assistant director pointed out that the crew was now moving in this same slow and steady rhythm, "I turned the damn thing off before the beat would louse up my schedule to say nothing of the budget. From then on I still used the different beats for every scene but kept it in my head." Tiomkin recognized this when he saw the final cut and "said to me that I [had] dictated the rhythm of his score, scene for scene, right up to the various chases." As he watched the film, Tiomkin began rattling off long strings of numbers. "Both Geri and I knew what he was doing," Lerner wrote. "He was quite surprised when we told him he was practicing the Schillenger [sic] System." With film, radio, the recording industry, and other midcentury media demanding large quantities of music composed quickly and at uniform levels of quality, professional musicians were attracted to Schillinger's promise of a compositional shortcut. According to the website of The Schillinger Society, his private students included George Gershwin, Glenn Miller, and Carmine Coppola.

Reviewers certainly noticed that something strange was going on. Bosley Crowther, who generally dismissed anything that might qualify as "cheap melodrama," noted the film's "oddly disturbing slow-beat rhythm and plenty of sleazy atmosphere." Another local critic, similarly unappreciative of yet another "dimwitted murder mystery," complained that "all the gunmen and women Mr. Scott meets hang out in dark, gloomy, brooding places and talk very slow and tough, see, as though each word is bursting with menace and meaning."[26] Perhaps he would have preferred a pacing other than largo?

Seeing him as another collaborator who could work quickly and efficiently, Lerner added Tiomkin to his unofficial production unit, where he joined Hirschfeld and Kerz on the next Laurel production, *Mr. Universe*. A comedy (rare at the time for an independent production), the film sets its slapstick action against a pervasive atmosphere of cynicism and corruption typical of early 1950s film noir. Jack Carson plays a charming liar and con man who decides to set up his naïve army buddy in modern America's biggest con: televised wrestling. In the ring he will play the good guy role of "Mr. Universe" in combat against Gorilla Hogan, Newton the Teuton, The Hoboken Turk, and other small-screen villains, all of whom appear as themselves. Also prominently featured was Dennis James, a popular wrestling announcer notorious for breaking chicken bones off-camera for added effect. Indeed, much of the film was shot at Sunnyside Gardens in Queens, where DuMont had been broadcasting live wrestling since 1946. While not the first feature film to take a poke at the new medium, parts of *Mr. Universe* are almost indistinguishable from the programming it satirizes. Indeed, the film itself became a local television favorite, where this author saw it many times during the 1950s. Bert Lahr, whose career ran from vaudeville and burlesque right through *The Wizard of Oz* and television commercials for Lay's potato chips, played Carson's rubber-faced partner, while Vince Edwards, a student at the American Academy of Dramatic Arts, made his big-screen debut in the title role, the only honest man in the film. Edwards later became famous as television's *Ben Casey* (1961–1966) but hated this role, which he thanklessly described as "a lousy way to make a debut in the movies."[27]

The slapstick elements in *Mr. Universe* channel the Three Stooges comedies that screenwriter Searle Kramer had been writing before the war, with Carson and Lahr playing Moe and Larry while Vince Edwards stands in as a kinder, gentler Curly Howard.[28] But the film noir atmosphere is more typical of Lerner. Everyone except Edwards is a chiseler: television is fiction, sporting competitions are rigged, athletes are the property of gangsters, and anyone who believes otherwise is not living in the real world. The big joke in the film is that Universe, as everyone calls him, fails to recognize this and spoils the show by dispatching his opponents right after the opening bell, whether he is scheduled to win or not. The gag would also seem to reflect the corrupt atmosphere of New York's film industry when Lerner was making this film. When I interviewed him in 1987, Lerner told me that he had offered the outside prop man $10 a week over scale if he would split the kickbacks he was receiving from prop houses.

> "I can't do that, Joe, 'cause I've got to make a living." (laughter) I'll never forget it. Same thing with the gaffer [chief electrician]. He says, "I'm going with Charlie Ross, we buy from Charlie Ross because their stuff is the best." I said, "OK, what's your kickback?" He says, "Fifteen percent." "I'll give you ten dollars a week over scale and I want to split that with you." "No, way, Joe!"

After seeing the transcript of our interview, Lerner wrote me that this had been a joke on his part, but the crew members in question don't seem to have thought it very funny. Nor were the police laughing. "Oh, you paid them off. And they were always around when anything was catered, so they could get free lunches!" Officers assigned by the city to help direct traffic or control crowds were generally quite helpful. "When we were shooting *Universe*, wherever we went they helped us, they really did. But we paid them off. And we paid them in cash. I'm sure it went all the way to the top because if you gave them less, the guy would say, 'How about the lieutenant?' So count the lieutenant as well." Of course, there needed to be some way of accounting for this in the budget. Lerner put in a line for "schmear," but the bank resisted. Nor would they accept "grease." Eventually they compromised on "incidentals." According to Lerner, this was just the way movies were made. This chain of corruption also involved the filmmakers because, "there was no way for the producer to make any money unless he was knocking down, he was getting his stuff out of the budget. Because you weren't making it out of the picture itself."

Production began at Sunnyside Gardens on May 1, 1950, with Lerner directing 178 extras and Chief Flying Mare, who had trouble getting his headdress through the ring ropes. The event was covered by the *New Yorker*, which otherwise only gave space to the production of films like *On the Town*. After ten days at the Gardens, Lerner would shoot the rest of the film at Fox Movietone.[29] As traditional in prize-fight films, the underworld demands a piece of the action, so in a move predating Mel Brooks, Carson and Lahr each sell controlling interest in Universe to gambler Robert Alda, leaving him with more than 100 percent and the boys with serious financial problems. In an interview given around the time he was producing *Mr. Universe*, Lerner suddenly began talking about the difficulty of financing independent films, suggesting that it was not only Jack Carson who was having money trouble. "Naturally, banking institutions came in for most of the heavy money," the article noted.

> They were not interested in the artistic stature of the picture, but had their sights set on the interest return and the amortization of the indebtedness. "This attitude on the part of the financiers is readily understandable," said Mr. Lerner, "but it causes a lot of headaches for the producer and director who wants to give the public something off the prescribed path."[30]

Rex Carlton, who was president of Laurel Films, had promoted a $400,000 loan from Chemical on August 22, 1949.[31] The money was to be repaid within eighteen months, which was then a standard financing agreement. Chemical's motion picture loans were managed by their vice-president, Edwin Van Pelt, who was also on the board of Republic Pictures; Milton Gettinger, an outside attorney frequently employed by Chemical to oversee the legal aspects of their film business, handled the paperwork, often partnering with Van Pelt.[32] There should not have been a problem here, especially since the films produced by Laurel all performed well. *C-Man* and *Guilty Bystander* (which were cross-collateralized) were distributed by Film Classics and ought to have been generating income for Laurel throughout 1950. But theater attendance had collapsed by then, and audiences had become far more selective. Low-end distributors like Film Classics were hit especially hard and scrambled to cover their own expenses; the producers whose films they handled suffered accordingly. Film Classics suddenly went out of business after a proposed merger with the slightly stronger Eagle-Lion fell apart in June but not before Eagle-Lion had changed its own name to Eagle-Lion Classics (ELC).[33] Distribution rights to the independent productions in the Film Classics package, many of which had also been funded by Chemical Bank and Trust, fell into dispute and would take years to untangle in court. Cash flow to several struggling independent producers, including Laurel Films, simply dried up.[34]

Mr. Universe had been shooting for about a week when the FC-EL merger was prematurely announced.[35] Despite the fact that the deal never went through, Chemical Bank leaned on the Film Classics producers to move their product over to Eagle-Lion Classics anyway, but Laurel, for one, resisted. Because Jack Carson had just signed a contract with Columbia, his new studio was eager to pick up *Universe* and made a handsome offer of $507,000 that Lerner and Carlton were inclined to accept. The bank, however, knew that Laurel's films were among the few valuable titles in the Film Classics catalog, which they were hoping to flip to United Artists.[36] They were not subtle about their intentions. Afraid that Gettinger and Van Pelt would seize the film, which was stored under bond at the De Luxe lab, Lerner came up with a plan of his own. "We took ten reels of negative, this is work print negative, and hid it," he told me. Unable to remove the film from the building without authorization, Lerner simply misfiled the ten reels, taking them from where De Luxe had stored them and putting them somewhere else. "Just stuck it in there, misfiled ten reels of negative. We knew where it was, but they didn't."

Lerner and Chemical eventually came to terms, and the bank sweetened the deal by agreeing to fund four more Laurel productions for ELC release, including a sequel to be called *Mr. Universe in Miami*.[37] Everything seemed fine on January 17, 1951, when *Mr. Universe* had its world premiere at the RKO Grand Theatre in Columbus, Ohio. But two weeks later, on February 2, Chemical Bank called their loan and foreclosed on *C-Man* and *Guilty Bystander*, citing the "eighteen month" clause in their contract. Not rolling over the loan, especially given the current circumstances, was highly unusual and seems to have caught Lerner and Carlton unawares. It would prove to be only the first of a series of foreclosures that would eventually tie up a dozen more independent features. *Mr. Universe* opened at the Palace in New York on March 22, to good business, and in April United Artists completed their purchase of the ELC library, as Chemical Bank always hoped it would.[38] The bank's agreement to finance additional films for Lerner suddenly evaporated, and those four New York films were never made, by him or anyone else. "That got us fairly disgusted, Geri and I, because the truth of the matter is we were looking forward to making something that we wanted to make, as opposed to making something that sounded like commercial product." Lerner quit producing his own films and sought work as a director for hire, on films of such low quality that he was embarrassed to use his real name. "We just walked away from it. We went into whatever was around. I became a whore. The only difference was I didn't peddle it in Eighth Avenue. When they waved a buck in front of me I lay down and hollered 'Roll 'em.'"

Rex Carlton was personally on the hook for these unpaid loans and declared bankruptcy in September 1952, citing liabilities of over $500,000 (although he felt that Lerner and Dorfmann were "also involved in running up this tally"). In his petition to the court he stated that he could not repay Chemical Bank because the bank had taken over all his assets.[39] He continued on the fringes of show business, most famously as writer-producer of *The Brain That Wouldn't Die*, which he made with Joseph Green in 1959. On May 7, 1968, he shot himself in his Hollywood apartment. Milton Gettinger continued negotiating film deals. In December 1952 he sold seventeen Film Classics pictures, which he claimed were all acquired "directly from the producers" to a sub-distributor. The list included *C-Man* and *Guilty Bystander*. He promised that additional FC product "will be picked up from time to time as it becomes available"—in other words, when the loan period expired.[40]

Carlton may have been blindsided by Chemical's move to foreclose on Laurel's assets, but the Lerners were traumatized. Claiming that they were "disgusted" and "just walked away" hardly describes the sudden turn in their fortunes after the bank took action on February 2, 1951. Laurel was then in postproduction on *Double for Della*, another spoof of New York television, this time focusing on a married couple who host a popular variety show and quarrel about starting a family (the airwaves were saturated with husband-and-wife teams like Tex and Jinx McCrary). The film reunited much of the cast and crew of *Mr. Universe*: Robert Alda and Janis Paige starred, with Gerald Hirschfeld, Leo Kerz, and Jimmy Di Gangi behind the camera. Searle Kramer again provided an original script and Gail Kubik was brought back from *Guilty Bystander*. Two weeks later the trades announced that Lerner was out of Laurel and had formed a new company of his own, North American Films, Ltd.[41] By the end of the month the Weisner brothers (Sidney and Irving), investors in the picture, had taken over the film and renamed it *Two Gals and a Guy*.[42] As a United Artists release it opened under that title in August, with neither Joseph nor Geraldine Lerner credited (Alfred E. Green was named as director, while the editor's credit was simply omitted).

Two Gals and a Guy is worse than it ought to be. Lerner had hired an excellent cast, with strong support from Lionel Stander, Arnold Stang, and James Gleason (standing in for Jack Carson).[43] But Searle's script clearly needed work, its television parody lacking the surreal edge of *Mr. Universe*. On the other hand, its dark elements hit much harder than the generalized attack on phoniness and corruption seen in Lerner's wrestling picture. The happily married small-screen couple does not just bicker in real life but disagree furiously on a hot-button issue generally avoided even in serious message pictures: the decision to have children. (The film is obviously modeled on the Betty Grable-Dan Dailey musical, *My Blue Heaven*, but in that case the issue was how to acquire children, not whether or not one should even have them around.) Citing their skyrocketing career, Alda's character flatly refuses to consider any sort of parenthood; Janis Paige storms around in mannish suits, seething at her inability to fulfill a woman's "natural" role, mumbling darkly about playing "second fiddle to a coaxial cable." Pushed to the breaking point, she quits the show and forces Alda and Gleason to replace her with a double (also Janis Paige, now channeling Judy Holliday). This character dynamic is both too painful and too realistic to mesh well with a series of slapstick routines involving drunkenness and mistaken identity that again seem left over from Searle's work with the Stooges. When combined with the film's general slackness in pacing and performance, it makes one wonder if anyone was actually in charge of directing and editing it.

Mr. Universe in Miami was never made, but in April and May 1952 Lerner did find himself at Miami's Ball Studios directing John Loder in *The Miami Story*, a nightclub thriller primarily designed to exploit the talents of stripper Lili St. Cyr. Rex Carlton and Irving Weisner were said to be backing the film, which again was shot by Gerald Hirschfeld.[44] The film seems to have had trouble finding a distributor and was regularly rejected by the Production Code Authority due to suggestive "costume and dance motion." In 1956 the title was changed to *Josette of New Orleans* and a PCA certificate was finally issued the following year.[45] Although Lerner's name had been associated with the film during production, on release the direction was credited to "Joseph Lee." A pressbook survives, but I have never spoken to anyone who claimed to have actually seen this film.

Lerner's friend Hazard Reeves had created the stereophonic sound system to be used in *This Is Cinerama*, a three-screen spectacle that would open in New York in September 1952. In his professional resume, Lerner wrote that he served as "associate producer and one of the directors" of this film, specifically "the trick introduction . . . with Lowell Thomas." But Walter Thompson was credited as "prologue supervisor" and Lerner's name again went unmentioned (and unrecorded in subsequent histories of Cinerama). Once a highly publicized engine of the local filmmaking community, Lerner was slowly becoming invisible.

In May 1953 a reporter from the *New York Times* visited the set of *The Hidden Woman*, perhaps the only film to have been shot at Eastern Teleproductions Studios, a bare-bones operation carved out of the old Alden Theatre in New Rochelle, recently renamed the Astor. Another sleazy vice-ring exposé (the female lead, Rosemary Pettit, also appeared in *Josette of New Orleans*), this claustrophobic film is set entirely in a rundown carnival operated by a cigar-smoking dwarf. The atmosphere of threadbare civic corruption is overpowering. Shot in the style of an early filmed television episode, there are no retakes for flubbed dialogue and the "sets" consist mainly of large swatches of tenting. The producer, Robert Presnell, boasted to the *Times* that Joseph Lerner was directing his $70,000 production, which would be distributed by Astor Pictures Corp., a specialist in race movies, reissues, and exploitation pictures (and also, apparently, the new owner of the building).[46] The cast was drawn from the usual mix of New York acting talent, including Broadway veteran Harry Bannister, television actor Richard Coogan (who created the role of "Captain Video"), and the reliable Frank Albertson, whose extensive film credits included both *It's a Wonderful Life* and *Psycho*. Sharp-eyed viewers can also catch another local television actor, Steve McQueen, swinging a heavy mallet while testing his strength at one of the carnival's few midway attractions.

When we spoke, Lerner admitted to having worked on seven "speed-up" jobs for Astor Pictures but refused to discuss them. "Don't look for them" was as much as I could get out of him, although he did recall taking over "a circus picture" when the original director had fallen "twelve days behind schedule" after the first two days' work (although it is hard to imagine this film having a schedule as long as twelve days in the first place). "Do I want to get involved in this garbage?" he asked his wife after reading the script. "Read the bankbook instead of the script," she answered. Still, Lerner seems to have done whatever he could to make the film visually interesting, shooting from odd angles and taking advantage of the carnival's theatrical lighting to cast intriguing shadows over otherwise mundane dialogue exchanges. As Jake Hinkson notes, the film "has an air of the grotesque that makes it more interesting than it has any right to be."[47] But unlike the modestly budgeted independent productions Lerner had previously been involved with, this is a classic exploitation film that would not even try for a Code Seal: noirish plot elements are frequently interrupted by a series of shabby burlesque numbers that take up almost a third of the running time. Evidence in the New York State Motion Picture Commission archives suggests the film was released as *Honky Tonk Burlesque* beginning in 1954 but existing prints refer to it as *Girl on the Run*.[48] Joseph Lerner is again credited as Joseph Lee.

After this the Lerners left the country and tried their luck in Europe, where Joe worked on the syndicated Italian television series *The Three Musketeers* and collaborated on film projects in Germany, Yugoslavia, Italy, and Greece, often anonymously or under aliases. Although he insisted that he had not been politically blacklisted, this career arc certainly resembles that of Joseph Losey, Bernard Vorhaus, Richard Wilson, Jules Dassin, and many other McCarthy-era film exiles. But he may just as easily have been lying low due to the continuing financial fallout caused by the Chemical Bank disaster, in which he had been "marked lousy" (a favorite expression of his) along with other local producers. When the Lerners returned to New York in 1956 Gerald Hirschfeld met them at the boat and offered Joe a position at MPO Videotronics, where he was able to reinvent his career as a prolific director of television commercials (including Buster Keaton's award-winning slapstick routines for the Ford Econoline van). Lerner remained active well into his eighties but never directed another American feature. He died on November 12, 2005, although the IMDb believes the date was 1976. Perhaps they were confusing him with someone named Joseph Lee.

Last of the Local Indies

The Lerners were not the only New York filmmakers who were essentially driven out of business when Film Classics collapsed and Chemical Bank swooped in to pick up the pieces. In addition to Laurel Films and Louis de Rochemont's RD-DR, two other local firms had managed to get multiple features before the cameras in 1949 and 1950.[49] We have already seen how the Danziger brothers produced an entire film, *Jigsaw*, working out of a small dubbing studio; in 1949 they followed it with *So Young, So Bad* and *St. Benny the Dip* a year later. Edward Leven also tried to follow the model established by *Close-Up* but with skimpier resources. The films he made in 1949, *Project X* and *Cry Murder*, have not been seen in seventy years. Although all of these producers were operating in the same low-budget universe, only the Danzigers would not get caught up in the Film Classics debacle. And what proved crucial here was that only the Danzigers were able to make their films with "no bank participation," a crucial lesson for all future independents hoping to make films in New York.[50]

So Young, So Bad began as a project developed by Hollywood director Bernard Vorhaus, inspired by a news account of a juvenile detention center for delinquent girls. Vorhaus enlisted writer Hugo Butler and his wife Jean Rouveral, who researched the subject and wrote a script called *Runaway*. Paul Henreid, an aging but still bankable leading man, would play the role of a supportive psychiatrist, and he agreed to appear on a participation basis. According to Vorhaus, "several studios were interested in financing it but held off because this was the beginning of the McCarthy period. Although the film was not political in any sense, anything that didn't present America as in every way the best of all possible worlds was suspect."[51] While there is some truth in this, it seems more likely that the studios backed away because Vorhaus, Butler, and

Rouveral had all been Communist Party members and few Hollywood studios were hiring Communists that season. Paul Henreid, never a party member, did belong to the Committee for the First Amendment, a group of Hollywood liberals who traveled to Washington in October 1947 to protest HUAC activities. He found himself blacklisted by all the major studios for the next five years.[52]

In February 1949, around the time Joe Lerner was wrapping up *C-Man* in New York, *Variety* reported that Edmund Dorfmann would finance *Runaway* and coproduce it with Henreid for UA release.[53] But Dorfmann failed to raise the cash and moved on to *Guilty Bystander*; the Danziger brothers then took over the project with the proviso that it be shot in New York, where their studio was located. They leveraged the deal by mortgaging *Jigsaw* and putting the resulting loan into *Runaway*, then budgeted at $550,000, with deferrals for Henreid and Vorhaus. "This will considerably reduce the sum Danzigers will be required to advance," *Variety* noted.[54]

Joseph Lerner had hired old friends like J. Edward Bromberg and Elliott Sullivan to work in *Guilty Bystander*, but the Danzigers were making *Runaway* top-heavy with party members and accused sympathizers (and is it just a coincidence that they also hired Elliott Sullivan, who appears in a small, uncredited role as a security guard?). When I asked Vorhaus about the Danzigers's politics he claimed, "They did not have any particular political interests although they both tended to be liberal in their attitudes."[55] As late as July 10, 1949, when the film had already been shooting for a week, they announced that the story and screenplay of their new film had been written by "Hugo Butler, Jean Rouverol and Mr. Vorhaus."[56] Butler did not receive screen credit, but the reason may not have been political; according to Jean Rouveral, Vorhaus had originally approached her husband (she had no screen credits), but "I don't think Hugo did anything," and she was left to write the script with Vorhaus.[57]

After writing and directing silent films in Hollywood, Vorhaus found himself directing low-budget talkies in Britain, returning in 1937 to produce and direct at Republic. During the war he made films for the Air Force Motion Picture Unit in Culver City, notably *Identification of the Japanese Zero Fighter* (1943), starring Ronald Reagan. Vorhaus remembered being sent to the SCPC in Astoria to make a documentary on the Yalta and Potsdam conferences, which was never released.[58] An experienced low-budget filmmaker, he had recently directed several features for Eagle-Lion, including the notable noir thriller, *The Spiritualist*. As with *Jigsaw*, the Danzigers avoided studio shooting and dubbed all the dialogue in postproduction. The main location during the seven-week shoot was the Yonkers campus of the Jewish Guild for the Blind, near the Sawmill River Parkway at 75 Stratton Street South. Some interiors were shot at the Ninety-Second Street YMHA, while other locations included the abandoned Ruppert Brewery; the laundry of the Vanderbilt Hotel; a potato patch in Wantaugh, Long Island; and the Carousel in Central Park.[59] All these locations were very well shot by Don Malkames, especially the hellish laundry sequences, which look like they belong to a much more ambitious film. Scenes involving fire and water (the girls attempt to burn down their dormitory and are later hosed down by a sadistic matron) were done under controllable conditions at the Fox studio. I do not know the location of the fictional "Faith Elliott Maternity Home," named after the film's script supervisor.[60]

Although *So Young, So Bad* functions as a Paul Henreid vehicle (and he gives much the same performance as in *Now, Voyager*), his character is poorly written and seems drawn from documentaries like *The Quiet One* or *Shades of Gray*. Worse, the film follows the general pattern of Hollywood "psychoanalysis" films in demonizing adult female figures while offering an adult male as sensitive and supportive of these abused young women. The evil matron shaves one girl's head and stomps another's pet bunny to death; Henreid's Dr. Jason, a paragon of understanding, takes the girls out of uniform and sponsors wholesome activities like dances and baseball games. But the scenes with the delinquent girls are all well written and often sensationally played by four young Broadway actresses: Anne Francis, Rosita (Rita) Moreno, Anne Jackson, and Enid Pulver. While Pulver soon turned from performing to playwriting, the other three went on to long and distinguished acting careers, Rita Moreno becoming only the third person to score an EGOT, winning the Emmy, Grammy, Oscar and Tony Awards. Although Moreno was the only one of the group to immediately land a Hollywood contract, the film's posters and advertising always featured the other three: the nymphomaniac (Anne Francis) and the apparent lesbian couple (Jackson and Pulver). Moreno's character, a good girl who is only sentenced to the Elmview Corrective School because she ran away from home, eventually hangs herself and is cut down by Paul Henreid's character. "I am sorry to report that the great actor used the scenes of cutting down my dead body as an excuse to run his hands over my breasts," Moreno wrote in her autobiography. "We did many takes, and, of course, being dead, I could not even flinch, let alone protest."[61] She writes this without apparent anguish or anger, the lines suggesting a weary shaking of the head at what is just another account of doing business in the movies in 1949.

Just as the film was about to go into national release, *Variety* reported that "indie producer" Harry Lee Danziger had been guest of honor at a May 23 Lions Club luncheon at the Savoy Plaza, where he received a letter of commendation from Mayor O'Dwyer "for his efforts in bringing back film-making to N.Y." O'Dwyer didn't show, but Clifford Evans, director of the city's television and motion picture unit, noted that the mayor "wants to keep TV flourishing here and also is eager to have more pictures shot in the area." Frank Lee Donoghue, director of the Department of Commerce, announced, "In the past year some 34 features were made either in whole or in part by Hollywood producers in N.Y., in addition to a number of other pix turned out by local filmmakers."

The hierarchy here is revealing. Television production is already more of a priority than feature filmmaking, while the work of visiting Hollywood producers seems of greater interest than the uncounted number of "other pix" produced locally. And this happened at an awards ceremony intended to honor a local producer who was about to start shooting his third feature (Donoghue did point out that New York made more short films than Hollywood).[62]

On release, the film was compared unfavorably to John Cromwell's *Caged*, with reviewers noting the similarity of various plot incidents in the two women-in-prison pictures. In fact, both films were shot simultaneously in July and August 1949. *So Young, So Bad* was released nationally on May 26, 1950, several weeks ahead of *Caged* (June 10). But *Caged* opened in New York two months earlier so most local critics saw Vorhaus's film as an imitation of the more elaborate Warner Bros. picture. Bosley Crowther dismissed it as a "miserably inept little item" that was "downright embarrassing to watch" and "much worse" than *Caged*, which the *Times*'s lead reviewer had already written off as overheated and unbalanced. Crowther, who was seldom driven to such emotional outbursts, was so incensed by the film that he suggested Vorhaus might soon "be requested to turn in his card by the Screen Directors Guild."[63] In fact, there was no need to do so. Beating it out of the country before they could be summoned to testify, Vorhaus and Henreid were already in France by the end of 1949, shooting a forgotten multi-language production called *Pardon My French*. Henreid eventually returned to Hollywood, but his days as a top star were over; he began a new career as a successful television director (two dozen episodes of *Alfred Hitchcock Presents* alone). Luckily for him, he owned 50 percent of the profits of *So Young, So Bad*, which had overcome its poor reviews to become a "minor sleeper," grossing twice its $500,000 negative cost.[64] His agent had warned him not to deal with "fly-by-night outfits," but "the picture did well and I made more money out of it than anything I've ever been connected with," he wrote in his autobiography. "The Danziger brothers treated me with complete honesty."[65] Bernard Vorhaus never worked in the United States again. Jean Rouverol and Hugo Butler went into exile in Mexico. Before leaving they had written an adaptation of *Robinson Crusoe* that the Danzigers planned to film on various Caribbean locations in 1950, with Jackie Robinson as Friday.[66] That never happened, but in Mexico they were able to sell the script to Oscar Dancigers (no relation), an itinerant European producer best known today for backing Luis Buñuel's Mexican films. Buñuel shot the Rouverol-Butler script in 1952, but Dancigers (unlike the Danzigers) would not allow the names of these blacklisted writers to appear in the screen credits.

The Danzigers' next picture was directed by Edgar G. Ulmer, another itinerant filmmaker, one who had been in and out of the New York film community since 1932. *St. Benny the Dip* is a comedy about three charming rogues who hide out in disguise as Protestant clergymen. Three years in gestation, *St. Benny* suffers from having passed through too many hands on its long and strange journey to the screen. Not only does it lack the topicality of *Mr. Universe*, but it isn't even very funny. As his biographer Noah Isenberg puts it, "comedy was not Ulmer's strong suit."[67] George Auerbach, a sometime writer and producer for MGM and Paramount now producing independently, launched the project with a bang in October 1948 by announcing that he had signed Marlon Brando. The star of *A Streetcar Named Desire* was already being pursued by every studio in Hollywood, but Auerbach won out with a personal pitch. "Mr. Brando was enamored and agreed to do it," the *Times* reported, although the promise of a healthy percentage seems to have helped. Roland Young and Louis Calhern were also attached, with the film set to start shooting in Hollywood, under Auerbach's direction, sometime after June 1, when Brando completed his commitment to *Streetcar*.[68] But Auerbach failed to locate a backer willing to let him direct the picture, and when June finally came he sold the package to the Danziger brothers for a reputed $100,000.[69] Unfortunately, the package no longer included Brando, who soon began work on his real first film, Stanley Kramer's *The Men*.

It is easy to see how Brando might have been attracted to this Runyonesque comedy, which would have allowed him to make his first screen appearance in a role as different as possible from that of Stanley Kowalski (and his appearance in the screen version of *Guys and Dolls* a few years later only confirms his interest in such characters). The Danzigers moved the project to New York and spent almost a year rewriting and recasting the picture. It took them until January 1950 to find a replacement for Brando, the popular crooner Dick Haymes—which of course meant the film had to be rewritten as a musical. After a series of delayed start dates production finally began on April 26.[70]

Unlike their earlier films, *St. Benny the Dip* features few exteriors and was shot mainly on sets at the Filmcraft studio in the Bronx (there is no art director credited, although Don Malkames was again behind the camera).[71] Ulmer was able to use Grace Church as a location and shot some interesting exteriors on the Lower East Side and at a pop-up "mission" the fugitives open near the South Street Seaport. But the one song written for Haymes barely qualifies the film as a musical, while the comedy content also falls short of genre expectations. The lengthy production delays meant that Brando was not the only actor missing in action by the time filming started. Although Roland Young was still featured, Louis Calhern had dropped out and was replaced by blacklisted actor Lionel Stander. On the first day of shooting there was still no female lead; after many months the Danzigers announced they had Beatrice Pearson, but she dropped out at the last minute and was replaced by Nina Foch.[72] *Force of Evil* and *Lost Boundaries* would remain Pearson's only screen roles. The Danzigers must have come close to losing Dick Haymes as well because a radio contract obliged him to fly back to Los Angeles every Friday night, returning on the red-eye two days later. According to the *Times*, "Mr. Haymes was complaining about feeling tired" and had lost seventeen pounds after the first ten round trips (there were three more to go). It was claimed that Haymes himself was paying the $8,500 airfare bill, although it seems more likely that the Danzigers were stuck with it.[73]

While Stander and Young appear to be enjoying themselves, Haymes and Foch both look as if they would rather be somewhere else. As usual in a New York production, the supporting cast consisted largely of Broadway and television actors, with a few European and Hollywood exiles thrown in. Former child star Freddie Bartholomew, last seen in a walk-on in *Sepia Cinderella*, was making his final film appearance, but perhaps the most interesting character actor here was Oskar (credited here as Oscar) Karlweis. Ulmer would have known Karlweis in Berlin, where he had starred in such important Weimar-era musicals as *Two Hearts in 3/4 Time* (1930). He plays the small role of Nina Foch's father, a classical musician having a hard time in an age of too many saxophones. In a confession to "Reverend Benny," he admits that he, too, has a religion: Mozart and Beethoven. One of the few personal touches in an otherwise colorless work, this must have come from the director of *Carnegie Hall*. Reviewers sensed that something had gone amiss, that the film "gives a semblance of not being quite the finished product it should have been."[74] But the Danzigers do not seem to have been unhappy, and in 1951 they hired Ulmer to direct their next film, *Babes in Bagdad*.

Like the Danzigers, Edward Leven had been operating on the fringes of the motion picture industry and felt that producing features would be the best way to get inside. As vice-president of Natco, then the third-largest manufacturer of 16 mm projectors, in 1946 he floated the idea of a chain of automatic, "employee-less" 16 mm theaters, small storefront operations that would run continuously on endless 16 mm loops. Natco would service the theaters by producing a biweekly package of feature and shorts shot in 16 mm at a cost of $45,000 per package. "Initially, well known stars will not be used, and the players will not be identified by name."[75] Leven had previously worked with Telenews Newsreel Theatres and must have seen the project as a logical development of the newsreel theater business.

The theater chain idea never worked out, but Leven soon partnered with Kenneth H. Granger and began producing low-budget features in New York, shooting *Project X* in April 1949 and *Cry Murder* in November. Don Malkames photographed both films, but neither carries a credit for production design or music, elements that Leven apparently considered low priority. It is difficult to say much about the quality of these films because I have not seen either of them, nor do I know of anyone who has since their original Film Classics release. Continuities deposited for censorship purposes with the New York State Motion Picture Commission tell us only that both made heavy use of first-person narration. "I must have sat there ten minutes," the hero of *Project X* tells us in voice-over while describing his visit to a nightclub used as headquarters by Soviet agents. "I couldn't take my eyes off her—she couldn't sing, but it didn't matter."[76]

Project X (also known as *Red Bait* and *Red Spy*) was the first feature directed by Edward J. Montagne, an SCPC veteran who had been making *This Is America* shorts for RKO-Pathé.[77] In an interview in the Screen Directors Guild newsletter, he criticized Hollywood producers who showed up in New York with "a script that is a perfect studio vehicle, but is in many cases impractical for location or documentary coverage." His film, because it was written specifically "to take full advantage of the city's wealth of backgrounds," allowed for a 60 percent cut in the budget, or so he claimed. Over a fifteen-day shooting schedule he is said to have worked on ten different "interior/exterior locations," suggesting that, like *Jigsaw*, the film was not shot in a proper studio but done entirely on exteriors and practical locations.[78] But Montagne may have been more forthcoming in a 1984 letter, when he wrote, "We made the picture in ten days and it cost very little. I don't think I ever got paid." Leven, he remembered, "ran out of money and the Danziger brothers bailed him out."[79]

Produced at the height of the Red Scare, *Project X* is a thinly disguised knockoff of *The House on 92nd Street*, with Communist spies in New York substituting for the Nazi agents in the original. Not much was made in that film of

7.2. Communist spymaster Gigi (Kit Russell) peddles her cigars and cigarettes to Keith Andes and Jack Lord in Ed Leven's *Project X*. Museum of Modern Art Film Stills Archive.

"Mr. Christopher," the female spymaster who dons male attire for a last-minute escape attempt, but here cross-dressing serves as a much more important plot point. Michael Radik, who runs the spy ring from that nightclub, spends most of the film as Gigi, a cigarette girl who uses her easy access to clients to further her spy business. When the hero finally pulls off her blonde wig, Gigi/Radik escapes and leads the police on a crosstown chase, dying in the gutter after a final gun battle. Kit Russell, who according to the *AFI Catalog* was a professional female impersonator, played the spymaster. Jack Lord, an Actors Studio trainee making his first film appearance, was a Communist recruiter.

Lord had a better part in *Cry Murder*, on which he also earned an associate producer credit (in lieu of salary?). The film was directed by Jack Glenn, an experienced *March of Time* staffer who had recently been working for Richard de Rochemont on the *Crusade in Europe* documentary series. Lord—who was himself a serious painter—plays a sinister Greenwich Village artist who blackmails a visiting Hollywood star and winds up a murder victim. Much of the film was shot on location in the Village, Gramercy Park, and at the main post office building, but the narrative was even more dependent than *Project X* on one character's interior monologue: "Time came to a stop . . . for how long, I didn't know. Then my eyes slowly opened. Where am I? Oooo—shambles. Who did that? Wait . . . careful . . . take a look. Dangerous. Tommy . . . something must have happened to Tommy. Without knowing why, I felt terror. Someone wearing checked pants. Who is this man? What was he looking for?"[80]

And so on. Both of Leven's films made it into theaters, but they were poorly reviewed by the few critics obliged to consider them. *The Hollywood Reporter* thought Don Malkames's photography of *Cry Murder* was "fairly well accomplished" but panned Jack Glenn's direction ("he never encourages his cast to do anything but stand about and stare at the camera while they deliver their dialogue"). Worst of all, "the records used as musical backgrounds do nothing to help the picture," the downside of not hiring someone to write a proper score.[81] Even the good parts, like the location work, failed to hold up on closer examination. "Most of the excitement occurs in the final scenes, where the villain, trapped by the police, shoots it out with them on the steps of New York's General Post Office building," *Harrison's Reports* concluded, "but even this sequence had a ludicrous touch because of the fact that the background shows several policemen directing traffic, completely oblivious to all the shooting taking place within one hundred feet of them."[82] Both films opened in New York on double bills at neighborhood theaters, where unlike the work of Joe Lerner and the Danzigers they were ignored by Bosley Crowther. I did find one review out of Pittsburgh, but critic Gene Januzzi still found only one bit worth commenting on: "The fact that many of its scenes on the city streets have been shot with no attempt to keep spectators from intruding on the action gives you an idea how bad this little piece is."[83]

Both of Ed Leven's films were caught up in the litigation surrounding the failed FC-EL merger. Perhaps Chemical Bank was involved as well. A note in the files of the New York State Motion Picture Commission from 1957 says that United Artists had lost its rights to *Project X*, which had reverted to Kenneth Granger.[84] But UA never seems to have distributed the film in the first place. Not held by any film archive or claimed by any distributor, *Project X* and *Cry Murder* simply vanished. On February 19, 1950, the *Times* reported that another Film Classics release, *A Game of Cards*, would begin filming in New York within a month. A Technicolor feature "in the tradition of such surrealist offerings as *Blood of a Poet* and *Dreams* [*That Money Can Buy*]," it would be written and directed by the poet and translator Richard Thoma and star the well-known dancer and choreographer Valerie Bettis.[85] Thoma was said to travel in the same circles as Jean Cocteau and Henry Miller; his brother Paul, responsible for such bizarre short subjects as the 1946 Gloria Swanson pilot, *Dear Miss Gloria*, was set to produce. According to the *Times*, the film dealt with "two men and a woman and a dancer, begins in a waterfront café, comes to a climax in a lonely villa and ends on a windswept beach." *A Game of Cards* was never released and may never even have gone into production; how big a part the collapse of its prospective distributor played in its demise is impossible to know.

Despite their apparent fiscal stability, the Danziger brothers disappeared as well, at least from New York. By the end of 1951 they were producing *Babes in Bagdad* in a Barcelona studio; the following year they turned up in London, where they founded "the most financially successful independent television production company in the UK."[86] In addition to some four hundred television episodes produced between 1953–1961 they also tossed off dozens of cheap features while further developing the cost-cutting strategies they had pioneered in New York—including offering work to blacklisted talent in no position to argue over salary. "I was introduced to the Danziger brothers," Joseph Losey remembered, "who wanted to know if I would supervise a television series without putting my name on it and direct some. So for most of 1953 I worked for the Danzigers and they paid me $100 a week under the table so I didn't have to pay tax on it, and that is what I lived on. . . . The television series were absolutely appalling, but at least it was work and I could live!"[87] True, the shows themselves may have been appalling, but the real value of the Danziger operation was its function as a talent incubator (Richard Lester was another early employee). What the Danzigers set up in London was not so different from what Roger Corman would be doing in Hollywood a decade later. But no such incubator started up in New York, where after the false dawn of 1950 the local film industry began to go downhill rapidly.

The fact that Mayor O'Dwyer never showed at the luncheon honoring the Danzigers for "bringing back film-making to N.Y." was probably a bad omen.

Instead, he had sent Frank Lee Donoghue, his Commerce secretary, to boast of the $5 million that the film industry annually spent here on salaries alone, while Manhattan Borough president Robert F. Wagner, Jr. touted the "great era of prosperity" that would result from the increased cooperation now being extended to film and television producers. O'Dwyer himself would soon be gone, replaced by Vincent Impellitteri, the City Council president. But would Impellitteri bother to run with this ball? Did he even understand what it meant that the labor situation in Hollywood had improved and that New York had still not delivered on the additional studio space producers had been clamoring for since 1946? And while the *Times* did not pick up on it in their coverage, *Variety* thought it important to note the splash of cold water that Donoghue himself tossed on the proceedings.[88] In return for the city's cooperation, he suggested, film producers ought to show New York in "its true light" and refrain from coming in with scripts that "louse up" the city. He seems to have been especially peeved at *City Across the River*, as well as *The Sleeping City*, an upcoming Universal-International crime thriller, shot at Bellevue Hospital, that pictured New York's most celebrated medical facility as a noirish hellhole. Why extend cooperation to films like that when you might be encouraging something more productive? From now on the city would be choosier about this film business. Producers reacted as one might expect: Hollywood suddenly began to look more attractive again, and even the Danzigers packed up and moved to Europe.

CHAPTER 8

JUST PASSING THROUGH

The delayed response to the success of *The Naked City* and the city's streamlining of its permit process peaked in 1949–1950. Despite the financing catastrophe that would soon take down a few unlucky independents, the city seemed more attractive than usual to visiting Hollywood companies, and a few local producers still managed to shoot some films of their own. Unfortunately, New York's newfound popularity was happening a few years too late. In 1948, American theaters sold an average of ninety million movie tickets every week; by 1950 the number had dropped to sixty million, a figure that would continue to fall for decades.[1] In response, the major studios cut overhead, reduced the number of films they handled every year, and made sure the ones that remained were filled with "must-see" elements like stars and spectacle. None of this played to the strengths of New York cinema, which may have owned the margins but was still lacking such basic elements as adequate stage space. New York filmmakers would create a response to these new conditions, a response that would revolutionize the way movies were made all over America. But that would take a few more years.

End of a Genre

There is probably no better example of the way these inflated expectations soon came to grief than in the abortive Yiddish film "revival" of 1950. That January two Yiddish-language features opened on Broadway, with two more in release soon after. The last such films had been made here in 1940, the genre being disrupted by the destruction of its European markets and a lack of access to raw stock that had put all producers of marginal cinema out of business for the duration. Joseph Seiden had pioneered the Yiddish talkie in the early 1930s, and as late as 1945 had been filming race movies at his Palisade Avenue studio in Fort Lee. But there were no new Yiddish pictures: not only had the old domestic and European markets collapsed, but a hoped-for "distribution in Palestine . . . was denied us because of the ban on Yiddish dialogue in favor of Hebrew, the country's national language."[2] Seiden seemed to have written off the entire genre in a May 1949 piece for the local Screen Directors Guild newsletter, admitting that "the audience for Yiddish films is dying out and most of the films I make today are used by Jewish organizations in fund-raising campaigns."[3] So what caused him to go into production on *God, Man and Devil* (*Got, Mentsh un Tayvl*) just a few months later?

Described by J. Hoberman as Seiden's best and most expensive film, *God, Man and Devil* was a throwback to the golden age of Yiddish theater, a Faust story detailing the corruption of a pious Jew.[4] Based on a 1900 Jacob Gordin play, the unusually stagy film was shot on a few small interior sets, probably at Seiden's current Cinema Studios operation at 106 West End Avenue.[5] On his first appearance, Satan wears a theatrical devil's costume straight out of Gounod or Spencer Williams. But its old school trappings mask a political subtext that, while not uncommon in early Yiddish films, seems downright radical for 1950. The film is a straightforward anticapitalist allegory, with a hero who begins modestly by copying Torah scrolls but then makes a fortune by opening a prayer shawl factory, essentially a *tallis* sweat shop.[6] This not only destroys his family but the artisanal community that had once done this work. His ultimate suicide (death by one of his own prayer shawls) is seen as a positive resolution, an indication that he had finally seen the error of his money-grubbing ways.

Although reviewed by the *Times*, which felt that the story "seems to have lost a great deal in its journey up from Second Avenue," *God, Man and Devil* was ignored by its intended audience—if such an audience even existed any longer. Historian Eric Goldman says that Seiden "was overwhelmed by the failure of his first 'big name' production. There no longer seemed to be any interest in Yiddish culture."[7] He was already in postproduction on his next film, *Three Daughters*, a sentimental piece of *shund* that looked back to the Yiddish cinema's other great tradition, the tear-jerking family melodrama. Described by Hoberman as "a mesmerizing spectacle of free-floating resentment and implicit self-loathing," it seems to have been released directly to the 16 mm market, bypassing conventional theater dates entirely.[8] The last dramatic Yiddish film produced during the classic period, it followed the last race movies by only a year or two.

But as with the race movie, music and comedy continued to keep this genre alive for at least another few months. Only a few days after *God, Man and Devil* opened to no business at the Stanley, a very different Yiddish film, *Catskill Honeymoon*, began a successful run a few blocks away at the Ambassador. The *Times* also reviewed this film, although it felt compelled to note that it was "not indeed a movie in the ordinary sense of the term."[9] More like an infomercial or a televised variety show, *Catskill Honeymoon* is an aggregation of music and comedy numbers designed to promote Ma Holder's Young's Gap Hotel in Parksville, New York, the heart of the borscht belt (straight up Route 17, so we are told). This is not necessarily a bad idea, as the shamelessly commercial montage that opens the film is probably the most interesting piece of work in it. After a few minutes spent with an elderly couple celebrating their fiftieth anniversary, *Catskill Honeymoon* follows with a series of songs and skits, not all of them in Yiddish, that serve to remind us that such hotels had already supplanted Second Avenue as a cultural center (its relative box office success may also have owed something to this bilingual element). The director, Josef Berne, had made one of the top Yiddish films of the 1930s, *Mirele Efros*, but spent most of the previous decade directing Soundies; his career never seems to have lived up to the promise of *Dawn to Dawn*, an impressive independent short he made in Hollywood in 1933.

Seiden saw the way this wind was blowing and assembled a compilation revue of his own, *Monticello, Here We Come!* The film may also have been released as *Borscht Belt Follies*. Or that might have been a different film entirely; sources are unclear.[10] By this time Seiden had assembled a significant archive of old Yiddish pictures, some of which he had made himself, others scavenged from rival producers. Over the years he kept this catalogue in constant release, in both 35 and 16 mm, and would also assemble compilation features created by dipping into the collection. Hoberman refers to *Monticello, Here We Come!* as "a veritable Seiden retrospective," revisiting footage he had shot as early as 1930.[11] If *Catskill Honeymoon* was an infomercial, *Monticello, Here We Come!* plays more like *That's Entertainment!*, a memorial to a cultural moment whose time had come and gone.

Yiddish pictures and race movies had served to anchor what remained of New York's feature film economy during the leanest period of its history, and race movies in particular were a major factor in the early postwar years. But by 1950 both genres had lost their audience and could never again support a revival of local feature film production. That would come through the documentary-inflected *policier* spun off of *The Naked City* itself—not just locally developed projects like *C-Man* and *The Tattooed Stranger* but a fistful of visiting Hollywood productions that followed directly in the wake of Hellinger's picture. Three of these films, all shot in 1949 on B-movie budgets, demonstrate how even a city with no usable stage space could still play a role in a major studio's release schedule: *Port of New York* (Eagle-Lion, directed by Laslo Benedek); *The Sleeping City* (U-I, directed by George Sherman), and *The Killer That Stalked New York* (Columbia, directed by Earl McEvoy).

Crime City

Port of New York was to have been one of two New York "documentaries" made for Eagle-Lion by the notorious "keeper of the Bs" Bryan Foy, and both this film and *Trapped* were supposed to be shooting there that summer.[12] But Foy seems to have moved *Trapped*, a Secret Service procedural, to Los Angeles, and by the time *Port of New York* was released he had already relocated to Warner Bros., having turned the project over to Aubrey Schenck. Phil Karlson had originally been announced as director, but before he left Foy brought in Laslo Benedek, a protégé of Joe Pasternak whose most recent film was the notorious Frank Sinatra musical, *The Kissing Bandit*.

Influenced by *T-Men* as much as *The Naked City*, *Port of New York* shows how Bureau of Narcotics and Customs agents destroy a drug smuggling ring masterminded by Yul Brynner. Eventually they track the drugs to the "Club Gay," a local nightspot where the MC does a killer impersonation of Charles Laughton's Captain Bligh. Benedek cast Brynner after seeing a screen test he had done for Fox; he liked him because he looked "strange" and was a new face.[13] Brynner would not be seen in another film until 1956, when he appeared in *The Ten Commandments*, *The King and I*, and *Anastasia*. "This is the Port of New York," the voice-over tells us over obligatory footage of the skyline and the harbor. All the exteriors were shot in New York, and the principal actors are seen at Penn Station (opening every locker with a passkey!), meeting informants at the Canal Street elevated station, and walking in and out of various public buildings. Benedek recorded no dialogue on location, and all interiors were done on Hollywood sets. The film does boast some excellent "agents at work" montage scenes, credited to John Hoffman, a Slavko Vorkapich protégé. But in a 1984 interview, Benedek complained about the "incompetent" New York crew he was forced to hire to cover the men he brought from Hollywood. "New York crews were known to be unreliable," he told me. His own cameraman, George Diskant, is best known for Nicholas Ray's *They Live by Night* and *On Dangerous Ground*, although the bulk of his career was spent shooting filmed television episodes.

Benedek felt that *Port of New York* was not film noir but just a crime story done in semidocumentary style. That put it squarely in the *Naked City* tradition, where the structures of civic society are not only dependable but incorruptible. The same could not be said of *The Sleeping City*, shot in New York in October and November as Universal's acknowledged follow-up to the Hellinger classic. Not only was Weegee once again hired to "expert" the picture, but exhibitors were shamelessly exhorted to "tie in *Sleeping* with *Naked*."[14]

On its release, *The Sleeping City* was awarded a certificate of civic merit by the Commerce Department, which cited it as "the first feature-length screen play to be made here in its entirety by a major West Coast producer within modern times."[15] There are a lot of qualifiers in that sentence, which carefully navigates around films like *Carnegie Hall* (not a major producer?), *The Window* (remember those collapsing tenement interiors?), and even *The Naked City* itself. But only a few months earlier it seemed more likely that *The Sleeping City* would instead bring down the wrath of Mayor O'Dwyer on the entire motion picture industry.

Produced as *Confidential Squad* (and also known briefly as *Web of the City*), *The Sleeping City* was based on an original story and screenplay by Jo Eisinger, whose script for *Night and the City* was being shot simultaneously in London by Jules Dassin. The U-I producer Leonard Goldstein, better known for the "Ma and Pa Kettle" and "Francis the Talking Mule" series, cloaked the entire production in mystery. "Nobody knows about this subject, and we will keep it a secret as long as we can," he announced to the *Los Angeles Times*, admitting only that "it will begin somewhere near where the late Mark Hellinger's famous film, *The Naked City*, left off."[16] Goldstein was used to working quickly, and perhaps some twist in Eisinger's story encouraged him to go into production as soon as it crossed his desk; it was very unusual for a modestly budgeted film to borrow both of its stars, Richard Conte and Coleen Gray, from a rival studio, leaving only one small role for a U-I contractee, Peggy Dow. The rest of the cast consisted largely of New York actors with little or no Hollywood exposure, U-I recruiting promising talent from such plays as *Detective Story, A Streetcar Named Desire*, and *Mr. Roberts*. Indeed, the *Times* reported that "all but three of the top roles in the drama . . . are performed by [local] theatre, radio and television personalities," with five to six hundred local extras also getting work.[17]

New York police are assigned to investigate the murder of a young intern at Bellevue Hospital, referred to here as "City Hospital." Undercover cop Richard Conte is planted among the new crop of interns and quickly discovers that the entire staff is overworked, depressed, and indebted to a garrulous old elevator operator/bookie named Pop (the Broadway veteran Richard Taber). "I swing hard, but there's nothing at the other end for my fist to smash into," mutters one of this hopeless crew. When they are unable to pay, Pop coerces his victims into providing him with stolen narcotics instead. Perhaps the most terrifying parts of the film occur when Detective Conte, pretending to be a doctor, administers injections and various other medical treatments to unsuspecting patients (an enormous amount of smoking also takes place). The big surprise comes when the potential love interest, Nurse Ann Sebastian (Coleen Gray, the heroine of *Kiss of Death*), is also revealed to be part of the drug ring. Despite protesting that she was only helping support a sick niece, Conte turns her over without batting an eye—an echo of Humphrey Bogart's treatment of Mary Astor at the end of *The Maltese Falcon*.

Bill Miller, the local cameraman on *The Naked City*, was brought back as director of photography on *The Sleeping City*, which was shot with an all New

York crew (although U-I made no known use of local labs, equipment houses, or studio facilities). This was possible because an agreement had been signed by the three regional cinematographers' Locals on August 16, 1948. When a film originated outside the jurisdiction of Local 644, the agreement stipulated that if at least two-thirds of it was being made in its territory, the entire crew would be composed of 644 members and no outside men would be brought in.[18] *The Sleeping City* may have been the only feature produced under this agreement, which was simply an accord among union locals and not binding on film producers. It was designed to prevent choice assignments like *Boomerang!* and *The Naked City* from automatically being filled by outsiders, but until Hollywood producers were comfortable with the work of New York cameramen it probably did more to discourage them from doing any extensive shooting here.

Miller used a range of wide-angle lenses to film inside claustrophobic interiors—office spaces and intern's quarters but also basements, mechanical rooms, and darkened hospital wards, where action always seems to be happening at night. Exteriors were shot at other recognizable New York landmarks—the Williamsburg Bridge, the Thirteenth Precinct police station, the Automat. "It's the only way to produce pictures," Miller had told a reporter from the *Times* a few months earlier. "Audiences get tired of dressed-up stuff. They want to see something real. There's never yet been a studio set that could give the same effect as the actual location."[19] Not only was dialogue recorded in situ, but the sound man, Corson Jowett, boasted that *The Sleeping City* was "the first full-length movie by a major studio to be recorded on magnetic sound-recording tape," a process he described in an interview with the *New Yorker:*

> You record something, play it back, and find out your mistakes, if any. The old sound film has to be developed and processed, and that takes a lot of time. We send a day's take out to the Coast on the night plane, and out there the sound is transferred to sound film, the tape is erased, and they send it back to us, ready to use again. We've used the same twenty thousand feet of tape about two hundred times now, and it gets better all the time.[20]

Jowett took advantage of his presence in New York to record fire engines and other authentic sounds of the city, not for use in this film but simply to add to the studio's library. His success in recording practical interiors on location demonstrated that filmmakers could now, quite literally, cut the cables that had bound them to studio soundstages. Unfortunately, George Sherman, a B-western specialist, was unable to get much out of the actors or the script, and the film was panned for missing a rare opportunity. Bosley Crowther may have been unfair in comparing it to the recently opened neorealist hit, *Bitter Rice*, but he still chided U-I for using "that magnificent place [Bellevue] as a background for nothing more than a routine cops-and-criminals film."[21] Crowther, it should be remembered, had not been all that impressed with *The Naked City*, either, which he dismissed as a superficial billet-doux. So it is surprising that he missed the very dark tone that colors every frame of *The Sleeping City*. Yes, the police do break up the drug ring, but the happy ending with Nurse Ann turns bitter, and nothing at all is done about the conditions at Bellevue that led to all the trouble in the first place: city hospital interns turning to crime as they attempt to make ends meet on $50 a month (some plan to marry into a wealthy practice, others give up the profession entirely). Miller's spooky lighting, and the amount of time spent in cramped tunnels and dormitories, lends visual support to Eisinger's unusually dark worldview.

When Mayor O'Dwyer first saw a cut of the film in May 1950 he "hit the ceiling," as *Variety* put it in a page one article. "His ire was particularly aroused by the fact that the pic includes in its story incidents showing cops and nurses stealing dope from the hospital shelves to peddle elsewhere." He summoned U-I's president, Nate Blumberg, to Gracie Mansion, along with Columbia's Jack Cohn and MGM's Nicholas Schenck, and announced that "the city would not cooperate any longer with Hollywood troupes if U did not tone down its film."[22] Universal, of course, capitulated immediately. First, they eliminated all traces of police involvement in drug trafficking, leaving the onus entirely on the nurses and interns. But they also agreed to append a ninety-second prologue to all prints of the film, in which Richard Conte, "dressed in white and accoutred [sic] with a stethoscope and other medical trappings, speaks directly to the audience to tell that the film does not describe any specific city in the U.S."[23] The mayor immediately ordered all departments to ignore his previous order and renew cooperation with Hollywood. The recut version proved so satisfactory that not only did U-I receive the civic citation mentioned above, but the studio reciprocated by bestowing a "gold-plated, pearl-handled .38 Colt service revolver" on the chief of detectives along with a citation of their own praising "the outstanding devotion to duty ... which characterizes the detective division of the New York Police Department."[24] The acting mayor, Vincent Impellitteri, attended the luncheon in place of O'Dwyer, who had been forced out of office a few weeks earlier.

The *Sleeping City* fiasco is more than just a bizarre footnote in this history. On an immediate level, the film's hoped-for authenticity was undercut by the insistence that it was all made up, simply a work of fiction. One out-of-town paper devoted their entire review to this issue. "The result is that a picture whose raison d'etre is reality spends great care in assuring you that what you're watching is just a fairy tale."[25] Producers would now have to reassess the value of this whole "realism" business, which seemed to carry with it a potential for unforeseen problems. New York's vaunted cooperation with the film community was also called into question, appearing now as a mercurial policy that could be on one week and off the next. And the fact that Bill O'Dwyer, who was well connected to the film industry, would no longer be around to guide this relationship added another element of uncertainty. As we will see, Hollywood's use of New York as a location dropped precipitously beginning in 1950, although it is hard to place the blame for that on any single incident or individual.

Finally, it is worth considering that curious prologue, in which Richard Conte (wearing the medical costume he wears in the picture when his character *pretends* to be a doctor) tells us about the real Bellevue he discovered while filming there—its dedicated staff, its excellence as a teaching facility, and the new buildings already under construction. Cutting a film for censorship reasons is an old and unremarkable story, but producing what is essentially a new film, intended to recontextualize (and to some degree reverse) the original, is rare. One suspects that Universal-International was not very happy about this, and the rest of Hollywood would also have taken note. In any case, the major studios would never allow the city to put them in a position like this again.

Less ambitious as a work of New York cinema—but more interesting for its use of New York history—was Columbia's *The Killer That Stalked New York*.

8.1. Evelyn Keyes contaminates a public drinking fountain in Battery Park. *The Killer That Stalked New York* was a melodramatic rendering of the city's 1947 smallpox epidemic. Author's collection.

The film imposes a now conventional tale of crusading Treasury agents onto a docudrama recreation of New York's March–April 1947 smallpox epidemic, combining two alien infiltration plots in one nightmarish urban melodrama. The last smallpox epidemic in American history, the disease had arrived in New York along with a tourist who became infected in Mexico. A dozen people came down with the disease but only two of them died, thanks largely to a massive vaccination program that inoculated five million people in two weeks. The film originated in a nonfiction magazine account of the epidemic, but screenwriter Harry Essex soon added a plot in which the carrier is not a tourist but a jewelry smuggler who has picked up both the disease and a shipment of stolen diamonds in Cuba. "It began on a November day in 1947," the narration tells us, a voice-over that functions equally well for both its documentary and film noir plot elements. Treasury agents and Health Department inspectors follow a trail of clues that wind up leading to the same person (Evelyn Keyes). Because the smallpox carrier thinks she is only being pursued as a smuggler, she does her best to hide from medical authorities, unknowingly giving the epidemic more time to develop. Then, in a disturbing noir twist, she learns that her husband, for whom she has smuggled the diamonds, has been carrying on an incestuous affair with her own sister. Keyes holes up in a Bowery flophouse run by her brother (Whit Bissell), picturesquely located near the Spanish-Portuguese Jewish Cemetery on St. James Street. She succeeds in wreaking vengeance on her two-timing husband, who has also dumped her sister, but by the end of the film is so ravaged by the disease that she looks more like Gloria Grahame at the end of *The Big Heat*.

Shooting in New York began on November 21, 1949, just after Universal's *Sleeping City* company had returned to Los Angeles.[26] O'Dwyer's municipal film production unit, now headed by Cliff Evans, documented the making of the film for a promotional short to be called *Hollywood Comes to New York*. Evans also planned to cover the filming of Fox's *Fourteen Hours*, but it is unclear if any such film was ever actually completed.[27] Of the principal actors, only Keyes seems to have made the trip, which also included visits to Battery Park, Chatham Square, Willard Parker Hospital (the city's infectious disease hospital, repeating the role it played in the actual epidemic), Penn Station, and Gracie Mansion.[28] The film is careful to give the mayor considerable credit for managing the vaccination program, hence the Gracie Mansion scenes, in which an unnamed Bill O'Dwyer is played by character actor Roy Roberts (who had just appeared as mobster Ben Tucker in *Force of Evil*).

The ending of the film credits both the New York and Los Angeles Departments of Health and Hospitals, and many of the locations were, in fact, shot in LA. The dramatic climax, where the villain falls to his death from a high building ledge, is obviously South Third Street in downtown Los Angeles, with the marquees of the Central and Cozy Theatres clearly visible. In one of those awful Hollywood coincidences, the film went into production just before Fox's bigger-budget Elia Kazan picture, *Panic in the Streets* (urban location: New Orleans; fatal disease: pneumonic plague). Columbia held up the release of its film, which had been completed first, until three months after *Panic in the Streets* had opened, but this was probably a futile gesture.[29] "Seventy-six minutes of decided unpleasantness," one trade paper said of it. "In the opinion of this critic, there is no reason why a picture based on such a harrowing and grisly theme should have been produced. In addition to the unpleasantness of seeing a horrible disease take effect, the picture offends good taste in another way: it is clearly implied that a sister had illicit relations with her sister's husband."[30] Columbia, attempting to sell a film that included distinct film noir and docudrama elements, appears to have succeeded in offending audiences on both accounts.

Of course, not everything being shot in New York in 1949 was either a rip-off of *The Naked City* or a Yiddish picture. Films as different as *Lost Boundaries* and *Guilty Bystander*, largely produced with local talent and independent financing, may not have seen themselves as part of a new wave of American regional cinema, but in retrospect that is clearly what they were. Yet their impact on critics and audiences was generally as modest as their budgets, and only a few trade papers thought much about them at all. What City Hall was focused on was luring some of those Hollywood production days back east, and all through 1949 most of the permits they issued went to what we might call legacy cinema—Hollywood films that just happened to use New York as their principal location. That includes *The Sleeping City* and *The Killer That Stalked New York*, of course, but also at least ten other major studio productions that came and went that season, among them half a dozen MGM features that worked in and around the city between April and September alone.

Fox was here first, with Joseph Mankiewicz bringing Richard Conte and Susan Hayward east for location inserts on *House of Strangers*, an immigrant saga set in Depression-era New York. Although Edward G. Robinson starred as the patriarch of a family of Italian-American bankers not unlike the Gianninis, it was Richard Conte, squeezing in another New York picture between *Cry of the City* and *The Sleeping City*, who featured in most of the location work. On March 6 the *Times* reported that Mankiewicz had "spent the wee hours of several days last week," shooting exteriors for the film: the Second Avenue Baths, a subway kiosk on Central Park West, and various locations in Little Italy were all featured.[31] Mankiewicz used quite a few local actors, many of them veterans of the city's Italian-language theater companies, but the film's "Hollywood Italians," hired on the West Coast, seem to have had some difficulty matching their accents.

The independent producer Benedict Bogeus sent Robert Florey's company to New York in July to film exteriors for his Damon Runyon adaptation *Johnny*

One-Eye.[32] Florey's photography of New York is striking, and the film begins with an intriguing ferryboat murder, the victim unceremoniously dumped into the harbor (Bill Miller shot the New York sequences while Lucien Andriot did the rest of the picture). The killing eventually catches up with gangster Martin Martin (Pat O'Brien), who staggers around Greenwich Village while slowly bleeding to death from a nasty gunshot. The film, which has been channeling Carol Reed's *Odd Man Out*, now shifts to full Damon Runyon mode, leaving Florey to cope with both a small child *and* a cute little dog, as well as "the most devastating 'Doll' in the Runyon gallery" (Dolores Moran).[33] Edward Dimendberg, one of the only writers to discuss the film, notes that the Village has replaced the midtown east locations of the original Damon Runyon story. The shift to an older, more horizontal, New York skyline reminds him of the precarious nature of this built environment, whose structures can be thought of as "imminent victims" of the city's skyscraper modernization.[34] But perhaps the streets and alleys around Washington Square also worked better as stand-ins for the Belfast locations so memorably documented in Carol Reed's film.

Around this same time Kirk Douglas was also in New York, filming location scenes for *Young Man with a Horn*, a fictionalized biography of jazz musician Bix Beiderbecke. Most of the film was shot in and around Los Angeles, but the dramatic climax is an extended sequence in which the despondent musician staggers around downtown Manhattan (Brooklyn Bridge, etc.) before collapsing in a drunken stupor and apparently breathing his last in an alcoholic ward. Except—surprise!—he manages to pull himself together and become the great man and great musician we all knew he was. At least this is what the narrator tells us—we never see it on screen. I don't know who was responsible for staging and photographing this nightmarish ending (perhaps it was the director of photography, Ted McCord, or his second cameraman, Ellsworth Fredericks). If there was a separate New York man on the picture, as with *Johnny One-Eye*, he went uncredited.

And again there was Leonard Goldstein, whose *The Sleeping City* would be honored as the first film by a Hollywood major to be shot entirely in New York "in modern times." It seems that Goldstein had prepared for that exercise by shooting quite a few segments of his previous film here. *Ma and Pa Kettle Go to Town* brought the rustic heroes of the *Egg and I* franchise all the way to New York, winners of the Bubble-O radio jingle contest. This gambit justifies a lot of "fish out of water" comedy, as well as a host of tourist-eye views of the city, from Grand Central Terminal to the Waldorf Astoria, Columbus Circle, Park Avenue, and Rockefeller Center. What is remarkable about these dopey vignettes is that Universal apparently recorded live dialogue on location. If not, then they certainly went to a great deal of trouble to carefully loop dialogue that had not actually been recorded there. This accomplishment was not only ambitious but technologically sophisticated, and one has to suspect that Goldstein did it mainly to practice recording strategies that would be used again on his all-location drama, *The Sleeping City*, which went into production only a few weeks after the Kettles returned to Cape Flattery.

The MGM Surge

When Mayor O'Dwyer summoned Hollywood executives to his office in May 1950 there was no one in attendance from Fox, whose interest in New York production had already begun to cool. Instead, his attention was directed at Nate Blumberg and Jack Cohn, whose studios were responsible for *The Sleeping City* (Bellevue) and *The Killer That Stalked New York* (Willard Parker). But there was a third executive present, Nicholas Schenck, president of MGM, who *Variety* said "is close to the mayor and an unofficial spokesman for the industry [and] has been trying to intercede and pacify both sides."[35] Schenck was also there because his own studio had shot far more films in the New York area over the past year than any of his Hollywood rivals. MGM's own medical film, *The Doctor and the Girl*, had managed to use both Bellevue and Columbia-Presbyterian Medical Center without suggesting that patients would do well to steer clear of either facility.

MGM's spurt of activity in New York had been managed by William D. Kelly, dubbed their "Eastern Trouble-Shooter" in a lengthy *Newsweek* profile. "Kelly acts as advance guard whenever one of his firm's production units moves East," it said. "In this capacity he must possess not only a supreme talent for being polite to city officials, but an unerring eye for the kind of legal booby trap that camera crews off the home lot have come to regard as a sort of occupational disease."[36] At the time of the interview, Kelly was supervising the work of four visiting MGM units simultaneously. To film one shot of Glenn Ford exiting a cab in front of Columbia-Presbyterian for *The Doctor and the Girl*, for example, Kelly had to wrangle permission "from the cab company, the hospital manager, the hospital police, the Screen Actors Guild, and the regular police." Kelly had been part of the industry group that worked with Edward Maguire to streamline the city's own filming regulations, but those were never the only permissions visiting filmmakers had to worry about. The fact that other studios seem to have lacked their own dedicated fixer may help explain why only MGM units were appearing so frequently on New York streets.

Of course, *The Doctor and the Girl* was hardly the sort of film noir thriller that would cause City Hall's switchboard to light up. Plotted somewhere between *Arrowsmith* and the "Dr. Kildare" series, the film was a conventional medical melodrama in which an idealistic young intern (Glenn Ford) must decide what sort of medicine he will choose to practice. Bellevue is not seen as gloomy or run-down—just a big public hospital where most of the patients are housed in wards, very different than the private hospital where Ford's snobbish father (Charles Coburn) is a powerful surgeon. As with *The Sleeping City*, there is some suggestion that one route to fame and fortune is to marry into a wealthy practice, but that dilemma is handled on a soap opera level and there are reasonable alternatives. Both Ford and his sister (Gloria DeHaven) resist their overbearing father, Ford falling in love with a penniless taffy-machine operator (Janet Leigh) while the sister makes good on her threat to move "somewhere in the Village, with a skylight." She does find a cute little spot on Patchin Place, but her misguided quest for independence eventually leads to pregnancy, abandonment, and death in a botched abortion (apparently self-induced, so no medical personnel are implicated). Ford settles down with Janet Leigh, opening his own practice above a delicatessen and below the Third Avenue El. *Showmen's Trade Review* indicated that the director, Curtis Bernhardt, was to spend two weeks on the location scenes but then reported him back in Hollywood only a week later.[37]

"Yes, this is my town ... the most exciting in the world," Barbara Stanwyck tells us in the voice-over narration that introduces MGM's *East Side, West Side*. But Stanwyck doesn't appear to have set foot in New York during the production, and all we really see of it, other than some back-projection plates, is the establishing shot of a car driving down East Eighty-Fourth Street near Gracie Square. This attractive, upscale Manhattan location also appears in films like *Gentleman's Agreement* and *The World of Henry Orient* (1964), popular because it dead-ends at the river and access could easily be controlled for filming purposes.

While Manhattan was often synonymous with "New York" in films made by visiting Hollywood companies, a few, like *Letter to Three Wives* or *Boomerang!*, would also venture off to the suburbs, some traveling as far as the outskirts of Princeton. *The Happy Years* was another MGM production managed by William Kelly that summer, a rare period film not shot on the studio's extensive back lot but in and around Lawrenceville, New Jersey, mainly at the exclusive Lawrenceville Prep School. The director, William Wellman, who specialized in the social dynamics of male groups under stress (*Wings, Wild Boys of the Road, The Ox-Bow Incident, The Story of G.I. Joe*), adapted a series of classic "coming of age" stories published by a Lawrenceville graduate in 1910. How do boys become men? After failing to discover enough capable local talent, Wellman cast veteran child actors Dean Stockwell and Darryl Hickman and spent two weeks in Lawrenceville with a Technicolor camera crew. "They were cordially received by the school authorities and the city officials who allowed a portion of Trenton's Main Street's macadam roadway to be covered with dirt to represent the dirt road that was known as the Trenton Turnpike in 1895," *Photoplay* reported.[38] Nostalgic, highly personal, and almost entirely out of alignment with the tastes and expectations of postwar audiences, *The Happy Days* lost

MGM over a million dollars and may have played a role in Louis B. Mayer's ouster from the studio the year after it was released.

George Cukor, who began his film directing career at Paramount's Astoria studio and spent some time at the Signal Corps Photographic Center during the war, had already returned for one postwar feature, *A Double Life* (written by Ruth Gordon and Garson Kanin). He would return again for three more Kanin films, a cycle of "New York" pictures that Patrick McGilligan feels "prodded Cukor away from artificiality and Hollywood clichés towards a naturalism and verisimilitude that were more in keeping with postwar tendencies and realities."[39] *Adam's Rib*, *The Marrying Kind*, and *It Should Happen to You* would all feature Judy Holliday, a Cukor protégé he had first directed in a small role in *Winged Victory* (1944). After years of working club dates and resort hotels she became an overnight sensation in Kanin's *Born Yesterday*, stepping into Jean Arthur's role when the star suddenly left the show just weeks before its scheduled Broadway opening in 1946. But translating this Broadway success into a film career was no sure thing, and while *Adam's Rib* is in many ways a conventional Tracy-Hepburn vehicle, it also functions as Holliday's screen test for the film version of *Born Yesterday*. (Harry Cohn, who at first refused to even consider "that fat Jewish Broad," would change his mind after seeing her play a remarkably similar character here.)[40]

Spencer Tracy and Katharine Hepburn stayed in Hollywood during the production of *Adam's Rib*, their "New York scenes" constructed entirely through the use of doubles or back projections. But the film does open with an engaging sequence in which Holliday's character stalks her husband (Tom Ewell) from a Bowling Green office building at 9 Broadway to a side street Brownstone at Lexington and Fifty-Second. She lurks behind candy stands and pops in and out of real subway entrances, although the trains and the station are strictly Hollywood backlot. The *Times* reported that filming the "dozens of takes" required for this business took from 10:00 a.m. until 4:00 p.m. on May 11 (I would be surprised if the rest of the location work took more than another day or two).[41] McGilligan writes that Holliday was "scared to death, and fumbling her lines and movements"; he blames her for the multiple takes. This was clearly not the case because there are no lines to fumble here. We do hear Ewell whistling Arthur Freed's "You Are My Lucky Star" as he walks up to the Brownstone, but even that would have been dubbed back at the studio. Holliday was still working in *Born Yesterday*, so she probably did ingratiate herself with the crew by handing out passes to the show, which had been running for three years on the strength of her knockout performance.[42] That one sequence (and a back-projected ride down East River Drive) is about all we see of New York in *Adam's Rib*, despite the fact that Cukor had announced on Bill Leonard's "This Is New York" program that "the entire production [was] to be made in the east."[43] It must have sounded better that way, and in any case, who would even notice?

Both Cukor and the Kanins liked working in New York, the Kanins because they lived there and Cukor because it gave him the opportunity for a subsidized visit to Broadway. In truth, there seems to be no other reason to have filmed any of *Adam's Rib* in New York or even to have set the picture there (unlike, for example, *A Double Life* or *It Should Happen to You*). So Cukor and MGM took advantage of the junket to scour the theater district for more acting talent. Tom Ewell was a busy Broadway actor who also starred in at least five Paramount Pacemaker comedies that season, one-reel comedies like *The Football Fan* (directed by Justin Herman) that were among the only traditional live action shorts still being made in the east. Other New York stage and screen actors signed for the picture by MGM included David Wayne, Jean Hagen, and Hope Emerson, but Cukor didn't even use them in the location sequences, which only feature Holliday and Ewell.

Far more rooted in the culture and geography of the city, and featuring almost nine minutes of principal photography, was MGM's reimagining of *On the Town*. A musical hit that established the careers of Betty Comden and Adolph Green (who had previously worked the club circuit with Judy Holliday as "The Revuers"), the property had been purchased by MGM even before its 1944 Broadway opening. The fact that it took five years to reach the screen was not especially unusual (*Pal Joey*, *Oklahoma!* and *Finian's Rainbow* all took far longer), but transplanting a wartime narrative into the postwar cultural scene forced a series of accommodations that significantly altered the character of the original show.

On the most obvious level, the bulk of the music composed by Leonard Bernstein was jettisoned and replaced by new Comden and Green numbers scored by Roger Edens. Opinions differ as to why this was done and what effect it had on the quality of the film, but the MGM version was certainly a far greater popular success. What interests us, however, is the decision to shoot parts of the film on location and the way this rare achievement was accomplished. In his otherwise authoritative history of Arthur Freed's production unit, Hugh Fordin inexplicably claims, "This was the first time any major studio sent a company to shoot musical sequences on public sites in New York."[44] But MGM had already sent a full musical unit here three years earlier, when they shot the signature number for *It Happened in Brooklyn*, to playback, on the pedestrian walkway of the Brooklyn Bridge. With Frank Sinatra. In uniform. Fordin's claim has been repeated by almost everyone who has written anything about *On the Town*, including the compilers of the *American Film Institute Catalog*.[45] It takes nothing away from the achievement of codirectors Gene Kelly and Stanley Donen to say that they were not the first to do this. Instead, we need to honor their tenacity because after *It Happened in Brooklyn*, MGM continued to film the numbers for such "New York" musicals as *Easter Parade* or *The Barkleys of Broadway* entirely on the back lot (and would continue to do so with films like *The Belle of New York* and *The Band Wagon*).

A second misconception is that the film was produced in the teeth of what Stephen Silverman calls "the mulish MGM mindset against shooting on location." Given that we are discussing *On the Town* in the context of the half-dozen MGM features that shot in the New York area in 1949 alone, the real question should be why codirectors Gene Kelly and Stanley Donen were not allowed to film more of the picture here. Silverman quotes Stanley Donen as putting the blame on J. J. Cohn, the studio's hard-nosed production manager.[46] But if Cohn approved all those other pictures (not to mention so many other MGM features shooting everywhere from Florida to the Cinecitta studios in Rome) there must have been something specific about *On the Town* that required Arthur Freed to intercede for a project most sources claim he did not much care for.

Perhaps Cohn was worried about the ability of his two novice directors to cope with something of such complexity so far from the studio. Perhaps he was thinking of *Portrait of Jennie* more than *It Happened in Brooklyn*. He needn't have worried. The single musical number that was shot in New York was so carefully planned that its genesis hardly resembled the creation of a typical Freed unit song and dance number. In fact, "New York, New York" is an outlier not only in this film but in the MGM musical canon in general, avoiding the painstaking rehearsals and retakes used to develop something like the "Day in New York Ballet" and substituting an intricate montage sequence for the long takes more typical of a back lot MGM musical. The film opens at dawn in the Brooklyn Navy Yard. Not the San Pedro docks or a back lot construction fleshed out with a Warren Newcombe matte shot but the actual Brooklyn Navy Yard. At a given moment (documented by a streaming zipper chyron at the bottom of the screen), a crew of sailors disembark for their twenty-four-hour shore leave. We will follow three of them—Gene Kelly, Frank Sinatra, and Jules Munshin.

What makes this number so unusual is not the fact that it was filmed on location but exactly *how* it was filmed. A fast-moving piece of ensemble work, it doesn't belong to anyone in particular—not the dancer (Kelly), the singer (Sinatra), or the comedian (Munshin)—but instead puts itself forward as the product of those creative people *behind* the camera. For a film that is otherwise committed to the traditional presentation of ballads or ballets built around the theatrical talents of its stars, "New York, New York" revisits the more self-consciously cinematic musical tradition developed by René Clair and Rouben Mamoulian. In films like *À nous la liberté* or *Love Me Tonight* the musical numbers were not simply the photographic record of a singer or dancer's dynamic performance but an exercise in cutting and camera placement that moved the real creative focus over to someone who wasn't even on screen. In an interview with Joseph Andrew Casper, Donen admitted that he loved the musicals of Clair, Lubitsch, and Mamoulian, found "some interesting things" in Busby Berkeley's films, and "didn't like [Vincente] Minnelli's musicals, except for *Meet*

8.2. Gene Kelly, Jules Munshin, and Frank Sinatra (in uniform) check the angle on Prometheus during a Rockefeller Center location shoot for *On the Town*. In the back row, Hal Rosson (cameraman) and Stanley Donen (director) with the Technicolor camera crew. Museum of Modern Art Film Stills Archive.

Me in St. Louis."[47] Purists sometimes bemoan the loss of Jerome Robbins's choreography, which was replaced in the film by Kelly and Donen's own ideas. But while Kelly was clearly calling the shots in the traditional dance numbers, "New York, New York" is Donen's opportunity, and he makes full use of it to channel Rouben Mamoulian, not just *Love Me Tonight*, but his innovative Broadway staging of shows like *Porgy and Bess* and *Oklahoma!* What we might have seen if the team had been able to film the whole picture in New York (or even most of it) can only be imagined.

This famous number, which takes up almost the first five minutes of the film, soon leaves the Navy Yard for a breathless tour of storybook New York: Brooklyn Bridge (the second time for Sinatra), Wall Street, Chinatown, Little Italy, the Statue of Liberty, Washington Square, Grant's Tomb, Cleopatra's Needle, and Rockefeller Center. Filming required not only a very loud playback system but a heavy Technicolor camera, albeit without the cumbersome silencing blimp required when shooting live sound. Many of these locations appear for only a few seconds, informational montage units slotted into a prerecorded score. Of course, a limited amount of improvisation was possible even here. "The other day we took a walk through Central Park and saw some people riding horses, and we decided to get a shot of the three of us riding horses, instead of that old rowboat corn," Kelly told a reporter from the *New Yorker*.[48] Then again, a few ideas couldn't be worked out exactly as planned. The open-topped double decker Fifth Avenue bus, which had made a (back-projected) appearance in *The Clock*, had been discontinued in 1946; a brief shot taken as the trio rides past the Atlas Statue in Rockefeller Center was actually made on a flatbed truck (look carefully for the folding chairs in the back of the shot). When this was pointed out to him at the time, all Kelly could say was "Our picture is timeless."[49]

None of this happened without a great deal of preparation. William Kelly, as usual, was looking after MGM's interests (although Fordin says that the company's "experienced, well-respected unit manager" was somehow "out of commission" by the time of principal photography).[50] Silverman reports that Roger Edens was in town for most of January, when he "laid the groundwork for the shoot" while also handling delicate negotiations with Leonard Bernstein.[51] The second-unit director, Andrew Marton, followed in April. Comden and Green told the *Times* that his unit was "shooting background stuff at the Brooklyn Bridge, the Brooklyn Navy Yard, Grant's Tomb and Carnegie Hall," suggesting that Marton was not only filming inserts and back-projection plates but functioning as a location scout, checking the best angles and lighting for a laundry list of potential locations.[52] The main unit came to town on May 5 and left on May 23, a tight schedule for a very intricate location trip.[53]

While Munshin was bored and Sinatra annoyed by the strain of filming on location (the crooner's disappearance at key moments almost proved disastrous), Gene Kelly was energized by filming in front of the crowds.[54] "This is like dancing in a theatre," he told one reporter. "There's nothing to equal the impetus you get from a couple of thousand eyes watching you, instead of a bunch of electricians. It makes you feel like a round actor again."[55]

A return to the Navy Yard ends the film where it began, with a four-minute sequence in which the boys bid farewell to their girls and three new sailors get off the ship. The camera rises up on one of the Yard's immense cranes, leaving us with a dramatic view of an overcast skyline and the traditional MGM end title: "Made in Hollywood, USA." The ninety minutes in between make use of Marton's inserts and back-projection plates in an attempt to maintain a semblance of location authenticity. But the visual clash between the Navy Yard and, say, the studio-bound Coney Island episode, can hardly be dismissed as just a charming theatrical conceit. Once we have seen that 360 degree pan from the top of 30 Rock, it is jarring to be pulled back to Culver City's version of the Empire State Building. As Betty Comden said, "The opening part of the picture was great. The rest wasn't."[56]

The film's commercial success suggests that audiences thought otherwise. So did Arthur Freed, once he had seen what Kelly and Donen delivered. After running the musical sequences he wrote his directors to say "they were the most inspiring works I have seen since I have been making moving pictures. Pressburger and Powell can't shine your shoes—red, white or blue."[57]

So why was Comden so disappointed with the film? After all, she cowrote the screenplay and all the new musical numbers. But now she and Adolph Green were no longer in the show, and there were other cast changes, notably the presence of the dynamic Gene Kelly, a dancer and a star whose character would need to be central. Frank Sinatra was also a star, but he was not directing the picture, which was being produced as a dance musical. Beyond the impact of such casting decisions, the five years that had gone by since the show first opened might as well have been a generation. The filmmakers not only had to write some new pop songs in a more fashionable style but also had to accommodate the cultural shift in gender roles that quickly followed the end of the war. To be blunt about it, the trio of self-reliant women the sailors encounter, who have been making their own way on the home front since Pearl Harbor, are now considered ancient history. In the film, the men have to ask Brunhilde Esterhazy why she is still driving a cab, a wartime fact of life in New York that now seems a curious anachronism. The character herself, previously accepted at face value, becomes a comic eccentric, not the representative of an uneasy sexual revolution. To judge this for ourselves, we can look at *Army-Navy Screen Magazine #1*, a military magazine reel produced at the Signal Corps Photographic Center in 1944. The end of this episode features a piece of Hildy's big number, "Come Up to My Place," as played by original cast members Nancy Walker and Cris Alexander.[58] Betty Garrett and Frank Sinatra do a great job with this in the film, but one can sense that an edge has been rubbed off here, and it was probably this edge that Betty Comden missed when she saw what time, and MGM, had done to her show.

Oddly enough, it would seem that MGM's previous New York picture, *Side Street*, may actually have grown edgier in the course of production, thanks to director Anthony Mann, a recent recruit from Eagle-Lion already responsible for such powerful noirs as *T-Men* and *Border Incident*. Hedda Hopper had reported that MGM was preparing "a documentary on the New York police department," which made it sound like another fact-based location melodrama highlighting the good work of America's law enforcement agencies.[59] The voice-over narration is delivered by a police captain (Paul Kelly), which suggests a cop's point of view, and the force did a lot more than simply keep the crowds at bay, supplying ten police cars for the film's climactic cross-town action sequence.[60] But this is no *Naked City*, and the cops in *Side Street* are little more than background characters, the focus here being entirely on one hapless delivery boy who sinks deeper and deeper into a black pit of duplicity, alienation, and despair. In fact, the narration here is not only misleading but illogical, as Kelly describes actions of which the police are unaware—something that would not have been an issue for omniscient storyteller Mark Hellinger in the earlier film.

If *The Sleeping City* is a more conventionally dramatic version of Hellinger's film, *Side Street* goes off in yet another direction, channeling the French poetic realist movement so bluntly that it is surprising to discover that the script is an original, not the remake of some depressing prewar French masterpiece (like *The Long Night* [1947], which revisits Marcel Carné's *Le jour se lève* [1939]). Farley Granger plays a war veteran who has "lost the gas station" and will soon have three mouths to feed, the birth of his child halfway through the film being a key plot element. An ordinary working-class type who might have been played by Jean Gabin in the original, Granger falls prey to a moment of temptation and decides to steal $200 so that his wife (Cathy O'Donnell) will not have to give birth in a charity ward. There is no femme fatale goading him, gambling debts to be paid off, or a plan for life on easy street. All he wants is a private room, a matter of proper medical care and income inequality also at issue in one of MGM's other current productions, *The Doctor and the Girl*.

But the package he steals actually contains $30,000, the proceeds of a blackmail scheme being run out of the office of a crooked attorney. Taking some time to consider his options, he asks a friend to hold the package; of course, the friend immediately looks inside and runs off with the money. There is no working-class solidarity in this picture. Because he is a good person, Granger foolishly confesses his theft to the lawyer. For the rest of the film he runs around New York looking for the friend, with both the murderous blackmailers and the police in hot pursuit (the cops know nothing of the $30,000, and only want him for a couple of killings—there is a high body count in this film). The climax comes when those ten police cars converge on a taxicab racing down Wall Street, which then flips over right at the foot of George Washington's statue.[61] Granger is wounded badly enough to pass muster with the Production Code Administration, which would have insisted on some degree of punishment for his having given in to temptation earlier in the picture. Some critics dismiss this as a happy ending, but that only works if we discount Granger's legal jeopardy, broken bones, and hopeless job prospects. This is really quite a dark film.

In most traditional examples of Hollywood film noir, what audiences saw was the arbitrary intervention of *fate*, which periodically stuck out a foot to trip up the hero of Edgar G. Ulmer's *Detour*, for example. Here Farley Granger's problem is not just one bad choice springing from a moment of weakness but the overbearing effect of *destiny*: it is pretty clear that he has been sliding in this same direction his entire life. Think Paris in the 1930s (*Le Quai des brumes*), not Berlin in the 1920s (*Die Strasse*). We see this even in the decor—less shadowy and exaggerated, more lived in, and unarguably real.[62] In noir terms, this is something like the difference between *Scarlet Street* and *Sunset Boulevard*. Accordingly, as the camera looks straight down at its piers and office buildings, narrator Paul Kelly starts the film by describing New York as "an architectural jungle, where fabulous wealth and the deepest squalor live side by side." We never see the usual skyline panorama but instead a topographical map marked by deep canyons and spiky office towers. It is almost too easy to describe this as the maze through which our hero will soon be racing. The end for these characters is not controlled by the whim of some god but by the pattern of the maze.

The characters played here by Farley Granger and Cathy O'Donnell seem intended to evoke the roles they created two years earlier in Nicholas Ray's *They Live by Night*. Adrift in a great cruel world to which they have never been properly introduced, this attractive young couple is not destined for success. But while Granger runs with a criminal gang throughout *They Live by Night*, he merely succumbs to a moment's temptation in *Side Street*, a crucial shift that only makes it seem more like a prewar French tragedy (Simone Simon as the young bride?). Ray's film had been shot two years earlier, but like *The Window* it was shelved by RKO's new owner, Howard Hughes, and not released until November 1949, just one month before MGM opened *Side Street*. Ordinarily, the commercially successful pairing of two stars might be expected to generate audience interest in seeing them "together again," but that could not have been the case here. It would be interesting to know the casting logic behind this, especially as both stars had to be borrowed from rival producers, an added cost that was never agreed on without good reason.

Although the *Brooklyn Eagle* wrote that MGM would make two-thirds of the picture in New York, the real figure was much lower (the *Times* reported a few weeks later that the unit had already "wound up a fast ten-day shooting schedule and moved West").[63] But the film gives the *effect* of having been shot almost entirely in New York, a remarkable achievement that even extends to most of the interior spaces. Visual cues in *The Naked City* make it relatively easy to tell studio spaces from practical interiors, but that game is much harder to play here, with nearly all interiors sharing the same cramped "location feel." The sound recording on both interiors and exteriors is remarkably sophisticated, and unlike the *On the Town* crew (which dubbed even nonmusical dialogue), Mann's company seems to have taken the trouble to record at least some live sound for their New York footage.

They also appear to have brought their own stunt men, Frank McGrath and Carey Lofton, who doubled for Granger and his nemesis (James Craig) in the taxicab scene. "McGrath, who has wrecked many a car during his hazardous career, was thoroughly disgusted by having to go through twelve 'takes' before he got the cab to do its flip-flop," the *Times* reported. Each take inflicted more damage, from dents and scratches to a series of flat tires and one entire wheel replacement. They did ten takes before lunch (fortunately, this was a Sunday morning), each time the cab rolling off the curb but then failing to wind up on its back. Dangerous for the drivers, the scene was also risky for the cameraman, Eddie Hyland, who was shooting from the ground—another low angle—with a rope tied around him to pull him to safety, just in case. After lunch two more takes were required before the cab managed to turn turtle, but even then it continued rolling and again wound up on all four wheels.[64] There had been filmed chases through the streets of New York for years, from silent movie days to *The Dark Corner*, but this was certainly the most spectacular to date, a worthy ancestor of the memorable *French Connection* chase two decades later. In a useful post to his "Crime Thriller Cinema" site, Max Alvarez documents all the downtown locations, showing how a sequence that begins on the studio's back lot "New York Street" turns into a relatively logical tour of Tribeca and the City Hall district.[65]

As with all the other films they shot in New York that year, MGM heavily promoted the use of locations, even exaggerating their importance whenever possible. *Side Street* shot at both Bellevue Hospital and the Stuyvesant Polyclinic, where Cathy O'Donnell's character gives birth. Saks Fifth Avenue, Bowling Green, and the Fulton Fish Market also appear, as do numerous Greenwich Village locations. Granger's odyssey justifies many of these locations: a tip sends him in search of nightclub singer Jean Hagen, but all he knows is that she used to work somewhere on Christopher Street.[66] He has no luck at Marie's Crisis Café—still a popular piano bar at 59 Grove Street—but eventually tracks her down to the fictitious Les Artistes (a studio set, where Hagen sings Cole Porter). But perhaps the most chilling bit of location realism involves the brief sequence where a police barge pulls a woman's body out of the East River. Filmmakers seem to have been fascinated with this issue of bodies in the river, a plot point in *The Naked City, The Sleeping City, Johnny One-Eye*, and various other New York location thrillers.[67] In the 1956 RKO-Pathé Screenliner short *Where Is Jane Doe?*, a missing-persons procedural that begins with the grim work of the Harbor Police, we are told that two hundred bodies are pulled out of New York waters every year. To prepare for the harbor scene in *Side Street*, police took William Kelly and other MGM staffers out for a trial run to see how this unit operated. "We actually found a body," Kelly reported to *Newsweek*, "a man's though—it had been drifting around in the river a couple of months."[68]

CHAPTER 9

PICTURES AND POLITICS

New York may have avoided the labor violence that disrupted film production on the West Coast just after the war, but by the 1950s so had Hollywood. Once the IATSE succeeded in turning back the challenge of the Conference of Studio Unions, producers would not have found Edward Maguire's promise of labor peace quite so impressive and would have looked instead at the quality of New York's work force and studio facilities. The steady employment of specialized workers characteristic of the American studio system had ended in New York back in the 1930s, when Paramount and Warner Bros. shut down their local studio operations. What replaced it was an early version of today's gig economy, with everyone from painters and teamsters to directors of photography employed by the individual job, the week, or even the day. Because of the broad jurisdiction of IATSE Local 52, these workers would move back and forth among a range of employment opportunities, from Broadway musicals and nightclubs to television commercials, newsreels, and the occasional theatrical motion picture. New York crews were forced to develop a wider range of craft skills than their peers in Hollywood, which was good, but they also lacked the single-minded dedication to one employer—or even one type of job—that gave their peers in Hollywood a different sort of edge.

In practice, this meant that visiting Hollywood production units could be very unhappy with the attitude of New York crews, who were not used to doing things the Hollywood way. Although the situation was different for the top men, lower-paid workers generally saw little chance of long-term opportunity in these infrequent gigs and found no reason to put themselves out for visiting producers who might never work here again.

The problem would reach a climax in April 1965 when director Delbert Mann held an angry news conference at the close of the *Mister Buddwing* shoot to announce that he "would never again come back to New York to shoot a film," due to "the most incredible example of non-cooperation by almost every local union concerned I have ever experienced."[1] A longtime supporter of New York production whose films included *Marty* (1955), *The Bachelor Party* (1957), and *Middle of the Night* (1959), Mann lashed out at the "uncooperative, sullen and arrogant attitude" of local union members who seemed determined to "take this company for every penny we can get."[2] This was not the first time a Hollywood producer had left in a huff, but Mann's status meant that the *Buddwing* affair could not go unanswered. A few years earlier he had praised his *Middle of the Night* unit as "comparable to any Hollywood crew. As a matter of fact, they pride themselves on their ability and the 'keep-'em-in-the east' kind of spirit and attitude. They're a crackerjack bunch, they really are. I can't see any difference between their abilities and that of the crews with whom I've worked on the coast."[3] But even then, Mann allowed that there was a clear difference between the crew he worked on in this all–New York picture and the technicians available during the one week of location work allotted to *Marty*. In that case, "a production coming in just for that limited period of time could only get men who were not otherwise engaged," he remembered, "so they were not top-notch quality all the way down the line. This we found out after the fact."[4]

The full story of the *Buddwing* fiasco is complicated, but strained relations between local unions and out-of-town producers certainly had plenty to do with it. Within months a new mayor, John V. Lindsay, would create a municipal Motion Picture Commission as one way of stopping the bleeding. "That was an embarrassment, I can tell you that. *Buddwing* was an embarrassment," admitted Sol Negrin, ASC, twice president of Local 644. Negrin, recalling his experience in the business since 1948, described to me a career in which the better element among the city's film workers had engaged in a constant uphill struggle against entrenched forces of nepotism and corruption.

> There was a lot of featherbedding and a lot of crap that goes on. An electrician can get a smoke, get a drink. He can walk off, and disappear from the job and he wouldn't be missed.... All of them can't do it, but if a guy wanted to go get a drink he wouldn't be missed, I can tell you that. And they had a lot of guys that were drunkards, and I mean drunkards. Would come back from lunch—drink like crazy—would come back and be impossible to work with. Dangerous.[5]

In this atmosphere, he felt, producers could easily distinguish someone who "wasn't a slouch" from the mass of deadwood around him, and despite the inevitable presence of featherbedding slackers, the skill and enthusiasm of the best technicians always made itself known. Happily, such bad behavior had all but vanished recently, at least in his experience, perhaps a function of the vast expansion in local production that had energized the entire business. "The attitude of the younger generation is completely different now [in 2016]. Very cooperative. The younger group are much more conscious of their craft and loving the craft, wanting to be part of the craft. These older guys—yeah, they were filmmaking people, but it was a job."[6]

Unfortunately, no matter how bad your work habits, it was almost impossible to lose that job in 1952, especially if you had been in the business forever and had deep union connections. That was the year the general manager of Warner News had written to Local 644's business representative to explain why they were terminating one cameraman whose job was otherwise protected by the union. The company was allowed to reduce staff for "reasons of economy" but needed to provide a litany of charges to explain why only this one man would be affected:

> He is no longer dependable. He normally is from three to four hours late in reporting for duty in the morning. When actively engaged in coverage he works extremely slowly and misses many scenes which the normal cameraman would get.
>
> He cannot work harmoniously with fellow employees. Many members of our organization have refused to work on assignments with him. His constant complaining and offensiveness make it undesirable to use him on a story requiring pleasant and courteous consideration of outside people.
>
> He fails to conform to the normal operating rules of our Company. He has at numerous times used a Company automobile on his personal affairs without permission and without the knowledge of the necessary parties. In one instance he cracked up a car which he had taken without permission. He has been constantly delinquent in filing his expense accounts. He has been regularly in debt. Your Union has frequently found it necessary to report to us his failure to pay his dues to the union.[7]

Even so, Warner News was only reducing his status from that of full-time employee to "one day per week guarantee" because this was all the union contract would allow.

Between 1946 and 1948 the trade papers had been filled with stories debating the pros and cons of New York as a potential film production site, but the situation had cooled way down by 1950. There were still no new studios, the union situation no longer seemed so advantageous, and the financing that had once backed independent producers like Laurel and RD-DR had evaporated. The precipitous drop in theater attendance affected the entire industry, but the way Hollywood reacted—making fewer and more elaborate films—was not a strategy designed to help low-budget producers on either coast.

And the industry's chief local booster, Bill O'Dwyer, was on his way out.

O'Dwyer had seemed ambivalent about running for reelection in 1949, issuing contradictory statements and confusing even his supporters. But brushing off the threat of several anticorruption investigations, he was reelected in a three-way race to a post he seemed to have little desire to actually hold. He was said to have suffered a heart attack soon after the election and in December flew south to recuperate in Florida. There he married socialite Sloane Simpson, with whom he honeymooned until February 1950.[8] When he did get back to New York his media interests seem to have shifted from movies to television, and he proclaimed the week of July 16, 1950, as "Television Week" in New York. There was nothing very strange about this. The city had established its own television production unit in 1949, and in economic terms the broadcast industry had already supplanted the production of filmed entertainment.[9] But what hurt was the mayor's prediction, in a telecast from the Waldorf Astoria, that by 1952 the American public would have deserted movie houses in order to stay home with their television sets, and "that's the way it should be."[10] If this wasn't bad enough, it looked as if O'Dwyer would be forced to testify before Senator Estes Kefauver's Crime Commission, then about to begin a series of televised hearings that would soon attract the largest audience in the history of the medium.[11] O'Dwyer's departure had been rumored for months, and in August he suddenly handed in his resignation, accepting a convenient presidential appointment as ambassador to Mexico. The mayor quickly made plans to leave the country but stayed around long enough to enjoy the ticker-tape parade his supporters staged for him.[12]

As it turned out, O'Dwyer found that he couldn't hide from Kefauver indefinitely. On March 19, 1951, he appeared to give testimony regarding his failure to pursue charges against mob boss Frank Costello following the death of Abe Reles, as well as a notorious 1942 meeting with Costello at which he was rumored to have sought Mafia assistance in winning the 1945 Democratic mayoralty nomination.[13] This sad affair interests us here not only because O'Dwyer had once been effective in promoting the city's film and television interests, but because his downfall would itself become a major media event, one of the first live entertainment spectacles to be splashed across screens both large and small all over the country.

Local viewers could choose to watch the testimony at home or on a newly developed network of theater television screens, from the New York Paramount to Century's Queens, a modest outer-borough picture palace. Most theaters projected the show using RCA's "instantaneous" video system, but the Paramount used that company's proprietary "intermediate" film system, which transferred the video feed into a projectable motion picture print, a technology that offered a brighter image at the cost of a slight time delay. The two competing systems were designed to present sporting events and live performances but also used newsworthy attractions like the Kefauver hearings as demonstration pieces. Some theaters let audiences in for free during the morning session, while "intermediate" playhouses seem to have held back the broadcast and run it during breaks between features. *Motion Picture Daily* praised the show as "the biggest hit yet on television" and reported audience response as "enthusiastic."[14]

But the vast majority of viewers still watched O'Dwyer's testimony right at home. The mayor had predicted that one day television programming would empty the nation's movie houses, and that is exactly what happened with the Kefauver hearings (that his own presence helped fuel this success was an irony he probably failed to appreciate). Twenty-two cities carried the live feed, and in New York, the nation's largest market, 70 percent of all sets were tuned in, double the ratings for the 1950 World Series.[15]

Because Costello had complained about the coverage, television cameras were only allowed to show his hands as he spoke, a bit of theatrical staging that made his testimony unforgettable. But O'Dwyer's appearance was also memorable, one broadcast industry magazine reducing the hearings to "the finger tappings of Costello, [and] the angry darting glances of O'Dwyer."[16] George Walsh, in his account of O'Dwyer's checkered career, found that by the end of the hearing, "O'Dwyer's hair, earlier carefully groomed, had become disheveled, his face was red with anger beneath the tan; the color of his shirt was limp with sweat. He was a man facing judgement."[17]

To add insult to injury, Fox Movietone quickly prepared an hour-long condensation of the hearing, produced by Edmund Reek from one hundred thousand feet of raw newsreel footage. Promoted as "A Great Public Service That Only the Exhibitor Can Perform for His Community," its posters ballyhooed the event as a literal face-off, with a column of "Investigators" (Kefauver, et al.) versus another of "Witnesses" (Frank Costello, Ambassador O'Dwyer, Anthony Anastasia, Virginia Hill, and Jacob "Greasy Thumb" Guzik, among others).[18] Putting O'Dwyer in this seedy company seems the equivalent of Emil Jannings returning to his hometown at the end of *The Blue Angel*, the unwilling star of a humiliating burlesque. But while O'Dwyer's reputation may have suffered, he was never convicted of any crime or even placed under indictment. Many of his close associates did not fare so well, including Police Commissioner William P. O'Brian, who had replaced Wallander in 1949 and was forced to resign not long after his boss left for Mexico, a scapegoat for all the gambling payoffs that police in Brooklyn had long enjoyed.

The new mayor, Vincent Impellitteri (the tabloids called him Impy), appears to have had less interest in the city's entertainment industry than any mayor since the 1920s. In February 1951 he returned Edward Maguire to the post of commerce commissioner (he had been serving as director of labor relations), but the film industry was no longer a priority at City Hall.[19] O'Dwyer seemed to have been right when he looked into the future and saw only television. As far as the public was concerned, the "golden age" of live-from-New York television was far more compelling, and media attention quickly turned away from the city's struggling theatrical motion picture business. During the early 1950s, Sidney Lumet, Arthur Penn, George Roy Hill, Robert Mulligan, Martin Ritt, John Frankenheimer, and Franklin Schaffner were all at work in New York, but they were directing television dramas, not motion pictures. Live music and variety shows tied up more local talent (Sid Caesar, Jackie Gleason). Producers even found a few rental studios capable of hosting such episodic series as *Man Against Crime* (live from 1949 and on film beginning in 1952). And the least glamorous aspect of this new medium, the filming of television commercials, proved to be a gold mine. "Production of TV commercials became the main source of Local 52's work in this period—its basic bread and butter—and retains this importance to this day," wrote Sam Robert, editor of IATSE Local 52's house paper in 1963. "Madison Avenue became to Local 52 what the major studios became to Hollywood—its creative source of work. (New York produced 70 percent of all TV commercials in 1962.)"[20]

With this sort of competition, whatever theatrical film production may have taken place during this period has never made it into the pages of most histories. Even the official history published by the the New York City Mayor's Office of Film, Theatre and Broadcasting in 2006 jumps almost directly from *On the Town* (1949) to *On the Waterfront* (1954), mentioning only a single film along the way, *Little Fugitive* (1953).[21] In reality, things were never as bleak as that. The Department of Commerce, which issued the city's motion picture permits in those days, was proud to announce that "portions of thirty-eight Hollywood films—a record number—were made in the city" in 1953, a 20 percent increase over the 1952 figure.[22] So why have historians had such a hard time getting a grip on whatever was happening here between 1950 and 1953?

Being distracted by the growth of local television production is only part of the answer. More significant was the lack of a compelling historical narrative. There was no Lindsay, O'Dwyer, or La Guardia leading a pro–motion picture campaign. There was no dominant genre—the last police procedurals of the *Naked City* era were shot in 1949—and no one studio seemed especially interested in filming here the way MGM had been in 1949, or Fox in 1945–1947. Instead, a lot of Hollywood filmmakers were just passing through, looking to add value to their productions through a quick dose of local color, something that can be said of anything from *How to Marry a Millionaire* to *Abbott and Costello Go to Mars*. Despite the figures offered by the Commerce Department, the use of the "million dollar back lot" for more than a few establishing shots had clearly fallen out of favor. Darryl F. Zanuck, once a major proponent of location work, now felt that the success of films like *Miracle on 34th Street* had come at too high a price. "It costs just as much to take a company on location as to build sets in our studios," he told columnist Hedda Hopper. "We got some wonderful atmosphere in *Kiss of Death*—but we paid for it."[23] Sam Fuller's *Pickup on South Street*, shot in September 1952, was exactly the sort of film that might have taken advantage of a week in New York to add a gloss of location realism; now it shot on the Fox lot and used downtown Los Angeles to double for Manhattan.

Zanuck was still sending crews to New York in 1950 but not for cops-and-robbers pictures. Henry Hathaway's work on the de Rochemont-influenced *Fourteen Hours* has already been discussed. Although Joseph Mankiewicz had come east to shoot parts of *Letter to Three Wives* and *House of Strangers*, he filmed most of the locations for *All About Eve* in and around the Curran Theatre in San Francisco. Only a second-unit crew worked in New York, where doubles were shot entering the John Golden Theatre, "21," and a few other recognizable local landmarks. Even for this quintessential Broadway picture, New York was no longer in the budget—a step back from Cukor and Kanin's *A Double Life* four years earlier.

More interesting was *I Can Get It for You Wholesale*, the adaptation of a 1937 novel by Jerome Weidman (also the author of *House of Strangers*). The story of a grasping Jewish hustler who exploits the garment industry workers he has organized, it appalled not only union activists but many influential figures in the Jewish community. According to one account, "a small group of Hollywood executives" pressured its publisher, Simon & Schuster, to pull it from bookstores. That plea was unsuccessful, but when he heard that his studio had bought the rights, Darryl F. Zanuck swore, "I'll be damned if I'll make a picture from an anti-Semitic book."[24] The solution was to hire Abraham Polonsky to write a script that would not only correct these problems but substitute an entirely new theme, something more appropriate for the postwar era. Polonsky dropped the union angle and changed the protagonist from a Jewish man to an Irish woman (Susan Hayward as an ambitious designer), avoiding accusations of anti-Semitism while creating one of the era's few investigations of what the author himself called "the woman question." Director Michael Gordon (who, like Polonsky, would soon be blacklisted for his political views) spent almost two weeks in New York with Hayward and costar Dan Dailey. They shot mostly garment district locations but also a few apartment houses (Sutton Place at Fifty-Sixth Street and 210 East Sixty-Second Street) and retail outlets like Bonwit Teller. According to a report in the *Times*, work was delayed when the unit discovered it had arrived during Yom Kippur, either an incredibly careless bit of advance work or a plot element left over from *The Lost Weekend*.[25]

Alfred Hitchcock also needed some New York footage that year and hired Bill Kelly to shoot second unit for *Strangers on a Train* (he may also have done the Washington, DC, footage). According to a 1959 résumé he filed with his union office, Kelly later worked in the same capacity on *The Trouble with Harry, The Wrong Man*, and *North by Northwest*, indicating that Hitchcock depended on the quality of his work throughout the decade.[26] But beyond a handful of gigs like these, major studio interest had clearly slacked off since the late 1940s. With the Hollywood studio system now in free fall, and both Louis de Rochemont and Joseph Lerner much less active, New York's future as a theatrical motion picture center seemed especially uncertain.

Ed Gardner was a radio veteran who felt he could make the move to independent film production more comfortably in the east. The creator and star of the popular radio series *Duffy's Tavern* (aired on various networks from 1941 to 1951), Gardner had moved the show to Puerto Rico in 1949 to take advantage of the favorable tax situation. He bought the rights to a paranoid mistaken-identity thriller called *The Man with My Face*, in which an American accountant working in San Juan discovers he has been replaced by a double. In a series of plot twists worthy of Cornell Woolrich, even his wife and dog fail to recognize him. The villains have spent five years cooking up this scheme, which involves a million dollars in stolen bonds and an especially vicious Doberman Pinscher.

The IATSE considered Puerto Rico neutral territory, not under the exclusive jurisdiction of any of the regional locals. Gardner, whose film experience was limited to an appearance in Paramount's 1945 *Duffy's Tavern* feature, produced the film himself, drawing crew members from both East and West Coasts. Camera and sound were handled by Hollywood teams with years of experience on westerns and B-pictures, where sound was often recorded on location under marginal conditions. But Gardner hired Edward Montagne (*The Tattooed Stranger, Project X*) to direct, and Montagne brought along the production manager Frank Mayer. Other New York personnel included Gene Milford (editor), Ira Senz (makeup), and Jack Shaindlin (music). Carole Mathews (*Cry Murder*) and Jack Warden (*12 Angry Men*) were among the New York actors, but the star—in a double role—was Hollywood veteran Barry Nelson.

Unlike *Sarumba*, shot three years earlier in Havana, production of *The Man with My Face* appears to have gone quite smoothly and led to Puerto Rico becoming a favorite location for New York producers searching for tropical backgrounds.[27] The film has no credited art director and appears to have been shot entirely on local exteriors and practical interiors, mainly offices and apartments. It climaxes with a dramatic chase through Morro Castle, but more significant was the amount of live sound recording accomplished by this ad hoc crew, a difficult issue even for companies that were better financed and equipped. Shot on a thirty-two-day schedule with a budget of $300,000, *The Man with My Face* received little critical notice but would have served as an object lesson for any independent producer worried about the problems, and costs, of location sound.[28]

Another lesson, less salutary, was offered by *The Big Break*. The Actors Laboratory Theatre, a left-wing theater company and acting school in Hollywood, had mounted a showcase production of Arnold Manoff's *All You Need Is One Good Break* in July 1948. The run was successful enough to attract Monte Proser and Joseph Kipness, the investors behind the musical hit *High Button Shoes*, who brought an expanded version to Broadway in February 1950.[29] The show soon folded in New York (*Times* theater critic Brooks Atkinson dismissed it as "meaningless and obsolete"), but Joseph Strick quickly picked up the film rights for $2,500.[30] Based in Los Angeles, Strick had made films for the U.S. Army Air Corps during the war and with Irving Lerner had produced an interesting local documentary, *Muscle Beach*, in 1948. He had the script of *The Big Break* (as he now called it) entirely rewritten, downplaying the political content and de-ethnicizing the main character, whose name changed from Rothman to Ross. The cast consisted entirely of unknown New York actors: James Lipton (later the host of *Inside the Actors Studio*) shares top billing with Gaby Rodgers (already employing the fine Bronx accent she uses in her only other film role, Lily Carver in Robert Aldrich's *Kiss Me Deadly*). Strick's version retained the original's proletarian ambiance, but the hero was now more of a dreamer than the "tenement wastrel" who had so annoyed Brooks Atkinson. The story became "the intimate narrative of two young people whose dreams far exceed their probability of attainment" and whose relationship is sorely tested after a series of melodramatic episodes.[31]

Strick is best known today for *The Savage Eye* (1960), which followed its disaffected heroine around a sharply etched city of Los Angeles. But at least one critic saw him doing the same thing here. "Most of the sets for this production are the streets, parks and buildings of New York," *Motion Picture Daily* reported, praising its "realistic photography" and the way Strick captured "the flavor of a youngster working as a shipping clerk in the garment center."[32] Production began on October 16, 1950, at Camp Fieldstone in Monroe, New York, where the Lipton and Rodgers characters meet cute at the Ramapo resort. Clearly deserted so late in the season, Fieldstone apparently provided accommodations in exchange for some heavy product placement. According to the *Times*, which devoted a column to the start of production, Boris Kaufman was behind the camera, which would have made this his first American feature.[33] But Kaufman seems to have been replaced by Bill Miller early enough for Miller to earn sole credit. Although produced on a budget of "under $100,000," Strick was not scrimping on the camera crew here; Kaufman and Miller were the top first cameramen in New York and the result was far more professional than the typical independent feature. Sound recording was also remarkably sophisticated, nearly all of it done directly on location, even on interiors.

The Big Break wrapped as scheduled on November 10, 1950, and was approved by the Production Code Administration two months later.[34] But like many other self-financed films that risked going into production without a distribution deal, the picture just sat on the shelf. Strick finally turned it over to Jack Rieger's Madison Pictures in September 1952, which offered it to low-end theaters needing something to fill out the bottom half of their double features.[35] The film did earn a few scattered commercial bookings, but the only reviews I could locate were the obligatory notices from trade papers. Although copies of the film are held by at least two American archives, *The Big Break* disappeared from public view soon after its original release and has been almost completely forgotten.[36] While not without its problems, Strick's film is interesting for the way it roots its coming-of-age narrative in the changing cultural and economic landscape of postwar Manhattan. In many ways it might even be said to prefigure the next generation of local indies, especially films like *Something Wild*, *The Small Hours*, or *The Greenwich Village Story*, all released between 1961 and 1963. Stanley Kubrick, after finishing production of *Fear and Desire* in 1952, was also stuck without a distributor. But Kubrick was either luckier than Joe Strick, or simply more patient. By holding on long enough he avoided Jack Rieger and managed to sell his picture to Joseph Burstyn instead.

But the most high-profile project shooting in New York in 1950 was neither a low-budget indie nor a traditional Hollywood studio production. *Teresa* was a high-end independent film developed by Fred Zinnemann and Arthur M. Loew, president of Loew's International Corporation. Loew "had been a staunch ally during the making of *The Search*," the innovative Lazar Wechsler production Zinnemann had shot in Germany in 1947.[37] That film had told the story of an American GI confronting the refugee crisis in postwar Europe. It was Loew who had the idea of producing what was in some ways a sequel, with a GI meeting and marrying an Italian war bride and bringing her home to a cramped New York apartment.

Zinnemann assembled a New York crew and filled most of the cast with New York actors discovered during open auditions held at the ANTA Playhouse on West Fifty-Second Street.[38] John Ericson, who played the soldier, was an acting student with no film or television experience. Ralph Meeker, Ed Binns, and Rod Steiger were also making their film debuts; all hoped that the same lightning that struck Montgomery Clift—a screen unknown when Zinnemann cast him in *The Search*—might work for them. The unit arrived in Italy in April 1950 and spent six weeks filming in and around Scascoli, a suitably picturesque town on the road from Florence to Bologna.[39] Bill Mauldin, the Pulitzer Prize–winning cartoonist famed for his coverage of the Italian campaign, played another GI and also served as technical adviser. Teenaged Italian actress Anna Maria Pierangeli (new name: Pier Angeli) was cast as the bride, although Loew failed in his stated intention of hiring Lamberto Maggiorani, star of *Bicycle Thieves*, to play her brother; he settled for Franco Interlenghi, one of the boys in *Shoe-Shine*.[40] The neorealist lineage was obvious, although the film is more closely rooted in the Lazar Wechsler tradition represented by *The Search*. And New York filmmaking was also a strong presence, not only in the cast but through the use of Bill Miller as cameraman and Louis Applebaum as composer (both from de Rochemont's *Lost Boundaries*) and Joseph Lerner veterans Leo Kerz (art direction) and Jim Shields (sound). The company returned to New York for another five weeks of location work, filming at the Bellevue maternity ward, Central Park, Jones Beach, and other recognizable spots. MGM's New York headquarters doubled as an unemployment office.[41] In his monograph on Zinnemann, Richard Griffith noted that "the New York interiors" were the only parts of the film not shot on location.[42]

Zinnemann had begun developing the project with Loew in much the same way he worked with Lazar Wechsler, personally researching the background issues and the stories of the characters. The war-bride issue would be central, and the damage to the main character should be less physical (as in Zinnemann's *The Men*) than psychological. Stewart Stern was brought in to develop a storyline that might unify all these elements, and he soon found a useful culprit: Mom. In a promotional piece that appeared in the *Times* just before the film opened, Zinnemann wrote directly about his main character, "the shy, weak, Philip, a victim of the scourge of 'Momism,' whose need for dependence upon someone else almost cost him his life as a soldier and his happiness as a man."[43] A few weeks later Bosley Crowther devoted an entire column to this scourge, which had suddenly popped up in both *Teresa* and *Fourteen Hours*. Crowther thought it worth noting that "the villains in the two most thoughtful American films so far this year are predatory mamas who tend to destroy the very ones they are supposed to love." He especially liked *Teresa*, a "fine little picture," praising its "poignant estimation of the torture and damage that can be innocently caused by 'mom.'"[44]

Today, the film seems at its best when concentrating on the fragile relationship of John Ericson and Pier Angeli but quickly runs off the rails when Mom takes over. "There was too great an emphasis on a minor facet of the story—the mother's dominance over the son," Zinnemann recalled in his autobiography. He claimed to have seen this coming in preproduction but lacked the authority to delay shooting until they could fix the script. By the time the crew arrived in Scascoli it was too late. He blamed Stern, a writer who "tends to dramatize his own personal experiences," a strategy that sometimes worked well but in this case drew attention away from the war-bride plot and left the film with a hero the audience perceived as weak and unattractive. Worse, he said, "I had failed to control the performance of the mother, the excellent actress Patricia Collinge." Zinnemann saw the handwriting on the wall when he realized they had "lost the audience at several crucial points" during the first Hollywood preview. But Loew refused to make any changes after a better-received preview for Nicholas Schenck and other executives in New York. Zinnemann vowed never again to go into production with an imperfect script, "a bitter lesson and one I remembered well on later occasions."⁴⁵

Whatever its flaws, *Teresa* was a landmark in New York production history, a proper climax to Bill Miller's lengthy career in features (although he continued to film shorts and television episodes) and an early milestone for Jim Shields, who a few years later would be doing sound for *On the Waterfront*. The way in which the *Teresa* project came together is also worth looking at. A well-funded production company (Coliseum Films spent $550,000 on the picture) is organized by Hollywood names (Zinnemann and Loew) and has a releasing deal with a Hollywood major (Loew's).⁴⁶ The cast consists mainly of New York actors with little or no film experience, while the technical crew has worked on everything from documentaries and industrial films to silent movies and ethnic pictures. Shooting in New York (and elsewhere) they work mainly on exteriors and avoid studio settings except when absolutely necessary. This business plan would serve as a template for New York's Lindsay-era motion picture renaissance a generation later where, to cite just one example, it was replicated almost exactly by the producers of *Midnight Cowboy* in 1968.

The Impy Era

What was happening in 1950 would set the tone for the rest of the Impellitteri administration. Between 1951 and 1953 Hollywood continued to send out a small number of crews every season. Some came only to film back-projection plates, while others arrived with principal actors in tow and a few even organized large casting calls for extras or small-part players. Independent producers continued to try their hand at local feature production, although the studio situation remained bleak and changes in the way films were being financed and distributed were clearly discouraging.

During this relatively quiet period it was Universal that seemed most interested in using New York as an extension of its own back lot. Their "Ma and Pa Kettle" franchise had already made an appearance, so producer Leonard Goldstein brought out the studio's talking mule for *Francis Covers the Big Town* in the summer of 1951. The credit sequence plays over footage of Francis and Donald O'Connor walking near the Helix approach to the Lincoln Tunnel, the skyline providing a readily identifiable background. We see them later in Central Park and, in the film's money shot, stopping traffic as they amble across Times Square. *Abbott and Costello Go to Mars* was proudly cited in one of the Commerce Department's annual reports, but in reality Universal only sent out John Fulton's special-effects crew, which shot background plates of midtown skyscrapers, the Statue of Liberty, the Brooklyn Bridge, and other local landmarks, including, yet again, the Lincoln Tunnel.⁴⁷ At the controls of a runaway rocket, Bud and Lou seem to fly under the Bridge, buzz the Statue, and zoom in and out of both ends of the Tunnel.

Jack Arnold, whose Oscar nomination for the labor docudrama *With These Hands* had won him a contract at Universal, was assigned to direct *Night Flowers*, a low-budget follow-up to *City Across the River* (it even copies that film's peculiar end-title sequence). The slum here is the lower east side, where everyone has a dead-end job and the goal of its residents is to escape to Astoria (the earlier film used Canarsie). Very little of *Girls in the Night*, as it was eventually called, was actually shot in New York, and authentic location footage is frequently mixed with studio scenes or Long Beach (California) exteriors.[48] As in most urban juvenile delinquency films, "a few views of littered, teeming slums are graphic and pointed illustrations of the locale of poverty, crime and delinquency."[49] Most of those views were packed into the final waterfront chase sequence, where the villain meets his end by falling onto high-voltage lines (a climax lifted from early drafts of *The Naked City*). Arnold still seems to be learning the ropes here, although the film is worth watching for Harvey Lembeck's energetic performance and an amusing "Miss Third Avenue" beauty pageant, apparently staged at the old Regent Theatre at 385 Third Avenue. Other Universal productions applying to the Commerce Department for a few days of second-unit work included *Flesh and Fury* (shot in 1951, with Tony Curtis as a deaf prizefighter) and *Playgirl* (Shelley Winters as the title character, 1953).

In what should have been a more ambitious effort, MGM shot some of *The People Against O'Hara* here in March 1951. Described by one of Spencer Tracy's biographers as "possibly the least interesting film of Tracy's postwar career," it featured a few shots of James Arness running through the streets in the shadow of the Williamsburg Bridge.[50] Tracy was cut into the action in much the same way he appeared in *Man's Castle* a generation earlier. The studio's major contribution was actually *I Love Melvin*, a modestly budgeted musical that reteamed two *Singin' in the Rain* cast members, Donald O'Connor and Debbie Reynolds. A company of nineteen spent four days shooting footage in Central Park (mainly the zoo), most of which was used in a two-minute chase sequence at the climax. But O'Connor—who plays a boyish *Look* magazine photographer—is also seen working a range of New York locations, from the Empire State Building to the Brooklyn Bridge.[51] The film's many musical sequences are well designed to show off, on a budget, the talents of the two stars. Indeed, one dream ballet even has a bit of fun at the expense of two bigger stars who are *not* in this picture, as Debbie Reynolds dances with a masked male chorus, all of them waxen clones of Gene Kelly or Fred Astaire. Unfortunately, like the rest of the film's musical numbers, this one was shot back in Culver City.

In fact, true musical numbers are quite rare in New York films of this period—with the exception of race movies, which always featured them. At a time when the Broadway musical was in its heyday, the talent and energy that otherwise might have gone into musical features could instead be found in band shorts and television revues. *Follies Girl*, *It Happened in Brooklyn*, and *On the Town* were rare exceptions, but the number that most directly channels New York's musical theater tradition lies at the heart of Lester Cowan's 1953 production, *Main Street to Broadway*. Cowan had made a deal with the Council of the Living Theatre, a nonprofit dedicated to expanding the audience for live theater, promising them a healthy fee and a cut of the profits if they could supply some big Broadway names. Tallulah Bankhead had the most significant continuing part, while Helen Hayes, Cornel Wilde, and both Ethel and Lionel Barrymore popped up among the supporting celebrities. The names behind the camera were also impressive: director Tay Garnett and cameraman James Wong Howe were working from a script by Robert E. Sherwood and Samson Raphaelson. Everyone seems to have felt they were about to repeat the success of *Stage Door Canteen*.

Most of the dramatic action in *Main Street to Broadway* was shot at the Goldwyn Studio in Hollywood.[52] But some scenes were done in Chicago and several important sequences really were shot in and around Broadway. Rex Harrison and Lilli Palmer were filmed on Forty-Fourth Street having a comic argument about the eating of triple-decker sandwiches. A Broadway opening, loaded with critics, celebrities, socialites, and other first-nighters, was shot at the Martin Beck. And the stage of the Martin Beck—available only for a two-week stretch before Arthur Miller's *The Crucible* moved in—was where the film's one musical number would be set. Modestly staged as a simple song rehearsal, Mary Martin sings Rodgers and Hammerstein's "There's Music in You," while the songwriting duo and the director, Joshua Logan, stand by as themselves. No one needed to be reminded that this was the team that created *South Pacific*.[53] Unfortunately, *Main Street to Broadway* was no *South Pacific*. "The whole picture has a faintly vulgar air," Bosley Crowther sniffed, dismissing the ambitious project as "a cheap and badly slipshod 'all-star' show in which a number of theatre personalities are dragged in."[54] Lester Cowan, previously responsible for hits like *The Story of G.I. Joe*, would never make another film. Garnett, writing in his autobiography, devoted just three words to the picture: "What a waste."[55]

A very different independent production was *The Thief*, produced by Harry M. Popkin as a non-dialogue feature—not a silent film, just one in which the characters "have nothing to say."[56] Before the war, Harry and his brother Leo were the biggest race movie producers on the West Coast, but sold out to Ted Toddy in 1941 when they moved up to B-pictures. They later teamed with writers Clarence Greene and Russell Rouse on a series of interesting low-budget thrillers, including *D.O.A.* (1950) and *The Well* (1951). *The Thief* is a Cold-War espionage melodrama in which scientist Ray Milland, who has been passing atomic secrets to a gang of foreign spies, is tracked from Washington to New York by FBI agents. It should be noted that this is not Louis de Rochemont's

9.1. Ray Milland filmed with hidden cameras in Penn Station for *The Thief*. Museum of Modern Art Film Stills Archive.

FBI: the Bureau fails to prevent the initial theft of our secrets, the agent tailing Milland manages to fall to his death, and the only reason the spy fails to make good his escape is because he has a sudden, massive, change of heart. The film was shot in eighteen days, five on location in Washington, five in New York, and the rest back at Motion Picture Center Studios in Hollywood. The cameraman, Sam Leavitt, had once been operator for George Folsey and Joe Ruttenberg when Paramount was still running the Astoria studio; he would later win an Oscar for shooting *The Defiant Ones*. This was his first credit as director of photography, and he was especially proud of two things: his ability to film the interior of Penn Station without additional lighting and the use of a handheld Éclair camera in the cramped confines of the Empire State Building's newly installed television mast. Unfortunately, a continuous tracking shot said to follow Milland down Broadway from Forty-Seventh to Forty-Second Street was broken up into fragments for a montage (the New York scenes take up about 40 percent of the running time).[57]

In a lengthy essay in *Theatre Arts*, Greene and Rouse defended their film against critics like Robert Hatch and Bosley Crowther, who had dismissed it as "an obvious and calculated stunt."[58] "We wanted to tell the story in the pure motion picture form," they argued, claiming that "the true values of the motion picture screen were being allowed to deteriorate" due to an overemphasis on dialogue. They provided numerous examples of how camera movement and camera placement (low in the first half of the picture and high in the second half, when the fugitive Milland is filmed "like a rat in a cage") allowed the camera to play a dramatic role in the action.[59] It is extremely rare to find such critical analysis coming from any traditional Hollywood studio filmmakers, much less those working on the low-budget fringe. While not mimicking silent film technique—there are no intertitles, for example—*The Thief* does carry a full orchestral score by Herschel Burke Gilbert. Gilbert realized that the lack of dialogue was for him a great advantage because the score would always "be audible and thus could truly speak for itself without submergence under dialogue," a reality that had been the bane of film music composers since the dawn of Vitaphone (the score was nominated that year for an Academy Award).[60]

Twentieth Century-Fox, which had opened many of its "New York" films to the strains of Alfred Newman's "Street Scene," did the same thing again in *How to Marry a Millionaire* in 1953. The first film shot in their new Cinema-Scope process (but the second to be released), it begins with Newman at the podium, conducting his music as if he were on stage at Carnegie Hall. Then a widescreen City Symphony montage takes us to Rockefeller Center, Central Park, and the Brooklyn Navy Yard (all spots familiar from *On the Town*) while a chorus rhapsodizes over "New York, New York, you high and mighty, bright and shiny, fabulous place."[61] After one last view of a street sign at the intersection of Fifty-Fifth Street and Sutton Place, we leave New York for the Fox stages at Movietone City. Films like these, where only a small portion of the overall footage would be shot in New York, could bring in a director of photography from the West Coast so long as a New York man was also hired at the equivalent rate of pay. Instead of just having him stand by, this might be accomplished by using the New York man as camera operator while paying him at the higher scale. On *How to Marry a Millionaire*, for example, Morris Hartzband was the operator, an uncredited position, but he was almost certainly being paid as if he were first cameraman.

Hartzband had functioned in the same capacity the year before on *Taxi*, Gregory Ratoff's remake of the 1951 Bernard Blier film, *Sans laisser d'addresse*.[62] Ratoff owned the rights and had intended playing the Blier role himself, but after he sold the project to Fox the part of the taxi driver was rewritten for Dan Dailey. Ratoff, who remained as director, told the *Times* that the film "has three stars—a boy, a girl and New York."[63] His unit worked there for six weeks in the summer of 1952, shooting a host of familiar New York landmarks but spending most of its time in unfamiliar Brooklyn and Queens waterfront neighborhoods. Fox claimed to have hired nearly seventy local actors, including Blanche Yurka, Stubby Kaye, and Geraldine Page. John Cassavetes made his first screen appearance as a cab driver (blink and you will miss him), while Ratoff himself appeared as a deli owner; both are uncredited. Page, still working in an acclaimed revival of *Summer and Smoke*, was originally announced as Dailey's costar but ultimately worked for only two days "somewhere in Queens."[64]

The actual costar of *Taxi* was Constance Smith, an Irish actress imported by Darryl F. Zanuck who worked in a number of postwar Fox films before returning to pick up her career in London.[65] Smith's character arrives in New York in search of her American husband, not seen or heard from since their whirlwind courtship and marriage the previous year. There is also a baby, and immigration problems raise issues of their own. Presented as a sweetly open and honest Irish countrywoman, her character makes a dramatic contrast to Dailey's irascible, even larcenous taxi driver, whose business plan involves taking every passenger on the longest route possible (Brooklyn to Manhattan via New Jersey?). A fractious depressive perpetually at odds with his mother, fellow cab drivers, and potential fiancée, he always seems about to let loose on someone—at least until things are suddenly papered over at the conclusion. "Dailey's change of type into a hard-boiled taxi driver probably will surprise his musical and dance-minded fans," the *Los Angeles Times* concluded. Indeed, a modern viewer might be more inclined to ride with Travis Bickel.

Another European innocent in America was at the center of Paramount's *The Stars Are Singing*, also shot in the summer of 1952. Part of a brief "melting pot" cycle that would include *Anything Can Happen* and *The Glass Wall*, it was intended as a showcase for their new star, the coloratura soprano Anna Maria Alberghetti. But the film was hijacked by the pop singer Rosemary Clooney ("Come On-a My House"), who had been signed only for a specialty number. Betty Hutton had just quit the studio, and the producer, Irving Asher, had a sudden brainstorm. "I realized here was a girl who really comes over on the screen," he told reporters. "We re-wrote her part, expanded her role into one of the star roles. She can do everything Hutton can."[66] Paramount moved her into Hutton's dressing room and cast her in *White Christmas*; Alberghetti, the loser in this classics-versus-jazz battle, was next seen in a western at Republic.

In *The Stars Are* Singing, Alberghetti played a Polish refugee who jumps ship in New York and hides from the authorities while searching for an old family friend. In Columbia's *The Glass Wall*, shot almost simultaneously in May and June 1952, Vittorio Gassman starred as a displaced person who jumps ship in order to find the American he saved during the war (an act that will give him preferential immigration treatment).[67] The project was developed by Ivan Tors, himself a Hungarian refugee who had arrived in New York in 1939. Best known at the time for the production of inexpensive science-fiction films (including *The Magnetic Monster* and *Riders to the Stars*), Tors was inspired by news events to make a film about "the displaced," stateless individuals who were "shuttling hopelessly from port to port" while being denied admission to countries like the United States.[68] The "glass wall" of the title is not some immigration ceiling but the modernist facade of the United Nations building itself. Gassman had been signed to a long-term MGM contract on the strength of his appearance in *Bitter Rice*, but the most interesting performance in *The Glass Wall* comes from the woman playing opposite him, Gloria Grahame. While Gassman is sweet, helpless, and obviously in need of all the assistance the UN can give him, Grahame's character is an incredibly tough cookie who has walked away from her $35-a-week job pasting tips on shoe laces. The pair meets while she is stealing someone's coat in the Automat, although her best scene shows her cadging two dimes from a pair of street urchins. Instead of dealing only with a needy immigrant gratefully acknowledging a helping hand from some generous Americans, *The Glass Wall* pairs him with a luckless New Yorker as much in need of Marshall Plan aid as he is.

The film uses a considerable amount of back projection and intercutting, especially around Times Square and Central Park, but efforts were made to establish Gassman in the footage as much as possible.

> Filming in crowded streets was done from a camera concealed in a packing box mounted on a hand truck pulled by two "grips." Mr. Gassman followed this odd vehicle from which two tightly packed cameramen photographed his ramblings. In an attempt to heighten realism, the producers dispensed with the usual roping off of location areas; hence the fluid movement of the crowds is completely natural.[69]

Tors did succeed in gaining full cooperation from United Nations personnel and was the first filmmaker to be allowed access to UN offices and meeting halls. The film's dramatic highlight is Gassman's impassioned plea to an empty Economic and Social Council chamber, more Stanley Kramer than Frank Capra, after which he attempts to throw himself off the top of the building. While somewhat preachy, the film's good intentions were immediately suspect on the political right. Isolationist Senator Patrick McCarran was "outraged" when he saw that "aliens are depicted in this picture as grand people while the Americans are portrayed in a most uncomplimentary manner."[70] For whatever reason, *The Glass Wall* was for many years the only commercial feature to enjoy this amount of access to the United Nations building. Alfred Hitchcock was denied permission to shoot portions of *North by Northwest* there in 1958 and was forced instead to steal whatever footage he could through the use of hidden cameras. "You see, someone had used that setting for a film called *The Glass Wall*, and after that Dag Hammarskjold prohibited any shooting of fiction films on the premises," he later admitted to François Truffaut.[71]

Like Hitchcock, George Cukor is not primarily thought of as a "New York director," but he would return here as often as possible in the years just after the war. He made *The Model and the Marriage Broker*, one of his most charming

New York stories, very quickly in June and July 1951, but only a bit of second-unit work was actually filmed there. As was becoming more common in Fox films of this period, the first sequence establishes the location while the rest of the picture will play out on studio sets. Here we begin at the Flatiron Building, as the character actress Helen Ford exits a subway station and walks into the iconic and easily identifiable landmark. This business lasts only long enough for the audience to recognize that we are in New York. Later, a few long shots show doubles for Jeanne Crain and Scott Brady catching a bus and walking along Beekman Place.

The documentary ambitions of *The Marrying Kind* were far more ambitious. Like Cukor's earlier Ruth Gordon-Garson Kanin property, *Adam's Rib*, it deals with the trials and tribulations of two married New Yorkers, this time a young working-class family played by Aldo Ray and Judy Holliday. Cukor and his producer, Bert Granet, arrived in New York in mid-August 1951 and spent a month casting and location-scouting.[72] Cukor films the couple's first meeting in Central Park, avoiding the need for direct dialogue recording by the use of some fancy voice-overs. His cameras show us where they live (Peter Cooper Village), where he works (the central post office building), and what else they do around town. *The Marrying Kind* earned a photo spread in the *New York Times Magazine*, highlighting some footage shot at the new Port Authority Bus Terminal.[73] But the film also shows us the city's Domestic Relations Court, where this young couple dissects their troubled marriage in a series of flashbacks (Cukor liked the idea of bringing veteran actors back to the screen, so the judge hearing their case is played by silent film star Madge Kennedy). A series of vignettes illustrating the highs and lows of a "typical" marriage, the film's casual narrative structure is often part of its charm. What is more surprising is how many of these vignettes appear to have been taken directly from King Vidor's *The Crowd* (1928), the Ur-film of American urban life, famously shot in this same town a little over twenty years earlier. In addition to the expected breakfast bickering, the film features a son's death, a jingle contest, a traffic accident, a family picnic, and a naive working-class couple stumbling as best it can through the fog of marriage. What the Kanins added was the jurist/therapist who helps husband and wife sort it all out, a very postwar improvement.[74]

After its release, the Commerce Department published some figures showing how much cash the producers of *The Marrying Kind* had left behind:

Payroll for local crew members, talent, extras	$36,000
Hotels and meals	$5,000
Purchase and rental of equipment	$7,500
Local transportation, taxis, trucks, buses, cars	$12,000

The total may seem modest, but the few weeks that Cukor and company worked in New York involved only a small amount of actual location footage and called for no new studio space or fiscal incentives.⁷⁵ To calculate its value in current dollars, the figures should be multiplied by a factor of ten.

Although requiring only "two weeks of arduous location work in New York" during the summer of 1953, *It Should Happen to You*, the last of the Cukor-Kanin films, was by far the most effective in the way it made use of the city.⁷⁶ Cukor shot some scenes in actual office interiors, and the opening Central Park sequence features a great deal of direct dialogue recording, demonstrating the new flexibility that was about to revolutionize location production on all levels. Garson Kanin had developed the project as *A Name for Himself* and intended it for Danny Kaye; it was Ruth Gordon who realized that the story worked better with a woman (*A Name for Herself*, so Judy Holliday again), although a last-minute change of title was entirely Columbia's idea and pleased no one on the creative team. Holliday plays Gladys Glover, a dreamer who purchases a Columbus Circle billboard on which she puts only two words: her own name.⁷⁷ Because New York is the self-promotional center of both the television industry and the advertising business, Gladys quickly becomes famous for being famous.

9.2. A shouting match between Heywood Hale Broun and Judy Holliday provides great footage for the documentary filmmaker Jack Lemmon in George Cukor's *It Should Happen to You*. Museum of Modern Art Film Stills Archive.

274 REVIVAL

Cukor always looked for fresh local faces in his New York films, and this time he came up with Jack Lemmon. Lemmon had appeared in only one film, *Once Too Often* (TF 20–1684, 1950) an army training film designed to warn recruits about the risk of off-duty injuries, mainly through a series of vignettes illustrating such procedures as the proper way of unscrewing a light bulb. Lemmon's familiar screen persona is already fully developed in *Once Too Often*, made at the Signal Corps Photographic Center by director Charles Turner.[78] Turner had found Lemmon playing piano at Paul Killiam's Old Knickerbocker Music Hall, a dinner theater on East Fifty-Fourth Street that burlesqued "old time movies" and theatrical melodramas (Killiam would also become an important member of New York's postwar film culture, distributing silent movies non-theatrically and even packaging them for television). The actor's subsequent popularity meant that the film played the military camp circuit for years, sometimes under alternate titles.

Here he plays a documentary filmmaker who runs into Glover during another meet cute scene in Central Park, but instead of just wandering around he is engrossed in a very appropriate New York project—shooting his own film with a 35 mm Eyemo. The friction between these two young people will stem from his devotion to what he sees as "real" and "valuable" and her instinctive attraction to the modern mantra of self-promotion. But the film, still a product of the early 1950s, will end with her surrendering her dream to his as the couple leave the city behind in search of something less artificial—yet another lovely shot of a car exiting the Lincoln Tunnel. Cukor's biographer, Patrick McGilligan, notes that this ending, which Kanin felt "a disaster," was concocted by Columbia, although Cukor appears not to have fought back too strongly.[79] Still, Penelope Houston, writing about the Cukor-Kanin films in *Sight and Sound*, had nothing but praise for their location work and the use of new faces like Lemmon, Tom Ewell, and Aldo Ray. "There is a quality of alert, tough-minded acuity, a suggestion of being immensely on-the-spot, that, although we don't often encounter it, we customarily regard as characteristic of the New Yorker."[80]

But the most impressive of all these Hollywood visitors was certainly the Rhedosaurus, an animated dinosaur created by Ray Harryhausen for *The Beast from 20,000 Fathoms*. A science-fiction fantasy clearly inspired by the work of Harryhausen's mentor, Willis O'Brien—primarily *King Kong* (1933) but with a few elements also borrowed from *The Lost World* (1925)—*The Beast* was a modestly budgeted independent production that would serve as the template for the entire *Godzilla* genre. A flash-frozen dinosaur released from its arctic tomb by an ill-considered nuclear blast heads straight for New York. Coming ashore near the Fulton Fish Market, it soon causes "the worst disaster in New York's history," with thousands of casualties and a $300 million price tag. While some model work was required to replicate the area around John Street, New York is mainly visible through second-unit footage shot in the summer of 1952. Stock shots of one of the city's civil defense preparedness drills, which had begun the year before, not only add spectacle value but underscore the film's own concern with nuclear weaponry. Modest crowds can be seen fleeing the East River waterfront, racing past Federal Hall (by now a favorite downtown location), and disappearing into a subway entrance in the shadow of the Municipal Building. Hollywood back-lot locations extend the illusion. Harryhausen's crew also shot a complex series of projection plates that were used for both back and front projection, a revolutionary advance that allowed him to sandwich the animated Rhedosaurus between two layers of live-action film. The monster is finally cornered in the "amusement district" of Manhattan Beach, but what we actually see is a portion of The Pike at Long Beach, Hollywood's usual stand-in for Coney Island (whose name is never mentioned in the film).

Local Boys

There were many reasons to shoot small parts of films like these in New York even after the *Naked City*-era fad for urban location work had cooled off. Films like *Pickup on South Street* and *The Band Wagon* were just as happy to avoid a long location trip entirely, and the future of New York as a feature film location might very well have resembled that of San Francisco, which was a nice place to visit but lacked both the talent and the infrastructure to support an indigenous film industry of its own.[81] The fate of Laurel Films and RD-DR may have scarred the local film community, otherwise occupied with theatrical shorts, sponsored films, and television programs, but the urge to crack the feature film market persisted.

Morris Engel was one local filmmaker who would attempt to reinvent feature film production in the early 1950s, and Stanley Kubrick was another. But in the months before *On the Waterfront* went into production at the end of 1953 a surprising number of features were produced in New York by local filmmakers who felt they could take advantage of the disruption that had staggered not just Hollywood but the Hollywood studio system itself. Not all of this work was very successful, either critically or commercially, and few of the films are remembered today even by specialists. But the innovative production strategies they helped pioneer would serve as models for the next generation of New York filmmakers, from Sidney Lumet to John Cassavetes.

Victor Komow was on the board of the Association of Documentary and Television Cameramen, a NABET affiliate not otherwise involved in theatrical film production. He was also "technical supervisor" at Motion Picture Stages, a commercial production house that operated four small stages at 3 East Fifty-Seventh Street, one of many such facilities scattered around the city.[82] Charles Vetter ran Motion Picture Stages, and Burgess Meredith was a board member.

In 1950 *Broadcasting* magazine announced they were "planning expansion in belief that dramatic shows on film will become [the] 'solid middle ground' of television."[83] I am uncertain as to when Komow and Vetter made *Death Tide*, for which they shared nearly all the production credits (Faith Elliott was the editor). It is also unclear if the film was intended as a "TV movie," a theatrical release, or something in between. Frank Silvera plays a seagoing jewel thief—essentially a pirate—who has robbed the passengers of an ocean liner and is trying to have the diamonds recut in New York. Most of the action involves a freelance photographer and his wife who recognize the gang and function as amateur detectives in the style of the popular "Mr. and Mrs. North" novels. There is a lot of filming on small boats near Sandy Hook and a few cheap interiors. The looping is amateurish, and the acting and staging hardly any better. The film may have been shot in 1952, 1953, or even a bit earlier.[84] *Death Tide* did play theatrically in the United States, appearing, for example, on the bottom half of a double bill in Philadelphia on June 12, 1955. But it was already on television there, in a one-hour time slot, as early as September 7.[85] The film was released in England as *Fools Rush In* (a forty-six-minute feature!), where it was dismissed by the *Monthly Film Bulletin* as "a crudely contrived thriller with its implausibilities further emphasized by the indifferent quality of the acting, direction and camerawork."[86]

Given the long-term impact of *The Naked City*, it might have been assumed that New York filmmakers would always specialize in murder mysteries and police procedurals, films like *Guilty Bystander* and *The Tattooed Stranger*. But when the popularity of location thrillers began to fade in the early 1950s they quickly shifted to a host of other genres, from war films to sports features and even one very peculiar puppet musical. This sort of flexibility was only possible because the local industry's well-developed infrastructure—while lacking adequate studio space—was well suited to accommodate almost any shift in exhibitor demand. *Guerrilla Girl*, shot in 1952, resembles some of the underground resistance films that were produced in many European countries after the war, films with a clear political agenda that sought to take control of the historical narrative before some rival political faction could put their spin on it first. The action begins in the Greek countryside during the Nazi occupation, introducing a range of characters we will meet again during the subsequent civil war. Where Nazis were the obvious villains in part one, their role is quickly filled by Communist insurgents in the postwar scenes ("There's no room for thinking in the people's democracy," they tell us). Helmut Dantine, whose once-busy career as a Hollywood Nazi derailed at the close of the war, plays an intelligence officer in the Greek resistance who battles both factions while finding himself at the center of a politically inflected romantic triangle. A serious film with a strong political message—everyone dies at the end of this internecine struggle—its level of technical competence is so far below its ambitions that Bosley Crowther felt it "can barely be considered in the category of professional films."[87] *Variety* found "no entertainment value" at all in the film, which it wrongly assumed was "lensed overseas."[88] How's that?

First of all, the participation of such local cameramen as Sid Zucker and George Stoetzel indicates that the film was made within the jurisdiction of IATSE Local 644. Even Bosley Crowther somehow learned it had been made in and around Newburgh, New York, which "may endow it with a certain interest for some."[89] While it is true that *Guerrilla Girl* incorporates some European stock footage, the fact that the nation's leading trade paper believed that this really was a Greek film makes it worthy of more than passing interest today. Who made this picture? And why? Who was "one John Christian," as Crowther referred to the film's credited writer-producer-director? IMDB says he was actually a Greek filmmaker named Giannis Hristodoulou, active there before the war, who returned to Greece after making this one American film in 1952. But could he also be the man whose commercial New York studio, John Christian Productions, made films like *The Pattern for Peace* under contract to the United States Information Agency (USIA) in 1958?[90] In fact, could this sober, entertainment-less action picture (produced by "Liberty Bell Motion Pictures") also have been made at the behest of the USIA? And while "John Christian" may have disappeared from New York's feature film scene after this one picture, one of his writers, William Kyriakys certainly stayed on. In 1956, with his partner Radley Metzger, Kyriakys began shooting a far better Greek film on the streets of Manhattan, *Dark Odyssey*. A classic example of postwar New York independent film, *Dark Odyssey* would take years to find a distributor—until Metzger released it through his own soft-core distribution outlet, Audubon Films.[91]

The production of two very different sports features in 1953, *Go Man Go* and *Roogie's Bump*, illustrates two very different production styles, one more institutional than the other, that coexisted in the New York film community for years. *Roogie's Bump* was a baseball film, made with the cooperation of the Brooklyn Dodgers, in which a handful of Dodger stars appear in small roles as themselves. A fantasy aimed directly at an audience of small boys, it centers on a fatherless eleven-year-old whose magically enhanced pitching arm allows him to throw with enough force to knock over Dodger catcher Roy Campanella (the pitchers Carl Erskine, Billy Loes, and Russ Meyer also have a few lines).[92] Probably the most interesting element of the film is a subplot involving the boy's exploitation by commercial promoters, who drag him before TV cameras and involve him in bogus endorsement deals. That concern echoes films like *Mr. Universe* and *It Should Happen to You*, but *Roogie's Bump* is itself stuffed with a range of outrageous product placements involving everything from airlines to bubble gum. At one point the boy's aunt, suddenly restless for a smoke, pulls out an entire carton of Phillip Morris. The film was shot very quickly at the end of the 1953 season, with production overlapping the start of the World Series, and it is doubtful that the players worked on it for more than a day or two.[93] Direction by Harold Young (*Citizen Saint*) is flat and uninteresting, but the B-movie slickness of this low-budget Republic release makes it seem far more professional than a more serious film like *Guerrilla Girl*. Much of the production crew, including George Justin, Charlie Maguire, and Jim Shields, were immediately hired by Sam Spiegel, who would start filming *On the Waterfront* in Hoboken only a few weeks after *Roogie's Bump* wrapped up in Brooklyn.

Roogie's Bump, whatever its merits, is a conventional Hollywood-style narrative that looks like any other Republic B-picture. But *Go Man Go* smells like a New York film, with a production unit that matched a visionary independent writer-producer with a frustrated Hollywood refugee (both touched by the blacklist) and channeled every local filmmaking tradition from newsreels and documentaries to race movies, street photography, and Yiddish pictures.[94] *Go Man Go* began with Alfred Palca, a publicist for Fox who noticed that newsreels of the Harlem Globetrotters seemed to delight everyone, even audiences who cared little or nothing for basketball. In 1950 he acquired film rights from Abe Saperstein, who created the team in the 1920s, and proceeded to sell the idea of a feature film about the Globetrotters to Columbia—this at a time when professional basketball was no big deal and the word most often associated with the sport was "fix."[95] But Palca was not happy with *The Harlem Globetrotters* (1951) and wrote another script that he vowed to produce independently. Born and bred in New York, Palca decided to shoot the new film right here, raising a budget of $175,000 and planning to sell the film himself once it was done (the original had cost $250,000).

To direct he hired James Wong Howe, a great Hollywood cameraman (*Yankee Doodle Dandy*, *Body and Soul*) whose career had stalled after his studio contract with Warner came to an end. Worse, he had spent an entire year fruitlessly trying to get a pet project called *Rickshaw Boy* off the ground and had also come under suspicion as a left-wing sympathizer.[96] *Go Man Go* would be the first feature handled by a Hollywood major (United Artists) to be directed by a member of a racial minority. Howe was stunned when he received the offer, leaving Hollywood so quickly he didn't even have time to tell his wife—he sent her the good news by Western Union. "I am the director for this picture. Yours and my dreams have arrived and I shall do my best for a fine film." He would be paid a fee of $5,000 and 2.5 percent of the profits, "if any."[97] Production began at the Movietone studio in May 1953, with games shot in Boston, Madison Square Garden, and the Teaneck Armory. Howe soon fired the original cameraman, Zoli Vidor, whose experience was limited to documentaries and television films, replacing him with feature film veteran Bill Steiner (*The Window*).[98]

Go Man Go is not the story of a basketball team but the story of the man behind it, Abe Saperstein. Set mainly in the 1930s, it serves as a prequel to

Palca's earlier Globetrotters film, showing how Saperstein came to organize a team of African American all-stars and the degree of prejudice that had to be overcome in order to win anything other than marginal play dates. The opening of the script suggests a sort of Dust Bowl documentary (although as with most 1953 films, attention to period detail is otherwise nonexistent).

Shot 20   LONG SHOT BLEAK HIGHWAY EXT DAY

It is a long hill gently sloping upward and along it chugs the sad car used in those days by the Trotters. . . ."[99]

Howe shot scenes like this against a vista of power lines reminiscent of Depression-era photography by Walker Evans or Arthur Rothstein. While not always given credit for the documentary quality of his work, Howe had pioneered the use of handheld Eyemos for studio photography in films like *Air Force* (1943). During the war he published an article, "The Documentary Technique in Hollywood," which began with a lengthy analysis of Soviet combat footage and predicted that 16 mm film "will take its place alongside 35 mm" in the postwar era.[100] Much of *Go Man Go* was scheduled to be shot in the cars and buses used by the Globetrotters as they traveled around the country, and their rise to fame would be marked, in part, by improvements in their mode of transportation. But "we had a problem with the scenes when they travel around by car," he later told the journalist Charles Higham. "We couldn't afford process shots."

> We took the wheels off the touring car and set the car on a trailer chassis, so there was room to put the camera on as well, then we drove around. But we had a problem because the trailer's diesel made a shattering sound and drowned out the dialogue. So we'd go to the top of hills, and let the trailer chassis go without the engine, and off the whole thing would go to the foot of the hills. So the Globetrotters were always going downhill in the picture! That is what's so good about low-budget pictures; you have to use your ingenuity, your imagination.[101]

This is one of only a handful of films credited to the great Broadway scenic designer Howard Bay, but even he could do only so much in the cramped confines of the Movietone stages. Interviewed by a reporter from the *Times* while on the set there, Palca seemed almost apologetic: "There's been lots of Grade B junk thrown together in the East in the guise of practicality. And if we come off with a good one instead, I hope to have made up in sincerity for what I may lack in talent."[102] Sincerity was clearly a goal. Talking to Bruce Weber years later, Palca described himself as an "old lefty" who "thought I could do something to help the blacks. . . . That mattered to me importantly. I could never write anything violent. I'm a softy in that regard, but politically I would do anything I could to help society, and as a Jewish fellow, I was for the underdog."[103]

Although both race films and Yiddish pictures were obsolete by this time, and *Go Man Go* is not generally considered part of either tradition, the film is built around a menu of elements drawn from both genres. The presence of Slim Gaillard, who performs the film's title song at a house party, as well as the casting of both Sidney Poitier and Ruby Dee, suggests more than a passing acquaintance with be-bop culture and the new generation of African American acting talent. On the other hand, the Jewish roots of Abe Saperstein and his family are emphasized throughout, not just in the religious ritual of Abe's wedding but in his choice of metaphor. His team of all-stars, he boasts, is like having "ten Heifetzs in the same orchestra." "It's like gefilte fish, Mr. Willoughby," he tells a skeptical promoter. "Without the freshest carp and the best eggs, where are you?" Unfortunately, his ethnic allusions may be lost on Willoughby, a villain who does everything he can to foil the Globetrotters by refusing to match them against better-known teams. (Remember that at this same time, films like *City Across the River*, *I Can Get It for You Wholesale*, and *The Break Break* took pains to efface or even delete the Jewish identities of their main characters.)

It is Poitier, a team member who is also Abe's right-hand man—and more like his brother than his employee—who quickly sees through Willoughby's excuses. He is the one who states the obvious: "We both know what the big hurdle is." So does the audience. Indeed, the second act of the film, in which a team of black men defeats a long string of all-white opponents while repeatedly being denied their chance at the big time, makes Palca's sincerity, and his intentions, crystal clear. So much so that *Variety* singled out *Go Man Go* and *The Joe Louis Story* as films that were being given "a cold shoulder by Southern exhibs." They reported that while *The Jackie Robinson Story* had played in the South without protest, *Go Man Go* "engendered demonstrations" in New Orleans, where it was pulled from exhibition in the middle of its run. The paper speculated that *Go Man Go*, like *Lost Boundaries*, "roused the South by hitting at an existing problem" in a way that *The Jackie Robinson Story* did not.[104] The specific references to Saperstein's Jewish identity—not to mention the reality of racism as another of the team's opponents—had gone unmentioned in the Hollywood version of the Globetrotters' story.

On June 10, 1953, Mayor Impellitteri presented both Palca and Howe with formal "Certificates of Appreciation," thanking them for producing *Go Man Go* in New York.[105] But when United Artists released the picture in January 1954 Palca's credit as writer and producer, and even the name of his production company, Alfred Palca Enterprises, were missing from the credits. He had been visited by the FBI repeatedly during the course of production, accused of Communist associations and pressured to name names. The agents were so persistent that he eventually sought to get even by pestering them to invest in the

9.3. Dane Clark and Sidney Poitier in James Wong Howe's *Go Man Go*. Alfred Palca, who wrote and produced the film, saw his screen credits disappear in the wake of the blacklist. Museum of Modern Art Film Stills Archive.

picture. Palca later admitted he had "joined all kinds of organizations, signed all kinds of things" but had never been a party member. He remembered that the FBI pointed to the presence of Sidney Poitier in the film as one of the strikes against it, but what seems more likely is that someone at the FBI identified the character Poitier played, as well as the film's overall picture of America's racial landscape, as undisguised liberal propaganda. No distributor would touch the film with Palca's name on it, so he gave his screen credits to his cousin and his brother-in-law. "The movie got out, but my career was phhhttt."[106] Palca's name never appeared on another film, although the Writers Guild of America did restore his credit on this one in 1997, the year before he died.

Oddly enough, Palca later dismissed the film. "I look at it now and I kind of wince," he admitted, laying some of the blame on James Wong Howe, who "was so nervous that he got terrible hives and was not much help."[107] For his part, Howe took advantage of his stay in New York to direct, produce, and photograph a fifteen-minute documentary, *The World of Dong Kingman*, which he shot in 16 mm Eastmancolor. The Chinese-American artist, a friend of Howe's, is shown creating a single watercolor, beginning on a street in Chinatown and finishing up in his Brooklyn studio. An extremely popular art documentary, it was distributed for decades by Contemporary Films. Describing the film to a reporter in July, Howe also revealed that he would soon be directing another local feature, "a baseball fantasy about a little boy who dreams about a bump on his arm which makes him into a great pitcher."[108] He said that *Roogie's Bump* would be produced by John Bash and Fletcher Smith (who operated a large commercial studio on East Forty-Fourth Street), with production due to start in August. Because he had done such a "fine job" on *Go Man Go*, Howe hoped to use Bill Steiner again as his cameraman. But Smith dropped out of the project, production was delayed until the fall, and Howe went back behind the camera. It would not, however, be the last time he shot film in New York.

While Sidney Poitier may have been the FBI's original subject of interest, he never seems to have suffered the degree of harassment that sank Palca's career. Poitier flourished in Hollywood, although his first screen work all took place in New York. He claims to have appeared as an extra in *Sepia Cinderella*, but his first real film performances were all in army training films. Charles Turner cast him as a hospitalized patient in *Time Out: Occupational Therapy in Tuberculosis* (PMF 5116A, 1949), and that same year he played the lead in the final segment of *From Whence Cometh My Help?* (TF 16–1556), an episodic film about the Army Chaplain's Office.

I interviewed Poitier on stage at the Museum of the Moving Image in 1989 and asked him about his appearance in the film, which had been directed at the Signal Corps Photographic Center by Broder Peterson. He remembered it the way most successful graduates of the SCPC recalled their army training-film experience—with a mixture of amused condescension and feigned embarrassment. "I remember clearly asking them for permission to come and look at it because I needed to see what I looked like on screen," he recalled. "This was my first crack and I did go and I saw it. It was quite an experience. It almost sent me back to the Caribbean [laughter from audience]."[109]

But I think that most people viewing the film today would instead agree with Richard Allen, an assistant cameraman on the picture who had once been an actor and later worked for years as a director at SCPC. "On this particular day we were preparing to film a scene in the Chapel," he remembered:

> A young black soldier, grief-stricken over the recent loss of his infant son, had come to see the Chaplain, seeking consolation. With a tear-stained face, he looked up at the Chaplain and pleaded: "Why'd God do this to me, Chaplain?"
>
> Suddenly to my utter amazement, a torrent of tears cascaded down my cheeks, as if someone had turned on a faucet. Cringing with embarrassment I turned away from the camera, quickly running the back of my hand over my wet face. I found myself staring at a group of grips, prop-men and electricians, all of whom were sniffling, coughing, staring up at the rafters, or reaching for a handkerchief. We were all profoundly embarrassed and caught off-guard. Suddenly everyone got busy changing lights, moving furniture, doing anything to avoid my tear-filled, blinking eyes. It is important to note that this was only a REHEARSAL, and the young actor spoke only ONE LINE and broke up the whole crew of seasoned veterans. The name of this actor: SIDNEY POITIER. . . . As a fledging actor myself, that experience taught me a valuable lesson: an awareness that the world is full of people with talent, but only a handful are gifted with a touch of genius! I will always feel privileged to have witnessed the emergence of such extraordinary artistry.[110]

Old Genres, New Directions

New York filmmakers won many postwar Academy Award nominations in the one- and two-reel short subjects and documentaries categories, but this success only applied to live-action shorts—short animated films were another story. Paramount's Famous Studios, the successor to the great prewar Fleischer studio, failed to receive a single Oscar nomination in this period, while the Terrytoons operation was similarly ignored after 1945.[111] Paramount did receive multiple nominations for its George Pal Puppetoons, but those were made on the West Coast. So how is it that New York's most significant postwar animated film, and its first-ever animated feature, was a puppet film? Indeed, according to historian Paul Mandell, *Hansel and Gretel* was "the most elaborate stop-motion animated film ever made."[112]

The film was the brainchild of Michael Myerberg, a theatrical producer best known for presenting *The Skin of Our Teeth* in 1942. Myerberg had previously worked as business manager for Leopold Stokowski and claimed credit for "producing the music" for both *One Hundred Men and a Girl* (1937) and *Fantasia* (1940), although he received no formal credit on either picture. Impressed with *Fantasia*, but believing that puppet animation was a better way of achieving the same effects, in 1942 he began working with Lou Bunin on what would have been a four-hour adaptation of Wagner's *Ring Cycle*. Only one sequence was filmed before the project was shelved three years later.[113] George Pal abandoned the popular Puppetoon series in 1947, but Jiří Trnka's award-winning *The Emperor's Nightingale* (1949, US release 1951) showed that a niche audience for high-class puppet animation might actually exist. In December 1952 Myerberg began work on *Hansel and Gretel*, an adaptation of the Humperdinck opera, moving his crew into an East Village banquet hall at 214 East Second Street.[114]

New York did have a strong tradition of stop-motion animation, but Myerberg insisted on a fresh approach (and Bunin's Punch Films, as it happened, was now very busy with television work).[115] Instead of experienced animators, he hired actors, puppeteers, and ballet dancers, whose understanding of body movement he felt would produce a more realistic effect. Myerberg had developed a new type of articulated puppet he called a Kinemin (Kinetic + Mannequin), which locked the figures into place through the use of electromagnets at their feet, power being turned on and off whenever the characters needed to be moved. A rubbery plastic material brewed up on site provided the synthetic flesh that made hands and faces especially realistic. "It looks like human tissue, feels like human tissue and acts like human tissue," the *Times* reported.[116] Some of the Kinemins were almost two feet tall, and the forest setting they performed in filled the entire ballroom of the old reception hall. In order to manipulate the Kinemins, holes were cut into the floor of the set, members of the crew popping up periodically to move the relevant figures a fraction of an inch. New hires received three weeks of on-the-job training.

The remarkable sets were the work of Latvian stage designer Evalds Dajevskis; John Paul, an actor who served as production manager on several of Myerberg's Broadway shows, was credited as director; the screen adaptation was by Irish poet and playwright Padraic Colum. None had ever worked on a film before; neither had Martin Munkácsi, the director of photography. Because his film consisted of "more than 117,000 single color shots," Myerberg felt that familiarity with motion picture technique was less important than the ability to light every one of those images perfectly.[117] Munkácsi had revolutionized fashion photography in the 1930s, although even then his contribution lay in the "spontaneity, informality, and documentary realism" that he brought to fashion from his work as a sports photographer, not exactly a skill that was required here.[118]

This would never have happened on the West Coast, where the producer would have hired the most experienced crew he could afford and pushed them to work as quickly and efficiently possible. Myerberg and his people had no idea how to do any of this work efficiently because everyone on the set was reinventing the wheel. They still needed to work quickly, however, but without an established management structure, speed could only be achieved by turning the screws. "Myerberg had his animators working day and night shifts, which kept activity buzzing for 24 hours around the clock," Paul Mandell notes. "On a typical day, the producer could be seen cracking the whip by casing the studio and demanding 'More footage, more footage!' The Barnum and Bailey atmosphere obviated any chance for quality control, and with the evening shift having to continue a scene started by the day shift, the animation was spotty at best."[119] But no matter how extravagant, eccentric, and uneven, Myerberg's circus still managed to find its audience.

Myerberg opened the film on his own at the Broadway Theatre, hoping to attract a distributor on the strength of good reviews. This is not always a great strategy for an independent production, but for once the gamble paid off. RKO's distribution deal with Walt Disney was coming to an end, but here was Michael Myerberg with *Hansel and Gretel*. Bosley Crowther put the film on his "honorable mention" list for 1954, while the *Philadelphia Inquirer's* Mildred Martin even compared it favorably with *The Emperor's Nightingale* (although she still found Trnka's film "more beautiful").[120] Myerberg announced that plans were moving ahead on *Aladdin, Lute Song*, and *The Ring of the Nibelungs*, but none of these films were ever made.[121]

If New York cinema was often operating at the margins, on the margins of those margins were the films Jonas Mekas referred to as "Hoboken movies." Discussing Alexander Singer's *A Cold Wind in August*, which he dismissed as "a Hollywood sex movie," Mekas claimed he had "seen still better actors in the Hoboken movies, actors from the streets, true realism. . . . The Hoboken movies are so much more realistic, uncompromising, spontaneous, to the point. Compared to any Hollywood sex movie, Hoboken movies are pure cinema."[122] Mekas was not praising the general run of sex exploitation films but a local variety whose spontaneous and realistic qualities he saw as models for the type of cinema he and his brother Adolfas were hoping to promote. The uncompromising part came from the genre's existence beyond the reach of Hollywood's Production Code, which may have limited its audience but at least allowed its makers to go about their business in relative freedom. Mekas was writing here in 1961, after the 1952 *Miracle* decision loosened local censorship regulations and helped launch a new wave of increasingly explicit independent cinema. The work of those filmmakers, such as Joe Sarno, is beyond the scope of this volume, but its roots can be traced back to at least the early 1950s, when the prewar exploitation cinema began to find new audiences in more mainstream (and more desperate) theatrical venues.[123]

Bud Pollard, an important figure in New York's postwar race film industry, was also a key player in the exploitation business. In September 1949 the local *Screen Directors Guild Bulletin* reported that *I Married a Savage*, which he had made "largely on location in Florida," would soon open on Broadway.[124] Zorita, a stripper whose act involved a very large snake, played a white jungle goddess who saves a shipwrecked USO entertainer from the wrath of local natives. A passing freighter soon rescues them and they are married by the captain before returning to New York. But her snake has become a problem (according to the *AFI Catalog*, "she spends most of her honeymoon keeping the snake company in the ship's hold"). Zorita refuses a commercial booking that would have required her to perform the sacred snake dance—at $1,500 a week—enraging the husband, now a hopeless alcoholic. The film ends with Zorita dead, the husband headed for the electric chair, and the snake nowhere to be found. Pollard's own credit was nowhere to be found on the finished film, which listed his longtime collaborator John E. Gordon as both director and cowriter.

Perhaps Pollard preferred to be associated with *Love Island*, which he shot in August 1949 at the Video Varieties studio, 510 West Fifty-Seventh Street. Location scenes were made not in Florida but at Point Lookout, a small beach community on the eastern end of Long Beach.[125] Video Varieties was the old West Coast Service Studio, a well-established commercial facility that had been used by Paramount, Fox, and Columbia before the war, and production credits were more professional than usual for a Pollard film (Sam Corso and William Saulter were credited as art directors). Another story of a marooned American falling for a sarong-clad jungle girl—Eva Gabor, complete with Hungarian accent—*Love Island* was shot in Cinecolor, making it the first all-color narrative feature ever produced in New York.[126] But an announced Eagle-Lion release failed to materialize and the film sat on the shelf for three years. As usual with Pollard, critics were unimpressed, *Daily Variety* damning it as "an unbelievably poor film which suffers from inept production, directing, acting and writing."[127] Currently available video copies are not even in color. Reviewing a "blurred colour" copy reissued by Astor a decade later, David Moller identified what we would now recognize as "the Pollard touch," a shameless incorporation of whatever convenient stock footage might have been handy. *Love Island*, he wrote in *Vision: A Journal of Film Comment*, "has two short sequences lifted from a documentary dealing with a totally different racial type, in a totally different part of the world, in which sequences one or two young girls expose their nipples to us."[128]

If our bar in this book is set at theatrical exhibition, the lowest level would have been filled by plotless "burlesque films." These features developed from short reels originally marketed to burlesque houses as filler to be projected during the interval between live performances. Burlesque films differed from the usual sex exploitation product because they depended on marketable stars—strippers like Lili St. Cyr and Tempest Storm, who needed to be paid top dollar and were often billed above the title. While first developed on the West Coast, early East Coast examples included William Alexander's *Burlesque in Harlem*, discussed earlier. Jerald Intrator's *Striporama*, shot in October 1953, starred Lili St. Cyr but is remembered today mainly for the brief appearance of pin-up icon Bettie Page. Not a professional stripper or exotic dancer, Page was an Irving Klaw pin-up model and student of Uta Hagen who read Stanislavsky and landed occasional bit parts in local television dramas and off-Broadway productions.[129] The assortment of burlesque routines in *Striporama* was excused by a flimsy frame story, but when Irving Klaw later produced his own burlesque features (*Varietease* [1954] and *Teaserama* [1955]) he abandoned this narrative fig leaf and returned to the traditional burlesque format. Klaw, who was later prosecuted by postal authorities for shipping his 16 mm "art studies" through the U.S. mail, saw the distinction between feature films and short stag reels as only a matter of scale. Lili St. Cyr, star of *Varietease*, described Klaw's "mode of operation" to historian Eric Schaefer as infinitely malleable:

> He would take these separate segments—one with me, and one with Betty Page, and all these other girls—then he would splice them together until he had enough time—fifty minutes or whatever—and make what he would call a full picture. But actually it was nothing but a bunch of segments of ten or twelve different girls doing their various acts. He'd piece them together in several different movies. The one I did he put into several other movies that I heard about later.[130]

Klaw's strategy resembled what had been happening in the race movie market during the late 1940s, where short subjects were sometimes extracted from existing features while new features might be created by assembling a collage of existing shorts. But while William Alexander had used the same master of ceremonies throughout *Burlesque in Harlem* to provide at least a semblance of dramatic continuity, the various performers in Klaw's "full pictures" are introduced by whoever happened to be hanging around the loft when the equipment was ready.

The ubiquity of strippers and exotic dancers was a constant factor in New York's postwar sex exploitation films—unlike the prewar era, where films like *Sex Madness* (1938) claimed the high ground while "promoting" sex education or exposing the evils of narcotics. Strippers allowed the presence of music (and in the pure burlesque films, comedy), and when some kind of narrative line was attempted the titillating grind house ambiance fit easily into common showbiz or urban gangster models. Hugh Prince's *Harlem Follies* (1949), for example, blends race movie and burlesque film tropes through the use of a plot that borrows liberally from such backstage musicals as *42nd Street* and *Footlight Parade*. Will nightclub impresario Max Granville be able to impress his backers and raise enough cash to put on his latest extravaganza? Prince was himself a writer and producer of burlesque shows, although he seems to have had no previous connection with the race film market.[131] It is hard to say where *Harlem Follies* was shot, although the presence of a chorus line from New York's Savannah

Club (a Genovese crime family operation at 68 West Third Street) suggests it was made locally. Prince may have used an all-black cast here as a ploy, realizing, as Thomas Cripps claims, that local censors often made allowances "for the arcana of black culture" displayed in race movies, especially in terms of comedy, music, and dancing, assuming that such films would only be seen by black audiences.[132] Records of the New York State motion picture censorship office do show that the film was submitted for review in several versions during the 1950s, indicating that it was recut over time as a way of appealing to different audiences. It would be interesting to know if *Harlem Follies* drew most of its support from white or black audiences.

Prince's next film, *The Strip-Tease Murder Case* (1950), places its strippers in a mob-infested nightclub (an inside joke?). It begins well enough, with atmospheric nighttime photography of West Fifty-Second street, while a narrator tells us that Abbott and Costello, Bert Lahr, and Phil Silvers all started in the burlesque business. Only about fifteen or twenty minutes of this film is devoted to a desultory love triangle and murder mystery plot, while the rest consists entirely of straight burlesque routines. Although that approach recalls the plot structure of several earlier race movies, the production values here are far lower, and Prince seems almost contemptuous of anything approaching narrative logic. The identification of the real killer is provided only by the voice-over narrator ("Oh say, I almost forgot to tell you who knocked Vince off."). This proves to be a minor character whose brief earlier appearance is then recalled for viewers by the insertion of a freeze-frame! As Eric Schaefer notes, "Not only are the story elements handled as an afterthought, they are shot as one too."[133]

It would be interesting to see Prince's last film, *I Could Not Marry* (1951), apparently a straight psycho-killer melodrama framed by the murderer's confession of his unholy obsessions to a prison psychiatrist. If independent features from this period have a poor survival rate in general, exploitation films are even harder to locate, and their traces exist mainly in press books and applications filed with local censorship offices. *I Could Not Marry* sounds promising on paper, with its Greenwich Village location and a troubled protagonist attempting to exorcise his demons through the creation of art. But Hugh Prince was no Fritz Lang (*Scarlet Street*), and it may be more rewarding to read about this film than to actually sit through it.[134] Prince himself is also a somewhat mysterious figure, and unlike Irving Klaw or Bud Pollard is not even well known to exploitation film specialists. All three of his films were produced by Arthur Jarwood for Futurity Films Corp. and released by Classic Pictures, Inc. Classic, which also released *I Married a Savage*, was a specialist in the most marginal cinema of the early 1950s. But their list included not only schlocky titles like these but worthy films that would not otherwise have been available through any distributor, like Jack Arnold's Oscar-nominated *With These Hands* (1950), Pierre Chenal's adaptation of Richard Wright's *Native Son* (1951), and George

Stoney's groundbreaking STD documentary, *Birthright* (1952). Strange bedfellows, indeed.[135]

Marvin Rothenberg made *Strip Tease Hold-Up* sometime in 1952, but I have never seen it and can only depend on the credit of a local cameraman, Fred Bornet, to establish it as a New York production (Bornet later shot *Purlie Victorious* for Ossie Davis). Willis Kent's *Strip Parade Follies* (1953) is even more of a question. Because these films were nearly all nonunion, more formal notions of union jurisdiction have little relevance. And can a Florida production count as a New York picture? A case in point was another Lili St. Cyr vehicle, *Josette of New Orleans*, which was shot at the Ball studio in Miami by a team of transplanted New Yorkers. As noted earlier, Joseph Lerner and Rex Carlton, and their regular New York crew (including Gerald Hirschfeld and Jim Shields) began shooting *The Miami Story* there in April 1952. While Lili St. Cyr provided marquee value, the presence of distinguished British actor John Loder was carefully noted in prerelease publicity, suggesting that Lerner was not making a burlesque picture but another edgy urban noir like *Guilty Bystander*. But Carlton, who was financing the film, declared bankruptcy in September and *The Miami Story* disappeared. Renamed *Josette of New Orleans*, it took five more years to finally reach its public. Surviving publicity material promises a "Sultry! Sexy! Sensational Striptease!" while billing only Lili St. Cyr (wrapped in a python apparently left over from *I Married a Savage*). Joseph Lerner hid behind his "Joseph Lee" pseudonym, a strategy he also followed with *Girl on the Run*, another misbegotten project that somehow crossed the line from hardboiled thriller to burlesque picture. He failed to mention the film at all when I interviewed him in 1987 and would have been pleased to learn that it is now considered lost.

One of the few such features that does still circulate is producer William Paul Mishkin's *Violated* (1953), the first effort in a lengthy career in sexploitation and gore (*The Orgy at Lil's Place* [1963], *Bloodthirsty Butchers* [1970]). But it is also the only feature film directed by the noted dance photographer Walter Strate, closely associated at the time with Valerie Bettis, José Limón, and Doris Humphrey. Strate had already directed three award-winning dance shorts, *The Desperate Heart* (1949), *The Moor's Pavane* (1951), and *Lament* (1952), but why he agreed to direct *Violated*—and take credit for it—can only be imagined.[136] Could Mishkin have known him because of the "figure studies" he exhibited or the course in "photography of the nude" he offered at The Camera Club on West Sixty-Eighth Street?[137] Perhaps the project sounded more legitimate when it was first proposed to him.

Violated is the story of a commercial photographer who works out of a loft at 144 Wooster Street (the film is well grounded in specific New York locations) and has not only been murdering attractive young women but also cutting off their hair. Mom is to blame for all this, of course, as we learn from a confession extracted under "truth serum" by an officious police psychiatrist. "It's one of the most cogent cases of subconscious passion I've ever seen," he tells us. Wim Holland, who coproduced the picture, stars as the psychotic photographer, a pathetic sort who spends most of the film mooning after a hard-hearted stripper (played by Lili Dawn) who alternately leads him on and humiliates him ("You make my skin crawl, you jerk!"). The *AFI Catalog* suggests that the film was shot in 16 mm, a distinct possibility given its obviously limited production circumstances. There are some interesting exteriors on a Hudson River ferry, in Central Park, and on the streets of Greenwich Village, where the villain takes one of his prospective victims for coffee at the Caffe Reggio. Most of the interiors are shot in the photographer's loft (we see him working there with a pair of ballet dancers), in a cheap approximation of a police station, and inside Ernie's, a nightclub at 76 West Third Street where Lili entertains the customers.[138] The club is name-checked more than once, and its neon sign is treated to a nicely lit close-up, suggesting it was made available in exchange for some prominent product placement. This Ernie's, of course, has nothing to do with the elegant San Francisco restaurant featured in Alfred Hitchcock's *Vertigo* (1958), but it did play a role in J. D. Salinger's *The Catcher in the Rye* (published 1951) as one of the spots visited by Holden Caulfield during his Manhattan odyssey. Holden drops in because his older brother used to take him there "before he went out to Hollywood and prostituted himself."[139] He also thinks it will be an easy place for an underage drinker to order a Scotch and soda. But the place is full of phonies and he doesn't stay long. *Variety*, spotting the film as part of the recent burlesque movie trend, was especially harsh, even finding the stripper "embarrassingly awkward." But they did praise the "thin documentary veneer" laid on by the location photography, as well as Tony Mottola's score, a jazz guitar solo that reminded them of his work on the current CBS television series *Suspense*.[140]

Violated was released in December 1953 and must have played somewhere in New York, although Bosley Crowther never reviewed it in the *Times*. I like to think that if it did play there, maybe down the street from the Rialto on Times Square, another local photographer might have been sitting in the audience, making mental notes. He was the sort of film buff who saw everything, and even the "terrible films on Forty-Second Street" were teaching him valuable lessons in what not to do.[141] He had also made a few shorts and had just released his first feature. Lately he had been spending a lot of time with ballet dancers and had recently moved in with a member of Jerome Robbins's company. In fact, Stanley Kubrick probably knew Walter Strate very well, at least by reputation. So when the lights came on and the men in trench coats shuffled back up the aisle, he would have realized just how lucky he had been to sign up with Joseph Burstyn.

PART III
RENAISSANCE

CHAPTER 10

CRIME ON THE WATERFRONT

The shooting season in New York ran from March through November, as it always had. No one wanted to be working outdoors in the winter, but things would soon be changing. On January 1, 1954, a midwinter dead spot in the local film industry's production calendar, Robert F. Wagner would succeed Vincent Impellitteri as mayor. While Tammany Hall celebrated, two feature film crews continued to struggle with a pair of very difficult shoots. Elia Kazan and Marlon Brando were braving the weather in Hoboken, and Stanley Kubrick was trying to hold his independent production company together over in the East Village. In retrospect, the success of these two projects may have seemed predictable, but things looked very different at the time.

> You don't have to be told who Elia Kazan is and what his artistic standing is in the m.p. world. Kazan is now making WATERFRONT, filming it right on the docks of New York and New Jersey. We are proud that Boris Kaufman, his camerman [sic], is using C-E equipment—a BNC camera, a dolly and dolly track, among other things....
>
> Stanley Kubrik [sic], of Minotaur Productions, used C-E cameras and equipment for a feature filmed entirely in New York City.[1]

Frank Zucker, the venerable head of Camera Equipment Co., had been a factor in the New York film business for forty years, catering to local producers who always needed to get their hands on some good professional studio equipment at a good price. He founded Camera Equipment Company in 1936 and was now publishing an irregular newsletter out of its offices at 1600 Broadway.[2] The sixteen-page sheet promoted his products and plugged the local producers who made use of them. In addition to the two films mentioned above, the second issue name-checked *Johnny Jupiter*, a puppet show being filmed for television by Soundmasters, and *William Tell*, an Errol Flynn project for which producer Barry Mahon had taken "our BNC Mitchell Camera" to Italy. One picture shows a smiling Flynn receiving "a warm reception from the office gals at Camera Equipment." Really not much to talk about that season, but business was about to pick up.

With the exception of *Hansel and Gretel*, *On the Waterfront* and *Killer's Kiss* were the only two features shooting in New York during the winter of 1953–54. The overlap in their production dates—Kubrick started *Killer's Kiss* in October, while *On the Waterfront* began in November—is pure coincidence, and the films differ significantly in everything from the way they were cast to how their sound was recorded. There are also major differences in style, budget, and theme. But what they do share goes beyond their association with Frank Zucker and his local equipment rental house. It is impossible to imagine either of these films being made, just as they were, at any other time or in any other place. These were the sort of films the struggling motion picture industry in New York had been preparing itself to make for the past twenty years.

The 1949 Pulitzer Prize for Local Reporting was awarded to Malcolm Johnson of the *New York Sun* for a series of twenty-four articles exposing "Crime on the Waterfront" in New York City (the drama prize that year went to Arthur Miller for *Death of a Salesman*). Johnson was not just a crime reporter; since the early 1930s he had also put in his time reviewing movies and club openings, and favorable quotes would occasionally find their way into display ads. The dying daily may have been trying to win new readers with the series, but the Pulitzer came too late to do the *Sun* any good, and it went out of business in January 1950. Johnson eventually landed on his feet at Hearst's International News Service, but by then the series had already been optioned by the Monticello Film Corporation.

Monticello had been incorporated in New York in the autumn of 1948 and purchased the rights to "Crime on the Waterfront" as early as May 1949.[3] It was the creation of Joseph Curtis, a vice-president of the Weiss & Geller advertising agency who was also the son of Jack Cohn, executive vice-president of Columbia Pictures and nominal head of their East Coast operations. Like many others that year, Curtis sought to take advantage of the promise of independent film production, and Monticello was only one element in a much more ambitious plan that even dabbled in theater acquisition. News of the project was broken by Hedda Hopper on June 2, Hedda eagerly promoting it as "a sock story, about all the water-front rackets and how they've been thriving, and would be ideal for Humphrey Bogart or Richard Widmark."[4] On June 15 the *New York Sun* reported that the film would be shot "in semi-documentary form . . . on actual locations in New York City," the accepted standard for "realistic" films of crime and corruption.[5] Johnson would write the screenplay himself, in collaboration with Henry Denker, a novelist who also wrote and directed radio plays. Indeed, Denker was also announced as director of the $500,000 production, which was scheduled to go before the cameras in September.[6] Since neither Johnson nor Denker had ever worked on a motion picture, Monticello apparently tried to acquire some sub-rosa expertise (probably on the cheap) by secretly negotiating with John Howard Lawson, most prominent member of "the Hollywood Ten." The blacklisted Lawson, who hadn't received a screen credit since *Smash-Up*, had long been a focus of FBI investigation, and on June 27 J. Edgar Hoover was informed of his plan to "work on a picture for the Montecello [sic] Film Corporation" dealing with "Crime on the Waterfront."[7] There is no further evidence of Lawson's connection to the project.

With no experience as a creative producer, Curtis seemed unable to lick the problem of transforming Johnson's episodic newspaper series into a single, coherent, dramatic narrative. A year later the *Los Angeles Times* announced that a "screen treatment" had been completed by Hollywood veteran Philip Yordan, with actor Robert Roark signed for the leading role, "a romantic ruffian," but nothing came of this version, either.[8] Then in October 1950 Universal-International released an unusual criminal melodrama called *Deported*. Director Robert Siodmak had shot the film in Naples and Rome during an extensive two-month location trip in 1949. Working with *Naked City* cinematographer William Daniels, Siodmak had created a peculiar hybrid of fiction and fact, a cynical tale of black-market waterfront activity that combined the most marketable elements of Italian neorealism and Hollywood film noir. It was also the last film Siodmak would make for a major Hollywood studio. Like many filmmakers of his generation, he was looking for a way to leave Hollywood as far behind as possible. "If you have ambition, that's always a liability in Hollywood," Siodmak later told a reporter from the *Times*, complaining about the "shopworn product" he had been "forced to manufacture" on the West Coast.[9]

Siodmak was obviously the man Joseph Curtis had been looking for, but before he could turn his attention to *Crime on the Waterfront* he needed to complete Louis de Rochemont's independent production of *The Whistle at Eaton Falls*—another film that Hollywood would never have produced. In the meantime, Curtis abandoned the Philip Yordan treatment and commissioned a new story from Edward McSorley, a specialist in Irish-American literature whose first novel, *Our Own Kind* (1946) had earned very favorable reviews and sold over 620,000 copies.[10] Its sequel, *The Young McDermott* (1949), did not fare so well, but the way it handled crime, politics, and ethnicity against a hardscrabble immigrant backdrop suggested that McSorley might be able to give *Crime on the Waterfront* the storyline Malcolm Johnson had left out.

Set in the Irish-American community of Providence, Rhode Island, in the early 1920s, *The Young McDermott* continued the story of Willie McDermott, now working his first real job as a reporter on the *Providence Herald* (McSorley himself had been a journalist; he later worked as a theatrical publicist). The novel is heavily plotted and stuffed with milieu detail. In following Willie's career we see him accused of being a "God-damn stool pigeon" when cousins of his are identified as bootleg hijackers, causing him to ponder how far clan loyalties should trump his obligations as a journalist.[11] Later on, after being radicalized, he sees police shoot down a striking Portuguese mill worker and takes part in a memorial march organized by union insurgents. He flees the city after refusing his publisher's order to clear himself with the corrupt union leader, John McArdle, a traitor to his class who arranges sweetheart deals with the mill owners while fiercely battling any opposition from "red agitators."

Edward McSorley's contribution to the development of *On the Waterfront* has been completely lost to history, largely because the man who followed him on the job, Budd Schulberg, wanted it that way. According to his own account, Schulberg was approached by Curtis and Siodmak to write the screenplay of *Crime on the Waterfront*, but what Schulberg always left out was that the screenplay he was supposed to write would be based on a story treatment written by Edward McSorley.

Like Siodmak, Budd Schulberg was another disgruntled Hollywood veteran. Now living on a farm in Bucks County, Pennsylvania, he was about to publish *The Disenchanted*, a roman à clef that implicated even more Hollywood insiders than his 1941 best-seller, *What Makes Sammy Run?* He loathed the movie business but agreed to sign on when told that he could do all of his work on the East Coast—and that his father, onetime movie mogul B. P. Schulberg, who "was living in my guesthouse working on his memoirs," would be brought on as a producer. Schulberg attributed his father's failure in Hollywood not to his own business decisions but to personal betrayal and the general atmosphere of shady business ethics, qualities he had already excoriated in his two Hollywood novels. He told Curtis and Siodmak that he hadn't left Hollywood but that "it had left me" after *What Makes Sammy Run?* was attacked by the "establishment" as "the work of a 'traitor.'"[12] What he may not have told them was that this same novel had also precipitated his explosive break with the Communist Party, the result of an attack largely orchestrated by the Hollywood chapter's leading figure, John Howard Lawson.[13]

We know that Schulberg was at work on this script by the end of 1950 because when Monticello's Sam Shaw submitted McSorley's "treatment—screenplay story" to the Breen Office on December 26 he boasted that while it was the work of "this prominent author," it was Budd Schulberg who was currently writing the screenplay.[14] McSorley's treatment is no longer available, but Schulberg's adaptation does survive, if only because Monticello circulated copies to prospective investors in 1951. In this earliest surviving draft we see no Crime Commission, no priest, no romantic story, and no focus on union corruption. Instead we follow a crusading reporter as he uncovers the evils of the shape-up, kickbacks paid to pier bosses by longshoremen desperate for work, and criminal loan-sharking schemes. All of this is seen to be masterminded by Bernard H. Burns, known as "Big He," described as "power-mad, vain and ruthless . . . king of the waterfront." Big He is not a union official but (operating as B. H. Burns Associates) controls the union and everything else connected to local shipping and transportation through a corrupt network of judges and politicians extending from Washington, DC, to the cop on the beat. Intimidation and violence are rampant, and a pre-credits sequence shows two of his thugs terrorizing the family of an insurgent longshoreman by dangling their screaming infant out a tenement window. Big He is a younger version of William J. McCormack, a mysterious real-life figure who began as a teamster but whose well-connected Penn Stevedoring operation eventually controlled the movement of goods shipped through the Port of New York. Malcolm Johnson was very clear that it was McCormack who was the evil genius behind all the corruption on the waterfront and obviously communicated this view to McSorley or Schulberg.[15] Robert Siodmak is listed as director on this undated draft, and while no specific actors are named, one can easily imagine the leading role played by Broderick Crawford, the memorable Willie Stark of *All the King's Men* (1949).

Although wealthy and powerful, Big He is still tied to the old neighborhood, where he lives with his mother in a walk-up apartment that provides easy access to his rooftop pigeon coop. "Some men are content to soar over their caged hopes on a pigeon's wing," a narrator tells us, but while Big He may have started small he has "clawed his way with a cargo-hook until he reached the top." Not an unattractive figure, he is keeping Kay Moran, an "ambitious and brittle beauty" whose career he promotes. Kay seems genuinely fond of Big He but is primarily concerned with material possessions. "I never want to smell the cabbage in the hallway again," she tells him, one of many specifically Irish touches suggestive of McSorley's work.

Another local, Joe Brush, has always loved Kay from afar, aware that he can never provide her with the creature comforts she desires (perhaps a role for Richard Conte, star of Siodmak's *Cry of the City*). During the course of the film he steps up as leader of the insurgents after the murder of Johnny Dutra, an outspoken waterfront agitator who is gored with his own hook. "He was going to bring these things out into the open. Name names," says a reporter. But Big He's goons set him straight. "He was a commie. They don't like commies on the waterfront...." The reporter (officially unnamed but referred to in a note as "M. Johnson" of the *Evening Sun*), is the most peculiar character in this version. He senses a story in this waterfront violence and spends most of the film gathering information by interviewing the other characters, who provide plenty of backstory. But he also serves as the narrator, delivering a voice-over commentary that makes clear anything else we might need to know or feel.

The script avoids any discussion of systemic union corruption, blaming everything on the William McCormack figure, the waterfront's "Mr. Big." When Dutra, and later Joe Brush, gather the men together for a mass meeting, it is not to vote anyone in or out but simply "to see what can be done about conditions on the waterfront." This meeting occurs on the same night as a glittering testimonial dinner honoring Big He, attended by VIPs from all levels of business and government. But at their meeting the longshoremen are attacked by thugs who beat all the minor characters senseless and kill the fleeing Joe Brush. The police take no action, and even two sympathetic detectives refuse to arrest Big He for ordering the killing (his culpability is apparently public knowledge), although they are outraged enough to start off for his apartment with the intention of working him over in the line of duty. But Kay has heard of Joe's death and gets there ahead of them, tracking Big He down to the pigeon coop we saw in the first reel. She restores her moral standing by firing a couple of bullets into him.

While this draft shies away from any direct criticism of the labor movement, it presents a far darker picture of police, judicial, and municipal corruption than anything yet seen in an American film. The Johnny Dutra character is an impotent agitator, the efforts of the men to improve their situation lead only to death, and there is no hope that the cops or the Crime Commission (not even mentioned here) will ever pay attention to this mess, much less act to correct it. Indeed, the reporter is still gathering his facts at the end of the script, and we never even see his story published. Only vigilante justice, it seems, can rid us of so powerful and well connected a villain.

It is hard to believe that any Hollywood studio would have considered a film in which the criminal lead is shown to control the judiciary and the police are spineless lapdogs. Even John Howard Lawson, a real Communist, would have turned Johnny Dutra into a Joe Hill figure around whose spirit the men could successfully rally. Monticello, unfamiliar with the ways of Hollywood, was about to learn an expensive lesson. Joe Breen responded to Shaw's submission of the McSorley treatment on January 4, 1951. The news was very bad. *Crime on the Waterfront* was "wholly and completely unacceptable" under the provisions of the Production Code, and Breen ordered Monticello to "dismiss from further consideration any plans for utilizing this material for motion picture purposes."[16] The reasons given in this letter are worth reprinting at length:

First of all, it is a story filled with a savage and primitive sort of brutality, violence, debasement, and corruption, so as to make the overall flavor of the material seem excessively low-toned and depraved.

Aside from the extreme cruelty and violence, large segments of the story suggest a wholesale breakdown of public order. It is indicated that police officers, judges, and public officials of every sort, up to the highest level, are completely at the mercy of the corrupting influence of the principal villain.

In addition, the story quite clearly indicates that the female lead is a complete sexual wanton. Not only is it suggested that she is living as the kept woman of the villain but, when the time comes, it is also indicated that she indulges in fornication with one of the principal sympathetic characters.

Lastly, there is a most offensive note in this story in that it is indicated that the completely loathsome, ruthless, obnoxious villain is a supporter of religion, who employs financial aid to the church in a hypocritical way, to build up his social standing. Such a suggestion would be immensely offensive to decent people.

The fact that Big He is shot in the last few seconds of the story not only does not balance the moral scales, but actually simply adds one more crime of violence to the closing minutes of the play. Furthermore, this accounts for only one of the criminals, thus leaving many others to go scot-free as far as the audience is concerned.[17]

Robert Siodmak had finished shooting *The Whistle at Eaton Falls* in November 1950, and over the next few months worked closely with Schulberg at the author's Bucks County farmhouse, helping turn McSorley's treatment into a workable scenario. The surviving script draft, completed by Schulberg subsequent to the submission of McSorley's treatment, would remove the material about Big He's financial contributions to the Catholic Church, which may have been too obviously modeled on Bill McCormack's role as "a pillar of the New York archdiocese and the universal church."[18] But the rest of this script hardly retreats at all from the bleak world view that shocked Joe Breen when he paged through McSorley's original.

On January 7, 1951, the *New York Times* reported that Schulberg and Siodmak were "whipping the script into shape" and hoped to start shooting in March. Siodmak said he would "concentrate on New York players" for his cast and "try to avoid plot as much as possible and make the most use of characterization and the wonderful waterfront backgrounds."[19] But that interview took place before Monticello received the bad news from Hollywood. Sam Shaw sent an angry telegram to Joe Breen on January 8, suggesting that no one at the MPPA had actually read the cover letter accompanying McSorley's treatment and demanding the immediate return of the manuscript.[20] A few days later Siodmak appeared on *The Lilli Palmer Show* on WCBS-TV. As he had no other film currently in release, he must have been there to talk about *Crime on the Waterfront*, and I would love to know what he had to say.

Largely ignoring Breen's suggestions, Monticello prepared a temporary production budget based on Schulberg's draft, calling for a tight twenty-five-day shooting schedule with a total negative cost of $367,500. This budget indicates a $10,000 payment for the "original story material" and $35,000 for the screenplay, although how this was to be divided among Johnson, McSorley, and Schulberg is unknown. Siodmak was also down for $35,000, with $50,000 set aside for an unnamed star and $25,000 for the rest of the cast.[21] While much less than what Elia Kazan's film would eventually cost, this figure compares well with the $350,000 spent by Sidney Lumet on another important New York film, *12 Angry Men*, five years later.[22]

With no distributor set, the picture was still being shopped around. Jack Curtis certainly hoped he might get lucky with his uncle, Harry Cohn, the head of production at Columbia Pictures (although Bernard Dick claims that Harry had little regard for his brother Jack's judgment).[23] And Siodmak still had a connection with Universal-International, for whom he had made a series of money-making films in the 1940s (among the noir classics he directed for them was producer Mark Hellinger's *The Killers*). According to his biographer, Deborah Lazaroff Alpi, "Universal's corporate newsletter announced that Siodmak would direct a film about dock workers in New York with a cast of complete unknowns."[24] The *Times* continued to report on the project, announcing on March 2 that "Harold Bayne, local musical comedy and nightclub singer," had been hired to appear in it.[25] Bayne was an obscure local talent most frequently heard on the Catskills resort hotel circuit, although he did have an uncredited bit as an intern in *The Sleeping City*. The announcement may simply have been a press agent's fantasy, but it would not be the last time someone suggested casting a lounge singer in Schulberg's waterfront picture. Indeed, the news may have sparked the imagination of Maxwell Anderson and Rouben Mamoulian, whose waterfront corruption musical *The Devil's Hornpipe* was announced for 1952. Never produced on Broadway, the property was eventually sold to Universal-International, which cast James Cagney as the grasping boss of a small Brooklyn local. Some scenes were shot along the DUMBO waterfront in late 1957, but *Never Steal Anything Small*, the last James Cagney musical, went unreleased until 1959.

At this point the exact sequence of events becomes even more cloudy. The decision was made to abandon McSorley's narrative and set Schulberg to work researching a completely different treatment of Johnson's material. Not only would Breen's objections need to be taken into account, but all of the plotting and characterization created by McSorley must also vanish without a trace. This required much more from Schulberg than the simple adaptation of another writer's manuscript.

Raised as a Hollywood princeling and familiar with the struggles of the working class only through his old Marxist study groups, Schulberg understood that he knew nothing of life on the waterfront. He realized it could take a year to research the subject properly and turned for help to Malcolm Johnson, who advised him to "go see Corridan—Father John, he really knows the score."[26] An activist Jesuit priest associated with the Xavier Labor School on West Sixteenth Street, Father John Corridan had been ministering to workers on the West Side docks since 1946. When he tried to raise public alarm at the crime and corruption he discovered there, he soon realized that he was fighting not only the mob-ridden union hierarchy, with its dense web of political connections, but the hierarchy of the Roman Catholic Archdiocese of New York as well.

Remarkably aware of the power of the media, Corridan published his own waterfront newsletter (*The Crusader*) and befriended key journalists and politicians who could help publicize his battle. He became a frequent source for print and broadcast journalists reporting on the situation, and in one letter to a fellow priest even claimed to have ghosted Johnson's final series of exposés, which had appeared in January 1949.[27] Corridan befriended Schulberg as well, introducing him to one of his own key sources, a battered insurgent longshoreman named Arthur Browne.[28] "Brownie" took Schulberg in hand, introducing him to the waterfront bars up and down the West Side, vouching for the presence of an obvious outsider. "In subsequent months my longshoreman friends and I sat in any number of water-front bars where killers were pointed out with the frequency of movie stars recognized in Dave Chasen's Hollywood restaurant," Schulberg remembered.[29]

Schulberg admired Corridan's courage and humanity, but he also valued his knowledge of waterfront issues and willingness to take on whatever establishment stood in his way. Even more impressive was the way in which Corridan managed to promote his social activism not as a left-wing crusade but as a form of anti-Communism, telling readers of the conservative *New York Sun* that "it is conditions such as prevail along the docks that promote the cause of Communism, not the American way of life."[30] Fascinated by the tough-talking, chain-smoking priest, Schulberg would eventually turn him into one of *On the Waterfront*'s central characters, delivering exactly what Corridan had asked for—"a *Going My Way* with substance."[31]

On April 14, 1951, Schulberg finished typing what he later came to consider the "first draft" of *Crime on the Waterfront* (that is, the first draft not based on McSorley's story idea). While still adhering to the revelations in Malcolm Johnson's articles, it featured a completely different narrative line. Over the years Schulberg would have plenty to say about the ups and downs of this project, which would become the most famous film he would ever be associated with. But he never told anyone exactly what was on his mind as he completed that draft, which is a pity because two days earlier his friend Richard Collins

10.1. Budd Schulberg at work. A Hollywood refugee, he agreed to adapt Malcolm Johnson's *Crime on the Waterfront* only if he could do all his work at home. Bison Archives.

had informed the House Committee on Un-American Activities that it was Budd Schulberg who had recruited him into the Communist Party. Collins also named two dozen others, including the directors Robert Rossen, Abraham Polonsky, and Frank Tuttle. These were big names, but it was Schulberg (author of a current best-seller) whose name came first when the *Washington Post* put the story on page one the next morning.[32]

Almost immediately, waterfront boss Joe Ryan ("Life President" of the International Longshoreman's Association since 1943) wrote to Malcolm Johnson's employer, William Randolph Hearst, Jr., smearing Johnson for his association with a reputed Communist. Johnson insisted that he had no knowledge of Schulberg's Communist associations, past or present. "If he is, or was, it will certainly hurt the prospects of our movie and that I shall regret for we had planned a hard-hitting, honest, documentary type film."[33] According to Schulberg, "once Siodmak and Father Corridan had approved [the script], out it went to tough Columbia honcho Harry Cohn, who turned it down, with an assist from Joe Ryan. He told Cohn it was the work of a 'commie'—me—based on the original series by another 'commie,' Malcolm Johnson."[34] Schulberg must have known, of course, that Columbia had just released a similar film of its own, *The Mob*, based on a *Collier's* magazine serial called *The Waterfront*. But that film, like Paramount's 1948 *Waterfront at Midnight* and similar waterfront exposés, had more to do with hijacking and said nothing about the role of union corruption.

Collins had been subpoenaed by HUAC in 1947 but was never called. If he had been, he claimed in his 1951 testimony, he would have refused to testify, but he felt differently about it now. His voluntary appearance before the Committee, and the sheer number of names he named, set a model for subsequent repentant Communists. (Edward Dmytryk, who had already gone to jail as one of the original Hollywood Ten, would testify voluntarily on April 25 and also produced a long list of names.) After seeing his name in the papers, Schulberg reached out to the Committee and took the stand on May 23. Outraged at being identified as a Communist—he claimed to have left the party in 1941—he demonstrated his bona fides by supplying his own list of names, including that of John Howard Lawson, a popular target also identified by fourteen other witnesses that season, including Collins and Dmytryk.[35] Did he know that Curtis had once considered bringing Lawson into the project, long before he himself had ever heard of it? Most of the friendly witnesses had agreed to testify because they had hopes of salvaging their careers in the motion picture industry. But the situation was different for Schulberg, who had written off his own Hollywood career years earlier. There was only one thing he needed to salvage: *Crime on the Waterfront*. But after the 1951 HUAC hearings were over, the ill-fated project seemed dead in the water.

In her biography of Siodmak, Deborah Alpi claims that these HUAC revelations were the primary reason that "Universal halted development of the project."[36] At the time, of course, Schulberg publicly ignored any fallout from the hearings and put most of the blame for the collapse of the project on Monticello. "The little film company was something less than a financial rock. In fact, it was unable to get up the 'scratch.' "[37] He also identified a more practical reason for Harry Cohn's sudden lack of interest in a film that all the creative participants insisted must be shot on location. "The subject matter was a little too hot to handle. If the longshoremen's locals were gangster run, how could our picture company get on the docks? Why not make a nice Western or a musical? Prospective backers backed away." Alpi refers to this more dramatically as "death threats from the Mafia."[38] Siodmak had also had enough and left for Europe to direct Burt Lancaster in *The Crimson Pirate*.[39] In a letter to Father Corridan that summer, Schulberg confessed that "our waterfront picture has hit a number of snags, the most recent one being the hesitancy of backers to go ahead without Ryan's approval for fear of AFL opposition to the picture."[40] After *On the Waterfront* was released in 1954 Siodmak was reported to have sued Sam Spiegel, the film's eventual producer, over his contribution to the script; according to Alpi, he was awarded $100,000 in damages.[41]

Schulberg's April 14, 1951, script draft, written before he, Collins, or Elia Kazan had testified before HUAC, can be found today among Kazan's papers at Wesleyan University, although it predates his connection to the project by many months. After Kazan came aboard the script would undergo a further series of revisions before the completed film was released, but this rough material is already recognizable as *On the Waterfront*—or at least a sketch of the main ideas that had attracted Budd Schulberg in the first place. It is a film about a crusading waterfront priest, Father Moran. Moran is radicalized following the suspicious death of the one honest longshoreman who would not play ball with the mob-controlled union bosses (he is crushed by a falling load of barrels). When Terry Monahan, a younger and more obviously rebellious longshoreman, is found floating in the river, Father Moran delivers a stirring eulogy in demand of justice. Terry's sister Edie also raises her voice, denouncing the racketeers and eventually convincing crusading newspaperman Al Chase to expose the horrors of the waterfront in the press. The virgin Edie has replaced the whore, Kay, and the outsider function of the reporter has largely been supplanted by another new character, the priest. Working with Kazan over the next three years, Schulberg would eliminate the character of the reporter entirely while gradually decreasing the importance of this priest, his Father Corridan surrogate (although he would build the character up again in the *Waterfront* novel he published in 1955).[42] Terry would eventually become the center of the film, and Edie would not be his sister but his love interest. The Waterfront Crime Commission would arrive like the U.S. Cavalry, offering real help to a working class incapable of freeing themselves from the grip of their corrupt union. The Big Bill McCormack figure would be reduced to a cameo, replaced by a union boss more recognizable as Joe Ryan. And the main character would achieve redemption by naming names. There would be good reasons for all these changes.

After his HUAC testimony Schulberg continued working on the project, soaking up more waterfront atmosphere and trying to find other publication outlets for this new obsession of his. He attempted to keep public interest alive (and dominate the discourse) through a series of articles in the *New York Times*, the *Saturday Evening Post, Commonweal*, and even *Holiday*.[43] That summer CBS broadcast a Peabody Award–winning radio documentary on "the slave conditions of the longshoreman," but the film had fallen off the radar.[44] By the end of 1951 the *Times* listed *Crime on the Waterfront* as one of several promising films that appeared to have "missed the boat."[45] On March 31, 1952, Schulberg wrote to Corridan that he was withdrawing from the Monticello deal because he had "lost faith" in Curtis and couldn't stomach his demands for "more violence and sex" in the script. In another month, he claimed, Monticello would lose their option on the property, and he was considering working on it directly with Johnson, "with the idea of finding sounder auspices for our script."[46] Breaking with Curtis may also have given Schulberg a financial reason to disown everything he had committed to print while under contract to Monticello. Whatever rights Schulberg subsequently acquired were challenged by Monticello after Curtis's death in 1954. Schulberg may have picked up rights to the newspaper stories, they argued, but Monticello claimed they still had a deal with him covering any script he might have written based on McSorley's treatment.[47]

His first move was to contact Edward Small. Known for decades as a producer and packager of inexpensive genre pictures, Small had recently been reissuing many of his older properties for sale to television, one of the first Hollywood veterans to do so. He was comfortable with low-budget film noir, having recently produced films like *Raw Deal, T-Men,* and *Scandal Sheet*—a reporter-centric noir from the pen of Sam Fuller. Small would have seen *Crime on the Waterfront* as a good fit, especially now that he was about to sign a releasing deal with United Artists calling for him to supply thirteen films over the next three years. Perhaps it was just a coincidence that announcements of the deal in the press linked his name to that of another independent producer, Sam Spiegel.[48] Small was interested, but cautious. On April 15 Schulberg sent him the latest draft of the script, which he immediately passed along to the Breen Office "before going ahead with any future plans on this project."[49]

"We realize that this present script represents very many changes over the original version of the story, which was presented to us and found to be utterly and completely unacceptable under the Code," Breen replied. Unfortunately, the current draft was still "a long way from what the Code requires." Although Schulberg had done what he could to scrub much of the sex and violence, the script still contained a suicide, two men who "both seem to be on the wanton side in their relationships with women," and "a number of criminals on the top" who go unpunished. Most significantly, "this is a story of great crime and corruption which is told without any seeming reference to law and order." While not as definitive as their earlier rejection, the Breen Office still concluded that "only a vast number of changes could make this material acceptable."[50] That sounded like a lot of hard work to Edward Small, who passed on Schulberg's project but immediately began production on two other violent urban noirs, *Kansas City Confidential* and *New York Confidential*.[51]

The Bottom of the River

On April 10, 1952, Elia Kazan appeared in public session before the House Un-American Activities Committee and offered up his own list of one-time Communist Party members.[52] A highly successful stage and screen director, Kazan was the most prominent of all the friendly witnesses, closely identified with such critical and commercial successes as *Death of a Salesman* and

A Streetcar Named Desire. Critics of his decision to testify claim that with such a track record Kazan would have had no trouble continuing his career—although maybe not in Hollywood. But what had he done lately? *Flight Into Egypt*, his first Broadway show since *Streetcar*, opened in March and closed in April. *Viva Zapata!*, Fox's most expensive black-and-white release of the season, had also just opened, and was also on its way to losing a lot of money. On March 20 the Academy of Motion Picture Arts and Sciences had snubbed Kazan's work on *A Streetcar Named Desire*, as had the Directors Guild of America (although he did better on the East Coast, winning the New York Film Critics Circle award as Best Director).

Under subpoena, Kazan had testified in closed session on January 14 but named no one. When news of his "secret" appearance was leaked to the *Hollywood Reporter* just before Oscar night, he knew the Committee would not be so easily satisfied. "Name the names, for chrissake," Darryl F. Zanuck told him. "Who the hell are you going to jail for? You'll be sitting there and someone else will sure as hell name these people."[53] Kazan returned to Washington and named those who had been with him in the Group Theatre's party cell in 1934–1936, including Clifford Odets and Paula Strasberg. In his autobiography, he recalls that the "storm of anger" following his testimony especially affected his wife Molly, who felt "I was being unfairly reviled." In response, she went off by herself and wrote a one-page statement defending his testimony, which he agreed to place as a display ad in the *New York Times*.[54]

There is a problem with this chronology. Kazan's April 10 testimony was released the following day and reported on page 8 of the *New York Times* on April 12. But the Kazans' display ad, which repeated verbatim much of that testimony, appeared on page 7 of the same edition.[55] Readers would have read both pieces the same day—indeed, if they were going through the paper in the usual way, they would have seen Kazan's ad first. The ad was not a response to the storm but instead was largely responsible for triggering it. It was the ad ("written by Molly") that "made people especially furious with me," Kazan remembered.[56] Instead of being just one more witness doing his best to cope with a subpoena, Kazan had gotten out in front of the Committee, arranging in advance to buy space in the *New York Times* in order to spin the story. As Victor Navasky put it, "Kazan's status, testimony, apologetic curriculum vitae, and advertisement, and rumors that he would make a big money deal with Spyros Skouras contingent on naming names—these collectively established him on the left as the ultimate betrayer."[57]

Skouras may or may not have offered him this Faustian bargain, but Kazan does describe the president of Twentieth Century-Fox urging him to film the anti-Communist exposé *I Led Three Lives* and pleading with him to go to Washington to clear himself before J. Edgar Hoover, an appointment he said he could arrange personally.[58] Kazan did neither of these things, but after his testimony

Skouras and Zanuck had no problem sending him to Bavaria to direct *Man on a Tightrope*, something that would not have happened had he made a show of refusing to name names. Fredric March would play a Czech circus owner who makes a break for the border—with his entire circus—in a film that has long been regarded as a public certification of Kazan's anti-Communist credentials. But what it really documents is Kazan's annoyance with the Communist Party's attempts to enforce cultural uniformity on its art workers—a complaint he shared with the author of *What Makes Sammy Run?* The March character boasts of having survived a decade of Hitlerite occupation and the aftermath of a world war, but by 1952 things have become intolerable. Not because he longs for greater political democracy or fears the growth of a police state but because the party has been trying to force him to rewrite his clown act. As the film suggests, artists are the same all over the world.

Kazan might have passed muster with Spyros Skouras, but most of his longtime collaborators felt differently about it. A few months after testifying he passed Arthur Miller and producer Kermit Bloomgarden while leaving his office in the Victoria Theatre. Neither man offered any sign of recognition. "Although I was to work with Art again ten years later, I never really forgave him for the snub," he wrote in his autobiography.[59] Edward Dmytryk eventually learned to take such things in stride, but Kazan came to believe that *he* was the injured party; the alienated director needed to find himself a new creative partner. Kazan had admired Budd Schulberg's stand against the party during the *What Makes Sammy Run?* affair and already had a printed copy of Schulberg's HUAC testimony, which had been handed to him at the time of his own closed testimony in January, a model of what the Committee eventually hoped to see from him.[60] At Molly's suggestion he reached out to Schulberg, hoping for a sympathetic ear. The two men and their wives bonded during a weekend in Bucks County, brought together by their shared history. "His closest friend had stopped talking to him as Miller had shunned me," Kazan wrote in his autobiography. "Now the 'progressives' had us both on their shit list."[61] Out of this shared sense of outrage and alienation they would develop a new project of their own. Kazan suggested looking into "The Trenton Six," a current civil rights case involving the same sort of forced confessions and procedural irregularities he had already dramatized in *Boomerang!* Schulberg researched the case but thought it would work better as "a Dreiserian novel."[62] Still emotionally committed to his waterfront project, he picked up a copy of one of his old drafts and handed it to Kazan. Only then did Schulberg learn that Kazan already had a waterfront script of his own.

As early as 1946, while Kazan was shooting *Boomerang!* in Stamford, Arthur Miller had told him about "exciting film material on the waterfront." They hoped to collaborate on such a project one day, Kazan remembered, "he to write, I to direct a waterfront film."[63] Miller was researching the story of Pete Panto, a left-wing union organizer whose 1939 murder was later tied to Albert Anastasia, boss of the Brooklyn waterfront.[64] During their subsequent work together on *All My Sons* and *Death of a Salesman*, Kazan continued to encourage Miller to complete this screenplay (he had never written one before) and in January 1951 they arrived in Hollywood with *The Hook*.[65] Both men were thoroughly committed to the film, which Kazan told Miller "should take off from the tradition of *Open City* and the other Italian neorealist films."[66] Kazan was still under contract to Twentieth Century-Fox, but Darryl F. Zanuck said he was unhappy with the "subject matter." Jack Warner also rejected it. A meeting with Harry Cohn at Columbia seemed to have gone better (perhaps because a new friend of theirs, Marilyn Monroe, "tagged along"), until Cohn insisted on having the script vetted by Roy Brewer. The IATSE president was a staunch anti-Communist and old friend of Joe Ryan. Brewer indicated that the gangsters and corrupt union officials needed to be identified as Communists, a requirement Kazan apparently thought he would be able to finesse.[67] Miller, fearing that this request was only the tip of a very large iceberg, withdrew the script, to Kazan's apparent surprise. By his account, he was in the middle of a budget meeting at Columbia when Miller called him with the bad news. A very unhappy Cohn cabled Miller in Brooklyn: "ITS [sic] INTERESTING HOW THE MINUTE WE TRY TO MAKE THE SCRIPT PRO-AMERICAN YOU PULL OUT."[68] "I could tell just by looking at him. . . . He's still one of them," Cohn told Kazan. "What about me?" the director asked. "You're just a goodhearted whore like me. . . . We'll find something else to do together."[69] As for Arthur Miller, the work he put into *The Hook* eventually helped shape his play *A View from the Bridge* (1955–1956), but his personal and professional relationship with Kazan was never the same. Kazan's subsequent HUAC testimony would practically put an end to it.

Schulberg claimed never to have seen a copy of Miller's script, which seems fair enough. Some of Miller's supporters detect similarities, but most waterfront crime pictures of the period deal with the same generic issues.[70] Yet *Crime on the Waterfront* and *The Hook* share a unique focus on labor issues, rare at any time, with Miller working from a popular-front perspective while Schulberg's approach seemed more influenced by the Catholic Worker movement.[71] And both scripts also share a concern with "the shape-up," an abusive hiring practice in which longshoremen milled about each morning, cattle call fashion, hoping to be selected for a day's work, an open invitation to favoritism and bribery. Indeed, a shape-up scene in which the pier boss hires only his favorites would be the only passage in the McSorley version that survived, nearly intact, all the way to the release print. And Father Corridan's famous "Christ in the Shape-up" sermon, of course, would be a centerpiece of every one of Schulberg's subsequent drafts.[72] Perhaps Schulberg was so fascinated by the shape-up because he recognized, even unconsciously, that this was the same way the early motion picture industry had hired film extras when his father was first establishing himself in Hollywood—a precedent of which Miller would probably have been unaware.

So Kazan went to Germany that fall to direct *Man on a Tightrope*, while Schulberg stayed behind to finish his research. He practically moved in with Arthur Browne. "I found myself writing down one Brownie quote after another, and, in time, they would find their way into the screenplay. Indeed, Brownie became 'Kayo Dugan,' one of the principal characters in the film."[73] One result of this research expedition was Schulberg's "Joe Docks, Forgotten Man of the Waterfront," published in the *New York Times*, in which he encouraged readers to turn away from the scandal's already familiar heroes and villains and consider the daily life of anonymous dock workers.[74]

In his autobiography, Kazan illustrates *Man on a Tightrope* with a photo of the associate producer, Gerd Oswald, conferring authoritatively with the cameraman while Kazan walks several paces behind with a "bemused" expression on his face. The difficult location shoot was making it clear to him that he "didn't have the vaguest idea how to direct an action movie," even after making films like *Panic in the Streets* and *Viva Zapata!* "Gerd Oswald directed more of this film than I did," he admitted.[75] But when he returned to New York he found that the experience had somehow energized him; he was "a new man," determined to take charge of his career and move it in a new direction. What he needed now was to find a new production team, the sort of crew he could never assemble in Hollywood.

In November, crime-busting Governor Thomas E. Dewey finally authorized the New York State Crime Commission to look into every aspect of racketeering and corruption on the waterfront, an action Father Corridan had been urging for years. "Crime on the waterfront" was big news again, and Corridan encouraged Schulberg to "incorporate the waterfront commission hearings in Manhattan into his script."[76] Soon the *New York Times* was reporting that Schulberg and Kazan would begin location filming of *Bottom of the River*—the title would keep changing—as early as May 1953. Two "major companies" were said to be interested, which meant that while Monticello was out of the picture, the film still had no financing and no distributor.[77]

But what probably triggered this piece—really just a statement released by Budd Schulberg—was the testimony of Anthony "Tony Mike" De Vincenzo before the Crime Commission on December 15, 1952. A longshoreman with twenty years' experience on the Hoboken docks, Tony Mike was the Commission's star witness, his firsthand account confirming the worst stories in Malcolm Johnson's original exposé. What was most surprising was that this break did not come from Manhattan's West Side docks—Corridan's stronghold and the focus of both Malcolm Johnson's reporting and Budd Schulberg's continuing research—but from Hoboken, whose ethnic communities "were just slightly less tribal and the efficacy of personal witness slightly more potent than across the river."[78] In other words, Tony Mike was willing to name names. Schulberg claimed to have attended every one of the Committee's public sessions and took Father Corridan's latest advice to heart. From that point on, every new draft of the script would reference the Committee's need for someone of courage to break the code of silence and tell the truth about what he had witnessed on the waterfront.[79]

Kazan was especially taken with Tony Mike. His 1953 appointment book shows many meetings with De Vincenzo, a man with whom he clearly identified. On the other hand, he did not share Schulberg's fascination with Father Corridan, whom he met with less frequently.[80] "What do priests really know about life? The waterfront priests know more, but they're still dealing in absolute right and absolute wrong," he told Jeff Young in 1971.[81] In eighty pages of text devoted to *On the Waterfront* in Young's oral history, the only time Kazan mentions Corridan—and not even by name—is to say he "smoked a lot and drank a lot of beer."[82] It was Tony Mike, who grew up on the dark side but then came to think better of it, whose story fascinated Kazan. "I did see Tony Mike's story as my own," Kazan wrote in his autobiography. When Terry Malloy taunts Johnny Friendly at the end of the film ("I'm glad what I done . . ."), "that was me, saying with identical heat, that I was glad I testified as I had."[83] De Vincenzo must have felt the same way, because he later sued the production for a million dollars, insisting that "his rights of privacy were violated when his life was depicted in the film," an assertion the filmmakers staunchly denied.[84]

Kazan still owed Fox another film, and despite the fact that Zanuck had rejected *The Hook* out of hand two years earlier, Kazan sent him the latest draft of his new waterfront script in January. Zanuck was interested but, like Harry Cohn, he was also afraid. He was afraid of what could happen on the docks if they went ahead without union support, and he was afraid of the same negative response from the State Department that he claimed had greeted *The Grapes of Wrath*. He thought there were too many speeches, and that something needed to be done to keep "the girl from looking like an amateur detective who is out to right the wrongs of the world." But he also told them to come out the following week to go over all this in person.[85]

Kazan was rehearsing his new play, *Camino Real*, which would open on Broadway March 17, so Schulberg made the trip on his own. After two lengthy conferences, Zanuck wrote that "we have solved all of the story differences between us with the exception of whether or not we keep Terry's son in the picture." He gave a number of sound dramatic reasons for eliminating this child—whom he felt "bursts into the story," and makes Terry seem more of a family man and less of a rebel—all of his arguments being carefully laid out in a remarkable fourteen-page memo. But he was not happy about the business arrangement they had proposed, a profit-participation deal tied to an unfinished original script, with no identifiable stars attached. The absence of Marlon Brando was evidently a problem. "If you could deliver me Marlon Brando," Zanuck wrote, "I would have a little more guts" in proposing the deal to Fox's board of directors. Indeed, Zanuck had a hard time seeing anyone but Brando in the role. "If you end up with Richard Widmark or Dana Andrews and people in this classification you may be wasting your time," he wrote. Burt Lancaster might work, but his availability was in question and "we are investigating further."[86]

Schulberg returned to New York. Another draft went out to Zanuck in April. Kazan was upbeat because an interim meeting with Spyros Skouras had ended with a handshake agreement, and on April 16 the *Times* headlined "Fox to Make Film on Pier Activities." *Water Front* was to be one of Darryl F. Zanuck's personal productions, the story said, and "Mr. Kazan will direct the picture in semi-documentary style," information obviously sourced from inside the studio.[87] A somewhat embellished version of the story appeared the same day in the *Los Angeles Times*, which emphasized the film's "documentary aspects" and connected them to the type of "headline feature" that had made Zanuck's reputation at Warner Bros. The paper even offered its own casting suggestions, naming Richard Widmark, Victor Mature, and Broderick Crawford. On the other hand, "Marlon Brando . . . could very well fit into *Water Front*, which it is said will be one of the last black-and-white films at the studio."[88]

Camino Real opened in New York as scheduled but closed on May 9 after only sixty performances. Finally, after an unexplained silence of several weeks, Zanuck once again summoned the men to the coast. Kazan assumed they were being brought out to discuss casting and budget, but when they arrived in Los Angeles Schulberg smelled a rat: there was no studio limo waiting for them at the station.[89] Even worse, "in our suite at the Beverly Hills Hotel . . . I noticed that there were no flowers. 'Flowers!' Gadge exploded, 'What are you—some kind of fruitcake? Who the hell needs flowers?' 'We're in trouble,' I said."[90]

On May 25 the men were ushered into Zanuck's office to hear the bad news. Zanuck suddenly didn't like anything about the picture. "Who gives a shit about longshoremen," he said, repudiating all the work and energy he himself had put into the story three months earlier.[91] The problem now was not HUAC, the unions, or even the lack of Marlon Brando. Now Zanuck talked only of CinemaScope, Fox's entry into the wide-screen revolution, a technological fix that he hoped would shore up the studio's flagging fortunes. Business had been very bad, and Kazan's last three Fox films had lost increasing amounts of money. On March 12 Zanuck had written to all Fox producers that the studio's future projects would "concentrate exclusively on subjects suitable for CinemaScope," namely, films that "enable us to take full advantage of scope, size, and physical action."[92] Then on May 7 he wrote another staff memo complaining bitterly about the public's rejection of such "excellent pictures" as *Viva Zapata!*

He could not point to a single recent success among "so-called propaganda" or "message" pictures. "I wonder what would have happened to *Pinky, The Snake Pit,* and *Gentleman's Agreement* in the present market.... When you think that a picture that says nothing like *Mississippi Gambler* can double the gross of *Viva Zapata!* and *Lili* then you must pause and take heed."[93]

To that list of unworthy successes Zanuck might soon have added *Bloodhounds of Broadway,* a Technicolor musical that was shooting on the lot the week Schulberg and Kazan arrived from New York. A low-budget *Guys and Dolls* imitation, it would gross $2 million on an $875,000 budget.[94] It had no longshoremen, but it did feature a Runyonesque mobster pursued by New York's "State Investigating Committee" and a subplot involving recalcitrant witnesses and a radio broadcast of the Committee's hearings. Filmed as far as possible from the real city, its stylized New York is amusingly theatrical. No message, and no difficulties with mobsters or trade unions, either (although the producers of the original *Guys and Dolls* apparently felt they had grounds for suit).[95] Explaining himself that day to Schulberg and Kazan, Zanuck rhapsodized about a film he did think could make money, Fox's upcoming adaptation of a popular comic strip, *Prince Valiant.* "Didn't he see that we weren't listening," Kazan remembered, "that we didn't give a damn about CinemaScope or his company's fate?"[96] Within a few days the studio announced Zanuck's cancellation of the project "because he does not believe it is adaptable to the wide-screen CinemaScope technique to which Fox has committed its entire output."[97]

Furious, the pair trashed the office they had been given on the Fox lot, stole the typewriter and office supplies, and retired to the Beverly Hills Hotel (still on Fox's tab) to plan their strategy. Schulberg wanted to go home and turn the script into a novel; Kazan thought it might work as a play. They sent copies of the script out to the other studios and watched as the rejections piled up. Finally Kazan blurted out, "God damn it, I'm going to stick with this thing if I have to get a 16 mm Eyemo and shoot it myself on the docks."[98]

CHAPTER 11

OBSESSED WITH FILM

Stanley Kubrick already had an Eyemo. Or at least he knew where to get one—from Frank Zucker at the Camera Equipment Company. Years later Kubrick would tell interviewers how it was Frank's son Burt who taught him how to operate the much more complicated Mitchell camera, spending an entire Saturday morning with him back in 1951, when he was about to shoot *Fear and Desire* ("that was the extent of my formal training in movie camera technique").[1] Zucker was not just being kind; Kubrick was renting the camera, but CECO needed to be sure the customer returned it in good order. Camera Equipment Company flourished in this period by targeting the nontheatrical and independent market, but their emphasis on personal service also appealed to filmmakers visiting from Hollywood.[2] The *Naked City* company, for example, had brought all their equipment with them from the West Coast, but maintaining this long supply line resulted in serious delays whenever anything broke down. By the 1950s producers understood that New York equipment houses, while still not at the Hollywood level, could be depended on to provide adequate professional support to visiting film crews. This established infrastructure gave New York an advantage over other cities that might otherwise have tried to pick up some of this location work. As noted earlier, both *On the Waterfront* and *Killer's Kiss* depended entirely on CECO for equipment and technical support.

Elia Kazan had taken the high road as he worked his way up the professional ladder: Williams College; Yale School of Drama; The Group Theater; Arthur Miller; Tennessee Williams; Darryl F. Zanuck. Kubrick's résumé began with Taft

High School in The Bronx and peaked with five years at *Look*, a postgraduate course that taught him more than Kazan would ever know about dramatizing life through a camera lens. Kubrick admired Kazan's work with actors but had no illusions about the rest of Hollywood cinema, vastly preferring Ophuls, Bresson, and Bergman to any of the American genre directors revered by the next generation of American cineastes. He studied the European masters at the Museum of Modern Art, but New York was filled with revival theaters and foreign-language houses (not to mention film clubs like Cinema 16 and The Huff Society).

"He was obsessed with going to see every film and very critical of films," remembered David Vaughan, who would later do the choreography for *Killer's Kiss*. "At the same time he would just see everything, that was all he really wanted to do. We would not only go to terrible films on Forty-Second Street, we would go to important movies as well."[3] Not impressed by most of what he was seeing, Kubrick decided he could master this new medium on his own. "I learned far more by seeing films than from reading heavy tomes on film aesthetics," he told critic Joseph Gelmis, although he seems to have done all the reading as well. Years later he could still hold forth on the distinction between Eisenstein's writings ("I still don't understand them") and Pudovkin's ("I would recommend his book to anyone seriously interested in film technique"). He felt that *Stanislavsky Directs* ("an excellent book") had taught him everything he needed to know about working with actors.[4] So while Truffaut and Godard were immersing themselves in Parisian film culture, Kubrick was educating himself in New York. Yet his tastes always seemed more *Sight and Sound* than *Cahiers du Cinema*, avoiding the edgier corners of Hollywood cinema: he never seems to have spoken about Ulmer, Preminger, or Nicholas Ray.

Odd, then, that his first recorded contact with any part of the local filmmaking community involved a brief appearance in a surrealist feature directed by avant garde pioneer Hans Richter. Richter began making abstract films in Germany as early as 1921 and was currently the director of the City College Institute of Film Technique, an influential local film program that the *Times* identified as the "largest documentary film center in the world."[5] Peggy Guggenheim, a patron of the arts whose largesse also extended to the avant garde film community, had awarded Richter a $6,000 grant "to edit a film consisting of excerpts from advance guard motion pictures of the past." But Richter and his friend Fernand Leger soon came up with a better idea: instead of simply anthologizing their classic films (along with those of Man Ray, Max Ernst, and Marcel Duchamp), they proposed making a new film to which each of these masters would contribute but whose episodes would be directed and assembled by Richter and his City College film students.[6] Alexander Calder, not previously a filmmaker, would also eventually participate.

Along with Guggenheim and Kenneth MacPherson, Richter formed Art of This Century Films (with capitalization of $25,000) and began shooting the

Leger episode in 1944, eventually taking advantage of some free studio space on Twenty-First Street made available by a former student.[7] The new film was shot on 16 mm Kodachrome by Arnold Eagle, another of his students now working professionally. "I started the picture as an adventure," Richter told Ezra Goodman, "not knowing whether I had enough money or what kind of story to make. But I knew one thing that was important. That is, in cinematography we have scratched only the surface of the art and that there are thousands of other possibilities in film."[8] Two years later the production of *Dreams That Money Can Buy* earned a three-page spread in *Life*, lavishly illustrated in color by one of their top photographers, Gjon Mili.[9] Richter assembled another collection of A-listers for his soundtrack (Paul Bowles, Darius Milhaud, John Latouche, Libby Holman, Josh White, John Cage, and David Diamond), blew the film up to 35 mm and sent it to Venice, where he took home "a beautiful little silver statuette (after Giovanni Bellini)" for "best original contribution to the progress of cinematography."[10]

Each of the top-lined collaborators had contributed an original episode, one way or another, but a framing story written by Broadway lyricist John Latouche ("Ballad for Americans," "Taking a Chance on Love") now provided both a central character and a rudimentary plot structure. What had originally been a bouquet of surrealist episodes now played out "in the offices of a 'heavenly psychiatrist' who sees each sequence as a vision of wish-fulfillment in the eyes of his patients."[11] Latouche also wrote "The Girl with the Pre-Fabricated Heart," sung here by Libby Holman and Josh White in the Fernand Leger episode, which impressed even Bosley Crowther as "a dandy song."[12] James Agee also liked the song but dismissed the rest of the film as "at once arch, snobbish and sycophantic. It is about as genuinely 'experimental' as a Chemcraft set, and not even its laziness is likeable."[13] Kubrick would probably have agreed with Agee, and his own film style would owe more to the vernacular surrealism of street photographers like Weegee than to anything he might have seen here.

But Kubrick's interest in *Dreams That Money Can Buy* was more than academic. It has always been known that his (future) second wife, the Balanchine ballerina Ruth Sobotka, was featured in the film's Man Ray episode, "Ruth, Roses and Revolvers." But only in 2019 did word spread on the internet that Kubrick himself was actually *in* the Richter film.[14] Anthony Frewin, a longtime friend and collaborator, recognized him in the audience of film buffs assembled for the screening of a Man Ray film, action that takes up most of *Dreams That Money Can Buy*'s Man Ray sequence. Kubrick had never mentioned the film to Frewin, which he found surprising. Even better, the woman seated next to Kubrick appears to be Toba Metz, his future first wife. And another member of this same audience (although never seen in the same shot) is Ruth Sobotka. Was this a coincidence? Or did all three already know one another as early as 1946?[15] Kubrick was taking a heavy schedule of liberal arts courses at City

College in the spring and fall semesters of 1946, but he never registered for a film class there.[16] How he connected with Richter's production is unknown. But while it may not have appealed to him stylistically, he certainly paid attention to the way the film had been produced ($15,000 and a lot of sweat equity), promoted (in *Life*), and marketed (it began a record-breaking fifteen-week run at the Fifth Avenue Playhouse on April 23, 1948).[17] Richter had made a highly personal feature film entirely outside the orbit of Hollywood's studio system and audiences were flocking to see it. Indeed, unlike most other films of the postwar avant garde era, *Dreams That Money Can Buy* was intended from the start as a commercial proposition, *Life* even noting with some amazement that its producers "expect to make money out of it."[18]

The *Times* reported that the film quickly recouped 75 percent of its production and distribution costs after playing only a few theaters in New York, San Francisco, and Los Angeles.[19] After a year it moved to the museum circuit and for decades was easily available in 16 mm from the Museum of Modern Art's circulating film library. But despite general recognition of Richter as a cinema pioneer whose students were highly visible in New York's burgeoning postwar film community, *Dreams That Money Can Buy* never achieved the canonical status of *The Quiet One* or *Little Fugitive*. "I felt that both modern

11.1. Seventeen-year-old Stanley Kubrick, one of an audience of film buffs in Hans Richter's *Dreams That Money Can Buy*. Frame enlargement.

art and the movies are an expression of our time," Richter told a reporter in 1948, "and that it would be interesting to combine the two."[20] Yet Maya Deren, Harry Smith, and the Whitney brothers were already demonstrating that film *was* modern art. By contrast, *Dreams That Money Can Buy* looked too much like the museum anthology Peggy Guggenheim had originally commissioned: a round-up of prewar avant garde tropes that almost everyone now regarded as obsolete. Agee's argument ("it is as formula-ridden as the worst junk peddled out of Hollywood") would seem to have carried the day.

Home movies included in Jan Harlan's 2001 documentary, *Stanley Kubrick: A Life in Pictures*, show that the Kubrick household had access to its own 16 mm camera by the mid-1930s. At a time when many other Bronx residents were lucky to raise the price of a movie ticket (and Elia Kazan and Ralph Steiner were making *Pie in the Sky* in a local landfill), Stanley's father, Jack, a successful local physician, was filming Stanley and his sister Barbara in the usual array of domestic activities, in both black and white and color. By the age of fifteen, Stanley was "fooling around" with his father's Graflex, a single-lens reflex considerably more sophisticated than the average snapshot camera.[21] No one knows if Stanley was involved, or even interested, in his father's filmmaking efforts, but he did learn to develop and print his own stills and quickly became staff photographer for the school newspaper. By the time he graduated from Taft in 1945 he was already working for *Look*.

Look was a biweekly picture magazine, and unlike its upscale rival, Henry Luce's weekly *Life*, the editors were not especially interested in breaking news. Instead, a team would be assigned some likely topic, and when the photos came back the editorial desk would organize them into a coherent picture story narrative. An important influence on the young Kubrick was Arthur Rothstein, the famed Farm Security Administration photographer of Depression days, who became *Look*'s director of photography in 1947. While the powerful social and political undertones of the FSA period were no longer in fashion, their narrative function—the idea that these images all had a story to tell—clearly appealed to Kubrick. But the fact that someone else made the crucial decisions regarding captioning, layout, and design eventually began to bother him, especially once he came to understand this editing process as representing a higher level of artistic control. By 1950 he had decided to abandon still photography and become a filmmaker. There, guided by his knowledge of Eisenstein and Pudovkin, he would do his own editing, knitting those solitary images together in the service of powerful montage schemes.

"A Middleweight Thriller"

Kubrick's move from magazine photographer to producer-director-cinematographer-editor of his own films is usually illustrated by tracing a line from

"Prizefighter," a photo essay published in *Look* on January 18, 1949, to *Day of the Fight*, a one-reel documentary he shot in the spring of 1950. The story features the promising middleweight Walter Cartier as he preps for an important match with Tony DeMicco (identified as D'Amico in the article). Cartier, who lived in Greenwich Village with his twin brother, Vincent, is shown relaxing with a girlfriend, training, and attending to a series of prefight rituals, ranging from a visit to St. Francis Xavier Church to the official weigh-in ceremony. These rituals are obviously what attracted Kubrick and his editors, as only two shots are devoted to the actual fight and one has to read the small print to learn that Cartier lost it on a TKO.

The DeMicco fight, which the story purportedly documents, was held at Croke Park in The Bronx on July 27, 1948. But the layout also includes at least one shot from Cartier's September 21 knockout of Jimmy Mangia in Jersey City, suggesting that Kubrick was following Cartier for months while assembling this story.[22] If Kubrick had coverage of Cartier's spectacular victory over Mangia, who was knocked out at 1:49 of the first round, why turn the apparent focus on one of his few defeats? In any case, Cartier quickly agreed when Kubrick approached him with the idea of turning the photo feature into a short documentary. The men lived within walking distance of one another in the Village, and would have continued to see each other around the neighborhood. Cartier and his brother lived with their aunt on West Twelfth Street, while Kubrick and his first wife, Toba Metz, were a few blocks away at 37 West Sixteenth Street. One of the unpublished photos Kubrick took of Cartier jogging in Washington Square shows him within shouting distance of the park's concrete chess tables, where Kubrick, an avid player, was still earning extra cash by hustling games at twenty-five cents a shot.[23] And Cartier may already have had acting ambitions—he would temporarily retire from the ring to play the continuing role of Private Dillingham on *The Phil Silvers Show* (1955–1957) and later had bit parts in films like *Somebody Up There Likes Me* and *A Face in the Crowd*.

Kubrick's friend Alexander Singer had told him that "there was apparently a fortune to be made in producing short documentaries," explaining that *The March of Time*, where he was then employed as an office boy, thought nothing of spending $40,000 to produce each episode. A few calls to labs and equipment houses convinced Kubrick that he could produce a similar reel for around $1,000, easily turning a fine profit on each production.[24] Singer later became a successful director of filmed television episodes, including *Lou Grant*, *The Fugitive*, and various *Star Trek* reboots, but his grasp of industry economics in 1950 was shaky. He should have known that the entire short-film market was on the verge of collapse and that *The March of Time* (which had never been profitable in the first place) was already on life support. He should also have known that MOT episodes were all produced by in-house staff.

Dismissing any thought of concocting an original film story, Kubrick turned directly to "Prizefighter," adapting it for the screen as if it were a preexisting literary property (which, in a sense, it was). The text, captions, and layouts of the original *Look* photo spreads served as a first draft of *Day of the Fight*, which would share many of the same dramatic incidents and much of its mise en scène. Kubrick emphasizes the "twinness" of Walter and his brother Vince and highlights their prefight attendance at St. Francis Xavier Church on West Sixteenth Street, down the street from his own apartment. "It's important for Walter to get Holy Communion, in case something should go wrong tonight," the narrator tells us. (One wonders if Kubrick knew that this was the headquarters of Father John Corridan, New York's famous "waterfront priest"?)

There were also changes, of course, notably the loss of extraneous characters like Cartier's girlfriend and little cousin. And due to the cost of film and camera rentals, it is unlikely that Kubrick would have been able to film very many of Cartier's bouts. Indeed, he may only have had one shot at filming Cartier in the ring. The Eyemo held 100 feet of film, but without an electric motor attachment it would only run for about twenty seconds before rewinding (only a still photographer would imagine he could film a prize fight in this manner). This was not long enough to cover an entire round, so Kubrick and Singer showed up at the Laurel Garden in Newark on April 17, 1950, with two Eyemos, one filming while the other rewound and reloaded (the two cameras, shooting from different angles, also allowed a bit of editorial flexibility). "Walter was fine in the scenes before the fight," Kubrick remembered. "But he made the fight itself too short. He finished the other guy in the second round. So, much later, we had to reshoot some of the fight scenes and it took some persuasion to get the other boxer and the referee and the handlers back for a retake."[25] It was Singer who got the money shot as Cartier knocked Bobby James out at 1:35 of the second round, an accident of fate that accounted for the biggest difference between Kubrick's two Cartier essays: a happy ending. For the photo essay, Kubrick had covered more than one fight and was able to choose which bout to feature. In the film, with less coverage to work with, the ending would be upbeat whether Kubrick liked it or not.

When Singer and Kubrick first considered entering the short documentary business there were several such series being produced locally, notably *The March of Time* (Fox), Paramount's *Pacemaker* series, and RKO-Pathé's *This Is America*. These would have been considered traditional "magazine style" documentaries, but most major distributors were also handling genre-specific shorts, usually musicals and sports reels. Columbia's *Cavalcade of Broadway* (1949–1951) visited various New York nightspots, such as *The Village Barn* (1950) and *Eddie Condon's* (1951), and Universal-International also released a few musical shorts made for them in New York, though most of these were little more than glorified band shorts. Sports reels were ubiquitous, and some of them appear to have been willing to accept material provided by outside producers.[26] While *Day of the Fight* is now thought of as a straight documentary, it is entirely possible that Kubrick and Singer originally hoped to sell it in the sports reel market.

But if their ambitions were higher, they might first have offered the film to Paramount's *Pacemaker* series (1946–1955), which would have looked like a very good fit. For example, their Oscar-nominated *Roller Derby Girl* (directed by Justin Herman in 1949) not only featured extensive footage of another popular local sport but also personalized it by profiling an ambitious newcomer (Jean Parker) who can only establish herself by surviving the physical and psychological intimidation of her chief opponent, Midge (Toughie) Brasuhn. As in *Day of the Fight*, we see real athletes appearing as themselves in a dramatically manipulated representation of their daily lives. There is no direct dialogue recording, only a poetic/proletarian third-person narration. And both films ultimately sell themselves on the quality of their photography, in this case the work of Boris Kaufman, a European refugee still mired in shorts and industrial films. Kubrick, who appears to have seen everything, would have probably been familiar with *Roller Derby Girl*, as well as such other Herman-Kaufman films as *The Lambertville Story* and *Neighbors in the Night* (also 1949), which resemble the sort of photo essays he had been doing for *Look*.

In a *New Yorker* profile Kubrick talked about receiving desultory offers of $1,500 and $2,500 from various distributors (probably the companies listed above), who dismissed his $40,000 *March of Time* story as "crazy." "The next thing we knew, *The March of Time* was out of business," he remembered.[27] That left *The March of Time*'s old rival, *This Is America*, whose finances were only marginally more stable. Jay Bonafield was now running the series, whose focus was domestic, not international, and whose stories tended to feature the everyday activities of ordinary citizens instead of the newsworthy behavior of the great and the good. The reel also avoided direct dialogue recording, typically relying only on Dwight Weist's signature narration and the music of Herman Fuchs.[28]

Kubrick had spent $3900 on *Day of the Fight* and was happy to accept Bonafield's offer of $4000. "They told me that was the most they'd ever paid for a short," he remembered.[29] Selling his film to *This Is America* was no disgrace. In June 1951 a number of episodes would be screened at Amos Vogel's prestigious Cinema 16 film society, described as "an important series of documentary-informational films."[30] And the deal seems to have been sweetened by a commission to make another short, *Flying Padre*. Two versions of *Day of the Fight* exist today. The generally available version, regarded by some as Kubrick's cut, runs only twelve minutes. But there is also a sixteen-minute cut, which appears to be the version that opened at the Paramount Theater in New York on April 26, 1951. As several writers have pointed out, this was *after* the scheduled March release of *Flying Padre*, which RKO-Pathé had issued through their less prestigious *Screenliner* series. In fact, *Flying Padre* was copyrighted on March 25, 1951, a week *before* the fight film (March 30). It would appear that the delay in releasing *Day of the Fight* was due to Jay Bonafield's addition of a four-minute prologue, consisting mainly of library footage, which sets a more jaunty tone while bringing the running time of Kubrick's picture up to the standard length of a *This Is America* release. Exactly why and how this occurred, and what degree of participation Kubrick may have had in the longer version, if any, has never been explained.

Whatever it was that happened with *Day of the Fight*, *Flying Padre* could never be considered anything other than a Kubrick assignment. The film was produced by Burton Benjamin, a fixture at RKO-Pathé who later spent twenty-nine years at CBS, becoming director of their news division in 1978. Other than Kubrick, every member of the crew was part of Benjamin's production unit: Bob Hite (narrator), Isaac Kleinerman (editor), Harold Vivian (sound recordist), and Nathaniel Shilkret (composer) all worked together regularly, and most would follow Benjamin as he worked his way up at CBS. On a structural level the film resembles one of Kubrick's photo-essays, but unlike *Day of the Fight* the visuals do little more than illustrate the voice-over: everything of importance here is conveyed through the narration. Significantly, it is the only Kubrick film without a writer credit.[31]

In accepting this assignment Kubrick was moving backward, professionally, but the deal with RKO-Pathé was obviously important to him (a licensed pilot, he must also have enjoyed the opportunity to film the aerial sequences). Rev. Fred Stadtmueller tends to his New Mexico flock by air, and Kubrick, or his camera, travels with him in the cramped cockpit of his Piper Cub as he flies to an isolated parish or rushes off to attend to a sick child. Kubrick seems to have spent much of his energy devising creative ways of filming Stadtmueller in the air, or at least giving the impression that he is in the air. On the ground, big close-ups of the gnarled faces of his aged parishioners suggest the influence of Arthur Rothstein and the FSA more than anything seen in *Day of the Fight*. Kubrick spoke with some pride about seeing his first film up on screen at the Paramount, but his only comment on *Flying Padre* was to dismiss it as "silly." (In compiling a full list of his credits in 1953, he was still referring to the film under its working title, *Skypilot*.)[32]

Shape of Fear

How would Stanley Kubrick have felt as he sat in the cavernous auditorium of the Paramount, waiting for *My Forbidden Past* to end so that the Kubrick film could start? He had just flown back from the West Coast, where he had both directed and photographed an entire theatrical feature—a rare accomplishment for any twenty-two-year-old. But in a 1966 *New Yorker* profile, Kubrick admitted that after *Flying Padre* wrapped there had been no offers to direct, and he was once again spending his time "playing chess for quarters in the park." He had succeeded in making a couple of short films for what he assumed was much less than the going rate; employing the same dubious logic, he decided he could also undercut Hollywood production costs while making a full-scale feature. In any case, "I felt I certainly couldn't make one worse than the ones I was seeing every week."[33]

Kubrick's ego had a lot to do with his assumption that he could pull this off, but there were precedents. He would have known about David Bradley, who had signed with MGM on the strength of two 16 mm features he made in Chicago with his classmate, Charlton Heston.[34] What someone like Bradley could do, he could do. Together with Howard Sackler, a budding poet and fellow Taft High School graduate who had gone on to Brooklyn College, Kubrick wrote a script called *The Trap*, a heavily symbolic wartime allegory clearly influenced by the European art films he and his friends had discovered in New York's revival houses. Beyond noting that he later won the Pulitzer Prize for *The Great White Hope* (1969), Howard Sackler's influence on Kubrick's early films has largely been overlooked. According to his entry in *American National Biography*, after writing *Desert Padre* (another alternate title for *The Flying Padre*?) he was awarded grants from the Rockefeller and Littauer Foundations that "allowed [him] to complete two more early screenplays for Kubrick, *Killer's Kiss* (1952) and *Fear and Desire* (1953)."[35] Although the dating is off, the information is intriguing: Sackler, whose early writing was heavily influenced by W. H. Auden, was just the sort of educated but approachable creative partner Kubrick would continue to seek out throughout his career. In 1954 he would win the Maxwell Anderson Award for verse drama—perhaps not so surprising for the author of *Fear and Desire*.

Kubrick took the project to Richard de Rochemont, who was now producing "video and informational films" at Vavin, Inc., one of New York's flourishing nontheatrical houses.[36] He might have been introduced to de Rochemont through Alexander Singer, or possibly through de Rochemont's wife, Jane, who worked as a photographic stylist for Kubrick's friend Bert Stern.[37] "He thought Stanley had talent," Jane told Kubrick's biographer, Vincent Lo Brutto. And also a lot of nerve. "Stanley looked very young and very skinny. Stanley felt quite a bit about himself, he was not exactly modest." But Kubrick's chutzpah appealed to de Rochemont, who soon became, in Lo Brutto's words, "Kubrick's benefactor, boss, and father figure."[38]

Lo Brutto also reveals that de Rochemont served as Kubrick's silent partner on the film, taking no credit but providing production services, running interference with the unions, and fronting an unspecified amount of cash. Kubrick had assumed he could make the film for $10,000, and tapped his wealthy uncle, Martin Perveler, for start-up costs. As late as December 1950 he was uncertain if he would shoot the film "this winter in California or next spring in the east."[39] But production circumstances made it imperative to start as soon as possible, and midwinter exteriors in upstate New York were not an option. Filming in the San Gabriel Mountains and other wilderness areas not far from Los Angeles meant that most of the cast and crew, as well as their equipment, had to be flown in from New York and billeted at the location, a considerable expense for a no-budget film. Indeed, this is the only example I can think of in this period where a "New York" company traveled to the West Coast to shoot their entire film. Perveler, a canny investor with significant local land holdings, failed in his attempt to tie Kubrick up to a lifetime contract, but he did insist that the film be shot on his own turf, not thousands of miles away back east.[40]

The *New York Times* ran a remarkable feature article on Kubrick in their January 14, 1951, issue, a time when neither of his shorts had been released and his prospective feature film was still unnamed. "If you think Stanley is nervous about the prospect of starting filming on his picture, as yet untitled, in March, then you are sadly mistaken," Thomas Pryor reported, taking note of "Stanley's" extraordinary self-confidence while simultaneously infantilizing him through the casual use of his given name.

> Stanley says that he has figured out every camera angle and that after he finds the proper location "in some wooded area of southern California" shooting should run smoothly and be concluded in fifteen to twenty-one days. He will bring four professional "but not well known name actors" out to the coast from Broadway, and because Stanley himself is not yet a member of the movie camera man's union, he will engage a professional cinematographer. The one requirement is that the camera man must agree in advance to follow the blueprint laid out by Stanley, who will direct and produce the film.[41]

With his wife Toba Metz and screenwriter Howard Sackler, Kubrick spent six weeks scouting locations in the San Gabriel Mountains and fleshing out the cast. His most important find was Frank Silvera, a veteran of the American Negro Theater who had recently appeared off-Broadway as Nat Turner.[42] A light-skinned African American, Silvera played all races and ethnicities. By the time *Fear and Desire* was released he would have been seen in at least four other films, but with the possible exception of *Death Tide* this was his first time before the cameras.[43] Virginia Leith, a model and aspiring actress, was discovered through an LA casting call. She spoke only one word in the film but would become the center of the distributor Joseph Burstyn's advertising campaign. Leith soon landed a contract with Fox, but she is best known today for her role as the disembodied head in the notorious East Coast exploitation film, *The*

Brain That Wouldn't Die.⁴⁴ The rest of the "not well known name actors" were all brought out from New York, including Paul Mazursky, then also living in Greenwich Village, who would later write and direct *Bob & Carol & Ted & Alice* (1969) and *An Unmarried Woman* (1978). "Our 'crew' consisted of three Mexican laborers who carried all the equipment."⁴⁵

He also brought with him the 35 mm Mitchell camera he had rented from Burt Zucker (at $25 per day), a set of four Baltar lenses, a few pieces of grip equipment, and "a tape recorder." According to one period account, this machine was not used to record location sound but only "memos" of some kind.⁴⁶ I find it hard to believe that Kubrick, given his limited resources, would have expended any amount of money on a costly instrument that could easily have been replaced by a pencil; it seems far more likely that he originally hoped to record actual production sound, or at least a wild track that could act as a guide to rerecording back in the studio. Years later Paul Mazursky remembered many problems with the sound (although he had a different recollection of the exact technology Kubrick was trying to work with). "The sound on the movie was terrible—the original sound. It was captured on a wire recorder. *Wire*. And it didn't work," he recalled. "And a year later, a *year* later, we had to loop the entire thing in New York."⁴⁷ Although wire recorders were being used in the field by experienced documentary and industrial film producers, the system proved more difficult for Kubrick to handle than he had expected.⁴⁸ The decision to dub the entire soundtrack would eventually add another $30,000 to the $9,000 cost of the location shoot.⁴⁹

The film follows the adventures of four soldiers, of undetermined nationality, whose small plane has crashed in a forest behind enemy lines. Although the chronology is strictly linear, Kubrick employs dramatic montage effects and a considerable amount of subjective narration, a series of internal monologues that shift throughout the film to represent the point of view of various characters (as well as an unseen third-person narrator, voiced by David Allen). One could argue that the film would have worked much better without so much "garrulity," as one critic called it, but Kubrick and Sackler seem very attached to the device.⁵⁰ There is one striking action sequence, staged and edited in the style of Pudovkin, but the film's most dramatic encounter features a captured female prisoner, tied to a tree, who is molested and killed by the most deranged member of the unit. As several reviews would point out, this is an extremely dark film, entirely lacking in comedy.

Although Kubrick had announced in the *Times* that he would be hiring a union cinematographer in California, this did not prove to be the case. Indeed, the completed film bears neither a union label nor an MPAA seal, an almost unprecedented act of independence that makes it remarkable that *Fear and Desire* was able to win any sort of commercial release in the United States. Lo Brutto, using records in Richard de Rochemont's files, documents $10,000 in "union settlement costs" as well as a protracted negotiation on de Rochemont's part with the American Federation of Musicians, which threatened to place the film and its producers on their "unfair list" over outstanding payments due for the recording of Gerald Fried's score. The fact that de Rochemont personally inserted himself into this argument suggests that he was more than just an interested party: Lo Brutto reports that on January 28, 1953, as the film was still slogging through postproduction, de Rochemont was officially assigned 2 percent of Kubrick's share of the profits.[51]

As might have been expected, shooting in the San Gabriel Mountains with an inexperienced company did not go as smoothly as Kubrick had hoped. Although Frank Silvera knew what he was doing, the rest of the cast were neophytes, and Kubrick's own efforts to guide them were inadequate. Kubrick came to hate the performances, but in later interviews would always blame himself. "I didn't know anything about directing *any* actors. I totally failed to realize what I didn't know."[52] Mazursky agreed. "Well, he knew nothing about acting. He never said much. I just did whatever I did. Stanley would just say, 'O.K., you've got her against the tree and you're—whatever—let's just do it and try it.'"[53] Virginia Leith, who spent much of the film tied to the tree, had her performance "constructed" by Kubrick in traditional Soviet montage style, each ambiguous close-up gaining significance only as juxtaposed with some other image. Otherwise, the actors were left to their own devices, sitting around in the forest doing whatever they could to keep busy. Frank Silvera, already set for the role of General Huerta in Elia Kazan's *Viva Zapata!*, would run his lines for Kazan's picture with Paul Mazursky.

Because the budget allowed for only so much film, the actors did the best they could in one or two takes, reminiscent of the way directors like Josh Binney would shoot race movies.[54] But unlike Binney, Kubrick spent extra time on the photography, perfecting the one element of the film (other than the tree scene) that always impressed its critics. Kubrick had not brought a great deal of grip equipment with him, and for tracking shots he is said to have improvised with a baby carriage, probably scavenged from the abandoned Boy Scout camp the crew had settled into. But other attempts at saving money worked out less well, like replacing a proper studio fog machine with an insecticide sprayer. A raft needed for the final sequence proved unavailable, and a substitute commissioned from a local woodsman sank beneath the actors.[55] The film began to run over schedule and over budget. Instead of fifteen or twenty days, Kubrick would report to de Rochemont that shooting had gone on for five weeks.[56] At one point he had to leave the location and drive down to his Uncle Martin's place, desperate for another $5,000, frustrated with the film's slow progress but "so determined that he spat at the windshield."[57] Perveler came up with the cash, and Kubrick eventually went back to New York with fifty thousand feet of negative, twice as much as he expected to use.[58]

Things would get even slower during postproduction. Kubrick would wait nearly two full years before *Fear and Desire* followed *Day of the Fight* into theaters. Some of this time was spent in on-the-job training, with Kubrick taking on the tasks of editing, mixing, and scoring a feature, all of which he insisted on handling himself. Besides the problems with the sound, there were "other things I did expensively and foolishly, because I just didn't have enough experience to know the proper and economical approach," he later admitted.[59] For example, in addition to renting a dubbing studio, he would now have to reassemble the actors and probably pay them again for their trouble (of course, the voices we hear may not be those of the actors we see; more on that later). Kubrick was a hard person to work for, but the young man's obvious enthusiasm for the medium clearly charmed many of the people he ran into while haunting the local production houses and equipment supply shops, many of whom seem to have done him small favors. "The New York City film community was good to Kubrick," Vincent Lo Brutto concludes, noting that, "Alan Friedman of De Luxe Laboratories extended him a modest credit during the production of the film."[60] One of the skills Kubrick was only now mastering was the negotiation of deferred payments, but he would be more conversant with "the proper and economical approach" this sort of financing represented on his next feature.

In a statement to de Rochemont dated August 12, Kubrick maintained that everything was finished except for the final sound mix and a few opticals, which would take a few more weeks and another $5,000, bringing the final cost to $53,500.[61] After that, nothing much happened with the film for many months. While he and his investors looked for someone willing to release it, Kubrick played a lot of chess in Washington Square Park, broke up with his wife, moved in with a ballet dancer, and took whatever anonymous film work friends like Richard de Rochemont could find for him. This would go on for over a year.

The most mysterious of these gigs was first revealed in a throwaway reference at the bottom of a single *New York Times* column. A. H. Weiler briefly noted that "the youthful producer-director" was still negotiating a release for his *fourth* film, then known as *Shape of Fear*. In addition to the two RKO shorts, Kubrick also claimed "a short on World Assembly of Youth made for the State Department."[62] The World Assembly of Youth had been created in 1948, probably by the CIA, as a response to the Eastern Bloc's World Federation of Youth. From August 5–16, 1951, it sponsored a heavily publicized "miniature United Nations" convocation at Cornell University.[63] Kubrick went uncredited on *World Assembly of Youth*, but the fact that he included it among his accomplishments suggests he was not just along for the ride but had played an important role on a project that had actually been completed.

In the fall of 1952, with *Fear and Desire* still on the shelf, de Rochemont assigned Kubrick to direct second-unit location scenes for *Mr. Lincoln*, a filmed, five-part miniseries that he was producing for *Omnibus*. After *The March of*

Time had ended, de Rochemont began promoting the idea of filmed television as a way of maintaining the residual value of quality programming that was then being transmitted live. Inexpensive filmed television already existed, but it was mainly for comedies and cop shows. De Rochemont felt that production efficiencies developed by *The March of Time* might be applied to the more prestigious "golden age" dramas as well, lowering their unit production costs while maximizing the income stream through reruns and ancillary market sales.[64]

Mr. Lincoln was a test case, underwritten by the Ford Foundation with an investment of $125,000. James Agee had been hired to write the scripts, and studio interiors were shot at the old Fox studio on West Fifty-Fourth Street. Royal Dano played Lincoln, Marian Seldes was Nancy Hanks, and Joanne Woodward appeared as Ann Rutledge, whose historical importance Agee vastly inflated. Agee had recommended Norman Lloyd as director, probably through their mutual connection to Charlie Chaplin. Lloyd shot the studio work and all the location scenes with the adult Lincoln in New Salem, Illinois. But with time becoming an issue, de Rochemont asked him if Kubrick might be allowed to direct the scenes of young Abe at their other location, Hodgenville, Kentucky, where the National Parks Service maintained a replica of Lincoln's boyhood home. As an audition piece, de Rochemont screened *Fear and Desire* for Lloyd, with Kubrick in the back of the room, "hunched down, looking rather dark."[65] After viewing the still unreleased feature, Lloyd decided that "the picture was not good, but the visual qualities were very strong."[66] Accordingly, he agreed that Kubrick could go to Kentucky and shoot the "mostly silent material of the cabin and its interior, the little boy learning to draw water from the well, riding in the wagon as black slaves went by, and the family sitting outside the cabin at night."[67]

Kubrick arrived in charge of three actors and a small crew. Marcel Rebière, the director of photography for the series, was assigned as cameraman (one wonders why he didn't stay with Lloyd and the first unit in New Salem). Rebière was a distinguished European documentary photographer and a contemporary of men like Boris Kaufman and Joseph Brun. He had shot *Mor Vran* for Jean Epstein in 1931 and more recently had been working for the de Rochemonts in Europe. He spoke no English, and in order to communicate with Kubrick he depended on the script supervisor, Sacha Lawrence, to act as translator. The unit was heavy with cameramen. Morris Hartzband was the camera operator and Sol Negrin was assistant cameraman, an entry-level position responsible for basic tasks like loading and unloading the camera.

Kubrick never worked well under any sort of bureaucracy. One day, according to Negrin, "we're shooting at Lincoln's house in Kentucky."

> And you're only allowed to work there from eight to five. Kubrick went wild....
> he had a pistol with him, a luger, and he went in the back, he had an argument
> with the people from the government, the National Parks Service, that we had

to get out of there. He got pissed off that we couldn't shoot. So he goes in the back of the house and we hear the gun going off. Boom! And he's yelling out our names! Hartzband—Boom! Rebière—Boom!⁶⁸

Kubrick may have been frustrated over some bureaucratic challenge, but the material he was turning in was excellent. Landscapes recall the work of the great *Life* photo journalist W. Eugene Smith, and close-ups of local extras channel Kubrick's mentor, Arthur Rothstein, or even Walker Evans, whose collaboration with James Agee on *Let Us Now Praise Famous Men* Kubrick certainly knew well. Still, Marcel Rebière, who thought that *he* was supposed to be photographing the picture, was less impressed. "He shoots everything like it's through a Rolleiflex," the cinematographer grumbled, an implicit criticism of Kubrick's background in magazine photography.⁶⁹

Worse, the director still had no facility with actors. One night at dinner, a drunken Crahan Denton, who played Lincoln's father and "couldn't stand" Kubrick, came up to him in a rage: "'Whoever called you a fucking director!' And he's calling him all kinds of names. And Kubrick, with that [Charles] Addams look that he had at the time, with the hair, and a black sweater, and a black . . . he just looked at him and said nothing. He just took all that shit and nothing. I thought the actor was gonna get fired. But he [Kubrick] was only second unit, you see."⁷⁰

Kubrick had no friends among the rest of the unit, either. Sol Negrin, who was only a few months younger, came from the same Bronx neighborhood, and shared the same religious and educational background, felt that Kubrick "thought he was a big deal. And not only that, but he was condescending. . . . We're sitting at lunch and we're talking about pictures. I had some question about a picture. 'What do you know about a picture? You're just an assistant.' I got pretty pissed off."⁷¹ While both men only had a few college credits, Negrin had studied for a year with Hans Richter. He later became president of Local 644, the cameramen's union, and was elected to the American Society of Cinematographers. And despite admitting the quality of some of Kubrick's later pictures, he remembered this insult for the rest of his life.

Norman Lloyd would have heard these stories one way or another, but what really aggravated him was a clipping from the *Louisville Courier Journal* that Marian Seldes sent him. This entertaining Sunday photo spread ("The Cameraman Spoke No English and the Director Knew No French" read one subhead) prominently featured Stanley Kubrick, who was identified as the director.⁷² "I found it very amusing because the indication was that he was making the picture," Lloyd remembered. This was a breach of protocol, as Kubrick's small role in the production did not even merit screen credit. Kubrick later turned up at the New Salem location and began criticizing the way Lloyd was setting up the shots. Oblivious to the effect of all this, he asked Lloyd for more work, "but on the basis of the clippings I said 'no thank you.' "[73] Lloyd, who was trying to establish his own career as a television director, needed no competition. "I knew he was going to be an enormous success; when you have an ego like that, at twenty-one, nothing will ever stop you."[74]

"Nancy Hanks," the episode on which Kubrick had directed second unit, aired on November 30, 1952. He had received no credit and was still without a distributor for his feature. Preview screenings were producing very mixed results. Mark Van Doren, a distinguished public intellectual whose class he had audited at Columbia, provided a remarkably personal blurb ("The future of Stanley Kubrick is worth watching for those who want to discover high talent at the moment it appears. . . .").[75] But Curtis Harrington, an independent filmmaker from Los Angeles who also attended one of the screenings, remembered a very different reaction. "The film was not well received," he told John Baxter. "In particular, Paul Mazursky's performance was laughed at. There were giggles in all the wrong places, and it seemed a bit overdone and overwrought. And afterwards, Stanley was in tears."[76]

Joseph Burstyn To the Rescue

On November 16, 1952, after a year of rejections from every other distributor, Kubrick sent his pitch letter to Joseph Burstyn: "Its structure: allegorical. Its conception: poetic. A drama of 'man' lost in a hostile world—deprived of material and spiritual foundations—seeking his way to an understanding of himself, and of life around him."[77]

If Burstyn was interested in this, he didn't tip his hand. Not until Kubrick, Perveler, and de Rochemont clarified their own relationship did Joseph Burstyn announce that he was taking on *Fear and Desire*.[78] Burstyn was an independent distributor of the old school who in the postwar period had learned that almost any European feature could be sold here at a profit by sexing up its advertising campaign. With his partner Arthur Mayer (known as "the merchant of menace" for his sensationalistic programming and promotion at the Forty-Second Street Rialto), this is the way he had handled *Open City, Paisan,* and *Bicycle Thieves*. On his own he distributed *Flowers of St. Francis* (subsequently retitling it *The Tyrant and the 13*), *Miracle in Milan,* and *The Ways of Love*. The last of these involved him in a landmark court battle (Burstyn v. Wilson) that proved crucial in demolishing the legal structures supporting local motion picture censorship. But how far to go in hyping such films was a very controversial matter, with some critics becoming suspicious of the entire art house project. "A thinly disguised art veneer covering a filthy sex picture," was the way one reviewer described yet another European import, and even the Museum of Modern Art film curator Richard Griffith admitted that the remarkable success of so many

Italian films "is due not to their merit but to the frankly pornographic advertising used to exploit them here."[79]

On March 31 Burstyn opened *Fear and Desire* at the Guild 50th, an intimate 450-seat theater tucked into the south side of Rockefeller Center. In art house fashion, it was supported only by a short, *Royal Destiny*, while newspaper ads featured that glowing blurb from Mark Van Doren, who praised the film as "brilliant and unforgettable" while also predicting that "the incident of the girl bound to a tree will make movie history."[80] His quote was prominently placed above the title, but an image of "the girl bound to a tree" dominated the advertising graphic. This strategy worked very well with the New York critics, most of whom fell for Kubrick's youth, as much as his cinematic audacity, and nodded indulgently at any shortcomings. "*Fear and Desire* is an unpolished production full of flaws," wrote the *Brooklyn Daily Eagle*. "But its mistakes are the result of its bold effort to discard old formulas and make a different movie, and in this it has been successful."[81] A. H. Weiler, who had been keeping *Times* readers abreast of the production for months, agreed: "If *Fear and Desire* is uneven and sometimes reveals an experimental rather than a polished exterior, its over-all effect is entirely worthy of the sincere effort put into it."[82] One man who didn't buy any of this was John McCarten of the *New Yorker*, whose sarcastic review (headlined "Amateur") mocked Kubrick's "towering thoughts" and dismissed the entire film as "a classic piece of malarkey." "I suppose I shouldn't kick around a horse that is as dead as this one, but it does seem to me that, considering the freedom of expression Mr. Kubrick obviously enjoyed, he should have done a hell of a lot better."[83]

Yet within a few years Kubrick himself had come around to McCarten's point of view, describing the film (to the *New Yorker*!) as "an exceedingly serious, undramatic, and pretentious allegory."[84] *Fear and Desire* soon fell out of theatrical distribution, although it continued to be distributed in the 16 mm market at least as late as 1966 (when this writer saw it in a film class at Hofstra University). Ranjit Sandhu, who has documented its early distribution history, cites a nationally publicized screening at UC Berkeley in March 1964, part of a Kubrick retrospective attended by his business partner, James B. Harris—but not the man himself.[85] This appears to be where the film was seen by Jackson Burgess, whose extended analysis in *Film Quarterly* was the first—and for a long time the last—serious effort to view this "honorable failure" within the larger context of Kubrick's cinema.[86]

After the reviews were in, James Agee is reported to have consoled Kubrick at a Greenwich Village coffeehouse. "There are too many good things in the film to call it arty," Gene Phillips quotes him as saying.[87] This could have happened. Both men lived in the Village and Kubrick might have known Agee from the *Mr. Lincoln* shoot. Agee was then involved in writing the script for *Noa, Noa*, an ambitious independent feature that David Bradley was about to film. Neither man could have known that, despite the talent attached and the front money already committed, *Noa, Noa* would never get off the ground. Unfortunately, this would be the fate of many independent films in the poststudio era. In retrospect, Kubrick might have considered himself lucky that *Fear and Desire* ever got released at all.

Burstyn's promotion for the second run was entirely different. On May 11, *Life* ran a two-page feature, not exactly on the film, but on Virginia Leith, "the girl bound to a tree." One page featured a Kubrick portrait of Leith leaning into a makeup mirror, her blouse open and breasts partially exposed. Two other photos showed Mazursky and Leith in the "tree incident."[88] This was pure cheesecake atypical of *Life* and a remarkable PR coup for someone in the Burstyn office. In New York the film went straight to the Rialto on Forty-Second Street, where it was double-billed with something Burstyn called *The Male Brute*. That was Jean Delannoy's *Le Garçon sauvage*, a film Burstyn had released the year before under the title *Savage Triangle*. Now the top-lined quote was from Walter Winchell, who noted, "The wolves are breathless about Virginia Leith."[89] This ran next to a more explicitly erotic shot of Leith, not from the film, but apparently part of the same Kubrick cheesecake layout offered to *Life*. Of course, the image of "the girl and the tree" was still there, only a bit smaller.

In retrospect, it is easy to criticize Burstyn for tarting up Kubrick's film as soon as it left the elegant precincts of the Guild 50th. But away from midtown Manhattan, critics and audiences understood that they had to put up with such foolishness if they ever expected to see anything of contemporary European art cinema or its American equivalents. This was the only way, it seemed at the time, to fill enough seats for a program like this. In Philadelphia, where the *Fear and Desire/Male Brute* double bill ran only with Burstyn's exploitation campaign ("a story of sin, sex and passion"), *Inquirer* film critic Mildred Martin praised the pairing of the "French master" with the "first effort" of young Kubrick as an event of "exceptional import" for thoughtful audiences.[90] The same sleazy layout used in the display ads reappeared, with a bit of color, in the poster art. Kubrick must have enjoyed this because he seems to have kept a copy of the poster in his archives (after his death, his estate included it in the massive traveling exhibition that has been touring internationally since 2004).

Kubrick's timing may have been better than he knew when he pitched his film to Joseph Burstyn. It was clear that there was still an audience for films like *Bicycle Thieves* and *Miracle in Milan*, but by 1953, at least according to Burstyn, European producers "had forgotten how to make artistic pictures." Returning that year from a buying trip to Italy and France, Burstyn had come back empty-handed. "I didn't see anything that seemed really good," he confessed. *Variety* reported that "Burstyn is worried about the future of the indie distribs and believes that it may be tied up with offbeat American pix rather than foreign lingualers."[91] Indeed, Joseph Burstyn, Inc. would only release three new features in 1953: Andre Cayette's *Justice Is Done*, Stanley Kubrick's *Fear and Desire*, and yet another offbeat American indie, *Little Fugitive*.

We have already seen how a number of hopeful postwar filmmakers decided to grab a camera, round up some friends, and get into the movie business. Stanley Kubrick had done this himself with *Day of the Fight*. But the mixed reception of films like *Dreams That Money Can Buy* indicated that producing a successful feature picture would be another matter entirely. *Little Fugitive* would prove the exception to this rule, an almost homemade feature that charmed both critics and audiences while inspiring young filmmakers around the world to pick up a camera and get out into the streets. But at first glance Burstyn did not really see *Little Fugitive* as his kind of picture.

He had already had one bad experience with a promising low-budget feature, *The Quiet One*, which despite international accolades and a pair of Oscar nominations had failed miserably at the box office in 1949. *The Quiet One* was directed by Sidney Meyers, whom the historian William Alexander thought may have been the most talented of the "very talented group of young artists" involved with Frontier, Nykino and the Film and Photo League in the 1930s.[92] Meyers's best-known prewar film was *People of the Cumberland* (1938), on which his collaborators included Elia Kazan and Jay Leyda. He went on to edit films for the Office of War Information, where he hired and trained Ralph Rosenblum. It seems to have been Leyda who introduced Meyers to Helen Levitt, a disciple of Henri-Cartier Bresson, who was planning a film on the Wiltwyck School for Boys, a progressive institution devoted to the emotional and psychological rehabilitation of disturbed urban youth.[93]

The film follows one troubled child and his course of treatment, while the "economic, social and emotional conditions which produce the damaged child," are illustrated through flashbacks of his life in the city.[94] Psychotherapy helps him confront the sources of his pain. Wiltwyck cannot eliminate them or even claim to repair his "malformed" psyche, but at the end of the film he succeeds in confronting his repressed feelings and is liberated "from the prison of his own personality."[95] Levitt and her producing partner, Janice Loeb, had written a basic plot outline—there never was a conventional script—and cast the main roles. Because the argument is dramatized through the presentation of one main character and his experiences, finding a non-professional able to take on this role was crucial. The lead here was not played by a Wiltwyck resident but a ten-year old Harlem schoolboy named Donald Thompson, "the complete opposite of the maladjusted child he portrays," according to Loeb. Unlike the illiterate and abandoned youth in the story, Thompson was a keen student whose father would not allow him to skip a day of class just for the sake of a film. As he was only available after school or on weekends and holidays, principal photography stretched out for five months.[96]

A photo published in the *New York Times* shows Levitt filming Thompson with a Cine-Kodak Special, Eastman's top-of-the line 16 mm camera, while Loeb shoots another angle with what appears to be a Bell & Howell Filmo, the 16 mm version of the Eyemo.[97] "Janice and I photographed the so-called documentary material of the streets and up at the school," Levitt remembered, "but the main story line was all photographed by [Richard] Bagley."[98] Bagley was a newsreel cameraman with combat film experience who had been trained at the Signal Corps Photographic Center. He would later film Lionel Rogosin's *On the Bowery*. *The Quiet One* was shot and edited entirely on 16 mm, and presented this way at various festivals. But when it was picked up for theatrical distribution by Arthur Mayer and Joseph Burstyn it was blown-up to 35 mm, a process with which Meyers would have been familiar thanks to his wartime documentary work.

It was only during the editing process, when Loeb saw that the film "seemed to fall apart in places," that the team called in James Agee, whom they had worked with earlier on a short film called *In the Street*. "It wasn't until Jim put in his commentary that the whole thing was stitched together," she remembered.[99] Indeed, Agee not only wrote the narration but initially recorded it; only when his performance was judged "too poetic" was Gary Merrill brought in.[100] There was a limit to the amount of money independent filmmakers could save by cutting or withholding salaries, but working in 16mm and avoiding the cost of direct dialogue recording—strategies closely associated with "documentary style"—were far more important in keeping down production costs. Throughout the 1950s and 1960s, Morris Engel, Stanley Kubrick, John Cassavetes and other exponents of New York's independent filmmaking community would build on lessons like these while struggling to get their own films made and released.

The line between fiction and non-fiction that Louis de Rochemont had blurred a decade earlier had by now faded almost entirely. The *New York Times*, which covered the film heavily both before and after release, first described *The Quiet One* as "not a documentary in the strictest sense of the word," but later referred to it as "a genuine masterpiece in the way of a documentary drama."[101] Uncertain of just how to pigeonhole it, Bosley Crowther compared it favorably to both the 1937 Pare Lorentz documentary, *The River*, and Vittorio de Sica's recent neo-realist drama, *Shoe-Shine*.[102] "In a sense, it might be reckoned the *Shoe Shine* of American urban life," he wrote in his original review.

But Vinicius de Moraes, a Brazilian poet and film critic who reviewed the film at length in *Hollywood Quarterly*, saw a clear distinction between the essential hopefulness of Italian neo-realism and the quiet desperation that always seems on the edge of breaking out here:

> More beautiful than *Shoeshine*, to which it is related in some respects, it is also a more excruciating social document. The young delinquents of Vittorio De Sica's picture do not suffer like the children of *The Quiet One* from the impos-

sibility of seeing their own faces in the mirror. For De Sica's children loneliness will come later, but at present their poverty is cheered by freedom to pursue vicious adventures through the sunlight streets of Rome. In *The Quiet One* [the boy] wanders on the sidewalks of Harlem in silence.[103]

The film was recognized and honored as a documentary on its release, winning the same International Prize at Venice in 1949 that Robert Flaherty's *Louisiana Story* had won the year before. And unlike Flaherty's film it was nominated by the Motion Picture Academy as Best Documentary Feature in 1948; then the following year it was nominated again, competing against films like *Paisan* in the Best Writing (Story and Screenplay) category. But in later years *The Quiet One*'s hybrid qualities often caused it to be overlooked by documentary historians. Eric Barnouw, for example, discusses it briefly in the same paragraph as *The House on 92nd Street* and *On the Waterfront*, other films he believes were labeled as "documentary" for a variety of irrelevant reasons.[104]

The Quiet One had a long and successful non-theatrical run, but only in 16 mm; Mayer and Burstyn probably regretted their decision to blow the print up to 35 for theatrical release. "The movie critics rallied to its support with the unanimously enthusiastic reviews which this gem of a picture so fully deserved," Mayer wistfully recalled. "Our final national gross was less than that of many Hollywood shorts!"[105] But three years later, with the quality of available European product falling short of expectations, Burstyn crossed his fingers and took another shot at this corner of the market.

While some young filmmakers had been looking to take advantage of new technologies that might help them put their ideas up on screen, the team behind *Little Fugitive* reversed the process and dreamed up a story idea that could highlight a technology they already had. Morris Engel was a New York Photo League veteran who had been a staff photographer for *PM* magazine, one of Weegee's favorite outlets. He first picked up a movie camera in 1939 when Paul Strand invited him to help out on *Native Land*. During the war he worked as a photographer for the navy, where he would have been introduced to the Cunningham Combat Camera, specially designed for military use in the field (meaning: under fire). The Cunningham was a handheld, electrically driven 35 mm camera, somewhat resembling a Thompson submachine gun. The cameraman would point it in the general direction of the action with the aid of a nonreflex telescopic sight and steady the camera with the aid of two handle grips and a rifle-stock support pressed against his chest. The army favored the use of Bell & Howell Eyemos for 35 mm handheld work, but those cameras, as Stanley Kubrick learned while filming the Cartier-James fight, could capture only twenty-second bursts of action without the addition of an electric motor; the Cunningham, with its two-hundred-foot magazines, could run for more than two minutes.[106]

Engel later credited Charles Woodruff, an engineer he had met in the navy, with reconfiguring this camera for civilian use. But sometimes he said that he had designed it himself (on *Little Fugitive*, the men share screen credit for "camera design"). By 1950, Engel was promoting *How America Lives*, a postwar update of *The March of Time* that would have featured the use of this camera, but he found no takers. Like Kubrick (a friend and fellow New York street photographer) he soon learned that the theatrical nonfiction market was shrinking, and television's embrace of the genre had yet to take hold. But there was still that camera, and not all the news was bad. Engel kept a copy of an internal memo in which one Curtis Publishing Company executive, while rejecting *How America Lives*, still noted that "Engel has developed something with his hand held movie camera which will help him as a photographer and *may eventually even have some effect on the taking of moving pictures generally*."[107] Ruth Orkin, later his wife and collaborator on *Little Fugitive*, wrote on the top of this page (which I found in her papers), "A Prophetic Memo."

As no one in the industry seemed interested in their ideas, they decided to become their own producers. Kubrick had started with some shorts before shooting *Fear and Desire* but Engel and Orkin felt they could skip those first steps. A limited partnership was created to produce a feature picture, *Little Fugitive*, consisting of twenty-eight investors who contributed a total of $81,009. Engel was the largest investor ($16,262.50) while Ruth Orkin contributed $8,250.[108] A third collaborator, Ray Ashley (Raymond Abrashkin), was brought on as the story man; he had been the education editor at *PM* but would later be better known as the coauthor of the "Danny Dunn" children's book series. Engel felt that he would be comfortable directing children, so the group prepared to develop a child-centered story, perhaps influenced not only by Ashley but by a wave of similar films already popular on the postwar art house circuit (not only *The Quiet One*, but *Shoe-Shine, The Fallen Idol, Germany Year Zero, The Boy with Green Hair, Forbidden Games*, etc.). But compared to those films, some of which are very heavily plotted, *Little Fugitive*'s storyline is so slight as to be almost nonexistent. A seven-year-old Brooklyn boy, the victim of a childish prank, becomes convinced that he has murdered his older brother. Boarding an elevated train to "escape" a policeman he winds up at Coney Island, where he spends a day and a night enjoying pony rides and eating hot dogs. The brother finds him the next day and they both get home before Mom notices anything out of the ordinary.

The film's simplicity was itself a great part of its appeal: no pointed moral, no dramatic character arc, no allegorical references to corruption, intolerance, World War II, or nuclear disarmament. Instead the audience is led on by the film's uncanny sense of observation—not just in terms of photographic imagery but in the way ordinary New Yorkers relate to one another, solve their little problems, and go about the mundane details of their everyday lives. Presented

11.2. Richie Andrusco at Coney Island in *Little Fugitive*, Ray Ashley, Morris Engel, and Ruth Orkin's landmark independent feature. Museum of Modern Art Film Stills Archive.

from a child's perspective, *Little Fugitive* obsesses over some issues—love that pony ride—while hardly noticing the magnitude of others. There is no sense, for example, that little Joey ever thinks of himself as *lost*; rather, his adventures in and around the boardwalk are just like those of any other *flâneur*. Joey is never without his Hopalong Cassidy gun belt, but there is also a real gun here (and live ammunition!) that his older brother and his friends enjoy taking turns shooting. Is it only my twenty-first-century sensibility that finds much of this hair-raising? On the Kino Video DVD commentary track, Morris Engel does admit that he was a bit worried about having the kids actually firing live rounds.[109]

This thematic simplicity is echoed by a pared down stylistic approach that makes the average neorealist picture look like a Cecil B. De Mille production. *Little Fugitive* was shot quickly and cheaply in about twenty-one working days between the Fourth of July and Labor Day during the summer of 1952. Engel reported a shooting ratio of 8:1 and a direct production cost of $33,000.[110] Additional crew, including a location sound man and a film editor, were let go after working on the film only a short time. Ruth Orkin, already a noted photographer in her own right (she sold her first photo to *Look* at the age of twenty-one), cut the film herself on a small moviola.[111] All the sound would be looped in the studio, but unlike *Jigsaw* or *Fear and Desire*, we hear so little dialogue (two thousand words) that *Little Fugitive* functions almost like a silent film. Guided by a two- or three-page story outline, the filmmakers developed their scenario while they shot the picture, usually a recipe for disaster but in this case a strategy that led to the film's only Academy Award nomination—for the writing of its original story!

Critics at the time commented on how this lack of resources forced the filmmakers to create imaginative workarounds for even the most basic procedures. For example, a musical budget of $1,000 meant that even a small orchestra was out; instead, composer Eddy Manson played the entire score himself on a three-octave harmonica. He saved even more money by composing the fifty minutes' worth of music in thirteen hours and recording the entire nine-reel picture live in a single day ("It took a week just for the swelling in my lips to go down").[112] His reward was that the film's main musical motif, "Joey's Theme," was covered on many recording labels and sold a great deal of sheet music.

Because the small team was so inexperienced they were always receiving helpful advice from more seasoned veterans, most of whom said that everything they hoped to do was impractical, impossible, or commercially inadvisable. Ruth Orkin was told that to assemble the film coherently would require approximately sixty opticals (dissolves, fades, etc.). Each optical cost money that the company would rather not spend. But Engel recalled seeing a recent Hollywood film—*The Snows of Kilimanjaro*, edited by Barbara McLean—that seemed to have hardly any opticals, so Orkin abandoned most of them in favor of straight cuts.[113] The popularity of innovative solutions like this soon caused a new generation to see the *Little Fugitive* team as role models, and their work was especially revered by young French directors like François Truffaut and Jean-Luc Godard, who studied everything from Engel's handheld camerawork to Orkin's avoidance of fades and dissolves. "Our new wave would never have come into being if it hadn't been for the young American Morris Engel, who showed us the way to independent production with his fine movie *Little Fugitive*," Truffaut told a reporter from the *New Yorker* in 1960.

> Not to be tied to tremendous sums of money serves the aesthetics of film very well. A working-class apartment in Montmartre is incomparably more real and intimate than anything one might create in a studio. Furthermore, a small crew is a great help for an actor, especially an inexperienced one. The fewer people he finds around him, the more natural he is. In shooting most of my scenes, I send away everyone but the cameraman.[114]

Of course, Engel, Orkin, and Ashley did not have the luxury of sending away excess staffers, because on *Little Fugitive* there weren't any.

Perhaps the most basic piece of advice the team was offered was not to stretch their story idea out to feature length but to shape it into a cute and compelling short. Later art house audiences would delight in films like Albert Lamorisse's *The Red Balloon* (1956), and even at the time Bosley Crowther saw *Little Fugitive* as reminiscent of *Sweeney Steps Out*, a 1942 Warner Bros. short in which a six-year-old boy wanders by himself in the Bronx Zoo.[115] But *Little Fugitive* was no vignette, and selling it as a feature-length picture proved nearly impossible. Every distributor passed on the film, including Joseph Burstyn. Then Burstyn took another look at the film, changed his mind, and sent it off to the Venice Film Festival, where it won the Silver Lion, a directing award.[116] True, it shared the award with five other pictures, including *Ugetsu monogatari* and *I vitelloni*, but *Little Fugitive* was still the most honored American film at the festival. Burstyn later gave the impression that he had "discovered" the film at Venice, but in fact he had placed it there very carefully, hoping that some "European art film" veneer might rub off on his offbeat American indie. He opened *Little Fugitive* in New York on October 6, 1953, but died suddenly on November 29, while the film was still playing first run at the Normandie. His company continued to distribute *Little Fugitive* (as well as *Fear and Desire*), but it seems unlikely that their promotional campaign could have been as aggressive as whatever Burstyn himself might have planned for it. Burstyn's death has been seen by some as a blow to the developing art house movement he helped create, but given the recent shift in his business plan (Kubrick and Engel instead of De Sica and Rossellini) it probably damaged New York's independent filmmaking community at least as much.

With *Fear and Desire* finally in theaters, Kubrick made a peculiar career move and took on one of the most commercial assignments available to a New York filmmaker: a commissioned industrial film. Why or how he agreed to direct a half-hour documentary on the Seafarers International Union (SIU) is unclear. The film was produced by Lester Cooper Productions, a small local shop headed by Cooper, who had been a writer in Warner's shorts department before the war and subsequently worked for the U.S. Army Signal Corps. He later wrote television documentaries for Mike Wallace and other local clients. The SIU was a maritime union, chartered in 1938, that organized sailors working on vessels operating out of American ports. It had been created by the American Federation of Labor to counter the more left-wing National Maritime Union affiliated with the CIO. Both unions were competing aggressively for membership, and SIU had already sponsored an eighteen-minute film, *This Is S.I.U.*, in 1949. That film showed "the function and operation of the [union] headquarters . . . thru the eyes of a 'rank and filer' home from a voyage."[117] It is probably no coincidence that *This Is S.I.U* was produced in the wake of Malcolm Johnson's Pulitzer Prize–winning exposé of waterfront corruption.

The new film, *The Seafarers*, would present itself as a third-person report "as told by" the respected CBS newscaster Don Hollenbeck, who appears as the on-screen narrator.[118] Kubrick shot the film during the summer of 1953—a pin-up calendar, coyly revealed through a slow tilt, indicates the month as June. There is not much that Kubrick could have done with this material, which allowed him even less creative control than he had on *Flying Padre*. The images are clearly subservient to the text, which reads like a promotional pamphlet (Will Chasan is credited as writer, with "technical assistance" from the staff of the union newsletter, *The Seafarers Log*). Kubrick scholars, hard put to find any stylistic signature here, usually point to a single lateral tracking shot in a seamen's cafeteria. But Kubrick clearly saw the film as a learning exercise; it was his first experience working in color and his first opportunity to work with 16 mm, which many then saw as the future of independent film production. *The Seafarers* was shot with the new Mitchell 16, a superior substandard gauge camera whose sophisticated movement might have appealed to Kubrick's exacting tastes.[119] Unfortunately, the photography lacks the dramatic quality of his earlier films and photo essays, most likely a fault of the slow speed of the color negative stock as well as his inability to control the lighting of scenes he was not actually staging.

There is no editor credited on this film, which suggests that Kubrick took on the job himself, another part of the learning process. Although he had edited *Fear and Desire* on his own, cutting 16 mm was in some ways more complicated. Kubrick was working out of office space at 1600 Broadway, a Times Square office building that functioned as the nerve center for New York's motion picture business. Vincent Lo Brutto refers to it as "Kubrick's self-styled film school," but today we might think of it as an ad hoc incubator, a nest of production houses crucial to the development of the city's independent film community. Like many other young filmmakers, Kubrick felt free to wander from one office to another "asking technicians, salesmen, and craftspeople about the mechanics of filmmaking." He appears to have spent considerable time with Faith Elliott (later Faith Hubley) "talking about his cinematic dreams and quizzing her about how films were made." Hubley would later become an Oscar-winning independent animator, but she was then working as an editor and script supervisor on industrial films and independent features. At one point Kubrick "asked Hubley to teach him how to match a 16 mm work print to the original negative so that he could prepare to cut the negative to make a print of a film," a technique he would only need to have mastered for *The Seafarers*.[120] As far as anyone knows, this was the first and last time Kubrick would work professionally in 16 mm.

While *The Seafarers* may lack much auteurist significance, its production is not unrelated to the work being done on another film focusing on the lives of local maritime workers, *On the Waterfront*. If the SIU had already produced a film celebrating the enlightened operation of its home office in 1949, why the need to do the job over again only a few years later? This is where Governor Dewey's Crime Commission fits in—especially the riveting testimony of his star witness, "Tony Mike" De Vincenzo, on December 15, 1952. Tony Mike's evidence, reinforced by the continuing stream of news stories documenting horrendous labor violence on the New York and New Jersey docks, tarred the public image of anyone and anything connected to the local maritime industry. In making this film, the Seafarers' Union was taking a proactive stance against any accusations of corruption or labor racketeering that might possibly come its way. We see nothing of the work of the seafarers and only a few shots of ships in the harbor. Instead, we see the union justifying itself as a union. The men have a health and education plan and their wives qualify for maternity benefits. Everyone seems clean and well dressed, with plenty of opportunity to enjoy the cafeterias, recreation halls, and even art exhibits sponsored by the SIU. Its election process claims to be the most democratic of any union in the country, and members speak up freely at open meetings. Most important, the operation of its hiring halls is shown to be both equitable and transparent. "Here, seafarers get their jobs not as a favor, but as a right," Hollenbeck tells us, a clear answer to the horrors of "the shape-up" being documented so forcefully by Father John Corridan and his allies. Kubrick may not have realized it, but with *The Seafarers* he was already addressing at least one element of the waterfront labor problem at a time when Budd Schulberg and Elia Kazan were still stuck in development hell.

CHAPTER 12

THE GOLDEN WARRIOR

Still smarting from his rejection by Zanuck, Elia Kazan met with his agent, Abe Lastfogel, in the Polo Lounge of the Beverly Hills Hotel. Also in attendance was another William Morris agent, Martin Jurow, who supervised the agency's motion picture interests on the East Coast.[1] But that afternoon he was just there to listen, while Lastfogel did his best to handle their client. "As Gadge finished his tale of woe, I noticed a man hovering nearby, devouring every word. He was Sam Spiegel, known earlier in his career as S. P. Eagle." According to Jurow, Spiegel "got right to the point, pleading with Gadge to let him produce *On the Waterfront*. He was certain he could get studio backing." Lastfogel, familiar with Spiegel's checkered financial history, put him off, and it was decided to decide nothing until Spiegel at least had a chance to read the script.

There is another version of this origin story, which first appeared under Budd Schulberg's byline in the *New York Times* even before the film had opened. "In our hotel was a wandering film man, Sam Spiegel," Schulberg remembered.

> Once in a while our doors would open at the same time and we could look briefly into each other's apartments and lives. One morning I went across the hall at my neighbor's invitation and paced up and down in front of Sam's bed. In Hollywood we have a rather charming tradition whereby writers rise early and tell stories to producers in their bedrooms or while they are shaving. Anyway, I did, and the rest is history or, at least the next best thing, a completed motion picture.[2]

This "open door" story was told and retold by both Schulberg and Kazan, with various layers of embellishment, over the next fifty years. Spiegel's association with the project came to be seen as a fortuitous coincidence, a chance encounter in a hallway leading Spiegel to ask, "Are you boys in trouble?"[3] In reality, as Jurow's recollection makes clear, Sam Spiegel already knew what had happened at Fox, and he first approached Kazan and Lastfogel downstairs in the Polo Lounge—a meeting at which Schulberg was not present. In his original article, Schulberg never says why he was invited to go across the hall and tell his story to Spiegel, and only in later accounts did he find various reasons to explain it. And all of those explanations are more entertaining than admitting that the William Morris Agency had something to with it.[4]

Memory can play tricks, and it is often easier to remember a good story than a true one. Just why was Sam Spiegel so eager to pick up this project, one he knew had been rejected by every studio in town (some of them more than once)? A logical answer might be that he was a good judge of talent and material who saw this as a potentially popular film that could be shot for under a million. Not much of a story there. So another part of the film's historical legend, especially when Schulberg was spinning it, is that Spiegel's primary motive was simple desperation. "He had a dismal flop on his hands, *Melba*, a movie about the old opera star Dame Nellie Melba that he literally couldn't give away. In his desperation, he told Kazan that if he could shoot my script on a B budget, in thirty-five days, he thought he could raise the money from United Artists."[5] But Kazan also remembered that *Melba* was " 'doing nothing' at the box office" just then, and even Jurow felt compelled to add that *Melba* "had played to empty houses," leaving its producer "at low ebb" the day they all met at the Polo Lounge.[6] Another good story, but also not true.

It is true that *Melba* would eventually lose a great deal of money, largely offsetting the profits Spiegel had expected to earn from *The African Queen*. But on May 25, the day Schulberg and Kazan walked out of Zanuck's office, the world premiere of *Melba* was still a month in the future, with the film's general release set for August 7. It would be many weeks before all those empty houses would get their crack at *Melba*. As far as anyone at the Polo Lounge that day knew, Sam Spiegel might have had another *Great Caruso* on his hands. Indeed, Spiegel was still completing postproduction on *Melba* when he ran into Schulberg and Kazan. Like a number of other producers (including *Shane*'s George Stevens), he was in the process of "modernizing" his latest picture by transforming it into an ersatz stereophonic, wide-screen release, despite the fact that it had not been shot that way.[7]

Spiegel went to work immediately—Schulberg remembered them flying back to New York together on the same plane.[8] Although its June 2 report of Fox's rejection hinted at an unnamed independent producer and distributor in the wings, by June 13 the *Times* was identifying the man as Sam Spiegel and the distributor as United Artists. Production of what was now called *The Golden Warriors* was scheduled to start "late in the summer or the fall," which left hardly any time at all to organize an all-location shoot with no studio infrastructure to fall back on.[9] Kazan was tied up with rehearsals for his new play, *Tea and Sympathy*, which would open its successful Broadway run on September 30. So it was now Spiegel who would work with Budd Schulberg to create a final shooting script, while supervising preproduction planning and completing negotiations with United Artists. Spiegel was depending on a residue of goodwill at UA because, in addition to producing *The African Queen*, he had served as intermediary between the original UA partners, Charlie Chaplin and Mary Pickford, and the incoming team of Arthur Krim and Robert Benjamin.[10] But Spiegel soon found that he had no friends at United Artists. "All the financial discrepancies that had been overlooked during his previous triumph were suddenly seized on when his operatic venture nosedived," his biographer, Natasha Fraser-Cavassoni, reports.[11] Perhaps if the returns on *Melba* had not been so dismal, Krim might have overlooked Spiegel's "shenanigans," but in the summer of 1953 he saw no reason to do so. This was when the "desperation" remembered by Schulberg may have kicked in.

All Spiegel really had to offer was his association with United Artists. The distributor had dutifully promoted its acquisition of *The Golden Warriors* all that summer, a story the *Times* continued to report as late as October 25.[12] But those announcements were a smokescreen intended to hide the film's real problems. Whatever deal Spiegel did have at UA suddenly unraveled when an "apoplectic" Krim finally lost patience and "insisted that Spiegel pay all his outstanding loans." With preproduction already underway in Hoboken, the project suddenly went into turnaround. Spiegel miraculously found a new distributor, but the announcement that Columbia would now handle the picture didn't come until November 30, followed by full-page trade ads on December 3. By that time the film had already been shooting for two weeks![13] The standard histories are vague on this detail, although Bob Thomas does indicate that Spiegel's deal was made directly with Abe Schneider and Nate Spingold of Columbia's New York office.[14] They could arrange this deal themselves because Spiegel's Horizon-American Corporation would be producing the film, not Columbia. Harry Cohn's input would be pro forma, so Spiegel could ignore his demand that the film be shot on the Columbia back lot (Jack Cohn was also out of the picture at this point). But Spiegel didn't need Schulberg and Kazan telling him that the film must be shot in the east; a European refugee of the old school, he "loathed Los Angeles," a desert community lacking decent cafés or a good ballet company, where the culturally deprived inhabitants "lived and breathed the film business."[15] This was not going to be one of Harry Cohn's pictures. So when Kazan screened the final cut for him months later, Cohn fell asleep about a third of the way through and snored through the rest of the film.[16]

Schulberg had been working on the film since 1950, and it reflected the creative input of everyone from Robert Siodmak to Darryl F. Zanuck (in a telegram to Kazan, Zanuck later reminded him that four of his "major suggestions" were still in the film, but that "I am not asking for screen credit. . . .").[17] As their producer, Sam Spiegel would now have his say on the script, forcing Schulberg to "open it up" again and again. "Spiegel was a taskmaster," Schulberg remembered. "A bear for structure. He thought it was overlength and sometimes discursive. Lots of times he was right."[18] When he thought Spiegel wasn't right, Schulberg would fly into rages at their St. Regis Hotel script conferences, accusing Spiegel and Kazan of conspiring against him. One day his wife asked him why he was up and shaving at three thirty in the morning. "I'm driving to New York to kill Sam Spiegel!"[19]

Spiegel was not simply trying to cut expensive sequences out of the film but to speed up the narrative so as to move more quickly through those sequences Darryl F. Zanuck might have described as "message propaganda." According to Fraser-Cavassoni, it was Spiegel's idea to shift the focus away from the investigative journalist, an outsider, and concentrate on the waterfront characters.[20] "I can't say why or how Sam knew so much about screenplay construction," Kazan remembered. "But he did have an instinctive story sense; he knew it had to be unrelenting as it unfolded, that it should never let up tension and always aim for the end."[21] Schulberg felt especially threatened by Spiegel's attack on what was, to him, the core of the film, the "Christ in the Shape-up" monologue. The sermon was far too long, Spiegel insisted, more suitable for a stage play than a motion picture. Kazan explained that he "would keep it visually interesting by cutting to reaction shots," which seemed to satisfy him, at least for the moment.[22]

The Hoboken Team

Regardless of who was distributing, planning for the production had to move forward. The first person hired by any producer is usually the production manager, who will be responsible for all business aspects of the shoot, including budgeting, contracting with vendors and technical crews, travel and transportation, permits and releases, and the creation of a shooting schedule. It is the production manager's job to keep the film on budget and on schedule, and Sam Spiegel would not have made this hire without serious thought. He had never made a film in New York before and could not afford expensive surprises, so he turned for advice to someone he knew and respected, Robert Aldrich. Aldrich had been the production supervisor on Spiegel's last Hollywood film, *When I Grow Up*, and had also worked as assistant director on the one before that, *The Prowler* (the assistant director is the point man who executes many of these responsibilities on the set, working closely with the director and the cinematographer). He was a director himself now, for both film and television, and had just finished seventeen episodes of *The Doctor* (1952–1953), a half-hour anthology series produced in New York by Marion Parsonnet.[23] He didn't want the job, but he did know two local people who might. On Aldrich's recommendation, Spiegel hired George Justin as production manager and Charles H. Maguire as assistant director.[24]

Justin was a Signal Corps veteran who had spent the war photographing army training films in Astoria. Since then he had worked as cameraman or director on a string of industrial films, taught film production at Brooklyn's New Institute for Film, and served as production manager on locally produced pilots and television series, including *The Doctor* and *Janet Dean, Registered Nurse*.[25] Charlie Maguire was born into the business, his father, Charles J. Maguire, having worked in the New York film industry since silent movie days. Charlie worked his way up from prop man, but it was Aldrich who "tutored" him and recommended him to Sam Spiegel. Justin and Maguire were already functioning as a team, having just completed work on the Brooklyn Dodgers feature, *Roogie's Bump*; they would work together again on *A Face in the Crowd*, *The Fugitive Kind*, and *Middle of the Night*. Both men continued their careers in Hollywood, where Justin was put in charge of production management at Paramount in the 1970s—a position Maguire would fill in the 1980s.

Justin would be *On the Waterfront*'s "outside man," guiding the flow of production and serving as intermediary between Sam Spiegel and the beleaguered crew. Schulberg considered Maguire "a stand-up guy physically and mentally" but displayed less affection for Justin: he later described him as a "moneyman," someone who "fussed about excessive petty expenditures and revealed his creative side in humorously written exhortations to the crew to bend more manfully to the oars in the interest of 'keepin' 'em [film productions] in the east.' "[26] Maguire worked more intimately with the director, acting as a personal assistant to execute his commands and screen him from irrelevant distractions. In Hollywood Kazan would have had an entire studio apparatus to help with this, but in Hoboken there was only Charlie Maguire. He quickly become Kazan's friend and confidant and later produced *Splendor in the Grass* and *America, America*, earning high praise in the director's autobiography.[27] Justin, on the other hand, must have struck Kazan as the "bad cop" in this partnership; he does not mention him in his book and they would not work together after 1957. But he seems to have been the right man for Sam Spiegel. Sol Negrin, later the president of Local 644, remembered him as a hard man to deal with. "He became very big as a producer," Negrin recalled. "But he was also a—. If he could cheat you out of your money, he'd cheat you out of your money [laughs]. 'Whataya mean, overtime!' You had to argue with him or bargain with him."[28]

12.1. George Justin on the set of *Mr. Rock and Roll*, an Alan Freed musical he produced at the Biograph/Gold Medal studio in 1957. Photo by Muky Munkacsi. George Justin Collection, Museum of Modern Art Film Stills Archive.

When *The Naked City* and *Portrait of Jennie* were shot here, local crews were never seriously considered for any of the key technical assignments—camera, sound, editing, or design. *The Window* and *Lost Boundaries*, which did depend mainly on local crews, were marginal productions made on low budgets by

B-list talent. *On the Waterfront* would be the first major New York production in decades in which all these departments were fully staffed by local talent—although that doesn't seem to have been the original intention. After failing with Aldrich, Spiegel brought in none of the key technicians who had worked on his earlier films and seems to have left such hiring decisions to Kazan. But Kazan, still tied up with *Tea and Sympathy* and facing what he already knew would be a difficult shoot, had no interest in breaking in an entirely new crew; he made the obvious decision and asked for the production designer and cinematographer responsible for the look of his most successful Hollywood film, *A Streetcar Named Desire*.

Compared to the other members of the team, Richard Day's work here has received very little attention from critics or historians. Despite the fact that he won Academy Awards for designing both *A Streetcar Named Desire* and *On the Waterfront* (the only such awards ever accorded a Kazan picture), Kazan fails to mention him in his autobiography. Duly honored in all histories of motion picture art direction—he won seven Oscars and was nominated twenty times—his work on this film is often seen as out of character. Charles and Mirella Affron cite *Waterfront*, in passing, as a "location" picture, hard to compare to one of his "studio" productions, like *Dodsworth* or *How Green Was My Valley*.[29] Leon Barsacq and Elliott Stein praise both *Streetcar* and *Waterfront* as containing "his best sets," but only because "the sets look like extensions of the real locations," an odd thing to say about a film, *On the Waterfront*, that was shot entirely on such locations.[30]

Only Beverly Heisner identifies the significance of Day's contribution, reading his years of work in the studios against a record of location shooting that could be traced back from *Cry Danger* (an LA noir shot in 1951) to Erich von Stroheim's *Greed*. Day had entered the film industry as a close associate of von Stroheim, designing the realistically detailed sets called for by the director in films like *Foolish Wives* and *The Wedding March*. But in 1924 they filmed *Greed*, an adaptation of Frank Norris's *McTeague*, not just on the streets of San Francisco but in practical interiors that the actors were ordered to live in during the shoot.[31] "Day, long expert at finding locations, had come up through the various schools of realism that held sway in Hollywood," Heisner concludes, "and was uniquely prepared to interpret the new brand of street realism forwarded by Kazan and other directors in the [postwar] decade."[32]

In a sense, Day was an obvious choice because of his prior association with Kazan on both *Streetcar* and *Boomerang!* He had also worked on *Miracle on 34th Street* and *Force of Evil*, and was as familiar as any West Coast designer with the potentials and pitfalls of New York location shooting. But Sam Spiegel was not going to fly in Richard Day from Hollywood just because of that. After many years as supervising art director at Fox, Richard Day had been freelancing and had not worked in Hollywood since *Hans Christian Anderson* wrapped in May 1952. In fact, he was now living in New York, having moved there to work on "color TV experiments" for NBC.[33] It would be many years before he worked in Hollywood again.

Kazan did not have to reach as far back as *Streetcar* in looking for a costume designer. Anna Hill Johnstone had done the costumes for *Tea and Sympathy*, so she was an easy choice for wardrobe supervisor for *On the Waterfront*. She would become Kazan's designer of choice on most of his future stage and screen projects and soon established herself as a key figure in the New York film renaissance, working with Sidney Lumet, Frank Perry, and Arthur Penn, and winning Oscar nominations for *Ragtime* and *The Godfather* (there was no Costume Design nomination for *On the Waterfront*, probably because the costumes looked too much like "the real costumes"). Although this was her first solo feature film assignment, she had assisted Lucinda Ballard on *Portrait of Jennie* six years earlier. In a film career that stretched over nearly forty films, she would barely set foot in Hollywood.[34]

Harry Stradling, the man who shot *Streetcar*, was also at the top of Kazan's list, but here the situation in New York was not so accommodating. Photographing a motion picture in New York fell under the jurisdiction of IATSE Local 644, which was trying to defend local jobs by putting up barriers intended to discourage the importation of Hollywood cameramen, members of West Coast Local 659. If a producer did insist on bringing in a non-644 director of photography, the union required him to hire a standby from their own active list at union scale, effectively doubling the cost. Hollywood excluded East Coast workers in the same way; in fact, it was probably the first to institute such barriers. Ironically, Stradling had once been a member of the New York local, in the 1920s, but had long since aligned himself with 659.

Sam Spiegel was not about to pay for a redundant cameraman, and despite working at it all summer he was unable to charm the union into seeing things his way. As late as September 28, Kazan was still hoping to overcome these "union problems" and bring in Harry Stradling.[35] But there were few local alternatives; some of the available men were too old, others too inexperienced. Don Malkames, ASC, had shot many low-budget features and television episodes, but he was not about to leave his secure studio assignment filming the *Man Against Crime* series in exchange for an opportunity to spend the winter outdoors in Hoboken.[36]

There was one man, however, who had been campaigning for the job since April, when the project was still being touted by Fox. Boris Kaufman had arrived in America in 1942, one of many European film refugees, but Local 659 would not accept him. So he remained in the east, working first for the National Film Board of Canada and then the Office of War Information. After the war he took whatever work was available, shooting documentaries, industrial films, and occasional two-reelers in the Paramount Screenliner series. New York cameramen were frequently called on to film screen tests of local hopefuls, and one of the tests shot by Kaufman was for Elia Kazan for *Viva Zapata!* Kaufman was given an hour to conjure the atmosphere of an old Mexican church out of "a column, a bench and some old drapes dragged from the basement of the Fox studio."[37] Kazan may not have used the services of the actress he tested that day, but he appears to have remembered the cameraman.

When publicity began appearing on the new film, Kaufman sent Kazan a two-page job application ("I have heard about your intention to make a picture about New York Waterfront"), reminding him of the *Zapata!* test, citing some of his recent documentaries (like *Capital Story* and *A Better Tomorrow*), and providing a résumé of his prewar work in France.[38] He had shot nearly twenty features there, working with directors like Abel Gance and Christian Jacques, as well as all the films of the great French master, Jean Vigo. He was especially proud of *L'Atalante*, where he had done "my best to express the less spectacular but nostalgic waterfront in Paris."[39] Kazan was interested but noncommittal, suggesting that Kaufman drop in on him at Fox's New York office in a few weeks (Zanuck had not yet killed the project). "I would be eager to talk with you about Jean Vigo, never having seen one of his pictures," Kazan wrote. "Can't you get one for me to see? Do you know whether the Museum of Modern Art has one? Perhaps we could see it together if they have—and talk about it afterwards."[40]

They never managed to find a copy of *L'Atalante*, but Kazan agreed to hire him anyway. Kaufman got the job not because of his experience in features (he had not shot a feature film since 1939) but because of what he had been doing lately: filming outdoors in all kinds of weather, making good use of practical interiors, and getting quality results with modest resources. Kazan may not have been completely serious when he vowed that he would shoot the film himself with a handheld camera, but hiring Boris Kaufman must have seemed like the next best thing. Kaufman's value at the moment lay almost entirely in his nonnarrative, nonstudio experience, the only work he had been able to find for the past decade. Some writers ascribe at least part of this quality to the influence of his brothers Mikhail and Denis (aka Dziga Vertov), who stayed behind to work in the Soviet film industry. But Boris Kaufman was still quite young when he left Russia and, according to a 1978 interview with Donald Crafton, had seen little of Vertov's work, remembering only *A Sixth Part of the World* and a few *Kino Pravda* episodes, and these not until after his arrival in Paris.[41]

After a visit to Hoboken on October 24, Kazan sat down with Spiegel, Kaufman, and Richard Day for a key production meeting on October 30.[42] There was plenty to discuss: the script was still fluid, key roles had not yet been cast, and everyone was still coming to terms with Hoboken. Because just as Arthur Miller's script had been tied to the Red Hook section of Brooklyn, where Pete Panto had operated, all of Schulberg's work had focused on the West Side piers in Manhattan. His main sources, Father Corridan and Arthur Browne, were West Siders, and he had spent most of his drinking time in waterfront saloons in Chelsea, not Hoboken and Jersey City. Tony Mike's testimony had drawn attention to the situation in New Jersey, but neither the script, nor the numerous essays Schulberg would publish around it, ever saw Hoboken as central.[43] Its name is not even mentioned in the finished film, and Schulberg made clear at the time that the film had not been written with Hoboken in mind—a possibility that seems to have aroused a good deal of local concern. "Mayor John J. Grogan said he had the assurances of the movie making firm that Hoboken will not be mentioned as the locale for most of the film unless the city desires it," one local paper reported. " 'We are assured that there will be nothing detrimental to the city shown in the production,' said Grogan."[44] But local sensitivity was not the only reason because when he later came to novelize his story, Schulberg still took pains to set it in "the grubby harbor town of Bohegan," a generic waterfront community directly across the Hudson from the gleaming "seaport metropolis" of New York.[45]

James Fisher suggests that the filmmakers were not pulled to Hoboken as much as they were pushed there, forced to leave their location of choice.[46] Joe Ryan had been ousted as head of the International Longshoremen's Assocation, but there was little reason to think that the threat of violence that had intimidated Darryl F. Zanuck and Harry Cohn had also gone away. Indeed, as late as 2017 the *New York Times* reported that "the fundamental relationship between the waterfront and the mob remains unchanged since *On the Waterfront*," and quoted the current executive director of the Waterfront Commission as saying, "The only difference is now, it's in color."[47] Working conditions on the West Side would have been rough, but they certainly were no worse than what the crew found in Hoboken. And remember that Martin Ritt was able to shoot much of *Edge of the City* on the West Side in April 1956, even in the snow.[48] Nevertheless, Fisher points out, "Working piers do not simply make themselves available to filmmakers." In a tremendous stroke of luck, Spiegel was able to take advantage of the fact that the operator of Pier 1 in Hoboken, Frank Nolan of the Jarka Corporation, had just been indicted for bribery.[49] The Port Authority owned all the old German Lloyd and Hamburg-America piers in Hoboken and quickly took advantage of the opportunity to close that pier for "renovation," thus making it available for Spiegel's exposé of waterfront corruption; Father Corridan, functioning as the project's "technical adviser," apparently helped arrange the deal with his friend Austin Tobin, executive director of the Port Authority.[50]

Once the problems of writing the script, finding someone to fund and distribute the picture, and deciding where to shoot it had been worked out, the most intractable problem still remained: Who would play Terry? As far back as February, Zanuck had told Budd Schulberg that if he could really deliver Marlon Brando, he was willing to green-light the project immediately.[51] This did not happen, though, because Brando had been so traumatized by Kazan's HUAC testimony that he refused even to look at the script. He continued to refuse to look at it for the rest of the summer. When Spiegel took over the project in June he said nothing about Brando but announced that the part was being offered to Montgomery Clift. Apparently considering Clift's casting a done deal, the *Los Angeles Times* reported a few days later that the news was "lacking only formal confirmation."[52] But the star of *From Here to Eternity* seemed as disinterested as Brando. Unwilling to give up on him, Spiegel continued to pursue Clift until just before the start of filming, sending him yet another draft of the script as late as October 7.[53]

In the meantime, Kazan began promoting a younger product of the Actors Studio, Paul Newman. "He's a really wonderful prospect, handsome, rugged, sexy and somehow turbulent inside," he wrote to Spiegel on August 1. "He looks quite a lot like Brando."[54] Karl Malden reports that Kazan had him work up a scene with Paul Newman and Joanne Woodward in an effort to sell the little-known actor to Spiegel, but the producer was adamant.[55] He was not interested in a television actor with no film experience—even if he did look like Marlon Brando—whose only theatrical credit was a small role in Joshua Logan's current production of *Picnic*.

And then there was Frank Sinatra. In September, Edwin Schallert, the entertainment editor of the *Los Angeles Times*, interviewed Sinatra and Ava Gardner by phone in New York. The point of the call was to squelch rumors of their impending breakup, but the pair also took the opportunity to plug some of their upcoming projects. On September 19 Schallert published "Priest Role on Slate for Sinatra," revealing that the singer "will probably star in *Waterfront*" as "a rugged waterfront priest." Eight days later he ran more of the same interview, with Sinatra describing his role as "a priest but utterly different from *The Miracle of the Bells*. The new feature would call for me to act a rugged waterfront personality."[56] Sinatra would never have said this to Schallert unless it was clear to him at the time that he was set to play Father Barry. It was a strong supporting role, as good as Sinatra's current part in *From Here to Eternity*, and could be seen as a variation on his Father Paul in *Miracle of the Bells* (an echo of Bing Crosby doing both *Going My Way* and *The Bells of St. Mary's*?).[57] Although every Hollywood leading man from Brando to Victor Mature had been suggested for the role of Terry, no one had ever brought up the name of Frank Sinatra. But time was running out for Sam Spiegel, who had no interest in Paul Newman and whose October 7 approach to Montgomery Clift had once again come up short. So sometime in October Sam Spiegel offered the part of Terry Malloy to Frank Sinatra. "Ironically, Sinatra had the same political leanings as Brando," notes his recent biographer, Richard Muti, "but he wasn't about to let that get in the way of a good movie role."[58]

In his autobiography, Kazan writes about how Spiegel kept him and Schulberg in the dark about all sorts of legal and contractual issues. "I never knew what the hell he was doing with *Waterfront*—despite the fact that I owned twenty-five percent of the film."⁵⁹ Spiegel apparently had not consulted with Kazan about his casting of Sinatra in *either* role. "One day Sam told me he'd 'set' Frank Sinatra and that I might have a chat with him about his costumes."⁶⁰ On October 21, Kazan composed a memo to Spiegel after studying George Justin's latest shooting schedule, which allowed just thirty days for shooting, assuming no difficulties with the weather, or the actors:

> Now, I want to go on record with you. I'm delighted to do the picture with Frank S. I'd still prefer to do the picture with Paul Newmann [sic]. I leave the decision to you. You have just told me on the phone you have gone ahead with Frank S. . . . I'm now speaking officially. Officially too I give you absolutely no hope of getting thru with him in twenty days or twenty-four days. George can tell you on the adjusted schedule how many days underlined it will take with Sinatra. For ME it is not worth the gamble that Sinatra might be taken away from us in the midst (accurately: towards the end) of our shooting. I underlined would not take that gamble. I do not agree to make that gamble good. I will do my best to make a creditable picture as fast as I can make it creditable. That's all.⁶¹

If what Kazan writes here can be believed, he would have been happy to do the picture with Frank Sinatra, a Hoboken native whose recent acclaim for his appearance in *From Here to Eternity* had not only revived his career but suddenly given him dramatic credibility in nonmusical roles.⁶² A week later Hedda Hopper reported that "Sinatra leaves [LA] shortly for New York to make a picture with his pals Elia Kazan, Lee Cobb, Julie Harris, and Karl Malden."⁶³ But Kazan presents so many obstacles that it is clear he is doing his best to manipulate Spiegel into finding someone else for the role. One final shot for Paul Newman? So with the start of production only a few weeks away, Spiegel swept down and finally worked his magic on Marlon Brando. "Sam had conned Marlon into making the film, and I let him do the dirty work and said nothing. I wouldn't have done what Sam did, but I was glad he did it; it was what I really wanted. I turned my face the other way as S. P. Eagle informed Sinatra's agency, William Morris, that Frank was out."⁶⁴ Karl Malden suggests that all this public focus on finding someone else to play "a role that Marlon knew in his heart belonged to him" may have raised his competitive instinct to such a degree that he finally "put his political ideals aside" and allowed himself to be persuaded.⁶⁵ He would make an exception, just this once. Nothing personal here, only business.

On November 1, Kazan wrote down "Sinatra Arrives" in his appointment book, later adding "for Waterfront."⁶⁶ A few days later the singer was back in Los Angeles, at Capitol Records, laying down tracks for a new album. Among the songs he recorded was "They Can't Take That Away from Me," a bittersweet ballad that somehow prefigured the big news that broke later that week: Marlon Brando had just been signed for the lead in Sam Spiegel's new picture.[67] Everyone involved with the film has told a different story of how and why Brando changed his mind and agreed to work again with Elia Kazan—some of them several different stories—although Spiegel's seductive negotiating style is the common element in most of them. Spiegel clearly had solid business reasons for continuing to pursue Brando. As Schulberg remembers, "U.A. wouldn't put up more than $500,000 for Frank," but with Brando on board, Spiegel could get a far better deal ($800,000, eventually raised to $880,000), more than justifying Brando's $100,000 salary.[68] As for Sinatra, Kazan made sure his wrath was not directed in his direction, apparently writing the singer a letter (a copy of which is not present in Kazan's papers at Wesleyan) assuring him of their personal friendship. Sinatra responded on December 8. "For me to tell you I was not deeply hurt would not be telling you my true feelings," he wrote. "However, with the passing of time and re-reading your letter, how could I do or say anything other than that I, too, want to be friends with you. We can discuss it again the first time we see each other." On the back of this letter, Kazan later wrote, "In re how Spiegel OOZED him out of Waterfront & Brando in."[69] Sinatra did not want to be friends with Sam Spiegel, however, and sued the production for $100,000 (settling later for $18,000).[70] Spiegel's biographer reports an incident at Romanoff's, years later, where Sinatra, after having congratulated Spiegel on the success of *Bridge on the River Kwai*, felt snubbed by the producer's tepid response. Calling out the producer as "Hey, fat man," Sinatra punched Spiegel on the shoulder twice, trying to attract his attention. "You're lucky that I bother to speak to you at all," Spiegel answered. Sinatra declined an invitation to settle the affair outside.[71]

Although Kazan may be more firmly connected to Brando in the public imagination, he had a longer (if not deeper) professional relationship with Karl Malden. In 1953 Malden was given the responsibility of casting *Tea and Sympathy* while Kazan finished postproduction on *Man on a Tightrope*, and he appears to have worked in a similar capacity on *Waterfront*.[72] Indeed, Malden's name had first been connected with the picture back in February, when Darryl F. Zanuck suggested him for the role of the priest; Malden was Serbian, but Zanuck liked him for the role because he thought he was Irish.[73] In a strange coda to the Sinatra debacle, Malden recounts how the singer, having been dumped as Terry, then asked to return to the role of Father Barry, a role that Kazan had already promised Malden. "Fortunately for me," Malden wrote in his memoir, "Kazan stuck by his promise and despite all his screaming and carrying on, even Sam Spiegel acquiesced to Kazan."[74]

Hiring Brando did not resolve all of the film's casting problems. Less than a week or two before the start of production, Kazan wrote an impassioned memo to Spiegel complaining that Sam was pressuring him to cast an unsuitable actress as Terry's love interest simply because she was available (could this have been Julie Harris, as Hedda Hopper had just reported?). Even worse, the casting of Terry's brother Charley hadn't been finalized either. "Don't tell me: it will work out! or GOD is over us!" Kazan fumed.[75] The fact that Lawrence Tierney had been the preferred choice for Charley was public knowledge at the time, but this memo suggests that a deal with Rod Steiger was not finalized until the very last moment. Tierney was the most intimidating actor in Hollywood, both on-screen and off, frequently under arrest for drunkenness or brawling when not starring in films like *Dillinger* (1945) or *Born to Kill* (1947). He was still playing roles like this when Quentin Tarantino cast him in *Reservoir Dogs*. Steiger remembered that Tierney was cut because he demanded too much money (odd for an actor who worked almost entirely in B-pictures), but it seems more likely that Kazan did not care to have another loose cannon on board.[76]

To imagine Lawrence Tierney as Charley is to imagine a very different film (Tierney and Brando in the taxicab scene?). Steiger had played a sympathetic VA counselor in his only previous film, *Teresa*, but was best known for his performance as the inarticulate Bronx butcher in *Marty*, a television broadcast of May 24, 1953 (he claimed to have appeared in 250 such programs between 1948 and 1953).[77] Tierney would have been perfect casting as a member of a waterfront gang—according to standard Hollywood thinking—but going with the softer and more introspective Rod Steiger helped turn the project from a film about a bunch of mobsters pillaging a community into a film about the tortured relationship of two brothers.[78]

The final last-minute addition to the cast was Eva Marie Saint in the role of Edie, once Terry's sister, but since Zanuck and Spiegel had had their say, now his love interest. Kazan considered many actresses for the part, and Malden reports that in the last weeks before the start of shooting he had been instructed to work with two of them, "one in the mornings, the other in the afternoons."[79] Elizabeth Montgomery was only twenty years old, a graduate of the American Academy of Dramatic Art with a good bit of television experience, much of it gained on her father's dramatic anthology series, *Robert Montgomery Presents*. On October 13 she had opened in her first Broadway show, *Late Love*, a conventional drawing-room comedy in which she played the ingénue lead opposite Cliff Robertson. Kazan, or possibly Sam Spiegel, must have seen her in this and set Karl Malden to work. Although "a fine actress," Montgomery "looked like exactly what she was: a girl from Beverly Hills with the confidence that came from the prep school education she had actually had," Malden remembered.[80]

Eva Marie Saint was nine years older than Elizabeth Montgomery and had slowly been working her way up in the industry, from modeling and radio acting to a continuing role in the video version of *One Man's Family*, a prime-time soap opera. Like Steiger and Montgomery (and Paul Newman and James Dean, for that matter), she was frequently seen on live television in 1953 and was lucky enough to have landed a small role in Fred Coe's March 1 NBC broadcast of *The Trip to Bountiful*. Coe decided to take the acclaimed production to Broadway, restaging it with the original cast (Lillian Gish) and director (Vincent J. Donehue). This was another show Kazan was sure to see, if only to catch Jo Van Fleet, whom he had directed in two recent plays (*Flight Into Egypt* and *Camino Real*) and would soon cast as James Dean's mother in *East of Eden*.

The Trip to Bountiful did not run as long as *Late Love* but got much better reviews. Brooks Atkinson praised Saint's "sweet characterization of a soldier's wife . . . whose senses of pride and sympathy are nicely balanced."[81] Kazan liked what he saw and what Saint showed him in the material Karl Malden prepared with her (she also had the advantage of Actors Studio training, almost obligatory on this film). But *On the Waterfront* was scheduled to begin shooting in Hoboken on November 17, and *Bountiful*, which had just opened on November 3, was expected to enjoy a good run. Saint would not only have to take on the role of Edie at the last minute but do so while appearing in her first Broadway show. As it happened, Marlon Brando had already provided the solution. As a sweetener in his contract, Spiegel had agreed to let him leave the set by four o'clock every afternoon for an appointment with his psychoanalyst. Because nearly all of her scenes were with Brando, this meant Saint would have plenty of time to get back to Henry Miller's Theatre before the evening curtain (the play would run until December 5). The entire cast finally assembled for the first full run-through at the Actors Studio on Sunday, November 15.[82] The next day, songwriter Jimmy Van Heusen discovered his house guest, Frank Sinatra, on the floor of his New York apartment, covered in blood and with his left wrist deeply slashed; the incident was dismissed at the time as an accidental cut.[83] *On the Waterfront* began production as scheduled on Tuesday. Ironically, much of the action would be filmed in and around the area known today as Sinatra Park.

CHAPTER 13

KISS ME, KILL ME

Fear and Desire attracted a surprising amount of critical attention but did nothing at the box office, and Kubrick busied himself with *The Seafarers* in the summer of 1953. "There were still no offers from anybody to do anything," he admitted to the *New Yorker* in 1966. "So in about two weeks a friend and I wrote another script . . . nothing but action sequences, strung together on a mechanically constructed gangster plot."[1] The unnamed friend was Howard Sackler, who had also collaborated with Kubrick on *Fear and Desire*. Sackler's participation was acknowledged in prerelease press accounts, and he was also a profit participant, cut in for one-twelfth of the net profits.[2] But by the time the film was ready for release, Sackler's name would disappear from the credits. Some attribute this to a lack of generosity on Kubrick's part, while others believe that Sackler suddenly thought better of having his name attached to "a mechanically constructed gangster plot" at a time when he was winning Foundation grants and prestigious literary awards. But given the fact that he had already been outed in the *New York Times*, does it make sense that an ambitious young writer would recoil from screen credit on a United Artists picture? Still, Sackler had by now become deeply involved with Caedmon Records, the pioneer of spoken word recordings, and over the next few years would direct two hundred recording sessions devoted to theater and poetry.[3] Among the actors he would use was Frank Silvera, who supported Burgess Meredith in Caedmon's *Everyman* (TC 1031, 1955) and played the lead in *Othello* (SRSM-225, 1960). After the success of *The Great White Hope*, for which he won Pulitzer and Tony Awards in 1969, Sackler returned to screenwriting (*Jaws 2*, 1978) but died suddenly in 1982.

Kubrick and Sackler may have started with a conventionally generic gangster plot, but they also had a gimmick to tie these action sequences together, one that might even support the love interest they had neglected to offer in *Fear and Desire*. Kubrick remembered Walter Cartier, the prizefighter he had profiled in his 1949 *Look* magazine photo essay, and how he had turned that feature story into *Day of the Fight*. In shrinking the print version down to a twelve-minute film Kubrick managed to retain Walter's twin brother Vince, but he had eliminated all the other characters in Walter's life—his aunt Eva, nephew Charlie, and current girlfriend Dolores Germaine. Now he realized he could bring back the girlfriend character and use her as part of a romantic triangle, a way of linking the prizefighter to the gangster plot.

The original script may have been written quickly, but Kubrick continued to work on it until just before release. Changes in the title suggest some of this flexibility. First called *Along Came a Spider* and subsequently referred to as *The Nymph and the Maniac*, it would eventually go into production as *Kiss Me, Kill Me*. The released version, *Killer's Kiss*, is a flashback narrated by Davey Gordon, a second-rate prizefighter with a glass jaw, who is contemplating the events of the past three days as he paces back and forth in Pennsylvania Station. Preparing for what turns out to be his final bout, Davey catches sight of a young woman getting dressed in an apartment across the way (their windows face each other across an airshaft). Using traditional montage strategies, Kubrick will compare and contrast the lives of these two characters throughout the film. The neighbor (Gloria Price) works for small-time hood Vince Rapallo in a taxi dance hall on Times Square. That night Gloria and Vince watch Davey lose the fight on television, a voyeuristic spectacle Vince experiences as a sexual turn-on. He later shows up at her apartment in an even more aggressive mood, and Gloria's screams bring Davey running to the rescue. After filling in each other's backstories (Gloria through a flashback of her own in which she narrates the story of her ballet-dancing sister, played by Ruth Sobotka), the pair decide to leave New York and move to his Uncle George's farm outside Seattle. This does not work out as easily as they hoped. Vince orders his thugs to work Davey over, but through a series of melodramatic coincidences they mistakenly kill his manager instead. Davey then fails to free Gloria, who has been kidnapped by Vince and tied to a chair in an empty loft. After a rooftop chase, Davey and Vince battle it out in another industrial loft, which is stuffed with nude female department store mannequins that are quickly weaponized. The flashback ends and returns us to Pennsylvania Station, where Davey ties up a lot of messy plot threads and wonders if he will ever see Gloria again. In a nominally happy ending, rare in this sort of noir or any Stanley Kubrick picture, Gloria rushes through the crowded station and into his arms.

To make this new film, Kubrick incorporated Minotaur Productions on August 13, 1953. He was president and owned fifty shares of Minotaur stock; Morris Bousel (like Martin Perveler, a wealthy pharmacist with some extra cash to invest) was treasurer and owned the other fifty shares. At first the company had no space of its own and worked out of the offices of its legal counsel, Stillman and Stillman, 1 East Forty-Second Street.[4] It was here on September 17 that Minotaur entered into a chattel agreement with De Luxe Laboratories, Inc., in which De Luxe agreed to defer billing for its services until Kubrick and Bousel could get the film completed and sold. The contract called for "delivery of photoplay, fully synchronized, scored, cut and edited and finished in all details, not later than ninety days from the date of this agreement."[5] Minotaur also agreed to deliver, *within ten days*, all necessary releases, distribution agreements, insurance certificates, musical cue sheets and censorship approvals, plus a final continuity script and a stack of related paperwork. If they defaulted on the terms of the contract, De Luxe would own the film. Much of this was pure boilerplate, of course, setting out a production schedule all parties knew could never be met, but it allowed De Luxe an extraordinary degree of control. In the end, Kubrick would not deliver on these contracts until July 12, 1955, seventeen months late.

If De Luxe Labs was paying for this film, at least in part, why were they so casual about enforcing the terms of their contract? A few years earlier, producers like Joseph Lerner had been driven out of business when they ran afoul of bankers and bank loans. But Stanley Kubrick had not gone to a bank for the bulk of his financing. Instead, Minotaur and De Luxe were in bed with each other, and Ellis Smith, who signed off for De Luxe, would have seen no benefit in kicking Kubrick out and seizing the assets. If *Kiss Me, Kill Me* fell behind schedule it would be in De Luxe's interest to makes things *easier* for Kubrick to finish the picture, not only because De Luxe wanted to be sure of an eventual repayment but because, in a time of decreasing production across the industry, it needed to cultivate even the fringes of its local client base. With De Luxe taking the lead, Titra Sound Corporation, Frank Zucker's Camera Equipment Company (CECO), and Consolidated Film Industries would sign similar deferment agreements, classic independent cinema contracts that prefigure the way all such films might one day by financed.[6]

Because the film did not yet exist, De Luxe was gambling on the package Minotaur had assembled: the contract specifically referenced using Kubrick and Sackler's script, Kubrick's services as director, and the casting of actor Frank Silvera in the principal role. While Silvera's name on the marquee might not be expected to sell a lot of tickets, he was a known quantity whose participation in the project gave it an aura of credibility. Silvera had appeared in four films in 1952, including Elia Kazan's *Viva Zapata!* and had given the best received performance in *Fear and Desire*. In a peculiar coincidence, the week that *Fear and Desire* had opened at the Guild 50th Street, Silvera was working a few blocks away in Kazan's Broadway production of *Camino Real*. He was also developing a career as a voice actor (something Howard Sackler would pick up on), having recorded the narration for Irving Jacoby's *The Lonely Night* in 1952. On December 17, 1953, with *Kiss Me, Kill Me* still shooting downtown, the Museum of Modern Art premiered the American version of Albert Lamorisse's *White Mane*, for which Silvera read James Agee's narration.[7] Silvera was not only crucial in getting Kubrick's project financed, but he would receive star billing on the film's main title. This was highly unusual for a heavy lead but does suggest that Kubrick and Sackler considered Vince Rapallo's character dramatically central. In a 1984 review, Richard Combs argued that it was Vince "to whom also goes the sense of injustice, of something out of joint in his own destiny."[8] Vince is a flawed man with a flawed plan but in retrospect is obviously the character in whom Kubrick is most interested. After Vince, casting the young lovers was a secondary concern.

Walter Cartier was still fighting, but he had acting ambitions—between 1955 and 1957 he would appear in fifty episodes of Phil Silvers's *Sgt. Bilko* show. Unfortunately, 1953 was a bad year for Cartier in the ring (he lost three out of four bouts, his worst record ever), and he may not have wanted the distraction of acting in a feature. Or perhaps Kubrick had had his fill of eager nonprofessionals. He turned instead to a young actor named Jamie Smith, who not only looked a lot like Walter Cartier but had almost as much acting experience as Frank Silvera. Smith had studied drama at Carnegie Tech (later Carnegie Mellon University) and played leads at the Pittsburgh Playhouse in 1946–1947. After graduation he toured in road companies of *All My Sons* and *Joan of Lorraine* and was part of José Ferrer's rep company at the Civic Center in 1948. According to an interview he gave his home town paper in 1952 (the source of what little information circulates about Smith's early career) he then went to study at the Sorbonne but instead found work "as assistant director and did narration on several documentaries and became a member of Orson Welles's company." While working with Welles, Smith was spotted by veteran Polish film director Józef Lejtes and given the starring role in *Faithful City*, that of "an American who takes a job at a children's settlement in Israel and learns about rehabilitating young war victims."[9]

Faithful City was released in the United States by RKO and opened in New York at the Park Avenue Theatre on April 7, 1952. RKO was also the distributor of Kubrick's two theatrical shorts, so he certainly would have been aware of it at the time. But this would not have been his only exposure to Smith's work in 1952–1953. As soon as he returned from Europe, the young actor, like so many others in New York, found plenty of work in the city's burgeoning television industry. Oddly enough, none of this experience was mentioned in the film's official publicity. In the press book maintained in Kubrick's own archives (a British press book), Smith is described only as a "ruggedly handsome actor from Pennsylvania" and a 1939 Golden Gloves finalist. The film's "realism" is emphasized at the expense of the professional expertise Smith actually brought to the role. We are told that he trained for months at Stillman's Gym under the supervision of Whitey Bimstein and Irving Cohen (Rocky Graziano's manager), losing twenty pounds during the course of production.[10] I have found no evidence of Smith's participation in the Golden Gloves, and he never made such a claim in his own publicity.

Silvera and Smith, experienced in European and Hollywood films, live television, voice acting, and every conceivable level of theater from touring shows to Broadway, were not box office names but were typical of the professional performers available to Kubrick and other film producers looking to cast their films in New York. In the early 1950s no other city in the world, including Hollywood, could compare in the richness of its variegated performance venues and the quality of its acting, writing, and directing talent.[11] Kubrick would have had a lot of young actors to pick from, although Smith, with his Welles experience, might have seemed more interesting than most. According to one reporter, he "ought to write a book about his experiences with Orson Welles's acting company in Paris. They're fabulous. . . ."[12]

As it happened, Jamie Smith was not the only graduate of Carnegie Tech to play a crucial role in Kubrick's new film. By the time he formed Minotaur, the director had already broken up with his first wife, Toba Metz, and moved in with Ruth Sobotka, a dancer and designer with the New York City Ballet. Sobotka, who emigrated from Vienna with her family in 1938, had been an art student at Carnegie Tech during the war, around the time that Jamie Schmitt (as he was then known) was there as a theater student.[13] She subsequently joined George Balanchine's Ballet Society in New York and appeared in the Man Ray "Ruth, Roses and Revolvers" episode of Hans Richter's *Dreams That Money Can Buy*. As noted earlier, Kubrick was well aware of this film, the reputations of the people who made it, and the cultural cachet Sobotka enjoyed from having appeared in it.

By the time he moved into her apartment at 222 East Tenth Street, Ruth Sobotka was already enjoying a taste of the artistic acclaim Kubrick clearly hoped might one day be his. In the summer of 1951, while he was struggling to edit his *Fear and Desire* footage and working as a chess hustler in Washington Square Park to make ends meet, Ruth Sobotka was being heralded for her work on Jerome Robbins's "The Cage," a bizarre dance novelty acclaimed by the *New York Times* as "easily the most important work of the season."[14] Sobotka had created the costumes for this ballet, performed to Stravinsky's *Basler Concerto*, which illustrated the mating habits of a series of predatory insects: the males are quickly discarded after having their heads crushed between the legs of their female partners. "Its characters are insects," wrote the *Times*. "It is without heart or conscience, and its opinion of the human race is not a high one."[15] The piece remained in New York City Ballet's repertoire for years, described simply as "the Robbins-Stravinsky-Sobotka 'Cage.' "[16]

Kubrick made space for her in the film, dancing alone on the stage of the Theatre de Lys on Christopher Street in a number choreographed by David Vaughan to music by Gerald Fried. The number is frequently dismissed as a vanity role created for the director's girlfriend, or even a clumsy way of pushing the film's footage count closer to that of a conventional feature.[17] Neither strategy seems typical of Kubrick, and in fact this sequence, a flashback recalled by her sister, plays an important role in the parade of contrasts that structure the film, emotionally colored to emphasize the gulf between a lost world of classical elegance and the tawdry dance hall where much of the action is set.

David Vaughan, who moved out of the apartment so that Kubrick could move in, was also part of the Balanchine circle and more Ruth's friend than Stanley's. To Vaughan, Kubrick was a strange character, an obsessive, badly dressed film buff with no sense of humor. "He wasn't exactly a stylish dresser. He looked like somebody from a Jewish family in the Bronx," Vincent Lo Brutto quotes him as saying, quite a contrast to the "extremely stylish" ballet dancer he was living with. In Vaughan's telling, Sobotka becomes the most interesting of Kubrick's wives, a woman who matched his creative drive and was already launched on a fulfilling career of her own. "Ruth really wanted to be his collaborator, not just his girlfriend or wife," Vaughan remembered.[18] Unfortunately, there was room for only one creative genius in the Kubrick universe. The pair separated in 1958 and divorced three years later.[19]

Stanley Kubrick would never be known as a woman's director, but he needed a woman in this picture and, as with *Fear and Desire*, lack of stage or screen experience would not be a problem. Instead of a traditional casting call he turned to Bert Stern, his friend since his days at *Look*. "I need a girl with a haunting quality about her," he told Stern over dinner. "A beautiful young thing who can evoke a feeling of loneliness."[20] Stern was now working as art director for *Flair* and knew every actress and model in the city. Later he himself would become one of the great Madison Avenue portrait photographers, noted for his remarkable images of Sophia Loren, Twiggy, Elizabeth Taylor, and the "Last Sitting" Marilyn Monroe sessions (1962).[21] Stern's photographs of Sue Lyon for Kubrick's *Lolita* would serve as the basis of that film's entire advertising campaign. So when Bert Stern told Kubrick he had found just the girl for *Kiss Me, Kill Me*, Stanley Kubrick paid attention.[22]

Irene Kane, as she would be billed in the film, would later be better known as Chris Chase, an author and journalist covering the entertainment industry. She was born Irene Greengard, the daughter of Benjamin Greengard, a vaudeville

13.1. Frank Silvera and Irene Kane take direction from Stanley Kubrick, who is simultaneously operating the camera on *Killer's Kiss*. Bison Archives.

comedian, but all of the contracts and correspondence in the Kubrick Collection at University of the Arts London refer to her as Christopher Kane.[23] She remembered that Stern brought Kubrick over to see her at "a little place I had in the Village," a few blocks from Kubrick's own apartment. According to a handwritten list of contact addresses in the Kubrick Collection, half of the production unit lived within walking distance of Washington Square Park. Christopher Kane was at 25 Fifth Avenue, a magnificent prewar apartment she paid for by "modeling some."[24] Kubrick showed up with the script "bulging out of his pocket," but Kane's reaction was diffident, to say the least. In her memoir she claims to have hidden behind the television set. "Your friend's pretty," she recalled Kubrick saying to Bert Stern, "but she's a little odd." Kubrick returned the next day and "showed me a soliloquy which went on for about six minutes, with the heroine's explaining her incestuous feelings for her father, her guilt about the death of her sister, [and] her idea of expiation—living in a crummy place with toast all over the floor, though she's only recently dwelt in marble halls on Long Island."

Kane had never acted before and felt that her "little boy voice" would be a problem. This did not seem to bother Kubrick, who told her the voice would make her famous and that "kids would imitate it the way they did Marlon Brando's." "He was enraptured," she recalled. "It was like a Betty Grable movie, the scene where Betty takes off her glasses and she's beautiful." Her memoir is the work of an entertainment journalist telling her own story, ironic and self-deprecating in the style of the 1970s. But like the biographies she wrote (or ghosted) for Betty Ford, Rosalind Russell, and Josephine Baker, it is both smarter and edgier than what one might expect. She had no illusions, for example, about the young director or the film he had just released. "All I remember about *Fear and Desire* was that a girl was tied to a tree, and later on she drank water out of a soldier's hand," she recalled. "All the soldiers were on both sides. Something like that."[25]

As it turned out, Kane would also find herself tied up and menaced in this film, and Kubrick would direct her with the same finesse he had used with Virginia Leith and Paul Mazursky. "The other day I was playing a love scene with a guy named Jamie Smith," she wrote to her sister, "when, in the middle of a kiss, he suddenly reached up and grabbed my left chest very firmly, as the camera ground away."

> I leaped to my feet screaming and calling Jamie and Stanley bad names (they'd clearly set the whole thing up behind my back) and Stanley gave me the foreign markets lecture. It goes, "No darling, we'd never show it that way in this country, but in Europe, everybody's broad-minded."
>
> "Bully for Europe," I said, "but I'm narrow-minded, and I want you to burn that film." Naturally, many promises were made, and I went home crying with the cameraman following me downstairs, earnestly explaining that "they" did feel different about things in Europe, especially the Germans and the French.

With financing arranged, a script in hand, and principal actors selected, Kubrick spent three weeks scouting locations in and around New York. While doing so he would have seen Phil Karlson's *99 River Street*, a "New York noir" about a washed-up prizefighter involved with an actress, which opened at the RKO Palace on October 2. The film may have seemed generically similar (the boxer even watches his old fights on television), but the only lessons Kubrick would have learned here involved things to avoid.[26] On a tight budget, Karlson was forced to recreate New York on a familiar Hollywood back lot. Kubrick, with even less money to spend, would distinguish his film by working almost entirely on location. "I wanted to film the smell, the feel and the colour of the city," he said in a statement published in the film's British pressbook (which accounts for the spelling). "I caught the atmosphere and authenticity, but it cost me a lot of worry and tension."[27]

One location he had already found was the Laurel Garden Arena at 457 Springfield Avenue in Newark. This is where he had filmed Walter Cartier in 1950, but the Garden had fallen on hard times; now used only for wrestling, it would soon close entirely. Of course, this time the fight would be fully staged, and Davey would go down for the count, his career "one long promise without fulfillment," as the fight announcer puts it. But while the arena is the same as in *Day of the Fight*, the audience is missing. Kubrick could arrange to shoot at this venue but couldn't afford to fill it with fans, so instead of a documentary record what we get is a highly subjective impression, and the only people watching are Gloria and Vince, on television. Two earlier long shots that do show a fight audience appear to be outtakes from *Day of the Fight*.

Pleasure Land, the taxi dance hall, is supposed to be just off Times Square on Forty- Ninth Street, but interiors were shot at a dance hall in Brooklyn. All we see of the street entrance is a doorway adjacent to a storefront displaying dress mannequins, obviously an insert. The many location shots establishing the Forty-Ninth Street area, done without permits, are all taken from automobiles or with hidden cameras.[28] Viewers never notice that there is not a single shot tying this doorway to the busy Times Square area, a relationship that is inferred solely through editing. The mannequin factory was on Greene Street in downtown Manhattan, but exteriors for that sequence were shot in Brooklyn, on Plymouth Street near Adams, and on various rooftops in what is now called DUMBO.[29] The film asserts that this place is near the "loft off Twenty-Fourth Street" in which Gloria is being held, but of course that isn't the case either.

The romantic leads live in the same Bronx apartment building and their windows face one another across a courtyard or airshaft (the distance seems only a few feet). Exteriors, and possibly a few staircase interiors, were shot at 3156 Perry Avenue in The Bronx, near the D train stop at 205th Street.[30] The building was also home to Kubrick's producing partner, Morris Bousel, which presumably helped with access to rooftops, stairwells, and bathroom facilities.[31] But Kubrick needed a very specific layout in order to emphasize the doubling of these characters (whose personal and professional problems mirror one another), as well as the undercurrent of voyeurism that also runs through the plot.

He rented loft space in the East Village (either Third Street or Fourth Street, depending on who is telling the story) and constructed the two apartments so that the actors, and the audience, can look easily from one into the other.[32] The bill for "Studio Rental & Electric" came to $904.75, while the "Cost and Rental of Sets" totaled $392.88. Charges for props and costumes soared to $3,316.75, due to all the damage to mannequins in the warehouse scene.[33] Although Kubrick himself claimed to have written, directed, photographed, and edited the film, one task he did not take credit for was the job of art director. In fact, there is no one credited for this job, even though someone must have been in charge. Was it the production manager, Ira Marvin, just at the start of a long and successful career with MPO? Or could it have been Ruth Sobotka, who would be credited as art director on Kubrick's next film, *The Killing*, and whose work at New York City Ballet had already won her a place in United Scenic

Artists Local 829?³⁴ Was there a union problem here that forced Kubrick to leave her name off the picture?

Although she later felt somewhat different about it, Chris Chase was awash with youthful enthusiasm during her first day on that set. "I nearly died of happiness," she wrote.

> I skipped through Washington Square Park on my way to the studio on Third Street, and the sun was shining. . . . I remember, too, moving around the set that was my room, the room where the girl I was playing was supposed to live. I touched every prop, every dish, every bobby pin. I listened to the musical powder box. I went and put my hands against the walls. And I thought, Nothing will ever be this good again.³⁵

Nat Boxer had a look at this set, too, but his response was considerably less enthusiastic. Boxer (sometimes listed as Nathan Boxer) had been hired because Kubrick did not want a repeat of the sound recording problems he had faced on *Fear and Desire*. A graduate of the film program at the New School for Social Research, one of several postwar film schools in New York, Boxer had trained as a cameraman but soon began working as a boom man, the specialist in charge of sound recording on the set. He later worked on many of the key New York productions of the 1970s and 1980s and was associated with Francis Ford Coppola on *The Godfather Part II*, *The Conversation*, and *Apocalypse Now* (for which he shared an Oscar). His connection to Kubrick, on the other hand, was brief.

> We were in some loft in New York's Greenwich Village, around 4th Street, and he was lighting the back room for the first scene. He wouldn't let us in there, and then he finally did. It was very handsomely lit, but when we went in and placed the microphones where we normally would, there must have been seventeen shadows in the picture. What do still photographers know about the problems of a movie?
>
> Well, he looked at the set and said, "Is that the way you do it? You mean you're going to put the microphone *there*? But that's impossible." "But that's the way we do it," I said. And then the actor started moving and all the shadows started moving and Kubrick yelled, "Cut! You don't make a movie that way. You guys are all fired!"³⁶

Boxer notes that Kubrick then decided to shoot the entire film nonsync, recording a wild track on "a little school audio-visual tape recorder," similar to his use of the wire recorder on *Fear and Desire*. Photos in the Kubrick archive do show the sound crew hanging a microphone over the set, as well as at least one picture of Kubrick working a small, consumer-grade tape recorder, what looks like a Revere TS-300.

Nat Boxer was not the only one to remain unimpressed by Kubrick's inexperience, boyish looks, and unprofessional demeanor. "My whole picture of Stanley is standing tall, wearing a sloppy kind of sweater outfit with the shirt hanging over, in need of a shave and his hair uncombed," one crew member confessed to Vincent Lo Brutto years later. "I never thought he would make it. I didn't think what the hell he was doing made any sense to me, but then he made it and I didn't, so he was way ahead of me. I just had a general feeling that this guy was not going to be a wheel of any kind."[37] Or as Chris Chase put it, "I'm in the hands of a lunatic who looks fully seventeen years old, has black hair that grows down over his neck, quotes widely from Henry Miller—the dirty parts—and takes time out from shooting to discuss with his girlfriend the sex habits of some canaries who are living in her apartment."[38] The general impression of shagginess, and grudging acknowledgement of his subsequent success, echoes Sol Negrin's recollection of working with Kubrick the year before on *Mr. Lincoln*.

Although Kubrick was the film's director of photography, he hired two other professional cameramen, Jesse Paley and Max Glenn, who are credited as camera operators. It is unknown if they worked together as a team or were employed individually at various times during the shoot. Paley's name appears on the original crew list; another local, he lived at 124 West Eleventh Street with his wife, the author and activist Grace Paley.[39] Kubrick knew Max Glenn from his days at Titra. "I loaded and threaded the camera," he told Vincent Lo Brutto. "I did the actual shooting but he directed. He was right next to me. He knew the composition that he wanted and where the camera should be set."[40] Glenn was a freelancer who had served on the executive board of the Association of Documentary and Television Film Cameramen, which represented many technicians working in nonfiction or nontheatrical production.[41] The history is complicated, but this local union, whose membership at various times included Ricky Leacock, Alexander Hammid, and Robert Flaherty (and probably Nat Boxer and Jesse Paley), had for some years been negotiating a middle ground in the jurisdictional battle between rival international unions struggling to organize all moving image production. A full page ad in *Variety* touting its accomplishments listed *Louisiana Story*, *The Quiet One*, *Dreams That Money Can Buy*, and *All My Babies* as productions on which its members had worked—something very different than anything a Hollywood union might claim.[42] But in 1954, just as *Killer's Kiss* was wrapping up, its three hundred members voted to abandon their association with NABET, primarily a television and radio union, and join the IATSE, which controlled theatrical work.[43] Because the IA was much more serious than NABET had been about allowing its members to associate with nonunion productions, Minotaur now found itself operating under strict IA rules, and Kubrick found himself a member of Local 644 (unlike *Fear and Desire*, the main title of *Killer's Kiss* proudly bears the IA union label). This issue may explain the added $222.50 in "union fees" as well as a mysterious $5,000 "Settlement with Union" cited in the "Schedule of Costs."[44]

Stills of the production, most of which were shot by Alexander Singer, show Kubrick working outdoors with a Mitchell camera, inside the apartment set with an Arriflex, and at various locations operating a handheld Eyemo. Max Glenn seems to have loaned this Eyemo to Kubrick, but it was stolen when someone broke into Kubrick's car; according to Glenn, Kubrick never made good on the loss.[45] United Artists, after they picked up the film, did try to promote Kubrick's photography as one of its key selling points. One ad, headed "SELL STANLEY KUBRICK," featured nine noirish stills (probably Alexander Singer's work) and positive quotes from two New York papers highlighting the "CHALLENGING PHOTOGRAPHY." *Killer's Kiss* is described as "The astounding new motion picture by the famous LOOK camera artist STANLEY KUBRICK!" How many in the audience—or even in the business—would have associated Kubrick with his former employer is unclear.

More interesting is Glenn's recollection of Kubrick paying off the police while filming on downtown streets. "A lot of cops came by and he was prepared for this. He had a whole flock of twenty-dollar bills in his pocket and everybody came to be paid off. Everybody got a twenty-dollar bill. One of the guys came back and said, 'Listen, the sergeant couldn't make it, he had to stay in the office.' Twenty to him too."[46] The "Schedule of Cost of Production" includes an additional $2,440 for "Location Rental & Gratuities." How much of this was paid out in twenty-dollar bills is unknown. Ben Hecht, discussing his budgeting for *Miracle in the Rain* in 1956, stated directly that the cost of production in New York was inflated not only by hotel rentals, per diems and the "required employment of standby crews," but by " 'envelopes' for police details."[47] Years later, the former Local 644 president, Sol Negrin, still recalled a system plagued by widespread graft and corruption. "The police were also corrupt," he remembered. What was worse, this institutionalized bribery was not even centralized. "You went into another precinct, you had to pay *them* off." And he was talking about films that already *had* permits.[48]

When Kubrick spoke about the "worry and tension" that gathering this location footage caused him he might have been thinking about the cost of gratuities, but he was probably more concerned about the weather. Across the river, the same problem would bedevil Elia Kazan and his crew in Hoboken. A season that had begun with unusually mild, even springlike temperatures was followed by a brutal cold spell in December and January. Kubrick shot most of his Times Square footage in late November, as we know from the films being advertised on the local marquees: *Queen of Sheba* at the Astor and *How to Marry a Millionaire* at the Globe, as well as *The Man Between* and *Take the High Ground*, all of which had opened in New York by November 20. Two rollicking conventioneers make off with Davey's scarf, and he chases them past the Globe. But

13.2. Stanley Kubrick, hand in pocket, waiting to resume work on *Killer's Kiss* while a crew member confers with a New York policeman. Bison Archives.

when he returns with it a few minutes later *Beachhead* is now playing the Globe and *Elephant Walk* is at the Astor. The passers-by no longer wrap themselves in heavy winter coats. Suddenly it's spring. Or more specifically, sometime after May 2, because that's when *The Flame and the Flesh* opened at the Loew's State.

Why the delay? Matching the weather conditions may have had something to do with it, but availability of actors was another factor. Chris Chase remembered Frank Silvera grumbling that "there was an off-Broadway play he could be doing right this minute, or at least reading for, if he didn't have to stay down in the gutter with the rest of us."[49] Indeed, Silvera would open on Broadway on January 6, appearing with Julie Harris and Eli Wallach in Jean Anouilh's *Mademoiselle Columbine*, directed by Harold Clurman. Jamie Smith opened in John Houseman's production of *Coriolanus* two weeks later, opposite Robert Ryan and Mildred Natwick.[50] According to Chase, neither actor seemed happy spending the winter huddling on freezing rooftops with Stanley Kubrick when they might have been working with Clurman or Houseman.

With Silvera and Smith off on paid gigs and inclement weather adding problems of its own, production must have shut down for most of the winter. Kubrick was lucky to have been able to reassemble enough of the cast to complete principal photography in the spring. This would have included not only the shots of Davey in Times Square returning with his scarf, but his rendezvous with Gloria in Pennsylvania Station, where Chris Chase and everyone else is suddenly dressed for much warmer weather. Of course, that would suggest that the opening scenes of Penn Station may also have been shot at the end—or perhaps "grabbed" would be a better word, because the footage clearly has an unauthorized quality to it. Stills in the Kubrick Archive show that scenes for the film were also shot at the Continental Trailways counter of the Port Authority Bus Terminal.[51] Were they discarded in favor of using the more impressive Penn Station locale?[52]

Although the Kubrick Archive lacks either a copy of the script or any sort of shooting schedule, it does include a considerable amount of financial information for this film. These figures allow us to see how Kubrick and his producing partner, Morris Bousel, succeeded where many other hopeful independents had failed: by deferring half the costs and securing the balance from private investors, they were able to get the film made without committing themselves to the sort of financing arrangements that had crippled other local producers.

Three documents make this especially clear. A "Schedule of Cost of Production" as of July 31, 1954, which indicates committed charges as of that date; a handwritten ledger detailing "Cash Costs," organized in the same categories, but only acknowledging money actually paid out (this runs from July 31, 1954, through June 30, 1955); and a final "Statement of Profit and Loss" as of July 30, 1960, at which time Minotaur Productions, Inc. appears to have been closed down. These records all agree that the "Total Cost of Production" for *Killer's Kiss* was $89,188.64. But a quick comparison of the "Cash Costs" with the "Schedule of Costs" shows that about half that amount—nearly all the laboratory, sound recording, and equipment rental costs—had not been paid out by June 30, 1955. In other words, those costs had been deferred by the various local supply houses who had signed on to Minotaur's project in September 1953.[53] What was left roughly matches the figure of $40,000 frequently claimed by Kubrick as the amount of cash he and Bousel needed to raise in order to make the picture.[54]

More about these deferments can be gleaned from an "approximate deferment breakdown" prepared on July 7, 1954.[55] Postproduction was still ongoing, but the figures given are close to the final amounts: they included De Luxe ($8,500), Titra ($14,500), and CECO ($20,000). However, this memo also indicated that some of the cast and crew were also working on deferment: Frank Silvera ($14,500), Jamie Smith ($14,700), Chris Kane ($8,040), the composer Gerald Fried ($8,000), the lyricist Norman Gimbel ($1,500), and the choreographer David Vaughan ($750). The difference is that these amounts do not show up on the "Schedule of Costs" memo, meaning that they were unsecured and

370 RENAISSANCE

there was no obligation to pay them unless the film began showing a profit. As of June 30, 1955, the amount actually earned by the film's production personnel and performing talent was as follows:

Producer-Director	$700.00
Production Manager	$1,893.59
Cameramen	$2,425.36
Grips & Electricians	$2,687.47
Sound Men	$407.52
Script Girl	$385.07
Editors & Cutting	$1,423.40
Contract & Bit Players	$3,551.45
Extras	$430.00
Additional Dubbing Costs	$320.00

Another $5,000 had been spent on musicians and arrangers for performing the score, but nothing for those who wrote it, whose fees were entirely deferred.

"We spent a year working on that movie, mostly in alleys with big signs that said NO TOILET, and on rooftops and city streets and deserted warehouses, and before it was done I was cold and tired and sick of it, with it, from it," Chris Chase remembered, no longer innocent in the ways of the movie world.[56] In order to get the film made, Minotaur had asked everyone from Frank Zucker to Frank Silvera to work on deferment, with the promise of a real payday once their project could get before an audience. The difference was that CECO knew this trick from experience and had made sure their debt was secured. The actors were not so clever.

> All the actors in that picture were working on what is called "deferral." I think it's illegal. It means you get paid a certain percentage of your salary every week, and the rest out of profits. If any. For instance, Frank Silvera, who played the villain, was getting $1,000 a week on paper, and drawing $100. I was contracted for $650, and took home what was left out of $65 after taxes.[57]

This explains why only $3,551.45 was ever paid out to the actors. Frank Silvera's $14,500 was "pie in the sky," but as an experienced professional he understood the gamble he was taking. The deal was not illegal, but it certainly violated the spirit of standard labor contracts—which is why Kubrick began shooting the picture nonunion. Vincent Lo Brutto relates a strange story, told to him by Norman Lloyd, who claimed that Kubrick had called him long distance and asked him to play a role in *The Nymph and the Maniac*.

I said, "Stanley, is this a union picture?" And he said, "No, no." I said, "Well, I can't do a non-union picture, I'm in the Screen Actors Guild," and he said, "Well, Frank Silvera's going to do it, he doesn't give a damn." I was a great admirer of Frank Silvera. I think he was one of the best actors in the business, but at that time Frank was breaking any rule he could he break. So I said, "I just can't do this."[58]

For her part, Chris Kane was too starry eyed to realize what she had agreed to, but she learned quickly. "He drove me home the other night," she wrote to her sister about Kubrick, "after a huge scene on the set—scene by stage-hands, not actors—in which everybody complained of cold, tiredness, lack of funds.... And Stanley listened to the whole thing, then very sweetly told everybody to take off, we were finished for the day. After we got in the car, I asked him how he could be so patient, and he grinned. 'Baby, nobody's going to get anything out of this movie but me.'"[59]

CHAPTER 14

"AND THE WINNER IN NEW YORK IS..."

November 17, 1953, the first day of shooting, seemed almost like a holiday in Hoboken. Reporters and local politicians crowded onto the roof of 105 Hudson Street, where Kazan would film Brando, Leif Erickson, and Tommy Hanley in front of a pigeon coop the art department had constructed there. Leif Erickson went way back with Kazan. He was currently playing one of the leads in *Tea and Sympathy* but had begun his career with the Group Theatre (although his was not one of the names Kazan had given the Committee in 1952). Now he was playing Eddy Glover, an agent of the Crime Commission; Brando's character would refuse to cooperate with him, at least until he decided he would. Tommy Hanley was a fourteen-year-old neighborhood boy who lived in this very building and had gone up to the roof one day to see what was going on. The film crew hired him to "watch" the coop, in effect a bribe not to set it on fire. As it happened, one of these men was Schulberg's waterfront connection, Arthur Browne, who recognized Hanley and knew that his father had been murdered on the docks years earlier. Realizing that Hanley and his mother were nearly destitute, "Brownie" arranged for the company to pay his fare to Manhattan and told him to see Schulberg and Kazan at the Actors Studio.[1]

While the acting company for this picture was assembled mainly from professionals who had studied the Stanislavsky method under Lee Strasberg and his disciples (or rivals), many smaller roles were filled by nonprofessionals cast for their value as local color. Longshoremen were hired to play longshoremen at their standard rate of $15 per day. Schulberg, a boxing fanatic, cast many retired prizefighters as low-level thugs and mobsters, including Tami Mauriello, "Two Ton" Tony Galento, Abe Simon, and Roger Donohue, who was said to have killed one of his opponents in the ring.[2] Hiring a neighborhood kid like Tommy Hanley to play Terry Malloy's acolyte—the next generation "golden warrior," a street gang Terry had founded years earlier—was not so different from Vittorio De Sica's hiring Enzo Staiola to play Bruno in *Bicycle Thieves*. And none of these nonprofessionals seem to have been intimidated by the Hollywood star power. "Sure, Brando's a good actor," Tony Galento admitted. "So what? I not only act, I do other things too. Ask around. I wrestled an octopus. I boxed a bear. I fight a kangaroo. How many actors you know can say that?"[3] "At the time I didn't even know who Brando was," Tommy Hanley remembered. "But the girls in my neighborhood knew who he was."[4]

Kazan should have been happy that his years of work on the project were finally coming to fruition, but happy he was not. As he climbed up to the roof he was greeted with a soupy overcast that obscured the New York skyline he hoped to use as a dramatic backdrop, the result of a freakish temperature inversion that blanketed the entire metropolitan region for the rest of the week.[5] "I didn't think much of my crew either," he later wrote. His cameraman, Boris Kaufman, "seemed on first view awfully soft for the job ahead of us and the place where the job was to be done. As for the crew, which had been haphazardly gathered, they already seemed uncertain and uncomfortable on the location, as well as shorthanded and perhaps the least bit timorous."[6] One person he did not see on the roof was Eva Marie Saint. Brando, Erickson, and Hanley are all listed on the call sheet for November 17, but the name of the actress playing "Edie" is left blank, her anonymous appearance demanded only for a special 11:00 A.M. rehearsal. One reporter was told that "an actress now being tested" will play "the girl who helps Brando find his conscience," but Spiegel would not officially announce the casting of Eva Marie Saint until November 24.[7] After ordering all onlookers off the roof—a request made three times before Sam Spiegel grudgingly left—Kazan finally had his film before the cameras.[8]

One reason that the crew might have been uncomfortable on this location is that nearly all of them commuted there from out of state. The crew sheet distributed by the production office provided contact numbers for twenty-six people, only three of whom lived in New Jersey.[9] George Justin was responsible for moving all of them, as well as the actors, back and forth to Hoboken every day. A bus left from Thirty-Ninth Street, between Ninth and Tenth Avenues, at 8:00 a.m. every morning; those not on the bus were given driving directions or instructed to take the #63 bus to Washington and First in Hoboken, then walk to wherever they were shooting that day. Although Marlon Brando is often said to have traveled to Hoboken on the Port Authority Trans-Hudson subway line, the production office did not advise the crew to take either the PATH tubes or the ferry to Hoboken.

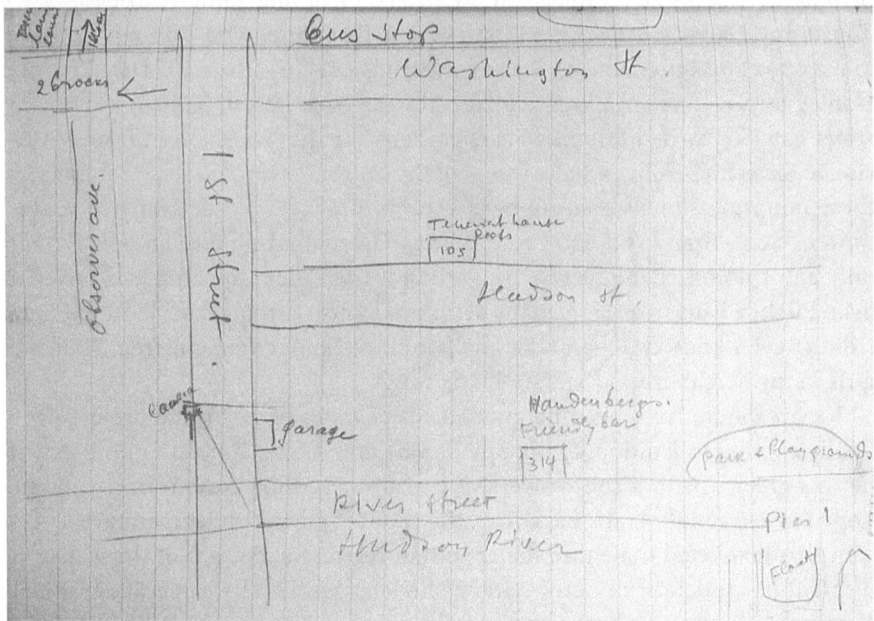

14.1. Boris Kaufman's sketch of Hoboken locations to be used in *On the Waterfront* includes the "Bus Stop" on Washington Street, the "Tenement house roofs" at 105 Hudson Street, and "Vandenberg's Friendly Bar" at 314 River Street. Notation at left indicates camera angle for filming exterior of taxicab scene. Boris Kaufman Collection, Beinecke Library. Courtesy of Andre Kaufman.

The pigeon coop had been built on the roof of 105 Hudson Street, while other action was planned for the nearby roof of 109. A Mrs. Lawler lived on the top floor of 105, and her apartment would be used as Edie's; Terry's room was on the top floor of 109, where a Mrs. Burmester lived.[10] By gaining permission to use these apartments the company also had access to the roof, but the apartments continued to be occupied during the shoot. "We couldn't even get rid of the tenants," Kaufman remembered. "We had to give them some place in the kitchen."[11] An assumption had been made that the crew could trek back and forth across the contiguous rooftops from 105 to 109, but the company neglected to make a deal with the people at 107, who subsequently denied them access to their portion of the roof. Kazan learned that "when we wanted to go from one roof to another, we'd have to go down the stairs of the building we were on, proceed along the street, and go up the stairs of the third building. This would apply not only to human traffic but also to equipment; it had to be carried down five flights, then up five flights."[12] Kazan tells this story as an illustration of how the tightwad Sam Spiegel was foolishly "chiseling," saving a nickel here but driving up costs by forcing the crew to work around one hold-out property owner. In fact, the company soon settled with this landlord, but Spiegel may have been right to try and hold the line. "Word soon got around that Spiegel was a walking mint and there was no stopping scores of petty grafters and local officials," *Time* reported. "In all, this monetary soup kitchen added an extra $30,000 to the *Waterfront* budget."[13]

The man who was supposed to deal with such problems was Arthur Marotta, director of the Department of Public Safety (less formally, the police chief). Marotta's help was essential, especially when it came to obtaining cooperation from the locals. Fifty years later, Leo Braudy tracked down Pepe Vandenberg, who still owned the saloon at 314 River Street that Kazan planned to use as a key location. Vandenberg had had no interest in renting the place to a movie company. "Then they came back with Marotta the police chief," he remembered. "I'm gonna chase the chief of police out?"[14] The Hoboken historian Sada Fretz reports that another saloon keeper

> raised his per-day rental from a hundred to a thousand dollars once the crew had started shooting there and established it as a location. Maybe that's why one bar scene, when Terry and Edie go for a beer and run into a wedding party, starts out in what is now [in 2004] Frankie and Johnnie's on the Waterfront at Fourteenth and Garden, but ends (although no switch is obvious) inside the old Meyers Hotel that stood at Third and Hudson.[15]

Every member of the company was instructed to call Marotta directly (Hoboken 3-2500) "should you need him."[16] Nevertheless, as Karl Malden remembered, "There were times we would spend one day working in a park, for example, and arrive the next day only to discover we had to move. Suddenly our permits had been revoked overnight."[17] The local police had been able to keep Kazan out of Bridgeport, but what was happening here had less to do with perceived damage to a town's image than with the simple reality of cold cash.

"There were things I can't tell [you] about corruption, about our paying off people—little black sacks, things like that," Kazan later told Stuart Byron and Martin Rubin.[18] Fearing that "the 'mob' was around, watching what we were doing" (hadn't Zanuck and Cohn warned him about this?), Kazan hired an armed guard, Joe Marotta—the police chief's brother—who "was never more than six feet away from me throughout the picture. One day some hoods pushed me up against a wall and, holding me there, began to berate me, their point being that I was making the people of Hoboken look bad—yes, they were that civic minded. But Joe walked up and they walked away."[19] In a more colorful account, Kazan said of his protector, "He got a hold of the guy who was going to hit me, and he murdered him, he beat the shit out of him. The atmosphere was that violent."[20] As Schulberg remembered it, Kazan, "had to shoot the picture in hostile territory, with police protection to guard him and the embattled company from an aroused underworld."²¹

In a memo to Spiegel sent just before the start of production, Kazan made clear just how important the need to spread cash around was to the success of the entire project. Marotta and Brownie had been insulted by being offered $100 as a sort of gratuity—like a no-show job you might dole out to a hapless relative. Their feelings were hurt. "I need these men," Kazan insisted. "They are part of my tools, my professional equipment. I am not going to go into a long song and dance about the Hoboken situation. There is a unique triangle which is the key to making this picture in Hoboken. Corriden, Brown and Marratta [sic]. We need them all. . . . It is not a laughing matter, and it's not a place to squeeze on the budget."²²

Kazan had been trying to get out from under the Hollywood studio system almost as soon as he got in. As early as 1947 he told a reporter from the *Brooklyn Daily Eagle* that he "would like to see far more [pictures] made away from studio sound stages and routine film studio sets."²³ He had done his best in *Boomerang!* and *Panic in the Streets*, but those films were also claimed (with some justification) by de Rochemont and Zanuck. In that same interview he also said that he hoped to see the same close connection between stage and screen work that existed in "London, Paris and Moscow." But the only place in America where all those elements had even a chance of coming together was New York. Or in this case, Hoboken.

Kazan was not the only important director to feel this way. While on a visit to New York in 1950, Vittorio De Sica said much the same thing himself. When a WNYC interviewer asked him if he had any plans to make a film in Hollywood, De Sica pointed to the basic structure of the Hollywood studio system. "The American film industry follows a pattern. It works according to a formula. It is this obedience to a pattern that I object to, but I would like to make a picture in Brooklyn," he announced. Brooklyn? "The atmosphere intrigues me. I do not have a story as yet, but I would like to make a picture using the Italian people in the media of Brooklyn."²⁴ De Sica and Kazan were clearly on the same wavelength, and both men understood that the two most important reasons for making films in New York had nothing to do with money. First, the city, its people, and its neighborhoods offered an endless array of stories. Second, it wasn't Hollywood.

Years later, after having directed films like *A Face in the Crowd* and *Splendor in the Grass* in New York, Kazan was even more certain in an interview with *Cahiers du Cinema*. "I do not think that an art can be organized like a commercial enterprise," he insisted. "In New York, everything is smaller, and poor. You do not have facilities, but the mentality is different." In New York you walk to the corner to get yourself a pack of cigarettes, he remembered. "In California, you are in a protected atmosphere, and at the end of a year, or two or three, you have lost contact with America."²⁵ He was getting that contact now, for better *and* for worse, and clearly drawing energy from it. New York was not just a convenient place to put down independent roots but a city with a vibrant cultural community and just enough "facilities" for first-class technical work. Within a few days, even the crews began to look good.

New York may have had few available studios, but there was certainly more than enough stage space to build the few modest interiors required by Schulberg's script. Yet some time during the last week of October the company arrived at a decision that would have tremendous consequences for the look and feel of the film. "During the selection of locations it was decided to shoot the interiors on real locations," Kaufman wrote in a 1973 tribute volume dedicated to Kazan:

> I had some experience in the matter during the war, shooting documentaries, where I developed precision lighting with very little help. Later, dragging equipment six floors up and squeezing it and the crew and actors into a tiny apartment, no regrets were voiced. . . . I don't believe an art director could have reproduced the feeling of the winter light mixed with artificial light and patina of the old tenement. Today it is taken for granted, but I think it was the first major production done entirely on real locations in U.S. [*sic*].[26]

By 1953, the incorporation of documentary elements into American features had been going on for almost ten years. But what had once been a mark of authenticity had gradually come to be associated with the cut-rate strategies of low-budget filmmaking. Kazan's desire to pursue this style was daring not because it was a new idea but because he was trying to reclaim a slightly tarnished genre. "For me a continuance," he told a reporter for the *Times*. "I started a sort of semi-documentary pattern . . . with *Boomerang*. This is the logical realization."[27] Jesse Zunser, one of the city's sharpest entertainment journalists, saw it as a group effort, a strategy growing directly from the earlier successes of writer, producer, and director. "Their idea was to make a documentary-styled fiction sizzler something like such Kazan successes as *Boomerang!* and *Panic in the Streets*, or Spiegel's *The Stranger* and *The Prowler*, or Schulberg's best-seller *The Disenchanted*."[28] But to achieve this style they all had to depend on Boris Kaufman.

A Hollywood cameraman, Kazan later wrote, was trained to greet the director with a crisp "Good morning, sir. Where do you want the camera?"

> But Boris did the artistic thing: he'd hook his arm to my elbow and stroll off with me in the manner of men-friends, in Europe, comrades in art, lead me away from the unit manager and his watch, away from the fretting crew, gently lead me into a quiet corner and there, after listening carefully to the notion I'd brought with me, nod respectfully, then say in his calm, cultured voice, "Now let's look at all the possibilities." Then we'd try to talk as artists and not as technicians with mechanical problems.[29]

Kaufman may have seemed like a European romantic to Kazan, but his papers reveal a technician with complete mastery of the physics, optics, and chemistry required for the job. In Kazan's notebooks we often find reference to the work of specific artists or composers. He began his notes for *Golden Warriors* with a few visual cues:

> *Visually* Ben Shahn
> —Desert of Brick and Space
> + A Feudal Kingdom[30]

These impressions are amplified in Kaufman's own notes, first under the heading "Spirit of the Picture."

> Mood of the Picture – Little Conventional Sun in Exter.
> Mostly Gray Days + Booster Lights for Day, Mist, Dusk, Rain, Night.
> Delicate Balance at Dusk—F.G. M.G. Back G.

Then under "Remarks Generally":

> Always a strong note, especially at night or low key or effect shots, somewhere in the scene, or actors. . . .
> —At Dusk—A Lighted Window, Lamppost, Chimnay [sic], House or Wall Stronger than the Average Gray of the Overall Scene.
> —Directional Light on Actors May Vary from 75 FC to 150 FC Limit. Some May Be Left Dim with Light Fill Only Against Lighter B.G. or Blending into B.G.[31]

Kaufman's greatest challenge with *On the Waterfront* was not the cold, or the use of practical interiors, but matching the photographic quality of scenes that had been filmed out of sequence in different weather conditions and would need to be edited together later on.[32] The smoggy haze during the first week of shooting, with the quality of light changing from minute to minute, was especially tricky, but reports from Consolidated Film Laboratories were encouraging. "Saw Horizon's rushes Thursday Friday and Saturday," Spiegel's lab contact cabled. "All OK. Appreciate difference in clear vs. hazy sky Wednesday vs. Thursday. Lab has done a good job of matching. . . . Kaufman doing good job under difficult sky changing conditions."[33] This was not a matter of luck, or innate artistic temperament, but the fruit of a lengthy series of preproduction tests Kaufman had run with Consolidated. There are pages of notes detailing his comparison of Du Pont and Eastman negative stocks, especially in regard to how effective they might be at low light levels when shooting at his preferred aperture of f2.8.[34] Kaufman was so concerned about lighting problems that he also ran latensification tests, what today would be called fogging or flashing. By manipulating the negative after exposure, but prior to development, one could greatly increase the apparent sensitivity of the film.[35] Latensification was touted as a miracle solution that could reduce, or even eliminate, the need to transport heavy electrical generators onto locations, but Kaufman labored over these tests because he knew the process could also introduce an unacceptable level of grain.

Bigger Is Not Always Better

One thing he did not worry about was the aspect ratio—the proportion of width to height in the final screen image. There is not one word about the aspect ratio of *On the Waterfront* in all the many boxes of his preserved notes, correspondence, and memorabilia.[36] This absence is significant because of what had happened to *Melba*. In the summer of 1953 a fad for wide-screen imagery had resulted in many films being projected in enlarged format, with the top and bottom of the image cropped off to produce a more horizontal effect. As we have seen, Sam Spiegel was among the first to prepare one of his films for projection in this way, regardless of how it had originally been shot, but *Shane*, *From Here to Eternity*, and *Julius Caesar* were also projected in this fashion during their first-run engagements that year. Joseph Mankiewicz was so angry when MGM began showing *Julius Caesar* in wide screen, "cutting off the heads and feet of anyone going up the steps of the Senate," that he engaged in a furious shouting match with the head of Loew's, Nicholas Schenck, who threw him out of his office and threatened to have him blacklisted.[37]

Some critics sneered, but once the fad had taken hold exhibitors (encouraged by distributors) insisted on running every film on these new wide screens. The Astor installed theirs as early as July 1, 1953.[38] *On the Waterfront* would open there a year later; across the street, the Loew's State was proudly presenting *Gone with the Wind* in wide screen and artificial stereophonic sound, seriously distorting every frame of one of the most carefully designed films in Hollywood history. *International Projectionist*, concerned that the men in the booth might be blamed if audiences had problems with any of this, warned its readers: "If a projectionist should change the proportions of any of the pictures now in circulation . . . he may in some cases find that he has sliced off somebody's head or feet, but the studios claim that the change can be accomplished without any real damage."[39]

It seems likely that *On the Waterfront* was shown at the Astor in some kind of wide-screen format, but there is no record of what ratio Kaufman, Kazan, and Richard Day had originally intended for the film. Soon after the opening Kaufman wrote to Kazan that he had seen the film three times, twice at the Astor, but said nothing about the photography.[40] It is true that by the end of 1953 cameramen working at certain Hollywood studios (including Columbia) had begun to compose their films with large "safe" areas, essentially visual dead spots at the top and bottom of each frame that would allow a film to be projected in various ratios without losing too much valuable image information. But Boris Kaufman was not a member of Local 659 or the Hollywood-based American Society of Cinematographers. He had not shot a theatrical feature anywhere since before World War II and had little or no direct knowledge of current production practices in Hollywood. Although a Columbia release, *On the Waterfront* was not a production of that studio and neither Harry Cohn nor Emil Oster, the head of their camera department, had any say in how it was shot.[41] Indeed, Kaufman had been shooting for two weeks before the crew even knew that Columbia would be their distributor. In a 1955 interview, when asked if current changes in the size and shape of the screen might affect the content of films, Kaufman replied that wide screens were good for "huge spectaculars and travelogues," not films of "dramatic substance," an answer that could have come from Darryl F. Zanuck. And while some subjects might be appropriate to a wide frame, "it is difficult to achieve intimacy without leaving too much empty space." His bottom line was that "the space within the frame should be entirely used up in composition," a conclusion that suggests he had not gotten the memo about leaving adequate amounts of "safe" space on his negatives.[42]

In the 2013 Criterion Blu-ray release of *On the Waterfront*, a visual essay titled "On the Aspect Ratio" of the film asserts that all Columbia features at this time were being photographed for projection in any ratio from 1.33 to 1.85:1, the result of careful preproduction planning and the incorporation of adequate "safe areas." But all that we really know is that this was what the studio said was happening (and, as noted, the film was not a Columbia *production* anyway). Sam Spiegel, of course, had made the very same statement about *Melba* some months earlier; it wasn't true, but it did make the film seem more up-to-date. Criterion also tells us that "the customary frame of European cinematographer Boris Kaufman. . . . split the difference at 1.66, so that all that was required was for him to leave extra room at the top and bottom of the frame and make sure nothing essential would be lost in wide-screen presentation."[43] This is wishful thinking at best, an inference for which there is no documentary evidence. On the contrary, there was no customary European ratio of 1.66:1 when Kaufman left France in 1941, and his rather firm assertion in 1955 about the need to use up all the available space in the frame suggests that he was not likely to be flexible regarding this "safe area" issue, even if he had been aware of it. Criterion, to their great credit, made a Solomonic decision and presented the film in three different aspect ratios.

How Cold Was It?

The Beinecke Rare Book Library at Yale preserves, among the boxes of Boris Kaufman's papers, a handwritten reminder to himself to purchase some boots with warm wool linings at Abercrombie's before starting work on *On the Waterfront*.⁴⁴ He may have been born in Bialystok, but Kaufman did not like cold weather and had been very unhappy when, newly arrived at the National Film Board of Canada, he was sent off to the frozen north to gather footage for documentaries.⁴⁵ Kaufman was prepared for the worst, not only for himself but his equipment. "Seventy-two percent of the shooting schedule of the picture was exterior work, with the company shooting in any kind of weather, mostly bad," it was reported at the time:

> When the weather got too cold the camera was wrapped in a heating pad and blankets. . . . The cold weather not only made it difficult for the camera crew but for the sound technicians as well. Electric heaters were focused on sound equipment, and the maximum life for a sound cable in wet and cold weather was 15 minutes before it was replaced and taken for a thorough drying.⁴⁶

But this same account concluded that it would have been "difficult to achieve the same quality and reality that is in *On the Waterfront* on a steam-heated stage." Kazan frequently emphasized the cold and the positive effects he felt it had on the film. "The bite of the wind and the temperatures did a great thing for the actors' faces: It made them look like people, not actors—in fact, people who lived in Hoboken and suffered the cold because they had no choice," he wrote in his autobiography. "In some scenes their breath was visible as they spoke, which made the scenes completely believable. Brando was occasionally difficult to bring out into the cold; I remember a few times going into the Grand Hotel and dragging him out. He remarked later that it was 'so cold out there that you couldn't overact.'"⁴⁷

Brando, for his part, reported that it was Kazan who stayed inside the hotel as much as possible, while the actors faced the brunt of the weather outdoors. Rod Steiger suffered as well. During the scene where Brando finds him in an alley, hanging on a hook like a piece of meat, it was so cold that "the camera froze, despite heat lamps to keep it warm, and filming had to stop to thaw it out." Steiger not only had to keep perfectly still, he needed to hold his breath so that it would not be visible in the glare of the lights. "I thought Marlon would never get me off the hook as he did his reacting and carrying on," Steiger remembered. He could finally take a breath once Brando slung him over his back, but "I still felt as though my lungs were going to burst."⁴⁸

Stories like this make the filming of *On the Waterfront* seem more like *Nanook of the North*. But while it can get quite cold on the Hudson River in midwinter, the company was actually very lucky with the weather for most of the shoot. The first day of production was the warmest November 17 in fifty-seven years, the temperature in Newark reaching 71 degrees.⁴⁹ November in general was two degrees warmer than normal, with one-third less rain.⁵⁰ December proved to be the third warmest in history, five degrees above normal, with December 3–12 setting a record for the warmest ten consecutive December days ever; flowering plants began to bloom in the Brooklyn Botanic Gardens.[51] The longshoremen, accustomed to much colder weather in November and December, must have been wondering what the film people were complaining about.[52]

But not every December day was so balmy. Right after that heat wave, temperatures fell briefly to 14.4 degrees, the coldest day of the year, causing the mechanical traffic light timing devices on Broadway to freeze solid; police had to be called out to direct traffic.[53] And the last few weeks of production more than made up for two months of relatively good weather. Between January 10 and 18 the temperature in New York seldom crawled above freezing. The heaviest snow in five years piled up in the streets, followed by a sudden jump in temperature that blanketed the region in a dense fog. A passenger ferry collided with a freighter in the harbor, the Coast Guard sent an icebreaker up the Hudson, and even the *Queen Mary* was late.[54] Living through those last few horrible weeks must have colored everyone's recollection of an otherwise unusually balmy location shoot. January 26 was the last official day of shooting, although there are no more daily call sheets in Kaufman's papers after January 8.[55]

14.2. Take five! A gloved hand holds the slate for Boris Kaufman's *Waterfront* camera, Hoboken, December 30, 1953. Frame enlargement.

It was one thing to shoot documentaries on location, where changing weather and lighting conditions only add to a film's feeling of authenticity—think of his work on Jean Vigo's *À propos de Nice* in 1930. But in a dramatic narrative, where scenes filmed out of continuity *must* cut together smoothly, being at the mercy of the elements could be a nightmare. The Kaufman Collection at Yale includes numerous Polaroid continuity photos shot on Hoboken rooftops (the instant photographic process was only introduced in 1947). "I like to do my shooting early in the morning or late in the afternoon," Kaufman wrote in 1956. "At those times the light comes from the sides rather than directly from overhead, giving me delicate modelings rather than harsh shadows. For distant shots, I like clear, sunny weather; for close-ups I think the diffused light of a hazy or overcast day is best."[56] There are stories of many great Hollywood films in which cast and crew could wait for just the proper arrangement of clouds, but given its constrained production circumstances, this would not be one of them. "Several times I had to shoot on overcast days when I wanted a bright, sunny effect, so it was necessary to bring artificial lighting onto the scene."

> For instance, the final scene of *On the Waterfront* required Marlon Brando to walk through a crowd of men up to a door and then to a pier. In the story, the time was early on a misty morning. But our production schedule didn't permit waiting for the proper time of day and weather conditions. The scene was actually shot at midnight. We lit our Hoboken pier to give the appearance of early morning and sprayed mist into the air to achieve what the weatherman wouldn't give us.[57]

Kaufman would preemptively hose down the streets before a scene, regardless of the weather, just in case it might have been raining when they returned to finish the scene some other day.[58] When filming on the rooftops he was not impressed by the landscape of "black tar paper, black hatches, black dull metal, soot covered pigeon coops, some TV antennas, and chimneys. So to bring it to life I used smoke, water, and a little paint—the last in order to break this blackness and bleakness of tar paper," transforming Hoboken into the (anonymous) waterfront city required for Kazan's social and political parable.[59] He used smoke again during the scene where Brando and Saint walk through a park—actually two different parks, several blocks apart.[60] Noticing some leaves burning in a basket at the first location, he brought in smoke pots to exaggerate the effect. "This device enabled me to continue the sequence through a different park which followed the first one and to make it flow. In other words, I tied the smoke over, and cleared only when we came to the iron fence facing the river. This is an example of positive exploitation of conditions," he told two interviewers from *Film Culture*. "I used the smoke not as an artifice but because I found justification for it: the mood of the scene and the need for maintaining continuity."[61] Hoboken residents recognized the "creative geography" here, but few others did.

For cinematographers in Hollywood, who believed that New York "newsreel photography" was a simple point-and-shoot business, Kaufman's manipulation of landscape and lighting was a revelation. They were used to doing such things within the controlled environment of a studio back lot or even a sound stage, with the aid of a small army of scenic artists and electricians. General audiences might accept what they saw in *On the Waterfront* as simple "realism," but industry professionals knew better, and could see that big changes were coming. This is why Kaufman, an outsider, won the Academy Award for black-and-white cinematography and was elected to the ASC.[62] On the other hand, it still didn't mean he would be allowed to work in Hollywood.

When George Justin assembled his *On the Waterfront* crew he was careful to draw from a small group of local technicians, many of whom would later move with him from one project to another, the so-called "first team" of the postwar New York film renaissance. Unlike a Hollywood crew, their credits were not limited to features but might also include everything from theater to television (both live and filmed), as well as every kind of nontheatrical and commercial work. So from his TV series *The Doctor* Justin brought not only Charlie Maguire but Jim Shields, a sound mixer whose feature film experience was limited to such local productions as *Guilty Bystander*, *Teresa*, and *Roogie's Bump*. Later he would work on *The Hustler*, *Long Day's Journey Into Night*, and *A Thousand Clowns*. The film's make-up man, Fred C. Ryles, had been trained by Wally Westmore on the West Coast, and his silent film credits included *King of Kings*, *The Last Command*, and *The Iron Mask*. He came to New York in 1929 to head the make-up department at Fox Movietone and the following year was elected first president of the Eastern Make-Up Artists. He had stayed in the east ever since, working on whatever happened to be shooting that week—Technicolor industrial films, Yiddish pictures, newsreels—a typical East Coast career. His recent films included *Carnegie Hall*, *Jivin' in Be-Bop*, and *Lost Boundaries*.

Brando's make-up needed to suggest years of battering in forgotten tank towns but without hiding the beauty of his face. And it couldn't take very long to put on. "His makeup on Brando as the ex-fighter is subtle therefore convincing," one journalist reported. "Scar tissue over his eyes from too many 'eggs,' and a scar from a deep cut on the left brow. It was done in plastic, and created through a series of plaster casts of Marlon's face."[63] Those who knew Brando were startled at the transformation. Robert Downing, who had worked with him in *Streetcar*, was hired for an uncredited bit. "A wardrobe man was 'aging' Marlon's shoes for the camera; daubing them with paint that quickly caked to resemble mud," he wrote in a fan magazine profile. "Brando's face looked strangely different beneath his 'pancake' movie make-up. I discovered that both his upper eyelids had been puffed out with putty just beneath the brows, to give the effect of a countenance that had survived several brawls."[64] Most viewers think of Terry primarily as a longshoreman, but Schulberg's protagonist is, above all, a fighter. And the beaten-up quality of his face has to reflect more than just his background in the ring—it needs to serve a double purpose, like the drifting smoke Boris Kaufman had added to the waterfront.

Anna Hill Johnstone, as noted earlier, would become the costumer of choice for many subsequent East Coast features. She dressed most of the male cast from the racks of a used-clothing store on Canal Street, distressing the already worn garments with Fuller's earth and the proper application of sandpaper and "a heavy file."

> For Brando, "original models" from the used clothing store were copied in triplicate, with the exception of one "new" jacket which was a ready made. Since he has his clothes torn in fights, and the picture was not filmed in continuity, this provided mobility as well as insurance against production delay should an accident occur to any.[65]

In Hoboken, the "Makeup and Wardrobe Room" was located in the Meyers Hotel at Hudson and Third, not far from most of the locations. The hotel also served as the local production headquarters, but as the winter grew more bitter ad hoc production offices sprang up in the nearest Hudson or River Street saloon. (The Meyers Hotel was also used for the scene where Terry and Edie dance and Terry receives his subpoena.)

A month into production, a *Times* reporter caught up with the company at the Bethlehem Steel Company pier in Brooklyn (ironically, not far from the would-be location of Arthur Miller's aborted *The Hook*). He found Johnstone, "a rangy, twinkling South Carolinian . . . happily at home, even on a slightly rolling deck."[66] They were filming the scene where Kayo Dugan is crushed by an avalanche of Irish whiskey and Father Barry (Karl Malden) delivers the "Christ in the Shape-up" sermon. Hoboken could provide the piers, but there were no suitable freighters available (the ships we see in the background there are mainly passenger liners, like the SS *Nieuw Amsterdam*), so the scene was staged on the *Rhadames*, a Dominican freighter docked in Brooklyn. It is the only scene in the film where the longshoremen are actually shown working on or in a ship.

"Christ in the Shape-up" had been the heart of Schulberg's story when the Father Corridan character was still at its center. But between Spiegel's concerns about its length and Kazan's general antipathy to its religious overtones, it was struggling to stay in the picture. Malden spent eleven days with Corridan ("who always liked to throw back a few beers with his meal") and consciously modeled his performance on the personality of this well-known public figure. He even bought the priest's hat and wore it in the picture.[67] Corridan told both

Schulberg and Malden that he first delivered the sermon after a long night of reflection, when a longshoreman he had inspired to stand up for his rights was beaten by thugs and thrown into the river. Earlier drafts had focused on the priest's moral and ethical dilemma in encouraging the men to risk their lives to challenge an entrenched evil, but the film was now more concerned with the ethics of informing. Nothing remains of Father Barry's anxiety and awareness of his responsibility for these actions, but the actions themselves are still in the picture, turning him into what Peter Biskind called "a ruthless crusader who manipulates others like chess pieces in the name of a higher good for which no price is too high, no sacrifice too great."[68] (In fact, the germ of this idea can be found in the McSorley version, when Kay confronts the reporter, who has been stirring up things on the waterfront. "Why don't you leave people alone? They're only another line in a story for you. You don't care what happens. . . .")

The night before shooting this scene, Kazan had taken Malden away from a dinner party in order to go over the entire speech three more times, "to get a sense of your pace." He seemed pleased that Malden had already "intended to do it at a fast clip" but was still prepared to cut away as often as necessary to keep Sam Spiegel happy. "I remember worrying frequently about the pace of the scenes," Spiegel later wrote in a Kazan tribute volume, "and urging dear Kazan to shoot added close-ups in order to enable us to speed up the scenes in the cutting room."[69] But if that wasn't enough, Kazan "came up with another way to up the ante of the scene." At the last minute he decided that someone needed to hurl a beer can at the priest, so the prop department produced one made out of rubber. When Charlie Maguire threw it at Malden it bounced off, so they decided to use a real can instead, an empty. That one floated down ineffectually, so Kazan ordered another try, with the can half full. "I'm not throwing that," the usually reliable Maguire insisted. Kazan climbed a ladder to throw the can himself. "A perfect aim. He cut my forehead wide open. But what was a little blood to a waterfront priest who smoked and drank."[70]

Malden and Kazan had worked together professionally for years, but with actors not trained at the Studio the director would avoid any talk of motivation. "I do it in terms of behavior, not psychology," he told Jeff Young. "You can screw them up by talking about feelings."[71] He gave one example in his autobiography:

> I had Tami Mauriello close to the camera, prominently featured, and no matter what happened, his face never fixed on anything, his eyes would always wander here and there, so that he gave the impression of indifference. I finally became desperate. Telling the camera operator to be ready, hand on switch, to roll the camera, I went over to Tami and suddenly whacked him as hard as I could with my open palm across the face, then, shouting "Roll!" I leaped back to the safe area behind the camera, close to Charlie [Maguire] and Joe [Marotta]. Tami was okay in that scene.[72]

But Kazan did not relate any stories regarding his direction of the neighborhood kids used in the film, the current members of "The Golden Warriors." None receive screen credit, but reporters identified at least three of them, including John McComb and Edward Stinson.[73] The only Warrior with significant screen time was Tommy, played by fourteen-year-old Tommy Hanley, the neighborhood kid who had originally been hired to "watch" the pigeon coops. Sent to the Actors Studio to audition, he began throwing chairs around when Kazan taunted him by suggesting his father had been murdered because he was a stool pigeon. He got the job. But on the set Kazan was still not seeing the level of emotion he needed. Before the "pigeon for a pigeon" scene, "they put me in a room with a big cop I didn't like. He started to get rough with me." When Hanley was suitably upset they took him up to the roof to shoot the scene, in which he appears shaken and tearful.[74]

Performers schooled in the Stanislavsky method were not subjected to this kind of physical and emotional bullying, a style of directing associated more with Erich von Stroheim than Elia Kazan.[75] For her first scene in the film, Eva Marie Saint was asked to use her training to conjure an emotional space far different than the Hudson Street tenement they were now working in. "I shall never forget the first day on the set," she told one reporter, "when I played a love scene with Marlon Brando, and how important Mr. Kazan's advice was to me. He wanted me to feel as if I had been lost in a forest, and that suddenly out of this dark wilderness I found something so wonderful as the love of this girl for the man."[76] Saint won the Oscar for this, her first film performance. Tami Mauriello never made another film.

The Hoboken historian Nicholas Acocella names many other local residents who appeared in the film, longshoremen playing longshoremen and cops playing cops. The one major exception was Frank Marnell, a gym teacher at the nearby David E. Rue School. Not only does Marnell play the shipping agent who says "Let's go to work!" at the film's dramatic climax, but he also appears as "Mr. Big," the shadowy puppet master who tells the servants not to take any more calls from Johnny Friendly.[77] Is the film suggesting, however obliquely, that there is a connection between these two? Newspaper reports had already identified the real Mr. Big as William J. McCormack, whose criminal web connected shippers, mobsters, and politicians on both sides of the river. Schulberg had long since abandoned the idea of building his script around so recognizable—and powerful—a local big shot. Like everyone else, he was right to be scared, so this bizarre piece of casting may be little more than an inside joke. But it does serve to remind us that, when it comes to politics, not everything in *On the Waterfront* is neatly laid out for us right on the surface.

Despite more than three years of work, the script was still in a state of flux as Kazan struggled not to fall behind schedule that winter. On November 23, Spiegel's office sent out a memo indicating several pages of cuts that everyone involved was to delete from their copies of the script; more cuts were promised "as soon as they come off the type."[78] This would have included all the scenes where Terry goes to confession and tells Father Barry, "I have blood on my hands." In Kazan's working copy of the script, the entire ending is a series of blue pages dated December 29, suggesting another round of significant changes at the last minute (and even that version ends with "Let's go to work," not "I'll be back!").[79] An undated script in George Justin's collection ends with Terry having been killed in the fight with Johnny Friendly, and the men moving forward on their own instead of simply following Terry onto the pier.[80] In a 1959 interview, Rod Steiger claimed that the Production Code prevented the use of this ending, where "the boy was supposed to float down the river on his face, dead," suggesting that the "dead Terry" ending was still under consideration during the time Steiger was on the picture.[81]

No film made under such stressful conditions could avoid being twisted and pulled in all directions by the force of circumstance, but what is remarkable about On the Waterfront is that it was not only able to absorb changes to its battle plan but benefit from them. To take one very small example, in the park scene between Brando and Saint (where Kaufman had already been inspired to do something with the burning piles of leaves), Schulberg had not provided any motivation for Edie to stay and listen to Terry's seductive patter. Her father had warned her about just this sort of thing, and her character would be expected to brush him off and walk away. "Eva was having a difficult time justifying her stopping to talk to him and understandably so," Malden recalled. Then Brando suggested, "Take off your gloves and while we're walking, drop one."[82] The gesture is crucial, but is this the true origin story? Kazan also suggests that the actors developed this improvised business in rehearsal, but Boris Kaufman remembered the moment as pure chance. "He knew how to use a location, including an accident," he wrote of Kazan. "When Eva Marie Saint accidentally dropped her glove and Brando picked it up this was the take used."[83]

"The Taxicab Scene"

A more significant example can be found in the famous "taxicab scene," one of the most frequently cited and heavily analyzed dialogue sequences in the history of American film.[84] For Kazan, "it is the perfect example of how this picture was made by a series of accidents and misfortunes that turned out well at the end."[85] The first fortunate accident was Lawrence Tierney's decision to reject the role of Charley, resulting in the more offbeat casting of Rod Steiger. But the best known is the solution the company found to an apparently insolvable problem that only popped up on the day of shooting. Kazan claimed, "My original intention had been to shoot the scene in a real taxi, an actual cab in traffic."[86] This could have been done but was still so difficult as to be extremely rare. Kazan would have known that Norbert Brodine, his cameraman on *Boomerang!*, had shot a brief dialogue exchange between James Cagney and E. G. Marshall for *13 Rue Madeleine* in a moving car. The camera operator had been strapped to the hood and illumination was provided by photofloods running off storage batteries.[87] Joseph H. Lewis (working for the King Brothers in 1949), had been able to film a longer dialogue sequence inside a moving car on *Gun Crazy*, but the dramatic significance of those words was not especially great and there was no need to cover the action in multiple takes in the first place (indeed, that was the whole point).

In Boris Kaufman's copy of the script this scene is described as "NY.B.G.," a reference to the need for an appropriate background plate of New York City, to which Kaufman has added "back projection?" in pencil.[88] Even in *Bicycle Thieves*, at the time the industry's benchmark of screen realism, whenever the characters board a car or truck, De Sica shoots the action against a filmed back projection. So the company prepared to film this sequence in the traditional manner. But where exactly? The Fox Movietone studio might have had all the appropriate facilities, but was returning to Fox really an option? According to Rod Steiger, the scene was shot "in an old broken-down TV studio at 85th Street in Manhattan."[89] But Nehemiah Persoff, who "drove" the cab, remembered it as "a CBS network owned studio on 58th and 9th Avenue [that] had once been a Borden Milk factory."[90] Other sources suggest different locations, but what is clear is that the crew was prepared to shoot inside a studio, the only such bit of movie magic in the entire picture. Yet somehow, on the day of filming, the appropriate cut-away taxi showed up but not the required back-projection equipment.[91]

Kazan blamed the lack of equipment on Spiegel's notorious desire "to save a big bill," while Steiger described, with relish, a titanic shouting match between them on the set.[92] Was Spiegel really so stupid as to arrange for a studio and a cut-away cab, but not the rear-screen technology that was the reason for their being there in the first place? Hard to believe of the man who produced *The African Queen*, a film that made extensive use of back projection to flesh out footage actually shot on location. Sol Negrin, who had been working in New York since 1947, told me later, "There was no such thing as rear-projection equipment in New York at that time. It had to come from this guy in California. . . . But maybe they didn't want to pay for it."[93] Could it really be true that New York had no back-projection facilities? Even in Marathon's *Close-Up*, an inexpensive film shot in November 1947, we see a well-handled back-seat conversation shot against rear-screen footage of the West Side Highway. Somebody dropped the ball here, but was it really Sam Spiegel? Kaufman, as his script notes indicate, would have been aware of the need for this footage, and it was his responsibility as director of photography to provide it. George Justin and (to a lesser degree) Charlie Maguire had the day-to-day responsibility of preparing for each day's shoot, be it studio or location. Did one of them lose track of something? The fact that Kazan made a whipping boy of Sam Spiegel does not necessarily prove that Justin or Maguire were not the guilty parties.[94] Unfortunately, I have been unable to locate the appropriate call sheet for that day's shooting or any production notes that might prove exactly what went wrong here.

As almost everyone familiar with *On the Waterfront* now knows, the situation was saved when one of the crew suggested they might simply block out the view from the back window by shutting it off with a louvered blind. In fact, many upscale pre-1955 cars came with a louvered rear-window option (Charlie Maguire remembered the one they were using was "like the old De Sotos that had the narrow windows."[95] If the equipment had materialized as promised, the scene would have looked like every other "Hollywood" location picture, where the actors work in front of a back projection of the city whenever the need to establish a location arises—a problem even for *Bicycle Thieves*. That potential flaw was gone now, but the blinds had created a new problem.

No proper back projection meant that there were also no views out the side windows, normally a factor in scenes like this—the crew couldn't put venetian

14.3. Rod Steiger and Marlon Brando in the taxicab sequence of *On the Waterfront*. Frank Serjack, the still photographer, captured this angle, unseen in the actual film, revealing the blank view out the cab's side window. Who forgot the back projection? Bison Archives.

blinds everywhere. So Kaufman had to bring the camera in much closer than usual, completely avoiding the edges of the cab where the side windows would have appeared. The resulting claustrophobia, already triggered by the blank, louvered wall behind the actors, focused the attention of the audience on one thing only. As with the burning leaves in the park, the solution was more than just a quick pragmatic fix but added a dramatic grace note that improved on the scene as presented in the script.

And unlike *Gun Crazy* or *Touch of Evil* (which would later feature a similar sequence) there are no visual pyrotechnics to distract us from the tragedy of these brothers. Indeed, there is not even an exterior shot of either man entering the cab—the actors play the entire scene within the confines of this back seat. Only toward the end do we see one brief view of the corner of First and River Streets, when the cab pulls over to let Marlon Brando's double get out. It is always a bit of a shock to see Nehemiah Persoff, another Actors Studio hire, suddenly pop into the frame to remind us that there is somebody else in that cab. Ignoring Charley's instructions to drive to "the Garden," he instead turns the corner and disappears into an underground garage at the fictitious "437 River Street." The cabbie turns out to be another of Johnny Friendly's henchmen, a plot point that seems borrowed from a silent movie serial—these villains are everywhere!—but the action is on and off the screen so quickly that audiences have no time to feel anything but surprise (as, we assume, does Charley).

Steiger claimed that the scene took eleven hours to film, which is not very likely given that Brando left at 4:00 P.M. to visit his analyst, and it had taken all morning to find the venetian blinds.[96] But because Steiger was the last man standing, his account of Brando's unprofessional behavior (and Kazan's facilitating of it) has marked most discussion of the scene.[97] Steiger never forgave Brando for leaving the set before his own close-ups had been shot, or Kazan for allowing him to do so. He would use this shocking disrespect (in his eyes) to fuel the emotion of his own performance. Nor did Steiger ever forgive Brando for the way he characterized their work in Truman Capote's notorious 1957 *New Yorker* profile. Brando had been discussing his concept of "the sensitive moment," something he felt that Elia Kazan was especially good at helping him reach. When asked to describe how this actually worked in the already famous taxicab scene, Brando responded as follows:

"Yes. Well, no. Well, let's see." He puckered his eyes, made a humming noise. "That was a seven-take scene, and I didn't like the way it was written. Lot of dissension going on there. I was fed up with the whole picture. All the location stuff was in New Jersey, and it was the dead of winter—the cold, Christ! And I was having problems at the time. Woman trouble. That scene. Let me see. There were seven takes because Rod Steiger couldn't stop crying. He's one of those actors [who] loves to cry. We kept doing it over and over. But I can't remember just when, just how it crystallized for me. The first time I saw *Waterfront* in a projection room with Gadge, I thought it was terrible. I thought it was so terrible I walked out without even speaking to him."[98]

The scene may indeed have required seven takes, judging from the variety of angles used by Kazan and his editor, Gene Milford, to piece it together. And Brando's problems with the script are well documented. But blaming Steiger for this seems ungenerous at best. According to Steiger, it was Brando who spoiled many takes by improvising away from the script ("Whataya think of the Yankees?"), apparently in search of that sensitive moment. Another interpretation has it that Brando felt the scene was unplayable so long as Charley had a gun in Terry's ribs. Time was running out and Steiger, in awe of Brando and at a loss as to where this "improvisation" was going, was starting to panic. "Buddy," the exasperated director finally had to insist, "stop the crap" (Brando was "Buddy" only to intimate friends). Brando and Kazan eventually found their moment (Terry's pushing the gun away appears to have been the solution), but Steiger still ended the day reading his lines to Guy Thomajan, the film's dialogue director. "I was lost, frightened, hurt, embarrassed," he remembered, shocked that Kazan had allowed Brando to leave for an appointment with his analyst before all of their joint performance was in the can. "At that time one of our strongest father images was Elia Kazan."[99]

Betrayal by the father is a recurrent theme in Kazan's cinema. Schulberg's early drafts had emphasized the parent-child relationship of Terry and his teenaged son, but that relationship had been eliminated, replaced by the relationship between brothers that now dominates the film's personal dynamic. Yet notes written in Kazan's copy of the script indicate that Johnny Friendly was still meant to function as a father figure to Terry—an orphan—but also as "a lover," making it especially painful when this parent humiliates him. Brando had already felt "betrayed" by Kazan when he learned the news of his HUAC testimony.[100] Now Kazan was dealing with *two* resentful actors, two men (playing brothers) both traumatized by the behavior of this same father figure—their director!

But the real father figure on the set, the focus of everyone's anxieties and insecurities, was Sam Spiegel. Kazan had ordered Spiegel off the set (literally, off the roof) on the first day of shooting. But the producer still made occasional appearances, usually in the early morning hours, stepping out of a limousine with a would-be starlet on his arm. "One day, fighting weather, fighting light, trying to hold together a crew so cold, miserable and contemptuously treated by S. P. Eagle that it was ready to mutiny," Schulberg wrote, Kazan received a personal visit from Sam Spiegel, who was there to complain that they had fallen one day behind schedule. Kazan walked away from Spiegel and turned to Schulberg. "Budd, I've had it. I warned that son of a bitch, if he came on this set once more and broke our concentration, I was gonna quit!"[101] Kazan did not quit, of course, but Karl Malden suggests that it was not just Spiegel's presence that outraged Kazan, but the presence of that presence:

> [Spiegel] would drive up in his limousine and step out of the car wearing a camel hair coat and fine leather gloves. Kazan tried to explain to him that this was insulting to all the real longshoremen who were working on the film as extras. Some of these men could barely afford a flimsy jacket, but they were working their tails off to help us in every way they could. Sam just didn't get it. Finally, Kazan just shut down work.... That Spiegel understood; time meant money."[102]

Rod Steiger recalled another night (or maybe it was the same night), with Spiegel haranguing Kazan in one room of their Hoboken headquarters while the actors in the next room could hear everything.

> What they heard was Spiegel saying, "I don't care about the actors. Beat them. Hit them. Kill them. Starve them, but get the goddamn picture done." With that, he came back into the room, lighting a cigar as he passed and climbed into his limousine waiting outside. "Good evening, ladies and gentlemen," he said as he left, as if nothing untoward had happened. The actors felt as if someone poured iced water over them.[103]

Kazan himself relates what he calls the "most famous" of these late-night appearances, when the crew had been trying to finish the scene where Brando and Saint are chased down an alley by a truck. It had started to snow, and in order to match the previous day's work, the crew had erected an awning over the alley, an awning that was rapidly filling up with snow and threatening to collapse. One grip had already fallen off a ladder and been taken away in an ambulance with a broken leg. The crew was taking a break, trying to get warm, when Spiegel, fresh from The Stork Club and wrapped in his camel hair coat, lit into them. "You're killing me," he told them, "You're absolutely killing me with your incompetence and your laziness."

> There was a little propman on that crew, Eddie Barr was his name, and he'd been working props for a million years, and he stood up and he said, "You Jew cocksucker!" Barr was a Jewish guy, and he could get away with that. "You Jew cocksucker, if it weren't for Charlie Maguire and that little guy outside ... we'd all be home. Nobody wants to be out here tonight. We don't need this kind of money. Now you better get your ass out of here if you want us to make this picture."[104]

Spiegel was lucky he was addressing the film crew, not the local extras. The longshoremen demanded their per diems promptly, and once when Spiegel was late with the money they turned to the man responsible for doling out their pay, Charlie Maguire, and dangled him over the edge of a pier. James T. Fisher, who reports this story, ends by quoting one line from Kazan's nostalgic recollection of his Hoboken adventure. "We were right in the midst of life on that picture, and it shows, doesn't it?"[105]

"Never Before Such Advance Acclaim for a Movie!"

The earliest crew sheets show that Gene Milford, the editor of *On the Waterfront*, was working on the picture from the start. Sam Spiegel wanted to get this film out as quickly as possible, so Milford would have been "working behind" Kazan, assembling the film as best he could from the footage piling up every day. Like Fred Ryles, Richard Day, Budd Schulberg, Elia Kazan, and Sam Spiegel, Milford had a lengthy Hollywood résumé, but after years of work on the West Coast had made a conscious decision to leave Hollywood behind. One coworker recalled him as a "progressive" who "got affected by the blacklisting. . . . Maybe that's one of the reasons he came to New York."[106] Milford's first screen credit as an editor was in 1926, for Columbia, where he stayed until moving briefly to RKO in 1942. In 1934, the first year the Academy gave an award for film editing, he was nominated for his work on *One Night of Love* (he came in second) and was a winner three years later for *Lost Horizon* (shared with Gene Havlick). But only a handful of the seventy-plus films he edited before the war are still remembered today, the vast majority being program pictures and B-westerns. During the war Milford worked under Sam Spewack as chief film editor at the Office of War Information, later taking a similar position with the Atomic Energy Commission.[107] For the OWI he assembled the documentary feature *The World at War* (1942) and around 1943 began working on sponsored films for the Princeton Film Center. His last Hollywood credit came in 1945, after which he turned to sponsored films and documentaries produced at the Film Center and other East Coast production houses. Among the most successful of these was *Battle for Survival*, made for the American Jewish Joint Distribution Committee in 1946.

According to Ralph Rosenblum, by 1952 Milford was "the person to call if you were an editor looking for work" in New York.[108] Milford got Rosenblum a job in television, and in 1955 (with Sid Katz) they would found MKR Productions, one of New York's busiest editing mills. The success of MKR grew directly out of the Oscar Milford won for cutting *On the Waterfront*. Milford returned to features, becoming a key member of Elia Kazan's East Coast production unit, editing *Baby Doll*, *A Face in the Crowd* and *Splendor in the Grass*. (In 1960 he produced and directed a notable New York noir of his own, *The Pusher*.) Rosenblum eventually took over MKR, building a reputation that would make him New York's most prominent film editor (*The Pawnbroker*, *The Producers*, *Annie Hall*). While Gene Milford and his work were highly respected inside the filmmaking community, unlike Rosenblum he never established a popular critical profile of his own. In 1987 he and Barbara McLean became the first recipients of the American Cinema Editors Career Achievement Award, but ten years earlier, when *Film Comment* published a special issue honoring the seventy-five most important film editors, Milford and his work were not even mentioned.[109] Because Milford had already assembled a rough cut, Kazan was able to finalize the editing of *On the Waterfront* very quickly. Boris Kaufman was off on his next assignment, so postproduction photography was handled by Hollywood cameraman James Wong Howe, whose own New York film, *Go Man Go*, had just opened at the Globe. Howe seems to have worked on the film in two separate stages. A letter from Horizon-American, dated March 10, 1954, contests his invoice for a ten-day per diem, arguing that their agreement had only called for five days of hotel reimbursement.[110] But two weeks later he seems to be back on the project, writing his wife that he will stay in New York for three additional days' work. He has now seen the picture, which he describes as "very really wonderful. . . . The cameraman did a fine job and they were blessed with the kind of weather that help [*sic*] the mood of the story."[111] Two days later he began to describe the assignment in greater detail:

> Darling, I have just returned from Hoboken, New Jersey's Water Front. Went there this A.M. to look for places to shoot. Its very interesting and full of wonderful character along the waterfront. Nice people if you don't bother them. . . . We will start photography on Monday, Tues or Wed. On Wed, I will make a wonderful opening shot of the New York water front from a Helicopter. We will start about three thousand feet over the harbor showing New York City in the background and then come down on a pier on the water front. That's how the picture 'Water Front' will open. They have a wonderful film and Marlon Brando is really at his best ever. I met some of the dock workers over there, and they are very quiet and untalkative at first. Hard to learn & know them right off. After a while they either like you or they don't. Some of those kids are really toughs, will tell you about them later.[112]

No helicopter shot was used in the finished film—in fact, New York City is barely visible in the picture at all. But Howe did recall one moment that does survive: in the scene where the badly beaten Terry Malloy leads the men onto the pier, he suggested a handheld camera be used to establish the character's point of view. "Howe had his camera operator stand where the scene was to begin and then turn in circles until he was dizzy. Finally, Howe gave the disoriented operator the camera and had him walk while filming. The unsteady, staggering result was perfect for a man in Brando's condition."[113] A year earlier,

Kazan had vowed to shoot the entire film on location with a handheld camera, but this one shot is as close as he got. Howe had already promoted the use of Eyemos in production photography in *Air Force*, and in *Body and Soul* he famously used one to shoot prize-fight sequences, inside the ring, on roller skates. Kaufman, despite his documentary experience, was always more comfortable shooting from a tripod, and that is how the film still opens.

Spiegel had been urging Kazan to speed things up during principal photography and continued to push him during postproduction. "Please Sam don't hurry my editing," Kazan snapped back at him in a memo.

> We hurried and hurried up to now—justifiably so with winter coming and the short days and the budget and so on. But I'm fed up with hurrying and I don't want to with the editing. If you're nervous or under some anxiety strain, why don't you take a vacation while I do this next job. I think most of the rush and push and hurry in our business is primarily habit. And I certainly have no intention of rushing a picture that I have spent months on to fit into the schedule of Lennie Bernstein or any other goddamn composer.[114]

Kazan eventually thought better of this and never sent the memo, but it does indicate the importance Spiegel attached to Leonard Bernstein's participation and Kazan's fresh annoyance at the appearance of a new celebrity collaborator.

Jon Burlingham, in his study of the film's score, suggests that Kazan's first choice as composer would have been Alex North, "the New York composer who Kazan had brought to Hollywood and who had won Oscar nominations for his brilliant music for Kazan's two [sic] previous films, *A Streetcar Named Desire* and *Viva Zapata!*" Unfortunately, Kazan's 1952 HUAC testimony had "destroyed his relationship with North, and the two never spoke again."[115] It was Spiegel, looking to add some last-minute marquee value, who came up with Leonard Bernstein. A crossover talent whose conducting skills had taken the concert world by storm, he was celebrated on Broadway for *On the Town* (1944) and *Wonderful Town*, which had opened at the Winter Garden in February 1953 and was still running. At first, Bernstein was not interested. He had never before agreed to write a film score (a chore he considered beneath him), although he did respect the film work of Aaron Copland and Sergei Prokofiev—not so much for what went on on-screen as for the concert pieces (like *Of Mice and Men* and *Alexander Nevsky*) they had later extracted from these scores. But there was another reason he didn't want to have anything to do with *On the Waterfront*. According to Bernstein's biographer, Humphrey Burton, he too was "reluctant to work with the director, Elia Kazan, who had been one of the most notorious and reviled informants to the House Un-American Activities Committee. The very subject of the film was the glorification of an informer."[116]

Spiegel did at least convince Bernstein to attend a screening of Kazan's rough cut. "It was down to length, but clumsy and uneven in details," Kazan remembered. This is the famous screening in which Brando got up and left without a word, "not even a goodbye" to his director, while badmouthing the film (and his own performance) to another of the attendees, Karl Malden. Even Spiegel seemed unhappy, Kazan suspecting he was "concerned that the film would be a box office failure and further lower his standing in the industry." Of course, Spiegel's negative attitude may have been just another ploy, an appeal to Bernstein's ego that only he could save this picture, but it had the effect of rousing Kazan to its defense. "This is a great picture!" he shouted, the first time this thought had occurred to him.[117] Yet Bernstein, one of the first outsiders to get a look at the film, immediately recognized what he was seeing. "I thought it a masterpiece of direction; and Marlon Brando seemed to me to be giving the greatest performance I had ever seen him give, which is saying a good deal. I was swept by my enthusiasm into accepting the writing of the score."[118] He quickly changed his mind and accepted Spiegel's offer of $15,000, the top of the scale for a Hollywood film score—so long as he could retain all rights to the "orchestral suite" he planned to extract from it.[119]

Sam Spiegel now had another problem on his hands. He had hired Bernstein for the value of his name, and the film's advertising campaign was set to award the composer the same broadsheet billing accorded Kazan, Schulberg, and Spiegel himself, a rare honor. But first he would have to clear Bernstein's name with whoever was in charge of those things at Columbia. Already well known for his left-wing sympathies, Bernstein's list of alleged "Communist Front" associations took up nearly two full pages in *Red Channels*. Lee J. Cobb, who played Johnny Friendly, had a one-page listing, but Cobb had already purged himself before HUAC in June 1953.[120] Sam Spiegel, working behind the scenes, somehow worked his magic again.

In New York, Bernstein was pretty much left to his own devices. Kazan gave him no instructions. Gene Milford put him in a room with a moviola, where he could run the film backward and forward, "measuring in feet the sequences I had selected for music, converting feet into seconds by mathematical formula, making home-made cue-sheets."[121] Most of the score was completed in New York, but by April Bernstein was in Hollywood, where his "home-made cue-sheets" were causing consternation. Burlingham reports "serious errors in timing, requiring that many cues be reconfigured." Bernstein gave up his original plan to produce his own orchestrations and even turned the conductor's baton over to the more experienced Morris Stoloff, head of Columbia's music department, despite having won the contractual right to conduct the score himself (although he does appear on the track, playing a twenty-second "piano juke box" cue during the scene where Terry and Edie have their first drink).[122]

Surprisingly, Bernstein was also present during the mixing phase, a painful experience he described at some length in the *New York Times*. Now having to take a back seat to Kazan, he "at least put up the semblance of a fight" when the director lowered the volume of his music to allow some dialogue to be heard, or even ordered a few passages eliminated entirely.[123] He was not used to working in so subsidiary a position and would never allow anything like this to happen again. Kazan was also unhappy and wrote to Spiegel on May 19, "I am getting some very bad reactions to the music."[124] Still, as Burlingham notes, Bernstein was "quite fortunate. Despite his public protestations, most of what he wrote wound up in the film."[125] Did Sam Spiegel get his money's worth? Few reviews even bothered to mention the music, which Budd Schulberg, diplomatically, thought was "too loud."[126] But the score was well regarded inside the film music community, even if it did lose the Oscar to Dimitri Tiomkin's *The High and the Mighty*. Bernstein premiered his "Symphonic Suite from *On the Waterfront*" at Tanglewood in 1955, but unlike his "Symphonic Dances from *West Side Story*," it never established itself as a concert favorite.

Kazan and Schulberg both expressed surprise when they found three hundred people lined up at the Astor Theatre at 9:00 a.m. on opening day, July 28, 1954. Schulberg later wrote that the film had opened "unheralded," suggesting that it had somehow snuck into town, only to prove a sleeper success.[127] In fact, Sam Spiegel had managed the prerelease publicity so well that the only surprise would have been if the film had failed to meet the very high expectations awaiting it. As the *Times* noted in their follow-up review, "The faint whisper some five years ago that the story of the crimes against the workmen of our wharves was to be filmed, gradually grew to what amounted to a tumult of tub-thumping and was climaxed last week by the opening of *On the Waterfront*. Most of our expectations were realized."[128]

"What brought them there?" Kazan wondered about that opening-day crowd. "My guess is that it's the theme."[129] Kazan was very clear about this theme. After synopsizing the plot at the beginning of his production notebook, he concluded, "This Motion Picture is about one thing only: a Young man, who has let his *dignity slip away, regains* it!"[130] Perhaps "the redemption of Terry Malone" (as some early poster art put it) really is what established *On the Waterfront* as a critical and popular favorite and kept it in the public eye well into the next century.[131] But what brought out the crowd that first day was Sam Spiegel's canny roll-out. Spiegel had elicited much of this advance publicity on the strength of his personality, his limousine, and his camel hair coat. The man was a walking success story, or so it seemed. But Abe Schneider, who had set up his deal at Columbia, knew better. He knew that Spiegel was "stony broke," and arranged for the producer to be put on the payroll at $500 per week to help with public relations in connection with the opening. Not surprisingly, Spiegel was indignant. "I tip more than that!"[132]

Two days before the film opened, a large display ad in the *Times* boasted "NEVER BEFORE SUCH ADVANCE ACCLAIM FOR A MOVIE!"[133] Most of the space was devoted to a series of exuberant promotional quotes, highlighted by Walter Winchell's prediction: "As far as I'm concerned, Columbia's Marlon Brando starrer *On the Waterfront* has already won every Academy Award. Hollywood doesn't even have to bother voting." Rave reviews from *Life* and the *Saturday Review* supported testimonials from potential rivals Sam Goldwyn and Humphrey Bogart. "A brilliant motion picture," said Bogart. "Wrap up all the Oscars, including mine, and send them over to Brando." Bogart had won his Oscar for Sam Spiegel's *The African Queen*. He might have won another for *The Caine Mutiny*, which had opened only a few weeks earlier, but the Academy would send that one to Brando instead. The rest of Winchell's prediction would also prove surprisingly accurate.

Hedda Hopper was not quoted in this ad, but the staunch anti-Communist did make it known that she also was impressed with Brando's performance. According to a report in the FBI's COMPIC files, an unnamed Bureau informant subsequently discussed this with her, "pointing out to her the damaging type of propaganda which this production could generate when distributed abroad, whereupon Hopper advised that she . . . had not realized what foreign distribution of such a picture could do to the efforts of our Government to sell democracy abroad and expressed the feeling that action should be taken to prevent the picture from being distributed in foreign markets." But as the film was already in distribution any such effort would have been futile. The same file also contains a précis of John Howard Lawson's attack on the film in the November–December 1954 *Hollywood Review* ("skillfully contrived anti-democratic, anti-labor, anti-human propaganda"), and a statement by "the Head of Paramount Pictures," that *On the Waterfront* could be used by Communists overseas "to the detriment of the American way of life."[134] Such comments were exactly what Darryl F. Zanuck had been afraid of.

As part of his Oscar campaign, Sam Spiegel took *On the Waterfront* to the Venice Film Festival, where it was entered in competition alongside Columbia's own dramatic contender, *The Caine Mutiny*. His film had just racked up the three greatest weeks in the history of the Astor Theatre and was still going strong.[135] Spiegel had his eye on the Festival's top prize, the Golden Lion, but this went instead to Renato Castellani's *Romeo and Juliet*. "How could a movie like that beat mine?" he complained, with some justification.[136] After all, the screening had been interrupted by applause five different times, and (as Spiegel proudly reported) the chairman of the Festival had told him, "*Waterfront* is the first Italian film made in America."[137] Considering how the aura of neo-realism and films like *Open City* and *Bicycle Thieves* had served to inspire the filmmakers, this was high praise indeed. But the film had to settle for the Silver Lion, a directing award that Kazan shared with Mizoguchi (*Sansho the Bailiff*),

Kurosawa (*Seven Samurai*), and Fellini (*La Strada*). *The Caine Mutiny* came up empty, as did Alfred Hitchcock's *Rear Window* and Luchino Visconti's *Senso*.

Sam Spiegel thought the results were fixed, probably for political reasons.[138] Certainly there were problems with the European left, as evidenced in Lindsay Anderson's notorious *Sight and Sound* essay, which dismissed *On the Waterfront* as "a bad film," denouncing its conclusion as "implicitly (if unconsciously) Fascist," because the men appear to have swapped one strong man for another.[139] When asked about this reaction, Boris Kaufman explained, "Naturally, in Europe they expected solutions. But this was not the scope of the picture. It exposed the problem instead of giving a cliché solution."[140] Yet even the *New York Times*, in an otherwise positive review, sensed a melodramatic lack of context, and wished that the film, "might, perhaps, have delved deeper into the terrible truths from which this dramatization stemmed."[141]

"Sam was often embarrassed by my crudeness and my hostility towards him, and he was right to be," Kazan later admitted. "But I always esteemed him as the man who produced this film when no one else would and the man who persevered against Budd's and my inertia until we had an excellent shooting script. I believe we would have had a failure without Sam, and a fiasco with Zanuck."[142] Spiegel was a hands-on producer who felt free to insert himself into any and every aspect of production. His "interference" had frequently driven Schulberg and Kazan to distraction, but both men eventually agreed that his contribution to their partnership was invaluable.

For a few years in the 1950s the Academy of Motion Picture Arts and Sciences ran a bicoastal Oscars ceremony, production centers in Los Angeles and New York sharing screen time courtesy of a transcontinental television hookup—an irony that appears to have gone unmentioned. On March 30, 1955, guests in Hollywood assembled at the Pantages Theatre while a smaller crowd in New York squeezed into a few camp chairs on stage at NBC's Century Theatre, an old Shubert house on Seventh Avenue that had been converted into a television theater. Bob Hope hosted the event in Hollywood, against a surreal depiction of Oscars in a landscape reminiscent of the dream sequence in *Spellbound*, while the more modest event in New York was anchored by Thelma Ritter and Conrad Nagel.[143]

That night *On the Waterfront* walked away with eight Oscars, a record then matched only by *Gone with the Wind* and *From Here to Eternity*. The total might have been nine, but Karl Malden, Lee J. Cobb, and Rod Steiger were all competing against one another in the Supporting Actor category, leaving an opening for Edmond O'Brien in *The Barefoot Contessa*. Joking with Marlon Brando, Hope noted, "Everybody in it got nominated except the pigeon." Spiegel, Brando, and Gene Milford accepted their awards in Hollywood, but the rest of the film's honorees were all sitting at the Century. With everyone fearful of running overtime, acceptance speeches that year were not so much short as perfunctory.

Gene Milford mumbled, "Thank you all" as he quickly snatched the trophy from Hope. Brando's was one of the longest ("It's much heavier than I imagined. . . .") as he took the time to thank "so many people" but no one in particular.

Years later Brando would refuse to show up to accept his *Godfather* Oscar, but by then he had already lost track of the one he did take home in 1955. "I don't know what happened to the Oscar they gave me for *On the Waterfront*," he wrote in his autobiography.

> Somewhere in the passage of time it disappeared. I didn't think about it until a year or so ago, when my lawyer called and told me that an auction house in London was planning to sell it. When I wrote a letter to them saying that they had no right to do so, they replied that they would abide by my wishes, but that the person who had put it up for sale wouldn't relinquish it because supposedly I had given it to him or her. This is simply untrue.[144]

Brando aside, a new mantra, "And the winner in New York is. . . ." rang out five times that night, the first and only time that ever happened. Schulberg, Kazan, Kaufman, and Richard Day all spoke briefly (Richard Day very briefly, a simple "Thank you, Hollywood."). Eva Marie Saint, nine months pregnant ("I may have the baby right here!") was the only recipient to deliver what a modern audience might expect from an Oscar acceptance speech, thanking Kazan, Spiegel, Brando, Malden, and "all the longshoremen."[145]

Within days, George Justin had placed a full-page "Thank You, Hollywood!" ad in *Variety*, acknowledging all the Academy Awards and pointing out that *On the Waterfront* had been "DIRECTED, PHOTOGRAPHED and PUT TOGETHER FROM STEM TO STERN in Little Old New York!" He signed off, "KEEP 'EM IN THE EAST."[146] The ad, placed not by the film's producer but by its production manager, must have seemed a bit excessive, if not presumptuous, to puzzled readers who may have noticed it in Hollywood. As far as they knew, *The Naked City* had been made in New York, and maybe one or two other films. So this one was better.

Hollywood had never really been paying attention to what may have been shooting in New York, an expensive location that most thought of as either a glittering backdrop or a costly junket. And how could you keep films in the east if everything had gone west back in the days of D. W. Griffith? But over the next ten years, with *On the Waterfront* as his poster child, George Justin would run a campaign that would correct that.

CHAPTER 15
===

HAPPY ENDING

The New York film community was not all that large in 1953–1954, so the rival Horizon and Minotaur production units would certainly have known about another independent feature being shot on the other side of the river. True, Kazan's budget was ten times what Kubrick had to spend and his film already had a distributor. But their crews would still have run into each other at 1600 Broadway or one of the local labs, and news of the rare production coincidence had already made the front page of Frank Zucker's house paper. One can easily imagine Frank Silvera, who had already worked for Kazan on both stage and screen, quietly slipping over to Hoboken to learn what he could about the director's plans for further production activity in New York.[1]

As for Stanley Kubrick, despite his already sizable ego, he never thought very highly of *Kiss Me, Kill Me* and would hardly have wanted anyone to see it as competition for *Waterfront* (both films would not settle on a final title until just before release). A decade later he even prohibited its inclusion in a Kubrick retrospective organized by the Museum of Modern Art.[2] But he certainly would have had Kazan on his mind as he and Frank Silvera struggled to complete their second picture together. In a 1957 interview in *Cahiers du Cinema* he named Elia Kazan as "without question the best director we have in America. And he's capable of performing miracles with the actors he uses."[3] Kubrick also knew and respected the work of Kazan's director of photography, Boris Kaufman. Some years later Kaufman wrote Kubrick directly after hearing he was considering producing another film in New York. As they had never met, Kaufman introduced himself by citing some of his most important American credits—three Elia Kazan films and two for Sidney Lumet. Kubrick didn't need the reminder and replied, "I am well aware of your work and have been a great admirer for quite a number of years."[4] Unfortunately, Kubrick did not make *Dr. Strangelove* in New York and never had the opportunity of working with Kaufman.[5]

As he moved into postproduction on *Killer's Kiss*, the sound again proved to be more of a problem than Kubrick had anticipated. He had expected to postsync the entire film, something he had been forced to do with *Fear and Desire*. But while that laborious task was the result of problems created by nonprofessionals unfamiliar with the use of a wire recorder in the field, the issue now was different: the sound recording here was (or would have been) fine, but it was the inexperienced cinematographer/director who was stymied by such mundane issues as microphone placement and boom shadow.[6] Fortunately, when Minotaur's original business plan was created back in September 1953 the Titra Sound Corporation had joined with CECO and De Luxe in offering the bulk of their services on a deferred basis.[7] Titra's core business, as it happened, was the postsynchronization of feature films for both major producers and independent distributors.

Titra Film Laboratories, Inc. had been established in New York in May 1943, the American branch of a French firm that pioneered a method of burning subtitles onto the release prints of foreign-language features. One of their early employees was Herman G. Weinberg, an important name in the New York film community whose job involved subtitling French and Italian art films.[8] Among the many he worked on were several of Joseph Burstyn's releases, including *Open City* and *Flowers of St. Francis*. Kubrick had known Weinberg since at least 1953, the year he took the portrait photo that appears on the cover of Weinberg's memoirs.[9] Weinberg had connections to the Museum of Modern Art Film Library and wrote for most of the serious film journals then in production, including *Films in Review, Sight and Sound*, and *Film Culture*, which he helped launch in 1954. Was it Weinberg who introduced him to people like Theodore Huff and Joseph Burstyn? Weinberg's papers at the New York Public Library show him to have been on a first-name basis with Kubrick (who signs his letters "Stan").[10] That Kubrick maintained a connection with local scholars and historians like Weinberg, Huff, and William K. Everson (in addition to his conventional film industry contacts), is typical of the cultural networking characteristic of the New York film scene during the postwar era.[11]

While Titra Film Laboratories continued with this subtitling operation, a separate facility (with the same address and telephone number) called Titra Sound Corporation was created to handle dubbing and synchronization work. This was the entity that had agreed to defer up to $9,000 in costs as part of Minotaur's organization plan, although only a legal fiction—and a single doorway—separated the Sound Corporation from the Film Laboratory. The film's original sound crew can be identified on a handwritten crew sheet preserved in the Kubrick Archive: Nathan Boxer (boom man), Willard W. Goodman (a mixer who later worked on films like *Andy* [1965] and *Alice's Restaurant* [1969]), and Robert Farren (an "assembly editor" whose films would include *Primary* [1960], *Gimme Shelter* [1970], and *Ciao, Manhattan* [1972]).[12] None of these men are credited on the release print, which instead lists only Walter Ruckersberg and Clifford van Praag as "sound recordists," names added to the crew after the start of production. Ruckersberg was Titra's managing director. I know little about van Praag, who later became president of a company that specialized in commercials and industrial films. "Titra Sound Studio" received a "Sound By" credit.

Kubrick spent at least a year working in Titra's offices (they had space at both 1600 Broadway and a few blocks south in the Paramount building, 1501 Broadway, another film industry center). Cameraman Max Glenn, who also worked at Titra, recalled meeting Kubrick there. He appears to have considered Kubrick a charity case and never seems to have realized that Titra was essentially an investor in his picture. "He had to have someplace to edit," Glenn told Vincent Lo Brutto. "He was a loose, sloppy-looking guy, and so he came to ask the owner if he could use the cutting room where there were moviolas. The owner looked at Stanley and said, 'Stanley, you look like a bum. Take a shave and I'll let you use the equipment.' He always looked like he needed a shave and a haircut. I just got the feeling he didn't shower very often."[13]

Not only did he do editing and sound recording at Titra, but Kubrick seems to have shot occasional inserts there as well. For example, during the fight in the mannequin warehouse an insert was needed to show a close-up of Davey's discarded gun. The brief shot shows a Luger lying amid a pile of junk, with the corner of a package barely visible. The package has nothing to do with mannequins or the garment business but is addressed from E. H. Jacobs of Motion Pictures for Television to Walter [Ruckersberg] of Tit[ra]. The package has either been carefully positioned as an inside joke or was simply an actual piece of debris tossed into a corner of the Titra offices. More interesting was another insert filmed at Max Glenn's home, where Kubrick "came up and shot some scenes right off my television set."[14] Few viewers notice that during the scene in which Gloria and Vince watch Davey's fight there is no establishing shot actually showing them in the same space as the television set. That is because their presence as "viewers" is constructed entirely through editing and a bit of flickering video light projected on their faces.

Kubrick claimed that the film had been shot in twelve weeks (in itself a great deal of time for a low-budget feature), but as we have seen this work was not continuous.[15] Most of the shooting could be divided into what we might call the "cold weather" phase in October and November 1953 and the "warm weather" sequences around May 1954, with time off in midwinter for inclement weather and Silvera and Smith's theater work. This means that twelve weeks of actual work were stretched out over seven months. Keeping the actors on board throughout this period was a remarkable accomplishment for a young filmmaker with little experience and less money. What degree of chicanery and charm Kubrick employed is impossible to say, but if he had fallen short in motivating the cast, the crew, and the financial participants, *Killer's Kiss* would have collapsed then and there.

It is worth noting here that a dating error in the *American Film Institute Catalog* entry for *Killer's Kiss*, which states that "production began Oct. 1954," has been repeated by even some of the most conscientious Kubrick scholars.[16] Getting that date wrong by an entire year means that these accounts fail to realize just how protracted (and potentially catastrophic) the film's extended postproduction period really was. It also makes a hash of the film's historical context, positioning *Killer's Kiss* as part of the post–*On the Waterfront* wave of New York independent productions when in reality the two films were shot simultaneously.

Silvera and Smith signed release agreements covering dubbing, narration, and rerecording on April 26, 1954, work that would have taken place at Titra. By May 23, Kubrick was telling the *New York Times* that *Kiss Me, Kill Me*, a film he had cowritten with Howard Sackler, was currently being scored by Gerald Fried and "should be ready for release in six weeks."[17] That would have been around the time a telegram arrived from Chris Chase's lawyers. In her autobiography, Chase claimed that she was philosophically opposed to dubbing:

> I felt sure Duse wouldn't have dubbed. I was equally sure that *no* great talent could have borne to stand in that little studio and stare at himself on the screen and try to fit words, off what's called a loop script, into his own mouth, over and over again, until the mechanicalness of the process drove him mad. Not that I didn't try. For eight hours I tried, and then I threw my loop script on the floor and went to Florida.[18]

This account suggests that she gave it her best shot and walked away (she identifies Peggy Lobbin as the actress whose voice we actually hear in the film). But a June 12 telegram from the firm of Wizin and Halperin in the Kubrick Archives tells a different story. "This office represents Christopher Kane," it announces. "Her voice is available for use in motion picture now entitled KISS ME, KILL ME. Your contemplated use of a substitute voice is a violation of her rights and you will be held strictly accountable for any such unauthorized activity."[19]

By her account, Kubrick had originally been attracted to her voice, which she described as "funny." "People are always getting me on the phone and saying, 'Sonny, let me talk to your father.' " But the frustration she describes at her first (and only?) looping session seems to echo the panic attack she suffered when Bert Stern brought Kubrick over to her apartment and she "went and crouched behind a television set in the corner."[20] The discipline required to loop an entire feature was not an issue for professionals like Silvera and Smith, but for Chase, always more of a model than an actor, this exercise was too much of a challenge. Kubrick, still inexperienced in handling actors, would not have been much help. In any case, *Killer's Kiss* would fail to jump-start her acting career, and after a few stage appearances (and continuing roles in such locally produced television series as *Love of Life* and *The Doctors*) Kane/Chase successfully reinvented herself as an entertainment journalist. Billed as Chris Chase, she made her last film appearance in Bob Fosse's *All That Jazz* (1979), playing an entertainment journalist.

Replacing one actor's voice with another was just another day's work at Titra (they were especially proud of "the American version" of Fellini's *La Strada*, which they took credit for producing).[21] But few directors other than Orson Welles would go so far as this in an English-language production. Critics often talk about how much time Kubrick spent in laying down each gunshot and footstep for the *Killer's Kiss* soundtrack, but the fact that he substituted an entire vocal performance in this ultra-low-budget film is barely mentioned. Having Peggy Lobbin voice the role of "Gloria Price" is not exactly the same as Billy Crystal and John Goodman "appearing" in *Monsters, Inc.*, but it does prefigure issues of performance and directorial control that would continue to crop up throughout Kubrick's career.

Kubrick again turned to his friend Gerald Fried to compose and conduct the score, which consists of a series of discrete musical motifs underscoring each melodramatic plot point. Fried had been working in a Mambo band that summer, a gig that inspired the jazzy Latin rhythms associated with Vince's dangerous romantic cravings.[22] For the flashback (within a flashback) illustrating Gloria's tale of her sister's abortive ballet career, Fried wrote a classical pastiche interpreted on stage by Ruth Sobotka. And at a time when many noir films incorporated a theme song, Kubrick decided to feature "Once," with music by Arden Clar and lyrics by Norman Gimbel.[23] Fried orchestrated this romantic melody in various ways, with one violin passage apparently marked "molto shmalzando."[24] But the film never makes use of it as a *vocal*, despite Gimbel's urgings. "Dear Stanley," he wrote on the bottom of a cue sheet, "Pls let me know when the release date is to be. Is there any truth or near truth to the six weeks bit in the [May 23] NYT article? Do your best to have the lyric used. It will enhance the possibilities of a major recording. Keep in touch. P.S. This is the lyric . . . I will not change it."[25] Kubrick ultimately decided not to use the lyric, but Gimbel had better luck years later with the even more melancholy Roberta Flack hit, "Killing Me Softly with His Song."

Fried worked on deferral, and there is no record of what, if anything, Minotaur might have paid him. The musicians were paid $3,894.52 and another

$1,100 was spent on orchestrating, copying, and arranging the score. The budget allowed $11,195.25 for recording and mixing, but this was all deferred by Titra. Charges of $4,127.90 for negative cutting and editing equipment rental were also deferred, as were $13,527.12 in camera rental costs (CECO) and $7,939.60 in lab costs (De Luxe). With $4,000 in legal and accounting fees also deferred, the total cash outlay as of July 31, 1954 was $40,039.02. The only significant money paid out after this date included a $5,000 union settlement and $700 for an MPAA Code Seal.[26]

On the Waterfront had opened on July 28. Kazan and Spiegel managed to get their film into theaters just a few months after the close of principal photography, but in that case a distributor, Columbia, already had theaters ready and waiting to show it. Kubrick had no distributor, but by then he probably did have a reasonable work print to show anyone who might be interested. As early as July 5 Minotaur had written the Production Code Administration inquiring about a temporary Code Seal; Joe Breen immediately cabled back asking to see a basic story synopsis, but none was forthcoming.[27] Indeed, it appears that the PCA never received a script or synopsis, highly unusual for the time.

Kubrick had somehow survived the long months that *Fear and Desire* sat on the shelf with no distributor in sight, and now it was happening again. Joseph Burstyn had recognized *Fear and Desire* as a rare bird, an English-language production suitable for art house distribution (not unlike *Little Fugitive*), but the more commercially oriented *Kiss Me, Kill Me* had to compete with B-budget melodramas still pouring out of Hollywood studios. Roger Corman, another hopeful independent filmmaker just two years older than Kubrick, produced *The Fast and the Furious* in May 1954 (in nine days!) for $50,000.[28] Kubrick's film had to compete with dozens of others like this, but his cast was headed by Frank Silvera and Jamie Smith, while Corman offered Dorothy Malone and John Ireland (who also directed).

In August the Kubrick/Sobotka joint bank account was overdrawn and Manufacturer's Trust charged them a $1.73 fee.[29] That fall he drew $700 in cash from the Minotaur account, the only direct salary payment he would see from this picture. Although $500 had already been spent on printing and processing stills during production, another hundred dollars' worth of stills were printed up in November. Records show that in December and January Minotaur paid for office space at a cost of $75 a month, apparently at 165 West Forty-Sixth Street.[30] No longer just an artsy little operation run out of Ruth Sobotka's apartment in the East Village, Kubrick's project was now going professional. He had even gotten himself an agent.

Adeline Schulberg, ex-wife of Paramount executive B. P. Schulberg and mother of *On the Waterfront* screenwriter Budd Schulberg, was one of the best-connected literary agents in New York. She was also known to moonlight as a talent scout for Columbia, but on December 9, 1954, Ad Schulberg ran

Kiss Me, Kill Me for Max Youngstein, the head of advertising and publicity for United Artists. Youngstein was impressed, and the next morning sent off a very enthusiastic memo to UA president Arthur Krim. Along with Robert Benjamin, Krim had pioneered the strategy of licensing product from independent producers when they worked at Eagle-Lion (Youngstein was another veteran). Tino Balio sees their work at Eagle-Lion, where they distributed such films as *Close-Up, Port of New York* and *Mr. Universe*, as an "indispensable" prelude to their successful reimaging of United Artists in the 1950s.[31]

Youngstein reminded Krim that Kubrick was the same young man who had shown them *Day of the Fight* years earlier. His new film was

> [N]ot an ordinary picture and doesn't have the usual commercial elements. It is too long in spots, it has to be cut, its photography is often too dark, there is much that you will think is bad but, for me, it has most unusual plus qualities and I think you ought to see it as soon as possible next week. The print is in the projection booth.

Youngstein suggested that this was the sort of film that could be "entered into some of the foreign film festivals and win important notices." He noted that "Mrs. Schulberg asks $150,000 for the picture world wide," but "I think it can be gotten for less." Yet what really seems to have attracted him was not the quality of this one off-beat film, but establishing a relationship with a discovery of great potential importance. "Kubrick needs money badly," Youngstein concluded. "This kid is about 25 years of age. I certainly haven't seen anything that shows this much talent in years."[32]

Ad Schulberg appears to have been the one who sold Stanley Kubrick to United Artists, but nothing in any records I have seen indicates what sort of fee she might have earned. Indeed, the online inventory of her papers at Dartmouth does not even show Stanley Kubrick as one of her clients. Was this some sort of personal favor? In any case, word traveled fast. Frank Zucker wrote to Minotaur on February 17, after hearing that United Artists was negotiating to purchase the film for a rumored $75,000 with a further $37,000 payable out of potential distribution profits. Zucker noted that Minotaur was indebted to CECO in the amount of $20,361.42; he proposed that CECO receive $15,000 of the initial $75,000, with the balance payable out of those later profits. Titra followed with a similar letter on February 23.[33] De Luxe had just struck three prints of the film, and surviving notes to the negative cutter indicate that Kubrick suddenly trimmed it by several minutes, perhaps at UA's request. On March 16 Sol Konecoff of United Artists, acting as if he was already the distributer, shipped a copy to the Motion Picture Association of America, a necessary step in acquiring a Code Seal. *Fear and Desire* had never received a Code Seal. It was handled by a distributor who was not a member of the MPAA and was exhibited only in theaters outside the control of any of the Association's member companies. The lack of a Seal limited its circulation, for the most part, to independent theaters specializing in exploitation or art house product. United Artists, an MPAA member, would not distribute the film without a Code Seal, so nothing could be finalized until the PCA had spoken and Kubrick had accepted whatever it was they demanded.[34] Not until all these details were attended to would *Motion Picture Daily* report UA's acquisition of the film on July 27; the first promotional screenings were held on August 8.[35]

Cinematic Beginnings

Budd Schulberg and Elia Kazan had spent years developing the script of *On the Waterfront*, but only a few short months of postproduction were required before opening the film on Broadway. The situation with *Killer's Kiss* was exactly the opposite: a reputed two weeks for Kubrick and Sackler to string together their "mechanically constructed" plot line, but one and a half years between the end of principal photography and the day United Artists finally got the film into theaters. So while Kazan was being prodded by Sam Spiegel to lock the film up quickly, Stanley Kubrick had a lot of time on his hands and nothing much to do but stare at a moviola. What happened during those months was not so much a polishing of the script he and Sackler had written in 1953 but an extended learning experience in which Kubrick taught himself how a film might be created in the editing room, a private space in which he alone could exercise the power of creation, locked away from actors, investors, disgruntled crew members, inclement weather, and grafting police officers.

A director like Kazan would have been scornful of the old Hollywood nostrum that any troubled film could be saved in the editing room. Could a mechanical process really overcome the defects of a poor script and an uninspired performance? Kubrick lacked Kazan's artistic pedigree, but he had read Pudovkin, whose analysis of film technique convinced him that the editing room was exactly where the art of film really happened.[36] Pudovkin studied with the first master of Soviet montage, Lev Kuleshov, who "maintained that film-art does not begin when the artists act and the various scenes are shot—this is only the preparation of the material." Considering the material Kubrick had to work with, this advice could only be heartening. "Film-art begins from the moment when the director begins to combine and join together the various pieces of film. By joining them in various combinations, in different orders, he obtains different results."[37] So Kubrick began to combine and recombine the material he had prepared, learning his craft by literally taking a page from the history of silent cinema.

"My sort of fantasy image of the movies was created in the Museum of Modern Art, where I looked at Stroheim and D. W. Griffith and Eisenstein," he told an interviewer while shooting *Full Metal Jacket*.[38] Their work was what had inspired him to become a filmmaker, and it was based, as often as not, on effects created through the juxtaposition of iconic images. Kubrick may have been the first postwar filmmaker to draw inspiration not only from his immediate cultural environment but also from a cinematic legacy largely laid down before he was even born. "I think that silent films got a lot more things right than the talkies," he admitted to Michel Ciment.[39]

So instead of developing the psychology of one or two major characters, Kubrick follows the masters and indicates character through juxtaposition, a not-so-simple compare and contrast exercise he picked up during long sessions at the Museum of Modern Art. Unlike *Fear and Desire*, very little in *Killer's Kiss* depends on the spoken word, and the film expresses itself largely through editing and cinematography. The frequently noted issue of doubling, for example, is developed almost entirely through Kubrick's juxtaposition of one set of actions or characters with another (compare this to *Little Fugitive*, for example, where the narrative line sticks to one character and one adventure). Davey and Gloria are both in the business of offering their bodies for the amusement of strangers and function more like mirror images than a typical romantic couple. When they leave for work they travel down parallel staircases and exit by the same door. At home, their apartment windows have only one view: the other person's apartment. Gloria's life as a taxi dancer is an echo of her sister's career, while Davey's attraction to Gloria differs from Vince's obsession mainly in its lack of fatal passion (this is the first Kubrick film in which the least emotional characters emerge as the survivors but certainly not the last). Vince may be an old man who "smells bad," but Davey, a veteran whose career has been "one long promise without fulfillment," is facing a similar set of issues. Kubrick uses classical montage strategies to build these associations, such as when he intercuts Davey's losing fight with the simultaneous wrestling match between Gloria and Vince. From Kuleshov he understood that just as editing can place a Brooklyn dance hall in Times Square or provide Vince Rapallo's office with a TV set, it can also generate character and emotion. As with Virginia Leith in *Fear and Desire*, Chris Chase's "performance" while she is tied to a chair in Vince's warehouse is constructed entirely through editing.

During those long months at the Moviola (subsidized by Titra's deferment), Kubrick had time to try all sorts of combinations. "Everything we did cost so little that there was no pressure on us—an advantage I was never to encounter again," he told Alexander Walker.[40] He could put things in, take a bit of time, and then maybe take them out again. Some sources describe a fantasy sequence in which Davey dreams of walking along Forty-Second Street wearing nothing but his trunks and boxing gloves. Was this intended as a parody of the landmark print ads Maidenform had been running since 1949? Or possibly an homage to a similar dream sequence in George Cukor's *The Marrying Kind*

(1952)? David Hughes suggests that Kubrick dropped the scene because the nearly naked prizefighter failed to elicit enough of a reaction from Broadway bystanders.[41] Whatever the reason, he certainly had plenty of time to come to a decision.

In another example, Kubrick shot footage of Davey on the subway, opening and reading a letter from his Uncle George and Aunt Grace in Seattle. As this is still the early 1950s, they are farmers. The letter, photographed in situ so that we can read it, begins like this: "We all hope you have been well. We try and follow your career as best as we can out here. . . ." But back at Titra's dubbing studio weeks or months later, Kubrick decided on a completely different voice-over: "We still haven't heard from ye yet this month and we wondered if everything was still all right with ya. . . ." The voice actor reading these lines adopts a stereotypical hayseed accent (which sounds nothing like Davey's) that seems intended to emphasize the gulf between the cynicism and corruption of the city and the corn-fed purity of Davey's country roots—a convention of nineteenth-century melodrama. Kubrick had established this even earlier through the farmhouse photographs placed around Davey's apartment. The hero and heroine hope to escape to this rustic Eden—indeed, this is Davey's main concern as he narrates the film to us from Pennsylvania Station. Again, this is quite a contrast to *On the Waterfront*, where Edie Doyle, raised by nuns in the countryside, tries to get Terry to escape the crime and corruption of the city with her. "Out west some place. A farm." To which he (and the audience) replies, "A farm?!" It seems that crickets make him nervous.

Flash forward twenty years to Martin Scorsese's *Taxi Driver* (1976), a film more influenced by *Killer's Kiss* than *On the Waterfront*, where Travis Bickle hopes to send little Iris back to the purity of her own family farm, another idyllic retreat conjured through black-and-white photographs and the heavily accented reading of "letters from home" (Iris, by the way, is also the name of Gloria's sister in *Killer's Kiss*). Of course, while Kubrick and Scorsese leave their audiences wondering just how happy that resolution actually might be, Kazan simply has his main character blow off the whole idea.

And then there is the ending, the one part of the film that many critics see as out of character for a Stanley Kubrick film, a noir film in general, and this violent and cynical exercise in particular. The troubled hero waits at the train station for his blonde femme fatale—and as the film pulls out of its final flashback she runs down the stairs and into his arms like someone in a David Lean picture. According to Vincent Lo Brutto, "concerns about box office potential weakened Kubrick's resolve for the film's conclusion. Doomed lovers of film noir never find happiness. The hero never finds peace. . . . The gloomy tone of the film was established but not sustained to its conclusion. Kubrick's film noir adventure was truncated."[42]

Chris Chase wrote her sister during production about the fluidity of the film's conclusion. "We have shot a bunch of endings for this plate of hash, and by now I don't know if I'm a bad guy or a good guy. There's one version where I kill the villain, there's another version where I try to seduce him, there's been more killing and resurrection than you'll find in the Bible."[43]

In the Stanley Kubrick Archive are a number of stills showing Vince, Davey, and Gloria all lying among the shattered mannequins in the warehouse, with Skippy Adelman—seen briefly in the released version as the warehouse manager—surveying the carnage. Was the film to have ended here? Is this where she killed the villain? If so, how did she get to this second warehouse? Or was it always a second warehouse and not simply another corner of the original warehouse, the one where she was tied to a chair? In that case, there would have been no need for the action sequence across the rooftops, leading from warehouse one to warehouse two. And maybe even no need for the Penn Station sequence at all (a late addition to the film, in any case). While the writing of *On the Waterfront* generated three years' worth of script drafts for historians to ponder, not a line of any *Killer's Kiss* script has so far turned up, making it impossible to know just how much of the film was there on the page all along and how much was created in the editing room at Titra.

Fear and Desire is essentially a literary text (at times approaching blank verse) dramatized by striking cinematography and targeted at the art house market. *Killer's Kiss* was something else entirely, a conscious pastiche of action sequences played out against a generic gangster movie plot. Roger Corman could make a gangster melodrama like *Machine Gun Kelly* (1958) with a straight face, but Kubrick was no Roger Corman. What still makes the film interesting to modern audiences is the distance the filmmaker establishes between himself and his material. While not an outright parody, *Killer's Kiss* is extremely self-conscious regarding its place in the continuing history of stage and screen melodrama. Traditionally, melodrama is seen as a strand of popular theater, developed during the Victorian era, which dealt with the interaction of types (in simplest form, a hero, heroine, and villain) rather than the exploration of psychologically individuated characters. An emotional form, it employed music (*melos*) not just metaphorically but as a practical element, with musical sequences frequently deployed throughout. Melodrama also emphasized spectacular action and reveled in such tricky plot devices as coincidence, all of which would be rejected by theatrical modernists like Ibsen and O'Neill. Endings tended to be positive, suggesting that in the final analysis this world is both rational and just. In the twentieth century, Hollywood movies would corner this dramatic market. Like most of Kubrick's films, *Fear and Desire* is not a melodrama, but *Killer's Kiss* certainly is.

Critics and audiences sensed these melodramatic roots in *Killer's Kiss*, but it was still too early to fully absorb the self-consciousness. *Variety* felt that "the yarn too frequently is reminiscent of old fashioned mellers which had the hero dashing up in the nick to save his beloved from the villain."[44] Exactly. A more modern interpretation, summarized by James Naremore, asks us to think of the film as a fairy tale, "a story about a fair maiden who is rescued by a kind of knight errant from the clutches of an ogre."[45] While *Killer's Kiss* certainly contains many elements identified with the film noir cycle, the fit is not especially neat. In trying to shape their material for a popular market, Kubrick and Sackler (art film devotees with scant interest in the routine of Hollywood genre film production) would have tried to understand the sources of contemporary screen melodrama and looked there for inspiration. Given what we see on screen, one likely source would have been A. Nicholas Vardac's influential 1949 study, *Stage to Screen: Theatrical Method from Garrick to Griffith*.[46] Vardac's book argued that a straight line could be drawn from the increasingly mechanized theatrical spectacles of the nineteenth century (like *Blue Jeans*) through David Belasco's concern with naturalistic staging techniques to the early film melodramas of D. W. Griffith. The book is heavily illustrated with nineteenth-century theatrical advertisements and early-twentieth-century motion picture stills, offered as visual evidence of this aesthetic continuity. I have not found Kubrick citing Vardac directly, but he did frequently reference the theoretical work of Sergei Eisenstein, whose seminal "Dickens, Griffith, and the Film Today" essay also pointed to these same conclusions.[47]

Kubrick certainly knew he was working in this tradition, and one can find clues even in the simplest elements of decor. Minor-league mobster Vince Rapallo has an office in the back of his dance hall, the walls adorned with not one, but four or five Victorian-era theatrical melodrama posters: *The Cherry Pickers, The Winning of Barbara Worth, A New York Girl,* and at least two for *Blue Jeans*, one of which features the classic "buzz-saw" scene, with the hero tied to a log and the heroine bursting through a door just in the nick. Once, when Vince is feeling especially humiliated, Kubrick cuts to a poster of two laughing vaudevillians (Weber and Fields?) not previously established in the room. The function of the posters in this film, we must assume, is more reflective than decorative.

Of course, it is also possible that Kubrick put those posters there just because he liked them. One of his most interesting *Look* magazine assignments involved aspiring showgirl Rosemary Williams, whom he documented for an unpublished 1949 photo essay. Like Walter Cartier, she is seen at home, at work, on the street, in church, and in her own kitchen. Rosemary's kitchen (more a tiny kitchenette) is decorated with not one but two posters from Charles Callahan's *The New Fogg's Ferry*.[48] Kubrick's *Look* photos are notorious for their theatrical staging, with Kubrick posing figures and redecorating environments in order to achieve certain narrative effects. We can believe that Rosemary Williams and

"Vince Rapallo" both had a passion for Victorian melodrama posters. Or we can believe that they shared the same decorator: Stanley Kubrick.

This is not to say that Kubrick, whose idea of a great film was anything directed by Ingmar Bergman, had any regard for the unsophisticated worldview of theatrical melodrama (as noted earlier, he was embarrassed by the film). Characters may become older and wiser because of their experiences, but no one in *Way Down East* or *Killer's Kiss* develops, emotionally or psychologically, because of the events in the plot. Hero or villain, they are the same person in the end as they were in the beginning. This, of course, is the opposite of what happens in *On the Waterfront*, where the whole point of the film, as Kazan wrote in his production notebook, was the restoration of the hero's dignity.[49] For reasons of their own, Kubrick and Sackler had chosen to work in a different tradition here, which privileged action and plot over character and psychology. Nor did they want to pursue the socially conscious route followed by something like Edward McSorley's original *Crime on the Waterfront* draft, where economic and cultural forces call all the shots. Instead, they opted to work within the dependable tradition of *Blue Jeans* or *The Streets of New York*, where stereotypical characters played out conventionalized dramatic conflicts, and style was *everything*. Which is why they made a melodrama, complete with happy ending, and probably why Sackler, also embarrassed, thought better of having his name attached to it. When it finally issued the film an MPAA Seal, the Production Code Administration filled out an "Analysis of Film Content" form for its own files, characterizing the themes, locations, characters, and plot elements. At the bottom of the first page, under "ENDING," are some boxes to check. The analyst put a big X in the one marked "HAPPY."[50]

One of the most interesting things about this detailed multipage form, which was compiled internally in an effort to assemble information about general industry trends, is that it gives us the length of the film at the moment it was approved by the PCA. Records in the Kubrick Archive show that on February 15, 1955, the lab invoiced Minotaur for three 35 mm prints, each with a length of 6,678 feet (seventy-four minutes). One of those prints was certainly the one shipped to the MPAA on March 16 by United Artists, already acting as the film's distributor. The print was received on March 18, and Geoffrey Shurlock responded on March 22 with a series of suggested cuts.

He had three major issues. In the fourth reel of the film the love scene between Davey and Gloria needed to be recut "so that it ends before the boy pushes the girl down on the bed," in order to excise the "unmistakable indication of a sex affair." In the sixth reel, "the young man looking at the apartment is obviously a 'pansy.' Such a characterization is unacceptable under the Code and would have to be eliminated." This refers to a character played by Shaun O'Brien, who receives screen credit but is no longer visible in the film. His role had already attracted attention, as evidenced by a handwritten note on a lab report, dated March 16, 1955, stating cryptically that "censor cut end of Shaun scene."[51] Once Shurlock looked at the film, the entire scene was eliminated. The final point involved the film's dramatic climax: "It is our opinion that the concluding sequence among the mass of nude mannequins is unacceptable as now edited. Certain portions of these scenes seem to go too far in their exploitation of the nudity of the mannequins. We feel that considerable elimination would be required in order that final Code approval could be rendered."[52] Kubrick accepted these cuts on May 18, also informing the Motion Picture Association that the title of the film had been changed from *Kiss Me, Kill Me* to *The Killer's Kiss*. Five days later the Association issued the film certificate #17520 at a length of 6,323 feet (seventy minutes).[53]

These PCA cuts had totaled nearly four minutes. But by the time the film was shown to the trade in August it was down to sixty-seven minutes, approximately 6,030 feet of film. I have no idea how or why this already short film was further reduced by another three minutes and twenty seconds after it had already been passed by the Production Code Administration.[54] Perhaps if we could find one of the three seventy-four-minute prints of *Kiss Me, Kill Me* struck by the lab in February? Such precensorship cuts were almost never preserved, but in this case one of them appears to have survived at least until 2005, when Taschen published *The Stanley Kubrick Archives*. The book includes many frame enlargements drawn from prints in Kubrick's own collection, including one showing the main title superimposed over the introductory shot of Penn Station. The name of the film is *Kiss Me, Kill Me*.

The figure of $75,000 for "Sale of *Killer's Kiss*" is repeated in Minotaur's "Statement of Profit and Loss" dated July 30, 1960. But as the "Cost of Production" is given as $89,188.64, the tally shows a loss of $14,188.64 on the sale. Beyond that, additional indirect expenses of $5,508.13 are also listed, despite the fact that nearly all of those charges had already been included in the $89,188.64 "Cost of Production." The corporate loss then totaled $19,696.77, which would seem to have effectively cut out any unsecured participants.[55]

In general, the industry trade papers were supportive and praised what the UA pressbook hoped they would, namely the location filming and photographic genius of Stanley Kubrick. "Filmed in and about New York City, Kubrick lets the camera tell the story, using a minimum of dialogue to good effect," noted *Motion Picture Daily*.[56] But the trade papers had to review everything. Other critics, under no such compulsion, simply ignored the film, which (unlike *Fear and Desire*) was not reviewed by the *New York Times*, the *New Yorker*, *Newsweek*, *Theatre Arts*, or the *Saturday Review*. British critic Gavin Lambert may have been the film's strongest early supporter, praising its "neorealist approach to human behavior, a feeling for the place and the moment, [and] the apparently trivial or commonplace which yields up dramatic meaning." In an earlier notice he had singled out the scene of Davey watching Gloria from across the

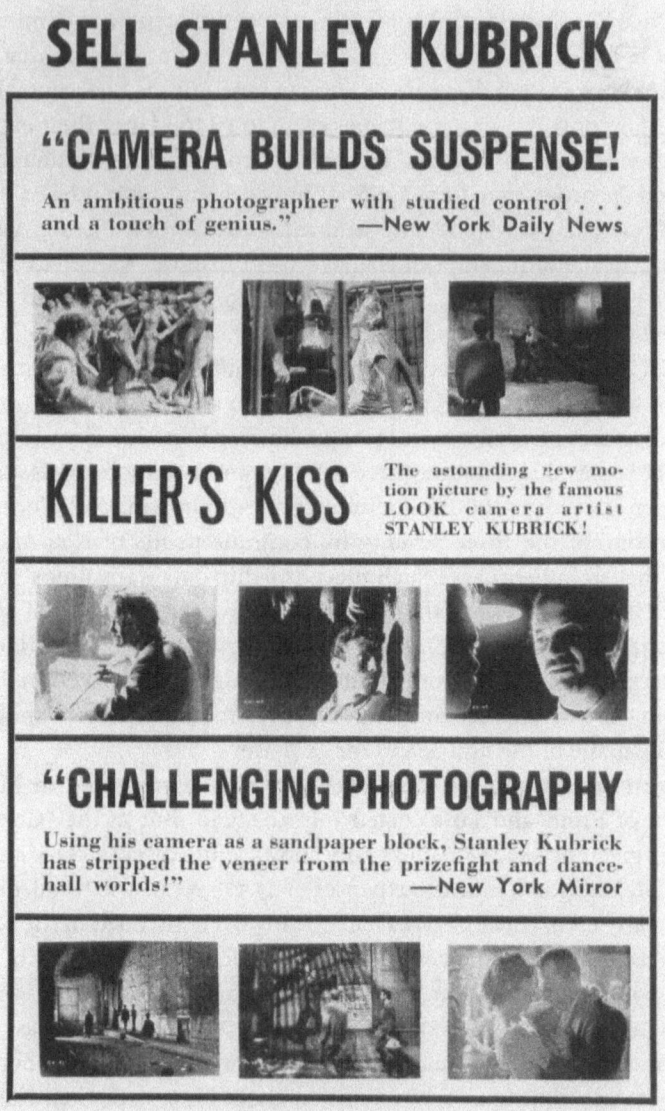

15.1. United Artists' publicity for *Killer's Kiss* focused on Stanley Kubrick's astounding camera artistry. Courtesy John McElwee/Greenbriar Picture Shows.

courtyard as having "an almost Zavattini quality."[57] It is hard to imagine the definition of neorealism Lambert is trying to apply here; he senses something of importance is going on but can't quite find the words for it.

Minotaur's cumulative profit and loss statement of July 30, 1960, says very clearly that the only income the corporation saw from *Killer's Kiss* was the

$75,000 payment from United Artists, leading to the losses described earlier. I have not seen the actual UA contract, which may or may not have included a clause allowing for a share of distribution receipts. Although the Kubrick Archive retains numerous daily receipt forms from theaters throughout the United States during its 1955–1956 run, the documents do not seem complete and no cumulative total for *Killer's Kiss* appears to survive there.[58] John McElwee cites figures showing only 3,130 bookings for the film (as opposed to 7,284 for *GOG*, a low-budget science-fiction film UA released in 1954). According to McElwee, this limited release brought in $130,285 domestically and $143,993 in foreign revenue.[59] Even if these figures include television, nontheatrical, and other ancillary revenue (and allowing for the cost of prints and advertising), one would have expected a few extra dollars left over for Minotaur's financial participants.

The few people who actually saw *Killer's Kiss* during its domestic theatrical release would have run into it as a supporting feature, the bottom half of a double bill headed by a more important UA release. Although it was occasionally paired with Charles Laughton's *Night of the Hunter* (great programming), *Killer's Kiss* was more frequently attached to a second or third run of David Lean's *Summertime*. But just how much of the picture did those audiences actually see? Like *On the Waterfront*, *Killer's Kiss* was an independent production shot in New York but released to theaters by a major distributor. There is no direct evidence that either film was photographed with "safe areas" at the top and bottom of each frame, suggesting that both were shot in the conventional 1.37:1 ratio. But that may or may not have influenced how theaters actually projected them. *Summertime*, according to the American Film Institute, was made almost a full year after *Killer's Kiss* and shot in the wider 1.85:1 ratio. The small number of theaters that actually booked Kubrick's film along with it might have changed their screen masking, lenses, and aperture plates to accommodate a different aspect ratio for this second feature (and then changed everything back again), but that seems like a lot of work for no practical benefit. Because of the late release of this film (1955–1956), it seems more likely that audiences at all 3,130 bookings sat through *Killer's Kiss* with the top and bottom of each frame cut off.[60] It could be argued that viewing it this way today would replicate the original performance experience, but that is not an experience I would care to sit through. The Criterion Collection, which released Blu-ray editions of both films, made no definitive decision about *On the Waterfront* but issued *Killer's Kiss* in 1.37:1 only.[61]

Kubrick appears to have leveraged UA's moderate interest in *Killer's Kiss* into a production deal. As early as June 26, 1955, the *New York Times* reported that he and a new producing partner, James B. Harris, would make *The Clean Break* for United Artists, and that filming would "start here in the fall."[62] Harris was the same age as Kubrick but much better positioned within the industry. He and his father, Joseph Harris, ran Motion Pictures for Television, Inc., "the market leader in the television distribution of feature films" (remember the shipping case that Kubrick casually positioned in an insert?), and James was president of Flamingo Films, a similar operation he hoped to use as the springboard for a move into production.[63] Harris-Kubrick Pictures Corporation would be the vehicle for a series of ambitious films the men would work on together, including *Paths of Glory* and *Lolita*. At first it looked as if they would continue to be based in New York. Kubrick approached Richard Sylbert (like the two partners, also born in 1928) to function as their production designer. Sylbert was primarily involved in local television production and had already designed one or two films, but Kubrick never followed up.[64] In September, just as *Killer's Kiss* was sneaking into a handful of neighborhood theaters on the Loew's circuit, the *Times* reported that Sterling Hayden would star in the new film, which "will go before the cameras in Manhattan, at the Biograph studio in the Bronx and at a racetrack here, starting next month."[65] The Biograph studio had been built for D. W. Griffith in 1913 and would soon be hosting the next generation of New York filmmakers, including Elia Kazan and Richard Sylbert. But Stanley Kubrick never worked there; a month later Harris-Kubrick relocated *The Killing* to Hollywood.[66]

CHAPTER 16

THANK YOU, HOLLYWOOD!

George Justin knew that the success of *On the Waterfront* would transform the New York film industry, lifting all boats in a busy regional production center whose creative personnel still spent most of their time filming nontheatrical subjects, documentaries, and television commercials. It would just take a little time. Boris Kaufman, for example, would finally be able to shoot features again, something he had not done since 1939. He would spend much of the next decade working on films like *Baby Doll, 12 Angry Men, The Fugitive Kind,* and *Splendor in the Grass*, not only establishing a visual signature for the coming New York film renaissance but training the camera crews that would carry the style forward for the next fifty years. Always a busy man, Kaufman finished work in Hoboken in January 1954 and by the time *On the Waterfront* opened six months later had already completed four more films. It would be nice to say that his career immediately turned a corner and that his inbox was suddenly filled with offers to shoot films like *The Group* or *Long Day's Journey Into Night* as soon as the quality of his achievement began to get around.

But in order for this to happen, one of two things needed to take place first. Either the Hollywood unions had to open their registration rolls to East Coast cameramen, or George Justin's campaign to "Keep 'em in the East" needed to gain a lot more traction. Initially, it was the first alternative that seemed more promising. When Kaufman arrived in the United States in 1942 his goal, like that of every other refugee filmmaker, was to find work in Hollywood. While that didn't happen, he did succeed in landing a job with the National Film

Board of Canada (1942–1943) and followed that with a two-year stint at the Office of War Information.[1] Out of a job when the OWI closed down, Kaufman revived his campaign to establish himself as a Hollywood cameraman and pulled what strings he could to test the waters. Unfortunately, the directors he had worked with in France were not the ones who had subsequently established themselves in Hollywood (Jean Renoir, Julien Duvivier, Anatole Litvak), so Kaufman turned to some of his OWI contacts instead. As it happened, many of these men were working on the fringes of the Hollywood industry in the same sort of marginal genres that were already flourishing in New York.

One of the people he knew was LeRoy Robbins, a Farm Security Administration photographer who had shot stills for the major studios and was branching out into documentaries.[2] Robbins had recently returned to Los Angeles and had made a few inquiries about the possibility of bringing out a cameraman with Kaufman's background and skill set. The response was not good. Indeed, "the answers have all been about the same—that it is now too late. During the war, they say, some permits were given out but now that it is over and men are returning the thing is closed tighter than ever before."[3] The problem was not with the producers but with the union. The business manager of Local 659 did not turn him down out of hand but instead told Robbins that a "board of review" would pass on the qualifications of any such person, something he did not find encouraging. The only possibility of winning a union card was to relocate to California, find a producer willing to promote you, and "spend a little time here and put up a fight." And even this slim chance applied only to work in the documentary field. The fact that Kaufman stayed in New York—where he would eventually become the biggest fish in a much smaller pond—may have been the luckiest thing that ever happened to him.

But Kaufman also knew several important East Coast documentarians, including Willard Van Dyke, Alexander Hammid, and Henwar Rodakiewicz, who hired him to shoot such films as *Journey Into Medicine* (1946) and *Land of Enchantment: Southwest U.S.A.* (1948). He became a naturalized U.S. citizen in 1947 and joined Local 644 the following year, a credential that allowed him to work on whatever theatrical films might be available in New York.[4] He teamed with the director Justin Herman on a series of Paramount Pacemaker shorts, including *The Lambertville Story*, *The Football Fan* (a 1949 Tom Ewell comedy), and the Oscar-nominated *Roller Derby Girl*, films that should have established his reputation as a fast, agile, and elegant cinematographer. But for some reason he seemed unable to move up to features. He began work on *The Big Break* in October 1950 but was replaced by Bill Miller.[5] *On the Waterfront* would be Kaufman's first screen credit on an American feature but, as noted earlier, he was at best the third choice. When Kazan saw him on the roof in Hoboken he immediately had second thoughts about his new cameraman, worried that Kaufman might not have the physical strength to survive there an entire winter. Instead, he soon realized he had found "the best cameraman I have ever worked with."[6]

Indeed, Kazan wrote to Kaufman on May 25, 1954, just before the start of shooting on his next film, *East of Eden*: "I tried to get you out here [to Hollywood] to photograph this picture for me. I made a strong effort and was completely blocked by the union here and also by the studio." He described an industry screening of *On the Waterfront*, after which "everyone there has called me remarking on how beautifully photographed the picture is and how unusual and new your work is." The reaction seemed general throughout the industry. "My secretary, who was at the showing, remarked, 'It's true.' So you should feel good and I should feel grateful, and I do." But the most important information in the letter was Kazan's revelation that "having made one picture in the east and found it worked out fine, I think in the future I'll put most of my time in there."[7]

Kaufman—who had no agent and was accustomed to making his career as a freelancer—responded with equal amounts of flattery, camaraderie, and self-promotion. He told Kazan that he had finished two more features and a "very interesting" short since *On the Waterfront*, but what he didn't say was that one was a documentary on tuberculosis, the second was a nudist film, and the third was, in all essentials but language, a Yiddish picture.[8] This sort of work was very typical of life in the East Coast film industry, but leaving such marginalia behind had been his main career goal for the past decade.

Kaufman seemed most proud of the documentary, *Within Man's Power*, which he had shot for the National Tuberculosis Association at an industrial film studio in Washington. Working with producer-director Nicholas Webster he created an "impressionistic" lighting scheme in which optical fades and dissolves were replaced by a complex series of lighting cues (as many as eighteen per scene). This allowed real-time scene changes on the film's numerous and highly stylized sets, which consisted mainly of props and furniture shot against black velvet.[9] This sort of lighting would have been more familiar on stage or live television, and Kaufman clearly enjoyed the opportunity to do something that seemed as different as possible from the open-air realism of *On the Waterfront*. It was the one film he hoped to be able to show Kazan the next time they met.

He was not so keen on *Garden of Eden*, which he shot March 15–25 at the Lake Como Club outside of Tampa. A job is a job, but one wonders why Kaufman agreed to do a nudist film as his immediate follow-up to *On the Waterfront*. In his letter to Kazan he says only that he has shot a film "in Eastman Color with very happy results colorwise but ludicrous story."[10] Perhaps he was in need of a Florida vacation (he and his wife both stayed at the camp)? Perhaps he was talked into it by the director, Max Nosseck, whom he probably knew from their days at Joinville Studios in Paris before the war? Indeed, judged as part of Kaufman's filmography, the nymph-in-the-woods footage here does recall his 1935 short, *La fontaine d'Arethuse*, an art film he once shot for Dimitri Kirsanoff.

When a West Coast talent agency wrote to Kaufman soliciting him as a client after a screening of *On the Waterfront*, they themselves brought up *Garden of Eden*. "We, of course, will see it and would very much like to use this as a further example of the quality of your work."[11] That never happened. Not as salacious as other nudist films, *Garden of Eden* offers a sincere defense of nudism as both natural and therapeutic but still faced monumental censorship hurdles. It did not open in New York until December 1957, when the *Times*, noting Kaufman's contribution with some surprise, dismissed it as a "limp dramatic ritual with all the flair of a television commercial."[12] Years later Kaufman often felt he was losing assignments because the industry had labeled him a black-and-white cameraman; perhaps he had seen this coming in 1954 and jumped on the first opportunity that came by.[13]

The third film Kaufman referenced, in which "I had some fun with a dream sequence," was *Singing in the Dark*, a nightclub musical involving a gangster (Lawrence Tierney), a Borscht Belt comedian (Joey Adams), and an amnesiac Holocaust survivor (Moishe Oysher). A subplot involves a psychiatrist whose use of narcohypnotic therapy helps Oysher access his repressed traumas. Max Nosseck, who had brought Kaufman into *Garden of Eden*, not only directed but produced, in partnership with Oysher and Adams. Nosseck had made *Overture to Glory* in 1939, one of the last prewar Yiddish pictures, in which Oysher played a cantor who abandons his religious calling for a concert career. *Singing in the Dark* again provided Oysher an opportunity to explore both sides of his repertoire—religious as well as secular—but the use of the Holocaust as little more than a plot device to explain the cantor's current nightclub gig is uncomfortable at best. Kaufman did not shoot the film's European location footage but worked on interiors at the Movietone studio beginning on May 3; his contract called for fifteen days of work at $150 per day, his usual rate. I suspect he also shot the film's wonderfully fogbound credit sequence, which may be the dream sequence he mentioned to Kazan.[14] Unimpressive in terms of acting and directing, *Singing in the Dark* is notable as one of the first films to deal with the effect of the Holocaust on its survivors, although a more sophisticated account would have to wait for *The Pawnbroker*—which Kaufman himself would shoot a dozen years later.

In traditional East Coast style, Kaufman then signed with IMPS, Inc., an independent producer of documentaries and industrial films that was looking to break into the feature picture business. They had a script, *Crowded Paradise*, a "semi-documentary on the life of Puerto Rican immigrants in New York City," which was set to begin filming at Movietone on May 12 (a schedule that would have overlapped with that of *Singing in the Dark*).[15] The director was Fred Pressburger (son of the émigré Austrian producer Arnold Pressburger), sets had been constructed by Richard Sylbert (his first film work), and Zoli Vidor had been hired as cinematographer. But according to Sylbert, "the company ran into serious money problems and closed down until the financing could be straightened out."[16] Sylbert left town for another project and was surprised to learn that the film had been revived during his absence and that Boris Kaufman was now behind the camera. In late July, while reporting to Kazan on the opening of *On the Waterfront*, Kaufman noted that he had just finished *Crowded Paradise*, "a feature about the Portoricans [sic] in the New York jungle. I think it can be a good picture if it isn't messed up in editing."[17]

Crowded Paradise is one of the most striking examples of the postwar immigrant saga, as well as a textbook example of New York independent cinema. The story focuses on a young Puerto Rican immigrant played by Mario Alcade and the class-based prejudice he faces inside New York's established Puerto Rican community (his prospective father-in-law, played by Frank Silvera, refuses to allow his daughter to marry the penniless newcomer). But the film is stolen by Hume Cronyn, whose portrayal of the building's janitor—a racist alcoholic—recalls his sadistic Capt. Munsey in Mark Hellinger's *Brute Force*. Although Kaufman thought he had finished with the film in July, a year later the *Times* reported that the production still had two weeks of shooting to go, with Boris Kaufman still behind the camera.[18] The protracted shooting of an underfunded independent picture—something that Frank Silvera would certainly have been familiar with—was all too common in New York. In his memoir, Richard Sylbert recalled that he never saw the film and couldn't remember if it was ever released. In fact, *Crowded Paradise* opened in New York two years after Kaufman first thought he had finished with it. *Singing in the Dark* was on the shelf nearly as long, while *Garden of Eden* took three and a half years before it opened at the Rialto. All three of these films took even longer to reach local screens than Stanley Kubrick's *Killer's Kiss*. If Kaufman thought that any of them might serve as further examples of the quality of his work he was in for a long wait.

As soon as *On the Waterfront* opened in New York—July 28, 1954—Kaufman received a letter from Bernard Sindell of the Jaffe Agency in Hollywood.[19] Sindell was soliciting Kaufman as a client, but despite noting that his "contribution to the film was outstanding," he offered little hope that he might be able to shoot a film in Hollywood. "It appears that this is most difficult to accomplish," he wrote, because the New York Local had recently turned down a West Coast cameraman's request to shoot a film in the east and Local 659 was not in a cooperative mood (could he possibly be referring to the rejection of Harry Stradling as photographer of *On the Waterfront*?). Indeed, when Sindell checked with the Local he received the same dismissive reply that LeRoy Robbins had gotten in 1945. Kaufman would have to write a letter making his case and wait for a response from "the local board." But even this could not be done without a firm offer in hand, and Sindell advised Kaufman "to do nothing about this until we have a bona fide offer acceptable to you to work here." Such an offer never came.

Kaufman was nominated for membership in the Hollywood-based American Society of Cinematographers on September 14, but this was an honorary society and not a union.[20] Six months later Sindell appealed to the ASC for help in getting their new member work on the West Coast, but was told that they "had arrived at the irrevocable conclusion that no out-of-state cameraman or non-members would be given special dispensation for employment here."[21] He advised Kaufman to contact the New York Local to see if they might be able to coordinate some sort of reciprocity deal. Nothing doing. Nine days later Kaufman won the Academy Award for filming *On the Waterfront*, but that still did nothing to change his outsider status as far as Local 659 was concerned.[22]

It was now pretty clear that the dream of working in Hollywood was a fantasy, at least as far as Boris Kaufman was concerned. But Plan B, George Justin's plan, was suddenly beginning to catch fire. Back in New York the new Oscar winner began work on Rod Serling's *Patterns*, a United Artists feature that Michael Myerberg and Jed Harris were producing.[23] A filmed version of Serling's first hit teleplay, *Patterns* was an early example of a new genre, the prestigious adaptation of some golden age New York television drama (other examples would include *Marty,12 Angry Men, Requiem for a Heavyweight*, and *The Miracle Worker*). While more successful critically than commercially, the cycle would still keep local crews busy for the better part of a decade.

And then Elia Kazan came back.

16.1. Budd Schulberg, Elia Kazan, Boris Kaufman, and Richard Day, just some of New York's Oscar winners that year, line up with their statues at the Century Theatre, March 30, 1955. Bison Archives.

Just before starting production on *East of Eden*, Kazan had written Kaufman about his hopes of returning to New York to make movies. Four months later, with his last Hollywood film in the can, he wrote a memo to his legal team outlining exactly how—and why—he proposed to accomplish this. While other filmmakers were forming their own production companies largely for the capital gains benefits, Kazan insisted that all he really wanted was a way of achieving "complete artistic and operational control."[24] He listed in detail the degree of control he wanted over scripting, casting, editing, and advertising. And he returned, again and again, to his overwhelming desire to escape the Hollywood studio system and all the waste, aggravation, and compromise that came with it. He wanted the power to decide for himself, "when and where and how," he would make his films. "I will no longer allow myself to get into a Zanuck situation," he wrote. "I have discovered that I cannot have complete artistic control unless I have complete operational control." His new company would develop "strong subjects and strong stories, [with] unusual and fresh personalities." Stars would be used as appropriate. Budgets would be medium or modest, "in the neighborhood of ON THE WATERFRONT." "I am not interested in spectacles or spectacular productions."

> My crews will all, I hope, work out of New York City and the locals there. I am sick of the over manning of productions here. The locals here are pushing simply to get jobs for as many of their members as possible. That's all. It seems to me that the piling on of electricians and grips here is shameless. This is one of the main reason [sic] costs here are so foolish. EAST OF EDEN is foolish at one million, seven. Double negative cost is 3 million four. How will I ever make any money out of that? I don't say it's all extravagant crews, but the WATERFRONT crew *was* much much smaller than even our smallest Eden crew.

For an independent producer, Hollywood simply did not make economic sense, at least according to Kazan's figures. Studio overhead and excessive labor charges were murderous, a lesson that Louis de Rochemont had already learned. But working in New York with George Justin and Charlie Maguire had revealed another way of making movies that—regardless of its own headaches—was neither foolish nor extravagant.

> The entire operation will be an autonomous unit operating in New York City. It will be organized in New York. The deal will be written in New York. The offices of the production unit will be entirely in New York City. The script preparation will be in New York City. The casting and the signing of actors will be in New York City. Ditto the art work. Ditto all editing. And scoring, and post syncing, and dubbing etc. etc. There are facilities in New York available for all this today.

If Kazan felt he needed to escape from Hollywood, he also knew he had an alternative waiting in New York, a functional production center that already boasted whatever technical facilities and creative personnel he needed to make his own films the way he wanted to make them. The man who had once threatened to shoot *On the Waterfront* guerilla-style, filming on the streets with a handheld camera, made no reference in this memo to the city's notorious shortage of studio space. That was just a real estate issue. What did concern him was finding a creative partner, but he had already taken care of that. In outlining his plans for the future he doesn't mention Budd Schulberg or Marlon Brando or Tennessee Williams, naming only one man as irreplaceable. "I want to use as my cameraman Boris Kauffman [sic], who is a member of the New York local and not acceptable or admissible to the Hollywood local. He is on the whole the best man I have ever worked with."

After a European vacation and a successful return to Broadway with *Cat on a Hot Tin Roof*, Kazan created Newtown Productions and by the end of 1955 had begun shooting *Baby Doll* on location in Mississippi. No longer working with Zanuck or Spiegel, he now served as his own producer and gathered together as many *On the Waterfront* veterans as he could, not just Boris Kaufman but Karl Malden, Charlie Maguire, Gene Milford, Anna Hill Johnstone, and even the script supervisor, Roberta Hodes. Richard and Paul Sylbert, new to the Kazan unit, designed the film. In February 1956 the company shot interiors for *Baby Doll* at the newly reopened Vitagraph studio in Flatbush, where Kaufman had shot *Patterns* the previous summer.[25] Vitagraph was soon joined by the refurbished Gold Medal (Biograph) studio in the Bronx, and Kazan found himself competing with directors like Sidney Lumet, Delbert Mann, and Robert Rossen for the city's top camera crews and design teams. Alliances were made, dissolved, and reestablished.

Kazan eventually soured on George Justin, for example, but formed an even closer relationship with Charlie Maguire. And after *Baby Doll* he even split briefly with Boris Kaufman, not simply because of "your famous 'slowness,'" but because he felt that Kaufman's constant "correcting," "fussing," and "improving" of the lighting had become a "grave nuisance," disturbing his ability to develop scenes with the actors. It was for these reasons, he wrote Kaufman, that he would not be using him on *A Face in the Crowd*.[26] Kaufman, for his part, blamed the production manager, Johnny Johnston, and the fact that the unit had been working in Mississippi without a proper gaffer (electrician).[27] But when Kaufman was nominated for an Academy Award for his work on the film all was forgiven, and the *Baby Doll* team reunited for *Splendor in the Grass* in 1960.

The pool of top creative talent in New York was not all that large in the 1950s and 1960s, so many of these same names, along with a few others, would dominate the credits of New York's most important films well into the 1970s.

By then most of the generation that had laid the groundwork for this postwar renaissance had died off, retired, or like George Justin himself, relocated to Hollywood. But the men and women they had trained, and the infrastructure they established, remained in New York, primed for a Lindsay-era film renaissance that no one, on either coast, had ever predicted.

During the 1980s, the Mayor's Office of Motion Pictures & Television would run a promotional "Why [blank] makes films in New York" campaign, featuring such prominent locals as Sidney Lumet and Martin Scorsese. They all had good reasons, but Woody Allen's were the most personal and the most relevant to an understanding of how and why New York could support an indigenous motion picture industry in the first place. "I like to make films in New York," he said, "because I live in New York and all my friends are here and I like to eat and sleep in my own home." Thirty years earlier, Elia Kazan had had the same idea.

SAT POST	*Saturday Evening Post*
SDGB	*Screen Directors Guild Bulletin*
STR	*Showman's Trade Review*
TA	*Theatre Arts*
TO	*Take One*
SD	*Screen Director*
SW	*Screen Writer*
TVD	*Television Digest*
VAR	*Variety*
WAA	*Washington Afro-American*
WP	*Washington Post*
WSJ	*Wall Street Journal*

NOTES

1. Not Just Another Location

1. "La Guardia Visits First Film Studio," *NYT*, September 22, 1938.
2. Thomas Pryor, "Astoria's Annual Upturn," *NYT*, September 3, 1939.
3. "Movie Trend East Is Noted by Mayor," *NYT*, January 9, 1940.
4. "Mayor to Start Film Firm Here If Others Balk," *NYHT*, November 12, 1939.
5. Frank T. Farrell, "Furnish Studio to Attract Movie Makers," *NYWT*, December 2, 1939.
6. "Once-Famous Movie Studio Here Is Formally Taken Over by Army," *NYT*, September 23, 1942.
7. "Mayor Asks Film Industry to Return to New York Where It Started," *NYT*, October 17, 1939.
8. Douglas Churchill, "Still More on the New York-Hollywood Tie-Up," *NYT*, December 17, 1939. See also Pryor, "Astoria's Annual Upturn." The working title of *Beyond Tomorrow* was *And So Goodbye*.
9. The phrase was Jesse Lasky's. "Paramount to Create Complete Production Center in New York," *EXHW*, October 26, 1929, 45.
10. [A.]F. Edouart, "The Paramount Transparency Process Projection Equipment," *JSMPE*, June 1943, 368–73.
11. A. F. Edouart, "Paramount Triple-Head Transparency Process Projector," *JSMPE*, August 1939, 171–84.
12. "Artful Camera Illusions," *NYT*, November 26, 1933.
13. "Of Local Origin," *NYT*, September 26, 1939.
14. "Minor Producers Will Get No More 35 MM Film," *IP*, October 1942, 22. Independent productions released through major distributors were not affected by this ban.
15. "WPB Clarifies Set-Building," *FD*, May 6, 1942, 1.
16. "*Follies Girl* Starts at Jersey City [*sic*] Studios," *FD*, October 1, 1942, 2.

17. An insert of the theatrical playbill for the show being produced reads "*Follies Girl* with Lew Hearn, Cliff Hall, Weidman Dance Group." All three subsequently perform. Thanks to Robert Kosinski of the Charles Weidman Dance Foundation, Inc., for identifying Charles Weidman on screen here. Email to author, June 17, 2014.
18. "*Follies Girl*," *MPD*, September 15, 1943, 10.
19. "William Rowland Forms Associated Producers," *FD*, August 5, 1942, 8.
20. "P.R.C.," *INDEFB*, July 9, 1945, 26.
21. "Associated Filmakers, Inc.," *The 1945–46 Motion Picture Almanac* (New York: Quigley, 1945), 427–28.
22. "Filmakers Seek Own Studios," *MPH*, December 19, 1942, 18.
23. "Astor Releases *Meadville Patriot*," *STR*, March 25, 1944, 8. The print I screened, in the Library of Congress, ran only thirty-nine minutes and lacked the back story explaining why the reporter has come to Meadville.
24. "Yonkers Studio Planned by Associated Filmakers," *FD*, November 23, 1945, 1.
25. "*The Meadville Patriot*," *EX*, May 31, 1944, 1516.
26. "*The Meadville Patriot*."
27. "Manhattan Bound," *NYT*, January 10, 1943. Not all of these stars appear in the film as released.
28. Thomas M. Pryor, "By Way of Report," *NYT*, July 9, 1944.
29. Carlo Gaberscek, *Sentieri del Western. Dove il cinema he creato il West II* (Gemona: Cineteca del Friuli, 2000).
30. Harold Conrad, "Gotham Grapevine," *BDE*, January 5, 1942.
31. "Along the Rialto," *FD*, July 15, 1942, 4. The film is discussed under its working title, *The Light of Heart*.
32. John Russell Taylor, *Hitch* (New York: Berkley, 1980), 184.
33. "Shadowing Mr. Hitchcock's *Shadow*," *NYT*, November 1, 1942.
34. George Turner, "Hitchcock's Mastery Is Beyond Doubt in *Shadow*," *AC*, May 1993, 62–67.
35. "Shadowing Mr. Hitchcock's *Shadow*."
36. Bill Krohn, *Hitchcock at Work* (London: Phaidon, 2000), 50.
37. Norman Lloyd has an excellent account of John Fulton's contribution to these scenes in *Stages: Of Life in Theatre, Film and Television* (New York: Limelight, 1993), 72–78.
38. At a cost of $1,987, according to Krohn, *Hitchcock*, or $2,979, according to Turner, "Hitchcock's Mastery." In any case, comfortably below the government cap.
39. Ed Sikov, *On Sunset Boulevard* (New York: Hyperion, 1998), 219–21. There is no truth to the assertion by James Sanders in *Scenes from the City* (New York: Rizzoli, 2006), 32, that "the harrowing [Third Avenue] sequence" was filmed on "a single Sunday—New Year's Day, 1944." Not only was this months before Wilder began shooting the film, but New Year's Day in 1944 was a Saturday.
40. Ezra Goodman, "Adventures of a New York Movie Camera Man," *NYT*, March 23, 1947.
41. "Construct *Weekend* Sets," *STR*, September 30, 1944, 25. One of the locations doubled in Los Angeles was P. J. Clarke's saloon, at the northeast corner of Third Avenue and 55th Street.
42. Paramount had set up the liquor store in an empty storefront rented for the occasion. Unfortunately, it was obvious on screen that it was adjacent to St. Agnes's Roman Catholic Church, a municipal violation. "Location New York," *NWSWK*, April 25, 1949.
43. Sikov, *On Sunset Boulevard*, 220.
44. Tom Wood, *The Bright Side of Billy Wilder, Primarily* (New York: Doubleday, 1970), 89; Gene D. Phillips, *Some Like It Wilder* (Lexington: University of Kentucky Press, 2010), 76; Maurice Zolotow, *Billy Wilder in Hollywood* (New York: GP Putnam's, 1977), 129–31.

45. Sikov, *On Sunset Boulevard*, 217.
46. Zolotow, *Billy Wilder*, 131. Italics in the original.
47. "London Acclaims G.I. Screen Star," *NYT*, May 15, 1944.
48. Edwin Schallert, "British Emissaries Due for Talent Search," *LAT*, April 11, 1945; Anthony Slide, *Banned in the U.S.A.* (London: I. B. Tauris, 1998), 154.
49. Michael Powell, *A Life in Movies* (New York: Knopf, 1987), 520; "Canterbury Tale Remake Awaits American Star," *BO*, June 23, 1945, 41.
50. Paul Tritton, *A Canterbury Tale: Memories of a Classic Wartime Movie* (Maidstone, UK: Tritton), 2000, 143–44.
51. Kim Hunter interviewed by Tom Weaver, posted on "The Powell and Pressburger Pages," accessed December 28, 2017.
52. Tritton, *Canterbury Tale*, 144. Laurence was a PR representative for J. Arthur Rank and had previously been a production executive for Goldwyn.
53. Reduced from 124 to 95 minutes, the "American version" was not released until January 1949, and even then it still failed to find an audience. Unfortunately, this cut supplanted the longer version even in England, and audiences did not see the original again until a 1977 restoration. Now it is the American version that is hard to find.
54. "Eastern Shooting Schedules Rise," *MPH*, May 24, 1947, 28.
55. James Sanders, *Celluloid Skyline* (New York: Knopf, 2003), 79, 287–89. The settings for *Week-End at the Waldorf* were even more elaborate; see 291.
56. Goodman, "Adventures."
57. Goodman, "Adventures."
58. "Of Local Origin," *NYT*, October 10, 1945.
59. Goodman, "Adventures." *Duffy's Tavern* and *Easy Come, Easy Go* were among the other Hollywood films said to have been shooting background plates in New York in the autumn of 1945, just as the war ended. See "N.Y. Making Some Inroads On Hollywood," *WP*, June 29, 1947.
60. "Fontaine May Star in New Film at RKO," *NYT*, June 29, 1945; "News of the Screen," *NYT*, August 14, 1945.
61. Rebecca Prime, *Hollywood Exiles in Europe* (New Brunswick, NJ: Rutgers University Press, 2014), 26.
62. "In Hollywood," *MPH*, May 12, 1945, 11.
63. "Prominent Figures Attend *92nd St.* Screening," *FD*, September 17, 1945, 7.
64. *SD*, January 1948, 1.
65. "Texas to Cite WB for *San Antonio*," *MPD*, May 28, 1945, 8.
66. Chas. A. Alicoate, "Production Facilities in and About New York," *FDYBK* (1947), 181.

2. The Pathé Studio: Miniature Hollywood or Just Another False Dawn?

1. "5 Movie Studios Crippled," *BDE*, October 14, 1945.
2. Ralph B. Austrian, "A Complete Motion Picture Production Plant for Metropolitan New York," *JSMPE*, July 1946 [paper presented October 17, 1945], 12–21.
3. "63 percent Valuation Cut on East Side Plot," *NYT*, April 13, 1946.
4. "RKO Pathé Opens East's First Post-War Studio," *FD*, December 13, 1946, 1.
5. Austrian, "Complete Motion Picture Plant," 12.
6. "Neal—Schmidlapp Plan Studio in Mt. Vernon," *FD*, June 25, 1945, 1.
7. "Yonkers Studio Planned by Associated Filmakers," *FD*, November 23, 1945, 1.

8. "Allied Opens Greatest Meeting," *INDEFB*, September 16, 1946, 11; "Allied Undecided on Production Venture," *MPD*, September 17, 1946, 6.
9. "No Theater Okays Last Week," *FD*, August 20, 1946, 1.
10. Colonial Film Corporation, which shared the same Rockefeller Center address and telephone number, continued to appear in industry trade directories until at least 1952. Stanley Neal was president of both Colonial and Associated.
11. "RKO-Pathé's New Studio in New York Opens Aug. 1; Feature Prod. Due," *VAR*, July 3, 1946, 20.
12. The Forty-Fifth Street building was sold to Transfilm, Inc. in May 1946. "Concerns Acquire Business Parcels," *NYT*, May 3, 1946 (although this report refers to the firm as "Tranfilm").
13. Chester L. Franke, "Pathe Beckons Production East," *MPD*, May 29, 1947, 5.
14. "Incursion," *NY*, April 5, 1947, 25–26.
15. "[Sponsor's Box]," unidentified newspaper clipping in New York Public Library "Pathé Studio" file, c. December 1946.
16. "Bell Centennial Picture," *BSM*, VIII(2) (1947), 23–24.
17. Franke, "Pathe Beckons."
18. "Eva Marie Saint Interviewed by Robert Osborne," TCM/YouTube, accessed June 26, 2020.
19. "The Good Old Days," *FD*, April 25, 1947, 4.
20. Richard Meran Barsam, " 'This Is America': Documentaries for Theaters," *CJ*, Spring 1973, 22–38.
21. Phil Reisman, Jr., "Guts, Honesty Top Documentary Ingredients," *FD*, April 25, 1947, 6.
22. "Warner Brothers Buys Pathe News," *NYT*, July 28, 1947.
23. Sale price from Douglas Gomery, *The Hollywood Studio System: A History* (London: BFI, 2005), 151.
24. *STR*, May 3, 1947, 38.
25. "Nun's Career Reviewed," *NYT*, July 8, 1946. See also "Studio Plans Film of Mother Cabrini," *NYT*, June 3, 1946, which states that Bryan Foy of Eagle-Lion is negotiating with Irene Dunne to star in such a film. According to the *AFI Catalog*, both Bing Crosby and Edgar G. Ulmer had also announced Cabrini films.
26. "15,000 See Cabrini Film," *NYT*, July 8, 1946; see also *MPD*, July 15, 1946, 2.
27. "Along the Rialto," *FD*, April 30, 1947.
28. "Of Local Origin," *NYT*, January 16, 1947.
29. This was a rare theatrical screening for *Seeds of Destiny*, produced by David Miller for the United Nations Relief and Rehabilitation Administration at the Signal Corps Photographic Center in Astoria. It won the Academy Award as Best Short Documentary of 1946. See Irene Kahn Atkins, *Seeds of Destiny*: A Case History," *Film & History* (May 1981), 25–33.
30. *MPD*, April 28, 1947, 28 ("inept"); *STR*, May 3, 1947, 38 ("poorly written").
31. "*Citizen Saint*," *STR*, November 8, 1947, 24.
32. "Elliott Enlarges *Saint*," *FD*, August 13, 1947, 8; "More Scenes for *Citizen Saint*," *BDE*, August 31, 1947; "*Citizen Saint*," *STR*, May 22, 1948, 11.
33. "*Portrait of Jennie* to Be Filmed Here," *NYT*, January 31, 1947.
34. Selznick quoted in Ronald Haver, *David O. Selznick's Hollywood* (New York: Knopf, 1980), 380.
35. Haver, "Selznick's Hollywood," 377.
36. Haver, "Selznick's Hollywood," 380.
37. Haver, "Selznick's Hollywood," 380.
38. "New York Lens-Leased to Hollywood Units," *FD*, June 17, 1947, 8.

39. "*Portrait* Trouble in N.Y.," *STR*, March 29, 1947, 31.
40. "Finished Portrait," *NY*, July 26, 1947, 18–19.
41. Rudy Behlmer (ed.), *Memo from David O. Selznick* (New York: Viking, 1972), 371–72. Memo dated May 1, 1947.
42. "*Jennie* Still Around," *STR*, June 14, 1947.
43. Edwin Schallert, "*So Evil* Trio Completed," *LAT*, March 28, 1947.
44. "Pathe Set Designers Hit Stride in Harlem," *FD*, April 25, 1947, 10.
45. Franke, "Pathe Beckons."
46. "Finished Portrait," *NY*.
47. Quoted in David Thomson, *Showman: The Life of David O. Selznick* (New York: Knopf, 1992), 499.
48. "Finished Portrait," *NY*.
49. Robert Selltitz, "Big Time Movies," *WSJ*, March 10, 1947.
50. "Finished Portrait," *NY*.
51. "Location Trips Setting New High for Hollywood Studios," *STR*, July 12, 1947, 28. They were still in New York at that date, shooting locations at the Cloisters. But Ron Haver (382) claims that after returning to the coast, "the bulk of the exterior shooting was done on the Culver City stages."
52. "Los Angeles," *STR*, October 4, 1947, 27.
53. Thomas Brady, "Hollywood Reacts," *NYT*, September 14, 1947.
54. Thomson, *Showman*.
55. Selltitz, "Big Time Movies" and Franke, "Pathe Beckons."
56. Franke, "Pathe Beckons."
57. Sumner Lyon, "The Other End of the Rainbow," *SW*, June 1947, 12–13.
58. Robert Pirosh, "Outside USA," *SW*, January 1948, 27–29.
59. Philip K. Scheuer, "Rene Clair Cites Ills of Hollywood," *LAT*, August 24, 1947.
60. "French-US Film Ready," *NYT*, May 16, 1947.
61. *FD*, March 28, 1947, 2.
62. "Pathe Set Designers Hit Stride in Harlem," 10.
63. *FD*, October 24, 1947, 3.
64. René Clair, *Four Screenplays* (New York: Orion, 1970), 108–10.
65. Philip K. Scheuer, "M. Chevalier Back on Screen," *LAT*, December 29, 1947.
66. "Vertical Lot Buzzes with Busy Personnel," *FD*, April 25, 1947, 2; "Incursion," *NY*.
67. "Eastern Trek Spurred by Pathe Studio as Gotham Lot Tees Off," *FD*, April 25, 1947, 9.
68. "Ullman Leaves Pathe to Produce for RKO," *FD*, July 10, 1947, 5; "Of Local Origin," *NYT*, August 1, 1947.
69. A. H. Weiler, "Notes About Pictures and People," *NYT*, October 26, 1947.
70. Ezra Goodman, "Motion Picture Photographer to Director," *AC*, March 1948, 84, 102.
71. "Production in Manhattan," *FD*, November 19, 1947, 5.
72. "RKO Saves $ Million on *Window*," *VAR*, December 8, 1947. Citing "modern sources," the *AFI Catalog* gives the cost of the film as $210,000, a remarkably low figure. On release, *Time* (May 23, 1949) said it cost under $750,000.
73. "N.Y. Prod," *VAR*, December 17, 1947, 23.
74. The tenement interior set, built to match the New York footage, collapsed accidentally "when struck by a hard wind," suggesting that weather-related production problems were not unique to New York. See "Production Piles Up," *STR*, January 10, 1948, 30.
75. "The News of Radio," *NYT*, May 12, 1948. NBC's upcoming five-year lease was announced immediately after the Hughes sale, so it must have been under negotiation for some time before this.

76. "RKO-Pathé's NBC Video Lease No Crimp to Eastern Prod. Hopes," *VAR*, May 19, 1948, 7. The headline is much more optimistic than the actual article.
77. For a summary of Hughes' first months at RKO, see Betty Lasky, *RKO: The Biggest Little Major of Them All* (Englewood Cliffs, NJ: Prentice Hall, 1984), 204–20.
78. *STR*, September 18, 1948, 32.
79. "F. Ullman Jr., 45, a Film Producer," *NYT*, December 27, 1948.
80. Selltitz, "Big Time Movies."
81. "*The Window*," *STR*, May 14, 1949, 18.
82. Thomas M. Pryor, "Posing a Question," *NYT*, August 14, 1949 (Hitchcock); "*The Window*," *NYT*, August 8, 1949 (Ullman).
83. Selltitz, "Big Time Movies."
84. "Marathon Pictures Moves to New York," *MPD*, September 16, 1947, 3.
85. Brady, "Hollywood Reacts."
86. "N.Y. OK for Filming," *VAR*, September 10, 1947, 20.
87. Brady, "Hollywood Reacts."
88. See page 150.
89. Hitler's private secretary, Martin Bormann, did die in Berlin, but his remains were not identified until 1973, and his fate was still a topic of discussion in 1947.
90. "Kollmar and Satenstein Join," *NYT*, July 10, 1946.
91. Production information from "Local Job," *NYT*, November 30, 1947; Patti Alicoate, "Production in Manhattan," *FD*, December 4, 1947, 6; "Virginia Wright," *LADN*, February 5, 1948.
92. Alicoate, "Production in Manhattan."
93. Mortimer's review, along with that of Cecelia Ager and several others, in *HR*, April 9, 1948.
94. "Film Rights to Marathon," *MPD*, July 12, 1948, 2.
95. "*Crime Lab*," *FD*, June 7, 1948, 6.
96. "*Crime Lab*," *Cumulative Copyright Catalog, Motion Pictures 1940–1949* (Copyright Office: The Library of Congress, 1953), 79.
97. "Filming Has Begun. . . ," *BDE*, August 6, 1949.
98. According to "modern sources" cited by the *AFI Catalog*.
99. "*The Tattooed Stranger*," *MS*, June 1950, 20.
100. A. H. Weiler, "*The Tattooed Stranger*," *NYT*, February 10, 1950.
101. Carl Macek, "*The Tattooed Stranger*," in *Film Noir: An Encyclopedic Reference to the American Style*, ed. Alain Silver and Elizabeth Ward (Woodstock, NY: Overlook, 1979), 282.
102. Herm., "*The Tattooed Stranger*," *VAR*, February 1, 1950, 20.

3. Now It Can Be Told: Louis de Rochemont, Henry Hathaway, and the Birth of Docudrama

1. De Rochemont later boasted that he had been criticized for "reenacting" news events as far back as 1915, when he was working as a newsreel stringer in Portland, Maine. Maurice Zolotow, "Want to Be a Movie Star?" *SAT POST*, March 29, 1952, 24ff.
2. Thomas M. Pryor, "Down the Homestretch," *NYT*, June 30, 1940.
3. See, for example, Carlo Celli, *National Identity in Global Cinema* (London: Palgrave Macmillan, 2013), 140, or Scott Eyman, *The Speed of Sound* (New York: Simon & Schuster, 1997), 171.

4. Raymond Fielding, *The March of Time* (New York: Oxford, 1978), 281–82.
5. Col. Darryl F. Zanuck, *Tunis Expedition* (New York: Random House, 1943), 78.
6. For a sense of Zanuck's impatience with the debilitating "luxuries" of postwar studio shooting, see Rudy Behlmer (ed.), *Memo from Darryl F. Zanuck* (New York: Grove, 1993), 141–44.
7. Fielding, *March of Time*, 275–76.
8. Behlmer, *Memo*, 63; Fielding, *March of Time*, 284.
9. "The FBI Front," *FD*, September 23, 1942, 7.
10. Thomas M. Pryor, "Blazing a Trail," *NYT*, April 1, 1945.
11. Director Henry Hathaway quoted in Pryor, "Blazing a Trail."
12. Richard B. Gehman, "De Rochemont—a Pictorial Journalist Who Records the American Scene on Film," *TA* (October 1951), 58–59, 80–81.
13. Fielding, *March of Time*, 246.
14. Scott Eyman, "I Made Movies," *TO* 5.1 [September–October 1974], 6–12. Robert Webb was the director originally scheduled. Rudy Behlmer (ed.), *Henry Hathaway. A Directors Guild of America Oral History* (Latham, MD: Scarecrow, 2001), 209.
15. Eyman, "I Made Movies."
16. Pat Casey to Walter A. Lang, February 12, 1945, Local 644 records, NYU Tamiment Library, Box 6, "Twentieth Century 1960–1930s" file.
17. Walter Lang to Pat Casey, February 16, 1945, Local 644 Records, NYU Tamiment Library, Box 6, "Twentieth Century 1960–1930s" file.
18. This note is written on a copy of a March 6 letter that Lang had received from Fox regarding preparations for the picture. Local 644 Records, NYU Tamiment Library, Box 6, "Twentieth Century 1960–1930s" file.
19. Henry Hathaway to Richard Koszarski, Los Angeles, October 1984.
20. The building was owned by a plastic surgeon ("mostly nose jobs") who lived upstairs and had his offices and operating rooms on the first two floors. Behlmer, *Henry Hathaway*, 210–11.
21. Herb A. Lightman, "*13 Rue Madeleine*: Documentary Style in the Photoplay," *AC*, March 1947, 89.
22. Lightman, "*13 Rue Madeleine*."
23. Philip K. Scheuer, "Cameras Use FBI Haunts for Adventure in Reality," *LAT*, July 22, 1945.
24. Scheuer, "Cameras Use FBI Haunts."
25. Behlmer, *Henry Hathaway*, 209.
26. Pryor, "Blazing a Trail."
27. Pryor, "Blazing a Trail."
28. "FBI Filmed Nazis with a Telephoto," *NYT*, September 13, 1945.
29. Hathaway claimed that making "Mr. Christopher" a woman was one of the ideas he and Zanuck cooked up to add "a little more showmanship" to de Rochemont's project. Behlmer, *Henry Hathaway*, 210.
30. For an account of the events surrounding this espionage trial (which does not take *The House on 92nd Street* very seriously), see Peter Duffy, *Double Agent* (New York: Scribner, 2014).
31. *AFI Catalog, The House on 92nd Street*.
32. T. M. P. [Thomas M. Pryor], "At the Roxy: *The House on 92nd Street*," *NYT*, September 22, 1945.
33. Even so, Fox was still using plates from their prewar stock. A back projection of Childs' Restaurant and the Republic Theater seen briefly in *The Dark Corner* appears identical to one used five years earlier in *I Wake Up Screaming* (1941).

34. We know that Hathaway directed this location footage because his name is visible on a camera slate dated October 19, 1945, seen in New York publicity photographs. While on the trip a few other locations were also photographed, including 500 Fifth Avenue, which appears as "The Grant Building," where Clifton Webb somehow manages to throw William Bendix out a window. Wendell Jamieson, "Right Out of Film Noir, A Shadowy New York," *NYT*, December 2, 2005.
35. The only Fox films to outgross *The House on 92nd Street* that year were *The Dolly Sisters* and *State Fair*, a pair of vastly more expensive Technicolor musicals. Aubrey Solomon, *Twentieth Century-Fox: A Corporate and Financial History* (Metuchen, NJ: Scarecrow, 1988), 221.
36. Behlmer, *Henry Hathaway*, 212–13.
37. Thalia Bell, "Hollywood," *MPD*, January 14, 1946, 5; Hedda Hopper, "Watch Mark Stevens," *MS*, April 1946, 78. *The Dark Corner* failed to earn back its negative cost, unusual for a modestly budgeted crime thriller. See Solomon, *Twentieth Century-Fox*. Mark Stevens apparently took the fall for this.
38. Behlmer, *Henry Hathaway*, 216.
39. "All-Air Location Trip," *FD*, April 12, 1946, 2; "20th-Fox Halts '13 Rue M,'" *FD*, June 1, 1946, 32. Non-flier Cagney was unaffected, as he had already gone on ahead.
40. Fred Stanley, "Hollywood Off on OSS Cycle," *NYT*, March 31, 1946.
41. "'13 Rue' Back in Hollywood," *STR*, August 17, 1946, 39; "20th Completes '13 Rue M,'" *STR*, August 24, 1946, 40.
42. "20th Century-Fox," *INDEFB*, August 5, 1946, 31. But according to Aubrey Solomon, *Twentieth Century-Fox*, the film still cost twice as much as *The House on 92nd Street*.
43. Lightman, "13 Rue Madeleine," 88.
44. Behlmer, *Henry Hathaway*, 215–16. Indeed, he also claims in this interview that de Rochemont's participation in the project was seriously compromised due to his chronic alcoholism, which suggests one reason for his reputation as a "hands off" producer.
45. Zolotow, "Want to Be a Movie Star?"
46. Anthony Abbot [pseud. Fulton Oursler], "It Was a Perfect Case," *The Rotarian*, December 1945, 14–16, 48. The credits say the film is based not on this story but on Abbot's later *Reader's Digest* condensation (for reasons explained below).
47. "Freed of Murder Charge," *NYT*, May 28, 1924.
48. See *STR*, July 23, 1946, 8 and July 27, 1946, 19.
49. "Bridgeport," *STR*, June 16, 1946, 30.
50. Thomas M. Pryor, "Stamford Doubles as Movie Set," *NYT*, September 29, 1946.
51. Pryor, "Stamford."
52. Quoted in Richard Schickel, *Elia Kazan, a Biography* (New York; HarperCollins, 2005), 143.
53. Edwin Schallert, "Fortune Smiles on Player Who Put Home Life First," *LAT*, September 29, 1946.
54. For a photo of Miller in the lineup, see "Movie of the Week: *Boomerang!*" *Life*, March 24, 1947, 92.
55. Elia Kazan, *A Life* (New York: Knopf, 1988), 319.
56. Pryor, "Stamford."
57. Quoted in Schickel, *Elia Kazan*, 144.
58. Elia Kazan, *A Life*, 316.
59. Darryl F. Zanuck to Elia Kazan, telegram, December 2, 1946. Reid Cinema Archives, Wesleyan University, Elia Kazan papers, File B18-F1. He argued that if they knew the identity of the killer, the audience would feel smarter than the DA and the police.

As this is often the case in detective fiction, Zanuck's concerns here seem more political than dramatic.

60. When he saw that film again while preparing his autobiography, "it filled me with nostalgia for those warmhearted but naïve days." Kazan, *A Life*, 105.
61. Stuart Byron and Martin Rubin, "Elia Kazan Interview," *Movie* #19 (Winter 1971–72), 3.
62. Kazan, *A Life*, 318.
63. Eli Willis, "Movie Analysis," *HM*, April 1947, 225, 244–45.
64. "Balance Sheet," *DNL*, August-September 1947, 113.
65. Only two other neorealist films were reviewed by the *New York Times* before 1949: *Vivere in pace* (Luigi Zampa, November 25, 1947) and *Tragic Hunt* (Giuseppe de Santis, October 22, 1948).
66. Philip K. Scheuer, "Hollywood Takes Stock as Year Draws to Close," *LAT*, December 22, 1946.
67. Peter Lev, *Twentieth Century-Fox* (Austin: University of Texas Press, 2013), 139.
68. "Gunn Shots," *SW*, December 1947, 26.
69. "*Bicycle Thief* Art Studied by Film Men," *LAT*, January 29, 1950.
70. Bosley Crowther, "An Absorbing Episode," *NYT*, November 28, 1945.
71. Bosley Crowther, "*Open City*. A Powerful New Film from Italy Points a Line of European Appeal," *NYT*, March 3, 1946.
72. "Swiss Producer 1st Indie to Be Coined By Floating Public Stock Issue in U.S.," *VAR*, January 30, 1946, 5.
73. Charles Affron and Mirella Jona Affron, *Best Years: Going to the Movies, 1945–1946* (New Brunswick, NJ: Rutgers University Press, 2009), 214.
74. Rebecca Prime, "Cloaked in Compromise," in, *"Un-American" Hollywood*, ed. Frank Krutnik, Steve Neale, Brian Neve, and Peter Stanfield (New Brunswick, NJ: Rutgers University Press, 2007), 146.
75. William Lafferty, "de Rochemont, Louis," in *Internet Dictionary of Films and Filmmakers* (2001), accessed October 29, 2015.
76. Louis Berg, "New England Makes a Movie!" *LAT*, January 21, 1951.
77. Lipsky received an Academy Award nomination for Best Story that year, losing to *Miracle on 34th Street*.
78. Richard Koszarski interview with Henry Hathaway (October 1984). The *AFI Catalog*, citing studio figures, gives the cost as $2,523,000; Aubrey Solomon, *Twentieth Century-Fox*, also citing studio sources, says $1,525,000, although this may not include prints and advertising.
79. Richard L. Coe, "Club's Extras Help Hollywood in N.Y. Scenes," *WP*, April 6, 1947.
80. *Kiss of Death* publicity handout quoted in Kingsley Canham, *The Hollywood Professionals* (London: Tantivy, 1973), 164.
81. Sources disagree on whether Louise May Alcott did or did not write parts of *Little Women* at her uncle's house at 130–132 MacDougal Street in 1868.
82. "Local 'Hollywood,' " *NYT*, March 16, 1947; Thomas M. Pryor, "Manhattan Doubles as Movie Set," *NYT*, May 11, 1947. For a later visit to the locations, see Jamieson, "Right Out of Film Noir."
83. "Movie of the Week: *Kiss of Death*," *Life*, September 22, 1947, 143–44, 46.
84. Canham, *Hollywood Professionals*, 164. The Fox press release quoted here also claims that "the zoom lens was employed to great effect [in the film], saving on trucking." While no conventional "zoom shots" are visible in the released film, the use of a variable focal length lens in this period was seen as a way to allow both close-ups and long shots to be filmed from the same setup, saving the trouble of repositioning the camera.

85. Pryor, "Manhattan Doubles as Movie Set."
86. Pryor, "Manhattan Doubles as Movie Set." This Charles Hall should not be confused with the art director Charles D. Hall.
87. Ezra Goodman, "Life of a Local Lily Gilder," *NYT*, July 27, 1947.
88. "Studio Roundup," *STR*, April 12, 1947, 45.
89. Edwin Schallert, "Cummings Will Portray Star," *LAT*, February 28, 1947. Schallert notes that Morison's character "double-crosses her spouse" while Mature is in prison, suggesting an additional level of duplicity in the film. But Eddie Muller, discussing the film on TCM (December 20, 2020) claims that Morison's character was raped by Henry Brandon's character, which could help explain why both roles were eliminated.
90. Philip K. Scheuer, "Informer Vindicated," *LAT*, August 14, 1947. Scheuer felt that this was the first time a film had sympathetically presented "the case for the 'squealer,' the stool pigeon."
91. Behlmer, *Henry Hathaway*, 221.
92. Curiously, Charles Hall described a very similar episode, set to be staged outside a hotel on Central Park South, being cancelled at the last moment when the hotel reneged on permission. How this action may have related to the ultimate ending is unclear. Pryor, "Manhattan Doubles as Movie Set."
93. Pryor, "Manhattan Doubles as Movie Set."
94. Behlmer, *Memo*, 163–64.
95. "Coming-Going," *FD*, January 22, 1946, 2.
96. According to Solomon, *Twentieth Century-Fox*, *Boomerang!* earned $2.25 million domestic, against a negative cost of $1.14 million, a slightly better return on investment than *Call Northside 777* ($2.7 million against $1.44 million).
97. Zanuck to Reynolds, March 19, 1947, reproduced in Behlmer, *Memo*, 123–24.
98. See the March 1, 1947 column in James Agee, *Agee on Film* (New York: Beacon, 1958), 242–43.
99. Zanuck to Lang, Reynolds and Leonard Hoffman, March 5, 1947, reproduced in Behlmer, *Memo*, 122–23.
100. For an account of the original case and its filmic version, see Arnie Bernstein, *Hollywood on Lake Michigan* (Chicago: Lake Claremont, 1998), 315–19. The real number to call was GRO-1758.
101. According to the *AFI Catalog*, *The Street with No Name* had originally been announced as de Rochemont's follow-up to *The House on 92nd Street*.
102. *Cry of the City* pressbook, NYPL, Billy Rose Theatre Collection.
103. "A. H. Weiler, "Cry of the City," *NYT*, September 30, 1948.
104. "On Location," *NYT*, March 21, 1948.
105. Thomas F. Brady, "Hollywood Buzzes," *NYT*, September 28, 1947.
106. A. H. Weiler, "By Way of Report," *NYT*, January 1, 1950.
107. "Youth 11 Hours on Ledge Leaps 17 Floors to Death as Thousands Watch Him," *NYT*, July 27, 1938; Daniel Blum, *Pictorial History of Television* (Philadelphia: Chilton, 1959), 9.
108. Joel Sayre, "The Man on the Ledge," *NY*, April 16, 1949, 34ff.
109. "Inside Stuff—Pictures," *VAR*, June 21, 1950.
110. Philip K. Scheuer, "On Sand, Sea or Skyscraper Ledge, New Films Tell Hathaway Versatility," *LAT*, April 1, 1951.
111. Hathaway interviewed by Charles Higham, Columbia University Oral History Project.
112. Philip K. Scheuer, "On Sand, Sea or Skyscraper Ledge."

113. All information on Lacovara from Thomas M. Pryor, "High Above Lower Broadway," *NYT*, June 11, 1950.
114. Quoted in Canham, *Hollywood Professionals*, 149.
115. "Miss Skouras Dies in Fall," *NYT*, July 18, 1950. According to the *AFI Catalog*, principal photography ran from early June through early August, 1950, and the *New York Times* had reported on the filming of the New York exteriors on June 11. Charles Skouras's apartment was atop the Fox West Coast Theatres corporate office building on West Washington Boulevard. It is possible that rushes of the New York footage had been screened there, especially because Dionysia's father, Spyros, had taken her to the West Coast himself before leaving her with his brother the week before. Would Dionysia, a New Yorker, have been invited to see a cut of this sequence? One hopes not.
116. Canham, *Hollywood Professionals*, 149.
117. Four other directors, including Howard Hawks, were already said to have turned the script down before Hathaway agreed to take it on. Canham, *Hollywood Professionals*, 150.
118. "Movie of the Week: *Fourteen Hours*," *Life*, March 12, 1951, 114–18.
119. A. H. Weiler, "Movies for the Classroom and Other Items," *NYT*, March 16, 1947; "De Rochemont Pact with UW Is Signed," *FD*, May 26, 1947, 1; "School Pix to Fore at Three Chi Meets," *FD*, July 8, 1948, 8. Eventually there were thirty-six titles in this series.
120. "Connors into Ad Film Distribution," *MPD*, April 14, 1948, 1. De Rochemont and his award-winning credentials were prominently mentioned in connection with the film.
121. Zolotow, "Want to Be a Movie Star?"
122. "Studio Size-Ups," *INDEFB*, February 16, 1948, 13.
123. "De Rochemont Plans 'Digest' Series," *MPD*, March 16, 1948, 3.
124. "Digest-de Rochemont Will Make MGM Shorts Series," *FD*, July 27, 1948, 7.
125. "MGM to Handle Film on Negro Problems," *MPD*, August 10, 1948, 3. An earlier "Negro problem" film, a version of Howard Fast's *Freedom Road* starring Paul Robeson, was at one time scheduled for production "in an eastern studio" in May 1947. "Robeson Seen Playing in Pro-Negro Picture as Cry vs. Prejudice," *VAR*, January 29, 1947, 1. That version was never produced, but Jan Kadar later directed a three-hour TV movie of Fast's novel, starring Muhammed Ali, in 1979.
126. Thomas Cripps, *Making Movies Black* (New York: Oxford, 1993), 352n32, suggests that MGM backed out because of opinion-sampling results; only 55 percent of audiences in Dallas expressed an interest in seeing such a film.
127. Thomas F. Brady, "The Hollywood Wire," *NYT*, November 14, 1948.
128. Zolotow, "Want to Be a Movie Star?"
129. Pryor, "Hoeing His Own Row: A Case History of Louis de Rochemont and His New Film, *Lost Boundaries*," *NYT*, June 26, 1949. Hyman and Levine, operating under the corporate name Telinbest, were said to have put up $300,000, while de Rochemont raised another $200,000 by mortgaging most of his assets.
130. Pryor, "Hoeing His Own Row."
131. *Strange Fruit* ran for sixty performances in the winter of 1945–46. Staged and directed by Jose Ferrer (no relation), the cast also featured Juano Hernandez, Ralph Meeker, and Murray Hamilton. Melchor Ferrer played one of the white characters.
132. Al Weisman, "He Passed as a Negro," *ND*, October 1951, 16–20.
133. "Production on *Lost Boundaries* Finished," *SD*, April 29, 1949, 3–6.
134. Pryor, "Hoeing His Own Row."
135. "*Lost Boundaries*," *STR*, July 2, 1949, 14.

136. William Greaves, who appeared in the film, felt that "the family had deluded themselves into thinking they had passed. To some people they may have, but not to others. It was just that some of the white people didn't think it was important enough to make a fuss about." Greaves quoted in Scott MacDonald (ed.), *A Critical Cinema 3* (Berkeley: University of California Press, 1988), 47.
137. Donald Bogle, *Toms, Coons, Mulattoes, Mammies, and Bucks* (New York, Viking, 1973), especially 147–50.
138. Bosley Crowther, "Issues of the Day," *NYT*, July 3, 1949.
139. The film suggests that this is not really so marginal an issue. Canada Lee's character says that eight million American Negroes are light enough to have to consider whether or not to pass. The same figure is cited in "Passing," *Ebony*, May 1949, 23ff.
140. Weisman, "He Passed as a Negro."
141. Cripps, *Making Movies Black*, 227.
142. Weisman, "He Passed as a Negro."
143. Weisman, "He Passed as a Negro."
144. William Greaves, "A Black Filmmaker Remembers Louis de Rochemont," *FLQ* (12.4) 1979, 13–15. At this time, Greaves was also a student in Hans Richter's filmmaking program at City College, studying with Leo Seltzer and Lewis Jacobs.
145. Greaves quoted in MacDonald (ed.), *A Critical Cinema 3*, 45–47.
146. Weisman, "He Passed as a Negro."
147. Daniel Leab, *Orwell Subverted: The CIA and the Filming of "Animal Farm"* (University Park: Pennsylvania State University Press, 2007), 33.
148. Quoted in Ira H. Carmen, *Movies, Censorship and the Law* (Ann Arbor: University of Michigan Press, 1966), 46.
149. Robert Sklar, *Movie-Made America* (New York: Vintage, 1976), 127–28.
150. Carmen, *Movies, Censorship and the Law*, 46–53. Although remembered as a liberal supporter of civil rights issues, Black had joined the Ku Klux Klan in the 1920s, a political decision he came to regret in later years.
151. "Studio Size-Up," *INDEFB*, January 30, 1950, 19; A. H. Weiler, "Random Notes About People and Pictures," *NYT*, June 25, 1950.
152. "Siodmak's 'Whistle,' " *NYT*, October 14, 1951.
153. It is unclear if Siodmak participated in *Cry of the City*'s brief New York location shoot in 1948.
154. [Christopher Lambert], "Robert Siodmak," in *World Film Directors, Volume One*, ed. John Wakeman (New York: Wilson, 1987), 1004.
155. "Siodmak's 'Whistle.' "
156. Harry Niemeyer, "Progress Note," *NYT*, November 6, 1949.
157. Irving Drutman, " 'Whistle (Sounds) at Eaton Falls,' " *NYT*, November 12, 1950.
158. Weiler, "Random Notes," June 25, 1950.
159. Drutman, " 'Whistle (Sounds).' "
160. Gehman, "De Rochemont." It is unclear who first brought up the issue of "Rossellini's practice" in this interview.
161. A. Barton Palmer, *Shot on Location. Postwar American Cinema and the Exploration of Real Place* (New Brunswick, NJ: Rutgers University Press, 2016), 242–43.
162. "Siodmak's 'Whistle.' "
163. Miriam Teichner, "Dorothy Gish Makes a Rare Movie Appearance," *NYT*, June 17, 1951.
164. Zolotow, "Want to Be a Movie Star?"
165. "Siodmak's 'Whistle.' "
166. Gehman, "De Rochemont."

167. Gehman, "De Rochemont."
168. Bosley Crowther, "Laboring a Point," *NYT*, October 21, 1951.
169. "*The Whistle at Eaton Falls* Blows Little Entertainment," *INDEFB*, August 13, 1951, 8.
170. "Documentary Below DeRochemont's Par," *HR*, August 1, 1951, 3.
171. Quoted in Leab, *Orwell Subverted*, 33.
172. Leab, *Orwell Subverted*, 34.
173. According to the IMDB, on May 26, 1951, de Rochemont and *Reader's Digest* released a nineteen-minute color short called *A Day with the FBI*, in which Hoover himself appeared.
174. Zolotow, "Want to Be a Movie Star?"
175. Tony Shaw, *Hollywood's Cold War* (Amherst: University of Massachusetts Press, 2007), 57.
176. "Walk East on Beacon," *NYT*, May 29, 1952.
177. "Sen. Mundt Lauds 'Pro-Americanism' of *My Son John, Walk East on Beacon*," *MPD*, May 7, 1952, 2. Mundt praised both films after a screening of *My Son John*, which he called, "a picture which has stirred America more than any other film since *Birth of a Nation*."
178. Zolotow, "Want to Be a Movie Star?"
179. Leab, *Orwell Subverted*, 21.
180. Gehman, "De Rochemont."

4. Race Movies: New York's Original Independent Cinema

1. A poster collector, Kisch maintains the online *Separate Cinema* archive. With Edward Mapp, he is the author of *A Separate Cinema: Fifty Years of Black Cast Posters* (New York: Farrar, Straus & Giroux, 1992).
2. *FDYBK* (1944), 945–47; "Negro Theatre an Expanding Field," *MPH*, April 12, 1947, 18.
3. "Minor Producers Will Get No More 35 MM Film," *IP*, October 1942, 22.
4. For a more extended history of Soundies, see Maurice Terenzio, Scott MacGillivray, and Ted Okuda, *The Soundies Corporation of America* (Jefferson, NC: McFarland, 1991).
5. "Long Island City Studio Makes Industrial Training Films," *QueensBorough*, June 1941, 34. There were rival producers and manufacturers in the motion picture jukebox business, but Soundies so dominated the field that the name became generic.
6. As late as 1945, RCA was taking full page ads promoting 16 mm projectors it was not allowed to sell. "Because of military demands these new RCA projectors are not available now for civilian use. But plan to see the new RCA projector before you purchase postwar equipment." *BSM*, VI, 3 (1945), 5.
7. See filmography in Terenzio, et al., *Soundies*, 25–176.
8. "How Movies Are Made," *Ebony*, March 1947, 40–43.
9. Henry Brown, "Sun Tan Studios Train Nation's New Starlets," *CD*, July 31, 1948. Sun Tan Studios also trained models and operated a "School of Exotic Dancing."
10. "See Tele-Film Interests Acquiring Bronx Studio," *FD*, March 17, 1948, 6.
11. "Negro Movies Hit Pay Dirt," *Ebony*, September 1946, 42–44.
12. Thomas Cripps, *Making Movies Black* (New York: Oxford, 1993), 132, 140.
13. "How Movies Are Made." The concept seems borrowed from the 1945 Rita Hayworth musical, *Cover Girl*.
14. "Louis Jordan," Wikipedia, accessed July 14, 2015. But when accessed on May 8, 2020, Wikipedia, using a different metric, placed him only at number five.

15. "Louis Jordan's *Caldonia, Beware* Pix, a 3-Way Payoff," *BB*, June 8, 1946, 35.
16. "Glucksman Sets 12 All-Negro Shorts," *MPD*, December 26, 1944, 8.
17. John Chilton, *Let the Good Times Roll: The Story of Louis Jordan and His Music* (Ann Arbor: University of Michigan Press, 1992), 110.
18. Stephen Koch, "*Caldonia*—Louis Jordan (1945)." loc.gov/National Recording Preservation Board, accessed July 12, 2015.
19. "Glucksman Sets 12 All-Negro Shorts"; "*Caldonia* via Astor," *FD*, May 3, 1945, 8; "*Caldonia*," *STR*, September 22, 1945, 45.
20. "Negroes Due for Break in Films with New York as Own Hollywood," *CD*, April 27, 1946 (Southern theater); "Along the Rialto," *FD*, April 22, 1946, 5 (Oriental).
21. "Louis Jordan, Berle Adams Contract New Movie Deal," *BB*, January 26, 1946, 16.
22. "Negro Movies Hit Pay Dirt."
23. "Negroes Due for Break."
24. The 1933 date comes from Savini's entry in the 1945–46 *MPA*. Anthony Slide, in *The New Historical Dictionary of the American Film Industry* (Lanham, MD: Scarecrow, 1988), 16, puts it at 1925. For an industry tribute to Savini, see Sherwin Kane, "Half-a-Century in the World of the Screen," *MPD*, August 30, 1954, 5–27.
25. In 1944 Astor released *Jimmy Steps Out*, their version of *Pot O' Gold*, a 1941 James Stewart musical that had been produced by James Roosevelt's Globe Productions—the first link between Astor and the world of Soundies.
26. "Astor to Produce Two," *MPD*, September 26, 1945, 8. The announcement suggests that both films were to be made at Filmcraft, but this proved not to be the case.
27. Less elegantly, another tenor saxophonist, Wardell Gray, is reported to have told Jordan, "Fuck you, Uncle Tom, I ain't going to work for you." Chilton, *Let the Good Times Roll*, 144.
28. Chilton, *Let the Good Times Roll*, 145.
29. "Negroes Due for Break."
30. Chilton, *Let the Good Times Roll*, 118.
31. "Astor Making Negro Pix," *FD*, October 31, 1945, 2, announces that production has started at the "American studio" in Fort Lee, probably the same location as the "All-American Studio" then being used by E. M. Glucksman for his own line of race movies.
32. Tag Gallagher, *The Adventures of Roberto Rossellini* (New York: Da Capo, 1998), 185, 195–96.
33. Donald Bogle, *Toms, Coons. Mulattoes, Mammies and Bucks* (New York: Viking, 1973), 72–75.
34. Elizabeth Oliver, "The Eyes Have It: Charlie Chan's Right-Hand Man," *WAA*, February 5, 1957.
35. "Elicker Joining Astor," *FD*, January 4, 1946, 3.
36. "Negro Movies Hit Pay Dirt."
37. "Denied Percentage in Negro Houses, Savini Plans to Roadshow with 16-mm," *STR*, December 7, 1946, 11; "Astor Will Roadshow Two 16-mm Negro Productions," *STR*, February 1, 1947, 16.
38. "*Alice in Wonderland* on 16 mm," *FD*, August 11, 1931, 2.
39. "Most-Played Juke Box Race Records 1946–1947," *BB*, April 3, 1948, front cover.
40. "Film Ready for Astor," *MPD*, October 29, 1946, 8. Don Malkames was again the cameraman.
41. Johnson later appeared in *No Way Out* (1950) and *The Joe Louis Story* (1953).
42. "Negroes Due for Break."

43. "*Reet, Petite and Gone*," *American Film Institute Catalog* online. Accessed May 22, 2013.
44. "Astor Completes Four Negro Films for World Release," *MPH*, September 13, 1947, 44. *O'Voutie O'Rooney* was a Slim Gaillard short handled by Jack Rieger.
45. "Film Ready for Astor." The film is referred to by its original title, *Wham, Sam*.
46. "Rank May Produce His Educational Films in NYC," *FD*, March 6, 1946, 9; "Rieger Joins Lafayette Tele & M.P. Studios," *FD*, March 13, 1946, 5.
47. "Still and Brent Join Lafayette Television," *FD*, May 3, 1946, 4.
48. For information about Still, a forgotten pioneer of independent television, see A. W. Bernsohn, "Meet Bill Still!" *Televiser*, Fall 1944, 55; T. R. Kennedy, Jr., "Man in the Window: Bill Still Sets Up His Own Television Station Over in Queens," *NYT*, November 25, 1945; and "Early Television Stations: W2XJT Jamaica New York" at earlytelevision.org (accessed July 28, 2015).
49. "Robert M. Savini," *STR*, March 6, 1948, 12.
50. "Astor to Publish Songs," *MPH*, January 10, 1948, 22.
51. Patrick McGilligan, *Oscar Micheaux: The Great and Only* (New York: HarperCollins, 2007), has the best account of the making of *The Betrayal*, but he does not realize that the "former radio news station on Twenty-ninth Street" (329) where the film was shot was in fact the All-American studio at 2901 Prairie Avenue.
52. Al Monroe, "All American News Shooting Full Length Feature Here," *CD*, October 16, 1948. The flicker he refers to is *The Joint Is Jumpin'*, not *The Betrayal*.
53. "First Negro Roadshow Pix Also in Three Installments," *FD*, February 9, 1948, 7.
54. July 3, 1948 *Amsterdam News* review, quoted in Pearl Bowser and Louise Spence, *Writing Himself Into History* (New Brunswick, NJ: Rutgers University Press, 2000), 218.
55. Al Monroe, "Thousands of Dollars Wasted Annually On Production Of Negro Films," *CD*, July 17, 1948, 9. Monroe felt the film, "is hardly what you'd expect of a movie. Its continuity is poor, its lines ill-timed and tasteless and the directing also by Mischeaux [sic] is faulty to say the least. . . . As it is the picture misses the boat and the actors, who show spasmodic signs of reaching a standard surface, are dragged to the bottom with the flicker."
56. "*The Betrayal*," *MPH*, July 10, 1948, 4233.
57. Cripps, *Making Movies Black*, 147 ("flop"); Bowser and Spence, 218 ("few days").
58. McGilligan, *Oscar Micheaux*, 342–43.
59. "NOTICE," *STR*, September 17, 1949, 27.
60. For a tribute to Savini's long career, see Sherwin Kane, "Half-a-Century in the World of the Screen," *MPD*, August 30, 1954, 5–27.
61. McGilligan, *Oscar Micheaux*, 270–72.
62. Claims that Alexander created or controlled this newsreel seem to have been exaggerated by later historians. See the discussion of All-American News below.
63. "Glucksman Sets 12 All-Negro Shorts."
64. G. William Jones, *Black Cinema Treasures* (Denton: University of North Texas Press, 1997), 155–57.
65. "Apollo, N.Y.," *VAR*, March 13, 1946, 58; "Offer Negro Short to Majors," *FD*, March 21, 1946, 11.
66. "Negro Movies Hit Pay Dirt."
67. "Astor, Associated Close 3-Film Deal," *MPD*, June 20, 1946, 4.
68. Richard Koszarski, "Joseph Lerner and the Post-War New York Film Renaissance," *FH* VII:4 (1995), 456–76. All quotes from Lerner are taken from this 1987 interview.
69. No copies of *The Fight Never Ends* appear to survive. My comments are based on a "censorship script" in Folder 11 of the Ted Toddy Collection, Margaret Herrick Library.

After initially distributing the film on his own, Alexander turned *The Fight Never Ends* over to Toddy for subsequent release.

70. "Loew's Books Joe Louis Film Into 4 N.Y. Nabes," *VAR*, February 18, 1948, 6.
71. "*The Fight Never Ends*," *STR*, February 28, 1948, 22–23.
72. Josh Binney, "Movies for and with Negroes," *SD*, December 10, 1948, 2–4.
73. Ruby Dee and Ossie Davis, *With Ossie and Ruby* (New York: Quill William Morrow, 1998), 174.
74. Dee and Davis, *With Ossie and Ruby*, 173, 175.
75. Four episodes available at SMU.SCHOLAR suggest the series may have been underwritten by the Republican Party or the Eisenhower for President Campaign.
76. Pearl Bowser, "Pioneers of Black Documentary Films," in *Struggles for Representation*, ed. Janet Cutler (Bloomington: Indiana University Press, 1999), 26. Did he mean OSS or OWI?
77. Joseph Clark, "Double Vision: World War II, Racial Uplift, and the All-American Newsreel's Pedagogical Address," in *Useful Cinema*, ed. Charles Acland and Haidee Wasson (Durham, NC: Duke University Press, 2011), 263–88.
78. "Sportcast Productions Signs Bob Elson," *MPH*, November 22, 1941, 16.
79. "Senate Fails to Restore OWI Fund," *MPD*, August 1, 1943, 1; "OWI Won't Aid Empty Houses, Newsreels Told," *MPD*, August 4, 1943, 1.
80. "Glucksman and Loewy Head All American," *FD*, June 23, 1944, 2; "Glucksman Sets 12 All-Negro Shorts."
81. See ad in *BAA*, July 6, 1946, 16. A surviving episode of All-American News shows Bud Pollard signing Ida James for an upcoming All-American feature.
82. "Through Harlem," *CD*, July 14, 1945, 14 and "Broadway Bound," *CD*, July 28, 1945, 14.
83. "Set Stepin Fetchit All-Negro Indie Pic," *VAR*, August 15, 1945, 7. All-American had footage of Fetchit being signed in vol. 3, no. 145, of their newsreel. See *STR*, August 4, 1945, 36.
84. For example, see the February 1946 exchange between John Ford and Darryl F. Zanuck quoted in Charlene Regester, "Stepin Fetchit. The Man, the Image, and the African American Press," *FH* 6:4 (1994), 521n109 and 521n110, in which Zanuck rejects Ford's request to use Fetchit in *My Darling Clementine* because White had, in effect, blacklisted him.
85. "Stepin Fetchit: Lincoln Perry Says He's No Uncle Tom," *BAA*, May 26, 1945, 5.
86. "All-American Will Produce Features," *MPD*, December 5, 1946, 5.
87. Joseph Clark, email to author, October 23, 2015.
88. J. Hoberman, *Bridge of Light* (New York: Museum of Modern Art, 1991), 216 (garage); Eric Goldman, *Visions, Images and Dreams* (Teaneck, NJ: Holmes and Meier, 2011), 120 (loft).
89. See Elva Diane Green, *Eddie Green* (Albany, GA, BearManor Media: 2016), 59–88. The other titles were *What Goes Up, Comes Midnight*, and *One Round Jones*.
90. "Cinema Studios Reopened," *FD*, January 16, 1945, 3.
91. FDYBK (1947), 560.
92. I have seen no evidence of where Binney's All-American Streamlined features were shot. Although he lumped them in with his East Coast films in an article for *The Screen Director* ("Movies for and with Negroes," December 10, 1948), they may have been made in Chicago, in whole or in part.
93. "Josh Binney Arrested," *VAR*, January 31, 1924, 19; "Hollywood Producers Arrested in *News* Expose," *MPN*, November 1, 1930, 26, 33. The *News* article is an especially detailed account of how such scams operated (although Binney was later released for lack of evidence).

94. "New Negro Film in Work," *MPD*, January 31, 1947, 8; Binney, "Movies for and with Negroes." Do not confuse Binney's feature with the 1934 Paramount short *Cab Calloway's Hi-De-Ho*, or Calloway's 1937 Vitaphone short, *Hi De Ho*, both also made in New York.
95. Quoted in the American Tap Dance Foundation's "Jeni LeGon" page. ATDF.org, accessed September 7, 2015.
96. "Apollo, N.Y.," *VAR*, October 2, 1946, 20.
97. The Library of Congress holds a seventy-seven-minute 16 mm print of the film (FCA 5722–23) that includes the entire Fletcher number and Calloway's brief introduction of the act.
98. For a period discussion of the wide popularity of this song, see George Frazier, "Jocks, Jukes and Disks," *VAR*, January 29, 1947, 33.
99. " 'Richard' Subject Completed," *MPH*, February 22, 1947, 40. As an indication of how fast distributors like Glucksman turned to innovative distribution strategies for films like this, see the large ad on page 214 of the May 1947 issue of *MM*, offering 16 mm prints of the film for sale only weeks after it was shot.
100. "New Acts. Dusty Fletcher," *VAR*, June 19, 1946, 50; see also "Zanzibar, N.Y.," *VAR*, December 18, 1946, 60.
101. Mel Watkins, *Stepin Fetchit. The Life and Times of Lincoln Perry* (New York: Vintage, 2006), 249.
102. "Texas Film Starts Soon," *MPD*, October 24, 1946, 4. Red River Dave did make two short musical westerns that were distributed by Universal in 1948, *Echo Ranch* and *Hidden Valley Days*. But these were directed by William Forest Crouch at a dude ranch in Hidden Valley, NY, near Lake Luzerne. "Movies Produced Here Distinguished for Reality," *NYWT*, October 30, 1947.
103. "*Merry-go-round*," *MFB*, May 31, 1948, 60. The reviewer also noted a "very blurred soundtrack."
104. Geoff Brown, email to author, June 15, 2015.
105. "Coming and Going," *FD*, December 11, 1947, 4, reports Binney's return from London, while "N.Y. Prod," *VAR*, December 17, 1947, 23, reveals that *Killer Diller* had started that Monday.
106. Binney, "Movies for and with Negroes."
107. "Captain Fulmer Named New Chicago Censor," *FD*, May 4, 1948, 2. The film is said to be distributed by Screen Guild, a creation of rival producer Jack Goldberg.
108. The scene where Dusty Fletcher and "Moms" Mabley kill a rabbit for dinner, which will not be described here, is even farther removed from what the PCA would have considered appropriate for comedy.
109. "Apollo, N.Y.," *VAR*, March 31, 1948, 55.
110. "National Minstrels' Debut Over Network," *CD*, July 10, 1948. See also "Summer Premieres," *VAR*, July 7, 1948, 20 and "NBC to Launch Minstrel Show for Summer Season," *CD*, June 12, 1948.
111. "Fans Divided on Cancellation of 'Radio Minstrels,' " *CD*, July 24, 1948.
112. "The News of Radio," *NYT*, July 28, 1948.
113. "Swingtime at the Savoy," *VAR*, August 4, 1948, 24. This review says that it sounds as if NBC had simply wired the Savoy Ballroom for sound, which suggests a live remote.
114. "Lucky Millinder to Remain in New York Until Winter Season," *CD*, September 11, 1948.
115. Although NBC had leased the building's stages for television as of July 1, the two smaller stages were not available to them until November. "The News of Radio," *NYT*, May 12, 1948. It should also be remembered that NBC was broadcasting Millinder's radio show.

116. Binney, "Movies for and with Negroes."
117. "*The Joint Is Jumpin'*," *American Film Institute Catalog*.
118. Al Monroe, "All-American News."
119. The *AFI Catalog* entry for *The Joint Is Jumpin'* makes this claim, to which Monroe's article adds additional support.
120. Al Monroe, "All-American News."
121. Binney, "Movies for and with Negroes."
122. Binney, "Movies for and with Negroes."
123. Binney, "Movies for and with Negroes."
124. "Start *Go Down, Death*," *FD*, November 1, 1943, 2; "Negro Feature Completed," *FD*, April 11, 1944, 6; "Sack Acquires *Of One Blood*," *FD*, August 5, 1944, 2. Although made earlier, the *AFI Catalog* suggests that these films were not released until 1945 or later.
125. "Goldberg-Sack to Make Seven Negro Cast Pix," *FD*, May 20, 1946, 1, announces that a series of films will be shot in New York or Hollywood but processed and edited at Harlemwood in Dallas. On November 13, 1946, 12, *FD* reported that *Dirtie Gertie from Harlem, USA* has been filmed entirely at Harlemwood, but lab work was handled in Los Angeles ("Sack's *Dirtie Gertie* Shot in Dallas Studios").
126. "Complete First 2 of 6 Sack Shorts," *MPD*, January 23, 1945, 6; "Increases Number of Negro Musical One-Reel Shorts," *MPH*, February 24, 1945, 54. The oldest of the group, Jordan's *The Outskirts of Town*, had been released as far back as October 19, 1942.
127. "Sack Amusement Buys Rights to Negro Pix," *FD*, April 16, 1947, 4.
128. "Bob Howard Papers," New York Public Library Archives and Manuscripts, accessed July 26, 2015. A new edition of the show was being filmed at a studio on East Fortieth Street in 1956. Pinky Herman, "Television—Radio," *MPD*, February 15, 1956, 6.
129. Visconti also shares credit with a New York cameraman on *Murder with Music*.
130. See the full page ad for Howard's WHN radio show in *Broadcasting*, July 2, 1945, 41. His television show was featured in "Coast to Coast in Television," *RM*, April 1949, 52–53.
131. "Hollywood Films to Produce in East," *MPD*, March 25, 1946, 4.
132. "Negroes Due for Break."
133. "Tells How Music Was Added to Josephine Baker's Film," *CD*, November 9, 1929. This scoring was done at the Recording Studios of America in New York.
134. Judith Weisenfeld, *Hollywood Be Thy Name* (Berkeley: University of California Press, 2007), 286n29. Smith would later appear in several of Goldberg's race movies.
135. "800 Negro Theatres in 32 States Point to Growing Demand," *MPH*, August 15, 1936, 27.
136. A. H. Weiler, "Ticket for the Chariot," *NYT*, August 3, 1941; "Negroes Movie Conscious; Support 430 Film Houses," *MPH*, January. 24, 1942, 33.
137. Cripps, *Making Movies Black*, 136–40; Weisenfeld, *Hollywood Be Thy Name*, 163–203.
138. "New Goldberg Producing Firm May Buy Studio," *FD*, March 14, 1944, 2; "Negro Marches On, Inc.," *Motion Picture Production Encyclopedia* (Hollywood: Hollywood Reporter Press, 1950), 697.
139. Konrad Nowakowski, "A Few Historical Remarks on *Boogie-Woogie Dream*," at www.colindavey.com, accessed August 14, 2015.
140. For example, the bill did above-average business at the Majestic in Providence. "'Janie', 'Angels' Take Providence Spotlight," *MPD*, September 18, 1944, 8.
141. "3-Min. Video Shorts," *VAR*, October 4, 1944, 9. By 1944 television was already seen as likely to supplant the Soundies market.
142. "Independent," *INDEFB*, April 10, 1945, 44; "Budget $600,000 for 12 Negro Pictures," *MPD*, April 11, 1945, 9.

143. "Sack Will Distribute Six Goldberg Features," *FD*, March 19, 1946, 4; "Plans Dallas Studio for Negro Cast Productions," *FD*, April 16, 1947, 7; "Goldberg-Sack to Make Negro Cast Pix," *FD*, May 20, 1946, 14. As part of the deal, Sack also acquired "all rights" to *Boogie-Woogie Dream, Harlem on Parade,* and *We've Come a Long, Long, Way* ("Sack Acquires Three," *MPH*, April 20, 1946, 45).
144. "Form Herald to Produce Negro Pix," *FD*, August 21, 1946, 2.
145. "Critics Label Sheila Guyse of Stage Another Lena Horne," *CD*, April 12, 1947.
146. Noah Eisenberg, *Edgar G. Ulmer: A Filmmaker at the Margins* (Berkeley: University of California Press, 2014), 177.
147. Vintage posters for *Boy! What a Girl!* feature Gene Krupa's name above the title or in far larger type than the nominal stars.
148. Sidney Poitier, *This Life* (New York: Knopf, 1980), 124.
149. "Screen Guild to Release Herald's Six Negro Pix," *FD*, August 12, 1947, 2.
150. "16 mm Mobile Units to Show Negro Films," *FD*, May 22, 1947, 7.
151. "Goldberg Plans 12 Negro Films," *MPH*, January 11, 1947, 53.
152. "Movie-Making Industry Back in Brooklyn," *BDE*, January 19, 1947. The address is given here as 152 South Oxford Street.
153. "*Miracle in Harlem* on Lot," *CD*, September 13, 1947.
154. William Greaves quoted in Watkins, *Stepin Fetchit*, 248.
155. Juanita Hall would later create important roles in two Rodgers and Hammerstein classics, *South Pacific* (1949) and *Flower Drum Song* (1958).
156. This includes the three Herald pictures for Goldberg and Joseph Seiden's *Stars on Parade* (1946). He died a few weeks before *Miracle in Harlem* was released. "'Vincent Valentini,'" *VAR*, April 21, 1948, 63.
157. "Herald Pictures Granted 20 Permits for Harlem Filming," *MPD*, September 9, 1947, 6; "Along the Rialto," *FD*, September 9, 1947, 4. Perhaps even more surprising was the fact that a press release was issued about this. Filming had started the day before.
158. "Goldberg Signs Shaindlin," *FD*, January 9, 1948, 3. It was to be recorded at RCA by a twenty-five-piece orchestra.
159. "*Miracle in Harlem*," *MPD*, August 13, 1948, 4.
160. Thomas Cripps reports the *Amsterdam News*' observation that Harlem audiences in 1939 preferred "sex and glamour rather than social realism or religious allegory." *Making Movies Black*, 330n16.
161. "*Miracle in Harlem*," *FD*, August 11, 1948, 5; "*Miracle in Harlem*," *STR*, August 21, 1948, 14.
162. "*Miracle in Harlem*," *VAR*, August 11, 1948, 8.
163. "*Miracle in Harlem* on Lot," *CD*, September 13, 1947; Al Monroe, "Thousands of Dollars Wasted Annually."
164. Watkins, *Stepin Fetchit*, 247.
165. "Canada Lee, Lena Horne Making Tolerance Short," *VAR*, September 10, 1947, 1.
166. Ralph Wilk, "Hollywood Vine-Yard," *FD*, October 10, 1947, 6.
167. "Herald Pictures to Make Six in West for SGP," *FD*, November 5, 1947, 2; "Goldberg Transferring Product to Coast," *FD*, November 10, 1947, 2.
168. "E-L Says 'No,'" *INDEFB*, February 16, 1948, 13; "Jack Robinson Biopic, K.O.d by Eagle Lion, May Become a Cause Celebre," *VAR*, February 25, 1948, 4.
169. "Bs, Westerns, Planned for Miami Airport," *STR*, August 13, 1949, 8.
170. "Robinson Wins $14,500 Lawsuit," *CD*, January 16, 1954.
171. "Toddy, Ted," *International Motion Picture Almanac* (1945–1946), 389.
172. "Toddy to Make Colored Features in East," *FD*, November 23, 1945, 6; "Toddy Line-Up Calls for Ten Features, Shorts Series," *FD*, December 12, 1945, 4.

452   4. Race Movies

173. Bill Robinson and Eubie Blake starred in Jack Goldberg's *Harlem Is Heaven* here in 1932, and in 1936 Oscar Micheaux made *Temptation* and *Underworld* for Alfred Sack. The studio, which occupied a prime site overlooking the Hudson at Eighty-Eighth Street and Boulevard East, burned down in 1953.
174. "Dewey (Pigmeat) Markham, Vaudeville and TV Comedian," *NYT*, December 16, 1981.
175. Kliph Nesteroff, "Last Man in Blackface: The World of Pigmeat Markham," *WFMU's Beware of the Blog*, accessed August 1, 2015.
176. "Astor to Start Second Negro Musical on Monday," *FD*, November 28, 1945, 3; "Toddy Signs Markham," *FD*, December 5, 1945, 10.
177. Herman Abrams at Tyler, Texas, Black Film Collection seminar, SMU, February 1985, quoted in G. William Jones, *Black Cinema Treasures*, 164.
178. If so, by 1949 Markham was up to his old tricks with the "love making bureau" skit in William Alexander's *Burlesque in Harlem*.
179. "Negroes Due for Break."
180. "Toddy Will Release 10 Features in '46," *MPD*, January 30, 1946, 3.
181. An exhaustive listing of Newfield's work can be found in "The Films of Sam Newfield" at DukeFilmography.Com, accessed August 2, 2015. But I cannot agree that *Mantan Messes Up* was the first of Newfield's East Coast productions.
182. "Eastern Production Looks Up," *FD*, September 10, 1947, 149.
183. DukeFilmography.Com
184. Dee and Davis, *With Ossie and Ruby*, 160.
185. "Toddy to Distribute," *MPD*, April 30, 1947, 9.
186. One of the few discussions of this film can be found in Weisenfeld, *Hollywood Be Thy Name*, 103–7.
187. Eugene Chadbourne, "Wesley Wilson," AllMusic.Com, seems the source for much of the available information on Wilson and Grant. Last accessed May 10, 2020. Unfortunately, neither Chadbourne nor Judith Weisenfeld seem aware of their participation in *Going to Glory, Come to Jesus*.
188. "Negro Theatre an Expanding Field," *MPH*, April 12, 1947, 18.
189. "Negro Theatre an Expanding Field."
190. Author's Interview with Sol Negrin, ASC, who worked on both films as Hartley's assistant cameraman, December 3, 2016 (in person), and December 8, 2016 (on the telephone).
191. "Distribution," *STR*, October 23, 1948, 4.
192. Binney, "Movies for and wth Negroes."
193. Greaves quoted in Jones, *Black Cinema Treasures*, 165.
194. Binney, "Movies for and with Negroes." The $48,000 would be the producer's share of a hit film generating $80,000 at the box office.
195. Jack Jackson, "The Brass Tacks of Efficient Theatre Management," *STR*, July 2, 1949, 16.
196. The Filmcraft/Edison Studio eventually became a center for television production, hosting such series as *You Are There*, *Man Against Crime*, and *The Hunter*. See "Film Studio Here Engaged by CBS," *NYT*, July 8, 1955.
197. Al Monroe, "Thousands of Dollars Wasted Annually."

5. Eight Million Stories

1. *Tall, Tan and Terrific*, *Beware*, *House-Rent Party*, and *Fight That Ghost* were made by two different producers in three different New York and New Jersey studios.
2. "Horne-Deutsch Mull Prod. East," *VAR*, March 13, 1946, 9, 22. Caldwell's novel, which they had acquired before publication, proved to be the best-selling fiction title of 1946.

3. "Lessers' Crime Newsreel Series with L. J. Valentine," *VAR*, October 17, 1945, 4; "Lesser Bros. Plan N.Y. Feature Production," *VAR*, March 13, 1946, 9. The Lessers' films were said to be produced at the "Filmcrest" (Filmcraft?) studio.
4. "N.Y. Making Some Inroads on Hollywood," *WP*, June 29, 1947. See also Ezra Goodman, "Adventures of a New York Movie Cameraman," *NYT*, March 23, 1947.
5. "Universal," *INDEFB*, May 13, 1946, 25, 30.
6. This would be the last credited screenplay of John Howard Lawson, most notorious of the soon-to-be-blacklisted "Hollywood Ten." He worked from an original story by Dorothy Parker. See Gerald Horne, *The Final Victim of the Blacklist* (Berkeley: University of California Press, 2006),166–69.
7. Matthew Bernstein, *Walter Wanger, Hollywood Independent* (Berkeley: University of California Press, 1994), 217.
8. Bernstein, *Walter Wanger*, 233.
9. A. H. Weiler, "Random Notes on the Film Scene," *NYT*, May 19, 1946.
10. Weiler, "Random Notes on the Film Scene."
11. "Eight Rolling at MGM," *STR*, June 1, 1946, 32. "Location shooting will start shortly in Brooklyn . . . with six weeks set aside for the work."
12. "Metro Is 'Shooting' Sinatra B'klyn Film," *BDE*, July 25, 1946; "Metro to Film More Backgrounds in N.Y.," *VAR*, May 2, 1947, 1.
13. Douglas Gilbert, "And Crowds Flock to Toss in the Color," *NYWT*, July 21, 1947.
14. "Morros, LeBaron, Form Federal Films, Inc.," *FD*, September 11, 1945, 2.
15. Boris Morros, *My Ten Years as a Counter-Spy* (New York: Viking, 1957).
16. These were the most frequently mentioned titles, although *The Wandering Jew* and Thomas Mann's *The Woman of a Hundred Faces* were also floated in the trade press. See "LeBaron—Morros Plans," *MPD*, November 21, 1945, 8; "Morros and LeBaron Start Here August 5," *MPD*, July 22, 1946, 7; "*Carnegie* Will Be Made in East," *MPH*, July 27, 1946, 45; "Filmed in Gotham," *NYT*, December 22, 1946.
17. "Eye Public Reaction to *Carnegie* Music," *FD*, September 12, 1946, 10.
18. Other names floated in the press included Vladimir Horowitz and Duke Ellington. Several reports claimed that Morros had gone to Rome and filmed the Vatican Choir, while Ulmer later claimed, "You don't even see the Toscanini sequence which I made, which was cut because Mr. Morros failed to pay." Peter Bogdanovich, "Edgar G. Ulmer: An Interview," *Film Culture* #58-59-60 (1974), 231.
19. Bogdanovich, "Edgar G. Ulmer."
20. "Chase to Do Screenplay for *Carnegie Hall*," *FD*, October 26, 1945, 6. Chase was one of the great writers of westerns, including *Red River* and *The Man from Laramie*. He wrote *I've Always Loved You* as *Concerto*, but the title was changed before release because, as *Variety* put it, "90 percent of exhibitors canvassed nixed the long-hair tag" ("Borzage's Top Republic Pic Does Titular Segue," October 31, 1945, 9). Morros probably should have paid more attention to this.
21. "Little Headlines," *FD*, June 18, 1946, 6.
22. Bogdanovich, "Edgar G. Ulmer," 231.
23. *Reveille with Beverly* is also an extreme example of the "classics vs jazz" motif, with Ann Miller's musical tastes winning out over those of classical DJ Franklin Pangborn, who is associated with the obsolete music of Beethoven and Mendelsohn. The people making *Carnegie Hall* would have been very aware of this film.
24. See, for example, Tony Tracy, " 'The Gateway to America': Assimilation and Art in *Carnegie Hall*," in *Edgar G. Ulmer: Detour on Poverty Row*, ed. Gary Rhodes (Plymouth, UK: Lexington, 2008), 211–24.
25. "Morros-LeBaron to Make Four Musicals for U.A.," *FD*, March 5, 1946, 1, 7.

26. See Paul A. Cantor, "Film Noir and the Frankfurt School," in *The Philosophy of Film Noir*, ed. Mark T. Conard (Lexington: University Press of Kentucky, 2007), 139–61.
27. Many of these same classics-vs-jazz issues had already been treated by Ulmer, in more sketchy form, in *Jive Junction* (1943). See Noah Isenberg, *Edgar G. Ulmer: A Filmmaker at the Margins* (Berkeley: University of California Press: 2014), 141–44.
28. "Carnegie Hall," *MPH*, May 24, 1947, 48.
29. "Stereophonic Sound Via *Carnegie Hall*," *FD*, July 22, 1946, 1, 13.
30. "Along the Rialto," *FD*, August 16, 1946, 3.
31. "Record *Carnegie Hall* Music with Aid of New Equipment," *BDE*, August 4, 1946.
32. "New Recording System, *NYT*, September 1, 1946.
33. When Academy Award nominations were announced that year, neither the music nor the sound recording of *Carnegie Hall* were judged worthy of recognition by the Academy.
34. "Studio Situation Threatens Commitment Conflict, *FD*, March 19, 1946, 9.
35. "Morros and LeBaron Start Here Aug. 5," *MPD*, July 2, 1946, 7.
36. "Pathe's New Studio, OK for Shorts, May Be Small for H'wood Features," *VAR*, December 18, 1946, 15.
37. "City Hall Mayor—*Carnegie Hall* Player," *FD*, August 6, 1946, 7.
38. "The Mayor Takes Over the Direction of a Motion Picture," *NYT*, August 6, 1946; "'On Location' in Carnegie Hall," *NYTM*, September 1, 1946, 48–49.
39. "UA Halts Some Features," *STR*, October 5, 1946, 42.
40. "Plenty of Equipment for N.Y. Production," *FD*, August 23, 1946, 1, 16.
41. "Morros and LeBaron for Eastern Studio," *FD*, October 21, 1946, 1, 6.
42. "Along the Rialto," *FD*, October 28, 1946, 18.
43. "Bricken on *Carnegie*," *MPD*, August 27, 1946, 8.
44. "*Carnegie Hall* Shatters a Myth," *FD*, special *Carnegie Hall* supplement, October 30, 1946, 11–18.
45. "Critics Label Sheila Guyse of Stage Another Lena Horne," *CD*, April 12, 1947.
46. "Filmed in Gotham," *NYT*, December 22, 1946.
47. "N.Y. Good for Some Pix," *VAR*, October 30, 1946, 7.
48. "Carnegie Hall," *FD*, October 28, 1946, 11.
49. Bosley Crowther, "The Screen," *NYT*, May 3, 1947.
50. James Agee, *Agee on Film* (New York: Beacon, 1958), 251, reprints his May 10, 1947, review of *Carnegie Hall* from *The Nation*.
51. Olin Downes, "*Carnegie Hall* May Be Milestone Despite Story," *NYT*, May 25, 1947. Downes reported that several weeks into the run it was still difficult to get seats for the film on a Sunday evening.
52. Financial information from United Artist Corporations records, U.S. Mss 99AN Series 3A, Box 12, folder 1, Wisconsin Center for Film and Theater Research, courtesy of Mary Huelsbeck.
53. "N.Y. Symph Plays 2D Role, in RKO Film," *VAR*, April 16, 1947, 37.
54. Thomas F. Brady, "Looking in on Hollywood," *NYT*, June 22, 1947.
55. "No N.Y. Exhib Bloc in Mayoralty—Brandt," *VAR*, September 19, 1945, 4.
56. "N.Y.'s New Mayor O'Dwyer to Ballyhoo Gotham as World's No. 1 Amus. Capital," *VAR*, January 2, 1946, 1.
57. One of the killings Reles was due to talk about was that of waterfront organizer Pete Panto. The death of Panto inspired Arthur Miller to write a waterfront corruption film script for Elia Kazan, *The Hook* (see pages 307–8.).
58. The incident later appeared in another New York production, *Murder, Inc.* (1960). But that film featured only Turkus and Reles and failed to mention either O'Dwyer or Costello.

59. See George Walsh, *Public Enemies: The Mayor, the Mob and the Crime That Was* (New York: Norton, 1980).
60. "NYC Theatres Reopen After Shutdown," *VAR*, February 13, 1946, 1
61. "N.Y. Theatremen Appeal Both to Dewey and O'Dwyer on New Tax, *VAR*, February 27, 1946, 19; "NYC Exhibs Protest Proposed 5 Percent Ticket Tax," *FD*, March 11, 1946, 1; "Amusement Tax Levy out of O'Dwyer's Tax Bill," *FD*, March 13, 1946, 2.
62. "O'Dwyer Draws N.Y. Nix by Show Biz," *VAR*, February 20, 1946, 1.
63. "Commercial-Pictures Group Promotes New Move for Eastern Production," *VAR*, February 6, 1946, 9; "Eastern Indies Chill O'Dwyer on Brushoff," *VAR*, February 27, 1946, 19; "Indies Seek N.Y. Mayor O'Dwyer's Aid in Recapturing Par (L.I.) Studio," *VAR*, April 3, 1946, 3; "Despite Studio Shortage Majors Don't Favor Prod. Shifting to East," *VAR*, April 17, 1946, 10.
64. "Commercial-Pictures Group Promotes New Move."
65. "O'Dwyer Takes Hand in UNO Tele Camera Row," *FD*, April 1, 1946, 1; "Withdraw Video Coverage of UNO," *MPD*, April 4, 1946, 6.
66. "Johnston, O'Dwyer Busy with Denials," *MPD*, July 9, 1946, 4.
67. "City Hall Mayor—'Carnegie Hall' Player," *FD*, August 6, 1946, 7.
68. "Publicity Barrage," *STR*, August 10, 1946, 20.
69. Malvin Wald, "Afterword," in Malvin Wald and Albert Maltz, *The Naked City* (Carbondale: Southern Illinois University Press, 1979), 135–37, 144.
70. Jim Bishop, *The Mark Hellinger Story* (New York: Appleton-Century-Crofts, 1952), 328–29.
71. Bishop, *Mark Hellinger*, 328.
72. "Little Headlines," *FD*, October 8, 1946, 8.
73. "N.Y.'s Homicide Bureau in Crime Pic Via Hellinger," *VAR*, October 9, 1946, 13.
74. Ed Baldwin interviewed by Richard Koszarski, June 5, 1979. Museum of the Moving Image Oral History Collection.
75. "Strikes, Costs Cue Prod. Move Away from Hollywood," *VAR*, October 30, 1946, 7.
76. "N.Y. Good for Some Pix."
77. "Sun, Smiles Beam on Macy's Parade," *NYT*, November 29, 1946.
78. Gavin Lambert, *Natalie Wood, A Life* (New York: Knopf, 2004), 45.
79. Zanuck to William Perlberg and George Seaton, November 6, 1946, in *Memo from Darryl F. Zanuck*, ed. Rudy Behlmer (New York: Grove, 1993), 119–20.
80. All of this casting was last minute; just a few weeks earlier the studio had seen this as a Victor Mature picture, with Nancy Guild playing "a young lady of character who becomes involved in a postwar marriage not altogether happy, but who maintains her personal integrity in the midst of various disturbing events." Edwin Schallert, "Nancy Guild to Reveal Her True Personality," *LAT*, September 15, 1946.
81. A. H. Weiler, "Random Notes About People and Pictures," *NYT*, December 8, 1946. This article also cites the use of a third-floor apartment at 253 West Fifty-Eighth Street for some portion of the parade coverage. A mail handling scene was shot inside the main post office, and exteriors of the New York State Supreme Court were used to support courtroom interiors shot back at the studio. See also Irene Kahn Atkins (interviewer), *Arthur Jacobson, The Assistant Director* (Metuchen, NJ: DGA and Scarecrow, 1991), 162.
82. Thomajan was a longtime associate of Elia Kazan as both actor and dialogue director; Albertson, an Oscar winner for *The Subject Was Roses* (1968), became a familiar face on such television series as *Chico and the Man* (1974–1978). Thelma Ritter, another New Yorker, made her film debut here as a Macy's shopper. All these actors were uncredited.

83. Maureen O'Hara, with John Nicoletti, *'Tis Herself* (New York: Simon and Schuster, 2004), 116. O'Hara remembers this happening during the suburban home scene near the end of the film, where Natalie Wood calls out, "Stop! That's it!"
84. Atkins, *Arthur Jacobson*, 162–63. Some store interiors, especially those requiring more complicated setups or extended dialogue, were shot on sets built to match back in California.
85. Neither Jacobson, Klune, nor Hall received screen credit, but the *American Film Institute Catalog* lists them in these roles for *Miracle on 34th Street*.
86. Edwin Schallert, "*Miracle on 34th Street* Decisively Out of World," *LAT*, June 14, 1947.
87. Figures from Aubrey Solomon, *Twentieth Century-Fox, A Corporate and Financial History* (Metuchen, NJ: Scarecrow, 1988).
88. Atkins, *Arthur Jacobson*, 162.
89. *Miracle on 34th Street*, American Film Institute Catalog.
90. Zanuck to Perlberg and Seaton, in Behlmer, *Memo*, 119–20.
91. Lambert, *Natalie Wood*, 45.
92. Atkins, *Arthur Jacobson*, 164.
93. Philip K. Scheuer, "Motherhood Is Woman's Real Career, Star Declares," *LAT*, June 8, 1947.
94. O'Hara, *'Tis Herself*, 118
95. *Miracle on 34th Street* won Oscars for Story and for Screenplay, as well as Best Supporting Actor (Edmund Gwenn). Fox was pushing another film that year, *Gentleman's Agreement*, which also won three. *It's a Wonderful Life* won nothing.
96. M. E. Freedgood, "Movies: By the Dawn's Early Light," *NYT*, July 8, 1951. According to the *AFI Catalog* the film also shot in Central Park, on a midtown bus, and at the Magistrate's Court on East Fifty-Seventh Street.
97. Bosley Crowther, "The Screen in Review," *NYT*, April 4, 1952. Based on a memoir that described events of twenty years earlier, the film had been updated to the Cold War era.
98. Thomas M. Pryor, "200 in Hollywood Screened in Loyalty Test by Studios," *NYT*, May 23, 1952.
99. "*Triumph* Scenes to Be Made Here," *NYT*, November 5, 1946; "*Arch* Filming Here," *MPD*, Novenber 8, 1946, 2.
100. Ezra Goodman, "Adventures of a New York Cameraman." Years later Clint Eastwood used digital technology for a similar effect in *Sully* (2016).
101. Richard L. Coe, "Club's Extras Help Hollywood in N.Y. Scenes," *WP*, April 6, 1947. This article also claims that "background shots" for *The Snake Pit* were then being shot in Brooklyn. See also A. H. Weiler, "Random Notes About Pictures and People," *NYT*, March 9, 1947. Other *Hucksters* scenes to be shot by Waters included views of Sutton Place and "the approaches to Jones Beach" (but not the beach itself).
102. "N. A. Rockefeller, Aides Quit as City's Business Advisers," *NYT*, May 18, 1947.
103. "Car of O'Dwyer Aide Kills Man on 8th Avenue," *NYT*, May 11, 1946.
104. Paul Crowell, "Pier Case Grows," *NYT*, May 23, 1947; William Conklin, "Action to Be Swift," *NYT*, May 24, 1947; William Conklin, "Cruise Line Official Renews His Charges Against Sanders," *NYT*, May 25, 1947.
105. "Film Liaison in Coordinating Plans," *MPD*, May 8, 1947, 1. Members included Local 52 head Sal Scoppa; Steve Fitzgibbons of Fox Movietone; Harold Lewis of RKO-Pathé; and O'Dwyer's "municipal labor conciliator," Edward Maguire.
106. "O'Dwyer Urges More Production in N.Y.," *MPD*, May 1, 1947, 1.
107. "Plans for City Film Co-Ordinator Stalled," *VAR*, May 23, 1947, 1, 6.
108. "Tendency to On-Location Shooting Part of New Concept for Economics," *VAR*, April 9, 1947, 3, 52.

109. Malvin Wald, "Cops and Writers," *SW* (December 1947), 23–26.
110. Malvin Wald to Mark Hellinger, October 11, 1946, USC Cinema-Television Collection. Cited in Carl Richardson, *Autopsy: An Element of Realism in Film Noir* (Metuchen, NJ: Scarecrow, 1992), 97.
111. Wald, "Afterword," 138–39.
112. Wald, "Afterword," 140.
113. Luc Sante, "New York Plays Itself," in Criterion Collection *The Naked City* Blu-ray insert, 4.
114. Mark Hellinger, "Handsome Boy," in *Moon Over Broadway* (New York: William Faro, 1931), 99–105.
115. Herb A. Lightman, "*The Naked City*: Tribute in Celluloid," *AC*, May 1948, 153.
116. Hellinger, *Moon Over Broadway*, 28–33.
117. *FD*, Oct. 21, 1946, 3 (proud); *FD*, September 11, 1947, 5 (option).
118. Wald, "Afterword," 141.
119. Brooks quoted in Wald, "Afterword," 141.
120. Wald, "Afterword," 140–44.
121. Cynthia Grenier, "Jules Dassin, an Interview," *S&S*, Winter 1957–58, 142.
122. Colin Burnett, "The 'Albert Maltz Affair' and the Debate Over Para-Marxist Formalism in *New Masses*, 1945–46," *Journal of American Studies* 48:1 (February 2014), 223–50. The "Maltz affair" is central to most histories of the Hollywood left. See, for example, Larry Ceplair and Steven Englund, *The Inquisition in Hollywood* (Urbana: University of Chicago Press, 2003), 232–37.
123. Among the actors working in Hellinger's Universal-International productions were Howard Duff, Jeff Corey, Roman Bohnen, Hume Cronyn, Albert Dekker, and Art Smith, all of whom were subsequently blacklisted or greylisted.
124. Quoted in Rebecca Prime, "Cloaked in Compromise: Jules Dassin's *Naked City*," in *"Un-American" Hollywood*, ed. Frank Krutnik, et al. (New Brunswick, NJ: Rutgers University Press, 2007), 148. Prime appears to have been the first to establish a link between this film and the writings of the Soviet theorist and filmmaker Dziga Vertov (who happened to be the brother of Boris Kaufman).
125. Richardson, *Autopsy*, 108.
126. Richardson, *Autopsy*, 107–9.
127. Prime, "Cloaked in Compromise," 308n49.
128. Dassin continued trying to help his friend, convincing Darryl F. Zanuck to allow him to film Maltz's novel *The Journey of Simon McKeever* (1949). But Maltz's premature announcement that he had "broken the blacklist" with this assignment scuttled the project. Patrick McGilligan and Paul Buhle, *Tender Comrades* (New York: St. Martin's, 1997), 207–8.
129. "U Shooting 2 in N.Y.," *VAR*, June 4, 1947, 6.
130. *The Naked City, a Screenplay by Albert Maltz and Malvin Wald* (Carbondale: SIU, 1979), 129–30.
131. "Notes on Chase Sequence—*The Naked City*," Mark Hellinger to Julie [Dassin], n.d., Criterion Collection *Naked City* DVD insert.
132. Hellinger felt that Jack Warner and Hal Wallis had cheated him out of his producer credit on this film, leading to a lifelong enmity with both studio executives. See Bishop, *Mark Hellinger*, 252–55.
133. Thomas F. Brady, "John Ford to Do a Film in Ireland," *NYT*, May 29, 1947, and "Inside Stuff: Pictures," *VAR*, June 11, 1947, 18.
134. Jacquelyn Judge, "Shooting *The Naked City*," *Photography*, Winter 1947, 94. This article is illustrated with twenty-three photographs credited generically to Weegee, Clemens

Kalischer, and Universal-International. The only image ascribed to anyone in particular is a single shot by Weegee of children playing in a hydrant stream.
135. Available in the *Look* magazine collection at the Museum of the City of New York.
136. Arthur Fellig [Weegee], *Naked City* (New York: Essential, 1945). See also Anthony Lee and Richard Meyer, *Weegee and "Naked City"* (Berkeley: University of California Press, 2008). *Weegee's New York* (1948), an impressionistic 16 mm film assembled by the photographer, has even less connection with Hellinger's film.
137. For example, James Agee's April 24, 1948, review in *The Nation*, reprinted in *Agee on Film*, 301.
138. Daily Call Sheets in Mark Hellinger Collection, USC, cited in Richardson, *Autopsy*.
139. Judge, "Shooting *The Naked City*," 94–98, 106, 108.
140. "Kaufman to Direct Film Scenes Here," *NYT*, June 2, 1947; "Studio Roundup," *STR*, June 21, 1947, 33.
141. "N.Y. Making Some Inroads On Hollywood," *WP*, June 29, 1947.
142. A. H. Weiler, "By Way of Report," *NYT*, June 1, 1947.
143. *NYT*, May 28, 1947. The Greenwich was part of a small chain that played what might be called recent revivals; these films were several years old.
144. Kazan, *A Life* (New York: Knopf, 1988), 331.
145. A. H. Weiler, "By Way of Report," *NYT*, June 1, 1947; "*Gentleman's Agreement* Crew Back for More Shooting," *FD*, August 7, 1947, 2.
146. "The Picture-Hanger Corrects the Artist," *WP*, May 31, 1947.
147. Kazan wanted a script from Paul Osborn, who later wrote *East of Eden* and *Wild River* for him. Kazan, *A Life*, 331.
148. Bishop, *Mark Hellinger*, 336–45.
149. Selznick later identified Hellinger's sudden death as one of the key elements that "frustrated" his operational plans for the Selznick Releasing Organization. He had counted on Hellinger to provide three films a year to feed the SRO pipeline. Rudy Behlmer (ed.), *Memo from David O. Selznick* (New York: Viking, 1972), 293–94.
150. "Of Local Origin," *NYT*, August 16, 1947.
151. Edward Dimendberg, *Film Noir and the Spaces of Modernity* (Cambridge, MA: Harvard University Press, 2004), 273n76.
152. John Francis Lane, "I See Dassin Make *The Law*," *Films and Filming*, September 4, 1958, 28, quoted in Richardson, *Autopsy*, 104.
153. *Naked City* Daily Production Report, Mark Hellinger Collection, July 29, 1947. But Bruce Goldstein, a neighborhood resident, tells me that it was really 252 East First Street. Email to author, August 20, 2020.
154. "Millions Fill Beaches Here in 87° Heat," *NYT*, September 1, 1947.
155. "Eastern Prod.'s Labor 'Saving,' " *VAR*, August 6, 1947, 7, 31.
156. Gilbert, "And Crowds Flock to Toss in the Color."
157. Malvin Wald's commentary track, Criterion Collection *The Naked City* DVD edition.
158. For information on these dates and locations see Richardson, *Autopsy*, 89–92.
159. The local unions did not appreciate this sort of flexibility, and the business manager of Local 644 sent a strongly worded telegram to the production manager, Gilbert Kurland, on September 30. NYU Local 644 files, Box 6, "Universal-International Pictures" file.
160. Miklós Rózsa, *A Double Life* (New York: Wynwood, 1989), 152–53. I believe that this unnamed composer was George Bassman, with whom Dassin had worked on four films at MGM. Blacklisted as a Communist Party member, he later testified before HUAC as a friendly witness.

161. Bishop, *Mark Hellinger*, 359–60.
162. Rózsa, *A Double Life*, 153–54.
163. Rózsa, *A Double Life*, 154. But in his Criterion Collection DVD commentary, Malvin Wald claims that it was Skinner who did the first, rejected, score.
164. "O'Dwyer at Rites on Coast," *NYT*, December 25, 1947.
165. Thomas F. Brady, "No Changes," *NYT*, January 18, 1948.
166. Dassin reported this to Rebecca Prime, "Cloaked in Compromise," 149–50.
167. Jules Dassin interviewed by Bruce Goldstein at LACMA screening (2004) on Criterion Collection *Naked City* DVD.
168. Grenier, "Jules Dassin, an Interview."
169. The January 21, 1948, *Variety* review refers to a January 20 screening of the final ninety-six-minute cut.
170. Jules Dassin interviewed by Bruce Goldstein.
171. Richardson, *Autopsy*, 106.
172. Wald, "Afterword," 145–46.
173. Rebecca Prime writes that Dassin left Hollywood in November. She also says he told her that on *Naked City* he spent "the least amount of time in the cutting room," of any of his films, which would contradict his 1957 interview with *Sight and Sound*. Prime, "Cloaked in Compromise," 309n60.
174. Maltz and Wald, *The Naked City, a Screenplay*, 5.
175. Prime, "Cloaked in Compromise," 150, 310n64.
176. Quoted from Bishop, *Mark Hellinger*, 355–57. An almost identical version appears in Goodman's own book, *The Fifty Year Decline and Fall of Hollywood* (New York: Simon and Schuster, 1961), 421–22.
177. "Top Grossers of 1948," *VAR*, January 5, 1949, 46. Universal's highest grossing release in 1948 was *Hamlet* ($3.25 million), a British film they distributed for J. Arthur Rank. *Tap Roots* grossed $2.5 million (but was seen as a loss because of its excessive production costs), and *The Naked City* was third at $2.4 million.
178. Kay Sullivan, *Parade*, March 7, 1948 [realistic]; Kahn., *VAR*, January 21, 1948 [tabloid].
179. *Cue*, March 6, 1948.
180. Howard Barnes, "On the Screen," *NYHT*, March 5, 1948.
181. *New Movies*, April 1948; James Agee, *The Nation*, April 24, 1948, reprinted in *Agee on Film*, 301.
182. *NY*, March 13, 1948.
183. Bosley Crowther, "*Naked City*, Mark Hellinger's Final Film, at Capitol," *NYT*, March 5, 1948; Bosley Crowther, "Tales of Two Cities," *NYT*, March 14, 1948.
184. Wald, "Afterword," 147.

6. The O'Dwyer Plan

1. Edward Ellis, "Film-Making Is Big Splash on N.Y. Scene," *NYWT*, November 1, 1947. This is the final installment in a six episode series on the local film industry that Ellis published beginning October 27.
2. "New York Beckons to Movie Industry," *LAT*, November 17, 1947.
3. "Story," *MPH*, June 7, 1947, 8.
4. "Mayor to Fly to Coast," *NYT*, June 28, 1946; "Film Biog Slated on Mayor O'Dwyer," *VAR*, June 4, 1947, 5.
5. "Mayor O'Dwyer's $200,000 Pix Price," *VAR*, October 6, 1948, 1.

6. "Maguire to Resign City Post on Aug. 31," *NYT*, June 9, 1947; "Maguire's Service Praised by Mayor," *NYT*, August 5, 1947.
7. "Mayor Names Maguire City Film Co-Ordinator," *FD*, July 10, 1947, 2;
8. "City Would Lure Movie industry," *NYT*, July 10, 1947.
9. "Coordination," *NY*, January 3, 1948, 16–17.
10. Richard Koszarski, *Hollywood on the Hudson* (New Brunswick, NJ: Rutgers University Press, 2008), 211.
11. Herb A. Lightman, "*A Double Life*: The Camera Goes Back Stage," *AC*, April 1948, 133.
12. A. H. Weiler, "By Way of Report," *NYT*, August 31, 1947.
13. "Along the Rialto," *FD*, September 5, 1947, 6.
14. "Coordination," *NY*.
15. A. H. Raskin, "Movie Unions Sign Peace Pact Here; City to Aid Industry," *NYT*, August 28, 1947 (floodlights); "Eastern Film Labor Pact Signed with O'Dwyer," *FD*, August 28, 1947, 1 (most dramatic).
16. "NYC to Introduce New Filming Permit," *MPD*, September 9, 1947, 1.
17. "N.Y. Seeks to Level Production Hurdles in City," *STR*, September 20, 1947, 6, 8.
18. "N.Y. City Fathers Deny Film Indie's Graft Charges," *VAR*, September 17, 1947, 3.
19. Edward C. Maguire, "New York Motion Picture Production," *JSMPE*, January 1948, 4–7.
20. Edward Ellis, " 'Come Home!' City Tells Movies," *NYWT*, October 27, 1947.
21. Maguire, "Motion Picture Production."
22. Bosley Crowther, "Hollywood Versus New York," *NYTM*, August 3, 1947, 10, 17–18.
23. Bosley Crowther, "Luring Hollywood," *NYTM*, November 5, 1939, 19.
24. Crowther, "Hollywood Versus New York."
25. Mayor William O'Dwyer (as told to Ed Sullivan), "Our Town," *MS*, January 1948, 28.
26. "Pathe Lot to Get O'Dwyer O-O on East Prod. Survey," *FD*, July 22, 1947, 1.
27. "Eberson Readies Telecity Plan for Mayor," *FD*, July 23, 1947, 1.
28. Chas. Alicoate, "Production Facilities in and About New York," *FDYBK* (1947), 181–84; "Fort Lee Studios Sold to Long Island Group," *FD*, September 26, 1947, 1, 7; Ezra Goodman, "On Its Way Out—Fort Lee—on Its Way In," *NYHT*, October 26, 1947.
29. "Skyscraper $20,000,000 Studio in N.Y. Insists Pix Majors Pledge Co-op," *VAR*, October 22, 1947, 3; Edward Ellis, "Ghosts Flicker in Fort Lee Studios," *NYWT*, October 29, 1947.
30. Koszarski, *Hollywood on the Hudson*, 486–88.
31. Ellis, "Ghosts Flicker."
32. This author remembers working with Tom and Nancy Hoving on a NYSCA-funded development plan for the derelict Astoria Studio in 1977. A glass-enclosed observation deck, from which the public could observe film and television production activity, was discussed at some length before being dismissed over tenant privacy concerns.
33. "N.Y. Studio Project Interests 2 Majors," *FD*, October 31, 1947, 1.
34. Ellis, " 'Come Home!' "
35. "RKO-Pathe's NBC Lease No Crimp to Eastern Prod. Hopes," *VAR*, May 19, 1948, 7.
36. Thomas Brody, "Academic Approach to Films," *NYT*, June 20, 1948. An earlier report by Edwin Schallert, "Goetz to Start British Invasion This Summer," *LAT*, April 5, 1948, claimed that "about a third of the actual production will be shot in actual locales."
37. Pearson had been in Hollywood for a year without winning a single assignment. See Gladwin Hill, "Starting at the Top," *NYT*, September 12, 1948.
38. Paul Buhle and Dave Wagner, *A Very Dangerous Citizen: Abraham Lincoln Polonsky and the American Left* (Berkeley: University of California Press, 2001), 108.
39. "*Body and Soul*," American Film Institute Catalog.

40. Thomas F. Brady, "Enterprise Gets *Tucker's People*," *NYT*, April 5, 1948.
41. Polonsky interviewed in Eric Sherman and Martin Rubin, *The Director's Event* (New York: Atheneum, 1970), 20.
42. "N.Y.C. *Numbers Racket* Footage Shot Silently," *FD*, August 2, 1948, 3.
43. Other locations included Trinity Churchyard and stretches of Riverside Drive between 136th and 151st Streets, although the latter may only have been used for back projections.
44. "Resume Shooting Here on *Numbers Racket*," *FD*, July 29, 1948, 3.
45. Philip Scheuer, "Polonsky, Meteoric Writer of Script, Wins Right to Direct *Tucker's People*," *LAT*, June 13, 1948.
46. John Schultheiss and Mark Schaubert (eds.), *Force of Evil: The Critical Edition* (Northridge, CA: Center for Telecommunications Studies, 1996), 176.
47. Lindsay Anderson, "The Last Sequence of *On the Waterfront*," *S&S*, January–March 1955, 127–130.
48. Andrew Sarris, *The American Cinema* (New York: Dutton, 1968), 220.
49. Ann Lewis, "Production Parade," *STR*, October 2, 1948, 28,
50. The famous phrase is from "Awake and Sing," a piece of 1930s agit-prop by Clifford Odets.
51. Edwin Schallert, "*Amboy Dukes* Cast Set," *LAT*, September 17, 1948.
52. James S. Barstow, Jr., "Brooklyn's the Happy Shooting Ground for a Producer," *NYHT*, April 3, 1949. Other locations included Prospect Park, the Marine Parkway Bridge, and Boys High School.
53. "Studio Roundup," *STR*, October 2, 1948, 28.
54. Herb A. Lightman, "Documentary Style," *AC*, May 1949, 161, 174–75.
55. A. H. Weiler, "Random Items About People and Pictures," *NYT*, April 3, 1949.
56. Display ad, *BDE*, April 5, 1949.
57. "A Tempest That Brewed in Brooklyn Blew 'Disparaging' Words from Movie Foreword," *NYT*, April 12, 1949.
58. "NYC Filming Report Submitted to Mayor," *MPD*, December 18, 1947, 1.
59. "Three More Hollywood Companies Join Those Shooting Location Sequences in New York," *FD*, May 12, 1948, 7. The other companies were those making *Force of Evil* and *You Gotta Stay Happy*, for which James Stewart and Eddie Albert were filmed getting in and out of airplanes at Newark Airport ("By Way of Report," *NYT*, May 2, 1948).
60. "Eastern Film Production's Biggest Impetus Aimed at Television Market," *VAR*, December 31, 1947, 1.
61. Sam Zolotow, "Danzigers May Do Spewacks' Comedy," *NYT*, July 25, 1947.
62. "Mrs. Danziger Divorced," *NYT*, July 16, 1950.
63. "Eastern Sound Studios to Dub Para., UA Films," *FD*, October 31, 1944, 1.
64. "Sue for 150G, Charge Film Appropriated," *VAR*, January 12, 1949, 5.
65. "U.S. Consul in Havana Preparing Handbook to Guide Yank Producers," *VAR*, May 28, 1947, 6.
66. Wonder had worked in the Ziegfeld Follies and danced in a number of 1940s Hollywood musicals. Doris Dowling was better known as a dramatic actress; she played one of Ray Milland's drinking buddies in *The Lost Weekend* and the murder victim in *The Blue Dahlia*. After *Sarumba* she moved to Europe, where she appeared in such films as *Bitter Rice* and Orson Welles's *Othello*.
67. "*Sarumba* with Michael Whalen, Doris Dowling and Tommy Wonder," *HAR*, March 25, 1950, 47.
68. "Astor Snares *Sarumba* from Ed Danziger," *VAR*, September 3, 1952, 5.
69. A. H. Weiler, "By Way of Report," *NYT*, May 2, 1948.

70. Mark Barron, "New York Is Location for Danziger Movies," *WP*, April 8, 1950.
71. Norman Keane, "*Jigsaw* Filmed Without Sound or Sets," *AC*, December 1948, 412, 427–28.
72. Keane, "*Jigsaw*."
73. Christopher Sterling (ed.), *Museum of Broadcast Communications Encyclopedia of Radio* (New York: Fitzroy Dearborn, 2004), 1512.
74. Weiler, "By Way of Report," *NYT*, May 2, 1948; "Of Local Origin," *NYT*, June 3, 1948.
75. "Franchot Tone in *Numbers Racket*," *LAT*, July 31, 1948.
76. Philip K. Scheuer, "*Jigsaw* Gives Serious Subject Odd Treatment," *LAT*, March 30, 1949.
77. Keane, "*Jigsaw*."
78. "*Jigsaw*," *HR*, March 8, 1949.

7. Joe Lerner's New York Noir

1. Unless noted, direct quotations in this chapter are from my July 16, 1987, interview with Joseph and Geraldine Lerner, and our 1984–1996 correspondence. An edited version of the interview appeared as "Joseph Lerner and the Post-War New York Film Renaissance," *FH* (1995), 457–78. Audio of the complete 1987 interview is available at https://www.bynwr.com/articles/joseph-lerner-speaks.
2. "To Show Olympic Feature," *FD*, January 15, 1948, 6.
3. "*Kings of the Olympics*," *MPD*, January 24, 1948, 49.
4. Arthur Daley, "Sports of the Times," *NYT*, March 29, 1948.
5. Walter Winchell, "Gossip of the Nation," *PI*, May 21, 1948.
6. Leni Riefenstahl, *A Memoir* (New York: St. Martin's, 1993), 356.
7. "Carlton-Lerner's 150G Indie Pic Made in N.Y.," *VAR*, December 29, 1948, 7. This announcement claims the film would be shot "at the Fort Lee studio" beginning January 12, but *C-Man* was shot at Reeves instead. It was described as completed by *VAR* on February 2 ("Edith Atwater Finishes First Screen Assignment," 49).
8. "Magnetic Recording," *BSM* X:5 (1949), 44–45. The first film to use the Magicorder was a documentary made by Alexander Hammid at Princeton. See illustrations in "The Princeton Movie," *Princeton Alumni Weekly*, November 26, 1948, 5.
9. Hazard Reeves, "Adding the Sound to Cinerama," in *New Screen Techniques*, ed. Martin Quigley (New York: Quigley, 1953), 129.
10. He also became one of the first Local 644 men to work in Hollywood, shooting films like *Young Frankenstein* (1974) and *Two-Minute Warning* (1976).
11. Saulter's name is misspelled in the credits ("Salter") as is the name of assistant director Sal Scoppa, Jr. (Scappa). I don't know if this is just sloppiness or a statement of some kind.
12. Frederick W. Sternfeld, "Gail Kubik's Score for *C-Man*," *HQ* IV:4 (Summer 1950), 360–69, is an especially thorough analysis of this landmark score.
13. Everett Helm, "Gail Kubik's Score for *C-Man*: The Sequel," *QFRTV* (Spring 1955), 263–82, compares the two versions.
14. Herm., "*C-Man*," *VAR*, April 20, 1949.
15. William K. Everson, "Guilty Pleasures," *FC*, November–December 1979, 31.
16. "Dorfmann Coin Backing Indie Pix for 20th-Fox," *FD*, July 15, 1948, 6. Dorfmann announced that he would be backing a large number of independent productions, but *Guilty Bystander* appears to have been the only one actually released.
17. "*Guilty Bystander*," *HR*, February 8, 1950.

18. Jake Hinkson, "The New Yorkers: Joseph and Geraldine Lerner and the East Coast Poverty Row," *Noir City* (Summer 2015), 33–38.
19. Edwin Schallert, "Scott, Emerson Star in *Guilty Bystander*," *LAT*, August 8, 1949; "Mystery Film to Use Gowanus as Background," *BDE*, August 6, 1949. Both reports claim that Juanita Hall, star of *South Pacific*, would also be in it, but she does not appear in the film as released. According to the *Chicago Defender*, she had written the music for "Love Can Hurt You," lyrics by Langston Hughes, which she was to introduce in the film (" 'Bloody Mary' Writes Song for Picture," September 10, 1949). Could the Hughes lyrics have been related to his poem "Lament Over Love"?
20. "Close-Up: Dede Allen," *FE*, June 1968, 2, 6, 8.
21. "Mystery Film to Use Gowanus as Background"; "Lerner, Director of *Bystander*, Lauds N.Y. as Film Scene," *MPD*, March 6, 1950, 6.
22. A. H. Weiler, "Notes on the Film Scene," *NYT*, September 4, 1949.
23. "Lerner Lauds N.Y."
24. Kubik instituted a lawsuit over this. "Composer Sues for 10G in Laurel Pact Breach," *VAR*, August 15, 1951, 7.
25. Philip and Teresa DiTullio, "The Woodshed: The Power of Permutation," at schillingersociety.com, accessed December 3, 2018.
26. Bosley Crowther, "An Involved Hunt," *NYT*, April 21, 1950; Seymour Peck, "Note of Sympathy to Faye Emerson & Zachary Scott," *New York Compass*, April 21, 1950.
27. George Carpozi, Jr., *Vincent Edwards* (New York: Belmont, 1962), 56–61. This book does not mention Lerner and claims that Hal Wallis cast Edwards in the part!
28. See especially the wrestling gags in Kramer's *Grips, Grunts and Groans*, directed by Jack White in 1937.
29. "Broadway," *VAR*, May 3, 1950, 62; "Foolproof," *NY*, May 13, 1950.
30. Edgar S. Van Olinda, "Producer of *Bystander* Played Stock in Albany," unidentified clipping included in *Guilty Bystander* pressbook, courtesy of Joseph Lerner.
31. "Carlton's $504,385 Liabilities in Bkptcy.," *VAR*, October 1, 1952, 7.
32. "Easier Loans Indicate Banks' Confidence," *FD*, September 17, 1948, 1. "UA in Bank Tieup to Audition Prod. Packages on Coin," *VAR*, November 12, 1952, 5, shows Gettinger and Van Pelt working as a team in setting up bank financing for United Artists.
33. Tino Balio, *United Artists, the Company That Changed the Film Industry* (Madison: University of Wisconsin Press, 2009), 35; "ELC's 'Clean Slate' as Old EL Folds," *VAR*, September 20, 1950, 7.
34. See Supreme Court of the State of New York, Appellate Division, First Department, "Irving Kaufman, as Assignee for the Benefit of Creditors of Film Classics, Inc., plaintiff, against Eagle-Lion Classics, Inc., et al., defendants," especially affidavit of Thomas Capek, November 4, 1954, which unpacks some of the connections among Chemical Bank and Trust, Film Classics, Laurel Films, and various other entities contesting the rights to these films. Thanks to David Pierce for pointing this ruling out to me.
35. "E-L Merger with F-C Close to Inking Stage," *INDEFB*, May 8, 1950, 17
36. "ELC Aims Lasso at UA Prods.," *VAR*, September 13, 1950, 5; "Growing List of Banks Doing Biz with ELC," *VAR*, September 20, 1950, 7.
37. "Of Local Origin," *NYT*, August 30, 1950. The first of the new films, *Live This Life*, was due to start shooting in New York on October 2. According to James Fenwick, Rex Carlton wrote to Stanley Kubrick on August 8, 1950, attempting to lure him into the growing Laurel-Chemical Bank imbroglio. He proposed that Kubrick, an unemployed twenty-two-year old still trying to find a distributor for *Day of the Fight*, invest fifty thousand dollars in a film of Ibsen's *An Enemy of the People* that he would then be allowed to both

produce and direct. Kubrick declined the offer. Fenwick, *Stanley Kubrick Produces* (New Brunswick, NJ: Rutgers University Press, 2021), 16–17.

38. *Mr. Universe* subsequently passed to United Artists, but I have also seen posters and other promotional materials crediting Eagle-Lion and even Pathé Industries. The "Mr. Universe" character was popular enough to appear in five issues of his own comic book in 1951, first as a television wrestler, later as a GI fighting in Korea.
39. "Carlton's $504,385 Liabilities in Bkptcy."
40. Inside Stuff—Pictures," *VAR*, December 17, 1952, 13; "Beverly, Gettinger in Distribution Deal," *MPD*, December 8, 1952, 3. Lerner always suspected that Gettinger and Van Pelt foreclosed on the loans so they could gain control of the films and package them for the growing television market. In fact, Chemical Bank, working through Gettinger & Gettinger, was a pioneer in leasing packages of foreclosed independent features to local television stations. See "Chemical Bank Now Leasing Films, 10 Foreclosed Pix Going to WCBS-TV," *VAR*, January 23, 1952, 1, 20.
41. "New Lerner Company to Produce Six," *MPD*, February 16, 1951, 3. Needless to say, those six films were never made.
42. Weisners Take Over Laurel's *Della*," *VAR*, February 21, 1951, 7.
43. Another future star, Patty McCormick, makes an uncredited appearance at the very end.
44. See Louella Parsons, *PI*, April 17, 1952; *AC*, May 1952, 230; "Coral Gables as Vidpix Center," *VAR*, May 7, 1952, 20.
45. *Josette from [sic] New Orleans*, AFI Catalog.
46. A. H. Weiler, "The Local Screen Scene," *NYT*, May 10, 1953.
47. Hinkson, "The New Yorkers," 38.
48. New York State Motion Picture Division License Application Files, case number 59823, *Girl on the Run*, aka *Honky Tonk Burlesque* (1954).
49. RD-DR, which shot *Lost Boundaries* in 1949 and *The Whistle at Eaton Falls* in 1950, is a slightly different case in that it grew out of de Rochemont's prior association with several Hollywood studios, notably Fox. None of the other producers mentioned shared such a history. See full discussion in chapter 3.
50. "Danzigers' End 100G Gets Them U.S. Rights to Italian-Made *Capri*," *VAR*, August 3, 1949, 4.
51. Vorhaus quoted in Patrick McGilligan and Paul Buhle, *Tender Comrades* (New York: St. Martin's, 1997), 677.
52. Paul Henreid, *Ladies Man* (New York: St. Martin's, 1984), 180–88. Other stars on that same trip, including Humphrey Bogart and Danny Kaye, were not blacklisted; Henreid suggests he was targeted because he was the only naturalized citizen in the group.
53. "Agnew's Sales Outfit to Handle *Prejudice*," *VAR*, February 16, 1949, 5.
54. "Dorfmann Out, Danzigers Take Over Henreid Pic," *VAR*, May 25, 1949, 9.
55. Bernard Vorhaus to Richard Koszarski, December 23, 1985.
56. A. H. Weiler, "By Way of Report," *NYT*, July 10, 1949.
57. Jean Rouverol quoted in McGilligan and Buhle, *Tender Comrades*, 167.
58. McGilligan and Buhle, *Tender Comrades*, 657–81.
59. Location information from *So Young, So Bad* pressbook (NYPL Billy Rose Theater Collection); Thomas Pryor, "Random Notes About Pictures and People," *NYT*, July 31, 1949; and "New York Filmmakers," *NYT*, April 16, 1950.
60. The New York film community was now large enough to support such inside jokes. A poster for Joe Lerner's *Guilty Bystander* can be seen on a wall in his subsequent film, *Mr. Universe*.

61. Rita Moreno, *Rita Moreno: A Memoir* (New York: Celebra, 2013), 81.
62. "N.Y. Pitches Again for Eastern Prod., Lauds Danzigers," *VAR*, May 24, 1950, 25. See also "Stress Films' Value to Economy of City," *NYT*, May 24, 1950.
63. Bosley Crowther, "The Screen in Review," *NYT*, July 24, 1950; T. M. P. (Thomas M. Pryor), "Bleak Picture of a Women's Prison," *NYT*, May 20, 1950.
64. "Danzigers Huddle with Todd to Film *Girls Go* with Marx," *VAR*, September 20, 1950, 7.
65. Henreid, *Ladies Man*, 189–90. The Danzigers made a loose remake some years later in England called *So Evil, So Young* (1961).
66. A. H. Weiler, "Danzigers Plan *Robinson Crusoe* Movie," *NYT*, July 16, 1950.
67. Noah Isenberg, *Edgar G. Ulmer: A Filmmaker at the Margins* (Berkeley: University of California Press, 2014), 215.
68. Louella Parsons, "Brando Set for Debut in Movies," *PI*, October 20, 1948; A. H. Weiler, "Coup," *NYT*, October 24, 1948; *Screenland*, February 1949, 55.
69. "Of Local Origin," *NYT*, June 17, 1949.
70. "Robert Young Says 'No' to Role in Film," *NYT*, January 27, 1950; "Of Local Origin," *NYT*, April 26, 1950.
71. Thomas M. Pryor, "Crowded Notebook," *NYT*, June 18, 1950.
72. "New York Filmmakers."
73. Pryor, "Crowded Notebook."
74. "*St. Benny the Dip*," *FD*, June 13, 1951.
75. "500 16-mm Theatres to Open Sept. 15th," *STR*, May 25, 1946, E-14.
76. New York State Archives, Motion Picture Division, *Project X* (casefile 53563).
77. After finishing *Project X*, Montagne returned to Pathé to direct *The Tattooed Stranger*.
78. Lloyd W. Durant, "It Can Be Done," *SD*, June 10, 1949, 9–11.
79. Edward J. Montagne to Richard Koszarski, March 12, 1984.
80. New York State Archives, Motion Picture Division, *Cry Murder* (casefile 54054).
81. "*Cry Murder* Fails to Come Across," *HR*, February 7, 1950.
82. "*Cry Murder*," *HAR*, February 11, 1950, 24.
83. Gene Januzzi, "*Cry Murder*," *PPG*, March 27, 1950, 22.
84. Note from United Artists dated November 1, 1947, New York State Archives, Motion Picture Division, *Project X* (casefile 53563).
85. A. H. Weiler, "Random Notes About Pictures and People," *NYT*, February 19, 1950.
86. "By Way of Report," *NYT*, December 9, 1951; "Danzigers, The," BFI ScreenOnLine, accessed December 17, 2018.
87. Michel Ciment, *Conversations with Losey* (London: Methuen, 1985), 134.
88. "N.Y. Pitches Again for Eastern Prod., Lauds Danzigers;" "Stress Films' Value to Economy of City."

8. Just Passing Through

1. "Industry Statistics," *FDYBK* (1953), 127.
2. Joseph Seiden, "First Generation Talkies," *SD*, May 13, 1949, 6.
3. Seiden, "First Generation Talkies."
4. J. Hoberman, *Bridge of Light* (New York: Museum of Modern Art, 1991), 336. Eric Goldman, *Visions, Images and Dreams* (Teaneck, NJ: H&M, 2011), 135–36, notes that Seiden paid some of the better known actors $300 or even $500 to appear in the film.
5. The *New York Times* said the film was made "here and on location upstate." "Yiddish Drama," November 13, 1949.

6. Seiden opened the film at the Stanley, a modest theater on West Forty-First Street known at the time mainly as a screening venue for postwar Soviet films. This may only be a coincidence.
7. Goldman, *Visions*, 137.
8. Hoberman, *Bridge of Light*, 339–40, suggests that the film, "even more claustrophobic" than *God, Man and Devil*, may have been filmed in Seiden's apartment on Riverside Drive.
9. "At the Ambassador," *NYT*, January 28, 1950.
10. Hoberman, *Bridge of Light* (338), says it was released first as *Borscht Belt Follies* in April 1950, but the 1951 *FDYBK* lists it only as *Monticello, Here We Come!*, released by Seiden's Cinema Service Company on September 22 (218).
11. Hoberman, *Bridge of Light*, 338.
12. "E-L Studios Will Resume on Feb. 16," *MPD*, Jan. 18, 1949, 1; "New York Shooting for Several Hollywood Features," *SDGB*, June 17, 1949, 3; *VAR*, "N.Y. Production," June 29, 1949, says filming was to start on July 5.
13. Laslo Benedek to Richard Koszarski, telephone interview, 1984. Benedek is better known today for the films he made with Stanley Kramer, including *Death of a Salesman* (1952) and *The Wild One* (1954). Subsequent quotes from Benedek are all from this interview.
14. "TIE IN *SLEEPING* WITH *NAKED*," *INDEFB*, September 25, 1950, 18–19. "'Weegee' Stays Awake to Find 'Psychic Shots,'" *WP*, September 25, 1950, revealed that Weegee was in D.C. in connection with the opening of the film, but the studio otherwise did a good job of keeping his connection to it under cover.
15. "Movie Industry Honored by City," *NYT*, September 12, 1950.
16. Edwin Schallert, "U-I Launching Mystery Project," *LAT*, September 26, 1949.
17. A. H. Weiler, "By Way of Report," *NYT*, October 30, 1949.
18. Matthew Levy to Walter Lang, November 11, 1949. NYU Tamiment Library, Local 644 Papers, Box 19, "Prod. Contract Negotiation 1949–51."
19. "Irving Drutman, "The East Is His Camera Preserve," *NYT*, May 29, 1949. Miller was speaking about his current project, *Lost Boundaries*.
20. "Horn-Happy," *NY*, December 31, 1949, 12–13. The recording was on Western Electric equipment, not the Reeves Magicorder that had been used earlier that year for *C-Man*. And postproduction sound here was still being done the traditional way, using optical tracks.
21. Bosley Crowther, "On Location," *NYT*, September 24, 1950.
22. "N.Y.'s Mayor O'Dwyer Plenty Hot at Unsympathetic Gotham Film," *VAR*, May 31, 1950, 1.
23. "O'Dwyer Burn Salved on Film Stinging N.Y.," *VAR*, June 7, 1950, 1.
24. "Movie Industry Honored by City."
25. R. L. C., "You Mustn't Recognize Bellevue: Hospital Story Hushes Realism," *WP*, September 28, 1950.
26. *DV*, November 15, 1949.
27. "N.Y.'s Municipal Film Unit Aims Its Cameras at Visiting H'wood Crews," *VAR*, June 7, 1950, 18.
28. One scene said to represent New Yorkers lining up for their vaccinations appears instead to be footage of the line to get into Radio City Music Hall.
29. "20th *Panic* Forces Col. to Delay *City* Till Dec.," *VAR*, August 16, 1950, 5. The film had been trade shown as *Frightened City* in May and was reviewed under that title by some monthlies, even playing a few dates under that name in October.

30. "*The Killer That Stalked New York*," HR, December 2, 1950, 192.
31. A. H. Weiler, "By Way of Report," NYT, March 6, 1949.
32. Thomas M. Pryor, "Random Notes About Pictures and People," NYT, July 31, 1949.
33. "Keep Your Eye on Damon Runyon's *Johnny One-Eye*," MS, April 1950, 15.
34. David Dimendberg, *Film Noir and the Spaces of Modernity* (Cambridge, MA: Harvard University Press, 2004), 90–98.
35. "N.Y.'s Mayor O'Dwyer Plenty Hot."
36. "Industry: Location New York," NWSWK, April 25, 1949, 92–93.
37. See STR, April 23, 1949, 30, and April 30, 1949, 24. On the other hand, the *Brooklyn Daily Eagle*, "Metro's 'On the Town' in Brooklyn," April 23, 1949, reported that the film has already been shooting in Manhattan for ten days. The *AFI Catalog* adds that Bernhardt worked on Forty-Second Street from a camouflaged truck and filmed diners in a coffee shop through "a fake wall."
38. "Real-Life Prep Studes 'Not the Type', Sez M-G," VAR, June 8, 1949, 20; "The Happy Years," PHOTO, September 1950, 29.
39. Patrick McGilligan, *George Cukor: A Double Life* (New York: Harper Perennial, 1992), 194.
40. McGilligan, *George Cukor*, 201.
41. "Men at Work," NYT, May 15, 1949.
42. McGilligan, *George Cukor*, 201. Holliday was replaced by Jan Sterling on May 28, just before the film crew returned to Los Angeles ("The New Billie Dawn," NYT, May 29, 1949).
43. SD, May 27, 1949, 2.
44. Hugh Fordin, *The World of Entertainment!* (Garden City, NY: Doubleday, 1975), 263–64.
45. Fordin's book is entirely focused on the work of the Freed unit, and any achievements by rival MGM musical producers, like Jack Cummings or Joe Pasternak, are dismissed with faint praise, if mentioned at all. This attitude is also reflected in studies of Gene Kelly, Stanley Donen, and Vincente Minnelli. I suspect that if *It Happened in Brooklyn* had been produced by Freed instead of Cummings the pioneering status of this number would not have been forgotten so easily.
46. Stephen M. Silverman, *Dancing on the Ceiling: Stanley Donen and His Movies* (New York: Knopf, 1996), 104–5.
47. Joseph Andrew Casper, *Stanley Donen* (Metuchen, NJ: Scarecrow, 1983), 24.
48. "Rush," NY, May 28, 1949, 22–23.
49. "Rush." See also "Open 5th Ave. Bus Near End of Trail," NYT, November 25, 1946.
50. Fordin, *World of Entertainment*, 264.
51. Silverman, *Dancing on the Ceiling*, 105.
52. "Migration," NYT, April 17, 1949. Around this same time MGM produced a two-reel Technicolor short (#4083) in their James Fitzpatrick travelogue series, *Mighty Manhattan, New York's Wonder City*. The film showed many of the same highlights visited by the sailors in *On the Town*, and costar Ann Miller appeared as one of the sights. "*Mighty Manhattan*," STR, May 28, 1949, 30.
53. Silverman, *Dancing on the Ceiling*, 112.
54. See "Rush" (Munshin bored) and Silverman, *Dancing on the Ceiling*, 115–16, for an account of Sinatra's irresponsible behavior during the Navy Yard shooting.
55. "Rush."
56. Silverman, *Dancing on the Ceiling*, 118. Casper (*Stanley Donen*, 28) refers to this clash of visual textures as "schizophrenic."
57. Fordin, *World of Entertainment*, 262. The fact that *The Red Shoes* was Freed's standard of excellence is telling.

468   8. Just Passing Through

58. https://archive.org/details/TheArmyNavyScreenMagazineNo1NavyEdition. The Signal Corps produced live musical subjects of its own to add interest to this reel, bringing the performers out to their studio in Astoria. These usually featured performances by individual stars, like Bea Lillie or Dooley Wilson, but occasionally a number from a current Broadway hit, such as *Bloomer Girl* or *On the Town*, would be filmed for the edification of its GI audience. Richard Koszarski, *The Astoria Studio and Its Fabulous Films* (New York: Dover, 1983), 108–11.
59. Hedda Hopper, "Actress Buys Rights to *Medal for Mom*," *LAT*, February 15, 1949.
60. "*Side Street* New York Film," *BDE*, May 7, 1950.
61. Russell Stewart, "Taxi Acrobatics in Wall Street," *NYT*, May 8, 1949.
62. See Dudley Andrew, "Poetic Realism," in *Rediscovering French Film*, ed. Mary Lea Bandy (New York: Museum of Modern Art, 1983), 119.
63. Lew Scheaffer, "Metro's *On the Town* in Brooklyn," *BDE*, April 23, 1949; Stewart, "Taxi Acrobatics."
64. Stewart, "Taxi Acrobatics."
65. https://crimethrillercinema.wordpress.com/author/alvarezmax/ accessed May 30, 2019. Alvarez claims that the company returned to New York for retakes in June.
66. Jean Hagen, best known as Lina Lamont in *Singin' in the Rain* (1952), also had a small part in *Adam's Rib*, although it is unclear if any of her footage in either film was actually shot in New York.
67. Early drafts of *On the Waterfront*—which once had the working title "Bottom of the River"—featured numerous floating bodies. See chapter 10.
68. "Industry—Location New York."

9. Pictures and Politics

1. Eugene Archer, "Criticism of Moviemaking Here Troubles Film Union and City," *NYT*, April 24, 1965.
2. "Delbert Mann Halts Filming in Dispute with a Crew Here," *NYT*, April 19, 1965.
3. Delbert Mann, February 1959, Columbia University Oral History Program.
4. Delbert Mann, Columbia University Oral History Program.
5. Sol Negrin interviewed by Richard Koszarski, December 3, 2016.
6. Sol Negrin interviewed by Koszarski.
7. Walton C. Ament, Warner News, Inc. to Jay Rescher, Local 644 IATSE, December 1, 1952. NYU Tamiment Library, Local 644 records, Box 7, "Warner Bros. Pictures" file.
8. Chris McNickle, *To Be Mayor of New York: Ethnic Politics in the City* (New York: Columbia University Press, 1993), 82–83.
9. Leo Seltzer, "New York City Goes Into Film Production," *TSD*, May 27, 1949, 8–9. The unit would produce its own documentary films and "serve as a liaison between the various city departments and local TV outlets."
10. "Production Party," *INDEFB*, July 31, 1950, 12. Unimpressed by the amount of time O'Dwyer had been spending out of town, this paper referred to him as "Mayor of New York and Florida." See also "N.Y. 'TV Town,' " *BROAD*, July 24, 1950, 64.
11. Thomas Doherty, "Frank Costello's Hands," *FH* 10.3 (1998), 359–74.
12. Warren Moscow, "Naming of O'Dwyer as Envoy to Mexico Is Imminent," *NYT*, August 15, 1950.
13. George Walsh, *Public Enemies: The Mayor, the Mob and the Crime That Was* (New York: Norton, 1980), 206–24.

14. "O'Dwyer Stars on 5 Theatre TV Screens," *MPD*, March 20, 1951, 1.
15. Eric F. Goldman, *The Crucial Decade—and After* (New York: Vintage, 1961), 194–95; see also Doherty, "Frank Costello's Hands."
16. "Be Careful on the Air," *Sponsor*, September 24, 1951, 79.
17. Walsh, *Public Enemies*, 216.
18. "Film Kefauver Hearings as Full Feature," *MPD*, March 27, 1951, 1 (see also back page ad in this issue). The film played on Broadway, at both the Astor and the Palace, from March 28.
19. "Maguire Takes Oath as Commerce Head," *NYT*, February 1, 1951.
20. Sam Robert, "The New York Studio Mechanics," *IABUL*, Spring 1963, 18–22.
21. James Sanders (ed.), *Scenes from the City: Filmmaking in New York 1966–2006* (New York: Rizzoli, 2006), 274–77.
22. Arthur Gelb, "Municipal Cooperation Pays Off," *NYT*, January 18, 1953.
23. Hedda Hopper, "Key to Film Future Told by Zanuck," *LAT*, October 5, 1947.
24. Paul Buhle and Dave Wagner, *A Very Dangerous Citizen* (Berkeley: University of California Press, 2001), 151–53.
25. A. H. Weiler, "Random Thoughts Concerning People and Pictures," *NYT*, September 24, 1950.
26. William James Kelly to Jay Rescher, November 21, 1959, Tamiment Library, Local 644 Papers, Box 23, "William Kelly" file.
27. For example, *Crowded Paradise* (1956) and *Frankenstein Meets the Space Monster* (1965).
28. "Fox to Release Short Film Made by Amateurs," *NYT*, August 13, 1950.
29. Sam Zolotow, "News of the Stage," *NYT*, September 12, 1949.
30. Brooks Atkinson, "At the Theatre," *NYT*, February 10, 1950; "Legit Bits," *VAR*, July 5, 1950, 52.
31. A. H. Weiler, "Boy Meets Girl in Monroe, N.Y., Starting Tomorrow," *NYT*, October 15, 1950.
32. "*The Big Break*," *MPD*, April 2, 1953, 6.
33. Weiler, "Boy Meets Girl."
34. *NYT*, November 8, 1950.
35. *HR*, September 2, 1952.
36. Thanks to David Pierce for pointing me to the 35 mm print in the Al Dettlaff Collection at the Library of Congress. The Academy Film Archive, which holds Joseph Strick's own 16 mm print, was disinclined to make it available to me because Strick hated it. He believed he had destroyed the negative and all other prints and is said to have told them, "I don't want it to be seen." Forwarded email from Mark Toscano, Academy Film Archive, to Jan-Christopher Horak, UCLA Film Archive, July 9, 2019.
37. Fred Zinnemann, *An Autobiography* (New York: Scribner's, 1992), 87.
38. Gladys Hall, "It Could Happen to You!" *Screenland*, August 1950, 40–41, 63–66.
39. Thomas F. Brady, "Hollywood Digest," *NYT*, February 11, 1951.
40. Edwin Schallert, "*Teresa* Bosses Seek Star of *Bicycle Thief*," *LAT*, April 22, 1950.
41. Brady, "Hollywood Digest."
42. Richard Griffith, *Fred Zinnemann* (New York: Museum of Modern Art, n.d (c. 1957), 12
43. Fred Zinnemann, "A Film Is Born," *NYT*, March 25, 1951.
44. Bosley Crowther, "Concerning Mamas," *NYT*, April 15, 1951.
45. Zinnemann, *An Autobiography*, 90–94.
46. Budget figure from Brady, "Hollywood Digest." $140,000 of that amount was spent in Italy. In "Americans in Rome," *NYT*, May 14, 1950, Jane Cianfarra quoted Zinnemann as saying that the film would have cost "almost twice as much" if the Italian sequences had been faked in the U.S.

47. Gelb, "Municipal Cooperation Pays Off."
48. Dana M. Reemes, *Directed by Jack Arnold* (Jefferson: McFarland, 1988), 20.
49. A. W., "*Girls in the Night* Arrives at Loew's State," *NYT*, January 6, 1953.
50. Larry Swindell, *Spencer Tracy* (Cleveland, OH: New American Library, 1969), 220.
51. "By Way of Report," *NYT*, June 1, 1952. Could this character have been suggested by Stanley Kubrick, a real *Look* magazine photographer who was three years younger than boyish Donald O'Connor. See chapter 11.
52. Ann Ronell, "So You Want to Be a Music Director? Notes on *Main Street to Broadway*," *FM* (May–June 1953), 3–9.
53. "News and Gossip Gathered on the Rialto," *NYT*, November 30, 1952, says the number will be filmed on December 2. The song was later inserted into the 1997 television production of Rodgers and Hammerstein's *Cinderella*, where it was sung by Whitney Houston.
54. Bosley Crowther, "The Screen: Three Films Begin Engagements," *NYT*, October 14, 34.
55. Tay Garnett, *Light Your Torches and Pull Up Your Tights* (New Rochelle, NY: Arlington House, 1973), 286.
56. Clarence Greene and Russell Rouse, "It Had to Be Told Without Dialogue," *TA*, October 1952, 74–75, 82.
57. Herb Lightman, "*The Thief*—A New Trend in Films?" *AC* (October 1952), 432–33, 448–49. The film was shot in May and June 1952 and released in October.
58. Bosley Crowther, "Tours de Force," *NYT*, October 19, 1952.
59. Greene and Rouse, "It Had to Be Told Without Dialogue."
60. Herschel Burke Gilbert, "*The Thief*," *FM* (November–December 1952), 4–5.
61. The most creative of all these introductory overtures is the opening of Jean Negulesco's *Woman's World* (1954).
62. NYU Tamiment Library, Local 644 Collection, Box 22, "Morris Hartzband" file. Hartzband reports here that he worked as camera operator on a string of visiting features, including *Francis Covers the Big Town*, *The Marrying Kind*, and *The Joe Louis Story*.
63. A. H. Weiler, "Random Observations of People and Pictures," *NYT*, July 13, 1952.
64. "Of Local Origin," *NYT*, July 18, 1952; Edwin Schallert, "Tennessee Williams Find Set for *Taxi*," *LAT*, July 22, 1952.
65. In film circles, Smith is probably best known for twice having stabbed filmmaker and historian Paul Rotha; the second time (1968) she was convicted of attempted murder. The pair married in 1974. She is the subject of the 2018 documentary *Constance Smith—Hollywood Tragedy* by Brian Reddin.
66. James Bacon, "Hutton Goes, Clooney Wins Her Roles," *PI*, August. 31, 1952.
67. "Realists," *NYT*, June 8, 1952, says the film has just completed seventeen days of location shooting in New York.
68. John Beaufort, "UN Quarters Used as Film Setting," *CSM*, November 11, 1952, 6.
69. Beaufort, "UN Quarters."
70. "*The Glass Wall*," Communist Influence of the Motion Picture Industry, D—Memorandum, January 3, 1956, IV, 30–31. McCarran's comments are as reported by the columnist Sidney Skolsky, who suggested that "something should be done about the picture." The memo claims, without source, that "the script . . . was originally inspired by the information branch of the United Nations which asked that the picture be made for distribution in Europe."
71. François Truffaut, *Hitchcock* (New York: Simon and Schuster, 1967), 192.
72. *NYT*, August 19, 1951, and September 8, 1951 (says production will start on September 17).

73. "Stage Set: New York," *NYTM*, September 30, 1951, 48. This photo essay identifies Aldo Ray as "John Harrison," the name Columbia intended to use for their new star before thinking better of it.
74. In 1981 Bruce Goldstein was working for Richard Schwarz at the iconic New York revival house, the Thalia, when Ruth Gordon and Garson Kanin showed up for a screening, unannounced. "Richard rushed to the lounge and the first thing out of his mouth was addressed to Garson: 'Is it true you stole *The Marrying Kind* from *The Crowd*?' Ruth's face pursed up, and she turned beet red, ready to explode. She pointed to a seat as far away from Richard as possible. 'Garson, sit over *there*!' I don't remember Garson saying one word the whole time." Bruce Goldstein to Richard Koszarski, email, May 2, 2020.
75. Gelb, "Municipal Cooperation Pays Off."
76. Patrick McGilligan, *A Double Life: George Cukor* (New York: Harper Perennial, 1992), 214.
77. The Columbus Circle billboard was attached to the International Theatre, then being used as an NBC Television studio. Later replaced by the New York Coliseum, the site is now occupied by the Time Warner Center. If still in place today, Gladys Glover's self-promoting billboard would face the Trump International Hotel.
78. Ronald S. Magliozzi, "Witnessing the Development of Independent Film Culture in New York: An Interview with Charles L. Turner," *FH* XII:1 (2000), 72–96.
79. McGilligan, 214–25.
80. Penelope Houston, "Cukor and the Kanins," *S&S* (Spring 1955), 186–91, 220.
81. Geoffrey Bell shows how San Francisco's active silent film industry collapsed in 1930. Because it never produced the marginal film genres that survived in New York, it never experienced the theatrical film revival that occurred there just after World War II. Bell, *The Golden Gate and the Silver Screen* (Rutherford, NJ: Fairleigh Dickinson University Press, 1984). Indigenous film production in San Francisco would not revive for another twenty years.
82. *FDYBK* (1951), 829, 555.
83. "Film Report," *BROAD*, May 29, 1950, 15.
84. In some 1959 union paperwork, Komow wrote that he made *Death Tide* before joining the IATSE in 1954. NYU Tamiment Library, Local 644 Collection, Box 23, "Victor Komow" file.
85. *PI*, June 12, 1955, and September 3, 1955. A later broadcast listing cited Betsy Palmer as the star, despite her very small role—further evidence that the film was produced much earlier in the 1950s, before Palmer's fame as a television personality. *PIPL*, January 27, 1957.
86. "Fools Rush In," *MFB* #264, January 1, 1956, 129. But the *AFI Catalog* lists the film as sixty-nine minutes. My comments are based on the short version.
87. Bosley Crowther, "The Screen in Review," *NYT*, July 7, 1953.
88. Brog., "*Guerilla Girl*," *VAR*, April 29, 1953, 6, 18.
89. Crowther, "Screen in Review."
90. See Arriflex advertising insert in *BSM* 8:19 (1958), n.p.
91. For details, see *AFI Catalog* listing for *Dark Odyssey*.
92. *Rookie of the Year*, a 1993 Fox release, is essentially an uncredited remake of *Roogie's Bump*.
93. The *BDE*, October 2, 1953, reported that *Roogie's Bump* was "now being filmed right here in Brooklyn."
94. Although commas, quotation marks, and exclamation points were often used on the film's publicity and advertising material, the main title on the print, as well as the copyright registration, reads simply *Go Man Go*.

95. Herbert Mitgang, "Picture Package from Palca," *NYT*, April 8, 1951. More specifically he sold it to Sidney Buchman; it was the last film Buchman made for Columbia before he was blacklisted.
96. His biographer Todd Rainsberger suggests that Howe was greylisted because of his association with John Garfield, Robert Rossen, Lewis Milestone, and other Hollywood leftists. *James Wong Howe, Cinematographer* (La Jolla, CA: Barnes, 1981), 23–25.
97. James Wong Howe to Sonora Babb, March 19, 1953. Margaret Herrick Library, James Wong Howe Collection, Folder 224b.
98. Vidor's assistant, Sol Negrin, told me that this team had been filming games at Madison Square Garden until they were summarily dismissed and replaced by Bill Steiner's crew. Negrin to Koszarski, December 3, 2016.
99. *Go Man Go*, original screenplay by Alfred Palca, revised April 10, 1953. Margaret Herrick Library, James Wong Howe Collection.
100. James Wong Howe, "The Documentary Technique in Hollywood," *AC*, January 1944, 10, 32.
101. Charles Higham, *Hollywood Cameramen* (Bloomington: Indiana University Press, 1970), 92–93. Six months later the makers of *On the Waterfront* would have a similar problem with back projection, for which they chose a different solution. See pages 388–92.
102. Howard Thompson, "Saperstein and Howe," *NYT*, May 17, 1953.
103. Bruce Weber, "A Film by Alfred Palca," *NYT*, August 20, 1997.
104. "South Still Snubs Negro Films," *VAR*, April 7, 1954.
105. Howe's copy can be found with his papers at the Margaret Herrick Library (22-f.273).
106. Weber, "A Film by Alfred Palca."
107. Weber, "A Film by Alfred Palca."
108. A. H. Weiler, "Random Observations on Pictures and People," *NYT*, July 19, 1953.
109. See full interview at www.movingimagesource.us/Poitier. Poitier was not always so shy about discussing his army training films. Interviewed on the set of *No Way Out*, he joked with a reporter from the *Chicago Defender* about the bulky "wad of money" he had just received for his Signal Corps work. "Tough, But Fair, Says Poitier," *CD*, December 3, 1949.
110. *Alumni News US Army Pictorial Center* (number 14, February/March 1991), 7.
111. For a discussion of Paramount's Famous Studios, see Leonard Maltin, *Of Mice and Magic* (New York: NAL, 1980), 305–16. Maltin sees the quality of these cartoons as dismal. "That the studio survived until 1967 is positively miraculous and offers some indication of how little anyone cared about the quality of theatrical cartoons." *Mighty Mouse in Gypsy Life* (1945), a Terrytoon distributed by Fox, was the last New York cartoon of the studio era to earn an Oscar nomination.
112. Paul Mandell, "Epics of Animation: *Hansel and Gretel*," *Cinemagic* 28 (Winter 1984), 22–25, 62–63.
113. Mandell, "Epics of Animation."
114. Meyer Berger, "Screening Some Science-Sired Super-Puppets," *NYT*, October 18, 1953.
115. Michael Sporn Animation—Splog, "Puppet Animation Lou Bunin," June 17, 2006. Accessed August 9, 2019.
116. Berger, "Screening Some Science-Sired Super-Puppets."
117. Berger, "Screening Some Science-Sired Super Puppets."
118. Nancy Hall-Duncan, *The History of Fashion Photography* (New York: Alpine Books, 1979), 68.
119. Mandell, "Epics of Animation," 25, 63.
120. Bosley Crowther, "Ten Best of 1954," *NYT*, December 26, 1954; Mildred Martin, "*Hansel and Gretel* Opera Timely on Stanton Screen," *PI*, December 24, 1954.

121. A. H. Weiler, "Of Pictures and People," *NYT*, April 11, 1954; William Brownell, "Hollywood Bulletins," *NYT*, August 1, 1954. Myerberg had produced *Lute Song* on Broadway in 1946.
122. "On the Classical Beauty of Hoboken (Blue) Movies, September 7, 1961," reprinted in Jonas Mekas, *Movie Journal* (New York: Macmillan, 1972), 33.
123. While not especially involved with the "blue movie" aspect of New York's independent film scene, the Mekas brothers are known to have worked under aliases on several of Sarno's films, including *The Love Merchant* (1965), which Adolfas edited as George Binkey.
124. "Bud Pollard Picture to Open on Broadway," *SDGB*, September 1949, 2.
125. "Eastern Production Includes Feature Being Directed by SDG Member," *SDGB*, August 12, 1949, 3; Danton Walker, "Gossip of the Nation," *PI*, July 18, 1949.
126. Both *The Middleton Family at the 1939 World's Fair*, an industrial film, and Hans Richter's avant-garde exercise, *Dreams That Money Can Buy*, had been released theatrically in color. But neither could be considered conventional screen narratives—a bar that Pollard's film does barely manage to cross.
127. "*Love Island*," *DV*, July 17, 1952, 3.
128. David Moller, "Nuderama," *Vision: A Journal of Film Comment* I:2 (Summer 1962), 18–20.
129. Karen Essex and James L. Swanson, *Bettie Page: The Life of a Pin-Up Legend* (Los Angeles: General, 1996), 146, 162–63.
130. Eric Schaefer, *"Bold! Daring! Shocking! True!" A History of Exploitation Films, 1919–1959* (Durham, NC: Duke University Press, 1999), 65. St. Cyr refers to Klaw filming in a studio, possibly the same loft at 212 East Fourteenth Street, above his Movie Star News operation, that he used to shoot his figure studies. The spelling of Page's given name was never very consistent.
131. See *VAR*, March 9, 1949, 55.
132. Thomas Cripps, *Making Movies Black* (New York: Oxford University Press, 1993), 128.
133. Schaefer, *Bold! Daring! Shocking!* 83.
134. See *AFI Catalog* entry for an extensive plot summary taken from New York State censorship files.
135. The 1951 *FDYBK* (p. 538) lists Max Rosenberg as president of Classic Pictures and Doris Wishman as the company's booker. Wishman later became a noted producer-director of nudies and "roughies," working in New York in the 1960s on films like *Bad Girls Go to Hell* (1965).
136. "Dance Film," *NYT*, June 14, 1959, announces an upcoming screening of the three films.
137. "Club Courses," *NYT*, February 1, 1948.
138. This is a few doors down from Club Savannah, which had supplied the chorus line (and possibly a filming location?) for *Harlem Follies*.
139. J. D. Salinger, *The Catcher in the Rye* (Boston: Little, Brown, 1951), 104.
140. "*Violated*," *VAR*, December 16, 1953, 6.
141. Vincent Lo Brutto, *Stanley Kubrick, a Biography* (New York: Donald Fine, 1997), 93.

10. Crime on the Waterfront

1. "Camera Bye-Talk," *Camera Talk* I: 2, n.d., 5.
2. "Cinematographers Honor Film Pioneer," *BSM* 23:1 (1962), 96.
3. "Chartered," *FD*, September 8, 1948, 6. Sam Goldwyn and Ida Lupino were also said to have been interested. See Haynes Johnson's "Foreword" to Malcolm Johnson, *On the Waterfront* (New York: Chamberlain, 2005), xxiv.

4. Hedda Hopper, "Water-Front Story Suited to Two Stars," *LAT*, June 2, 1949.
5. James T. Fisher, *On the Irish Waterfront*," (Ithaca, NY: Cornell University Press, 2009), 120.
6. "By Way of Report," *NYT*, June 19, 1949; "Eastern Feature Production Up," *SDGB*, June 24, 1949, 4. Denker's subsequent film scripts included *Time Limit* (1957), which he adapted from his own play, and the Korean War drama *The Hook* (1963), not related to Arthur Miller's unproduced waterfront corruption project.
7. Gerald Horne, *The Final Victim of the Blacklist* (Berkeley: University of California Press, 2006), 227.
8. Edwin Schallert, "Elizabeth Scott to Play *Raiders* Lead," *LAT*, June 15, 1950; "Romantic Ruffian," *LAT*, July 5, 1950. Yordan had recently written the script of *House of Strangers* (*q.v.*). A few years later he would write and produce the film version of Budd Schulberg's novel *The Harder They Fall* (1956).
9. "Siodmak's *Whistle*," *NYT*, October 14, 1951.
10. Lawrence J. McCaffrey, "His Own Kind: Edward McSorley and the Providence Irish," *Working Papers in Irish Studies* 06-1 (2006), Winthrop University, Rock Hill, SC, 4–5. McCaffrey compares McSorley favorably to John O'Hara and James T. Farrell
11. Edward McSorley, *The Young McDermott* (New York: Harper, 1949), 113.
12. Budd Schulberg, "Introduction" to Malcolm Johnson, *On the Waterfront*, xxxiv–xxxv.
13. For Lawson's side of this affair, see Horne, *Final Victim of the Blacklist*, 134–37.
14. Sam Shaw, Monticello Film Corporation, to Joseph Breen, director of Production Code Administration, December 26, 1950, *Crime on the Waterfront* PCA file, Margaret Herrick Library.
15. Fisher, *On the Irish Waterfront*, 41–50, sees McCormack's role as crucial in understanding the corrupt power dynamic revealed in Johnson's articles, but he is unaware of the existence of the McSorley-Schulberg script.
16. Joe Breen to Sam Shaw, January 4, 1951. *Crime on the Waterfront* PCA file.
17. Breen to Shaw, January 4, 1951.
18. Fisher, *On the Irish Waterfront*, 48–49.
19. "By Way of Report," *NYT*, January 7, 1951. But a later news report suggests that Schulberg was by then writing the script for Siodmak in Hollywood. Hedda Hopper, "*Ransom of Red Chief* Likely Clifton Webb Vehicle," *LAT*, January 25, 1951.
20. "THE LETTER WHICH ACCOMPANIED IT WOULD HAVE COVERED MOST OF TOUR [sic] COMMENTS IF WE HAD BEEN FORTUNATE ENOUGH TO HAVE HAD SOMEONE IN YOUR OFFICE READ IT." Telegram, Sam Shaw to Joe Breen, January 8, 1951. *Crime on the Waterfront* PCA file.
21. *Crime on the Waterfront*, "Temporary Production Budget," Mills Collection, Museum of the Moving Image. Thanks to Barbara Miller for pointing this collection out to me.
22. Sidney Lumet, *Making Movies* (New York: Vintage, 1996), 26.
23. Bernard Dick, *The Merchant Prince of Poverty Row* (Lexington: University Press of Kentucky, 1993), 83–88.
24. Deborah Lazaroff Alpi, *Robert Siodmak* (Jefferson, NC: MacFarland, 1998), 179. There is no date or source given for this claim.
25. "Paramount Buys Odets' New Play," *NYT*, March 2, 1951.
26. Schulberg, "Introduction," xxxv.
27. Fisher, *On the Irish Waterfront*, 102.
28. The name is sometimes given as Brown, but I will refer to him as Arthur Browne because that is the way Schulberg spelled it in the dedication to his novel, *Waterfront* (a dedication he shared with Malcolm Johnson and Father John Corridan).

29. Budd Schulberg, "Drama in Hoboken," *Holiday*, August 1954, 82–85.
30. Fisher, *On the Irish Waterfront*, 111.
31. Fisher, *On the Irish Waterfront*, 125. Years later, when the film finally appeared, Columbia's publicity campaign would do its best to establish a connection to this most popular of Hollywood's "religious" films. The line, "a story that is as warm and moving as *Going My Way* (with brass knuckles)," was used in the trailer and some of the poster art.
32. Murrey Marder, "Film Writer Names 25 as Once Reds," *WP*, April 13, 1951.
33. Joseph Ryan to William Randolph Hearst, Jr., April 17, 1951, and Malcolm Johnson to Seymour Berkson, April 23, 1951, quoted in Fisher, *On the Irish Waterfront*, 135. See also Haynes Johnson, "Foreword," xxv.
34. Schulberg, "Introduction," xxxvii.
35. *Annual Report of the Committee on Un-American Activities for the Year 1952*. House Report No. 2516, December 29, 1952. A transcript of Schulberg's testimony appears in Nicholas Beck, *Budd Schulberg: A Bio-Bibliography* (Lanham, MD: Scarecrow, 2001), 77–133.
36. Alpi, *Robert Siodmak*, 179. The source of this information is not credited.
37. Budd Schulberg, "*Waterfront*: From Docks to Film," *NYT*, July 11, 1954.
38. Schulberg, "*Waterfront*." See also Alpi, *Robert Siodmak*, 179.
39. Edwin Schallert, "Pact Stymies Curt," *LAT*, July 22, 1951.
40. Schulberg to Corridan, August 9, 1951, quoted in Fisher, *On the Irish Waterfront*, 135.
41. Alpi, *Robert Siodmak*, 179.
42. Budd Schulberg, *Waterfront* (New York: Random House, 1955).
43. Several pieces by Schulberg are reprinted in Malcolm Johnson, *On the Waterfront*, sharing space with a collection of Johnson's original *New York Sun* articles.
44. John Crosby, "Crime Series Qualifies for Big Salute," *WP*, August 31, 1951.
45. A. H. Weiler, "Promissory Note," *NYT*, December 30, 1951.
46. Fisher, *On the Irish Waterfront*, 193.
47. "Suit Filed Here Over 'Waterfront' Rights," *MPD*, October 19, 1954, 2; "Joseph Curtis Rites; Son of Jack Cohn," *MPD*, August 3, 1954, 1, 3. Curtis died of a heart attack at the age of thirty-seven.
48. "UA in Deals with Small and Spiegel," *MPH*, May 24, 1952, 32. Spiegel's deal, it was reported, would begin with *Melba* and be followed by *The Witness*, in which he planned to star Marlon Brando and Ingrid Bergman. But according to Arthur Laurents, who Spiegel hired to adapt *The Witness*, Brando "had never heard of the picture I was writing for him." Arthur Laurents, *Original Story By* (New York: Knopf, 2000, 292).
49. Ben Hersh, Edward Small Productions, to Joseph Breen, MPAA, April 21, 1952. Margaret Herrick Library, PCA file, *Crime on the Waterfront*.
50. Joseph I. Breen to Edward Small, April 25, 1952, Margaret Herrick Library PCA file, *Crime on the Waterfront*.
51. Small began shooting *New York Confidential* in the summer of 1954, just as *On the Waterfront* went into release. A very violent film in which all the main characters are murdered or commit suicide, it features a government Crime Commission investigating massive corruption schemes run by the New York syndicate. Although not dealing specifically with the waterfront, the general air of civic collapse suggests that someone had read McSorley's manuscript. Broderick Crawford and Richard Conte starred, but the film was shot in Hollywood, leading *FD* to complain that "some of the New York backdrops and street scenes smack of phoney sets" (February 17, 1955).
52. "C. P. Trussell, "Elia Kazan Admits He Was Red in 30's," *NYT*, April 12, 1952.

53. Elia Kazan, *A Life* (New York: Knopf, 1988), 453–55.
54. Kazan, *A Life*, 464–65.
55. In an odd coincidence, considering the role of Italian neorealism in all this, Kazan's "Statement" ran alongside another *NYT* ad announcing that Vittorio De Sica would be signing autographs in the lobby of Loew's State "today only," promoting his appearance in *Tomorrow Is Too Late* (*Domani è troppo tardi*).
56. Kazan, *A Life*, 468.
57. Victor Navasky, *Naming Names* (New York: Penguin, 1981), 206. The "apologetic curriculum vitae" was a list Kazan gave the Committee of twenty-five films and plays he had directed, annotated to emphasize the anticommunist elements in each one. The list did not appear in either his display ad or the *Times*' news report of the testimony.
58. Kazan, *A Life*, 451–52.
59. Kazan, *A Life*, 461.
60. Kazan, *A Life*, 456–57, 445–46.
61. Kazan, *A Life*, 487.
62. Schulberg, "Introduction," xxxvii.
63. Kazan, *A Life*, 319.
64. Stephen Schwartz, "Arthur Miller's Proletariat: The True Stories of *On the Waterfront*, Pietro Panto, and Vincenzo Longhi," *FH* 16:4 (2004), 378–92.
65. My summary of this trip is drawn from Kazan, *A Life*, 401–13, and Arthur Miller, *Timebends* (New York: Grove, 1987), 299–308. There are significant inconsistencies in their detailed recollections, but both men agree on the overall result of the trip.
66. Miller, *Timebends*, 195.
67. According to the FBI's COMPIC files, "Communist Influence in the Motion Picture Industry," Running Memorandum summary dated January 3, 1956, pages IV: 20–21, an unnamed source advised the Bureau that "the picture would be exceedingly detrimental to the labor movement in the United States and would be good propaganda of a Communist nature. As a result of objections to portions of the script, Miller reluctantly agreed to make changes desired and delete objectionable portions while Kazan was agreeable to any script changes since he did not want to direct such a picture because he is 'pro-labor and anti-Communist.' " The source also advised that although the studio had paid Miller $50,000 for the story, "at the present time 'The Hook' is not scheduled for production."
68. Miller, *Timebends*, 308.
69. Kazan, *A Life*, 414.
70. For a critique of those who see too many similarities, see Schwartz, "Arthur Miller's Proletariat," 379–80.
71. Fisher, *On the Irish Waterfront*, 214–15.
72. For background on this sermon, see Fisher, *On the Irish Waterfront*, 97–100.
73. Schulberg, "Introduction," xxxvi. It should be noted that a likely Browne surrogate named Knobby already existed in the McSorley version.
74. Budd Schulberg, "Joe Docks, Forgotten Man of the Waterfront," *NYTM*, December 28, 1952, 3, 28–30. The article is a valuable summary of Schulberg's understanding of the waterfront situation and the sources that informed his thinking.
75. Kazan, *A Life*, 480.
76. Fisher, *On the Irish Waterfront*, 193.
77. A. H. Weiler, "By Way of Report," *NYT*, December. 21, 1952.
78. Fisher, *On the Irish Waterfront*, 191.
79. Fisher, *On the Irish Waterfront*, 195.

80. See Kazan's 1953 appointment book, "Personal F 110-F119," Elia Kazan papers, Reid Cinema Archives, Wesleyan University. Among the many clippings devoted to waterfront crime in his research files (B31-F9) is a well-worn copy of Tony Mike's May 1953 *True Magazine* article, "The Mob Said They'd Kill Me for My Story," cowritten with Richard Carter.
81. Jeff Young, *Kazan: The Master Director Discusses His Films* (New York: Newmarket, 1999), 129.
82. Young, *Kazan*, 159.
83. Kazan, *A Life*, 500.
84. "Stevedore Files *Waterfront* Suit," *MPD*, December. 2, 1954, 2. Perhaps Tony Mike found out that Father Corridan had been paid five thousand dollars for use of his "likeness, personality, activities and career." Fisher, *On the Irish Waterfront*, 246. De Vincenzo is said to have collected twenty-three thousand dollars. See Sada Fretz, "Hoboken's Waterfront" in *On the Waterfront, Starring Hoboken, New Jersey* (Hoboken Historical Museum, 2004), 8.
85. Zanuck to Kazan, February 4, 1953, in *Memo from Darryl F. Zanuck*, ed. Rudy Behlmer (New York: Grove, 1983), 224.
86. A shortened version of this memo appears in *Memo from Darryl F. Zanuck*, where it is dated February 12 (pp. 225-28). But a longer version, dated February 10, can be found in Kazan's papers in the Reid Cinema Archives, Wesleyan University, file B31-F8.
87. Thomas M. Pryor, "Fox to Make Film on Pier Activities," *NYT*, April 16, 1953.
88. Edwin Schallert, "Zanuck Resumes Headlines with *Water Front*," *LAT*, April 16, 1953.
89. Kazan, *A Life*, 507.
90. Budd Schulberg, "Afterword," *On the Waterfront, the Final Shooting Script* (Hollywood: Samuel French, 1988), 146.
91. Kazan, *A Life*, 508.
92. Zanuck to Philip Dunne, et al., March 12, 1953, quoted in Aubrey Solomon, *Twentieth Century-Fox* (Metuchen, NJ: Scarecrow, 1988), 86-87. *Water Front* was named as one of only two exceptions.
93. Zanuck to Philip Dunne, May 7, 1953, quoted in Solomon, *Twentieth Century-Fox*, 71-72
94. Figures from Solomon, *Twentieth Century-Fox*, 224, 247.
95. *Bloodhounds of Broadway* (1952), American Film Institute Catalog.
96. Kazan, *A Life*, 508.
97. Thomas M. Pryor, "Westward, Again, in Covered Wagon," *NYT*, June 2, 1953. The article ends with the news that Schulberg and Kazan were already negotiating with "an independent producer who has a major distribution company outlet," i.e., Sam Spiegel.
98. Schulberg, "Afterword," 147-48. The Bell & Howell Eyemo was a 35 mm camera; their 16 mm model was called the Filmo. (Zanuck, who had used them both in North Africa, would have known the difference.) But in Kazan's own book he claims that he said this, or something like it, not to Schulberg, but to Abe Lastfogel. In that version he also says he will make the film "with the cheapest producer in town" and mentions the King Brothers, producers of such interesting low-budget films as *Gun Crazy* (1950). *A Life*, 509.

11. Obsessed with Film

1. Joseph Gelmis, *The Film Director as Superstar* (Garden City, NY: Doubleday, 1970), 314.
2. Frederick Foster, "Equipment Source for Film Producers," *AC*, October 1954, 502-03, 518-20.

3. Vincent Lo Brutto, *Stanley Kubrick: A Biography* (New York: Donald Fine, 1997), 93.
4. Gelmis, *Superstar*, 315–16.
5. "Many Co-Eds Study Technique of Film," *NYT*, September 25, 1949. Richter boasts in this article that 25 percent of the program's incoming students are women.
6. Ezra Goodman, "Musical Fantasy Filmed in Manhattan Loft," *NYT*, April 11, 1948. See also Cleve Gray (ed.), *Hans Richter by Hans Richter* (New York: Holt, Rinehart and Winston, 1971), 51–54.
7. This address is variously described as the back room of "an old New York house," ("Surrealist Movie," *Life*, December 2, 1946, 86–88) or a loft belonging to one of his students (Goodman). The mailing address of Art of This Century Films in 1947, which may or may not have been the same location, was 34 East Twenty-First Street.
8. Goodman, "Musical Fantasy."
9. "Surrealist Movie."
10. "Of Local Origin," *NYT*, October 17, 1947; Hans Richter to Frank Stauffacher, October 13, 1948, quoted in Scott MacDonald, *Art in Cinema* (Philadelphia: Temple University Press, 2006), 184.
11. Goodman, "Musical Fantasy."
12. Bosley Crowther, "The Screen," *NYT*, April 24, 1948.
13. James Agee in *The Nation*, July 24, 1948, reprinted in *Agee on Film* (New York: Beacon, 1964, 309–10).
14. See, for example, "Stanley Kubrick on Screen 1947," posted on YouTube by the Stanley Kubrick Appreciation Society on June 2, 2019. The date of this filming was actually 1946.
15. The 1946 *Life* article begins with a Gjon Mili photo of the very scene that Kubrick, Metz, and Sobotka appeared in, although the picture only shows the audience from the back.
16. Dave Davidson email to author, March 12, 2020. Kubrick's record indicates that he studied French, Philosophy, Hygiene, and Economics and was allowed to transfer 15.5 credits from Taft. But he registered for only one course in spring 1947 and withdrew before the end of the semester.
17. "Art Pays Off," *NYT*, September 26, 1948.
18. "Surrealist Movie."
19. "Art Pays Off."
20. Goodman, "Musical Fantasy." But Richter later wrote, "The film never earned money for us, in fact, it lost every penny put into it." *Hans Richter by Hans Richter*, 51–54.
21. Thomas M. Pryor, "Young Man with Ideas and a Camera," *NYT*, January 14, 1951.
22. Walter Cartier's professional record from boxrec.com, accessed July 23, 2017.
23. "Walter Cartier Running in Washington Square Park." Museum of the City of New York, 24U39YDA.
24. "How About a Little Game?" *NY*, November 12, 1966, 71.
25. Saul Pett, "Movie Maker Cuts Costs," *Winona Republican-Herald* (AP), December 27, 1950.
26. Among the sports reels then in production were *Sports Parade* (Warner), *Sportscope* (RKO-Pathé), *Sports Review* (Fox), and *World of Sports* (Columbia).
27. "How About a Little Game?" 71.
28. Richard Meran Barsam, "*This Is America*: Documentaries for Theaters, 1942–1951," *CJ*, Spring 1973, 33.
29. Gelmis, *Superstar*, 312.
30. Scott MacDonald, *Cinema 16: Documents Towards a History of the Film Society* (Philadelphia: Temple University Press, 2002). The films included *I Am an Alcoholic* and *Street of Shadows* but not *Day of the Fight*.

31. David Hughes, *The Complete Stanley Kubrick* (London: Virgin, 2000), 9, credits Kubrick with the screenplay, but others suggest it is actually the work of Howard Sackler (see note 35).
32. Stanley Kubrick to Ted Huff, February 17, 1953. George Eastman Museum, *Fear and Desire* file. For *Flying Padre*, see James Fenwick, *Stanley Kubrick Produces* (New Brunswick, NJ: Rutgers University Press, 2021), 21–24.
33. "How About a Little Game?" 71–72.
34. Bradley had been active since before the war. After a stint in the Signal Corps, which included a posting at the SCPC in Astoria, he completed a 16 mm version of *Julius Caesar* ("The Noblest Roman," *MM*, March 1950, 103). Profiles of Bradley emphasized his youth and self-confidence, occasionally alluding to the career of Orson Welles, elements Kubrick would have identified with. See, for example, William Howe, "He Knew What He Wanted," *MM*, June 1953, 150–51, 161. Other youthful outsiders attempting to crash the theatrical feature market included twenty-year-old Raymond Rohauer (J. H. Schoen, "Hollywood Genius," *HM*, April 1947, 216–17, 240–42).
35. "Howard O. Sackler" in *American National Biography: Rousseau—Simmons*, ed. John A. Garraty and Mark C. Carnes (New York: Oxford University Press, 1999), 185–86.
36. "Vavin, Inc.," *BSM* 18:1 (1957), 114.
37. Lo Brutto, *Stanley Kubrick*, 77.
38. Lo Brutto, *Stanley Kubrick*, 77, 87. "You know, we're really Dick's children," Kubrick later admitted to Jane.
39. Pett, "Movie Maker Cuts Cost"; Iris Owens, " 'It's Movies for Me,' " *MP*, September 1953, 85.
40. Lo Brutto, *Stanley Kubrick*, 78–79.
41. Pryor, "Young Man with Ideas." Throughout the article, "Stanley" is referred to as "a young man from the Bronx," "a funny kid" and "no ordinary tyro," bolstering the "boy genius" narrative that Kubrick clearly encouraged.
42. "Peters' Play Being Offered," *NYT*, November 28, 1950.
43. If the *AFI Catalog* is to be believed, while still on the West Coast Silvera would work in Budd Boetticher's *The Cimarron Kid*, Elia Kazan's *Viva Zapata!*, Herbert Kline's *The Fighter*, and Michael Curtiz's *Miracle of Our Lady of Fatima*. All were shot after *Fear and Desire* but released earlier.
44. Philip K. Scheuer, "Girl from 'Art' Film Wins Contract at Fox," *LAT*, June 11, 1953.
45. Gelmis, *Superstar*, 313.
46. Iris Owens, "It's Movies for Me," 98.
47. Justin Stewart, "Kubrick's First Feature: Paul Mazursky Q & A on *Fear and Desire*," *FC*, March 26, 2012 (accessed August 9, 2017).
48. Use of the wire recorder for low-budget filmmaking is described in Tinkham and Boyers, "A Magnetic Sound Recorder of Advanced Design," *JSMPE*, January 1947, 29–35.
49. Gelmis, *Superstar*, 313.
50. John McCarten, "Amateur," *NY*, April 11, 1953, 129.
51. Lo Brutto, *Stanley Kubrick*, 81–82, 86.
52. "How About a Little Game?" 72.
53. Stewart, "Kubrick's First Feature."
54. Josh Binney, "Movies for and with Negroes," *SD*, December 10, 1948, 2–4.
55. Saul Pett, "Broadway," *Rocky Mount [NC] Telegram* (AP), September 9, 1952, 22.
56. Lo Brutto, *Stanley Kubrick*, 81.
57. Stewart, "Kubrick's First Feature."
58. The fifty-thousand-foot figure comes from Iris Owens, "It's Movies for Me," 98; the fact that this was double what he had expected is from Pett, "Broadway."

59. Gelmis, *Superstar*, 313.
60. Lo Brutto, *Stanley Kubrick*, 80.
61. Lo Brutto, *Stanley Kubrick*, 81.
62. A. H. Weiler, "By Way of Report," *NYT*, June 24, 1952. In a letter to his friend Ted Huff just before the release of *Fear and Desire*, Kubrick listed "Misc. television and state dept. trivia" among his credits. Stanley Kubrick to Ted Huff, February 1953, George Eastman Museum, *Fear and Desire* file.
63. Warren Weaver, Jr., "63 Nations' Youth in a Miniature U.N.," *NYT*, August 6, 1951.
64. Val Adams, "Different Approach," *NYT*, December 14, 1952.
65. Lo Brutto, *Stanley Kubrick*, 83.
66. Norman Lloyd interview, Archives of American Television, part 3 of 6. Accessed July 12, 2017.
67. Norman Lloyd, *Stages: Of Life in Theatre, Film and Television* (New York: Limelight, 1993), 145.
68. Richard Koszarski interview with Sol Negrin, December 3, 2016.
69. Lo Brutto, *Stanley Kubrick*, 83, says Rebière reported this to Norman Lloyd.
70. Negrin interview.
71. Negrin interview.
72. Paul Hughes, "The Lincoln Story Breaks Into TV," *LCJ*, October 26, 1952.
73. Norman Lloyd interview, Archives of American Television, part 4 of 6. Accessed July 12, 2017; Lo Brutto, *Stanley Kubrick*, 85.
74. Lloyd, *Stages*, 145.
75. Kubrick sent a copy of Van Doren's blurb, which was dated June 1952, to his friend Ted Huff on July 3. Van Doren refers to the film as *Shape of Fear*. George Eastman Museum, *Fear and Desire* file.
76. John Baxter, *Stanley Kubrick* (New York: Carroll & Graf, 1997), 54.
77. Norman Kagan, *The Cinema of Stanley Kubrick* (New York: Holt, Rinehart Winston, 1972), 9. Kagan does not reveal the source of this letter, which has subsequently been reprinted by most of those writing about this film.
78. The Burstyn deal was announced by A. H. Weiler in "By Way of Report," *NYT*, March 15, 1953. But Kubrick was using the title *Fear and Desire* even before Burstyn entered the picture. See Pett, "Broadway."
79. Barbara Wilinsky, " 'A Thinly Disguised Art Veneer Covering a Filthy Sex Picture.' Discourses on Art Houses in the 1950s," *FH* 8:2 (1996), 143–58.
80. *Fear and Desire* display ad, *NYT*, March 31, 1953.
81. Jane Corby, "Newcomer to the Film Field Makes Harsh Picture of War," *BDE*, April 1, 1953.
82. A. W., "The Screen in Review," *NYT*, April 1, 1953.
83. McCarten, "Amateur." Years later, Cecile Starr still found the shortcomings of Kubrick's film critically useful. In a negative review of another independent New York feature, *Guns of the Trees*, Starr wrote that at least it was better than *Fear and Desire*, with its "phoney representations of phoney ideas." "New York Letter," *S&S* (Winter 1961–62), 15.
84. "How About a Little Game?" 72.
85. "UC Spring Cinema Series Including Kubrick Films," *BO*, March 23, 1964, reproduced at rjbuffalo.com/fear_and_desire, accessed August 5, 2017.
86. Jackson Burgess, "The 'Anti-Militarism' of Stanley Kubrick," *FQ*, Fall 1964, 4–11.
87. Gene Phillips, *Stanley Kubrick, A Film Odyssey* (New York: Popular Library, 1975), 16.
88. "A Silent Virginia Is Discovered," *Life*, May 11, 1953, 122, 125.

89. "Walter Winchell," *Syracuse Herald-Journal*, April 4, 1953. Winchell goes on to ask, "How did the censors pass that scene where she drinks water from a lad's hands?" He had previously mentioned Virginia Leith on March 30. Two plugs from Winchell in less than a week might have been a greater achievement than the *Life* layout. Both columns are reproduced at rjbuffalo.com/fear_and_desire.
90. Mildred Martin, "2 New Film Dramas at the Studio," *PI*, July 25, 1953.
91. "Europe Losing Its Artistic Drive?" *VAR*, October 7, 1953, 4, 71.
92. William Alexander, *Film on the Left* (Princeton, NJ: Princeton University Press, 1981), 83.
93. John Wranovics, "The Makers of *In the Street* and *The Quiet One*," in *Agee at 100*, ed. Michael Lofaro, (Knoxville: University of Tennessee Press, 2012), 201–27.
94. The phrase comes from a proposal sent by Loeb to the Wiltwyck board on September 19, 1946. Wranovics, *The Makers*, 214.
95. Press information quoted in Wranovics, *The Makers*, 215.
96. Thomas M. Pryor, "Prelude to *The Quiet One*," *NYT*, January 9, 1949.
97. Jean Cocteau, "Focus on Miracles," *NYT*, October 24, 1948. Cocteau's article lauds the low cost and flexibility of 16mm as the answer to the cinema's current creative problems. Although he does not mention any specific films, the *Times* illustrated his piece with production shots from *The Quiet One* and *Dreams That Money Can Buy*.
98. Wranovics, *The Makers*, 216.
99. Wranovics, *The Makers*, 217.
100. Wranovics, *The Makers*, 217.
101. "Success Story," *NYT*, November 14, 1948; Bosley Crowther, "*The Quiet One*, Documentary of a Rejected Boy," *NYT*, February 14, 1949.
102. Bosley Crowther, *The Quiet One*," *NYT*, February 20, 1949.
103. Vinicius de Moraes, "The Making of a Document: *The Quiet One*," *HQ*, IV, 4 (Summer 1950), 375–84.
104. Eric Barnouw, *Documentary: History of the Non-Fiction Film* (New York: Oxford University Press, 1974), 185.
105. Arthur Mayer, *Merely Colossal* (New York: Simon and Schuster, 1953), 232.
106. Ironically, there are very few shots in *Little Fugitive* that run anywhere near twenty seconds and only one long take (seventy seconds) showing Joey in a batting cage.
107. Bruce Gould to John Morris, August 4, 1950. Ruth Orkin Scrapbook #1, Margaret Herrick Library. Italics in this quote represent words underlined by Ruth Orkin.
108. "Inside Stuff—Pictures," *VAR*, June 23, 1954, 16.
109. On the same commentary track, Engel notes that the drowning victim seen being carried off the beach by lifeguards was a real drowning victim, fortuitously caught by the production's remarkably mobile camera.
110. Information from Morris Engel and Ruth Orkin discussion following *Little Fugitive* screening at MOMA, November 30, 1984, author's notes. But in an undated Billy Rose column ("We Aren't Poor Enough") found in the Ruth Orkin scrapbooks, Ray Ashley tells Rose that the cost was eighty-seven thousand dollars, slightly more than the amount of money subscribed. That figure may include later postproduction charges.
111. Program note, "Cineprobe Special: Morris Engel and Ruth Orkin," Museum of Modern Art, November 30, 1984.
112. Eddy Manson, "The Music for *Little Fugitive*," *FM*, January–February 1954, 8–14.
113. Morris Engel, commentary track.
114. "On Film," *NY*, February 20, 1960, 36–37.

115. Bosley Crowther, "Small Film, Big Hopes," *NYT*, October 18, 1953; "Sweeney Steps Out," *FD*, October 5, 1942, 8.
116. Burstyn ordered the team to cut five minutes—any five minutes—out of the eighty-minute film before release. Current video releases have restored these cuts, so the film is now longer than originally shown (Morris Engel, commentary track).
117. "*This Is S.I.U.*," *EFG* (1953), 354.
118. Hollenbeck, like Douglas Edwards, was a familiar CBS newscaster. Neither man seems to have done any other credited motion picture voice-over work. Using well-known newsmen, instead of the usual anonymous narrators, was a way of enhancing the authority of these films. Loren Ghiglione, *CBS's Don Hollenbeck: An Honest Reporter in the Age of McCarthyism* (New York: Columbia University Press, 2008), 205.
119. An image of Kubrick using the Mitchell 16 can be seen in Jan Harlan's 2001 documentary, *Stanley Kubrick, a Life in Pictures*.
120. Lo Brutto, *Stanley Kubrick*, 73.

12. The Golden Warrior

1. Jurow's account is taken from Martin Jurow, *Marty Jurow Seein' Stars: A Show Biz Odyssey* (Dallas, TX: SMU Press, 2001), 33–37.
2. Budd Schulberg, "*Waterfront*: From Docks to Film," *NYT*, July 11, 1954.
3. Budd Schulberg, "Afterword," *On the Waterfront, the Final Shooting Script* (Hollywood, CA: Samuel French, 1988), 149. Kazan's version, which does at least reference Lastfogel, is in *A Life* (New York: Knopf, 1988), 510–11.
4. Another interesting question: Why was Sam Spiegel, who owned a fabulous Beverly Hills estate, staying at the Beverly Hills Hotel in the first place? According to Natasha Fraser-Cavassoni, he was "afraid of being arrested" over "unpaid debts," and his estranged wife, Lynne, had recently run amok in the mansion with a pair of scissors, cutting up everything from his underpants to his Picassos. *Sam Spiegel* (New York: Simon & Schuster, 2003), 147–48.
5. Schulberg, "Introduction" to Malcolm Johnson, *On the Waterfront* (New York: Chamberlain, 2005), xxxix.
6. Kazan, *A Life*, 511; Jurow, *Seein' Stars*, 34.
7. Thomas Pryor, "Hollywood Report," *NYT*, May 24, 1953; "Re-Record *Melba* for Stereo Sound," *MPD*, July 13, 1953, 5.
8. Schulberg, "Afterword," 150.
9. Thomas M. Pryor, "Spiegel and U.-I. [sic] Back Kazan Film," *NYT*, June 13, 1953. The headline mistakenly identifies Universal-International (U-I), although the article itself refers to United Artists. See also A. H. Weiler, "Random Observations on Pictures and People," *NYT*, June 14, 1953.
10. Fraser-Cavassoni emphasizes his function as intermediary (*Sam Spiegel*, 118–19), but Tino Balio makes no mention of Spiegel playing such a role in *United Artists, The Company That Changed the Film Industry* (Madison: University of Wisconsin Press, 1987).
11. Fraser-Cavassoni, *Sam Spiegel*, 144–45.
12. See the full-page UA ads in *MPD* on July 21, 1953, 8 and September 22, 1953, 5, as well as "The Local Screen Scene," *NYT*, October 25, 1953.
13. "Columbia to Release Eagle's *Waterfront*," *MPD*, November 30, 1953, 7; see also *MPD*, December 3, 1953, 5. Fraser-Cavassoni, *Sam Spiegel*, 149–50, quotes Leo Jaffe as saying that Columbia quickly "acquired the rights from United Artists" in a swap for another

property, *Trapeze*. This exchange was the price of disentangling Spiegel from his commitment to UA, something Spiegel apparently got Columbia to pay for.
14. Bob Thomas, *King Cohn* (New York: Putnam's, 1967), 346.
15. Fraser-Cavassoni, *Sam Spiegel*, 62.
16. Kazan, *A Life*, 528.
17. Zanuck to Kazan, July 15, 1954, Kazan papers, Reid Cinema Archives, Wesleyan University, F-116; also in Rudy Behlmer (ed.), *Memo from Darryl F. Zanuck* (New York: Grove, 1983), 229–30. Zanuck was not writing to congratulate the team but to complain that both had been bad-mouthing him for having abandoned the project due to a sudden lack of courage.
18. Schulberg, "Afterword," 151.
19. Kazan, *A Life*, 517–18, for example.
20. Fraser-Cavassoni, Sam Spiegel, 151.
21. Kazan, *A Life*, 517.
22. Karl Malden, *When Do I Start?* (New York: Simon & Schuster, 1997), 241–42.
23. Alain Silver and James Ursini, *What Ever Happened to Robert Aldrich?* (New York: Limelight, 1995), 323.
24. For Aldrich's recommendation of Justin and Maguire, see Howard Thompson, "George Justin: Local Movie Man on Our Town," *NYT*, November 26, 1961, and "Charles H. Maguire; Movie Producer," *LAT*, January 24, 2001.
25. Information from George Justin's professional résumé, courtesy of Susan Felleman.
26. Budd Schulberg, *A Face in the Crowd: A Play for the Screen* (New York: Random House, 1957), xxvi–xxvii.
27. Kazan, *A Life*, 519–24.
28. Sol Negrin interviewed by Richard Koszarski, December 3, 2016. This hard-nosed style of production management was not designed to win friends among New York's craft unions. For example, correspondence in Box 3 of Local 644's business records in the Tamiment Library at NYU ("Misc. 1949–55") reveals the exasperated business manager of Local 829 on the point of placing a picket line around Justin's studio on East Fifth Street because of his failure to employ union scenic artists or even accept his phone calls. Rudy Kanolt to Jay Rescher, September 9, 1955.
29. Charles Affron and Mirella Jona Affron, *Sets in Motion* (New Brunswick, NJ: Rutgers University Press, 1995), 25, 194.
30. Leon Barsacq, *Caligari's Cabinet and Other Grand Illusions*, rev. and ed. Elliott Stein (Boston: New York Graphic Society, 1976), 62.
31. *Greed* remained a touchstone of Hollywood realism for decades and the team behind *On the Waterfront* was clearly aware of it. On June 14, 1953, Schulberg dropped his work on the script to take part in a literary discussion of *McTeague* broadcast over WTOP. "Sunday Radio Highlights," *WP*, June 14, 1953.
32. Beverly Heisner, *Hollywood Art* (Jefferson, NC: McFarland, 1990), 271.
33. *TVD*, August 23, 1952, 7; see also *TVD*, August 29, 1953, 2.
34. Her only West Coast credit was *East of Eden*, and she may have done the bulk of her work for that film back in New York.
35. Elia Kazan to Boris Kaufman, September 28, 1953. Boris Kaufman papers, Beinecke Library, Yale University, Box 13, Folder 227.
36. This Don Malkames story, related by his great-grandson, Bruce Lawton, has been handed down from one generation to another in this family of cinematographers.
37. Kaufman's original manuscript, written for a Wesleyan Kazan tribute, Boris Kaufman papers, Box 16, Folder 362. Edited version published in *Working with Kazan* (Wesleyan University, September 1973).

38. In June 1946 these two OWI documentaries had been featured in the Museum of Modern Art's groundbreaking series, "The Documentary Film 1922–1945." *Museum of Modern Art Bulletin* XIII:2 (December 1945), 23.
39. Boris Kaufman to Elia Kazan, April 6, 1953. Boris Kaufman papers, Box 13, Folder 227. Kaufman did not mention the Paramount Screenliner series, not even the Oscar-nominated *Roller Derby Girl* (1948), and highlighted for Kazan only his most serious work.
40. Elia Kazan to Boris Kaufman, April 13, 1953. Boris Kaufman papers. Box 13, Folder 227.
41. Transcript of January 1, 1978 interview with Donald Crafton. Boris Kaufman papers, Box 16, Folder 334.
42. Elia Kazan 1953 appointment book, Kazan papers, Reid Cinema Archives. "1953" file in "Personal F110–F119" box.
43. For example, none of his 1952–1954 articles reprinted in Malcolm Johnson, *On the Waterfront*, contains more than a passing reference to New Jersey or Hoboken.
44. "Film Won't Hurt Hoboken." See also "De Sapio Jr. Asks Board to See If Marotta's Going Hollywood" and "Schulberg Credits Hoboken with Writing Movie Scene," all of them unidentified clippings in the collection of the Hoboken Historical Museum.
45. Budd Schulberg, *Waterfront* (New York: Bantam, 1956), 1.
46. Fisher, *On the Irish Waterfront*, 252–60.
47. Joseph Goldstein, "The Mob's Last Candy Jar," *NYT*, January 8, 2017.
48. Halsey Raines, "On Location in Gotham," *NYT*, April 15, 1956. Although this film is credited to Joseph Brun, Raines reports it as being photographed by "Boris Kaufman, noted for his prize-winning work on *On the Waterfront*." In fact, Kaufman was summarily fired by producer David Susskind on March 30. NYU Tamiment Library, Local 644 Collection, Box 23, "Boris Kaufman" file.
49. "Jarka Is Accused of $119,859 Bribery," *NYT*, October 21, 1953.
50. Fisher, *On the Irish Waterfront*, 258–59.
51. The promise was even codified in a memo (Zanuck to Schulberg and Kazan, February 12, 1953). See Behlmer, *Memo from Darryl F. Zanuck*, 226–27.
52. Pryor, *NYT*, June 13, 1953; Philip K, Scheuer, "Clift Practically Set for Kazan Venture," *LAT*, June 15, 1953.
53. Fraser-Cavassoni, *Sam Spiegel*, 154–55.
54. August 1, 1953, letter from Kazan to Spiegel, quoted in Fraser-Cavassoni, *Sam Spiegel*, 155.
55. Malden, *When Do I Start?* 236–37.
56. Edwin Schallert, "Priest Role on Slate for Sinatra," *LAT*, September 19, 1953, and "Is Equal Star Status Soothing Ava, Frankie?" September 27, 1953.
57. Although Martin Jurow, in his own memoir, *Seein' Stars*, suggests that Sinatra "forgot that when he played a priest in *Miracle of the Bells*, the movie was one of the turkeys that threatened to end his career" (35).
58. Richard Muti, *Cent' Anni. The Sinatra Legend at 100* (Woodland Park: North Jersey Media Group, 2015), 206.
59. Kazan, *A Life*, 514–15.
60. Kazan, *A Life*, 515.
61. Elia Kazan to Sam Spiegel, October 21, 1953. Reid Cinema Archives, Kazan Papers, F-116. This copy appears to be a draft of a telegram. Fraser-Cavassoni, *Sam Spiegel*, 154–55, quotes a portion of this document, sourced from Spiegel's papers, but misdates it as August. Presumably the underlined wording is a typographic instruction.
62. On March 25, 1954, Sinatra won the Academy Award for his performance in *From Here to Eternity*. However he won the part, Sinatra would have known that the role only

became available because the first choice for Maggio, Eli Wallach, could not get out of his commitment to Kazan's *Camino Real*. See Fred Zinnemann, *A Life in the Movies* (New York: Scribner's, 1992), 124.
63. Hedda Hopper, "Ava May Request Sinatra Divorce," *LAT*, October 28, 1953.
64. Kazan, *A Life*, 516.
65. Malden, *When Do I Start?* 236–37.
66. Kazan 1953 appointment book, Reid Cinema Archives.
67. Richard Muti, *Sinatra Legend*, 207. The Capitol recording sessions took place on November 4 and 5. See also Thomas M. Pryor, "Brando Will Star in Local Pier Film," *NYT*, November 7, 1953 ("The deal . . . was set this week in New York.").
68. Schulberg, "Afterword," 150; Kazan, *A Life*, 520. Did Columbia sign on before the deal with Brando, or after? Despite the volumes of material available on this film, the sequence remains unclear.
69. Frank Sinatra to Elia Kazan, December 8, 1953. Kazan papers, Reid Cinema Archives, Personal 1952–1984, file F-116.
70. Fraser-Cavassoni, *Sam Spiegel*, 160. According to this source, "a screening room was built at Sinatra's house" as part of the deal. Karl Malden heard that the bonus was "a magnificent painting, museum quality, of course." *When Do I Start?* 238.
71. Fraser-Cavassoni, *Sam Spiegel*, 160–61.
72. Kazan, *A Life*, 489.
73. Fisher, *On the Irish Waterfront*, 241.
74. Malden, *When Do I Start?* 238.
75. Kazan to Spiegel, undated (circa early November 1953). Reid Cinema Archives, Kazan papers F-116.
76. Rod Steiger Oral History, July 1959, Columbia University. See also Sidney Skolsky, "Hollywood Is My Beat," *NYP*, August 26, 1954.
77. Steiger claimed that Kazan instructed him to see Schulberg about the part "a few days after the TV showing of *Marty*," but if so, nothing was settled for many months. See Tom Hutchinson, *Rod Steiger* (New York: Fromm, 2000), 71, 80.
78. In Schulberg's 1995 Broadway production of *On the Waterfront*, Charley was played by James Gandolfini.
79. Malden, *When Do I Start?* 239–40.
80. Malden, *When Do I Start?* 239–40. Montgomery may have intimidated this crowd; a graduate of the Spence School, she had been presented at the Waldorf Astoria's 1951 Debutante Cotillion the year Schulberg was naming names before HUAC and Kazan was preparing his revolutionary epic, *Viva Zapata!*
81. Brooks Atkinson, "First Night at the Theatre," *NYT*, November 4, 1953.
82. Patricia Bosworth, *Marlon Brando* (New York: Viking, 2001), 106. Bosworth says that Saint was cast two days earlier.
83. Richard Muti, *Sinatra Legend*, 209. The fact that Sinatra was also being divorced by Ava Gardner that week did not make things any easier for him.

13. Kiss Me, Kill Me

1. "How About a Little Game?" *NY*, November 12, 1966.
2. A. H. Weiler, "Of Pictures and People," *NYT*, May 23, 1954. Agreement with Howard O. Sackler dated September 2, 1953, signed by Stanley Kubrick and Moe Bousel. Stanley Kubrick Collection, University of the Arts, London. SK/6/1/1/1-2. Subsequent

references to this collection only by the SK file number. Thanks to Cathy Surowiec for searching this archive for me.
3. "Howard O. Sackler" in John A. Garraty and Mark C. Carnes (eds.), *American National Biography: Rousseau—Simmons* (New York: Oxford University Press, 1999), 185–86.
4. Kubrick had by now left West Sixteenth Street and moved in with Ruth Sobotka, an American Ballet Theater dancer who lived at 222 East Tenth Street; Bousel was at 3156 Perry Avenue in the Bronx. SK/6/1/4.
5. Loan Agreement, Minotaur Productions, Inc. and De Luxe Laboratories, Inc., September 17, 1953. SK/6/1/4.
6. For its part, Titra agreed that the first $9,000 of their charges—nearly all of the film's expenses for sound recording and mixing—"shall be deferred and paid . . . out of the net receipts," a risky concession which assumed that the film would not only be sold but also show a net profit. Information on these agreements assembled from documents located in SK/6/1/1/1-2, SK/6/1/3, SK/6/1/4 and SK/6/1/5.
7. "White Mane," *VAR*, December 23, 1953, 16. On the currently available Criterion Collection edition of *White Mane*, the Silvera/Agee narration has been replaced by one spoken by Peter Strauss. *The Lonely Night* played the Venice Film Festival in 1952 but did not open in New York until 1954.
8. Richard Combs, "*Killer's Kiss*," *MFB*, January 1, 1984, 220–21.
9. Edith Rosenblatt, "Tech Drama Grad Returns," *PPG*, May 16, 1952, 25.
10. *Killer's Kiss*, British press book. SK/6/5.
11. I haven't been able to identify any radio dramas on which Silvera or Smith may have worked, but locally produced films like *Close-Up* (1948) were often stocked with experienced radio actors.
12. Harold V. Cohen, "The Drama Desk," *PPG*, May 17, 1952, 20.
13. See the picture of Sobotka as an art student in "Picturesque Clown at 71 Models for Tech Artists," *PPG*, October 23, 1942, 17.
14. John Martin, "Ballet by Robbins in Local Premiere," *NYT*, June 15, 1951.
15. Martin, "Ballet by Robbins."
16. John Martin, "Balanchine 'Bayou' in World Premiere," *NYT*, February 22, 1952.
17. The De Luxe contract called for a film of at least seventy minutes, often considered a dividing line separating B-pictures from grade A releases. Even with the ballet sequence, Kubrick's film still fell short.
18. Vincent Lo Brutto, *Stanley Kubrick: A Biography* (New York: Donald Fine, 1997), 92–94.
19. Or so she claimed in a letter to the *New York Times* (February 20, 1966), the point of which was to establish the date of their wedding as June 1955, therefore proving that the role in *Killer's Kiss* was not simple nepotism. No one denies that the pair was a couple at the time, but there is surprisingly little agreement on the date of the wedding. Lo Brutto (101) says January 15, 1955, while Sobotka's obituary in the *Times* (June 19, 1967) gives it as 1953. Her friend David Vaughan, who would have known, later wrote that Sobotka "was married to Stanley at the time" they all made *Killer's Kiss* (David Vaughan, "Kubrick's Vérité on 42nd Street," *NYT*, June 27, 2004).
20. *Killer's Kiss*, British press book. SK/6/5.
21. Also a noted photographer of jazz performance, Stern would later codirect *Jazz on a Summer's Day*, an impressionistic record of the 1958 Newport Jazz Festival.
22. Stern and Kubrick also shared an appreciation for the ballet, or at least for ballet dancers in George Balanchine's company. In 1959, when Kubrick was still married to Ruth Sobotka, Stern married Allegra Kent, another Balanchine dancer. Occasionally the two

women even danced on the same bill. See John Martin, "Ballet: Two Novelties," *NYT*, January 1, 1957.
23. The part remained credited to Christopher Kane throughout production, and as late as May 18, 1955, this was the name submitted to the Production Code Administration on the "official credits sheets." Confusingly, the *New York Times* was referring to her as "Irene Kane" as early as May 23, 1954, but then as "Christopher Kane" on September 11, 1955, just before release. Stanley Kubrick to Geoffry [*sic*] Shurlock, May 18, 1955, PCA Records, *Killer's Kiss*, Margaret Herrick Library. A. H. Weiler, "Of Pictures and People," *NYT*, May 23, 1954; A. H. Weiler, "Screening the Motion Picture Scene," *NYT*, September 11, 1955.
24. Subsequent quotations from Kane are from Chris Chase, *How to Become a Movie Star, or A Terrible Beauty Is Born* (New York: Harper and Row, 1974), 14–23, itself reprinted from her essay, "Now I'll Tell You How to Be a Movie Star," *NYT*, August 15, 1971.
25. Or as she wrote her sister during production, "Stanley's a fascinating character. . . . He's all for sex and sadism. Talks about Mickey Spillane, and how the public eats it up." *How to Become a Movie Star*, 21–22.
26. "To say this film is offensive would be kind; to point out that it induces an irritating boredom would be accurate," O. A. G., "Melodrama of Murder," *NYT*, October 3, 1953. The *Times* also found Karlson's film a "stale melodrama" and a "tasteless rehash."
27. *Killer's Kiss* British pressbook. SK/6/5.
28. Vaughan, "Kubrick's Vérité."
29. Locations for the film were identified at the time in A. H. Weiler, "Of Pictures and People," *NYT*, May 23, 1954.
30. Location identified by Juli Kearns. See http://idyllopuspress.com/idyllopus/film/killers_kiss_1.htm.
31. SK/6/1/4.
32. It is possible that this was simply a vacant loft, but it might also have been the small Biltmore Studio, located at 66 East Fourth Street, often used by local film and television producers in the 1950s. See "Television-Radio," *MPD*, August 31, 1955, 10. The television series *The Goldbergs* was filmed here.
33. "Minotaur Productions, Inc. Schedule of Cost of Production of 'Killer's Kiss.'" SK/6/2/1.
34. John Martin, "The Dance: Novelties," *NYT*, June 10, 1951.
35. Chase, *How to Become a Movie Star*, 18.
36. Fabrice Moussas, "The Art of the Boom: Nat Boxer," *FMN*, May 1976, 18.
37. Lo Brutto, *Stanley Kubrick*, 98. These are the recollections of Max Glenn, one of the film's camera operators.
38. Chase, *How to Become a Movie Star*, 21.
39. Among Paley's few other screen credits is the feature length 1964 documentary *The Inheritance*, which was produced locally by the Amalgamated Clothing Workers' Union.
40. Lo Brutto, *Stanley Kubrick*, 96–97.
41. "Arthur Florman Is 1950 President of Documentary TV Cameramen," *BSM* II:5 (1950), 39.
42. "Who Shot Pres. Eisenhower???" *VAR*, February 10, 1954, 47. Also listed are shorts, commercials, and filmed television material.
43. "In the Spotlight," *IP*, July 1954, 14.
44. SK 0233 (E) Box 022. I found no record of Kubrick's own union membership in the Local 644 archives at the Tamiment Library. But a July 22, 1954, letter to "Dear Brother

488   13. Kiss Me, Kill Me

Kubrick" in SK 6/7/1 informs him of the need to take certain steps now that his union has been absorbed by Local 644.
45. Lo Brutto, *Stanley Kubrick*, 97.
46. Lo Brutto, *Stanley Kubrick*, 97.
47. "Reasoning by Hecht," *VAR*, November 28, 1956.
48. Sol Negrin to Richard Koszarski, December 3, 2016.
49. Chase, *How to Become a Movie Star*, 22.
50. See Silvera's credits in Internet Broadway Data Base; also Brooks Atkinson, [*Coriolanus*], *NYT*, January 20, 1954.
51. SK/6/8/2 Contact Sheets. See especially SK-87.
52. Delaying that part of the shoot until May could have been a blessing in disguise. Herb Lightman, "*The Thief*—A New Trend in Films?" *AC*, October 1952, 432–33, 448–49, describes how difficult it was for anyone to film in Penn Station, even on a sunny day. Kubrick may have found it impossible to do so during his scheduled winter shoot.
53. Another $4,000, representing legal and accounting fees, also appears to have been deferred; possibly that was a contribution from one of Minotaur's private investors.
54. Joseph Gelmis, *The Film Director as Superstar* (Garden City, NY: Doubleday, 1970), 313.
55. SK/6/6/2 (i).
56. Chase, *How to Become a Movie Star*, 18.
57. Chase, *How to Become a Movie Star*, 16.
58. Lo Brutto, *Stanley Kubrick*, 95–96. If Silvera was already cast, what role was available for Lloyd? And after their run-in on *Mr. Lincoln*, did Kubrick really believe that Norman Lloyd would ever want to work with him again?
59. Chase, *How to Become a Movie Star*, 22. According to Alexander Singer, speaking to Jan Harlan for his film *Stanley Kubrick: A Life in Pictures*, there were other reasons for letting the crew go home early. "On Fridays he dismissed the company for a couple of hours, went to the unemployment line and collected his unemployment check, because that was what he was living on." On the other hand, Chris Chase (19) claimed that Kubrick was living off *Ruth Sobotka*'s unemployment checks.

14. "And the Winner in New York Is . . ."

1. Tommy Hanley, interviewed by Richard Koszarski at a dinner honoring Budd Schulberg, Fort Lee, NJ, November 2, 2007. The $250 he earned weekly was "a fortune" that got his family out of debt. In 2007 Hanley was still a union shop steward in Bayonne, but "can't afford to live in Hoboken" due to gentrification. According to an interview with Hanley on the Criterion Blu-Ray, it was the notorious waterfront mobster Cockeye Dunn who had murdered his father.
2. Richard Schickel, *Elia Kazan* (New York: HarperCollins, 2005), 302.
3. Jesse Zunser, "*Cue* Covers the Waterfront," *Cue*, February 20, 1954, 33.
4. Hanley to Koszarski.
5. "3-Day Smog Torments Entire East as Cold 'Lid' Traps Irritants in Air," *NYT*, November 20, 1953.
6. Kazan, *A Life* (New York: Knopf, 1988), 517.
7. A. H. Weiler, "By Way of Report," *NYT*, November 22, 1953; "Of Local Origin," *NYT*, November 25, 1953.
8. Kazan, *A Life*, 520.

9. Boris Kaufman Papers, Beinecke Library, Box 8. Spiegel, Kazan, Schulberg, and Day were not considered crew; the list does include Kaufman, Justin, Maguire, and other craft workers.
10. Kaufman papers, Box 8.
11. Mr. and Mrs. Robert C. Franklin, "Boris Kaufman Oral History," April 1959, Columbia University Oral History Program.
12. Kazan, *A Life*, 520.
13. *Time*, August 9, 1954.
14. Leo Braudy, *On the Waterfront* (London: BFI Publishing, 2005), 31.
15. Sada Fretz, "Hoboken's Waterfront," in *On the Waterfront, Starring Hoboken, New Jersey* (Hoboken Historical Museum, 2004), 10.
16. Crew info packet, Kaufman papers, Box 8. His name is spelled "Maratta" here.
17. Karl Malden, *When Do I Start?* (New York: Simon and Schuster, 1997), 244.
18. Stuart Byron and Martin Rubin, "Elia Kazan interview," *Movie* #19 (Winter 1971–72), 8.
19. Kazan, *A Life*, 521.
20. Byron and Rubin, "Elia Kazan interview."
21. Schulberg, "Afterword," *On the Waterfront, the Final Shooting Script* (Hollywood: Samuel French, 1988), 152.
22. Kazan to Spiegel, undated memo, c. early November 1953. Reid Cinema Archives, Wesleyan University, Kazan collection, F-116. He does not say which Marotta he is referring to (and his spelling of all the names is casual at best).
23. "Director Kazan Won't Be Lured By Movie Luxury," *BDE*, April 13, 1947.
24. A. H. Weiler, "De Sica Favors Brooklyn," *NYT*, February 12, 1950.
25. Michel Delahaye, "A Natural Phenomenon," *Cahiers du Cinema in English* #9 (March 1967), 31.
26. Boris Kaufman, "Working with Kazan," Wesleyan University (1973).
27. Howard Thompson, "By Way of Report," *NYT*, December 20, 1954.
28. Zunser, "*Cue* Covers the Waterfront."
29. This is from a letter Kazan wrote to the Museum of Modern Art Department of Film on September 5, 1980, reproduced in the program note for a brief "Camera by Boris Kaufman" retrospective.
30. "Golden Warriors" notebook (started June 28, 1953). Reid Cinema Archives, Kazan collection, B31-F7.
31. Kaufman papers, "Lab Notes," Box 8. Initials refer to Foot Candles and Fore Ground/Middle Ground/Back Ground.
32. Boris Kaufman, "I Envy the Amateur," *Popular Photography*, December 1956, 178.
33. Teletype from Cushman to Dougherty, November 23, 1953. Kaufman papers, Box 8.
34. He settled on Du Pont. See the full-page ad touting the "realism" Kaufman achieved with Du Pont negative in *IP*, December 1954 and *AC*, November 1954.
35. Phil Tannura, "The Practical Use of Latensification," *AC*, February 1951, 54, 68–70; "By Hyper-Sensitization Du Pont Raises Speed," *AC*, November 1940, 499.
36. Kaufman would seem to have saved everything of value regarding the photography of *On the Waterfront*, down to the original instruction sheet included with the 35 mm Eyemo rented to film shots of pigeons flying off the roof. Kaufman papers, Box 7, Folder 104.
37. Kenneth Geist, *Pictures Will Talk* (New York: Scribner's, 1978), 234.
38. "Of Local Origin," *NYT*, June 16, 1953.
39. "Round-Up of the Wide-Screen Process," *IP*, July 1953, 5–6, 8.
40. Handwritten letter (draft?), c. August 1954, Kaufman to Kazan. Kaufman papers, Box 13.

41. The argument that the film's main titles look to be composed for wide screen is irrelevant; this postproduction work would have been handled by the studio on the West Coast, without Kaufman's input.
42. Edouard L. de Laurot and Jonas Mekas, "An Interview with Boris Kaufman," *Film Culture* I:4 (1955), 4–6. The earliest reference to aspect ratio I found in Kaufman's papers is a March 15, 1961, letter to Leslie Oliver of the British Technicolor lab, concerned that *Splendor in the Grass* was not being projected there in 1.75:1, as he had intended it to be shown. Box 9.
43. "About the Aspect Ratio and Transfer," insert booklet, *On the Waterfront* (Criterion, 2013).
44. Kaufman papers, Box 8.
45. Kaufman papers, Box 12, Folder 203.
46. "Hollywood Pro's [sic] at Work," *HM*, September 1954, 356.
47. Kazan, *A Life*, 521.
48. Tom Hutchinson, *Rod Steiger* (New York: Fromm, 2000), 89.
49. "At 69.5°, Flowers Bloom A La Spring," *NYT*, November 18, 1953. That day it was even warmer on the Jersey side than in Manhattan.
50. "Weather Summary," *NYT*, December 1, 1953.
51. "3d Warmest December Goes Into Records Here," *NYT*, January 5, 1954; "The Week's Events. City and Suburbs Report Unseasonable Bloom," *NYT*, December 13, 1953.
52. Although at least one period report found the longshoremen also suffering under the "murderous" weather conditions, especially in January and February. See Zunser, "*Cue* Covers the Waterfront."
53. "14.4°, Year's Low, Halts Midtown Traffic Lights," *NYT*, December 19, 1953.
54. See, for example "9-Inch Snow Halts 75 Percent of Cars Here" (January 12); "A 'Chance' of More Snow as Mercury Slips to 11°" (January 14); "Two Ferryboats Crash at Battery" (January 20); "Fog Cancels Flights, Delays *Queen Mary*" (January 21), all in *NYT*, 1954.
55. Date of the last official day of shooting from "Hollywood Pro's at Work." Did Kaufman leave the film early? A few period references report that some shooting was still going on in February.
56. Kaufman, "I Envy the Amateur."
57. Kaufman, "I Envy the Amateur."
58. Mr. and Mrs. Robert C. Franklin, "Boris Kaufman Oral History."
59. De Laurot and Mekas, "Interview with Boris Kaufman."
60. Church Square Park and Elysian Park were both used; see Nicholas Acocella, "Location: The Parks" at www.troop146.org, accessed July 11, 2016.
61. De Laurot and Mekas, "Interview with Boris Kaufman."
62. His ASC nomination was put forward by Frank Zucker on September 14, 1954. Kaufman papers, Box 12, Folder 174.
63. "Hollywood Pro's at Work."
64. Robert Downing, "Behind the Brando Headlines," *Screenland*, June 1954, 26–27, 64. Downing appeared in the church basement scene.
65. "Hollywood Pro's at Work."
66. Howard Thompson, "By Way of Report," *NYT*, December 20, 1953.
67. Jane Corby, "Karl Malden, *Waterfront* Priest, Had Expert Coaching," *BDE*, August 8, 1954. They were the same hat size, 7¼. But the rest of Malden's wardrobe was ordered from an ecclesiastical tailor.
68. Peter Biskind, "The Politics of Power in *On the Waterfront*," *FQ* (Fall 1975), 25–37.
69. Sam Spiegel, "Working with Kazan" (Wesleyan University, 1973).

70. Malden, *When Do I Start?* 242–43.
71. Jeff Young, *Kazan: The Master Director Discusses His Films* (New York: Newmarket, 2001), 167.
72. Kazan, *A Life*, 521–22.
73. See A. H. Weiler, "By Way of Report," *NYT*, November 2, 1953, and Ann X. Smith, "Hoboken's Like Hollywood These Days," *Newark Star-Ledger*, December 6, 1953, which gives Stinson's address as 115 Hudson Street.
74. Tommy Hanley interviewed by Richard Koszarski.
75. For accounts of von Stroheim's biomechanical directing style, see Richard Koszarski, *Von: The Life and Films of Erich von Stroheim* (New York: Limelight, 2001), 288–89.
76. Edwin Schallert, "Eva Marie Saint Puts Family Before Films," *LAT*, December 12, 1954.
77. Nicholas Acocella, "Location: The Local Players," at www.troop146.org, accessed July 11, 2016.
78. Memo, Sam Spiegel to "All Concerned," November 23, 1953, Kaufman papers, Box 8.
79. Annotated shooting script of *On the Waterfront*, Reid Cinema Archives, Kazan collection, Box 32.
80. I was shown this draft by Valerie Sharaff Justin in June 2008 but could not study it in detail. It was not a part of the George Justin papers she subsequently donated to the Museum of Modern Art.
81. Rod Steiger Oral History, July 1959, Columbia University. Terry also dies at the end of Schulberg's *Waterfront* novel, his body "found in a barrel of lime that had been tossed on one of the multi-acre junk heaps in the Jersey swamps" (New York: Bantam, 1956), 298.
82. Malden, *When Do I Start?* 245–46.
83. Kazan, *A Life*, 525–26; Kaufman, "Working with Kazan."
84. David Naylor's short documentary, "Contender: Mastering the Method," included on both the 2001 Columbia and subsequent Criterion release is excellent. But the repurposing of Schulberg's dialogue in Martin Scorsese's *Raging Bull* is even better at signaling the film's importance to future generations of independent New York filmmakers.
85. Kazan, *A Life*, 524.
86. Kazan, *A Life*, 524.
87. Herb A. Lightman, "*13 Rue Madeleine*: Documentary Style in the Photoplay," *AC*, March 1947, 88.
88. Kaufman papers, Box 8.
89. Rod Steiger Oral History.
90. John William Tuohy, *On the Waterfront: The Making of a Great American Film* (Lexington, KY: n.p., 2013), 280. I have been unable to identify an operating studio at either address. But both men remembered it as a television studio (not an industrial film facility), and Persoff also recalled playing the scene while seated on "a wooden milk cart," an odd bit of trivia that points to the CBS Broadcast Center on West Fifty-Seventh Street. CBS had acquired the old Sheffield Farms depot (not Borden's) in 1952, planning to install enough shops and office space to support ten large television stages. But in 1953 the facility was still unfinished and probably offered little more than four bare walls. "Sheffield Plant Resold to C.B.S.," *NYT*, May 17, 1952.
91. It is unclear exactly what was missing here: the rear-screen projector, the footage of an appropriate nighttime urban landscape, or the entire package? A proper facility would have prepared for this situation.
92. Kazan, *A Life*, 524; Hutchinson, *Rod Steiger*, 87–88.
93. Richard Koszarski interview with Sol Negrin, December 3, 2016. Negrin knew Kaufman's style and later worked with him on commercials and also, briefly, *The Pawnbroker*.

94. Sol Negrin, who later served two terms as president of Local 644, had his own suspicions. "It could have been George Justin. I hate to tell you. He's a cheap bastard, to a certain degree. I got a feeling that he didn't want to bring in the rear-screen projection." Negrin to Koszarski.
95. Peter Manso, *Brando* (New York: Hyperion, 1994), 365. For more information on the prevalence of such blinds, visit the website www.autovenetianblinds.com.
96. Hutchinson, *Rod Steiger*, 88.
97. See Steiger interview in Naylor, "Contender: Mastering the Method."
98. Truman Capote, "The Duke and His Domain," *NY*, November 9, 1957.
99. Rod Steiger in Naylor, "Contender."
100. See, for example, Denise Mann, *Hollywood Independents: The Postwar Talent Takeover* (Minneapolis: University of Minnesota Press, 2008), 152.
101. Schulberg, "Afterword," 153. In his copy of the script, Boris Kaufman noted, "The way to speed it up is to have next location set in advance," suggesting that a lack of production coordination was responsible for any delays, not foot-dragging by the cast and crew. Kaufman papers, Box 8.
102. Malden, *When Do I Start?* 243–44.
103. Hutchinson, *Rod Steiger*, 87.
104. Kazan, *A Life*, 523–24.
105. Fisher, *On the Irish Waterfront*, 264. The quote is from Rubin and Byron, "Elia Kazan Interview."
106. Sol Negrin interviewed by Richard Koszarski.
107. "Milford to Edit Film," *MPD*, July 26, 1943, 4.
108. Ralph Rosenblum and Robert Karen, *When the Shooting Stops . . . the Cutting Begins* (New York: Viking, 1979), 129.
109. "Prime Cut," *FC*, March–April 1977, 6–29.
110. Horizon-American Corporation to James Wong Howe, March 10, 1954. Margaret Herrick Library, James Wong Howe Collection, Folder 217.
111. Howe to Sonora Babb, March 25, 1954. James Wong Howe Collection, Folder 224b.
112. Howe to Babb, March 27, 1954. James Wong Howe Collection, Folder 224b.
113. Todd Rainsberger, *James Wong Howe, Cinematographer* (La Jolla, CA: Barnes, 1981), 116.
114. Kazan to Spiegel, undated carbon, c. January 1954, marked "not sent." Reid Cinema Archives, Kazan collection, Personal 1952–1984, File F-116.
115. Jon Burlingham, "Leonard Bernstein and *On the Waterfront*," in *On the Waterfront*, ed. Joanna E. Rapf (Cambridge: Cambridge University Press, 2003), 126. Burlingham forgets *Man on a Tightrope*.
116. Humphrey Burton, *Leonard Bernstein* (New York: Doubleday, 1994), 236.
117. Kazan, *A Life*, 526–27.
118. Leonard Bernstein, "Notes Struck at 'Upper Dubbing,' California," *NYT*, May 30, 1954.
119. Burlingham, "Leonard Bernstein," 127.
120. American Business Consultants, *Red Channels* (New York: Counterattack, 1950), 16–17, 37–38.
121. Bernstein, "Upper Dubbing."
122. Burlingham, "Leonard Bernstein," 130–31. The recording of the score was done on April 24, 27 and 28, 1954.
123. Bernstein, "Upper Dubbing."
124. Natasha Fraser-Cavassoni, *Sam Spiegel* (New York: Simon & Schuster, 2003), 147–48.
125. Burlingham, "Leonard Bernstein," 133.

126. Burlingham, "Leonard Bernstein," 140–41.
127. Schulberg, "Introduction," xl.
128. A. H. Weiler, "Dockside Violence," *NYT*, August 1, 1954.
129. Kazan, *A Life*, 528.
130. Elia Kazan, "Golden Warriors" production notebook. Reid Cinema Archives, Kazan Collection, B31-F7.
131. This preliminary poster art, from a time before Terry's name was changed to Malloy, reflects the more directly religious quality of Schulberg's early drafts. A copy can be seen in the photo section of the Criterion release.
132. Fraser-Cavassoni, *Sam Spiegel*, 158.
133. Display ad, *On the Waterfront*, *NYT*, July 26, 1954.
134. FBI COMPIC Files, "Communist Influence in the Motion Picture Industry," Running Memorandum summary dated January 3, 1956, pages II: 36–39.
135. "*Waterfront* Is Still Strong at Astor," *MPD*, August 19, 1954, 5.
136. Fraser-Cavassoni, *Sam Spiegel*, 159.
137. Robert F. Hawkins, "Venice Appraises the International Cinema," *NYT*, September 19, 1954; Fisher, *On the Irish Waterfront*, 291.
138. Fraser-Cavassoni, *Sam Spiegel*, 159.
139. Lindsay Anderson, "The Last Sequence of *On the Waterfront*," *S&S*, January–March 1955, 127–30. And this attack does not even raise the issue of informing.
140. De Laurot and Mekas, "Interview with Boris Kaufman."
141. A. H. Weiler, "Dockside Violence."
142. Kazan, *A Life*, 527.
143. Video of the 1955 telecast has been posted online by the Academy of Motion Picture Arts and Sciences.
144. Marlon Brando, *Brando: Songs My Mother Taught Me* (New York: Random House, 1994), 201.
145. The baby arrived two days later. By coincidence, Hope and Grace Kelly had been making *A Star Is Born* jokes about the nonappearance of nominee Judy Garland, whose own child had been born the day before.
146. "Thank You Hollywood!" *VAR*, April 6, 1955, 23.

15. Happy Ending

1. After his public testimony, Kazan was contacted by columnist Sidney Skolsky and asked for information on others he had worked with. Skolsky said he'd been "talking to the Coast and Frank Silvera's name came up. He's a bad one, I know. What about him?" This time Kazan took the high ground, saying that he only provided that kind of information "for the government." Elia Kazan, *A Life* (New York: Knopf, 1988), 471.
2. "How About a Little Game?" *NY*, November 12, 1966, 72. He also banned the showing of *Fear and Desire*. Indeed, "he would probably be just as happy if the prints were to disappear altogether," a fate that nearly did befall *Fear and Desire*.
3. Michel Ciment, *Kubrick* (New York: Holt, Rinehart & Winston, 1983), 4, from a July 1957 interview by Raymond Haine in *Cahiers du Cinema*.
4. Kaufman to Kubrick, May 7, 1962; Kubrick to Kaufman, May 9, 1962. Boris Kaufman Collection, Beinecke Library, Box 13. Kaufman may or may not have known Kubrick's work. In his letter he praises the freshness and expressiveness of *The Killers*, either misremembering the title of *The Killing* or confusing it with Robert Siodmak's film. It is

unlikely he was thinking of *Killer's Kiss*. Kubrick, who had probably faced this issue before, let it go.
5. According to Richard Sylbert, whom Kubrick had approached to design the film, the pair spent nearly a month investigating the possibilities of shooting *Dr. Strangelove* in New York before concluding that the city's lack of "a studio or a projection screen large enough" made the idea impossible. Richard Sylbert and Sylvia Townsend, *Designing Movies* (Westport, CT: Praegar, 2006), 43.
6. Fabrice Moussas, "The Art of the Boom: Nat Boxer," *FMN*, May 1976, 18–20.
7. Titra Sound Corporation, September 19, 1953. Stanley Kubrick Collection, University of the Arts, London, SK/6/1/5. Subsequent references only to the SK file number.
8. "Two New Film Firms Incorporated in N.Y.," *MPD*, May 18, 1943, 4; "Two New Imports," *MPD*, August 22, 1944, 11.
9. Herman G. Weinberg, *Coffee, Brandy and Cigars* (New York: Anthology Film Archives, 1982).
10. Herman G. Weinberg Collection, Billy Rose Theater Collection, NYPL. Kubrick to Weinberg, January 26 and February 4, 1959, concern Weinberg's promotion of an unknown for the role of "Lolita," as well as a response to Weinberg's criticism of the ending of *Paths of Glory* ("I don't see how the ending softens the execution," Kubrick insisted).
11. Weinberg was a founding member of the Theodore Huff Memorial Film Society, which Everson ran for many years. In a history of the Huff Society, Everson noted that the group could not claim to have nurtured as many talented filmmakers as the Cinémathèque française, but did identify Kubrick as one of the "successful directors who learned their basics with old film" at the Huff's weekly screenings. https://www.nyu.edu/projects/wke/notes/huff/huff_briefhistory.htm. Everson told me that Kubrick, after he returned to New York following the production of *Spartacus*, not only attended screenings but contributed a few days of photography to *Captain Celluloid and the Film Pirates*, a serial spoof on which various Huffians worked in the early 1960s.
12. SK/6/1/6 (f).
13. Vincent Lo Brutto, *Stanley Kubrick: A Biography* (New York: Donald Fine, 1997), 97.
14. Lo Brutto, *Stanley Kubrick*, 97.
15. A. H. Weiler, "Of Pictures and People," *NYT*, May 23, 1954.
16. For example, Lo Brutto, *Stanley Kubrick*, 94 and David Hughes, *The Complete Stanley Kubrick* (London: Virgin, 2000), 25.
17. Weiler, "Of Pictures and People."
18. Chris Chase, *How to Become a Movie Star* (New York: Harper and Row, 1974), 20.
19. SK/6/1/6 (a).
20. Chase, *How to Become a Movie Star*, 15–16.
21. See Titra's display ad in *MPD*, April 29, 1957, 15.
22. Lo Brutto, *Stanley Kubrick*, 104.
23. For example, see the use of "Slowly" in *Fallen Angel* or "I Can't Believe That You're in Love with Me" in *Detour*.
24. Christine Gengaro, *Listening to Stanley Kubrick: The Music in His Films* (Lanham, MD: Scarecrow, 2013), 14.
25. SK/6/2/2.
26. Schedule of Cost of Production (SK/6/2/1) and Cash Costs through June 30, 1955 (SK/6/6/2 [g]).
27. Margaret Herrick Library, Production Code Administration files, *Killer's Kiss* (subsequently PCA); also SK/6/7/2-13 (b).

28. And a few months before that, Corman had produced *Monster from the Ocean Floor* with no stars, for $12,000 plus deferments. Roger Corman, *How I Made a Hundred Movies in Hollywood and Never Lost a Dime* (New York: Random House, 1990), 19–25.
29. SK/6/6/1. Manufacturer's Trust Bank Statement, Stanley Kubrick or Ruth Sobotka, August 2–31, 1954.
30. Cash Costs through 6/30/55 (SK/6/6/2[g]).
31. Tino Balio, *United Artists, the Company That Changed the Film Industry* (Madison: University of Wisconsin Press, 2009), 9–39.
32. Max Youngstein to Arthur Krim, December 10, 1954. United Artists Corporation Records, MCHC82-046 Folder 1, Wisconsin Center for Film and Theater Research.
33. SK/6/6/1. The indebtedness to CECO seems to have increased since the original agreement.
34. United Artists did release *The Moon Is Blue* without a Seal in 1953, but despite the clout of producer-director Otto Preminger it was still banned from portions of the Loew's, RKO, and Fox West Coast theater chains. It is unlikely UA would have gone to the same trouble for *Killer's Kiss*. See *AFI Catalog* entry for *The Moon Is Blue*.
35. "UA Gets Rights to *Killer's Kiss*," MPD, July 27, 1955, 9. The *Killer's Kiss* file in the Billy Rose Theatre Collection of the NYPL holds an invitation to UA's August 8 promotional screening.
36. Joseph Gelmis, *The Film Director as Superstar* (Garden City, NY: Doubleday, 1970), 315.
37. V. I. Pudovkin, *On Film Technique* (London: George Newnes, 1933). See especially 138–41, an account of how editing can create performance regardless of the intentions or abilities of the actors!
38. Lloyd Grove, "Stanley Kubrick, at a Distance," WP, June 28, 1987.
39. Michel Ciment, *Kubrick* (New York: Owl, 1984), 174.
40. Alexander Walker, *Stanley Kubrick, Director* (New York: Norton, 1999), 16.
41. Hughes, *The Complete Stanley Kubrick*, 32.
42. Lo Brutto, *Stanley Kubrick*, 104.
43. Chase, *How to Become a Movie Star*, 22.
44. Gilb., "*Killer's Kiss*," VAR, September 21, 1955.
45. James Naremore, *On Kubrick* (London: British Film Institute, 2007), 65–66.
46. A. Nicholas Vardac, *Stage to Screen: Theatrical Method from Garrick to Griffith* (Cambridge, MA: Harvard University Press, 1949).
47. Sergei Eisenstein, *Film Form* (New York: Harcourt, Brace, 1949), 195–255.
48. See MCNY Blog: New York Stories, "The Sultry Showgirl," especially X2011.4.11448.62B. Accessed August 16, 2018.
49. Elia Kazan, "Golden Warriors" production notebook. Reid Cinema Archives, Wesleyan University, Elia Kazan Collection, B31-F7.
50. PCA files, *Killer's Kiss*, "Analysis of Film Content."
51. SK/6/3/1 (c). Who was this censor, who was already cutting the film before the PCA had even seen the print? Possibly an in-house agent employed by United Artists?
52. Geoffrey Shurlock to Sol Konecoff, March 22, 1955. PCA Files, *Killer's Kiss*.
53. See *Killer's Kiss*, "Analysis of Film Content" in PCA Files, and SK/6/3/1 (C).
54. The film's British press book gives an even shorter length of 5,828 feet (sixty-four minutes), a figure repeated in the *MFB* review of January 1, 1956, 29, and some of the secondary literature, including Gene Phillips, *Stanley Kubrick: A Film Odyssey* (New York: Popular Library, 1975), 182, and Walker, *Stanley Kubrick, Director*, 375. But a later review in *MFB* on January 1, 1984, 220–21 (of a 16 mm release), gives the length as sixty-seven minutes.

55. SK/6/2/1 (Schedule of Costs) and SK/6/6/2 (Statement of Profit and Loss). These figures are reported from the Minotaur side. But Tino Balio, who had access to figures from the UA side, reports that UA "paid $100,000 for the picture," and another $100,000 "to Kubrick" for a second film. *United Artists: The Company That Changed the Film Industry* (Madison: University of Wisconsin Press, 1987), 157.
56. "Killer's Kiss," *MPD*, July 27, 1955, 9.
57. G. L., "Killer's Kiss," *MFB*, January 1, 1956, 29; Gavin Lambert, "Killer's Kiss," *S&S*, Spring 1956, 198.
58. SK/6/4/1 "Theatre Runs"; SK/6/4/2 "Distribution Accounting Reports."
59. John McElwee, "Killer's + Killing + Kubrick," Greenbriar Picture Shows, posted October 1, 2011.
60. Thanks to Lou DiCrescenzo for a great discussion of period projection practice.
61. These decisions are always debatable. While the AFI considers *Night of the Hunter* (released by UA the same month as *Killer's Kiss*) a 1.85:1 film, the Criterion Collection release is 1.66:1.
62. "By Way of Report," *NYT*, June 26, 1955.
63. Eric Hoyt, *Hollywood Vault* (Oakland: University of California Press, 2014), 142; *TVD*, December 5, 1953, 6. The pair first met just after United Artists agreed to distribute *Killer's Kiss*. Kubrick had come to Harris's office to see about selling *Fear and Desire* to television, but the rights were already hopelessly tangled. Nick Pinkerton, "Interview: James B. Harris (Part One)," www.filmcomment.com, accessed January 10, 2021.
64. Sylbert discussed Kubrick's approach with Vincent Lo Brutto (*Stanley Kubrick*, 72–73). But if he was then working on *Patterns*, as he remembered, this was not as early as Lo Brutto suggests (the film was shot at the Brooklyn Vitagraph studio in June and July 1955).
65. A. H. Weiler, "Screening the Local Motion Picture Scene," *NYT*, September 11, 1955.
66. "Precedent," *NYT*, October 16, 1955. The article notes that Ruth Sobotka Kubrick will be the first woman to serve as art director on a Hollywood film. Sylbert, for the time being, stayed in New York.

16. Thank You, Hollywood!

1. The OWI employed him as both a motion picture director and photographer, rating his work as "very good" and "excellent" and paying him $5,600 a year. Boris Kaufman papers, Beinecke Library, Box 20, Folder 400.
2. Robbins may be best known today, if at all, as codirector of *Even As You and I* (1937), a Dadaist short that parodied both Hollywood cinema and the international avant-garde. See Jan-Christopher Horak, *Lovers of Cinema* (Madison: University of Wisconsin Press, 1995), 52, 376–77.
3. LeRoy Robbins to Boris Kaufman, October 25, 1945. Kaufman papers, Box 13, Folder 255.
4. Kaufman's January 15, 1948, application for membership in Local 644 was sponsored by Sidney Zucker and Morris Hartzband. It includes an extensive account of his prior professional experience. Local 644 Papers, NYU Tamiment Library, Box 23, "Boris Kaufman" file.
5. A. H. Weiler, "Boy Meets Girl in Monroe, N.Y.," *NYT*, October 15, 1950.
6. Elia Kazan to Boris Kaufman, March 14, 1962. Kaufman papers, Box 13. Kazan wrote this at the start of a letter informing Kaufman that he did not want to use him to shoot *America, America*.

7. Elia Kazan to Boris Kaufman, May 25, 1954. Kaufman papers, Box 13, Folder 227.
8. Boris Kaufman to Elia Kazan, undated (c. June 1, 1954). Kaufman papers, Box 13, Folder 227. This copy is a handwritten pencil draft.
9. William Bancroft Mellor, "Light Plays a Part in Set Design," *AC*, June 1954, 286–87, 298–99; Nicholas Webster, "Specialized Lighting and Set Techniques for a Non-Theatrical Production," *JSMPTE*, February 1956, 100–101. Webster later directed several features in New York, including *Gone Are the Days!* (1963) and *Santa Claus Conquers the Martians* (1964).
10. Kaufman to Kazan, c. June 1, 1954, Kaufman papers, Box 13, Folder 227. Jim Shields, the innovative *On the Waterfront* sound man, also recorded live dialogue for *Garden of Eden*.
11. Bernard Sindell to Boris Kaufman, July 28, 1954. Kaufman papers, Box 13, Folder 220.
12. "*Garden of Eden*," *NYT*, December 18, 1957.
13. In his June 1 letter to Kazan, Kaufman asked if *East of Eden* was being shot in Eastman Color or Technicolor, suggesting an ongoing concern with color technology. But he did not ask what wide-screen process (if any) was being used, another indication of his lack of interest in the ongoing ratio debate. Kaufman papers, Box 13, Folder 227.
14. Letter of agreement, Boris Kaufman and ANO Productions. Kaufman papers, Box 12, Folder 168. See also Box 19, Folder 390.
15. "On Location," *NYT*, May 9, 1954.
16. Richard Sylbert and Sylvia Townsend, *Designing Movies* (Westport, CT: Praeger, 2006), 37–39.
17. Boris Kaufman to Elia Kazan, n.d., [late July 1954]. Kaufman papers, Box 13, Folder 227.
18. "Of Local Origin," *NYT*, June 24, 1955.
19. Bernard Sindell to Boris Kaufman, July 29, 1954. Kaufman papers, Box 13, Folder 220.
20. ASC nomination petition, September 14, 1954. Kaufman papers, Box 12, Folder 174.
21. Bernard Sindell to Boris Kaufman, March 21, 1955. Kaufman papers, Box 13, Folder 220.
22. In November Kaufman became a member of the Academy of Motion Picture Arts and Sciences, another fine accolade but equally useless in helping him find work in Hollywood. George Seaton to Boris Kaufman, November 3, 1955. Kaufman papers, Box 12, Folder 168.
23. Herbert Mitgang, "Shaping *Patterns* for Pictures," *NYT*, August 14, 1955.
24. The following quotes are from a three-page memo, unaddressed but dated September 25, 1954. Reid Cinema Archives, Wesleyan University, Elia Kazan Collection. File F 113 "Personal."
25. Milton Esterow, "*Baby Doll* in Dixie and Flatbush," *NYT*, February 26, 1956.
26. Elia Kazan to Boris Kaufman, March 14, 1956. Kaufman papers, Box 13, Folder 227. The film was shot at the Gold Medal Studios by Harry Stradling, the man Kazan originally wanted for *On the Waterfront*. The screen credit was split with 644 member Gayne Rescher, his first as a director of photography. Now his own producer, Kazan was happy to pay the salaries of two men if it meant he could get the one he really wanted.
27. Boris Kaufman to Elia Kazan, March 16, 1956. Reid Cinema Archives, Kazan Collection, File F126.

INDEX

Entries in **boldface** refer to film and television productions made in New York or with the participation of New York crews.

13 Rue Madeleine, 55–56, 61–63, 66, 69–71, 73–76, 166–67, 389
16 mm film, 5, 53, 57–58, 70, 90, 95, 104, 111, 128, 132, 140, 142, 178, 227, 233–34, 279, 282, 287, 290, 312, 315–17, 322, 330, 333–34, 339
99 River Street, 363
Abbott and Costello, 288
Abbott and Costello Go to Mars, 259, 265–66
Abrams, Herman, 137
Academy Film Archive, 469n36
Acocella, Nicholas, 387
Actors Laboratory Theatre, 262
Actors Studio, 391
Adam's Rib, 245–46, 272, 468n66
Adams, Berle, 98–100, 105
Adams, Joey, 422
Adelman, Skippy, 412
Adler, Celia, 175
Adorno, Theodor, 153
Affron, Charles and Mirella, 67, 347
African Queen, The, 342–43, 389, 399

Agee, James, 66, 73–74, 158, 187, 315, 327–28, 330, 333
Air Force, 279, 396
Alberghetti, Anna Maria, 270
Albertson, Frank, 221
Albertson, Jack, 166
Alcade, Mario, 423
Alda, Robert, 217, 219–20
Alden Theatre, 221
Aldrich, Robert, 262, 344–45, 347
Alexander Nevsky, 396
Alexander, Cris, 250
Alexander, William (filmmaker), 96, 109–116, 140, 286–87, 332, 447n62
Alexander, William (historian), 332
Alice's Restaurant, 404
All My Babies, 366
All My Sons, 64, 308, 359
All That Jazz, 406
All That Money Can Buy, 41
All-American News/Studio, 107, 109, 116–118, 122, 124, 143

Allen, Dede, 213
Allen, Fred, 81
Allen, Richard, 282–83
Allen, Woody, 4, 427
Alpi, Deborah Lazaroff, 300, 303
Alvarez, Max, 253
Am I Guilty?, 136
Amboy Dukes, The, 199–201
American Ballet Theater
American Matchmaker, 16
American Negro Theatre, 83, 102
American Society of Cinematographers (ASC), 328, 380, 424
Amos 'n' Andy, 130
Anastasia, 235
Anastasia, Albert, 159, 308
Anastasia, Anthony, 258
Anchors Aweigh, 150
Anderson, Eddie "Rochester", 103, 136
Anderson, Leonard, 110, 115
Anderson, Lindsay, 199, 400
Anderson, Maxwell, 300, 322
Andes, Keith, 228
Andor, Paul, 90
Andrews, Dana, 60, 62–64, 159, 311
Andrews, Herb, 87
Andriot, Lucien, 242
Andrusco, Richie, 336
Andy, 404
Angeli, Pier, 263–64
Animal Farm, 89, 91
Anna Lucasta, 103
Annie Hall, 1, 395
Anouilh, Jean, 368
Anything Can Happen, 168, 270
Apocalypse Now, 365
Apollo Theater, 104, 110, 119, 123, 134
Arch of Triumph, 168
Army-Navy Screen Magazine, 250, 468n58
Arness, James, 266
Arnold, Jack, 4, 206, 266, 288
Arriflex camera, 367
Arthur, Jean, 245
Associated Filmmakers, 18, 19, 33, 67, 147, 160
Associated Producers, 18
Associated Producers of Negro Motion Pictures, 109–110
Association of Documentary and Television Cameraman, 275, 366

Astor Pictures, 18–19, 96, 100–110, 121, 203, 221, 286, 446n
Astor Theatre, 367–68, 379, 398–99
Astoria studio, 4, 7, 13–14, 34, 70, 112–13, 142, 151, 157, 160–64, 190, 223, 245, 254, 268, 345, 460n32
Astoria, NY, 13, 14, 69, 72, 94, 266
Atkinson, Brooks, 262, 355
Atlanta, Georgia, 84
Auerbach, George, 226
August, Joseph, 41–42
Austrian, Ralph, 32–33, 35, 147

Babes in Bagdad, 227, 230
Baby Doll, 394, 419, 426
Bachelor Party, The, 255
Back Door Man, 96
Back to the Sun, 133
Bagley, Richard, 333
Baker, Josephine, 129, 363
Balanchine, George, 315, 360–61
Baldwin, Ed, 163
Ball Studios, 220, 289
Ballard, Lucinda, 348
Bamboozled, 123
Band Wagon, The, 27, 246, 275
Bank of America, 12
Bankhead, Tallulah, 19, 267
Bannister, Harry, 221
Barefoot Contessa, The, 400
Barkleys of Broadway, The, 246
Barnes, George, 196–97
Barnes, Howard, 187
Barnett, Claude, 117
Barnouw, Eric, 334
Barr, Eddie, 393
Barrymore, Ethel, 41, 267
Barrymore, John, 20
Barrymore, Lionel, 267
Barsacq, Leon, 347
Bartholomew, Freddie, 131–32, 227
Basehart, Richard, 78–79
Bash, John, 282
Bassman, George, 458n160
Batfink, 119
Battle for Survival, 394
Baxter, Alan, 48
Baxter, John, 329
Bay, Howard, 279

Bayne, Howard, 300
Beale Street Mama, 130
Beast from 20,000 Fathoms, 274–75
Begley, Ed, 64, 156
Beiderbecke, Bix, 242
Belasco, David, 413
Bell, Thomas, 28
Belle of New York, The, 246
Bellevue Hospital, 22, 24, 231, 236–39, 243, 253, 264
Bells Are Ringing, 27
Bells of St. Mary's, The, 37, 196, 351
Ben Casey, 209, 216
Bendix, William, 440n34
Benedek, Laslo, 234–35, 466n13
Benjamin, Burton, 321
Benjamin, Robert, 343, 408
Beregi, Oscar, 168
Bergman, Ingmar, 314, 414
Bergman, Ingrid, 40, 168
Berkeley, Busby, 247
Berne, Josef 234
Bernhardt, Curtis, 244
Bernstein, Leonard, 246, 249, 396–98
Bernstein, Matthew, 149
Berry, John, 28
Best Years of Our Lives, The, 186
Betrayal, The, 107–109, 143
Better Tomorrow, A, 349
Bettis, Valerie, 230, 289
Beware, 100–104, 143
Beyond Tomorrow, 14
Bicycle Thieves, 52, 54, 66, 67, 263, 329, 331, 373, 389–90, 399
Big Break, The, 262–63, 420
Big Broadcast of 1938, 14, 152
Big Clock, The, 178
Big Heat, The, 240
Big Timers, 116–117
Binney, Josh, 5, 46, 113–14, 117–26, 141, 142, 325
Binns, Ed, 263
Biograph studio, 16, 86, 142, 346, 418, 426
Birth of a Baby, The, 113
Birth of a Star, The, 101
Birthright, 289
Bishop, Jim, 162, 180, 183
Biskind, Peter, 386
Bissell, Whit, 240
Bitter Rice, 237, 271

Black Rose, The, 76
Black, Justice Hugo, 84
Blackboard Jungle, The, 201
Blacklist, 88, 91, 185, 195–96, 199, 212, 222–23, 225–26, 230, 260, 278, 281, 295, 379, 394, 448n84, 458n160, 464n52
Blake, B.K., 18
Blaze of Noon, 168
Blier, Bernard, 269
Blood of a Poet, 230
Blood of Jesus, 97, 126, 139
Bloodhounds of Broadway, 312
Bloodthirsty Butchers, 289
Bloomer Girl, 468n58
Bloomgarden, Kermit, 307
Blue Angel (nightclub), 204–5
Blue Angel, The (film), 258
Blue Jeans, 413–14
Blumberg, Nate, 238, 243
Boarding House Blues, 122–24
Bob & Carol & Ted & Alice, 324
Body and Soul, 195–96, 278, 396
Bogart, Humphrey, 186, 236, 295. 399
Bogdanovich, Peter, 152
Bogeus, Benedict, 241
Bogle, Donald, 82, 103
Bohnen, Roman, 457n123
Boland, Mary, 212
Bonafield, Jay, 36, 49, 50. 320–21
Bonnie and Clyde, 213
Bonwit Teller, 260
Boogie Woogie Blues, 124
Boogie-Woogie Dream, 129
Boomerang!, 56, 62–66, 68, 70–71, 73–76, 79–80, 167, 179, 209, 237, 244, 307, 347, 376–77, 389
Border Incident, 250
Borgnine, Ernest, 87
Bormann, Martin, 438n89
Born to Kill, 354
Born Yesterday, 245
Borscht Belt Follies, 234
Borzage, Frank, 15, 19, 151
Bostic, Earl, 121
Boston, 40, 61, 90, 278
Bound Brook, N.J., 37
Bousel, Morris, 358, 364, 369
Bowery, 36, 178, 211, 240, 333
Bowles, Paul, 315

Bowman, Lee, 149
Bowser, Pearl, 116
Boxer, Nathan, 365–66, 404
Boy with Green Hair, The, 335
Boy! What a Girl!, 130–32, 143, 157
Bradley, David, 322, 330
Brady, Scott, 272
Brain That Wouldn't Die, The, 219, 324
Brando, Marlon, 48, 199, 226, 293, 311, 350–55, 372–73, 381, 383–93, 395, 397, 399–401, 426, 475n48
Brandon, Henry, 72
Brandt, Harry, 47, 48, 188
Brasuhn, Midge "Toughie", 320
Braudy, Leo, 375
Braun, Heywood Hale, 273
Braunstein, Cy, 115
Breckinridge, Paul, 123
Breen Office, 296, 298–300, 305, 407
Brenon, Herbert, 136
Brewer, Roy, 308
Bribery, 169, 181, 190, 308, 350, 367, 372, 375, 409
Bricken, Jules, 48, 156
Bridgeport, CT., 62–63, 375
Bridges, Lloyd, 86
Brief Encounter, 174
Broadway Theatre, 285
Brodine, Norbert, 55–57, 70, 389
Bromberg, J. Edward, 212–13, 223
Bronx, 67, 94, 131, 142–43, 226, 314, 317, 318, 328, 364, 418, 426
Bronx Botanical Gardens, 50
Bronx Zoo, 338
Brooklyn, 4, 17, 31, 106, 128, 130, 132, 147, 150, 160, 171, 188, 199–202, 269, 270, 278, 282, 300, 308, 349, 364, 376, 385, 410, 456n101, 496n64
Brooklyn Botanic Gardens, 382
Brooklyn Bridge, 20, 28, 29, 48, 150, 214, 242, 246, 248–49, 265–66
Brooklyn College, 7, 322
Brooklyn Dodgers, 277–78, 345
Brooklyn Museum, 205
Brooklyn Navy Yard, 50, 171, 247–49, 269
Brooks, Hadda, 124–25
Brooks, Louise, 113
Brooks, Mel, 217
Brooks, Richard, 173

Browder, Earl, 173
Brown, Geoff, 121
Browne, Arthur, 301, 309, 349, 372, 376
Brownsville, 200
Brun, Joseph, 90, 327
Brute Force, 162, 173, 174, 178, 182, 186, 423
Brynner, Yul, 235
Buchalter, Louis "Lepke", 159
Buck and Bubbles, 138
Buck, Jules, 185
Buckner, Robert, 85
Bunin, Lou, 284
Bunuel, Luis, 225
Burger, Hans, 129
Burlesque in Harlem, 286–87
Burlingham, Jon, 396–98
Burstyn, Joseph, 85, 263, 290, 323, 329–34, 338, 403, 407
Butler, Hugo, 222–23, 225
Buttons, Red, 61
By-Line Newsreel, 115–16
Byron, Stuart, 375

Cabin in the Sky, 18
Cabrini, Mother Frances, 37–38
Caedmon Records, 356
Caesar, Sid, 259
Café Zanzibar, 102, 103
Caffe Reggio, 290
Cage, John, 315
Cage, The, 360–61
Caged, 225
Cagney, James, 61–62, 66, 300, 389
Cahiers du Cinema, 314, 376, 402
Cahn, Sammy, 150
Caine Mutiny, The, 399–400
Calder, Alexander, 314
Caldonia, 99–102, 127
Caldwell, Taylor, 147
Calhern, Louis, 226
Call Northside, 777 55, 73–74, 76
Calloway, Cab, 5, 96, 99, 118–20
Camera Equipment Company (CECO), 293–94, 313, 358, 369, 407–8
Camino Real, 310–11, 355, 359
Camp Fieldstone, 262
Campanella, Roy, 277
Canarsie, 266
Canterbury Tale, A, 25–26

Capital Story, 349
Capitol Records, 45, 352
Capote, Truman, 391
Capra, Frank, 168, 214
Capt. Celluloid and the Film Pirates, 494n11
Capt. Video, 221
Captain from Castile, The, 76
Carlisle, Una Mae, 124
Carlton, Rex, 207, 217–20, 289
Carmichael, Hoagy, 96
Carne, Marcel, 251
Carnegie Hall (film), 29, 48, 124, 130, 150–59, 161, 163–64, 166, 178, 202, 227, 236, 384
Carnegie Hall (venue), 249, 269
Carpenter, Carleton, 86
Carradine, John, 208
Carson, Jack, 216–18, 220
Cartier, Walter, 318–19, 357, 359, 363, 413
Cartier-Bresson, Henri, 332
Casper, Andrew, 247
Cassavetes, John, 3, 269, 275, 333
Castellani, Renato, 399
Cat on a Hot Tin Roof, 426
Cat People, 26
Catcher in the Rye, The, 290
Catlett, Sid, 130
Catskill Honeymoon, 234
Cayette, Andre, 332
CBS, 35, 127, 161, 204, 290, 299, 304, 321, 339, 389
Central Intelligence Agency, 89
Central Park, 14, 39–40, 42, 50, 71, 164, 223, 241, 249, 264–66, 269, 271–74, 290
Central Park Zoo, 149
Century Theatre, 400, 424
Chaplin, Charlie, 327, 343
Chasan, Will, 339
Chase Bank, 18
Chase, Borden, 152
Chase, Chris (aka Irene Kane), 361–63, 365–66, 368–71, 405–6, 410, 412, 487n23
Chase, Ilka, 19
Chayefsky, Paddy, 3
Chekhov, Michael, 168
Chemical Bank and Trust, 207, 217–19, 222, 230
Chevalier, Maurice, 43–44, 119
Chicago, 5, 11, 38, 73–74, 95, 107, 109, 116, 122, 124–25, 267, 322

Chicago After Dark, 117
Chief Flying Mare, 217
Chilton, John, 101–2
Chinatown, 248, 282
Christian, John, 277
Chrysler Building, 69–71
Churchill, Savannah, 133
Ciao, Manhattan, 404
Cine-Kodak Special camera, 333
Cinema, 16 314, 320
Cinema City, 194
Cinema Studios, 118
CinemaScope, 76, 269, 312
Cinemasters, 94
Cinerama process, 95
Cinerama Holiday, 92
Citizen Kane, 205
Citizen Saint, 37–38, 169, 278
City Across the River, 195, 199–202, 266
City College, 314, 315–16
City Hall, 190
Civilian Production Administration, 33
Clair, Rene, 43–44, 247
Clar, Arden, 406
Clark, Dane, 281
Clark, Joseph, 116–17
Classic Pictures, Inc., 288
Clift, Montgomery, 263, 351, 354
Cloak and Dagger, 173
Clock, The, 26, 29, 31, 249
Cloisters, The, 437n51
Clooney, Rosemary, 270
Close-Up, 42, 47–49, 150, 202, 212–13, 222, 389, 408
Clouzot, H.G., 187
Clurman, Harold, 368
Cobb, Lee J., 352, 397, 400
Coburn, Charles, 244
Cocteau, Jean, 230
Coe, Fred, 355
Cohn, Harry, 245, 300, 302, 303, 308, 310, 343, 350, 375, 380
Cohn, J.J., 247
Cohn, Jack, 238, 243, 294, 343
Cold Wind in August, A, 285
Cole, Nat "King", 96, 119, 122
Coliseum Films, 265
Collinge, Patricia, 264
Collins, Richard, 301–2, 303, 304

Colman, Ronald, 189–90
Colonial Pictures Corp., 33
Colum, Padraic, 284
Columbia Pictures, 14, 15, 85, 88–89, 91, 112, 152, 171, 191, 196, 206, 213, 218, 234, 238, 239, 241, 270, 273–74, 278, 286, 294, 300, 302, 308, 319, 329, 343, 379–80, 394, 397–99, 407
Columbia-Presbyterian Medical Center, 243
Columbus Circle, 242, 273, 471n77
Comden, Betty, 246, 249–50
Come On, Cowboy!, 140
Communism (Communist Party), 64, 91, 173–74, 185, 196, 212, 223, 228–29, 276, 280, 296, 298, 301–2, 303, 305, 306–7, 308, 397, 399
Como Club, 421
Compton, Betty, 12, 163
Coney Island, 159, 249, 275, 335–36
Conference of Studio Unions (CSU), 31, 155
Confessions of a Nazi Spy, 54, 69
Connors, Tom, 60
Conroy, Frank, 174
Consolidated Film Industries, 358
Conte, Richard, 75–76, 236, 238–39, 241, 297
Contner, J. Burgi, 117
Convent of the Holy Angels, 69
Conversation, The, 365
Coogan, Richard, 221
Copland, Aaron, 396
Coppola, Carmine, 215
Coppola, Francis Ford, 365
Corey, Jeff, 208
Corman, Roger, 230, 407, 412
Cornell University, 326
Cornell, Katherine, 19
Corridan, Father John, 301–2, 303, 304, 308–10, 319, 340, 349, 350, 385
Corso, Sam, 45, 50, 99, 124, 286
Corwin, Norman, 204
Coslow, Sam, 95
Cossacks in Exile, 133
Costello, Frank, 5, 159–60, 257–58
Cotton Comes to Harlem, 209
Cotton, Joseph, 21–22, 39–42
Count Basie, 96, 120, 152
Cow Town, 121
Cowan, Lester, 267–68

Coward, Noel, 13, 174
Crafton, Donald, 349
Craig, James, 252
Crain, Jeanne, 272
Crawford, Broderick, 297, 311
Crawford, Cheryl, 199
Crawford, Joan, 179
Crime Lab, 49, 54
Crime Newsreel, 148
Crime on the Waterfront (newspaper series), 294–95, 302
Crimson Pirate, The, 303
Criner, Lawrence, 138–39
Cripps, Thomas, 83, 97, 288
Cromwell, John, 225
Cronyn, Hume, 423
Crosby, Bing, 351
Crossfire, 80
Crouch, William Forest, 95–96, 98–102, 105–6, 119, 121, 126–27, 136
Crowd, The, 15, 52, 272
Crowded Paradise, 422–23
Crowther, Bosley, 66, 67, 82, 89, 157–58, 187, 192–93, 202, 215, 225, 229, 237, 264, 268, 276–77, 285, 290, 315, 333, 338
Crucible, The, 268
Crusade in Europe, 229
Cry Danger, 347
Cry Murder, 84, 222, 227, 229–30, 261
Cry of the City, 29, 62, 75–76, 195, 214, 241, 297
Cuba, 203, 240
Cukor, George, 34, 190, 245–46, 260, 271–74, 410
Culkin, Father John, 7
Cummings, Homer S., 62
Cunningham Combat Camera, 334–35
Curran Theatre, 260
Currie, Finlay, 90
Curtis, Joseph, 294–96, 300, 303–5
Curtis, Tony, 200–201, 266
Curtiz, Michael, 129
Cushman, Robert, 86

Dailey, Dan, 220, 260, 269–70
Daisy Kenyon, 178–79
Dajevskis, Evalds, 284
Dancigers, Oscar, 225
Daniels, Billy, 131

Daniels, William, 85, 174–75, 177–78, 182, 200–201, 295
Dano, Royal, 327
Dantine, Helmut, 276
Danziger, Edward and Harry, 202–5, 222–31
Dare, Carla, 38
Darien, CT, 180
Dark Corner, The, 60–61, 68, 69, 76, 166, 253
Dark Odyssey, 277
Dassin, Jules, 66, 133, 173–85, 187, 222, 236
Davies, Marion, 196
Davis, Bette, 109–110
Davis, Ossie, 114, 289
Dawn to Dawn, 234
Dawn, Lili, 290
Day of the Fight, 318–21, 326, 332, 357, 364, 408
Day, Dennis, 123
Day, Richard, 195–96, 347–49, 379, 394, 401, 424
De Corsia, Ted, 175, 182
De Leon, Raoul, 44
De Luxe Laboratories, 156, 178, 218, 326, 358, 369, 403, 407–8
de Moraes, Vinicius, 333–34
De Rochemont, Louis, 4, 36, 51–66, 73–77, 79–92, 98, 112, 143, 156, 162, 166, 195, 200, 222, 229, 260–61, 264, 268, 295, 376, 425
De Rochemont, Richard, 322, 324–29, 333
De Sica, Vittorio, 52, 54, 67, 204, 333, 338, 373, 376, 389, 204, 333–34, 338, 373, 376, 389
De Vincenzo, Anthony "Tony Mike," 309–10, 340
Dean, James, 354
Dear Miss Gloria, 230
Death of a Salesman, 294, 305, 308
Death Tide, 276, 323
Decca Records, 98, 100, 104
Dee, Ruby, 97, 110–14, 138, 141, 280
Deep Waters, 68, 76
Defiant Ones, The, 268
DeHaven, Gloria 244
Delannoy, Jean, 331
DeMicco, Tony (aka D'Amico), 318
Denes Psychodramatic Theatre, 37
Denker, Henry, 295
Denton, Crahan, 328
Depinet, Ned, 52

Deported, 85, 295
Deren, Maya, 317
Desperate Heart, 289
Destination Tokyo, 173
Detective Story, 236
Detour, 131, 153, 158, 251
Deutsch, Armand, 147
Devil's Hornpipe, The, 300
Dewey, Thomas E., 198, 309, 340
Di Gangi, Jimmy, 48, 219
Diamond, David, 315
Dick, Bernard, 300
Dickens, Griffith and the Film Today, 413
Dieterle, William, 39, 41
Dietrich, Marlene, 204
Dillinger, 354
Dimendberg, Edward, 181, 242
Directors Guild of America, 306
Dirty Gertie from Harlem, USA, 127
Disenchanted, The, 296, 377
Diskant, George, 235
Disney studio, 6, 285
Dixie Film Exchange, 136
Doctor and the Girl, The, 243, 251
Doctor, The, 345, 384
Doctors, The, 406
Docu-drama, 54–55, 62, 66, 76–77, 79, 91, 240–41, 266
Documentary films, 4, 32, 35–37, 39, 41, 45, 49–50, 52–54, 56, 58, 60, 64–68, 76–80, 86, 91, 115, 149, 152, 162, 166, 176, 178, 183, 185, 201, 206–7, 223, 229, 234–35, 240, 250, 262, 272–75, 279, 282, 284, 286, 289–90, 295, 302, 304, 311, 314, 317–20, 324, 327, 333–34, 338, 364, 366, 377, 394, 396, 420, 421
Donehue, Vincent J., 355
Donlevy, Brian, 72
Donoghue, Frank Lee, 224–25, 231
Donoghue, William J., 159
Donohue, Jack, 48, 150
Donohue, Roger, 373
Donovan, Joseph, 171–72
Doran, D.A., 70–71
Dorfmann, Edmund L., 211, 219, 223
Dorsey, Jimmy, 96
Double Indemnity, 22
Double Life, A, 182, 190, 245
Douglas, Justice William O., 85

Douglas, Kirk, 242
Dover, NH, 90
Dow, Peggy, 236
Dowling, Doris, 203
Downes, Olin, 158
Downing, Robert, 384
Dream Girl, 178
Dreamer, The, 106
Dreams That Money Can Buy, 230, 315–17, 332, 360, 366
Dress Rehearsal, The, 118
Driscoll, Bobby, 45
Du Pont film stock, 378
Duchamp, Marcel, 314
Duel in the Sun, 39, 215
Duff, Howard, 174, 185
Duffy's Tavern, 261
DuMont, 216
Dunn, Rev. Robert A., 81, 87
Dunne, Philip, 72
Durbin, Deanna, 26
Durham, NH, 81
Duse, Eleanora, 405
Duvivier, Julien, 420

Eagle, Arnold, 315
Eagle-Lion, 49, 84, 135, 203, 207, 218, 223, 234, 235, 250, 286, 408
Eagle-Lion Classics, 218
East of Eden, 355, 421, 425
East River, 16, 20, 253, 275
East Village, 284, 293, 364, 407
Eastern Make-Up Artists, 384
Eastern Service Studios, 14, 94
Eastern Sound Studios, 203
Eastern Teleproductions Studio, 221
Eastman Kodak, 333, 378
Eastmancolor, 282, 421
Eastwood, Clint, 72
Eaves Costume Company, 214
Eberson, John, 194
Ebony, 97–98, 100, 104, 110
Ebony Parade, 98–99, 101, 106
Eckstine, Billy, 110
Éclair camera, 268
Edens, Roger, 246, 249
Edison studio, 94–96, 143
Edison, Thomas, 2
Edouart, Farciot, 15

Educational Pictures, 101
Edwards, Vince, 216
Egg and I, The, 242
Eisenstein, Sergei, 54, 314, 317, 409, 413
Eisinger, Jo, 236, 238
Elks Lodge, 106, 132, 147
Elliman, Lawrence,
Ellington, Duke, 96, 99 194
Elliott, Clyde, 37–38
Elliott, Faith (aka Faith Hubley), 3, 48, 213, 224, 276, 339
Ellis Island, 152
Ellis, Edward, 188
Ellison, Ralph, 83
Emerson, Faye, 212, 214–15
Emerson, Hope, 76, 246
Emperor Jones, The, 95, 102
Emperor's Nightingale, The, 284, 285
Empire State Building 27, 249, 266, 268
Empire Theatre, 190
Engel, Morris, 275, 333, 334–38
Enterprise Studio, 196
Epstein, Jean, 327
Erickson, Leif, 372–73
Ericson, John, 263–64
Ernie's (club), 290
Ernst, Max, 314
Erskine, Carl, 277
Essex, Harry, 240
Etra, Jack, 137
Ettlinger, Don 211
Evans, Clifford, 224, 240
Evans, Walker, 279, 328
Everett, Francine, 117, 127
Everson, William K., 210, 403, 494n11
Ewell, Tom, 245–46, 274, 420
Eyemo camera, 53, 165, 274, 279, 312, 313, 319, 333, 334, 367, 396, 477n98, 489n36
Eyman, Scott, 4, 55

Face in the Crowd, A, 318, 345, 376, 394, 426
Fail Safe, 209
Faithful City, 359
Fallen Idol, The, 335
Famous Studios, 283
Fantasia, 283
Farrell, James T., 173
Farrell, John, 87
Farren, Robert, 404

Fast and the Furious, The (1954), 407
Fast, Howard, 173
FBI Front, The, 54
FBI Story, The, 214
Fear and Desire, 313, 322–27, 329–32, 335, 337–39, 356–57, 359–61, 363, 365, 366, 403, 407–8, 410, 412, 415
Fear in the Night, 200
Federal Bureau of Investigation (FBI), 54–60, 75, 90, 151, 171, 268, 280–82, 295, 399
Federal Films, 150–51, 154, 156, 158
Federal Hall, 275
Federal Motion Picture Studios, 132
Feitshans, Fred, 156
Feldzug in Polen, 52
Fellini, Federico, 400, 406
Fennelly, Parker 81, 86, 87
Ferrer, Jose 168, 359
Ferrer, Mel, 81, 82–84
Fetchit, Stepin, 103, 117, 120–21, 132, 134
Fielding, Raymond, 53, 55
Fields, W.C., 120
Fifth Avenue, 17, 148, 150, 179, 249
Fifth Avenue Playhouse, 316
Fight Never Ends, The, 112–115, 140, 143, 206, 211
Fight That Ghost, 137, 143
Fighting Lady, The, 53
Filbert, Fatty, 118
Film Classics, 84–85, 207, 218–19, 222, 227, 230
Film Culture, 383, 40BI
Film noir, 50, 56, 59–60, 75, 85, 90, 134, 169, 173, 181, 190, 210, 216, 221, 223, 231, 235, 240–43, 250–251, 289, 295, 300, 305, 347, 358, 363, 367, 394, 406, 411, 413
Filmcraft studio, 95–99, 102, 105, 107, 112, 113, 118, 131–32, 134, 143, 160–61, 202, 226
Filmo camera, 333
Films in Review, 403
Finian's Rainbow, 41, 83, 130, 246
Fisher, James, 350, 394
Fitzgerald, Barry, 174, 177, 185, 186
Fitzgerald, Ella, 123
Fitzgibbon, Steve, 19
Flack, Roberta, 406
Flagstad, Kirsten, 152
Flaherty, Robert, 162, 334, 366

Flamingo Films, 418
Flamm, Donald, 18
Flatbush, 14, 142, 160, 202, 426
Flatiron Building, 272
Fleischer studio, 119, 283
Fleischer, Richard, 34
Flesh and Fury, 266
Fletcher, Dusty, 46, 103, 120–23
Flicker Flashbacks, 34, 35
Flight Into Egypt, 306, 355
Florence, Italy, 85, 263
Florey, Robert, 241–42
Florida, 5, 77, 94, 128, 130, 135, 140, 247, 257, 285–86, 289, 405, 421
Flower Drum Song, 451n155
Flowers of St. Francis, 329, 403
Flushing, NY, 71
Flying Padre, 320–22, 339
Flynn, Errol, 294
Foch, Nina, 226, 227
Follies Girl, 17–19, 28, 31, 113, 136, 267
Folsey, George, 268
Fonda, Henry, 178–79, 204
Fontaine, Joan, 27, 28
Fontanne, Lynne, 19
Foolish Wives, 347
Football Fan, The, 246, 420
Foote, Horton, 7
Footlight Parade, 287
Forbidden Games, 335
Forbidden Street, The, 76
Force of Evil, 81, 87, 195–99, 204, 226, 240, 347
Ford Foundation, 327
Ford, Glenn, 243–44
Ford, Helen, 272
Ford, John, 41
Ford, Paul, 175
Fordham University, 7
Fordin, Hugh, 246, 249
Fort Lee, 69, 70, 102, 104, 107, 117, 118, 137, 143, 194, 223
Fort Tryon Park, 50
Fosse, Bob, 406
Fourteen Hours, 4, 77–79, 240, 260, 264
Fox Movietone News, 51, 57, 258
Fox Movietone studio, v, 18, 19, 51, 57, 94, 130, 143, 147, 154, 156–57, 160–61, 163, 166, 213, 217, 224, 258, 278–79, 384, 389, 422

Fox studio, 156, 327, 349
Foy, Bryan, 37, 235
Francis Covers the Big Town, 265
Francis the Talking Mule, 236, 265
Francis Xavier Church, St., 318, 319
Francis, Anne, 87, 224
Franken, Rose, 149
Frankenheimer, John, 259
Fraser-Cavassoni, Natasha, 343, 344
Fredericks, Ellsworth, 242
Freed, Alan, 346
Freed, Arthur, 100, 245, 246–47, 250
Freedom Road, 443n125
Freeman, Kenneth, 138
French Connection, The, 1, 253
Fretz, Sada, 387
Frewin Anthony, 315
Fried, Gerald, 325, 361, 369, 405–6
Friedman, Alan, 326
From Here to Eternity, 351, 352, 379, 400
From This Day Forward, 28
From Whence Cometh My Help?, 282
Frontier Films, 88, 332
Fuchs, Herman, 320
Fugitive Kind, The, 419
Full Metal Jacket, 410
Fuller, Sam, 260, 305
Fulton Fish Market, 169, 253
Fulton, John, 22, 26, 148, 265, 274
Futurity Films, 288

Gaberscek, Carlo, 20
Gabin, Jean, 251
Gabor, Eva, 286
Gaillard, Slim, 106, 280
Galento, Tony, 373
Game of Cards, A, 230
Gance, Abel, 349
Gang's All Here, The, 150
Garbo, Greta, 178
Garcon Sauvage, Le (The Male Brute), 331
Garden of Eden, 421–23
Gardenia, Vincent, 55
Gardner, Ava, 81, 351
Gardner, Ed, 261
Garfield, John, 81, 151, 177, 195–99, 204
Garland, Judy, 27
Garmes, Lee, 14
Garnett, Tay, 267, 268

Garrett, Betty, 250
Gassman, Vittorio, 270–71
Gateway Productions, 194
Geiger, Rod, 103
Gelmis, Joseph, 314
General Artists Corporation, 98
General Electric, 107
General Post Office Building, 229
Generation of Vipers, A, 77
Genovese crime family, 288
Gentleman's Agreement, 80, 135, 179–80, 244, 312
George Washington Bridge, 58, 169, 197–98
Gershwin, George, 153, 215
Gertsman, Maury, 200–201
Gettinger, Milton, 217–19
Giannini, A.H., 12, 241
Gilbert, Herschel Burke 269
Gillespie, Dizzy, 112
Gilmore, Virginia, 48
Gimbel, Norman, 369, 406
Gimme Shelter, 404
Girl Crazy, 48
Girl in Room, 20 127
Girl on the Run, 221, 289
Girl with the Pre-Fabricated Heart (song), 315
Girls in Chains, 153
Girls in the Night, 266
Gish, Dorothy, 86–87
Gish, Lillian, 355
Glad, Gladys, 180
Glass Menagerie, The, 38
Glass Wall, The, 214, 270–71
Gleason, Jackie, 259
Gleason, James, 171, 220
Glenn, Jack, 229
Glenn, Max, 366–67, 404
Globe-Mills Productions, 94
Glucksman, E.M., 104, 107, 109, 116–25, 129, 142, 143
Go Down, Death!, 127
Go Man Go, 277–82, 395
God, Man, and Devil, 233
Godard, Jean-Luc, 314, 337
Godfather Part II, The, 365
Godfather, The, 1, 348, 400
Godzilla, 274

Goetz, William, 30
Going My Way, 185, 301, 351
Going to Glory, Come to Jesus, 139, 140
Gold Medal (Biograph) Studio, 346, 426
Goldberg, Jack, 117, 128–35, 142, 143, 157
Golden Gloves, 360
Golden, Edward A., 43
Goldman, Eric, 233
Goldstein, Bruce, 458n153, 471n74
Goldstein, Jonah, 30
Goldstein, Leonard, 236, 242, 265
Goldwyn, Samuel, 27, 148, 267, 399
Gomery, Douglas, 37
Gone With the Wind, 166, 379, 400
Goodman, Benny, 153
Goodman, Ezra, 45, 186, 315
Goodman, Willard, 404
Goofy Movies, 35
Gordin, Jacob, 233
Gordon, John E., 103, 107, 286
Gordon, Michael, 260
Gordon, Ruth, 245, 272–73
Gorilla Hogan, 216
Gotham Hotel, 77, 79
Governor's Island, 177
Gowanus Canal, 214
Grable, Betty, 53, 220, 362
Grace Church, 226
Gracie Mansion, 238, 240
Gracie Square, 179, 244
Grahame, Gloria, 240, 271
Gramercy Park, 229
Gran Torino, 72
Grand Central Terminal, 178, 242
Granet, Bert, 272
Granger, Farley, 251–52, 253 268
Granger, Kenneth, 227, 230
Grant, Leola (Coot), 139
Grant's Tomb, 248, 249
Grapes of Wrath, The, 53, 310
Gray, Coleen, 71–72, 236
Grayson, Kathryn, 150
Graziano, Rocky, 360
Great Caruso, The, 342
Great Neck, 56
Great White Hope, The, 322, 356
Greaves, William, 83–84, 132–33, 142, 143
Greed, 178, 196, 347
Green Fields, 133

Green Pastures, 102
Green, Adolph, 246, 249, 250
Green, Alfred E., 219
Green, Eddie, 118
Green, Joseph, 219
Greene, Clarence, 268
Greenwich Theatre, 179
Greenwich Village, 229, 242, 253, 288, 290, 318, 324, 330, 365
Greenwich Village Story, The, 263
Gregory, Dick, 136
Grey, Zane, 55
Greyhound Bus Terminal, 69, 70
Grierson, John, 162
Griffith, Bea, 106
Griffith, D.W., 1, 86–87, 149, 401, 409, 413, 418
Griffith, Richard, 264, 324
Grogan, John J., 350
Group Theatre, 212, 306, 313, 372
Group, The, 419
Guaranty Trust Company, 77–78
Guerrilla Girl, 276–78
Guggenheim fellowship, 210
Guggenheim, Peggy, 314, 317
Guild 50th Street Theatre, 330–31, 359
Guilty Bystander, 28, 84, 211–15, 218–19, 223, 241, 276, 289, 384
Guitry, Sacha, 43
Gun Crazy, 389, 391
Guys and Dolls, 226, 312
Guyse, Sheila, 130, 133, 157
Guzik, Jacob "Greasy Thumb", 258

Hackensack River, 21
Hagen, Jean, 246, 253
Hagen, Uta, 287
Halas & Batchelor studio, 89
Half Moon Hotel, 159
Hall, Charles, 69–70, 166
Hamilton, Murray, 87
Hamlet, 187
Hammarskjold, Dag, 271
Hammid, Alexander, 158, 366, 420
Hampshire House, 155
Hanley, Tommy, 372–73, 387
Hansel and Gretel, 283–85, 294
Happy Years, The, 244–45
Harlan, Jan, 317

Harlem, 32, 80, 96, 99, 102, 109, 110, 113, 115, 116, 128, 130, 133, 141, 332, 334
Harlem Follies, 115, 287–88
Harlem Globetrotters, 278–82
Harlem on Parade, 130
Harlem on the Prairie, 136
Harlemwood Studios, 127, 128, 140
Harrigan, William, 38
Harrington, Curtis, 329
Harris, James B., 330, 417–18
Harris, Jed 424
Harris, Julie, 352, 354, 368
Harrison, Rex, 267
Harryhausen, Ray, 274–75
Hart, Dorothy, 175
Hart, Moss, 179–80
Harten, Charles, 27
Hartley Productions studio, 140
Hartley, Irving, 140
Hartzband, Morris, 269, 327–28
Hathaway, Henry, 4, 51, 55–62, 68–73, 76–79, 178, 260
Haver, Ronald, 40
Havlick, Gene, 394
Hawley, Monte, 138
Hayden, Sterling, 418
Haydon, Julie, 38
Hayes, Helen, 19, 267
Hayes, Patrick Cardinal, 12
Hayes, Peter Lind, 178
Haymes, Dick, 226–27
Hays, Will, 30, 161
Hayward, Susan, 148–50, 241, 260
He Walked by Night, 90
Heard, "Crip", 123
Hearst, William Randolph, 11, 151, 152, 294
Hearst, William Randolph, Jr., 302
Heart of Spain, 162
Heatherton, Ray, 17
Hecht, Ben, 367
Heifetz, Jascha, 151, 152
Heisler, Stuart, 149
Heisner, Beverly, 347
Hell Gate Bridge, 69
Hell's Angels, 101
Hellinger, Mark, 5, 162–63, 168–78, 180–87, 193, 195, 199–201, 234–36, 251, 300, 423
Hemingway, Ernest, 172, 186
Hempstead, David, 40, 42, 169

Henderson, Fletcher, 139
Henreid, Paul, 222–25
Henry Miller's Theatre, 355
Hepburn, Katharine, 62, 151, 152, 245
Herman, Justin, 246, 320, 420
Heston, Charlton, 322
Hi De Ho!, 5, 118–22, 125, 143
Hickman, Darryl, 244
Hicks, Walter, 153
High and the Mighty, The, 398
High Bridge, 28
High Button Shoes, 262
Higham, Charles, 78, 279
Hill, George Roy, 90, 259
Hill, Virginia, 258
Hinkson, Jake, 212, 221
Hirschfeld, Gerald, 209–10, 213, 215, 219–20, 222, 289
Hitchcock, Alfred, 21–22, 25–26, 40, 47, 260–61, 271, 290, 400
Hite, Bob, 321
Hitler, Adolph, 158, 207
Hiveley, Jack, 182
Hoberman, J., 233, 234
Hoboken, 2, 278, 293, 309, 343–45, 348–52, 355, 367, 372–76, 378, 381–85, 387, 393–94, 395, 402, 419, 420
Hoboken Ferry Terminal, 49
Hoboken Movies, 285
Hoboken Turk, The, 216
Hodes, Roberta, 3, 426
Hoffman, John, 235
Hofstra University, 330
Hogan, Frank, 169
Holland, Wim, 290
Hollenbeck, Don, 339–40
Holliday, Judy, 220, 245–46, 272–74
Hollywood Comes to New York, 240
Hollywood Pictures Corp., 128–29
Hollywood Ten, 185, 295, 303
Holman, Libbey, 180, 315
Holmes, Taylor, 35
Holocaust, 422
Home of the Brave, 82, 86
Homesteader, The, 107
Homicide Squad, 171
Hook, The (script), 308, 310, 385
Hoover, J. Edgar, 30, 54, 56, 75, 90–92, 151, 294, 306

Hopalong Cassidy, 336
Hope, Bob, 400–401
Hopper, Edward, 196
Hopper, Hedda, 250, 260, 294, 352, 354, 399
Horizon-American Corporation, 343, 395, 402
Horkheimer, Max, 153
Horne, Hal, 147
Horne, Lena, 129, 135, 138, 141
Hotel Marguery, 69
Hotel Pennsylvania, 32
Hotel Progress, 185
Hough, Horace, 81
House of Strangers, 241, 260
House on 92nd Street, The, 4, 29, 30, 54–60, 62, 66, 67, 70, 75, 76, 79, 90, 160, 162, 166, 193, 202, 228, 334
House on Telegraph Hill, 62
House Un-American Activities Committee (HUAC), 75, 91, 185, 199, 212, 223, 302–8, 311, 350, 392, 396–97
Houseman, John, 368
House-Rent Party, 137
Houston, Penelope, 274
Hoving, Thomas and Nancy
How Green Was My Valley, 57, 347
How to Marry a Millionaire, 259, 269
Howard, Bob, 124, 127–28, 135
Howe, James Wong, 267, 278–82, 395–96
Hristodoulou, Giannis, 277
Hucksters, The, 169
Hudson Heights, NJ, 17, 136, 143
Hudson River, 2, 202, 290, 350, 381, 382
Huff Society, 314, 494n11
Huff, Theodore, 403
Hughes, David, 411
Hughes, Howard, 27, 46, 91, 252
Hughes, Langston, 123, 136, 463n19
Huie, William Bradford, 115
Humoresque, 151
Humperdinck, Engelbert, 284
Humphrey, Doris, 289
Hunt, Marsha, 130, 152, 155, 204
Hunter College, 161
Hunter, Kim, 25–26
Hustler, The, 4, 7, 213, 384
Hutton, Betty, 270

I Ain't Gonna Open That Door, 121
I Am a Fugitive from a Chain Gang, 53

I Am an Alcoholic, 36
I Can Get It for You Wholesale, 260, 280
I Could Not Marry, 288
I Led Three Lives, 306
I Married a Communist, 91
I Married a Savage, 285–86, 288, 289
I Want to Live!, 149
I Was a Male War Bride, 76
I've Always Loved You, 151, 152
Ibsen, Henrik, 412, 463n37
Ideal Studio, 17, 136, 143
Imitation of Life, 81, 82
Impellitteri, Vincent, 231, 238, 258, 265, 280, 293
In a Lonely Place, 124
In the Street, 333
Informing, 72, 198, 235, 386, 396, 399
Inner Sanctum, 35
Inside the Actors Studio, 262
Interlenghi, Franco, 263
International Alliance of Theatrical Stage Employees (IATSE), 31, 156, 161, 170, 191, 254, 259, 261, 277, 308, 348, 366
International Brotherhood of Electrical Workers (IBEW), 161
International House, 14
International Longshoreman's Association, 302, 350
International News Service, 294
International Sweethearts of Rhythm, 110
Intrator, Jerald, 286
Intruder in the Dust, 80
Invasion, 109
Invisible Man, 83
Ireland, John, 407
Iron Curtain, The, 75, 76, 91
Isenberg, Noah, 226
It Happened in Brooklyn, 48, 150, 161, 197, 246, 247, 267
It Happened on Fifth Avenue, 150
It Should Happen to You, 245–46, 273–74, 277
It's a Wonderful Life, 168, 221
Ivens, Joris, 162

Jackie Robinson Story, The, 135, 280
Jackson, Anne, 224
Jackson, Bull Moose, 123
Jacksonville, FL, 118

Jacobson, Arthur, 166–67
Jacoby, Irving, 359
Jaeckel, Richard, 200
Jaffe, Sam, 80
Jagger, Dean 208–210
Jamaica Radio-Television Mfg. Co., 107
James, Bobby, 319
James, Dennis, 216
James, Harry, 151, 153
James, Ida, 116, 119
Janie, 129
Jannings, Emil, 258
Januzzi, Gene, 229
Jarka Corporation, 350
Jarwood, Arthur, 288
Jason, Leigh, 135
Jaws, 2 357
Jenny Lamour, 187
Jersey City, 318, 350
Jewish Guild for the Blind, 223
Jezebel, 109
Jigsaw, 197, 202–5, 209, 222–23, 228, 337
Jive Junction, 162
Jivin' in Be-Bop, 111–12, 115, 143, 384
Joan of Lorraine, 359
Joe Louis Story, The, 280, 446n41
John Golden Theatre, 260
Johnny Jupiter, 294
Johnny One-Eye, 241–42, 253
Johnson, Albert, 34
Johnson, Dotts, 97, 102–3, 105
Johnson, Malcolm, 294–98, 300–302, 304, 309, 338
Johnson, Raymond Edward, 35
Johnston, Dr. Albert C., 82
Johnston, Eric, 185
Johnston, Johnny, 426
Johnstone, Anna Hill, 348, 385, 426
Joint Is Jumpin', The, 124
Jones Beach, 264
Jones, Jennifer, 39–41
Jordan, Louis, 98–107, 120, 127, 129, 131, 135, 138
Joseph, Lazarus, 47
Joseph, Robert L., 47
Josette of New Orleans, 289
Jour se leve, Le, 63
Jourdan, Louis, 27
Jowett, Carson, 237

Juke Joint, 127
Julian, Ray, 213
Julius Caesar, 379
Junction 88, 127, 137, 203
Jurow, Martin, 341–42
Justin, George, 3, 7, 278, 345–46, 352, 373, 384, 388–90, 401, 419, 424–27
Juvenile Jury, 105

Kamb, Karl, 152
Kanin, Garson, 62, 190, 245–46, 260, 272–74
Kansas City Confidential, 305
Karlson, Phil, 235, 363
Karlweis, Oskar, 227
Kaszner, Kurt, 168
Katz, Sid, 394
Kaufman, Boris, 3, 4, 6–7, 158, 262, 293, 320, 327, 348–49, 373–74, 378–85, 389–91, 396, 400, 402–3, 419–26
Kaufman, George S., 178
Kaufmann, Stanley, 7
Kaye, Danny, 101, 148, 273
Kaye, Stubby, 269
Kazan, Elia, 2, 3, 4, 7, 62–65, 77, 88, 179–80, 199, 206, 212, 241, 293, 300, 304–14, 317, 325, 332, 340–45, 347–55, 359, 367, 372–79, 381–403, 407, 409, 411, 414, 418, 420–27
Keaton, Buster, 222
Keel, Howard, 7
Keene, NH, 82
Keep em' in the East campaign, v, 3, 7, 346, 419
Kefauver Crime Commission, 257–58
Kegley, Kermit, 182
Keith, Charles, 109–110
Keller, Walter, 45
Kelly, Gene, 246–50, 266
Kelly, Paul, 250–52
Kelly, William (Bill), 23–24, 27, 148, 260–61
Kelly, William D., 243–44, 249, 253
Kemp, Jack, 131, 133
Kennebunkport, Maine, 81
Kennedy, Arthur, 64
Kennedy, Madge, 272
Kent, Willis, 289
Kenton, Stan 96
Kerz, Leo, 213–15, 219, 264
Keyes, Evelyn, 239–40
Kilgallen, Dorothy, 30, 48
Killer Diller, 46, 121–22, 124, 143

Killer That Stalked New York, The, 234, 239–41, 243
Killer's Kiss, 2, 5, 7, 29, 143, 171, 197, 294, 313–14, 322, 357–59, 361–71, 402–18, 423
Killers, The, 162, 171–73, 176, 181, 182, 186, 300
Killiam, Paul, 274
Killing, The, 364, 418
King and I, The, 235
King Brothers, 389, 477n98
King Kong, 15, 27, 45, 274
King of Kings, 384
King of the Zombies, 103
King, Henry, 68, 76
Kingman, Dong, 282
Kings of the Olympics, 206–7
Kino Pravda, 349
Kipness, Joseph, 262
Kirk, Andy, 122
Kisch, John, 93
Kiss Me Deadly, 262
Kiss Me, Kate, 72
Kiss of Death, 4, 55, 56, 68–73, 166–67, 169, 178, 198, 209, 211, 236. 260
Kissing Bandit, The, 235
Kitten with a Whip, 211
Kittery, Maine, 81
Klansman, The, 115
Klaw, Irving, 287–88
Kleinerman, Isaac, 321
KLM Royal Dutch Airlines, 208
Klune, Ray, 39, 166
Knock On Any Door, 113, 186
Knox, Mickey, 200
Kodachrome film, 53, 70, 315
Kohlmar, Fred, 60, 68
Kohner, Susan, 81
Kollmar, Richard, 48
Komow, Victor, 275–76
Konecoff, Sol, 408
Kramer, Searle, 216, 219
Kramer, Stanley, 82, 214, 215, 226, 271
Krim, Arthur, 343, 408
Krohn, Bill, 22
Krupa, Gene, 96, 130–31, 132
Kubik, Gail, 210, 214, 219
Kubrick, Stanley, 2, 3, 7, 177, 205, 263, 275, 290, 293–94, 313–33, 335, 338–40, 356–71, 402–18, 423, 463n37
Kuleshov, Lev, 409, 410

Kurosawa, Akira, 400
Kyriakys, William, 277

L'Atalante, 349
La Guardia, Fiorello, 11–15, 28–30, 160–61, 189, 191–92, 194, 259
Lacovara, Richard, 78
Ladd, Alan, 60
Lady from Shanghai, The, 204
Lady on a Train, 26
Lafayette Television and Motion Picture Studio, 106–7, 128, 130, 132
LaGuardia Airport, 176, 209
Lahr, Bert, 216–17, 288
Lait, Jack, 49
Lake Como Club, 421
Lambert, Gavin, 164, 167, 415–16
Lambertville Story, The, 320, 420
Lambs Club, 169
Lament, 289
Lamorise, Albert, 338, 359
Lancaster, Burt, 303, 311
Land of Enchantment, 420
Landers, Harry, 208–9, 213
Landis, Carole, 33
Lane, Priscilla, 22, 26
Lang, Fritz, 173, 288
Lang, Lester, 118
Lang, Otto, 73–74, 79
Lang, Walter, 55
Lardner Jr., Ring, 173
Lasky, Jesse, 13
Last Chance, The, 67
Last Command, The, 384
Lastfogel, Abe, 341–42
Latensification, 378–79
LaTouche, John, 315
Laughton, Charles, 168, 235, 417
Laura, 59–60
Laurel Films, 207, 211, 214, 215, 217–19, 222, 256, 275
Laurel Garden, Newark, 319, 363
Laurence, Jock, 26
Laurents, Arthur, 82
Lawrence, Gertrude, 19
Lawrence, Sacha, 327
Lawrenceville, NJ, 244
Lawson, John Howard, 173, 295, 296, 298, 303, 399, 453n6

Le Gon, Jeni, 119
Leab, Daniel, 84, 89
LeBaron, William, 150–58, 161
Lee, Canada, 82, 86, 103, 135
Lee, Joseph (pseud. Joseph Lerner), 220–22, 289
Lee, Spike, 123
Leonard, Arthur, 94, 110, 126, 130–31, 133, 135
Lerner, Geraldine, 206–10, 213, 215, 219
Lerner, Joseph, 112–15, 143, 206–23
Lesser, Erwin, 147–48
Let's Face It, 18
Letter from an Unknown Woman, 27
Letter to Three Wives, 202
Letter, The, 109
Lev, Peter, 66
Levene, Sam, 212
Leventhal, Leon, 18
Levine, Harry, 80
Lewis and White, 123
Lewis, Harold, 182
Liberace, Walter, 96
Liberty Bell Motion Pictures, 277
Liberty City Motion Picture studios, 129
Life magazine, 317, 328, 331
Life and Miracles of Blessed Mother Cabrini, The, 37
Life Begins at Eight-Thirty, 20–21, 27, 57
Limon, Jose, 289
Lincoln Theatre, 122
Lincoln Tunnel, 265, 274
Lindsay, John V., 1, 7, 181, 255, 259, 265
Lindsay, Powell, 110–111, 115
Lipsky, Eleazar, 69
Lipton, James, 262
Little Carnegie Theater, 147
Little Foxes, The, 109
Little Fugitive, 5, 259, 316, 332, 334–38, 407, 410
Little Italy, 241, 248
Litvak, Anatole, 63
Lives of a Bengal Lancer, 55
Lloyd, Harold, 15, 27–28
Lloyd, Norman, 22, 26, 327–28, 370
Lo Brutto, Vincent, 322, 324, 325, 326, 339, 361, 366, 370, 404, 411
Lobbin, Peggy, 405, 406
Local 161, 213
Local 52, 155, 161, 194, 254, 259

Local 644, 27, 148, 237, 255–56, 277, 328, 345, 348, 366–67, 420, 423–24
Local 659, 348, 380, 420, 423–24
Local 829, 365
Loder, John, 220, 289
Loeb, Janice, 332–33
Loes, Billy, 277
Loew, Arthur M., 263–65
Loew's, Inc., 113, 132, 196, 206, 263, 265, 379, 418
Loewy, Joseph, 116
Lofton, Carey, 252
Logan, Joshua, 268, 351
Lolita, 361, 418
Lonely Night, The, 359
Long Beach, L.I., 286
Long Day's Journey Into Night, 384, 419
Long Night, The, 63, 251
Look magazine, 177, 266, 314, 317–20, 336, 357, 361, 413
Lookout Sister, 107
Lopez, Vincent, 99
Lord, Jack, 50, 228–29
Loren, Sophia, 361
Lorentz, Pare, 92, 333
Losey, Joseph, 222, 230
Lost Boundaries, 68, 76, 79–86, 88–89, 97, 108, 226, 241, 264, 280, 346, 384
Lost Horizon, 394
Lost in the Stars, 83, 130
Lost Weekend, The, 22–24, 27, 29, 31, 57, 70, 73, 76, 148, 193, 199, 260
Louis, Joe, 112–14, 135, 140
Louisiana Story, 334, 366
Love in Syncopation, 110
Love Island, 286
Love Me Tonight, 247, 248
Love of Life, 406
Lower East Side, 226
Lubitsch, Ernst, 34, 247
Luce, Henry, 51, 317
Luciano crime family, 159
Luciano, Charles "Lucky", 85
Lucky Gamblers, 117
Lucky Millinder, 123
Lucky Star Productions, 138
Lumet, Sidney, 3, 4, 259, 275, 300, 348, 403, 426–27
Lunt, Alfred, 19
Lupino, Ida, 20

Lured, 178
Lyceum Theatre, 190
Lyddy, John, 63
Lyon, Sue, 361
Lyon, Sumner, 43
Lyons, Leonard, 204

Ma and Pa Kettle Go to Town, 242
Mabley, "Moms", 46, 97, 122–23
Machine Gun Kelly, 412
MacMahon, Aline, 41
MacPherson, Kenneth, 314
Macy's, 164–67
Maddow, Ben, 162
Mademoiselle Columbine, 368
Madison Pictures, 263
Madison Square Garden, 278
Mafia, 257, 303
Maggiorani, Lamberto, 263
Magnetic Monster, The, 270
Maguire, Charles J., 345
Maguire, Charlie, 278, 345, 384, 386, 389–90, 393–94, 425, 426
Maguire, Dorothy, 180
Maguire, Edward C., 5, 46, 161, 189–95, 202, 243, 254, 258
Mahon, Barry, 294
Main Street to Broadway, 267–68
Malden, Karl, 61, 64, 71, 156, 351, 352–55, 375, 385–86, 388, 393, 400, 401, 426
Malkames, Don, 27, 38, 94, 99, 102, 112, 118, 128, 133, 203, 205, 224, 226–27, 229, 348
Malone, Dorothy, 407
Maltz, Albert, 173–74, 185–86, 187
Mamoulian, Rouben, 247–48, 300
Man About Town, 43–44, 169
Man Against Crime, 259, 348
Man On a String, 92
Man On a Tightrope, 307, 309, 353
Man on the Eiffel Tower, 204
Man Ray, 314, 315, 360
Man With My Face, The, 261
Man's Castle, 15, 24, 27, 266
Mandell, Paul, 283, 285
Mangia, Jerry, 318
Manhattan, 14, 16, 19, 22, 24, 49, 60, 163, 164, 168, 176–77, 187, 190, 194, 195, 204, 231, 242, 244, 260, 263, 277, 309, 331, 349, 364, 372, 389

Manhattan Beach, 275
Manhattan House of Detention, 214
Mankiewicz, Joseph, 202, 241, 260, 379
Mann, Anthony, 190, 250–52
Mann, Delbert, 255, 426
Manoff, Arnold, 262
Mansfield Theatre, 108
Manson, Eddie, 337
Mantan Messes Up, 138
Mantan Runs for Mayor, 138
Mantz, Paul, 169
Marathon Pictures, 47–49, 188–89, 389
March of Time, 4, 36, 51–54, 57, 64, 74, 90, 91–92, 118, 129, 162, 229, 318–20, 335
March, Fredric, 307
Margie, 74, 76
Marie's Crisis Café, 253
Marked Woman, 69
Markey, Enid, 175
Markham, Dewey "Pigmeat", 96, 97, 103, 115, 120, 127–28, 136–38
Markle, Fletcher, 202, 204–5
Marley, John, 184
Marnell, Frank, 387
Marotta, Arthur, 375, 376
Marotta, Joe, 375, 386
Marrying Kind, The, 245, 272, 410
Marshall, E.G., 55, 61, 389
Martin Beck Theatre, 268
Martin, Dean, 119
Martin, Mary, 268
Martin, Mildred, 285, 331
Marton, Andrew, 249
Marty (film), 255, 424
Marty (TV), 354
Marvin, Ira, 364
Marvin, Lee, 115
Marx, Groucho, 137
Mask of Dimitrios, The, 212
Mathews, Carole, 261
Matter of Life and Death, A, 25–26
Mature, Victor, 71–73, 75–76, 311, 351
Mauldin, Bill, 263
Mauriello, Tami, 373, 386, 387
Mauvaise Graine, 23
Mayer, Arthur, 47, 329, 333–34
Mayer, Frank, 261
Mayer, Louis B., 65, 245
Mayo, Virginia, 148

Mayor's Office of Motion Pictures and
   Television, 1, 259, 427
Mazursky, Paul, 324–25, 329, 331, 363
McCarey, Leo, 128
McCarran, Sen. Patrick, 271
McCarten, John, 330
McCarthy, Sen. Joseph, 222
McComb, John, 387
McCord, Ted, 242
McCormack, William "Big Bill", 160, 297–98, 299, 304, 387
McCracken, Boots, 63
McCrary, Tex and Jinx, 219
McDonald, Miles, 160
McDowell, Hugh, 81
McElwee, John, 417
McEvoy, Earl, 234
McGilligan, Patrick, 108, 245, 274
McGrath, Frank, 252
McHugh, Frank, 155
McKinney, Nina Mae, 138
McLean, Barbara, 337, 395
McQueen, Butterfly, 122
McQueen, Steve 221
McSorley, Edward, 295–301, 305, 386, 414
McTeague, 347
McVea, Jack, 120
Meadville Patriot, The, 18–19
Medford, Kay, 212, 213
Meeker, Ralph, 263
Meet Me in St. Louis, 247–48
Mekas, Jonas and Adolfas, 285, 473n123
Melba, 342–43, 379–80
Mellett, Lowell, 17
Memphis Belle, The, 210
Men, The, 264
Menschen am Sonntag, 23, 85
Mentone musical shorts, 116
Mercury Summer Theatre of the Air, 204
Meredith, Burgess, 204, 275, 356
Merrill, Gary, 333
Merry-go-round, 121
Metropolitan Museum of Art, 26
Metz, Toba, 315, 316, 318, 323, 360
Metzger, Radley, 277
Meyer, Russ, 277
Meyers Hotel, 375, 385
Meyers, Sidney, 332–33
Mezzrow, Mezz, 139

Miami, 129, 135, 220, 289
Miami Story, The, 220, 289
Micheaux, Oscar, 82, 97, 107–109, 110, 133
Middle of the Night, 255, 345
Middleton Family at the New York World's Fair, The, 19
Midnight Cowboy, 1, 265
Midnight Menace, 117
Mildred Pierce, 212
Miles, Vera, 79
Milestone, Lewis, 168
Milford, Gene, 4, 261, 392, 394–95, 397, 400–401, 426
Milhaud, Darius, 315
Mili, Gjon, 315
Milland, Ray, 22–24, 267–69
Miller and Lee, 140
Miller, Arthur, 64, 268, 294, 307–9, 313, 349, 385
Miller, Bill, 27, 48, 156, 178, 182, 236–37, 242, 262, 264–65, 420
Miller, David, 38
Miller, Flournoy, 138
Miller, Glenn, 215
Miller, Henry, 230, 366
Miller, Wade, 211
Millinder, Lucky, 123
Million Dollar Productions, 136
Mills Brothers, 112, 113
Mills Novelty Company, 94–96, 99
Mills, Gordon, 95
Minnelli, Vincente, 27, 247
Minoco Productions, 94
Minotaur Productions, 293, 358, 360, 366, 369–70, 402–3, 406–8, 414–16
Miracle decision, 85, 285
Miracle in Harlem, 132–35, 138, 143
Miracle in Milan, 329, 331
Miracle in the Rain, 367
Miracle of the Bells, 351
Miracle on 34th Street, 20, 76, 164–68, 180, 196, 259, 347
Miracle Worker, The, 3, 7, 28, 424
Mirele Efros, 234
Mishkin, Paul, 289
Mississippi Gambler, 312
Mistaken Identity, 127
Mister Buddwing, 255
Mitchell camera, 294, 313, 324, 339, 367

Mitchell, Cameron, 9
Mizoguchi, Kenji, 399
MKR Productions, 4, 394
Mob, The, 303
Model and the Marriage Broker, The, 271–72
Moke and Doke, 120
Mole-Richardson, 205
Momism, 77, 264, 289–90
Monogram studio, 100, 103, 139
Monroe, Al, 124–25
Monroe, Marilyn, 308, 361
Monroe, NY, 262
Monroe, Vaughn, 151
Monsters, Inc., 406
Montagne, Edward, 50, 228, 261
Montgomery, Elizabeth, 354
Monticello Film Corporation, 294–300, 303–5
Monticello, Here We Come!, 234
Moon Over Broadway, 172
Moon Over Harlem, 133
Moonlight and Pretzels, 14, 18
Moontide, 173
Moor's Pavane, The, 289
Moore, Tim, 130
Moorehead, Agnes, 77
Mor Vran, 327
Moran, Dolores, 242
Moreland, Mantan, 102–3, 106, 136, 138–40
Moreno, Rita, 224
Morison, Patricia, 71–72
Morris, Newbold, 30
Morros, Boris, 92, 150–52, 154–58, 161
Mortimer, Lee, 49
Motion Picture Association of America (MPAA), 161, 185, 324, 407–409, 414–15
Motion Picture Stages, 275
Motion Pictures for Television, 404
Mottola, Tony, 290
Mount Vernon, NY, 33
MPO Videotronics, 222, 364
Mr. Bell, 34–35
Mr. Blandings Builds His Dream House, 202
Mr. Lincoln, 326–27, 330, 366
Mr. Lucky, 179
Mr. Rock and Roll, 346
Mr. Smith Goes to Washington, 64
Mr. Universe, 215–20, 226, 277, 408, 464n38
Muller, Eddie, 442n89

Mulligan, Robert, 259
Mundt, Sen. Karl, 91
Municipal Building, 275
Munkacsi, Martin, 284
Munkacsi, Muky, v, 346
Munshin, Jules, 247–49
Murder with Music, 127
Murder, Inc. (film), 454n58
Murder, Inc. (syndicate), 30, 159–60, 189
Murnau, F.W., 153
Murphy, Dudley, 95
Murphy, George, 90
Murphy, Richard, 62
Murray, John "Rastus", 137
Muscle Beach, 262
Musicals, 3, 6, 14, 17–18, 33, 44, 48, 94–112, 115–34, 136–40, 147, 150–59, 168, 197, 203, 220, 226–27, 233–35, 246–50, 254, 259, 262, 266–70, 276, 287–88, 300, 312, 319, 337, 346, 412, 422
Muti, Richard, 351
Mutual decision, 84–85
My Blue Heaven, 220
My Darling Clementine, 76, 448n84
My Forbidden Past, 321
My Immortal Beloved, 151, 158
Myerberg, Michael, 283–85, 424

Nagel, Conrad, 400
Nagra magnetic recorder, 208
Naked City, The, 5, 29, 41, 48, 49, 65–66, 85, 87, 115, 133, 170–78, 180–88, 193, 195, 200–202, 210, 232, 234–38, 241, 250, 252–53, 259, 266, 275–76, 295, 313, 346, 401
Naked Spur, The, 75
Namczy, Frank, 102, 131
Nanook of the North, 381
Naremore, James, 413
Natco, 227
National City Bank, 149
National Film Board of Canada, 84, 348, 381, 419–20
National Legion of Decency, 211
National Minstrel Show, The, 123
Native Land, 88, 162, 334
Native Son, 288
Natwick, Mildred, 368
Navasky, Victor, 306
NBC, 46, 77, 123, 140, 143, 155, 348, 355, 400

518 Index

Neal, Stanley, 18, 160–61
Negrin, Sol, 255, 327–28, 345, 366, 367, 389
Negro Marches On, Inc., The, 129
Negro Soldier, The, 129
Neighbors in the Night, 320
Nelson, Barry, 261
Neo-realism, 4, 47, 52, 63, 65–68, 85, 86, 103, 149, 171, 237, 263, 295, 308, 333, 336, 399, 415–16, 441n65
Never Steal Anything Small, 300
New Deal, 12, 92, 201
New England, 80–82, 85–86, 88–89
New England Story, The, 85
New Jersey, 18, 37, 112, 117, 133, 136, 140, 293, 340, 350
New London, CT, 52
New Orleans, 6, 77, 241, 280
New Rochelle, 221
New School for Social Research, 365
New Tobacco Land, 79
New Tombs, 214
New York City Ballet, 360, 361, 364
New York City Office of Cultural Affairs, 7
New York Confidential, 49, 305
New York Film and Photo League, 332, 334
New York Film Critics Circle, 187, 306
New York Girl, A, 413
New York Philharmonic, 159
New York Public Library, 403
New York State Crime Commission, 309
New York State Motion Picture Division, 38, 221, 227, 230, 288
New York Sun, 294–95, 298, 301
New York Transit Museum, 214
Newark, 22, 319, 363, 381
Newburgh, NY, 277
Newcombe, Warren, 247
Newfield, Sam, 136–38
Newington, NH, 61, 68, 80, 82
Newman, Alfred, 60, 73, 179, 269
Newman, Paul, 351–52, 354
Newsreels, 2, 4, 11, 18–20, 24, 32, 34–37, 45, 48–49, 51–52, 56, 64, 68, 76, 79, 107, 109, 115–18, 122, 124, 129, 148, 161, 176, 178, 190, 200–201, 227, 254, 256, 258, 278, 333, 384
Newton the Teuton, 216
Newtown Productions, 426
Night and the City, 76

Night of the Hunter, 417
Night Song, 159
Nightmare Alley, 75
No Place Like Home, 36
No Way Out, 83
Nobody Lives Forever, 177
Nolan, Doris, 17
Nolan, Frank, 350
Nolan, Lloyd, 57, 61, 90
Norris, Frank, 347
North by Northwest, 261, 271
North, Alex, 214, 396
Nosseck, Max, 421–22
Nothing Sacred, 15
Notorious, 45
Now, Voyager, 224
Nykino, 332

O'Brian, William P., 258
O'Brien, Edmund, 400
O'Brien, Pat, 188, 242
O'Brien, Shaun, 414
O'Brien, Willis, 274
O'Connell, Arthur, 87, 175, 198
O'Connor, Donald, 265, 266
O'Donnell, Cathy, 251–53
O'Dwyer, William, 5–6, 30, 38, 46–47, 49, 133, 147, 154–55, 157, 159–64, 168–70, 177, 181, 184, 188–95, 202, 215, 224, 230–31, 236, 238, 240, 243, 257–59
O'Hara, Maureen, 165–68
O'Keefe, Dennis, 190
O'Neill, Eugene, 412
O'Voutie O'Rooney, 106
Odd Fellows Temple, 32
Odd Man Out, 242
Odds Against Tomorrow, 3, 199
Odets, Clifford, 306
Of Human Bondage, 109
Of Mice and Men, 396
Of One Blood, 127
Office of Alien Property, 206
Office of Civilian Defense, 13
Office of Policy Coordination, 89
Office of Strategic Services, 60–61, 116
Office of War Information, 109–10, 116, 158, 332, 348, 394, 210, 394, 420
Oklahoma!, 246, 248
Old Kickerbocker Music Hall, 274

Oldwick, NJ, 40
Oliver, Gordon, 18–19
Olympia, 206–7
Omnibus, 326
On Dangerous Ground, 235
On the Bowery, 333
On the Town, 217, 246–49, 252, 259, 267, 269, 396
On the Waterfront, v, 2–4, 6–8, 88, 143, 171, 196, 198–99, 259, 265, 275, 278, 293–313, 334, 339–44, 347–55, 372–401, 405, 407, 409, 411–12, 414, 417, 419–24, 426; Taxicab scene 388–92
Once Too Often, 274
One Hundred Men and a Girl, 283
One Man's Family, 354
One Night of Love, 394
One Third of a Nation, 15
Opatoshu, David, 175
Open City, 66–67, 174, 186, 308, 329, 399, 403
Open Secret, 47
Open the Door, Richard, 120, 123
Ophuls, Max, 314
Orgy at Lil's Place, The, 289
Orkin, Ruth, 335–37
Orlob, Harold, 38
Ormandy, Eugene, 159
Orwell, George, 89
Oscar (Academy Awards), 3, 4, 7, 8, 35, 41–42, 51, 62, 148, 151, 168, 180, 182, 196, 224, 266, 268, 283, 288, 306, 320, 332, 339, 347–48, 387, 394, 396, 398–401, 420, 424
Oster, Emil, 380
Oswald, Gerd, 309
Othello, 356
Our Own Kind, 295
Owen, Seena, 152
Oysher, Moishe, 422

P.J. Clarke's, 434n41
Pacemaker series, 246, 319, 320, 420
Page, Bettie, 287
Page, Geraldine, 269–70
Paige, Janis, 219–20
Paisan, 66, 97, 103, 105, 187, 329, 334
Pal Joey, 246
Pal, George, 151, 283–84
Palace Theatre, 218, 363
Palca, Alfred, 278–82

Paley, Jesse, 366
Palmer, A. Barton, 87
Palmer, Betsy, 471n85
Palmer, Lilli, 267, 299
Panic in the Streets, 62, 77, 241, 309, 376, 377
Panoram, 94–95, 100, 110
Pantages Theatre, 400
Panto, Pete, 307, 349
Paradine Case, The, 39
Paradise in Harlem, 102, 133
Paramount building, 404
Paramount Decrees, 193
Paramount Pictures Corp., 13–15, 22, 24, 27, 35, 53, 55, 70, 73, 95, 152, 168, 178, 203, 226, 257, 261, 270, 283, 286, 303, 345, 399, 407
Paramount Theater, 257, 320, 321
Pardon My French, 225
Paris, France, 43, 314, 349, 360, 376, 421
Parisi, Ted, 115
Park Avenue Theatre, 359
Parker, Jean, 320
Parksville, NY, 234
Parsonnet, Marion, 345
Parsons, Harriett, 159
Passing Parade, The, 178
Pasternak, Joe, 235
PATH subway, 373
Pathe Laboratories, 32, 37
Pathe News, 35–36
Pathe studio, 32, 37–39, 41–44, 47, 98, 121–22, 124, 143, 147–48, 154, 160–61, 163, 169, 171, 180, 182, 193, 202, 209
Paths of Glory, 418
Pattern for Peace, The, 277
Patterns, 424, 426
Pawnbroker, The, 4, 394, 422
Payne, John, 165, 167
Pearson, Beatrice, 81, 195–96, 198–99, 226
Pearson, Drew, 201–202
Peck, Gregory, 179–80
Pedi, Tom, 175
Peerce, Jan, 151, 154
Penn, Arthur, 7, 259, 348
Pennsylvania Station, 26, 235, 240, 267–68, 357, 369, 411, 412, 415
People Against O'Hara, The, 266
People of the Cumberland, 65, 162, 332
Perry, Frank and Eleanor, 7, 348

Persoff, Nehemiah, 389, 391
Perth Amboy, 148
Perveler, Martin, 323, 325, 329, 358
Peter Cooper Village, 272
Peters Sisters, 120
Peterson, Broder, 282
Petrie, James, 85
Pettit, Rosemary, 221
Philips, Mark, 70
Phillips, Gene, 24, 330
Piatigosky, Gregor, 151, 154
Pichel, Irving, 20
Pickford, Mary, 343
Pickup on South Street, 260, 275
Picnic, 351
Pie in the Sky, 185, 317
Pigmeat Throws the Bull, 96
Pinky, 82, 108, 135, 312
Pinson, Martha, 3
Pinza, Ezio, 151
Pirosh, Robert, 43–44
Piston, Walter, 210
Platt, Joseph, 41
Playgirl, 266
Plaza Hotel, 179
Plough That Broke the Plains, The, 91
Point Lookout, Long Island, 286
Poitier, Sidney, 84, 132, 280–82
Polaroid film, 383
Pollard, Bud, 101–105, 107, 109, 116–18, 126, 143, 285–86, 288
Pollard, Fritz, 96, 102
Polo Lounge, Beverly Hills, 341–42
Polonsky, Abraham, 195–99, 260, 302
Pons, Lily, 151
Popkin, Harry, 268
Popkin, Leo, 136, 268
Porgy, 102
Porgy and Bess, 248
Port Authority Bus Terminal, 272, 369
Port Authority of NY and NJ, 350
Port of New York, 234–35, 408
Porter, Cole, 18, 253
Portrait of Jennie, 38–43, 124, 169–70, 176, 178, 180, 193, 215, 247, 346, 348
Portsmouth, NH, 80–81, 83, 85–88, 90
Potemkin, 88
Powell, Michael, 25–26, 250
Powell, William, 178

Preminger, Otto, 77, 179, 314
Presbyterian Hospital, 176
Presnell, Robert, 221
Pressburger, Arnold, 422
Pressburger, Emeric, 25–26, 250
Pressburger, Fred, 422
Preview Music, 100, 102
Pride of New York, The (project), 188–89
Pride of the Marines, 173
Primary, 404
Prime, Rebecca, 68, 174, 185
Prince of Foxes, 76
Prince Valiant, 312
Prince, Hugh, 115, 287–88
Princeton Film Center, 394
Princeton, NJ, 244
Producers, The, 395
Production Code Administration, 25, 106, 186, 198, 220–21, 251, 262, 285, 298, 305, 388, 407–9, 414–15
Project X, 84, 222, 227–30, 261
Prokofiev, Sergei, 396
Proser, Monte, 262
Prouty, Jed, 35, 38
Prowler, The, 344, 377
Pudovkin, V.I., 314, 317, 324, 409
Puerto Rico, 261, 422, 423
Pulaski Skyway, 21
Pulitzer Prize, 210, 263, 294, 322, 338, 357
Pulver, Enid, 224
Punch Films, 284
Puppetoons, 151, 283–84
Purlie Victorious, 289
Pusher, The, 394

Quai des brumes, Le, 251
Quebec, 61, 75
Queens (borough), 200, 216, 269, 270
Queens Theater, 257
Queensboro Bridge, 16, 20, 60, 149, 180
Quiet One, The, 224, 316, 332–35, 366
Quigley, George, 127–28, 203
Quinichette, Paul, 101

Race movies, 4–5, 16, 30, 37, 83, 93–143, 147, 156, 203, 207, 221, 233–34, 266, 278, 288, 325
Radio City, 22, 27, 194
Ragtime, 348

Raines, Ella, 178
Rainey, Pat, 106
Ramparts We Watch, The, 52, 54, 55, 80
Raphaelson, Samson, 267
Ration Blues, 127
Ratoff, Gregory, 269–70
Raw Deal, 305
Ray, Aldo, 272, 274
Ray, Nicholas, 113, 124, 206, 235, 252, 314
RD-DR Corporation, 80, 84–85, 90, 222, 256, 275
Readers Digest, 80, 82, 90
Reagan, Ronald, 223
Rear Window, 400
Rebel Without a Cause, 200–201
Rebiere, Marcel, 327–28
Red Balloon, The, 338
Red Channels, 185, 397
Red Hook, Brooklyn, 349
Red River, 215
Red Shoes, The, 151
Ree, Max, 156
Reed, Carol, 242
Reek, Edmund, 258
Reet, Petite and Gone, 98, 105–6
Reeves Magicorder, 208, 210
Reeves Sound Studios, 153, 160, 207–9, 213
Reeves, Hazard, 207–8, 210, 220
Regan, Phil, 100
Regent Theatre, 266
Reinhardt, Max, 153
Reisman, Jr., Phil, 36, 49
Reles, Abe, 159–60, 257
Renoir, Jean, 420
Republic Pictures, 217, 223, 270, 278
Requiem for a Heavyweight, 424
Reservoir Dogs, 354
Return of Mandy's Husband, 103, 138
Reveille with Beverly, 152
Revere TS-300 magnetic recorder, 365
Revere, Anne, 179
Revuers, The, 246
Reynolds, Debbie, 266
Reynolds, Quentin, 73–74
Rhapsody in Blue, 153
Rhedosaurus, 274–75
Rheiner, Samuel, 156
Rhythm in a Riff, 110
Rialto Theatre, 47, 290, 329, 331, 423

Riano, Jack, 122
Richardson, Carl, 174
Richmond, June, 106
Richter, Hans, 314–17, 328, 360
Rickshaw Boy, 278
Riders to the Stars, 270
Riefenstahl, Leni, 206–207
Rieger, Jack, 106–7, 128, 263
Ring Cycle, 284–85
Ritt, Martin, 259, 350
Ritter, Thelma, 400
River, The, 92, 333
RKO Pathe, 32, 33–37, 42–43, 45–46, 49–50, 147, 195, 228, 319, 321
Roaring Twenties, The, 162, 176
Roark, Robert, 295
Robbins, Jerome, 248, 290, 360–61
Robbins, LeRoy, 420, 423
Robert Montgomery Presents, 354
Robert, Sam, 259
Roberts, Bob, 195–96
Roberts, Roy, 240
Robertson, Cliff, 354
Robinson Crusoe, 225
Robinson, Bill, 119
Robinson, Edward G., 241
Robinson, Jackie, 135, 141
Rocco Blues, 127
Rockefeller Center, 25–26, 179, 242, 248–49, 269, 330 check against Radio City
Rockefeller, Nelson, 169
Rockingham Hotel, 81, 86, 226
Rodakiewicz, Henwar, 420
Rodgers and Hammerstein, 133, 268
Rodgers, Gaby, 262
Rodzinski, Artur 151
Rogosin, Lionel, 333
Rolleiflex camera, 328
Roller Derby Girl, 320, 420
Roman d'un tricheur, Le, 43
Romance on the Beat, 116
Romeo and Juliet, 399
Roogie's Bump, 277–78, 282, 345, 384
Roosevelt, Elliott, 212
Roosevelt, Franklin, 12, 19, 36, 62, 92
Roosevelt, James, 94–96
Rosenbaum, Max, 206
Rosenberg, Julius and Ethel, 90
Rosenblum, Ralph, 3, 4, 332, 394–95

Ross, Anthony, 71
Ross, Charles, 216
Rossellini, Roberto, 66, 85, 86, 97, 103, 112, 143, 174, 204, 338
Rossen, Robert, 7, 195, 302, 426
Rosson, Hal, 248
Rothenberg, Marvin, 289
Rothstein, Arthur, 279, 317, 321, 328
Rouse, Russell, 268
Rouveral, Jean, 222–23, 225
Rowan & Martin's Laugh-In, 136
Rowland, William, 17–18
Royal Destiny, 330
Royal Family of Broadway, The, 190
Royal Gospel Productions, 139
Rozsa, Miklos, 182–84
Rubin, Martin, 375
Rubinstein, Artur, 151–52, 159
Ruckersberg, Walter, 404
Runyon, Damon, 172, 186, 226, 241–42, 312
Ruppert Brewery, 49, 223
Russell, Kit, 228–29
Russell, Rosalind, 363
Ruthless, 212
Rutledge, Ann, 327
Ruttenberg, Joe, 268
Ryan, Clendenin, 12
Ryan, Joe, 302–4, 308, 350
Ryan, Robert, 368
Ryles, Fred, 384, 394

Saboteur, 22, 26
Sack Amusement Enterprises, 96, 126–28, 136
Sack, Alfred N., 97, 126–30, 130, 134, 135, 139
Sackler, Howard, 322–24, 356–59, 405, 409, 413–14
Sadler, Dudley, 64
Saint, Eva Marie, 8, 35, 354–55, 373, 383, 387–88, 393, 401
Sak's Fifth Avenue, 179, 253
Salinger, J.D., 290
Salt of the Earth, 88–89
San Francisco, 11, 118, 260, 275, 290, 316, 347, 471n81
Sandburg, Carl, 91
Sanders, George, 161, 169–70, 189
Sanders, James, 26, 434n39
Sandhu, Ranjit, 330

Sandy Hook, 276
Sans laisser d'addresse, 269
Sansho the Bailiff, 399
Sante, Luc, 172
Saperstein, Abe, 278–80
Sarno, Joe, 285
Sarris, Andrew, 199
Sarumba, 203, 261
Satenstein, Frank, 47–49
Saulter, Howard, 34, 41, 44, 50, 209, 213, 286
Savage Eye, The, 262
Savannah Club, 287–88
Savini, Robert, 100–109, 129, 135, 138, 142, 203
Sayre, Joel, 77–78
Scandal Sheet, 305
Scarface, 101
Scarlet Street, 149, 252, 288
Scascoli, Italy, 263–64
Schaefer, Eric, 287–88
Schaffner, Franklin, 259
Schary, Dore, 36, 45–46, 80–81
Scheff, Fritzi, 17
Schenck, Aubrey, 235
Schenck, Nicholas, 238, 243, 264, 379
Schillinger, Joseph, 215
Schmidlapp, Horace, 18, 33, 147
Schneider, Abe, 398
Schuberg, B.P., 296, 407
Schulberg, Adeline, 407–8
Schulberg, Budd, 198–99, 296–312, 340–53, 372, 375, 377, 385–88, 392–94, 397–98, 400, 407, 409, 424, 426
Schulman, Irving, 199–201
Schumann, Robert, 151, 152
Schwartz, Maurice, 16
Schwarz, Richard, 471n74
Scoppa, Jr., Sal, 124
Scoppa, Sal, 161, 456n105
Scorsese, Martin, 411, 427, 491n84
Scott, Zachary, 212–15
Scoundrel, The, 15
Screen Actors Guild, 156, 243, 371
Screen Directors Guild, 30, 81, 125, 155, 202, 225, 228, 233, 285
Screen Guild Productions, 132–33
Screenliner series, 253, 321, 348
Sea of Grass, 62, 65
Seafarers International Union (SIU), 338–340

Seafarers, The, 339–40, 356
Search, The, 67, 263–64
Seaton, George, 21, 164–68, 180
Secret Life of Walter Mitty, The, 29, 148
Seeds of Destiny, 38
Seeger, Hal, 118–19, 122, 124
Seiden, Joseph, 117–18, 124, 126, 133, 233–34
Seitz, John F., 23, 27
Seldes, Gilbert, 35
Seldes, Marian, 327, 328
Selznick, David O., 27, 38–43, 45, 47, 81, 149, 169, 180, 184, 195
Senator Was Indiscreet, The, 178
Sennett, Mack, 171
Senso, 400
Senz, Ira 48, 261
Sepia Cinderella, 113, 130–32, 134, 143, 227, 282
Sepia-Art Pictures Co., 118
Serjack, Frank, 390
Serling, Rod, 424
Serpico, 213
Seven Brides for Seven Brothers, 7
Seven Samurai, 400
Sex Madness, 133, 287
Shades of Gray, 224
Shadow of a Doubt, 21–22
Shahn, Ben, 378
Shaindlin, Jack, 133, 261
Shakespeare, William, 132
Shamroy, Leon, 179
Shane, 342, 379
Shane, Maxwell, 200–201
Sharpe, Albert, 41
Shaw, Sam, 296, 298, 299
Shaw, Tony, 90
She's Too Mean for Me, 140
Shepperton Studios, 76
Sherman, George, 234, 237
Sherry-Netherlands Hotel, 180
Sherwood, Robert E., 267
Shields, Jim, 264, 265, 278, 289, 384
Shilkret, Nathaniel, 321
Shoe-Shine, 66, 263, 333, 335
Shor, Toots, 30, 180, 181
Showboat, 81, 82
Shuftan, Eugen, 156
Shurlock, Geoffrey, 414–15
Side Street, 60, 250–53

Signal Corps, 4, 52–53, 113, 202, 338
Signal Corps Photographic Center (SCPC), 4, 13, 112, 142, 157, 160, 164, 206, 209, 245, 250, 274, 282, 333, 345
Sikov, Ed, 23–24
Silence est d'or, Le, 43–44
Silvera, Frank, 276, 323, 325, 356, 358, 368–71, 402, 405–7, 423
Silverman, Stephen, 247, 249
Silvers, Phil, 288, 318, 359–60, 362
Simon, Abe, 373
Simon, Simone, 252
Simpson, O.J., 115
Simpson, Sloane, 257
Sin of Harold Diddlebock, The, 27, 148
Sinatra, Frank, 48, 150, 152, 235, 246–50, 351–53, 355
Sindell, Bernard, 423–24
Sing Sing prison, 69, 70, 72
Singer, Alexander, 285, 318–20, 322, 367
Singin' in the Rain, 266
Singing in the Dark, 422–23
Siodmak, Robert, 76, 85–89, 176, 295–97, 299–300, 302–3, 344
Sissle, Noble, 123, 127–28
Sixth Part of the World, A, 349
Ski Flight, 73
Skin of Our Teeth, The, 283
Skinner, Frank, 184
Skipper Next to God, 199
Skouras, Charles, 79
Skouras, Dionysia, 78–79
Skouras, Spyros, 30, 78–79, 306–7, 311
Slater, Bill, 207
Slattery's Hurricane, 77
Sleeping City, The, 231, 234–38, 240–44, 251, 253, 300
Slick and Slack, 124
Sloane, Everett, 204
Small Hours, The, 263
Small, Edward, 305
Smash-Up, 148–50, 161, 295
Smith, Al, 169
Smith, Bessie, 119, 139
Smith, Constance, 270, 470n65
Smith, Ellis, 358
Smith, Elwood, 131
Smith, Fletcher, 282
Smith, Harry, 317

Smith, Jamie, 359–60, 363, 368–69, 405–7
Smith, Mamie, 129
Smith, W. Eugene, 328
Smythe, Vanita, 96
Snake Pit, The, 312, 456n101
Sniper, The, 212
Snows of Kilimanjaro, The, 337
So Young, So Bad, 87, 213, 222–25
Sobotka, Ruth, 315, 357, 360–61, 364, 406–7
Social Register, 14
Society of Motion Picture Engineers (SMPE), 32–33, 192
Somebody Up There Likes Me, 318
Something Wild, 263
Song of Love, 151
Song to Remember, A, 151
Souls of Sin, 115, 143
Soundies, 94–100, 105, 110, 113, 119, 126–27, 130–31, 143, 152, 234
Soundmasters, 160, 294
South Pacific, 268
South Street Seaport, 226
Spanish-Portuguese Jewish Cemetery, 240
Speedy, 15
Spellbound, 196, 400
Sperling, Milton, 189
Spewack, Sam, 394
Spiegel, Sam, 6, 151, 278, 303, 305, 341–55, 373–80, 385–90, 392–401, 407, 409, 426
Spingold, Nate, 343
Spirit of Youth, 135
Spiritualist, The, 223
Spitz, Leo 184, 186
Splendor in the Grass, 3, 28, 345, 376, 394, 419, 426
Sportscope, 34
St. Agnes Church, 22, 434n42
St. Benny the Dip, 222, 225–27
St. Cyr, Lili, 220, 286, 287, 289
St. Francis Xavier Church, 318, 319
St. Louis Blues, 119
St. Patrick's Cathedral, 27
St. Raymond's Cemetery, 50
St. Regis Hotel, 344
Stadtmueller, Rev. Fred, 321
Stage Door Canteen, 19, 267
Staiola, Enzo, 373
Stamford, CT, 63–64, 65, 88, 307
Stander, Lionel, 220, 226–27
Stang, Arnold, 220
Stanislavsky, Konstantin, 287, 314, 372, 387
Stanwyck, Barbara, 244
Star Trek, 209, 318
Stars Are Singing, The, 270
Stars in My Crown, 80
Stars on Parade, 117–18, 124
Staten Island, 200
Statue of Liberty, 22, 170, 248, 265–66
Steichen, Edward, 53
Steiger, Rod, 199, 263, 354, 381, 388–93, 400
Stein, Elliott, 347
Steiner, Bill, 45, 50, 278, 282
Steiner, Ralph, 317
Stepanek, Karel, 90
Stern, Bert, 322, 361–62, 406
Stern, Stewart, 264
Stevens, George, 342
Stevens, Leith, 159
Stevens, Mark, 28, 60, 61
Stevens, Rise, 151, 154
Stewart, James, 75
Stewart, Slam, 130–31
Still, William Bundy, 107, 109, 128
Stillman's Gym, 360
Stinson, Edward, 387
Stockwell, Dean, 179, 244
Stoetzel, George, 57, 118, 277
Stokowski, Leopold, 151, 153, 283
Stoloff, Benjamin, 135
Stoloff, Morris, 397
Stoney, George, 289
Stork Club, The, 393
Storm, Tempest, 286
Stormy Weather, 150
Story of GI Joe, The, 244, 268
Strada, La, 400, 406
Stradling, Harry, 348, 423
Strand, Paul, 334
Strange Bargain, 46
Strange Fruit, 81
Stranger, The, 377
Strangers on a Train, 260
Strasberg, Lee, 199, 372
Strasberg, Paula, 306
Strasse, Die, 251
Strate, Walter, 289–90
Stravinsky, Igor, 360–61
Street of Shadows, 36

Street Scene (music), 60, 64, 73, 179, 269
Street With No Name, The, 75
Streetcar Named Desire, A, 199, 226, 236, 306, 347, 348, 384, 396
Streets of New York, The, 414
Strick, Joseph, 262–63
Strip Parade Follies, 289
Strip Tease Hold-Up, 289
Striporama, 286, 287
Strip-Tease Murder Case, The, 288
Stromberg, Hunt, 27, 178
Struggle, The, 149
Sturges, Preston, 27
Stuyvesant Polyclinic, 253
Styne, Jule, 150
Sullivan, Elliott, 212–14, 223
Summer and Smoke, 270
Summertime, 417
Sun Tan Studios, 96
Sunnyside Gardens, 216–17
Sunset Boulevard, 252
Suspense, 290
Swanee Shuffle, 104
Swanson, Gloria, 13, 113, 230
Sweeney Steps Out, 338
Sweet Surrender, 18
Sweet, John, 25–26
Swell Guy, 174, 184
Swing Parade of 1946, 100
Swingtime at the Savoy, 123, 140
Sylbert, Paul, 426
Sylbert, Richard, 418, 422–23, 426

Taber, Richard, 236
Taft High School, 313–14, 317, 322
Taking of Pelham One Two Three, The, 214
Talbot, Dan, 7
Tales of Manhattan, 151–52
Tall, Tan and Terrific, 102–4, 115, 137, 143
Tammany Hall, 160, 293
Tanglewood Festival, 398
Tarantino, Quentin, 354
Tarnished Lady, 190
Tarzan's New York Adventure, 20
Tattooed Stranger, The, 50, 54, 234, 261, 276
Taxi, 269–70
Taxi Driver, 411
Taylor, Don, 175, 182

Taylor, Elizabeth, 3612
Taylor, John Russell, 21
Tea and Sympathy, 343, 347, 348, 353, 372
Teaneck (NJ) Armory, 278
Teaserama, 287
Technicolor, 30, 55, 76, 151, 157, 230, 244, 248, 312, 384
Telecity studio complex, 194
Telenews Newsreel Theatres, 27
Television, 2, 3, 32, 35, 46, 67, 77, 79, 86, 90, 92, 95, 104, 107, 109, 118, 119, 124, 127, 128, 130, 132, 136, 138, 143, 150, 155, 161, 164, 193, 199, 202, 204, 209, 212, 214, 216, 219–22, 224–25, 227, 230–31, 235–36, 254, 257–59, 263, 265, 267–68, 273–76, 278, 284, 287, 290, 294, 305, 318, 327, 329, 335, 338, 345, 348, 351, 354, 357, 359–60, 362–64, 366, 384, 394, 400, 404, 406, 417, 418–19, 421–22, 424, 427
Television Center, Inc., 32
Television Motion Picture Company, 129
Temple, Shirley, 53, 101
Ten Commandments, The, 235
Tenney, Jack, 196
Teresa, 263–65, 354, 384
Terror of Tiny Town, The, 101
Terrytoons, 283
Tetzlaff, Ted, 45–47
Tevya, 16
Texas, 2, 94, 127, 139, 140
Texas, Brooklyn and Heaven, 43
That Man of Mine, 104, 110–12, 114, 115
That Old Black Magic (song), 131
That's Entertainment!, 234
Theatre de Lys, 361
They Live by Night, 235, 252
They Were Expendable, 41
Thief, The, 267–69
This Gun for Hire, 173
This Is America, 34, 35–36, 44, 45, 49, 50, 54, 228, 319, 320–21
This is Cinerama, 220
Thoma, Richard, 230
Thomajan, Guy, 166, 392
Thomas, Bob, 343
Thomas, Harry, 188
Thomas, Lowell, 220
Thompson, Donald, 332–33
Thompson, Walter, 220

Thomson, David, 42
Thousand Clowns, A, 384
Three Daughters, 233
Three Musketeers, The, 221
Three Stooges, The, 216, 220
Thunderbolt, 210
Tierney, Lawrence, 354, 388, 422
Tiffany's, 166
Tillman, Harrel, 111
Time Out: Occupational Therapy in Tuberculosis, 282
Times Square, 177, 265, 271, 290, 339, 357, 364, 367, 369, 410
Tiomkin, Dimitri, 214–15, 398
Titra Sound Corporation, 358, 366, 369, 403–12
To Kill a Mockingbird, 7
Tobacco Road, 115
Tobin, Austin, 350
Toddy, Ted, 97, 103–4, 134–40, 142, 447n69
Tone, Franchot, 204
Toot That Trumpet, 127
Tors, Ivan, 270–71
Toscanini, Arturo, 158, 453n18
Touch of Evil, 211, 391
Tracy, Spencer, 15–16, 24, 62, 245, 266
Trade unions (see also individual Locals), 2, 6, 12, 27, 31, 48, 55, 74, 86–89, 115, 142, 155–56, 161, 170, 191, 214, 237, 254–56, 260–61, 289, 296–98, 301, 303–4, 308, 310–12, 322–24, 328, 338–40, 348, 365–67, 370–71, 407, 419–21, 424
Trail of the Lonesome Pine, 55
Trapped, 235
Travers, Harry, 168
Treasure of the Sierra Madre, 187
Tribeca, 253
Triborough Bridge, 69
Trip to Bountiful, The, 355
Trnka, Jiri, 284, 285
Trouble With Harry, The, 22, 261
Truckline Café, 48
Truffaut, Francois, 271, 314, 337
Truman, Harry, 59
Tudor City, 40
Tumbleweeds, 101
Tunis Expedition, 53
Turkus, Burton, 159
Turner, Charles, 274, 282

Turner, George, 22
Turner, Nat, 323
Tuttle, Frank, 174, 302
Twedell, Frank, 50
Twelve O'Clock High, 77
Twentieth Century, The, 35
Twentieth Century-Fox, 20, 27, 32, 35, 52, 53–55, 57, 59, 60, 62, 68–69, 70–80, 83, 87–91, 98, 150, 164–67, 169, 173, 178, 195, 235, 240–41, 243, 259–60, 269–70, 278, 286, 306, 308, 310–12, 319, 323, 342, 347–48
Twentieth Century-Fox Hour, The, 79
Twiggy, 361
Two Gals and a Guy, 219–20

Ugetsu monogatari, 338
Ullman, Jr., Frederic, 33–36, 44–47, 49, 50
Ulmer, Edgar G., 16, 37, 130–31, 133, 150–58, 162, 163, 212, 225–27, 251, 314
Uncle Tom stereotypes, 101, 103, 117
Uncle Tom's Cabin, 101
United Artists (UA), 39, 84, 153, 158, 207, 218, 219, 223, 230, 278, 280, 305, 342–43, 356, 367, 408–9, 414–17, 424
United Nations, 161, 271
United States Information Agency (USIA), 277
Universal Pictures, 14, 17, 26–27, 116, 149, 194
Universal-International (U-I), 76, 85, 105, 177–78, 180–86, 190–91, 195, 199–200, 202, 206, 231, 234–40, 242, 265–66, 295, 300, 303, 319, 449n102, 459n177
University Club, 27
Unknown Soldier Speaks, The, 129

Valentine, Lewis, 147
Valentini, Vincent, 102, 117, 131, 133
Valentino, Rudolph, 13
Van Doren, Mark, 329, 330
Van Dyke, Willard, 420
Van Fleet, Jo, 355
Van Heusen, Jimmy, 355
Van Pelt, Edwin, 217–18
Vandenberg, Pepe, 375
Vanderbilt Hotel, 223
Vanderbilt Jr., Cornelius, 30
Vanities, The, 109, 110, 126
Vardac, A. Nicholas, 413

Varietease, 287
Vaughan, David, 314, 361, 369
Vavin, Inc., 322
Venice Film Festival, 315, 334, 338, 399
Venona intercepts, 151
Vertigo, 75, 290
Vertov, Dziga, 174, 349
Vetter, Charles, 275–76
Video Varieties studio, 286
Vidor, King, 15, 52, 272
Vidor, Zoli, 278, 422
View from the Bridge, A, 308
Vigo, Jean, 349, 383
Village Barn, The, 319
Violated, 289–90
Visconti, John, 128
Visconti, Luchino, 400
Visual Arts Productions, 112, 206
Vitagraph studio, 142, 160, 161, 426, 496n64
Vitaphone, 130, 269
Viva Zapata!, 306, 309, 311–12, 325, 349, 359, 396
Vivian, Harold, 321
Vogel, Amos, 320
von Fritsch, Gunther, 178
Von Stroheim, Erich, 178, 347, 387, 409
Voorhis, Westbrook van, 51, 90
Vorhaus, Bernard, 222–25
Vorisek, Richard, 153, 208
Vorkapich, Slavko, 235
Voskovec, George, 168

W2XBS, 77
W2XJT, 107
Wagner, Richard, 284
Wagner, Robert F., 7, 231, 293
Wald, Malvin, 161–74, 177, 182, 185, 186–87, 199, 200
Waldorf Astoria Hotel, 242, 257
Waldorf Declaration, 185, 196
Walk a Crooked Mile, 91
Walk East On Beacon, 86, 89–92
Walker, Alexander, 410
Walker, Jimmy, 12, 163, 194
Walker, Nancy, 250
Walker, Robert, 27, 151, 152
Wallace, Jean, 204
Wallace, Mike, 338
Wallach, Eli, 368, 485n62

Wallach's Department Store, 27
Wallander, Arthur W., 163, 169, 171, 177, 181, 182, 258
Waller, "Fats", 96, 107, 127, 128
Waller, Fred, 95
Walsh, George, 258
Walsh, Richard, 170
Walter, Bruno, 151
Wanger, Walter, 12, 148–49
Wantaugh, Long Island, 223
War Production Board, 5, 17, 21, 22, 94
War Refugee Board, 30
Warde, John, 77, 79
Warden, Jack 261
Warner Bros., 6, 14, 27, 30, 36–37, 45, 53–54, 129, 142, 153, 160, 177, 189, 212, 225, 235, 254, 278, 338
Warner News, 256
Warner Pathe News, 36
Warner, Jack, 177, 308
Washington Square, 242, 248, 318, 326, 360, 362, 365
Washington, DC, 38, 57, 61, 64, 90, 109, 116, 136, 223, 260, 268, 297, 306, 421
Waterfront at Midnight, 303
Waters, John, 169
Watkins, Mel, 121, 134
Way Down East, 414
Wayne, David, 41, 246
Ways of Love, The, 329
We Are the Marines, 53, 80
We've Come a Long, Long Way, 129
Weatherwax, Paul, 182
Webb, Clifton, 59, 440n34
Webber, George, 27, 113, 131, 133
Weber and Fields, 413
Weber, Bruce, 279
Webster, Nicholas, 421
Wechsler, Lazar, 67, 263–64
Wedding March, The, 347
Weegee, 177, 235, 315, 334
Weidman, Charles, 17
Weidman, Jerome, 260
Weinberg, Herman G., 403, 494n10
Weingarten, Shirlee, 86
Weisenfeld, Judith, 129
Weisner Brothers, 219–20
Weiss & Gallery Agency, 294
Weissmuller, Johnny, 20

Weist, Dwight, 320
Welk, Lawrence, 96
Well, The, 268
Welles, Orson, 24, 176, 184, 204, 205, 359–60, 406
Wellman, William, 244
Werker, Alfred, 81, 83, 90
Wesleyan University, 304, 353
West Side Highway, 389
West Side Story, 398
Western Electric, 13, 153, 208
Westerns, 4, 20, 22, 30, 55, 94, 107, 117, 121, 135–38, 140, 237, 261, 270, 303, 394
Westinghouse, 19
Westmore, Wally, 384
Whale, James, 131
What a Guy, 138
What Makes Sammy Run?, 296, 307
Wheeler and Woolsey, 137
Whelan, Arlene, 178
When I Grow Up, 344
Where Is Jane Doe?, 253
Where the Sidewalk Ends, 77
Whistle at Eaton Falls, The, 76, 85–91, 295, 299
White Christmas, 270
White Mane, 359
White Plains, NY, 63
White, Josh, 97, 315
White, Walter F., 117, 448n84
White, Walter L., 82
Whitney, John and James, 317
Widmark, Richard, 72, 209, 295, 311
Wild Boys of the Road, 244
Wilde, Cornel, 267
Wilder, Billy, 22–24, 26, 199
Wilder, Thornton, 21
Willard Parker Hospital, 240, 243
William Morris Agency, 341, 342, 352
Williams College, 313
Williams, Spencer, 97, 128, 134, 139–40, 233
Williams, Bert, 123
Williams, Clarence, 107
Williams, Larry, 20, 27, 57, 60
Williams, Rosemary, 413
Williams, Tennessee, 313, 426
Williamsburg, 200
Williamsburg Bridge, 175, 177, 180, 182, 237, 266

Willis, Bob, 107
Wilson, Frank, 102
Wilson, Irene, 139
Wilson, Richard, 222
Wilson, Wesley, 139
Wiltwyck School for Boys, 332
Winchell, Walter, 172, 207, 331, 399
Windjammer, 92
Window, The, 45–47, 49–50, 71, 121, 124, 236, 252, 278, 346
Winged Victory, 245
Winter Garden, 102, 396
Winters, Shelley, 266
With These Hands, 4, 88, 213, 266, 288
Witherspoon, Cora, 18
Within Man's Power, 421
Within Our Gates, 97
Wizard of Oz, The, 216
WNBT, 35, 155
Wolfert, Ira, 195, 198
Woman in the Window, 179
Wonder, Stevie, 98
Wonder, Tommy, 203
Wonderful Town, 396
Wood, Biddy, 116
Wood, Natalie, 165, 167
Woode, Henri, 110
Woodruff, Charles, 335
Woods, Milton (aka Milton Wood), 105–6, 117
Woodward, Joanne, 327, 351
Woolley, Monty, 20
Woolrich, Cornell, 45, 200, 261
World Assembly of Youth, 326
World Film studio 194
World of Dong Kingman, The, 282
World of Henry Orient, The, 244
Wright, Richard, 288
Writers Guild of America, 282
Wrong Man, The, 261
Wyatt, Jane, 62, 63
Wyler, William, 210
Wylie, Philip, 77

Xavier Labor School, 301

Yale, 6, 313, 380, 383
Yalta Conference, 223
Yankee Doodle Dandy, 278

Yiddish films, 16, 37, 117, 136, 156, 232–34, 241, 278, 280, 384, 421, 422
Yom Kippur, 23–24, 260
Yonkers, 33, 147, 186, 223
Yordan, Philip, 295
Yorke, Maine, 81
Young Go First, The, 206
Young Man With a Horn, 242
Young McDermott, The, 295–96
Young People's Film Festival, 7
Young Widow, 27
Young, Al, 131
Young, Harold, 37, 278
Young, Jeff, 310, 386
Young, Loretta, 15
Young, Roland, 226–27
Young, Victor, 151
Young's Gap Hotel, 234

Youngstein, Max, 408
Your World and Mine, 79

Zanuck, Darryl F., 52–53, 55, 59–63, 65, 68–80, 82–83, 91, 164–68, 180, 259–60, 270, 306–8, 310–13, 341–342, 344, 350, 353–54, 375–76, 380, 399–400, 425–26
Zavattini, Cesare, 171, 174, 416
Ziegfeld, Florence, 12, 180
Zinnemann, Fred, 263–65
Zolotow, Maurice, 24, 62, 80
Zoom lens, 24, 197, 441n84
Zorita, 285–86
Zucker, Burt, 324
Zucker, Frank, 293–94, 313, 358, 370, 402, 408
Zucker, Sid, 118, 277
Zukor, Adolph, 13
Zunser, Jesse, 377

FILM AND CULTURE

A series of Columbia University Press

Edited by John Belton

What Made Pistachio Nuts? Early Sound Comedy and the Vaudeville Aesthetic, Henry Jenkins
Showstoppers: Busby Berkeley and the Tradition of Spectacle, Martin Rubin
Projections of War: Hollywood, American Culture, and World War II, Thomas Doherty
Laughing Screaming: Modern Hollywood Horror and Comedy, William Paul
Laughing Hysterically: American Screen Comedy of the 1950s, Ed Sikov
Primitive Passions: Visuality, Sexuality, Ethnography, and Contemporary Chinese Cinema, Rey Chow
The Cinema of Max Ophuls: Magisterial Vision and the Figure of Woman, Susan M. White
Black Women as Cultural Readers, Jacqueline Bobo
Picturing Japaneseness: Monumental Style, National Identity, Japanese Film, Darrell William Davis
Attack of the Leading Ladies: Gender, Sexuality, and Spectatorship in Classic Horror Cinema, Rhona J. Berenstein
This Mad Masquerade: Stardom and Masculinity in the Jazz Age, Gaylyn Studlar
Sexual Politics and Narrative Film: Hollywood and Beyond, Robin Wood
The Sounds of Commerce: Marketing Popular Film Music, Jeff Smith
Orson Welles, Shakespeare, and Popular Culture, Michael Anderegg
Pre-Code Hollywood: Sex, Immorality, and Insurrection in American Cinema, 1930–1934, Thomas Doherty
Sound Technology and the American Cinema: Perception, Representation, Modernity, James Lastra
Melodrama and Modernity: Early Sensational Cinema and Its Contexts, Ben Singer
Wondrous Difference: Cinema, Anthropology, and Turn-of-the-Century Visual Culture, Alison Griffiths
Hearst Over Hollywood: Power, Passion, and Propaganda in the Movies, Louis Pizzitola
Masculine Interests: Homoerotics in Hollywood Film, Robert Lang
Special Effects: Still in Search of Wonder, Michele Pierson
Designing Women: Cinema, Art Deco, and the Female Form, Lucy Fischer
Cold War, Cool Medium: Television, McCarthyism, and American Culture, Thomas Doherty
Katharine Hepburn: Star as Feminist, Andrew Britton
Silent Film Sound, Rick Altman
Home in Hollywood: The Imaginary Geography of Cinema, Elisabeth Bronfen
Hollywood and the Culture Elite: How the Movies Became American, Peter Decherney
Taiwan Film Directors: A Treasure Island, Emilie Yueh-yu Yeh and Darrell William Davis
Shocking Representation: Historical Trauma, National Cinema, and the Modern Horror Film, Adam Lowenstein
China on Screen: Cinema and Nation, Chris Berry and Mary Farquhar
The New European Cinema: Redrawing the Map, Rosalind Galt
George Gallup in Hollywood, Susan Ohmer

Electric Sounds: Technological Change and the Rise of Corporate Mass Media, Steve J. Wurtzler
The Impossible David Lynch, Todd McGowan
Sentimental Fabulations, Contemporary Chinese Films: Attachment in the Age of Global Visibility, Rey Chow
Hitchcock's Romantic Irony, Richard Allen
Intelligence Work: The Politics of American Documentary, Jonathan Kahana
Eye of the Century: Film, Experience, Modernity, Francesco Casetti
Shivers Down Your Spine: Cinema, Museums, and the Immersive View, Alison Griffiths
Weimar Cinema: An Essential Guide to Classic Films of the Era, Edited by Noah Isenberg
African Film and Literature: Adapting Violence to the Screen, Lindiwe Dovey
Film, A Sound Art, Michel Chion
Film Studies: An Introduction, Ed Sikov
Hollywood Lighting from the Silent Era to Film Noir, Patrick Keating
Levinas and the Cinema of Redemption: Time, Ethics, and the Feminine, Sam B. Girgus
Counter-Archive: Film, the Everyday, and Albert Kahn's Archives de la Planète, Paula Amad
Indie: An American Film Culture, Michael Z. Newman
Pretty: Film and the Decorative Image, Rosalind Galt
Film and Stereotype: A Challenge for Cinema and Theory, Jörg Schweinitz
Chinese Women's Cinema: Transnational Contexts, Edited by Lingzhen Wang
Hideous Progeny: Disability, Eugenics, and Classic Horror Cinema, Angela M. Smith
Hollywood's Copyright Wars: From Edison to the Internet, Peter Decherney
Electric Dreamland: Amusement Parks, Movies, and American Modernity, Lauren Rabinovitz
Where Film Meets Philosophy: Godard, Resnais, and Experiments in Cinematic Thinking, Hunter Vaughan
The Utopia of Film: Cinema and Its Futures in Godard, Kluge, and Tahimik, Christopher Pavsek
Hollywood and Hitler, 1933–1939, Thomas Doherty
Cinematic Appeals: The Experience of New Movie Technologies, Ariel Rogers
Continental Strangers: German Exile Cinema, 1933–1951, Gerd Gemünden
Deathwatch: American Film, Technology, and the End of Life, C. Scott Combs
After the Silents: Hollywood Film Music in the Early Sound Era, 1926–1934, Michael Slowik
"It's the Pictures That Got Small": Charles Brackett on Billy Wilder and Hollywood's Golden Age, Edited by Anthony Slide
Plastic Reality: Special Effects, Technology, and the Emergence of 1970s Blockbuster Aesthetics, Julie A. Turnock
Maya Deren: Incomplete Control, Sarah Keller
Dreaming of Cinema: Spectatorship, Surrealism, and the Age of Digital Media, Adam Lowenstein
Motion(less) Pictures: The Cinema of Stasis, Justin Remes
The Lumière Galaxy: Seven Key Words for the Cinema to Come, Francesco Casetti
The End of Cinema? A Medium in Crisis in the Digital Age, André Gaudreault and Philippe Marion
Studios Before the System: Architecture, Technology, and the Emergence of Cinematic Space, Brian R. Jacobson
Impersonal Enunciation, or the Place of Film, Christian Metz
When Movies Were Theater: Architecture, Exhibition, and the Evolution of American Film, William Paul
Carceral Fantasies: Cinema and Prison in Early Twentieth-Century America, Alison Griffiths
Unspeakable Histories: Film and the Experience of Catastrophe, William Guynn
Reform Cinema in Iran: Film and Political Change in the Islamic Republic, Blake Atwood
Exception Taken: How France Has Defied Hollywood's New World Order, Jonathan Buchsbaum
After Uniqueness: A History of Film and Video Art in Circulation, Erika Balsom
Words on Screen, Michel Chion

Essays on the Essay Film, Edited by Nora M. Alter and Timothy Corrigan
The Essay Film After Fact and Fiction, Nora Alter
Specters of Slapstick and Silent Film Comediennes, Maggie Hennefeld
Melodrama Unbound: Across History, Media, and National Cultures, Edited by Christine Gledhill and Linda Williams
Show Trial: Hollywood, HUAC, and the Birth of the Blacklist, Thomas Doherty
Cinema/Politics/Philosophy, Nico Baumbach
The Dynamic Frame: Camera Movement in Classical Hollywood, Patrick Keating
Hollywood's Dirtiest Secret: The Hidden Environmental Costs of the Movies, Hunter Vaughan
Chromatic Modernity: Color, Cinema, and Media of the 1920s, Sarah Street and Joshua Yumibe
Rewriting Indie Cinema: Improvisation, Psychodrama, and the Screenplay, J. J. Murphy
On the Screen: Displaying the Moving Image, 1926–1942, Ariel Rogers
Play Time: Jacques Tati and Comedic Modernism, Malcolm Turvey
Spaces Mapped and Monstrous: Digital 3D Cinema and Visual Culture, Nick Jones
Anxious Cinephilia: Pleasure and Peril at the Movies, Sarah Keller
Film Studies, 2nd Edition, Ed Sikov
Hollywood's Artists: The Directors Guild of America and the Construction of Authorship, Virginia Wright Wexman
Absence in Cinema: The Art of Showing Nothing, Justin Remes
Bombay Hustle: Making Movies in a Colonial City, Debashree Mukherjee

GPSR Authorized Representative: Easy Access System Europe, Mustamäe tee 50, 10621 Tallinn, Estonia, gpsr.requests@easproject.com